WILLIAM MORRIS

WILLIAM MORRIS

WILLIAM MORRIS

EDITED BY LINDA PARRY

Philip Wilson Publishers
IN ASSOCIATION WITH
The Victoria and Albert Museum

Published to coincide with the exhibition
William Morris 1834–1896
held at the Victoria and Albert Museum, London
9 May – 1 September 1996

Exhibition sponsored by

Text and illustrations © the Trustees of the Victoria and Albert Museum 1996
First published in 1996 by Philip Wilson Publishers Limited
143–149 Great Portland Street, London W1N 5FB

ISBN 0 85667 442 7

Designed by Gillian Greenwood
Set in Palatino typeface
Printed and bound in Italy by Società Editoriale Libraria per azioni, Trieste

Title-page: E.H.New, *Kelmscott Manor, c.*1898
Cover design: Johnson Banks Design Limited

CONTENTS

PREFACE

The William Morris Centenary Exhibition is the first major display to be organised at the V&A during my term as Director and, although I can claim to have had little to do with either its inception or development, it is undoubtedly a particularly appropriate exhibition with which to start. Morris was much involved with the Museum in its early days, contributing to its collections (giving modest financial donations and, more importantly, his expertise) and also using those collections as a source for his designs. This was, of course, precisely the intention of the eminent patrons and scholars, led by Prince Albert and Henry Cole, who established the Museum in the wake of the Great Exhibition of 1851.

The idea that a museum can and should play a useful role in promoting good design, educating current artists and craftsmen through examples of the best work of different periods and different cultures, is one that has found favour again in recent decades. I like to think that the role of the V&A today is one that would be immediately recognisable to its founders; certainly the very wide range of our educational activities, from joint courses with the Royal College of Art to activities for hundreds of schools, indicates that the Museum is much more than just a treasure house of unparalleled richness.

William Morris also contributed to the fabric of the V&A when his firm received the commission in 1865 to decorate one of the new refreshment rooms. The Green Dining Room, known now as the Morris Room, is one of the many splendours of the Museum, reminding visitors that our exhibits start with our buildings. So it is in every way appropriate that the V&A should mark this centenary with what is certainly the most ambitious exhibition ever devoted to William Morris, and one of the largest on any subject ever mounted within the Museum. Such things do not happen by themselves; sponsors are needed and we are especially grateful to Pearson Plc for their very generous support. Many people within the Museum have contributed their time and expertise, above all Linda Parry, the Curator of the Exhibition and Brian Griggs the Designer. I am grateful to them, and to many others. In its own way the exhibition is a tribute to the spirit which founded the Museum and led William Morris to work in it. I have no doubt it will contribute to the excellence of contemporary design, as well as bringing pleasure to many.

Dr Alan Borg
DIRECTOR, VICTORIA AND ALBERT MUSEUM

SPONSOR'S PREFACE

It gives me particular pleasure that Pearson is returning to the Victoria and Albert Museum to sponsor the great exhibition to mark the centenary of the death of William Morris. Two years ago we sponsored the comparable exhibition devoted to the life and work of A.W.N.Pugin, the other pillar on which much of the glories of nineteenth-century design in this country rest. Their relationship was clear to Morris's peers, as Lewis F.Day wrote in his appreciation in *The Art Journal* in 1899:

> He it was that snatched from the hand of Ruskin the torch which Pugin earlier
> in the century had kindled and fired the love of beauty in us.

Moreover, both were men to whom design was only a part of a much fuller life. In Pugin's case his work was an expression of and sprang from a convert's passionate Roman Catholicism. Morris read theology, decided against taking Holy Orders, became famous as a poet and then towards the end of his life turned into an equally passionate socialist activist and writer. Yet at the same time he established the Kelmscott Press, which virtually recreated the book as an art object in its own right. Just before his death it was Longman, now part of Pearson, that became his last publishers and kept the more important titles of Kelmscott in print so, happily, we are associated with Morris as we were with Pugin.

Morris and Pugin were both immense supporters of what was originally the South Kensington and is now the Victoria and Albert Museum. Morris's knowledge of old textiles owed much to the Museum's collections and he was equally instrumental in helping it build up an unrivalled collection of middle eastern carpets. For him it was truly the national museum of art and design.

Great as are Morris's achievements in the field of design, it is perhaps his preoccupation with the nature and quality of work in an industrial society that is most original and striking today. He never reconciled his desire for every worker to be a creative force with the repetitive and often machine-dependent processes used for Morris & Co.'s products. That freedom is easier to grasp today and we at Pearson pride ourselves on nurturing the talent and originality of all the people who work within a group whose success ultimately depends on its continuing creativity.

Michael Blakenham

CHAIRMAN, PEARSON PLC

ACKNOWLEDGEMENTS

The publication of this book has only been possible through the expertise, co-operation, assistance and good wishes of many individuals, organisations and institutions. It is not possible to mention everyone by name, but heartfelt thanks are offered to everyone who has taken part.

Through their sponsorship Pearson Plc have demonstrated their support of the project, and I am particularly grateful to James Joll who first suggested the idea of a 1996 Morris centenary celebration many years ago. His knowledge and enthusiasm has been a constant encouragement.

A book of this size and scope could not have been completed without the considerable assistance of the authors, and I am grateful to all of them for offering so willingly and generously of their time and expertise both in the initial selection of exhibits and the publication. Many of them would like to acknowledge others for their help and I must apologise, as editor, for the need to group these together as one. This in no way diminishes their contribution nor our thanks to them.

I am grateful to the many societies, institutions and private lenders, listed on page 378, who have not only graciously allowed their precious objects to be lent for the exhibition but have gone to the trouble of allowing me and colleagues to visit them to view and photograph these. I would like to add my personal thanks to Helen and Sanford Berger; my extended study of their collection was both an enjoyable and edifying experience, the memory of which will remain with me for many years to come. Bryan Maggs, David Mason, Paul Reeves and Michael Whiteway have been particularly helpful in securing loans for the exhibition.

Many museum colleagues have provided invaluable assistance. Peter Cormack and Norah Gillow from the William Morris Gallery, Walthamstow, and Stephen Wildman from Birmingham Museums and Art Gallery have consistently and unselfishly shared their very considerable expertise with contributors, and many sections of this book could not have been completed without their help. I would also like to thank Glenys Wild from Birmingham Museums and Art Gallery, Howard Coutts of the Bowes Museum, Barnard Castle, Judy Rudoe and Christopher Date of the British Museum, Dr Scot McKendrick of the British Library, George Breeze of Cheltenham Museums and Art Gallery, Helen Webb and Don and Pat Chapman at Kelmscott Manor, Edward Morris from the Walker Art Gallery, Liverpool, Veronica Tongue of Maidstone Museum and Art Gallery, Wendy Evans and Alex Werner of the Museum of London, Secily Greenhill of the Society for the Protection of Ancient Buildings, John Cherry, Bernard Nurse and David Morgan Evans of the Society of Antiquaries of London, David Rodgers and Derek Baker of the William Morris Society and Frances Pritchard of the Whitworth Art Gallery, Manchester.

Richard and Hilary Myers whose own definitive research on Morris tiles is due to be published in 1996 have generously offered advice for the catalogue. Ros Allwood permitted her soon to be published manuscript *British Furniture: 1837–1887* to be read and Dawn Thorndycraft allowed information to be used from her dissertation, *A Royal Commission: Morris & Co., at St James's Palace*, (Royal Holloway College, 1993). I would also like to thank the following individuals for their help, The Reverend Christopher Armstrong, Tye Blackshaw, Dorothy Bosomworth, John Brandon-Jones, Jon Catleugh, the Church Wardens and members of the Parochial Church Council, St Edward the Confessor, Cheddleton, David Coachworth, Anthony Collieu, Phil Crook, Kate Eustace, Donald J.R.Green, Rowland and Betty Elzea, Irene Forrest, Albert Gallichan, Lucy Goffin, The Hon. Janet Grant, Michael Hall, Vikram Joshi, Paul Joyce, Peter Howell, Barbara Hutchinson, Richard Kingzett, Hans van Lemmen, Martin Levy, Sir Andrew Lloyd-Webber, Norman Machin, Robert Milner, Mary Oliphant, Jimmy Page, John Parry, Michael Parry of Arthur Sanderson & Sons, Mrs Reichmann, Peter Rose, Royal Holloway College,

University of London, Egham, John S.M. Scott, The Reverend Christopher Sharp, Robert Stone, Anthony Symondson SJ, Andrew Saint, Clare Thorn, Dawn Thorndycraft and Dr Jenny West.

This publication has proved a major undertaking for the Museum which, through the considerable efforts of many colleagues, has been completed with speed and efficiency. I would particularly like to thank the following: Anne Amos, Derek Balfour, Val Blyth, Tina Cogram, Sherry Doyal, Audrey Hill, Lynda Hillyer, Agnes Holden, Meryl Huxtable, Marion Kite, Vicky Oakley, Gill Owens, Elizabeth Martin, Tim Miller, Juanita Navarro, Albert Neher, Jane Rutherston, Helen Shenton, Nick Umney and Pauline Webber all from the Conservation Department. Also Alun Graves, Robin Hildyard, Oliver Watson from the Ceramics and Glass Collection; Tamsin Daniel of Collection Services, Sorrel Hershberg from Furniture and Woodwork, Amanda Robertson and Susannah Robson of the National Art Library, Glenys Evans and Martin Durrant of the Picture Library; Charles Newton, Moira Thunder and Mark Haworth-Booth of Prints, Drawings and Paintings; and Valerie Mendes and Emma Taylor of Textiles and Dress. An intensive programme of photography has been required for this book and I would like to thank James Stevenson, Ken Jackson, Christine Smith, Pip Barnard, Philip De Bay, Graham Brandon, Barry Chappell, Richard Davis, Sarah Hodges, Mike Kitcatt, Mike Larkin, Daniel McGrath, Dominic Naish and Paul Robins for providing such marvellous photographs.

The full-time administration and organisation of the exhibition and catalogue has involved a small band of staff and helpers. I am indebted to Linda Lloyd-Jones and Juliette Foy from Exhibitions, Brian Griggs and Sharon Beard, Colin Corbett and Mike Malham from Design and to Margaret Rose who has been very generous in devoting her own precious time for helping with research. To Ariane Bankes and Celia Jones for editing help and to Gillian Greenwood for designing the catalogue. Lastly, my special thanks go to Howard Batho, Juliet Bingham and Ghislaine Wood without whose excellent assistance the project could not have been realised. It has been a pleasure to work with them and all the other individuals mentioned.

Linda Parry

MAY 1996

NOTES ON THE CATALOGUE

All catalogue entries are illustrated unless stated
and all are written by specialist authors unless denoted by initials:

SA	Stephen Astley
MB	Mary Bennett
LP	Linda Parry
ET	Eric Turner
RW	Ray Watkinson

Measurements are in centimetres, height then width then depth

Exhib. references are to exhibitions held in the V&A

1934	*William Morris Centenary Exhibition*
1952	*Exhibition of Victorian and Edwardian Decorative Arts*
1961	*Morris & Co. Centenary Exhibition* (Arts Council)

Sources and References

Frequently used sources and references are abbreviated.
Full details can be found in the Bibliography, pages 376–7

THE MAN

INTRODUCTION

Linda Parry

William Morris was both a realist and a dreamer, a dichotomy that shaped his character and controlled his life. He hoped that his writing and his art, the fruits of his imagination, would help him escape from the mediocrity and injustices of modern civilisation that he claimed to hate, yet only the eclectic and tumultuous atmosphere of nineteenth-century England could provide the intellectual challenge and the practical means for him to influence change.

This constant tussle between his aspirations and actuality became the main spur for his work, but at times it also proved a great hindrance. He rose above his uneventful childhood by the power of his imagination, yet his idealised romance and marriage was, in reality, a nightmare. Through his own physical efforts he established himself as one of the most popular designers and manufacturers of his age, yet his belief in the sanctity of art and high standards of practice meant that his work was denied to many whose lives he wished to improve.

Such inconsistencies seen alongside the enormous range of his achievements make Morris a fascinating subject for study and a constant source of enquiry. This book and integrated catalogue provide a reassessment of the man, his work and his reputation one hundred years after his death and is published to accompany the Victoria and Albert Museum's 1996 exhibition *William Morris*. It is very fitting that this Museum should organise and house such a comprehensive display of Morris's work as its collections inspired and fascinated him throughout his life. The Museum also greatly benefited from a long and harmonious relationship with the designer, calling on his services firstly as a decorator and then as an expert adviser on the acquisition of exhibits. The Museum's curators working in this century have continued this close connection by reviving and maintaining an interest in Morris's art through publications and by a series of exhibitions held at the Museum in 1934, 1952 and 1961. As a fitting tribute to one of the most influential designers that Britain has produced, the scope of the present exhibition and publication attempts a more complete and comprehensive assessment of his artistic career than has been possible before.

Morris – The Man

Childhood to Marriage, 1834–60

William Morris was a Victorian in the true sense of the word, his life spanning all but a few years of Queen Victoria's reign. He was born on 15 March 1834 at Elm House, Walthamstow, the third child and oldest son of William and Emma (née Shelton) Morris. The Morrises, who eventually had nine children, were an affluent family with pretensions. William Morris Senior was a partner in a reputable firm of bill brokers in the City who in 1843 was granted his own coat of arms, an honour his eldest son was never to use. Successful speculation in the 1840s in a west-country copper-mining project, Devon Great Consols, provided not only increased prosperity and a larger home for the family but the foundation of young William's inheritance and the means by which he was 'sheltered from real hardships in the struggle for life', as Holman Hunt described it many years later. Morris was six years of age when the family moved to Woodford Hall, a large country house with fifty acres of parkland adjoining Epping Forest. Some measure of Morris's privileged childhood can be gained by comparing the annual rent of £600 for this house with the £180–£200 he was to pay for the rent of his not insubstantial home in Hammersmith, London, nearly forty years later.

The grounds and surrounding countryside of Woodford Hall provided the young Morris with an enormous playground and although he was close to his two eldest sisters, Emma and Henrietta, he spent much time by himself. Various popular story books in the home fed his imagination and Walter Scott's novels, in particular, provided the balance of heroes and swashbucklers needed by this impressionable boy. He enacted his early fantasies on solitary pony rides through the Forest and began to visit local Essex churches and other early buildings in the area. Morris thus developed an early affinity with historic romance, landscape and buildings and it is not surprising that his first sight of Canterbury Cathedral at the age of eight seemed like 'the gates of heaven opening'.

Morris was nine years old before receiving his first formal teaching at a local preparatory school and, following the untimely death of his father in 1847, he was sent as a boarder to the newly opened Marlborough College, which he attended between February 1848 and Christmas 1851, when he was removed following a riot at the school. Morris claimed to have learned nothing from his time here although it is likely that his knowledge of and interest in classical languages and literature dates from these years, and evidence suggests he was of average aptitude at this time. While away at school he continued to roam the countryside whenever he was able to. Wiltshire presented new experiences through the prehistoric monuments of Silbury Hill, Avebury and Pewsey Vale, and his passion for history developed.

Following his withdrawal from the school, Morris moved back to Walthamstow where the family now lived, and was tutored privately for Oxford entry by the Reverend Frederick B. Guy, a master from the local Forest School. At last Morris seemed to accept and delight in learning. Guy developed Morris's interest in history and the Classics and by the time he went up to Oxford in January 1853, to study for the Church, he was a well-read and confident scholar.

The strong personal views that were to set him apart in later life had also begun to make themselves known. It is said that he accompanied the family on a trip to the 1851 International Exhibition in Hyde Park but refused to go inside the glass building knowing that he would not like what he saw. Similarly, but for quite different reasons, he refused to travel to London to watch the Duke of Wellington's funeral in November 1852, preferring to spend the day at home and riding through Epping Forest.

Soon after arriving at Oxford, Morris met Edward Jones (later Burne-Jones), the first of a number of lifelong close friendships forged by Morris in his youth which satisfied his constant need for companionship and camaraderie. Burne-Jones's vivid reminiscences of the period give an indication of what Morris must have been like: 'From the first I knew how different he was from all the men I had ever met', Mackail quotes. 'He talked with vehemence, and sometimes with violence. I never knew him languid or tired. He was slight in figure in those days; his hair was dark brown and very thick, his nose straight, his eyes hazel-coloured, his mouth exceedingly delicate and beautiful.' It was soon after this time that Morris earned the nickname 'Topsy'; this was 'on account of his curls & cos he growed as he got bigger' (a reference to a character in Harriet Beecher Stowe's *Uncle Tom's Cabin* published in 1852).

Burne-Jones introduced Morris to friends from his native Birmingham who were students at Pembroke College. The bond of this small intimate group, which comprised Morris, Burne-Jones, William Fulford, Richard Dixon, Charles Faulkner and Cormell (Crom) Price was poetry, according to Dixon, but their interests covered all forms of literature. 'The Set' or 'the Brotherhood' as it became known, also dreamed and fantasised. Their favourite novels were romances, stories of chivalry, self-sacrifice and conscience, and both Burne-Jones and Morris had ideas to form a monastic order. Morris's passion for reading out loud began at this time as the group explored established works by Shakespeare, Milton and Tennyson, as well as the writings of the contemporary reformers Charles Kingsley and Thomas Carlyle. Such publications gave Morris his first conscious awareness of the deep division in contemporary society brought about by poverty and deprivation, and, as Fiona MacCarthy has suggested, the daily contact of his less affluent and more worldly Birmingham friends is likely to have further widened his horizons in this respect. How deeply Morris judged himself part of the class division in these early years is debatable. On coming of age in 1855 he inherited shares that provided him with a substantial income and, whereas Dixon described his early manners and tastes as aristocratic, he was keen not to be separated out because of his wealth and was generous, always happy to finance the projects that he and his less fortunate friends and colleagues were involved in.

Before coming up to Oxford Morris had read John Ruskin through the first two volumes of *Modern Painters*. With the publication of *The Stones of Venice* in 1853, Morris and Burne-Jones became ardent followers. Ruskin's chapter 'Of the Nature of Gothic' was particularly significant to the two who were developing a fascination for all things medieval. Visits to France and the Low Countries in summer vacations increased these passions. The French cathedrals they visited made an enormous impression on Morris and in churches and museums he was able to study at first hand paintings, sculpture, tapestries and other forms of early medieval northern European decoration, which became his greatest artistic influence.

Morris also developed an interest in modern painting and particularly the work of the Pre-Raphaelite painters Rossetti, Holman Hunt and Millais. He had first seen their work in the form of book illustrations and, encouraged by Ruskin's published reviews of their work, sought out their paintings in the few available local sources, such as the collection of Thomas Combe, the Oxford University Press printer.

Following their second tour of Northern France, Morris and Burne-Jones both realised that their intended futures lay not as clergymen but in art, Burne-Jones as a painter and Morris an architect. To appease his distressed mother, Morris took a pass degree in November 1855 but in the following January he pursued his own ambitions and became an articled pupil in the Oxford office of George Edmund Street, one of the most notable Neo-Gothic architects of his generation.

Morris had little talent or patience for architecture and only stayed with Street for eight months. He is said to have spent most of his time in the office drawing one building, but his preoccupation with other external projects may account for this lack of progress. On 1 January 1856 the first issue of the *Oxford and Cambridge Magazine*, had been published (cat.no.A.2). Suggested by Dixon and financed by Morris, this became a literary vehicle for Morris and the Oxford group. Based on the earlier short-lived Pre-Raphaelite journal, *The Germ*, the magazine included poetry, stories and reviews. Morris edited the first monthly issue then passed this task, with a salary, to William Fulford. Morris's first literary works were published in this magazine and he contributed eight prose tales, five poems and two articles to ten of the twelve volumes published. The magazine also provided the first contact with Ruskin.

Despite Morris's realisation that he would never make an architect, the experience of Street's office proved invaluable for his later work as a designer. It was here also that he first met Philip Webb, the first of a group of modest, unassuming colleagues who provided invaluable support in business and firm friendship for Morris throughout his life. Morris's gift for selecting friends was only matched by the loyalty and admiration that they, in turn, displayed to him.

By the time Morris joined Burne-Jones in lodgings in London he, too, nursed ambitions to become an artist and he began to buy paintings (cat.nos.A.3–5). The close association of the two with Rossetti, whom Burne-Jones had got to know when Morris was still in Oxford, proved to be very useful. Through him they attended drawing classes for the first time and worked in both Rossetti's and Ford Madox Brown's studio, meeting a number of other leading artists there. By attending exhibitions and meetings of such groups as the Medieval Society and Hogarth Club both became part of various fashionable artistic circles existing in London at that time.

Morris's Oxford background helped Rossetti to secure a commission to decorate the newly built Debating Room of the Oxford Union, and both Morris and Burne-Jones were part of the group of artists who set about transferring some of their favourite stories from the *Morte d'Arthur* to the upper walls of the room. Inexperience of mural painting and the difficult architecture of the buildings meant that the scheme was never successfully completed and faded quickly, although some restored evidence of the work remains to this day. However, the project proved to be important for two reasons. It was the first scheme that Morris, Burne-Jones, Rossetti and their colleagues had worked on together and they had clearly enjoyed not only the labour but the social aspects of the work. Secondly it led to the first meeting of Morris with his future wife Jane Burden. Rossetti and Burne-Jones had first met her while visiting the theatre in Oxford. She was startling to look at, tall, dark and slender and with a mass of wild, naturally curly hair, a long neck, large eyes and a generous mouth (cat. nos. A.7–8) – quite unlike the neat and conventional idea of beauty at that time, Rossetti immediately saw her potential as a model. Morris was smitten by her from their first meeting, 'Topsy raves and swares [*sic*] like or more than any Oxford bargee about a "stunner" that he

Fig. 1 Photograph of Jane Burden *c.*1858 (cat. no. A.8).

has seen', Crom Price wrote to his father in December 1857. From this point Jane became an icon, representing the perfect idealised beauty of the *avant garde* epitomised in Rossetti's paintings for the next thirty years.

Apart from her very arresting appearance and Morris's inherent promise of a secure future it is difficult to understand why Morris and Jane decided to marry, especially as there were very great social difficulties with the match. Jane was working class, the daughter of an Oxford stableman and, although Morris was keen to shun conventional behaviour whenever the opportunity arose, in a climate such as that of mid-Victorian England one cannot dismiss lightly the class differences that existed between them. A number of Morris's friends attempted to warn him off such a marriage but the two seemed determined, for quite different reasons, to go ahead. Jane found the group admiring and fun to be with and a future with Morris promised comfort and a continuation of this. Morris was now ready for romance and marriage and Jane represented for him the perfect mistress and chatelaine. She was also greatly admired by Rossetti, whose judgement Morris valued greatly. Morris and Rossetti's first drawings of Jane, done soon after they met her, make an interesting comparison. Morris's work (cat.no.G.8), is hesitant and poignant yet is, surprisingly, closer to her image than Rossetti's more confident piece, which attempts far more than a physical likeness. Here there is already a suggestion of the strong attraction of the artist for his model (cat.no.A.6).

Morris and Jane became engaged in the spring of 1858 and the same year Morris celebrated his new-found confidence in romance by painting her portrait in the guise of *La Belle Iseult* (cat.no.G.10) and with the publication of his first book of poetry *The Defence of Guenevere and Other Poems*. The volume included a number of works written earlier, although the title poem and 'In Praise of my Lady' show his newly found interest in and sympathy with the opposite sex. Published at Morris's expense, the book was not received well by critics and he waited a further nine years before submitting anything else for publication.

The marriage took place quietly in Oxford on 26 April 1859 and the two settled in rooms in Great Ormond Street, London, while waiting for their new house to be built. Morris had bought a plot of land at Bexleyheath in Kent. Surrounded by orchards and lying on the medieval route for pilgrims from London to Canterbury, the site was both beautiful and historically significant for Morris. Philip Webb designed the red-brick building to Morris's specifications, producing a modern house based on elements of English vernacular architecture that both he and Morris admired. Jane and William moved in to Red House in the late summer of 1860, and the decoration of the interior occupied much of Morris's time for the next two years. It was still not completed when circumstances compelled them to move back to London in 1865.

Red House: The Firm and Literary Fame, 1861–74

Red House soon became the social centre of the artistic and literary group that had begun to develop around the Morrises. Regular visitors included Webb, Jane's sister Bessie, Rossetti and his wife Elizabeth Siddal, Edward and Georgiana Burne-Jones, Charles Faulkner and his sisters, Lucy and Kate, and the poet Swinburne. Most of them took some part in the decoration of the house either by designing, painting or embroidering. Within two years of moving in Jane gave birth to two daughters, Jane Alice (Jenny), born in January 1861, and Mary (May), in March 1862.

The success of the decorations and the enjoyment experienced in completing the work persuaded the friends to try and start their own commercial company, and in April 1861 the firm of Morris, Marshall, Faulkner & Co. was formed. Morris's initial dream was of a workshop run on medieval lines from Red House. This was not realistic and even later plans to extend the house so that the Burne-Jones family could move in had to be abandoned. Instead the firm (as it became known) set up studios and a shop at 8 Red Lion Square, a few doors away from where Morris and Burne-Jones had shared lodgings a few years before.

The first notable display of the firm's wares was at the 1862 International Exhibition, and despite very mixed reviews they were encouraged enough to issue a prospectus for potential customers. Their range at this time concentrated on the type of decoration that had been prepared for Red House – wall painting and embroidery – with tableware and furniture supplied to their design by outside makers. Stained glass and tiles were soon added.

The first three important commissions came from the architect George Frederick Bodley, who Morris had met through G.E.Street. These were for the decoration of three newly built churches in Scarborough, Brighton and Selsley, and for many years church stained glass proved their most popular product. All of the partners – Morris, Burne-Jones, Webb, Rossetti, Ford Madox Brown, Faulkner and Peter Paul Marshall (who had been introduced to the group through Brown) – produced designs of one kind or another and were paid accordingly. The firm made very little money in their first five years and only Morris, with a private income, did not also need to seek out work elsewhere. By 1865 larger premises were taken in Queen Square and commissions for decorative work on such prestigious buildings as St James's Palace and the South Kensington Museum helped to increase popularity and sales. Morris was becoming totally absorbed with the firm's work, and although officially appointed business manager from the start he had also begun to take a strong directorial role. This made the move from Red House back to London inevitable and in the autumn of 1865 the family took rooms on the first floor over the shop and workshop at Queen Square. Jane must have been pleased to be back in London. She had become part of various fashionable circles there and had made a number of friends. She had also become Rossetti's favourite model and frequently visited his studio and house in Cheyne Walk (cat. no. A.14). At what point their relationship transcended friendship is debatable. When Morris became aware of this is even more difficult to determine. A series of cartoons published in *Punch* in March 1866 suggests that Rossetti's dalliances were already widely discussed, and the thinly veiled images of the unfortunate Lizzie Siddal, who had died tragically in 1862, and Jane proves this was common knowledge soon after Jane's appearance back in London.

Morris's response was to turn again to poetry and in 1867 he published *The Life and Death of Jason* which was greeted with great critical acclaim. This was one story of a eventual group of twenty-four that Morris spent five years preparing under the collective title of *The Earthly Paradise*. The final volume, published in 1870, was widely read and admired, not only by literary figures but by many who did not normally read verse. The success of this volume and the fame it brought to Morris cannot be overstated and its reputation remained until his death.

Morris's relationship with Jane worsened and even a holiday to Bad Ems in Germany in 1869, where she was able to take the spa waters in an effort to help relieve a reccurring and unnamed malady, did not seem to help. Caricatures drawn by Burne-Jones and Rossetti at the time give some insight into the separate lives they were beginning to lead (cat. nos. A.15–18). Morris was a bon viveur, he appreciated conversation, good food and wine, possessing what Jane described as '…that precious gift of enjoyment [which] is a gift and not an acquirement'. Burne-Jones's sketches concentrate on these social activities, most of which do not appear to have included Jane. Rossetti's drawings, on the other hand, are much more savage and concentrate on what he saw as Morris's egocentric behaviour and lack of attention to his wife. Both men emphasise Morris's preoccupation with poetry at the time, especially *The Earthly Paradise*.

While selecting stories for *The Earthly Paradise*, Morris first studied the Icelandic sagas and he soon became fascinated by the language and history of Iceland. From 1868 he worked on Icelandic translations with the scholar Eiríkr Magnússon, and in July 1871 he made the first of two visits to Iceland accompanied by Magnússon and Charles Faulkner, chronicling his six-week tour of the island in a journal (cat.no.A.19). Already enfeebled emotionally by the problems at home, Morris was deeply affected by the remote landscape and the people, and his comparison of the simplicity of life there and so-called civilised sophisticated British society roused in him his first political yearnings '…the most grinding poverty is a trifling evil compared with the inequality of classes', was how he summed it up in 1883.

Before travelling to Iceland, Morris had signed a joint tenancy with Rossetti on Kelmscott Manor, a sixteenth-century Oxfordshire manor house, and while he was away Jane, Jenny, May and Rossetti had spent much of the summer together there. The arrangement, under the circumstances, seems difficult to understand and suggests that Morris had decided to accept the situation rather than the emotional and social drawbacks that any alternative would bring. Much of his unhappiness

Fig. 3 A photograph taken about 1885 of May Morris in the grounds at Kelmscott, the Manor can be seen in the background.

at the time was expressed in letters to Georgie Burne-Jones, herself the victim of marital infidelity, and she remained his closest confidante throughout his life.

Kelmscott Manor became Morris's spiritual home and he visited it whenever possible, indulging in his hobby of fishing (cat.no.A.22) and enjoying the garden and surrounding countryside. However, life in London became busier and busier. He took up again his interest in calligraphy, an art form he had practised since the 1850s and to which he now devoted Sunday mornings. Ruskin described his gift for illumination as being 'as great as any thirteenth century draughtsman', and in all Morris produced approximately 1,500 illuminated and manuscript pages. A large number date from this time, including his own 'A Book of Verse' (cat.no.N.5) and, with Burne-Jones, exquisite versions of the *Odes of Horace* and *Virgil's Aeneids* (cat. nos. N.13–14). He also continued to work on Icelandic stories and published a number of translations, including *The Saga of Gunnlaug Worm-Tongue* (1869) and *The Story of Frithiof the Bold* (1871), both of which also appeared in calligraphic form.

In 1872 the family had moved from Queen Square to Horrington House in Chiswick High Street, which provided a more congenial home for Jane and the girls and also left extra space for the work of the firm. Morris's days were totally preoccupied in designing, learning manufacturing techniques and directing the business and workshops. He was now in full control and the inevitable split between partners, with Rossetti, Madox Brown and P.P.Marshall resenting his domination and Webb, Faulkner and Burne-Jones supporting him, finally occurred. In 1875 the firm was reorganised under Morris's sole direction and re-named Morris & Company. Rossetti had given up the tenancy of Kelmscott Manor in 1874, so now the break between the two men was complete. Further links with Morris's past life were also severed with the resignation of his directorship of Devon Great Consols.

Commercial Success, Politics and Conservation, 1875–85

The next ten years of Morris's life saw an even greater frenzy of activity than had been achieved before, including his debut as a public figure. So far his reputation had been based on his literary and artistic achievements and although these areas of activity continued to develop, other interests demanded an increasing amount of his time.

His most celebrated publication of the period was the four-part poem, *Sigurd the Volsung* (1876), described by George Bernard Shaw as 'The greatest epic since Homer', and a year later he was asked to stand for election as Professor of Poetry at Oxford, which, although he refused, gives some measure of his standing in literary circles.

This was also Morris's busiest period as a pattern designer. All forms of furnishing textiles – printed and woven cloth, lino and machine-woven carpeting – were added to the range of goods available, and these were made by contractors to Morris's very precise specifications. Morris's attitude towards production became more commercial and the firm prospered. A new shop was opened in fashionable Oxford Street in 1877, and was able to supply most of the furnishings needed in the home. Commissions to decorate the homes of a number of influential clients saw Morris and Webb working on houses in different parts of Britain.

Morris's expertise as a practising designer and knowledgeable art historian were also in demand. He already acted in an unofficial capacity as an adviser to the South Kensington Museums, and in 1876 was appointed an examiner of drawings at the School of Art established there. The first of many lectures on art and design was given in the winter of 1877 to the Trades Guild of Learning in London and entitled 'The Decorative Arts'.

In June 1876 Morris penned his first political letter to the Press. This concerned Turkish aggression in the Balkans, and he was particularly agitated by the British Government's lack of support for Bulgaria, where massacres had been reported. The letter, which was signed by the 'Author of the "Earthly Paradise"', created some interest and within a short time Morris was set on a course of action not only to improve the situation in Europe but also on his own doorstep. His conversion was gradual, however, and from membership of the Eastern Question Association he became Treasurer of the National Liberal League in 1879. His gradual disillusionment with Parliamentary politics brought on by British imperialistic activity in Ireland and against the Boers in Transvaal persuaded Morris to look outside organised politics for his answers, and by 1883 he had declared himself a socialist and joined the only existing radical organisation, the Democratic Federation.

Morris's public agitation at the time also involved his distress at the increased restoration of some of Britain's most significant early buildings. He was first alerted to this on seeing G.E.Street's restorations of Burford parish church, not far from Kelmscott, in the summer of 1876. His letter to *The Athenaeum* the following March protested at this general trend and in the same month the first meeting of the Society for the Protection of Ancient Buildings took place, with Morris as Secretary. The Society organised a system of registering and monitoring buildings in need of structural repair and offered advice. It also acted as a protest group against work planned or already in progress. Over the years Morris personally became involved in a number of national and international *causes célèbres*, including Canterbury Cathedral, St Mark's in Venice and Westminster Hall in London.

Although Morris continued to holiday in the countryside as frequently as possible, the importance of London as a base for his new public life increased. Despite Jane's diminishing attachment to Rossetti, elements of home life continued to worry Morris. In 1876 Jenny developed epilepsy, then seen as an incurable illness. Understandably, both parents were deeply distressed, especially Morris as it was inherited from his family. Morris's great affection for his daughters, especially the invalid Jenny, can be seen in the frequent letters he wrote to them. These also provide an invaluable source of information on his day-to-day life when away from home.

Neither Morris nor Jane enjoyed living in Horrington House, and in 1878 a lease was taken on a flat-fronted five-storied Georgian property overlooking the Thames at Hammersmith (cat.no.A.25). Called The Retreat, Morris soon re-named it Kelmscott House in honour of his country home. It was from this house that Morris's public activities for the rest of his life were centred. Within a short time of moving in he set up looms and produced his first tapestry and hand-knotted carpets, and with time it was to provide the meeting place for political discussion.

The need for greater space at Queen Square, combined with Morris's constant irritation at the mistakes made by contractors manufacturing goods for the firm made the search for new premises urgent. Morris longed for a country situation which would provide more space and pleasant surroundings. After visiting a few potential sites, his friend the potter William De Morgan found Merton Abbey, a disused factory on the River Wandle near Wimbledon, not far from London. In June 1881 production was moved there, and with the setting up of the stained-glass workshop, dye vats, printing tables and looms, Morris was at last able to have full control over the firm's work.

Morris's new radicalism also affected his attitude to art and its manufacture, although in the matter of making business profitable he was not able to provide the short hours and increased pay that he advocated for workers. George Wardle and the four sub-managers of Morris & Co. shared directly in the profits of the business, with the colour-mixer and foreman-dyer receiving bonuses. The rest of the staff received either fixed daily rates or piece-work: '…two or three people about the place are of no use to the business and are kept on the live-and-let-live principle', Morris explained in a letter of 1884, an indication that he was 'a benevolent rather than grasping employer' as defined by Harvey and Press. Some women and boys were employed by the firm, mostly for carpet knotting and tapestry weaving, and the works offered the only apprenticeships available for such work in Britain, with the boys living in a house on the site under the care of a housekeeper.

It is difficult to know how Morris found time for writing his political articles and for giving lectures and attending the various meetings of the Social Democratic Federation (as it became known), many of which were organised outside London. Yet his involvement proved pivotal in 1884, when a split in the leadership forced him and a number of supporters to resign and set up a new group which they called the Socialist League. Divisions also dogged this organisation from the start but Morris endeavoured to make it work. He financed the League's newspaper, *Commonweal*, which first appeared in February 1885 and he contributed articles to it for the next five years. He also became a frequent participant in street-corner oratory and on marches, constantly chiding authority who frequently turned a blind eye to his antics knowing that his fame would attract more publicity than was desirable. He was finally arrested for obstruction in July 1886 and let off with a fine, much to the amusement of the press.

The events of 'Bloody Sunday' on 13 November 1887, in which the police attacked a large contingent of marchers at Trafalgar Square, disillusioned many members of the Socialist League and membership declined. Morris remained an active member of its Hammersmith Branch which, in 1890, was re-named the Hammersmith Socialist Society. This group, which met in the coach house at Kelmscott House, became a forum for discussion and both Jenny and May Morris took part. In the last years of his life Morris made a number of attempts to reunite the various cells of the warring socialist movement. His efforts can be seen to have contributed to the foundation of the Independent Labour Party in 1892, but despite being asked to join the leadership of this new important organisation Morris insisted on remaining an independent, anti-establishment force.

Having established the firm at Merton Abbey and supervised the various sections of the workshops for the first few years of production, he began to visit less frequently leaving matters in the charge of his assistant Henry Dearle, his works manager George Wardle, his daughter May and his two business partners, F. and R. Smith. His last new textile designs were shown at the first Arts and Crafts Exhibition held at the New Gallery, Regent Street, in 1888. He continued his interest in tapestry, and for the last five years of his life was involved with Burne-Jones and Dearle on the planning, designing and weaving of a series of panels based on one of his favourite Arthurian themes, the Search for the Holy Grail.

Morris published a number of prose narratives during the last years of his life and two appeared posthumously. All are set in an imaginary past or future and, in the case of *News from Nowhere* (1890), in particular, greatly inspired by his own socialist aspirations. This book is Morris's vision of a simple and beautiful world in which art or 'work-pleasure' is demanded, practised and enjoyed by all. Although intended to be the future, it inevitably looks back to a utopian, medieval-inspired setting of Morris's own dreams. Not all of these publications were politically based, and in the case of *The Wood Beyond the World* (1894) he hoped it would be judged simply as a readable, enjoyable story.

Books had always been important to Morris as a reader, a poet, an author, a scribe and a publisher. As early as 1865 he had attempted to produce an illustrated version of the story of 'Cupid and Psyche' from *The Earthly Paradise*, and an ambition to print his own books dates from this time. This was finally achieved in 1891 with the foundation of the Kelmscott Press, set up in premises at 16 Upper Mall very close to Morris's London home. His simple intentions were described in a later lecture: 'I began printing books with the hope of producing some which would have a definite aim of beauty...they should be easy to read and not dazzle the eye, or trouble the intellect of the reader by eccentricity of form in the letters.'

Morris designed all of the sixty-six books issued by the Press, including typefaces, initial letters and borders, and Burne-Jones drew most of the illustrations. The first edition published was *The Story of the Glittering Plain*, one of twenty-three titles by Morris himself. Distributed by subscription, the undertaking proved far more popular that at first anticipated, with 21,000 books printed in all. *The Works of Geoffrey Chaucer*, which was finished just before Morris's death is, without doubt, the Press's masterpiece and it is unfortunate that *Froissart's Chronicles*, the second largest projected undertaking, was never realised.

For many years Morris had attempted to improve both urban and rural environments through his involvement with such groups as the Kyrle Society, a forerunner of the National Trust. In his last years he concentrated his energies on preserving the countryside. In *Under The Elm Tree, or Thoughts on the Countryside*, published in 1891, Morris articulates his deep feeling for nature which had provided both inspiration and pleasure throughout his life; one of his last public campaigns was an attempt to halt the felling of his beloved hornbeam trees in Epping Forest. In 1895 he made a pilgrimage there with a few friends. The brevity of the entry in his diary for 7 May very adequately reflects his feelings for the area, 'to Epping Forest with Webb, Lethaby, Walker, Ellis, Cockerell, nothing else' (see cat.no.F.14b).

Morris had been in bad health since 1891, for many years suffering from gout, but increasing kidney problems, diabetes and, as Fiona MacCarthy has recently suggested, signs of his inherited epilepsy proved far more debilitating. By the summer of 1895 he had become very weak but still insisted, whenever possible, on attending engagements. In December he caught a chill speaking at the funeral of the Russian revolutionary, Sergius Stepniak, which turned tubercular. He continued to write and attend to Kelmscott Press work and his last political speech was given in January 1896 at Holborn Town Hall. Kelmscott Manor was visited in April and May and Morris noted in his diary how medieval the garden was looking there. His doctors recommended a trip to Folkstone to take the air and in July Morris undertook a four-week cruise to Norway, travelling as far north as Trondheim.

Following his return in August, Morris hardly left Kelmscott House although he was constantly attended by his many friends. He was now very weak and even the playing of virginals by Arnold Dolmetsch on 21 September was not able to lift his spirits. A short walk to the garden the following day brought on a haemorrhage. He died on the morning of Saturday 3 October and Jane, who had been preparing herself for some time declared 'I am not unhappy though it is a terrible thing, for I have been with him since I first knew anything'.

Morris was buried in Kelmscott on 6 October, his plain coffin being transported from the station to the church on an open horse-drawn cart decorated with branches of bay. Philip Webb designed his simple tombstone which he affectionately described as 'a roof for the old man'.

Fig.4 *Home Again,* a caricature by Edward Burne-Jones, 1871 (cat.no.A.21).

A.1 *Quinti Horatii Flacci Opera* (The Odes of Horace)

Published by Whittaker, 1844
14.0 x 9.25 x 1.75 cm
Inscribed with various notes including the date
'March 21 1851'
Sanford and Helen Berger Collection

Morris's earliest known book. He attended the newly founded
Marlborough College from February 1848, when he was
thirteen years old, until the end of the Christmas term 1851,
when he was withdrawn following a rebellion in the school.
He claims to have neither enjoyed nor learned from his time
there describing it as a 'boy factory'. The notes in this book
show how he compensated for this with typical schoolboy
humour. The book has a number of pencil and ink drawings
added by him. As well as his name and the date 'March 21
1851' (presumably when he was given or bought the book),
the endpapers show a pencil drawing of a church steeple
and a man with a wooden leg holding up a placard reading
'W.Morris His Horace'. On page 73 the ownership is repeated
with the inscription 'Bill Morrace is Orace'.

Following Marlborough, Morris was tutored for a year in
Walthamstow by the Reverend Frederick Guy in order to
prepare him for the Oxford entrance examination. It was
from the time with Guy that Morris developed his great love
and knowledge of the classical literature. Burne-Jones
recounts sitting next to Morris for the Oxford matriculation
examination and seeing him finish a Horace paper early, so
confident was he of his subject. This work remained a
favourite and in 1874 he chose the subject for one of his most
beautiful illuminated manuscripts.   LP

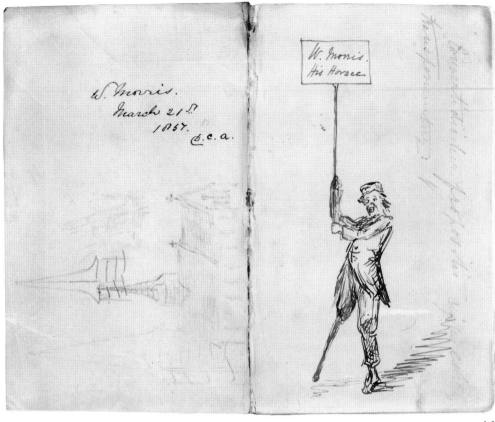

A.1

A.2 *The Oxford and Cambridge Magazine*

Published by Bell and Daldy, Number 5, May 1856
22.2 x 14.5 cm
William Morris Gallery
(London Borough of Waltham Forest) (K.689)

The publication of a magazine of 'mainly Tales, Poetry,
friendly critiques and social articles' was first suggested by
Richard Watson Dixon, a member of the Oxford set
(*Memorials*, I, p.115).

Burne-Jones described the venture in a letter to his cousin
Maria Choyce in the autumn of 1855, 'We have set ourselves
to work...and banded ourselves into an exclusive
Brotherhood of seven. Mr Morris is proprietor. The expense
will fall very heavily upon him, I fear, for it cannot be published under £500 per annum...he hopes not to lose more
than £300, but even that is a great deal' (*Memorials*, I, p.121).

The first issue of the magazine appeared on 1 January 1856
under Morris's editorship, a few months after he passed his
Oxford Finals. An initial 750 copies were printed and good
sales led to a further 250. For the second issue Morris handed
the job of editor to William Fulford. Although anonymously,
Morris contributed a number of articles (notably on Amiens
Cathedral), poems and prose stories for ten of the twelve
issues that were published including 'Riding Together' in
this, the May edition.   LP

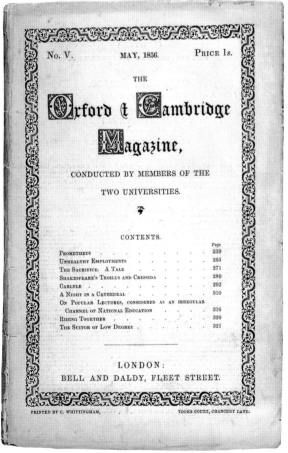

A.2

A.3 *The Hayfield*

Ford Madox Brown, 1855–6
Oil on panel, 24.0 x 33.2 cm
Signed, dated and inscribed:
'F. MADOX BROWN, HENDON 1855'
Tate Gallery, London (T01920)

'Yesterday', Madox Brown noted in his diary for Sunday 24 August 1856, 'Rossetti brought his ardent admirer Morris of Oxford who bought my little hay field for 40 gns, this was kind of Gaggy.' (Surtees, 1981). It was their first meeting. This moonscape was one of three small landscapes of the mid-1850s which explored differing effects of light, in this case the 'greeny greyness of the unmade hay…with lovely violet shadows and long shades of the trees thrown athwart all and melting away one tint into another imperceptibly…' It had been finally retouched that summer and was the most recent work available for sale. The other two landscapes were sold, but Morris may have seen some more expensive earlier works including the great *Jesus Washing Peter's Feet* (Tate Gallery, London).

In 1860 the artist got *The Hayfield* back in exchange 'for the work to be done at the Red House' but ultimately, in 1864, for cash, as this project evaporated (Madox Brown Account Book). He later sold the painting to Colonel Gillum. MB

A.5 *The Tune of Seven Towers*

Dante Gabriel Rossetti, 1857
Watercolour, 31.4 x 36.5 cm
Inscribed: 'DGR [in monogram] 1857'
Tate Gallery, London (3059)

Before he knew Morris, Rossetti had already started to replace Dantesque with Arthurian and ballad images. The poems and tales he had encountered in the *Oxford and Cambridge Magazine*, yet more his meeting with Morris in the summer of 1856, further stimulated this trend. Some of his new, brilliant, bizarre watercolours were made for Morris, who bought five examples including this, which he was desperately trying to finish for the exhibition of Pre-Raphaelite pictures at Russell Place in June 1857.

Morris's poem of the same name was written for it and appears in *The Defence of Guenevere and Other Poems*, published in 1858. From the endless flow of information filling English journals during the Crimean War (1854–6), Rossetti may have plucked the romantic name of Seven Towers which was a real fortress in Constantinople where the Sultan imprisoned foreign noblemen who displeased him. The symbolic scene refers to Rossetti's relationship with the sick Lizzie Siddal who posed for the seated female figure. The decorative details of the painting show the type of early furnishings being made at the time for Red Lion Square, including a chair with a box overhead and wall decoration and bed hangings of similar design to the early *If I Can* embroidered panels (cat. no. M.4). RW

A.4 *April Love*

Arthur Hughes, 1856
Oil on canvas, 88.9 x 49.5 cm
Signed and dated
Tate Gallery, London (2476)

This painting was exhibited at the Royal Academy in 1856 (578). It was greatly admired by Ruskin who had tried unsuccessfully to persuade his father to buy it beforehand, and in his *Academy Notes* he described it as 'Exquisite in every way; lovely in colour, most subtle in the quivering expression of the lips, and sweetness of the tender face, shaken, like a leaf by winds upon its dew, and hestitating back into peace'.

Morris was keen to buy the picture and Georgiana Burne-Jones recounts that 'after brooding upon the subject for a few days made up his mind to possess it'. As he was still spending his weeks in Oxford he asked Burne-Jones to 'nobble it' for him.

At the end of his life Arthur Hughes remembered Burne-Jones arriving at his studio with Morris's cheque, 'My chief feeling then was surprise at an Oxford student buying pictures'.

To buy this painting was a tremendous assertion by Morris of his freedom as patron to buy what moved him and it was also an indication of his readiness for love.   RW

A.4

A.6

A.7

A.10

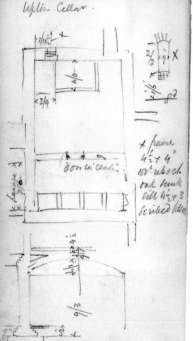

A.9

A.6 *Jane Burden*

Dante Gabriel Rossetti, October 1857
Pencil, 47.6 x 33.0 cm
Inscribed: 'D.G.R. Oxon primo delt Oct 1857' and 'JB.AETAT XVII'
Society of Antiquaries of London (Kelmscott Manor)

Rossetti was very careful to inscribe the sitter's age, the month and year on this, his most precious first drawing of her. It was completed soon after Jane was first encountered in the theatre of the Old Music Room in Oxford and persuaded to pose for the group then working on the Oxford Union murals.

Jane was soon to supplant Lizzie Siddal as the subject of many of Rossetti's paintings and poems. Yet this is not yet the supreme aesthetic beauty first seen in *The Blue Silk Dress* of 1867–8, now at Kelmscott Manor, though she can be recognised as the same girl depicted in Morris's contemporary drawing (cat. no. G.8).
Exhib. 1934 (335)   RW

A.7 *Jane Burden*

Herbert Watkins, Regent Street, 1858
Albumen print, 8.5 x 5.8 cm
V&A (Ph.1736-1939)   Given by Dr Robert Steele

A studio photograph of Jane Burden taken during a trip to London from Oxford in 1858. Her engagement to William Morris was announced in the spring of 1858 when she was eighteen years of age and this photograph may have been taken at the time. Their marriage took place on 26 April 1859 at St Michael's church, Oxford.

Given by May Morris's executor, the photograph originally belonged to the Morris family and is part of an album assembled by Gordon Bottomley (see cat. nos. A.8, 14).   LP

A.8 *Jane Burden*

Photographer unknown, *c.*1858
Albumen print, 9.3 x 5.9 cm
V&A (Ph.1735-1939)   Given by Dr Robert Steele
FOR ILLUSTRATION SEE FIG 1, PAGE 15

Photograph of Jane Burden leaning against the back of a chair. This is not a conventional studio photograph but has been posed, probably to be used as reference for a drawing or painting. Morris's first drawing of Jane in 1857 (cat. no. G.8) closely resembles her in this photograph and both works of art have the same provenance. Furthermore, Jane's mode of dress, conventional and inexpensive Victorian attire, suggests this picture dates from before her marriage and contrasts sharply with the sophisticated, artistic dresses she wore in 1865 for photographs posed by Rossetti (cat. no. A.14).

The donor was May Morris's executor and the photograph was originally owned by the Morris family and is part of an album assembled by Gordon Bottomley (see cat. no. A.7, 14)   LP

A.9 Notebook

Philip Webb, *c.*1859
Pencil and pen and ink, 30.0 x 8.0 cm (open)
Private Collection

A notebook containing details and rough sketches of Red House and the surrounding area. It includes a plan for the cellar (titled 'Upton Cellar'), a list of eighty trees in the surrounding orchards (all but four are identified, with apples, plums, cherries, damsons and hawthorns). Mackail claims that the house 'had been planned with such care that hardly a tree in the orchard had to be cut down; apples fell in at the window as they stood open on hot autumn nights'. The notebook also includes a receipt written out by Edward Russell, a local tradesman, in acknowledgement of £4 14s. 6d. paid by Morris for a wattle fence 'up to Plum Tree opposite Pantry of House'.

A.11

A.12

The writing is uncharacteristically untidy and this is likely to be the pocket book Webb used when visiting the Bexleyheath site when Red House was under construction.

In a note written at the time by Burne-Jones to his father (*Memorials*, I, p.211) he wrote 'I hate the country – apples only keep me in good spirits – Topsy's garden is perfectly laden with them'. LP

A.10 *Morris Presenting Miss Burden with a Ring*

Dante Gabriel Rossetti, 1857
Pencil on toned paper stained with various pigments, 35.8 x 25.4 cm
Birmingham Museums and Art Gallery
(verso of 273'04) Presented by Subscribers

Rossetti took with him to Oxford in August 1857 studies for his contribution to the Oxford Union murals *Lancelot's Dream of the Sanc Grael*, in which Queen Guenevere tempts him from the apple tree. This drawing of Morris giving a ring to Janey was made on the back of one of them. It has been thought to be an engagement ring but this is unlikely as it is being placed on her right hand. She looks down admiring and pleased: Morris is anxious that she should be, so it is more likely simply to have been a present, possibly brought back by Morris from his trip to Manchester at the end of September.

The drawing was originally owned by H.T.Dunn, Murray Marks and Charles Fairfax Murray. RW

A.11 *Red Lion Mary*

Dante Gabriel Rossetti, 1856–9
Pencil on toned paper, 12.4 x 8.8 cm
Inscribed in pencil, verso, by ?Charles Fairfax Murray: 'Mrs Nicholson Red Lion Mary the servant of W Morris and E B J at Red Lion Square'
Birmingham Museums and Art Gallery (250'04)
Presented by Subscribers

A drawing of Mary Nicholson ('Red Lion Mary'), the servant to Morris and Burne-Jones when they lived at 17 Red Lion Square between November 1856 and the spring of 1859. Jane Morris said this was a good likeness.

Georgiana Burne-Jones claimed her 'originality all but equalled that of the young men, and she understood them and their ways thoroughly. Their rough and ready hospitality was seconded by her unfailing good temper' (*Memorials*, I, p.169). Her friendly and often humorous rapport with Burne-Jones and the frequent visitor, Rossetti, did not include Morris. However, she seems to have been happy to work for him 'though he was so short-tempered I seemed so necessary to him at all times, and felt myself his man Friday' (op.cit.p.171). Her work not only included keeping house and occupants clean but delivering messages and embroidering hangings to be used on the walls of the lodgings. LP

A.12 Study of Morris as *David as King* for Llandaff Cathedral

Dante Gabriel Rossetti, *c*.1861
Pencil, 24.5 x 22.3 cm
Birmingham Museums and Art Gallery (261'04)
Presented by Subscribers

Rossetti, commissioned by John Pollard Seddon (1827–1906) to produce a reredos in Llandaff Cathedral which he was restoring, took some time deciding on the subject. *The Seed of David* was chosen in which, in the right-hand compartment, Morris appeared sumptuously robed and crowned as King David – and Jane's face replaced that of the original sitter Ruth Herbert, an actress admired by Rossetti, in the centre panel as the Madonna. Rossetti started work in 1858 and the painting was finished in 1864 but probably retouched in 1869.

Two of the three existing studies of Jane for the triptych are dated 1861 (one has an additional note of September) so it is likely that this drawing was done at the same time.

The drawing was originally owned by William Michael Rossetti and Charles Fairfax Murray.

Exhib. 1934 (331) RW

WILLIAM MORRIS.
Ellis and Green,   London.

A.13

Mʳ Morris reading poems to Mʳ Burne Jones

A.15

A.14

A.13 *William Morris*

Ellis & Green, London, *c.*1868–70
Carte-de-visite albumen print, 10.2 x 6.4 cm
V&A (Ph.1780-1939)   Given by Dr Robert Steele

One of the few conventionally formal photographs taken of Morris. This is the source of a small watercolour of Morris by Charles Fairfax Murray on the title-page of 'A book of Verse' (cat. no. N.5). A second version is in the National Portrait Gallery (NPG 3652)

Given by May Morris's executor, the photograph belonged to the Morris family.   LP

A.14 Album of photographs of Jane Morris

John R. Parsons, July 1865; later prints by Emery Walker
Original albumen prints with later gelatin-silver prints from the originals; album 33.0 x 51.0 cm open; original prints 19.6 x 13 cm; copy prints 25.7 x 20.3 cm

V&A (Ph.1735 to 1752-1939)
Given by Dr Robert Steele

Album of photographs of Jane Morris posed by D.G. Rossetti and taken in his garden at ' Tudor House', 16 Cheyne Walk, Chelsea. A letter from Rossetti to Jane postmarked 5 July 1865 ('Sunday Night') and stating 'The Photographer is coming at 11 on Wednesday', is in the National Art Library. The photographer, John Parsons, was a London studio professional recommended to Rossetti by his close friend Charles Augustus Howell.

Jane is shown in a number of different artistic poses standing, sitting and lying on a couch with backdrop decoration of a Japanese screen and awning. She is shown wearing two different artistic dresses, one belted and the other loose from the shoulders. These also appear in a number of later Rossetti paintings of Jane.

The album was assembled before 1933 by Gordon Bottomley for May Morris from framed prints owned by

William Morris. It is bound in *Bourne,* an early twentieth-century Morris & Co. printed cotton designed by J. H. Dearle. Each photograph is shown in the album with a later gelatin-silver print produced from the original negative by Emery Walker sometime before 1930. The negatives for the latter are in St Bride's Printing Library.

May Morris clearly felt these photographs to be of a personal nature, and a letter from her to Sydney Cockerell at the the time of the Museum's 1934 exhibition states her objection to Rossetti's photographs of her mother being reproduced and sold.   LP

A.15 Two caricatures of William Morris reading to Edward Burne-Jones

Edward Burne-Jones, *c.*1865
Pencil, pencil pen and ink,
7.5 x 9.3 cm, 9.3 x 12.6 cm
V&A (E.450-1976); British Museum (1939-5-13-12)
British Museum example inscribed with title
Given by Dr Robert Steele
SEE ALSO FIG 14, PAGE 44

After Morris had moved from Red House to Queen Square he got back into the habit of writing again and then reading what he had just written to the company in the evenings. His output at this time was epic both in subject and scale; *The Earthly Paradise* has over 40,000 lines. Morris chanted rather than declaimed his poetry. Georgie Burne-Jones wrote that she remembered '...often falling asleep to the steady rhythm of the reading voice, or biting my fingers and stabbing myself with pins in order to keep awake'. This drawing shows her husband failing to take such measures.

One of these drawings was originally owned by Jane Morris. The other belonged to Maria Zambaco, a sculptress with whom Burne-Jones was romantically entangled between 1868 and 1871.   SA/LP

A.16 *The Bard and Petty Tradesman*

Dante Gabriel Rossetti, 1868
Pen and brown ink, 11.4 x 17.9 cm
Inscribed with title and 'No 1 London',
'Published as Lord Campbell's Act forbids. One Penny'
British Museum (1939-5-13-5)
Given by Dr Robert Steele

Drawn on a letter to Jane Morris in May 1868 in which Rossetti writes 'I shall keep Wedy the 27th sacred to the Earthly Paradise. Will you tell Top that my soul expands to meet "large paper" but that meanwhile I extend my patronage forthwith to him and Ellis as one of the average public'.

An edition of twenty-five 'large-or-fine-paper' copies of the first part of Morris's *The Earthly Paradise* was published by F.S. Ellis soon after the book's initial publication in April 1868. Another letter from Rossetti to Jane, dated 7 May 1868, repeats this nickname for Morris as 'the bard and P.T. – I will not indulge him with his favourite title', by which he meant 'poet and designer'. The lower inscription refers to Lord Justice Campbell's 1857 act against obscene publications.   LP

A.17 Five caricatures of William Morris

Edward Burne-Jones, *c*.1870

a *Sed Poeta Turpiter Sitiens Canescit*
Pen and ink, 16.9 x 10.2 cm
Further inscription: 'To J.M. from E.B.J. the above
will be home about 2 tonight'
British Museum (1939-5-13-13)
Given by Dr Robert Steele

b *Morris Eating*
Pen and ink, 3.7 x 7.5 cm
British Museum (1939-5-13-14)
Given by Dr Robert Steele
FOR ILLUSTRATION SEE PAGE 376

c *Grace before meat Disgrace after meat*
Pen and ink, 15.0 x 11.2 cm
Inscribed with title
British Museum (1939-5-13-15)
Given by Dr Robert Steele
FOR DETAIL SEE PAGE 368

d *Back View of William Morris*
Pencil, 18.0 x 11.5 cm
V&A (E.449-1976)
FOR ILLUSTRATION SEE PAGE 378

e *Morris Playing Ping Pong*
Pencil, 10.1 x 15.5 cm
Private Collection
FOR ILLUSTRATION SEE CONTENTS PAGE

These drawings were produced from and for a circle of
close friends by an artist with a sharp eye. They are some
of many. The subject-matter of the untitled example
(A.17d) has been variously interpreted as Morris the out-
cast, one of many comments on Morris's increasing girth
at this period, or Morris urinating. The last is not unfeasi-
ble. Behind the badinage, and the rough and tumble of
an almost communal life, jokes had a cutting edge or
even a certain cruelty with Morris often cast as victim.
This drawing was owned by Maria Zambaco.   SA/LP

A.18 Three caricatures

Dante Gabriel Rossetti, 1869

Deeply affected by the close liaison of Janey and
Rossetti and worried by Janey's increasing bad health,
in the late summer of 1869 Morris took his wife to Bad
Ems, a fashionable spa town a few miles from Koblenz
in Germany so that she could take the waters. By all
accounts the six weeks spent there were miserable for
both of them. A group of caricatures sent by Rossetti in
letters to Jane give further insight into the relationship
between the three participants in what was to become,
for a time, an unhappy *ménage à trois*.

a *The M's at Ems*
Pen and brown ink, 10.9 x 17.6 cm
Inscribed with title
British Museum (1939-5-13-1)
Given by Dr Robert Steele

Enclosed in a letter dated 21 July 1869 with the comment 'The accompanying cartoon will prepare you for
the worst – which ever that may be the seven tumblers
or the 7 volumes'. The drawing shows Jane drinking the
spa waters while her husband reads to her from *The
Earthly Paradise*.

A.16

A 18a

A18c

A.18b

A.17a

b *Resolution or, The Infant Hercules*
Pen and brown ink, 20.5 x 13.2 cm
Dated: '14.8.69', and inscribed with title
British Museum (1939-5-13-8)
Given by Dr Robert Steele

Enclosed in a letter with the following description:
'Conceive if your cure were now to proceed so rapidly
that there remained a glut of surplus baths, and Topsy
were induced to express a thanksgiving frame of mind
by that act which is next to godliness! Give him my
love, and if he wishes to be revenged for the apposite
diaphragm – i.e. diagram, let him know that I have
bought the works of the poet Banting, that "idle singer
of a too full day".' In 1863 William Banting published *A
Letter on Corpulence* in which he advocated dieting to
lose weight. 'The idle singer of an empty day' is a quotation from *The Earthly Paradise*.

c *The German Lesson*
Pen and brown ink, 14.4 x 17.9 cm
Inscribed with title
British Museum (1939-5-13-2)
Given by Dr Robert Steele

This caricature accompanied a letter of 4 August 1869
with the comment 'I fear that the legitimate hopeless-
ness of the pictorial and ideal Topsy has somewhat
communicated itself to the german maid in the cartoon…The poetry and philosophy of the subject are I
hope complete, while you will see that even Scriptural
analogy has not been neglected'.   LP

No 85

A.20

A.19 'A Journal of Travel in Iceland'

William Morris, 1871
Vellum binding, hand-written,
33.6 x 22.7 cm closed, 33.6 x 48.0 cm open
Inscribed: 'Georgie from W.M., July 8th 1873'
Fitzwilliam Museum, Cambridge
Given by Sir Philip Burne-Jones and
Mrs Margaret Mackail
NOT ILLUSTRATED

This journal chronicles Morris's first trip to Iceland begun on Thursday 6 July 1871, when Morris, Charles Faulkner and Eiríkr Magnússon left King's Cross Station 'in a somewhat adventurous spirit' according to May Morris. An additional sheet of notes lists Morris's requirements for the journey.

The diary describes their progress through Scotland and the boat trip to Iceland via the Faroe Islands. Morris notes the places he visited (mostly on pony back), the weather and the people he met during his six-weeks' tour where he was called *skald*, or travelling poet.

The journal was rewritten and finished in June 1873 and this fair copy was given to Georgiana Burne-Jones. Despite Jane Morris's opposition to its publication 'Mr Morris did not think it well enough written as it stands…' (letter to S. Cockerell, NAL), sections were published and it appeared in its entirety in the *Collected Works* in 1911.

Morris discovered the Icelandic sagas while looking for tales to include in *The Earthly Paradise* and in 1868 was introduced to Eiríkr Magnússon. Together they worked on a number of the stories, with Magnússon providing literal translations from the Icelandic and Morris transposing these into Icelandic-English prose. The journey had an enormous spiritual effect on him, coming at a time of great emotional stress in his marriage. It was also to prove a turning point for him as a political thinker. He returned to the island only once more, in 1873, but retained a lifelong interest. LP

A.20 *Study of Jane Morris in Icelandic Dress*

Dante Gabriel Rossetti, 1872
Pencil, mount size 29.8 x 26.5 cm
Inscribed in pencil: 'No.85'
Fitzwilliam Museum, Cambridge
Given by the Friends of the Fitzwilliam Museum (835)

A sensual drawing of Jane Morris, possibly made at Kelmscott Manor. She wears an embroidered Icelandic smock which William Morris is likely to have brought back as a present from his first trip to Iceland in 1871. LP

A.21 *Home Again*

Edward Burne-Jones, 1871
Pen and ink, 17.5 x 11.5 cm
Mr and Mrs Christopher Hampton
FOR ILLUSTRATION SEE FIG 4, PAGE 22

Although not inscribed, this caricature is known by this title and is said to depict a tired, bored or possibly inebriated Morris recently returned from his first Icelandic trip. The representation of a sprig at the top of the drawing is said to signify that this was one of Burne-Jones's favourites.

The drawing was purchased from Sotheby's Belgravia on 29 June 1976 (336) and was originally owned by Maria Zambaco. LP

A.22 *William Morris Fishing in a Punt*

Dante Gabriel Rossetti
Dated 'Kelmscott 11 Sept 1871' with inscription 'Enter Morris moored in a punt, And Jacks and Tenches exeunt.'
Pen and brown ink, 18.2 x 11.0 cm
British Museum (1939-5-13-9)
Given by Dr Robert Steele

Morris loved to fish, and trips to Kelmscott gave him the opportunity to indulge in what was his only work-free pastime. In a letter from Rossetti to William Bell Scott written at Kelmscott on 15 September he mentions Morris's recent return from Iceland. 'One day he was here he went for a day's fishing in our punt, the chief result of which was a sketch I made…' LP

A.23 The Morris and Burne-Jones families

Frederick Hollyer, 1874
Platinotype photograph, 14.0 x 13.1 cm sight
V&A (Ph.1813-1939)
Given by Dr Robert Steele

One of a set of photographs of the Morris and Burne-Jones families taken in the garden of The Grange, the Burne-Jones's house on the North End Road in Fulham. LEFT TO RIGHT: Burne-Jones's father, Edward Jones, on a visit from Birmingham; Margaret, Edward, Philip and Georgiana Burne-Jones. Standing are May and William with Jane and Jenny Morris seated in front.

Hollyer took up photography about 1860 and became one of the most popular professionals within fashionable artistic and literary circles. He produced portraits of many eminent figures of the day as well as house exterior and interior views. From the mid-1870s he collaborated with Burne-Jones on a series of commercial reproductions of the painter's work and it is probable that his Pembroke Square studio was responsible for providing photographic services for Morris & Co., including the production of tapestry and stained-glass cartoons.

In the 1890s Hollyer became a member of The Linked Ring, an exhibiting society formed in opposition to the Photographic Society of Great Britain.   LP

A.24 William Morris in hat and working smock

Photographer unknown, *c*.1876
Albumen print, 13.3 x 9.3 cm
V&A (Ph.1808-1939)
FOR ILLUSTRATION SEE FIG 5, PAGE 33

Morris photographed in working clothes, possibly during the period when he was attempting to revive dye techniques with Thomas Wardle in Leek, Staffordshire. In March 1876 he wrote to May 'I had too much to do to be able to write yesterday or the day before. I dye in the dye-house with sabots and a blouse on: you would laugh to see me' (Kelvin 318).   LP

A.25 *Hammersmith from Barnes*

James Richard Marquis RHA (d.1885)
Oil on canvas, 43.0 x 63.5 cm
Signed and dated: 'Marquis 1881'
William Morris Society, Kelmscott House, London
Bequeathed by Leslie Paton Esq.

A view of the stretch of river at Chiswick and Hammersmith soon after the Morris family moved there. A lease was taken on The Retreat from April 1878 when it was re-named Kelmscott House.   LP

A.22

A.23

A.25

THE DESIGNER

Fiona MacCarthy

In the late spring of 1878 Morris was in Venice with his wife and his two daughters. All four went, like other tourists, on a day trip to Murano and stopped at one of the smaller glass-blowing work-shops, a dark shack which gave out a sudden dull red glow as the furnace door was opened. Outside was the glittering sunlight and a fig tree and the scent of the sea, 'all so primitive and pleasant', as recollected in her memoir of her father by Morris's younger daughter May. Morris swept aside the standard Murano glass the craftsman proferred and, picking up his stick (he suffered painfully from gout), he drew the outline of a tumbler on the dusty workshop floor. The 'bright-eyed friendly craftsman' used this design to produce a simple glass, slightly coloured, slightly bubbly in its texture, which pleased Morris greatly, although to his frustration he could not make the craftsman understand that he wanted to place a quantity order for his shop in Oxford Street.

That brief scene tells us a lot about Morris the designer: his high-speed assessment of technical parameters; his almost instinctive understanding of the potential of material and craftsman; his pragmatic efficiency in conveying his instructions; the way the design process permeated all his thinking, at home or abroad, on holiday or not. Morris never stopped designing, redesigning and improving. The encounter shows his grand impetuosity in action: Morris fertile, forthright, comically optimistic. It would make the perfect subject for a Burne-Jones cartoon.

William Morris was many kinds of man: visual artist, poet, political activist, Marxist theoretician. He was also many kinds of designer. Morris designed numerous special one-off objects that he either made himself, the design often evolving through the processes of making, or collaborated on with his craft workers and friends. He designed for one-off and small batch production in his early workshops and for relatively large-scale production runs in later days at his factory at Merton Abbey. To an extent that few people are aware of he designed other products to be made by sub-contractors and sold through his firm's showrooms. He acted as designer-buyer for his shops in the sense of searching out and commissioning new ranges to be sold alongside Morris, Marshall, Faulkner & Co.'s own products. On an earlier visit to Italy his travelling companion Edward Burne-Jones complained about Morris's obsessive 'merchandizing for the firm'.

As chief designer and overall controller of the firm's visual and technical standards Morris covered a stupendous range. In his neurotically energetic lifetime his interests and technical knowledge burgeoned outwards to include embroidery, furniture, stained glass, wallpapers and mural decorations; wood engravings, illumination and calligraphy; printed and woven textiles, high-warp tapestry. At the end of his life there was the final challenge of book design and type design at his own Kelmscott Press. William Morris saw things whole. His view of design was rich, complex, dominated by his reverence for buildings as repositories of history and keepers of the soul. The point of Morris's acutely detailed knowledge of individual processes and products was his passion for the total architectural *mise-en-scène*. He liked the completeness of designing for a church or domestic interior. He was as interested in gardens as in houses and, as we see at his own Red House, Morris had great feeling for the interflowing spaces. His generous concept of the role of the designer would eventually lead him to envisage whole communities, networks of productive and sociable semi-self-sufficient small country towns, precursors of the early twentieth-century garden cities. As expounded so sturdily in a famous lecture 'Art under Plutocracy' (1883), his view of art encompassed what we would now think of as total environmental planning: design for 'all the externals of our life'.

Morris argued that art was not merely a matter of painting and sculpture, architecture, 'the

Fig. 5 William Morris in working
smock, *c*.1876 (cat. no. A.24).

shapes and colours of all household goods', it also took in 'the arrangement of the fields for tillage
and pasture, the management of towns and our highways of all kinds'. He saw visual alertness as a
basic human function and the shared appreciation of beauty and design in everyday surroundings
and ordinary objects as the means of reconciling the artist with society. In his Utopian novel *News
from Nowhere* art has become so deeply embedded in the life of the community of Morris's new
England that it has no name.

Morris's strengths as a designer spring from the exactness of his observation. Even as a child
exploring gentle, quirky rural Essex, and his later expeditions as a disaffected schoolboy into the
countryside around Marlborough College, his sense of landscape was almost uncannily acute. In a
letter written after Morris's death, his daughter Jenny commented on his facility for grasping the
essentials: 'in half a dozen words Father could make one see a place exactly'. The details of known
landscapes stayed in his mind forever and he drew on what became almost a library of riverscapes

and tree forms, flowers, fruits and the little living creatures of the meadows and the woodlands: squawking starlings, robins hopping, kingfishers swooping, sleek and amiable rabbits (cat.no.M.56). They recur in his design work as vividly as they do in his poetry and prose. Morris was often caustic about the vapid, fashionable decorative designs of his contemporaries, citing Alma-Tadema's with particular venom: 'they appear to me too much made up of goose giblets and umbrellas.' His own idea of pattern embraced memory and nature, a theme he followed through in his 1881 lecture, 'Some Hints on Pattern Designing'. Morris's ideal pattern held 'unmistakable suggestions of gardens and fields'.

He reached out for solidity, the real, the unmistakable. Again, back in his childhood, he glorified the tactile, clinging to a rag at bedtime, recalling with precision a picture of Abraham and Isaac worked in worsted, a carved ivory junk with painted, gilded puppet figures, a particular Dutch toy town spread out satisfactorily upon the floor. Gradually, as a designer and a design theorist, he evolved a whole philosophy of things, arguing the strengths of well-printed books and splendid tapestries, beautiful and functional kitchens as a bulwark against social alienation and decay. What is fascinating is the scope of his intelligence. His great originality, a facet of his genius, is the way that Morris moves, apparently without self-consciousness, between the solid, 'manly' worlds of furniture and buildings and the soft, traditionally female textile crafts.

At a very early stage Morris had begun drawing. It was almost a compulsion, like his spurts of fluent writing. At Oxford in the middle 1850s his fellow undergraduates watched him pouring out his sketches of windows, arches, gables. A sketchbook of the Red House period, now in the British Library (cat.no.C.3), contains rapidly made drawings of knights in armour, flowers, medieval maidens, architectural detailing, suggesting the way in which Morris used these sketches to arrive at design concepts. Late in life he was still doodling, covering the notes for his lectures, adorning the sheets of his agendas for committees, with an endless profusion of patterns. Morris was his own best exemplar of the power of pattern to soothe and civilise. He would argue for drawing, and in particular for drawing from the human figure (hard as he himself always claimed to find it), as the central, essential discipline in a training for design. Morris recommended accurate drawing as the antidote to the 'sloppiness or vagueness' he so much disliked in the visual arts, as indeed in politics. The thousands of Morris's remaining working drawings, mostly for wallpapers and textiles, show his characteristic linear exactness reining in the deep sweep of his imaginative surge.

Morris absorbed colours with the poet's eye that made him the supreme colourist of the Victorian period. His precocious reading of Gothic stories and medieval mysteries taught him to see colour in terms of panoramic history. He would always be enraptured by the colours of banners, the insignia of battle, the dazzle of the novels of Sir Walter Scott. Morris's sense of history was creative and dynamic. He was immensely knowledgeable and was also adept, with the fanatic's sure-fire intuition, at recapturing the details and the atmosphere of medieval life: 'When I think of this', he said in his lecture 'The Hopes of Civilisation', 'it quickens my hope of what may be.' Morris took the colours of the past – the red of the knights, the purple of the emperors, the stern grey stonework of old village churches, the shrill blue that was the colour of ancient holidays – and gathered them into his own decorative palette. His use of colour is intensely reminiscent; it reminds one inevitably of the luminosity of colour in Morris's early poetry, the vivid violent narratives of *The Defence of Guenevere*. As so marvellously described by his disciple W.R.Lethaby, 'Morris's colourwork glows from within'.

As a designer his most radical departure was in his approach to materials and processes. He confessed in his lecture, 'The Aims of Art', he was never truly happy unless either making something or making believe to make it; and he developed a passionate attachment to the properties and potential of materials. Addressing the art students in Burslem in 1881 he entreated them 'try to get the most out of your material, but always in such a way as to honour it most'. Morris's views on right-making became the received wisdom of the (very gentlemanly) Arts and Crafts Movement. But in its day it was defiantly eccentric. As J.W.Mackail, Morris's first biographer, explains so valuably from his closer vantage-point, 'a poet who chose to exercise a handicraft, not as a gentleman amateur, but under the ordinary conditions of handcraftsman, was a figure so unique as to be almost unintelligible'. Mackail also made the comment, which was true, that the secret of the excellence of Morris's designs was that he never designed anything that he did not know how to

Fig.6 Oxford Union Debating Hall, showing a section of the murals.

produce with his own hands. Morris needed handwork psychologically. From the time he was at Marlborough, observed by his schoolfellows making nets for catching fish or trapping birds, with one end of the net fixed to the classroom desk, he relied on the rhythms of repetitive manual activity to control his inherent restlessness and edginess. Morris needed to feel himself literally in touch.

Handwork also brought a theoretical solution to the intellectual problems assailing him since Oxford, where Morris first read Ruskin's essay on art and workmanship in *The Stones of Venice*. Morris perceived that handwork could be a way of ending the deadly separation between the operative and the designer, and a means of challenging that vaster, more iniquitous divide between the labourer and the non-labouring employer. By the middle 1850s, still in his early twenties, Morris had embarked on stone carving, clay modelling, stained-glass design, mural decoration, painted furniture. In Oxford he had a frame made for embroidery, based on an old example, and supervised the special dyeing of his worsteds. His practical involvement in the techniques of production justified the detail of his glowering criticisms.

Fig.7 Merton Abbey Works.

It was once he moved to London in 1856 that Morris began to find himself as a designer. Sharing rooms in Red Lion Square with Edward Burne-Jones, he evolved his ideal of the interior as a place that was tidy but not too tidy (indeed, Red Lion Square had its elements of chaos, with its clutter of old armour, draperies and tapestry, and sketchbooks) and his concept of the home as spiritual space. As Morris would expound it in a later lecture, houses had to be fit for the 'noble creatures, tall, wide-shouldered, and well-built, with their bright eyes and well moulded features, those men full of courage, capacity and energy' who inhabit them. Already at Red Lion Square one detects the beginnings of the risky combination of the homely and heroic that became his mature decorative style.

This was the period of the 'Barbarossa' furniture. Morris had commissioned for Red Lion Square the series of large-scale, rough-hewn pieces described by Rossetti as 'intensely mediaeval... tables and chairs like incubi and succubi'. Morris, Burne-Jones and Rossetti painted the big bare panels with decorative scenes. This was the kind of co-operative venture Morris hymned in his later lectures on design. The Barbarossa furniture was hardly functional. There were other things at issue beyond mere practicality. Morris believed in resonance, the mystic, the spectacular. As a designer of furniture he had a sweeping arrogance: 'If you want to be comfortable go to bed.'

In the development of Morris the designer two early episodes were absolutely central. The first was the decorating of the Oxford Union through the summer of 1857 (fig.6). The second was the building two years later of Red House at Bexleyheath (fig.2), the home designed by Philip Webb for Morris on his marriage to Jane Burden, with Morris in the role of ultimate creative client. Both these architecturally distinguished brand new buildings were important in giving Morris his first real experience of practical design work: the building up of pattern, the layerings of colour, the controlled but exuberant approach to the interior that Morris was to perfect in his professional practice on a much more lavish scale. Both episodes confirmed his faith in the romantic concept of male creative teamwork, the band of brother artists, experts in different disciplines, that surfaced so hopefully (and ended so tragically) with Morris, Marshall, Faulkner & Co. Most crucially, Morris's own intense enjoyment of these working holidays gave a new conviction to his views on joy in

Fig. 8 The textile printing shed at
Merton Abbey.

labour. His heartfelt thesis that creative work gives pleasure and that life without pleasurable work is mere endurance can be traced back to the Union, the popping of the soda-water corks and Morris ebulliently pressing his thumb into the wet paintwork, leaving traces on the sandwiches the artists ate while they were working: 'This is mine and this and this.'

Morris, Marshall, Faulkner & Co., established in 1861, provided Morris with a framework for design activity that lasted, more or less unaltered, till his death. 'The firm', as it was called informally and jokily, consisted originally of seven partners, but much of the creative impetus was Morris's. The firm had been financed largely by himself and with loans from Morris's mother, and from very early days he himself was paid a salary as business manager. He was the partner permanently on the premises, fulfilling the role we would now call the art director's. Morris was responsible for overall design decisions and quality control. He became the designer who was also delegater over a wide spectrum. His daughter May, who later worked as Morris's assistant, described the degree of his involvement:

> He was in direct relation with the silk-weavers and carpet-weavers, dyers and blockers, with pattern-makers and block-cutters, with cabinet makers and carvers in wood; with glass painters, kiln men and labourers and with his wall-paper printers; and it was not as if he sat in an office and received reports from managers of different departments with the technical details of which he was unfamiliar: he had grasped the nature of those he employed – understanding their limitations as well as their capabilities.

For Morris designing was an exercise in fellowship.

From the early 1860s William Morris was also in direct relation with the public, in the form of the firm's professional and private clients and random visitors to the shop and showroom attached to the firm's workshops, first in Red Lion Square, then in Queen Square, Bloomsbury. Morris liked the idea of shopkeeping, imbuing with romance the discreet exchanges of small specialist traders. The expertise of London food merchants had intrigued him when he visited his father in the City as a boy. He saw shopkeeping as part of the whole cycle of designing, the personal fulfilment of the contract between the creator and end-user of the product. A visitor to the shop at Red Lion Square was at first a little startled to be shown around by the tousle-headed proprietor himself. When she chose two tumblers, Morris and his friend Val Prinsep wrapped them up in paper. The customer, Mrs Richmond Ritchie, went away 'very amused and interested, with a general impression of sympathetic shyness and shadows and green glass'.

By 1862, when the firm made its official debut at the International Exhibition at South Kensington, Morris was already immersed in the first and longest lasting of his great design enthusiasms, the revival of stained glass. This was partly pragmatism: the refitting of old churches and the building of new ones in the onsurge of ritual revival made it a commercially sensible development. But as always with Morris there was more to it than that. On his tours of Northern France as an undergraduate he had seen the medieval stained glass in the Gothic cathedrals. Its possibilities lay deep in his imagination. Stained glass appears in several of his stories of that time. He responded not just to the sparkle and the glamour but to the narrative qualities. Stained glass conveyed its message even to the illiterate. Morris felt he had discovered a truly populist art.

His contribution to the firm's stained glass was less that of designer of individual windows, though some of his own glass had a great clarity and sweetness. His chief role was to keep overall control over the colour and, in later years, also the leading of each window. The artists submitted their designs in cartoon form for the men in the workshop to 'glassify' as Morris directed them. His serious and selfless involvement in the project can be gauged by William De Morgan's description of Morris at Red Lion Square dressed in vestments and posed as if playing on a regal 'to illustrate points in connection with stained glass'.

Morris's sympathies were always with the recondite. His brilliance was in rescuing apparently lost causes, pulling forgotten processes out of their obscurity to give them a highly personal contemporary significance. In the middle 1860s it was wood engraving. Burne-Jones and Morris were working on a series of illustrations for Morris's 'Big Book of Stories in Verse', his *Earthly Paradise*. They based their style on Italian Renaissance woodcuts, particularly those of the *Hypnerotomachia*

Fig.9 Two-light stained-glass window *The Flight into Egypt*. St Michael and All Angels, Brighton, 1862.

Fig. 10 Design for *Bluebell* printed cotton, 1876 (cat. no. M.50).

Poliphili, printed in Venice in 1499. Morris attacked the task with an almost manic vigour, cutting over fifty blocks. Burne-Jones drew a famous cartoon of him in action, with his graver's tools around him, hunched up with energy (fig.102). By 1870 Morris was reviving lost techniques first of calligraphy and then illumination, laboriously learning the rudiments of Roman and italic scripts, rediscovering the ancient art of gilding. May remembered her father's study for years after strewn around with his experimental squares of gilding as Morris tried out ancient recipes given by Theophilus. He could not regard design work as a separate activity. Its cyclic concentrations dominated Morris's personal life and eddied through his homes.

The main thrust of Morris's life was integration. He worked passionately for an end to class divisions, both as a political thinker and as a practical socialist. As an early environmentalist he attempted to reconcile the country and the city. As a writer William Morris shifts conventional boundaries: his political polemic is poetic, in his poetry and novels the inventiveness masks hard political statement. He is always a great deal more complex than he seems. The importance of Morris the designer in his period, and indeed in any period, is the degree of integration he achieved between the visual design processes and the productive. The extent to which Morris designed through making, proposing and retracting, developing, adapting according to the progress of his technical experiments, is clear from his extensive, detailed, often agitated correspondence with his sub-contractor Thomas Wardle, the textile manufacturer of Leek.

For the whole decade from the middle 1870s Morris's energies were focused upon textiles. It is fascinating to watch his dogged progress as he masters the techniques in one area after another, gradually drawing in production under his own control. First we find him investigating vegetable dyeing, working in Leek with Wardle, his arms plunged in the dye vats, 'taking in dyeing at every pore'. Next he turns his formidable attention to weaving. Morris rising in the dawn through the summer of 1879 to work on the experimental loom set up in his bedroom at Kelmscott House in Hammersmith is as heroic a Victorian as Charles Darwin, driven by the same necessity to know. By the time Morris's workshops transferred to Merton Abbey in 1881 they were self-sufficient in dyeing, in weaving silk and woollen fabrics, in hand-knotting rugs and carpets, and were at the early stages of making the high-warp tapestry that had for so long been Morris's 'bright dream'. His technical confidence gave Morris's design work a new urgency, huge buoyancy. He produced at least thirty-two designs for printed fabrics, twenty-three for woven fabrics, twenty-one designs for wallpapers as well as designs for carpets and rugs, embroideries and tapestries between 1875 and 1885. At this period his productivity approached frenzy. He wrote to his friend Aglaia Coronio: 'I am drawing patterns so fast last night I dreamed I had to draw a sausage; somehow I had to eat it first, which made me anxious about my digestion: however I have just done quite a pretty pattern for printed work.'

Morris's test of a successful pattern was that it provoked thought and concentrated feeling. It spoke of shared human experience and 'ancientness'. It gave an intimation of things beyond itself. Perhaps one explanation for the increasing depths in Morris's magnificent patterns of this later middle period is the growing despair of his political analysis. Design was his own life blood. In one of his lectures, 'The Prospects of Architecture', Morris admitted he would die if deprived of what he called his 'special work', his proper work', by which he meant his routine production and supervision of designs. How to equate his own necessary quest for perfectionist excellence with his perception of civilisation on collision course, his bleak belief that art must go under in the end? Morris in the 1880s has been misrepresented. He could never be complacent about his continuing to manufacture luxury goods for the sophisticated bourgeoisie whilst so actively embroiled in the socialist cause. If Morris was much goaded he was his own chief goader: 'Am I doing nothing but make-believe then, something like Louis XVI's lock-making?' was his anguished question to Georgiana Burne-Jones. In the socialist turmoil Morris from time to time neglected his design work. But inevitably, and with poignant joy, he would return to it. Some of his designs of that period – for example the extraordinary *Woodpecker* tapestry (fig.13) – have the dignity of imperfectibility.

In January 1891 Morris was once again beaming with activity. He had rented a cottage at 16 Upper Mall in Hammersmith, where he was installing the Kelmscott Press. The Press, his last great opus in practical designing, has been interpreted as an old man's aberration, a softening, almost a reneging on his socialist fervour. In fact it should be seen as a triumphant culmination, a drawing together of many of the threads that had fascinated Morris throughout his life in the politics of art.

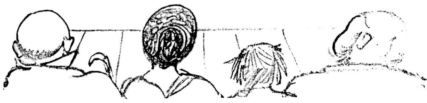

Fig. 11 A caricature by Burne-Jones showing Morris giving a weaving demonstration at the Arts and Crafts Exhibition, November 1888.

Morris, so endlessly, productively resilient, had recast his long experience as bibliophile and collector, his immersion in the book crafts of illumination and calligraphy, his own history as a reader avaricious for knowledge and for narrative. Morris began his Press with a very clear idea of what a book could do. Most of all it was the final illustration of his theory that 'Nothing should be made by men's labour which is not worth making, or which must be made by labour degrading to the makers'. The Press was not a revolutionary workshop: it was almost paternalistic in its structure. But it was the final expression of Morris's belief in community endeavour, his sense of the importance not just of what we make but of how we relate to one another while we make it. Its coherence and integrity of purpose and of product were to be influential in the whole development of twentieth-century European and American typographic and book design.

Reminiscing in the 1890s Morris's friend and chief collaborator Edward Burne-Jones summed up his career with exasperated fondness:

> When I first knew Morris nothing would content him but being a monk, and getting to
> Rome, and then he must be an architect, and apprenticed himself to Street, and worked for
> two years, but when I came to London and began to paint he threw it all up, and must paint
> too, and then he must give it up and make poems, and then he must give it up and make
> window hangings and pretty things, and when he had achieved that, he must be a poet
> again, and then after two or three years of Earthly Paradise time, he must learn dyeing, and
> lived in a vat, and learned weaving, and knew all about looms, and then made more books,

and learned tapestry, and then wanted to smash everything up and begin the world anew, and now it is printing he cares for, and to make wonderful rich-looking books and all things he does splendidly – and if he lives the printing will have an end – but not I hope, before Chaucer and the Morte d'Arthur are done; and then he'll do I don't know what, but every minute will be alive.

It is tempting to wonder what Morris would have turned to had he lived a few years longer. Metalwork is the prime candidate. There is only the one isolated example of the Arthurian armour he commissioned from a forge near Oxford Castle, the helmet of which trapped him inside it, 'dancing with rage and roaring' (the helmet is now at the William Morris Gallery, Walthamstow). Yet Morris's writings, in particular those late fantasy novels, show just how attuned he was to metalwork: they clatter with drinking cups and breastplates, swords and ankle clasps and hauberks. He admired the antique silverwork when he was in Iceland and brought back decorative girdles for his daughters. Morris's robust physique and confrontational character appeared to his contemporaries the model metalworker's: both in King René's Honeymoon Cabinet (cat.no.J.13) of the 1860s and Walter Crane's membership card for the Socialist League Hammersmith Branch of the 1880s Morris is depicted as a smith. Bernard Shaw bemoaned the fact that there was never a Kelmscott Theatre. It is more to the point to regret that there was never a Kelmscott forge or Kelmscott silversmithing workshop. Morris with his strength and grace could have made admirable metalwork. But very shortly after Burne-Jones spoke those words he died.

Fig. 12 *Brother Rabbit* printed cotton designed by Morris, 1880–81 (cat.no.M.56).

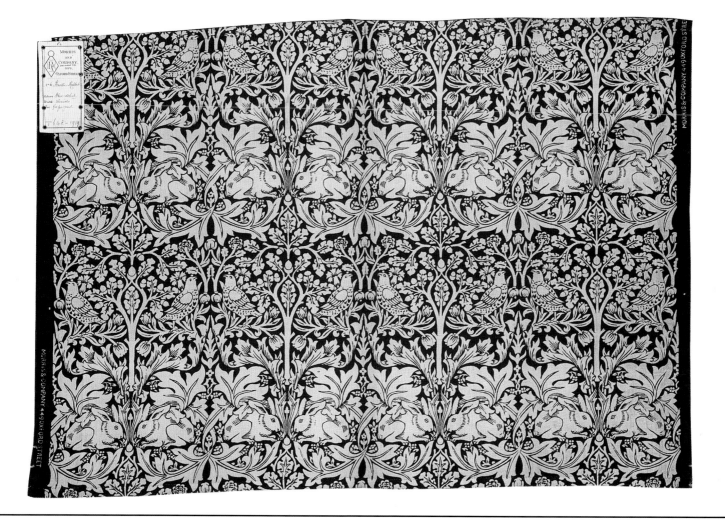

Fig. 13 The *Woodpecker* tapestry.
Designed by Morris 1885.

THE WRITER

Peter Faulkner

Fig. 14 Morris reading poetry to
Burne-Jones (cat. no. A.15).

Amidst all his other activities and commitments, Morris was a prolific writer. *The Collected Works*, splendidly edited by his daughter May between 1910 and 1915, run to twenty-four volumes, and she added two further bulky volumes in 1936. Subsequently there have been editions of his other writings, including letters, journals, diaries, lectures and journalistic articles, and a play: and there is plenty more, especially in the form of uncollected political material. His writings cover an enormous range, but their favoured form is the story, whether in verse or prose. Morris was already a story-teller when he was a schoolboy at Marlborough – the captain of his dormitory apparently found him 'an inexhaustible source' of the stories he wanted to hear – and on his death-bed Morris was correcting the proofs of his last story, *The Sundering Flood*, having enjoyed the completion of his Kelmscott edition of the works of Chaucer, the greatest of English story-tellers.

By the time he entered Oxford in 1854 Morris was already widely read, with the works of Scott early favourites for their combination of exciting narrative and attention to the earlier history of Britain. At Oxford he read Keats and Tennyson, together with such social critics as Carlyle and Ruskin, and socially responsible novelists such as the Christian Socialist Kingsley and the High Church Charlotte Yonge. His friends, knowing him as a rather boisterous young man with a wide range of enthusiasms, particularly for medieval history and architecture, were surprised by his presenting himself as a poet, suddenly in the autumn term of 1854. Much later R. W. Dixon was to recall, vividly, listening to Morris reading 'The Willow and the Red Cliff' to Burne-Jones and himself, and thinking the poem astoundingly original and impressive. When congratulated, however, Morris is said merely to have remarked, 'Well, if this is poetry, it is very easy to write'. This story, though it may have been simplified in memory and lends itself to presenting a Morris more naive than he actually was, does suggest something of his undoubted fluency and, more importantly, his eager and energetic imagination. His was a naturally creative sensibility, and one way in which this expressed itself was in telling a great proliferation of stories.

Almost all these stories are set in the past. Morris's imagination, guided by his wide reading, ranged freely back into history, and found its home there. He was of course not unaware of the condition of the country in which he was living and became more so as his experience expanded, but he discussed such matters largely in lectures and non-fictional prose. In his poetry and fiction the past provided him with a distance through which he could focus more readily on his subject-matter: human behaviour and society as revealed to an imaginative and historically informed mind. In *News from Nowhere* in 1890 he was to criticise, through the intelligent observations of the vivacious Ellen, the realist literature of his own day as having done nothing to liberate its readers from their social oppression – for having been, as recent critics have suggested, in collusion, however unconscious, with that oppression.

However that may be, Morris consistently rejected the present as the setting for his stories. There seem to be only two exceptions. In *The Oxford and Cambridge Magazine* (which was produced with the aid of Morris's recently inherited £900 a year in 1856) there is one story out of eight with a contemporary setting, 'Frank's Sealed Letter'. Later, in 1872, Morris was to start writing a novel in a modern setting, but he abandoned it as 'abortive'. 'Frank's Sealed Letter' is highly melodramatic, and cannot compare in quality with the other stories in the magazine with their dreamlike or vaguely medieval settings, and names such as 'The Hollow Land' and 'Gertha's Lovers'. The most disturbing of them is 'Lindenborg Pool', adapted from a story called 'The Sunken Mansion' in Benjamin Thorpe's *Northern Mythology* (1851). The narrator's experience is that of nightmare as he finds himself riding, in the costume of a thirteenth-century priest, to a great house, where he is taken to what he expects to be a dying man to whom he can minister – but who turns out to be a pig. The revelation is received with grotesque laughter by the hundreds of people present, while the narrator escapes, horrified. As he turns back, however, he sees that the castle has disappeared, and all that is left is a cloud of lime-dust and a deep black lake. The reader has been taken into a Gothic world like that of Edgar Allan Poe. It is an astounding story for the young Morris to have written, as indeed are the others, though none is so succinctly powerful and all are shot through with more positive qualities of hope, love and beauty.

However, the world of Morris's early writing is, for whatever reasons – psychological largely, we must suppose, since at this stage he was not deeply concerned with social issues – a sombre world of conflict and violence. This is equally true of his early poems, published as *The Defence of Guenevere and Other Poems* in 1858, when Morris was only twenty-four. The thirty poems in the volume show Morris employing a remarkable variety of poetic forms, adapted to the varying subject-matter. The title poem and the following three are taken from the Arthurian legends, which were one of the Victorians' favourite sources of material for both literature and painting. Tennyson's *Idylls of the King* (of which the first group was to appear in the following year, 1859) constitute the most elaborate handling of this material, always inflected by the Poet Laureate with a sense of duty and of morality. Morris's handling is very different. Guenevere is shown defying her accusers, offering her physical beauty as its own justification, and referring to her marriage to Arthur in dismissive terms. Everywhere in these poems Morris is interested principally in vivid and dramatic scenes or characters. By contrast with most other Victorian writers, he seems surprisingly disinclined to moralise. The violence and suffering are shown, both in the world of Malory and that of Froissart, who described the wars between England and France in the fourteenth century. A poem such as 'The Haystack in the Floods' gives a powerful picture of the failure of the loving Robert to save his beloved Jehane from the evil Godmar. Godmar's killing of Robert is chillingly described, as is Jehane's response, while the haystacks remain amid the rain and mud, as dreary as the human experience conveyed. There is also a group of more mysterious poems, with titles such as 'The Wind', 'The Blue Closet' and 'The Tune of Seven Towers' (the last two derived from water-colours by Rossetti which Morris had bought). They evoke a mysterious world of ghostly presences and threatening supernatural forces. The volume also includes 'Praise of My Lady', a love poem to Jane Burden, seeing her as a lady of romance and with as much awe as confidence.

The Defence of Guenevere was the first book of Pre-Raphaelite poetry to be published – neither Rossetti nor Swinburne had yet done so. It accordingly drew scorn from a critical establishment still uneasy about the influence of the Brotherhood founded ten years previously. *The Spectator* was representative in speaking of the 'faults of affectation and bad taste' in the poems, although there were a few favourable responses. What seemed affectation to conventional minds was what attracted younger readers to poems that carry the Romantic impulse strongly forward in the narrative form which, as we have seen, held the strongest appeal for Morris. These are some of the most powerful poems of the mid-century; but Morris was never to write in the same mode again. There is no direct evidence that he was affected by the reviews – few letters survive from the period and it was a busy one in other ways, so he may have had less time for writing. He started writing some poems on the fall of Troy, but they came to nothing. At all events, he was to publish nothing further until 1867, the longest gap in his writing career. However, during this period he married Jane Burden, moved into Red House, established the firm, began his career as a designer and fathered two daughters. His next poem was to be on a classical theme: *The Life and Death of Jason*, published with great success in 1867, tells the story of Jason and the Golden Fleece, devoting a good deal of attention to the heroine-enchantress Medea – as we have already seen, Morris was inclined to give female characters a good deal of attention in his poetry. *Jason* is a very long poem, in seventeen books, which is little read today, but it appealed to Victorian taste. The young Henry James reviewed it, praising its appeal 'to the jaded intellects of the present moment' as offering a world 'where they will be called upon neither to choose, to criticise, nor to believe, but simply to feel, to look, and to listen'. These may seem odd grounds for praise, but they suggest that the appeal of the poem lay in its remoteness from the social and political issues of the age. Morris had found a subject-matter which he could handle with confidence and fluency, and which appealed to the large and growing middle-class reading public.

Jason had originally been intended, before it grew so long, for inclusion in a larger poem, to be called *The Earthly Paradise*. The structure of this was based on such poems as Chaucer's *Canterbury Tales*, where a number of stories are brought together within a single work. In *The Earthly Paradise* there were to be as many as twenty-four stories, told alternately by a group of Northern Wanderers in the fourteenth century and their hosts in 'some Western land', where they settle in old age after lives spent vainly seeking an earthly paradise. The stories are taken from a variety of sources, classical, medieval, oriental and Icelandic, from 'Cupid and Psyche' to 'The Lovers of Gudrun'. Morris took pleasure in retelling these stories for the benefit of contemporary readers who might be unable to read them in the original languages, and the public received them with pleasure. Morris's later books were often published with the inscription, 'By the author of *The Earthly Paradise*'. The poem is structured around the months of the year, and each is introduced by a brief lyrical poem. Some of these, particularly that for November, express a deeply personal sense of suffering and doubt, as do other poems written at the time, reflecting the failure of Morris's marriage, as Jane turned towards the charismatic Rossetti. It seems extraordinary that a man so emotionally reticent as Morris should publish in *The Atlantic Monthly* in May 1870 a poem like 'May Grown A-Cold', which concludes: 'Thy love is gone, poor wretch, thou art alone.' However, it was not for such private poetry that Morris was admired, but rather for his narrative works.

Reference has already been made to 'The Lovers of Gudrun', a poem in the third part of *The Earthly Paradise* and often considered the most dramatic and powerful of all its stories. The subject-matter is taken from the Icelandic Laxdaela Saga, and this is evidence of the important turn Morris took at this stage towards the literature and culture of the North. In 1868 Morris met the Icelander Eiríkr Magnússon, with whose help he set about learning the language. Soon it was to become vitally important to him, and to lead to the publication of a number of translations: *The Saga of Gunnlaug Worm-Tongue* and *The Grettis Saga* in 1869, *The Story of the Volsungs and Niblungs* from the Volsunga Saga in 1870. Icelandic culture now became of central importance to Morris as he sought for positive values in a mid-Victorian world in which *laissez-faire* industrialism was eating up the countryside and creating its hideous towns. Iceland was first known to Morris through the sagas, but he visited the country in both 1871 and 1873. The 1871 Journals, though not intended for publication, contain some of Morris's most vigorous writing, as do the poems which commemorate his visits, especially 'Iceland First Seen'. The *Three Northern Love Stories* of 1873 show his continuing enthusiasm, which culminated, as far as literature is concerned, in *Sigurd the Volsung* in 1876. Morris wanted to make 'the great story of the North' available to English readers, believing it was as important as the tale of Troy so widely accepted in the culture. The result was his most energetic long narrative poem, told in hexameter lines which rhyme in couplets, with a good deal of alliteration. The story is that of the hero whom Wagner, employing the German account, was celebrating at the same time in *The Ring* (Morris did not like opera or consider it dignified enough to do justice to this material). Morris's poem is in four Books, 'Sigmund' (the father of Sigurd), 'Regin' (the early life of Sigurd), 'Brynhild' (in which Sigurd is tricked into forgetting Brynhild, whom he loves, and into marrying Gudrun, and is killed by Guttorm, driving Brynhild also to her death), and finally 'Gudrun' (with Atli's destruction of the Niblungs). Morris manages to convey the uncompromising spirit of the saga with great success; but it is a spirit that did not appeal to the Victorian public. The critics praised the poem, but the public did not buy it; there was no second edition until 1887. Whether as a direct result of this or not, Morris turned more to prose in his later years.

He had published another ambitious but not well received poem in 1872, entitled *Love is*

Enough. It is his most complex poetic structure; at its centre is a morality play about a king seeking love, which is performed before a newly married emperor and empress; the performance is framed between two peasant lovers and the royal couple, and there are a number of lyrical passages entitled 'The Music' which assert the theme of the centrality of love. However, the poem seems unsure of its own direction, and the Love (with a capital letter) that it celebrates hangs uncertainly between the divine and the human. *Love is Enough* shows unusual formal ingenuity on Morris's part, but perhaps this was a way of avoiding the difficult personal questions that the title suggests. Morris wrote nothing like it subsequently.

But his poetic energy did not subside. It expressed itself in the form of translations, notably *The Aeneids of Virgil* in 1876, *The Odyssey of Homer* in 1887–8, *Beowulf* (with A.J.Wyatt) in 1895, and *Old French Romances* in 1896. The range of Morris's ability and enthusiasms is remarkable, especially when we bear in mind his continuing work with Magnússon for the five volumes of the Saga Library, published between 1891 and 1895 (the sixth was in 1905, after Morris's death). Probably the Homer now reads most effectively: among the reviewers who praised it was Oscar Wilde, a good classical scholar, who saw it as expressing 'the fine loyalty of poet to poet'. However, by 1889 Morris was being criticised for the diction of his translations. R.Y.Tyrell accused his version of Virgil of possessing an inappropriate 'olde-world tone' because of its 'Wardour-Street English' – a reference to a street noted for its production of sham-antique furniture. Morris did deliberately employ a special vocabulary in his later work, aimed to take the reader away from the contemporary world into that of the historical text. We may regard this as a positive imaginative feat.

In the 1880s, however, much of Morris's formidable energy went into lecturing and political activity. Although he continued to write as much as ever, because of the subject-matter of these writings they are discussed in other sections of this book. But of course his remarkable literary ability contributed significantly to the success of his socialist writings, and the masterpiece *News from Nowhere*. But throughout his final decade – and along with the creation of the Kelmscott Press – Morris continued to create works of imaginative fiction, usually referred to as the prose romances because of their avoidance of contemporary subject-matter and of a realist mode of writing. The first of these is *A Tale of the House of the Wolfings* (1888) which dramatises (in a mixture of prose and verse) the conflict between the Romans and a Germanic tribe, or between commercial imperialism and the idea of community. *The Roots of the Mountains* (1889) deals with another Germanic tribal community under threat, this time from the Huns, some centuries later. Morris now wrote at greater length, and uniformly in prose, a carefully constructed prose whose diction is appropriate to the culture described. By the end, the Men of Burgdale have defeated the Dusky Men; these late romances contrast with the prose stories Morris had written as a young man at Oxford in their happy endings in which society and its leaders come together in a healthy unity. (The optimism contrasts strongly with the tone of the realist fiction of the era, that of Hardy and Gissing.)

As the years passed, and Morris became less directly involved in the socialist movement, the romances became less historical and more purely symbolic, as their titles suggest. In *The Story of the Glittering Plain* (1890) the hero finds himself in a sterile world, a nightmare version of an earthly paradise. He exclaims, 'I seek no dream, but the end of dreams'. In so far as he speaks for Morris, we may interpret this not as meaning that there will be a turn towards realism; rather it may suggest that he now felt able to look directly at reality because of his political hopes for transforming it. At all events, the late romances all culminate in success for their attractive central characters, both male and female (the latter in particular being endowed with an independence and vitality very unusual in Victorian fiction), and for the societies in which they exist and to which they contribute their abilities as leaders. The same qualities are celebrated in some of Morris's later poems, included in the 1891 volume *Poems by the Way*, such as 'The Folk-Mote by the River' or 'Mine and Thine'. The movement towards something like fairytale can be seen in a poem such as 'Goldilocks and Goldilocks', but this again culminates in an attractive social unity.

That Morris did not want his romances to be interpreted too crudely is made clear by his letter to *The Spectator* in 1895, telling its readers that in the volume that had been reviewed, *The Wood Beyond the World*, he had intended no political allegory: 'it is meant for a tale pure and simple, with nothing didactic about it.' But of course, stories have implications, even if the intention is not didactic, and the defeat of the evil Dwarf and his deceptively beautiful Lady by Golden Walter and the Maid must prove heartening to the reader who has sympathised with the latter pair throughout. More powerfully, in *The Well at the World's End* (1896) the eventual triumph of Ralph and Ursula is welcome to the reader because they have endeared themselves by their courage and humanity; again, it is notable that Ursula is as important a character as her partner. The symbolic world of the Dry Tree and the Well where the lovers drink together is finely rendered; as is their choice not to linger by the Well but to return together to their social responsibilities. In *Child Christopher and Goldilind the Fair* (1895) Morris produced a version of the fourteenth-century English lay *Havelock the Dane*, with a similar structure to his other romances. *The Water of the Wondrous Isles* (1897) is notable for having a female hero in a genre in which women are traditionally relegated (though not by Morris) to the roles of reward-for-male-courage or danger-to-be-avoided. Finally, in *The Sundering Flood* (of which Morris did not live to complete the final revision) the movement is again towards unity, as the river fails to prevent the lovers from coming together and creating a new society through their heroic efforts. When, towards the end, Steelhead responds to a monk's 'Go in peace, and All Hallows keep thee', with the words, 'We will not contend about it, but I look to it to keep myself', the reader feels close to Morris's humanism, with its note of Icelandic stoicism. The Steelhead, who 'therewith strode off into the night', speaks to us of and for Morris, whose writings constitute an important part of his extraordinary all-round achievement.

Fig. 15 Detail from from the manuscript: 'Bellerophon in Lycia' from *The Earthly Paradise* (cat. no. N.3).

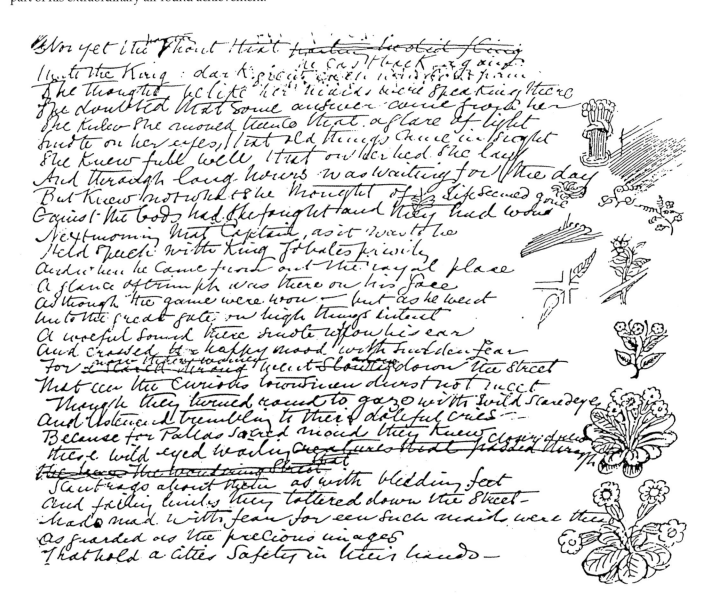

THE BUSINESSMAN

Charles Harvey and Jon Press

William Morris was from a commercial background, and he became familiar at an early age with both the rewards and tribulations of business life. He also acquired during his childhood a profound love of art, architecture and literature, especially that of the medieval period. In his youth, he studied theology, was articled to G.E.Street, one of the leading architects of the Gothic Revival, and tried his hand at painting at Rossetti's insistence. All of these experiences were to have a profound influence upon his subsequent career in the decorative arts.

The prestige of the decorative arts grew rapidly in the 1850s. Street insisted that decoration was integral to architecture and that architects should seize the potential of crafts such as stained glass, metalwork and embroidery. Ruskin likewise emphasised that every aspect of a building should form 'a great and harmonious whole', and his belief that the designer should be 'entirely familiar' with decorative techniques and materials made a great impression on Morris. The ideas of men such as Street and Ruskin struck a chord with a wide cross-section of Victorian society and Morris was not unusual in responding to them. What made him unique was the immense effort he made during his lifetime to give their ideas practical expression, and to extend them in important ways. This process began with the building and decoration of Red House, Morris's home at Bexleyheath, Upton, Kent, and led in turn to the formation of Morris, Marshall, Faulkner & Company (MMF & Co.) in April 1861.

There were six other partners in the firm: Dante Gabriel Rossetti and Ford Madox Brown were already famous; Philip Webb was an architect and Edward Burne-Jones had just begun a career in painting; Charles Faulkner was a mathematics don and Peter Paul Marshall an engineer and amateur painter. With supreme self-confidence, these young men set out on a commercial venture whose ultimate purpose was to transform the British public's appreciation of the decorative arts. The task was harder than they expected. It was as though they had gone out to start a revolution, only to find that it had already begun. From the outset, they faced strong competition from established firms such as Lavers & Barraud, Clayton & Bell, and Heaton, Butler & Bayne in stained glass, and Skidmores and Hardmans in ecclesiastical furnishings.

Clearly, the firm could only be successful by dint of much hard work; and the view later put about by Rossetti that MMF & Co. was 'mere playing at business' might well reflect his own attitude, but tells us little about the other members. Marshall, it is true, was a heavy drinker, and probably no great asset; but Morris, though blessed with a substantial private income, had a voracious appetite for work. Burne-Jones suffered all his life from anxieties about money and was keener than anyone that the firm should be a paying proposition. He needed work and income, not membership of a pleasant, civilised, unremunerative club. Nor is it likely that the practically minded Madox Brown would have given much time to the sort of casual business concern so airily described by Rossetti.

There was nothing casual or lighthearted in the thinking that caused the partners to band together. The firm's operations and finances were planned and worked out in detail. Morris was made business manager at a salary of £150 a year. Commissions were shared out according to the actual contributions made by individual members. This did not merely apply to the quantity of work done: the greater skills of Rossetti, Burne-Jones and Madox Brown were rewarded with higher fees than those of Morris and Marshall. The partners were well aware of the advantages that this type of association could confer: a group of artists working together could offer a much more

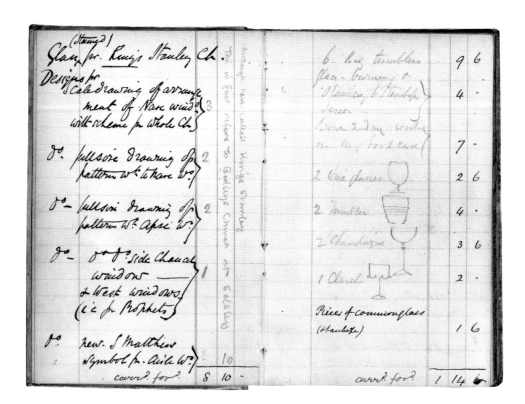

complete service than they could possibly do as individuals – a point emphasised in the firm's prospectus.

The establishment and development of the firm was based upon the partners' appreciation of the rapidly growing market for ecclesiastical products. During the early decades of Victoria's reign there was an upsurge of church building on a scale unknown since the thirteenth century. Between 1840 and 1876, the Church of England built 1,727 new churches and rebuilt or extensively restored 7,144, at a total cost in excess of £25 million. As the years passed, churches became more elaborate, decoration more lavish and costly. All kinds of furnishings were in demand, and stained glass for windows was particularly favoured. Morris and his friends made effective use of personal contacts in securing commissions, and efforts of this type were crucial to establishing the reputation of MMF & Co. Morris and Webb got work from Street, Bodley and other architects of their acquaintance. Rossetti, with his wide social circle and ready charm, also managed to win numerous contracts for the firm.

Within a few years of its formation, however, the firm ran into difficulties. It had become too dependent upon the stained-glass market, which declined sharply in the general depression of the late 1860s. Fashions changed, too, and several potential customers expressed a preference for more straightforward Gothic Revival work. The firm undertook some large secular projects in the mid-1860s, notably the St James's Palace commission and the decoration of the Green Dining Room at the South Kensington Museum in 1867. But while these projects were prestigious and very profitable, the market was necessarily small and unpredictable.

It was clear by the late 1860s that the business, in its existing form, could never provide large incomes for the partners. For some, this hardly mattered. Faulkner had returned to academic life at Oxford. Marshall, who always had to be chased for designs, had never given up his career in surveying. For Rossetti, the firm was never more than a sideline. It was Morris who was most affected by the changing fortunes of the firm. Just as sales began to slump, his once substantial unearned income from mining shares entered a terminal decline. It was through necessity that he became a committed man of business, intent on expanding trade and acquiring an income that would safeguard his financial future.

The principal lesson learned by Morris during his early years in business was that if MMF & Co. was to prosper, it would have to enter new markets and establish its reputation with the general public. This was easier said than done. A complete interior decorating service called for a whole new range of products of good quality and design. In the early 1870s Morris worked long and hard to produce fresh designs for wallpapers and chintzes and get suppliers to meet his needs. He was often disappointed with the results, but still managed to impart a characteristic style to his interiors. The wealthy responded with some enthusiasm. Webb introduced important clients, such as the fashionable George and Rosalind Howard. And friends such as the Ionides family, wealthy members of the Greek merchant community in London, gave their social blessing to the Morris venture.

Fame and financial success brought new problems in their wake. MMF & Co. remained a partnership, and each partner was legally entitled to an equal share of the profits, but Morris was no longer prepared to devote his life to generating profits for sleeping partners. In August 1874, he announced his intention to reconstitute the firm under his sole ownership. The result was a prolonged and acrimonious dispute with Madox Brown, Rossetti and Marshall. As risk-sharers, they felt entitled to an equal share of the profits and assets of the firm, just as they accepted 'joint and several' liability for its debts. They had a point, and it is possible that a court would have upheld their claims to substantial compensation.

Yet, even if one accepts the logic of their argument, it is hard to resist the conclusion that they got more out of the firm than they had put into it. Morris made the mistake of not acting sooner, before the furnishing and decorating business had really taken off. Even so, the balance of sympathy must lie with him, for while the others had been building their own careers he had devoted much of his time to reviving the fortunes of MMF & Co. In the end, fearing the damage an all-out legal battle might cause, Morris agreed to pay each partner £1,000, although Burne-Jones, Faulkner and Webb decided not to take their share. On 31 March 1875 it was announced that the partnership had been dissolved. Thenceforth the business traded as Morris & Company, with Morris as sole owner.

The years that followed were the most creative of Morris's career in business. Within a decade, his designs and products were admired throughout the western world. The strenuous efforts that he made to master such techniques as dyeing, fabric printing, weaving, tapestry making, and the high quality of the resulting products, are justly celebrated. The reasons for Morris's exceptional productivity deserve consideration. In the first place, he was powerfully motivated by the need to safeguard financial security; the freedom to work creatively was for him 'a dear delight'. The well-being of his family was also an important factor. Secondly, Morris's appetite for work was fundamental to his character. He derived tremendous pleasure from the anticipation of reaching a goal. Once a thing was done, it was quickly set aside in favour of the next challenge. It should not be thought, however, that Morris's appetite for new projects caused him to cut corners. He was dedicated to perfection. Only after the most meticulous research and testing would he begin the manufacture of a new range of products. The thoroughness of his approach ultimately made for a high level of personal efficiency. He was capable of carrying out many tasks in parallel while giving of his best to each.

The need for commercial success became even more pressing with the move to Merton Abbey in 1881. It was essential to take full advantage of Morris's years of experimentation, but it represented a substantial capital investment for a relatively small company. The old buildings had to be thoroughly overhauled and modified, and new tools and equipment acquired. Many months were to pass before the works were fully operational; block printing, for example, did not begin in earnest until late in 1882.

Of course, the commercial success of Morris & Co. did not depend simply upon the energy of its owner and excellence of its designs and products. Morris was acutely aware of the importance of marketing, and did not intend to leave matters to chance. He made a big effort to win favour with the public. The firm's brochures developed the theme that beautiful design, colouring and originality, though expensive, represented good value for money, and that product quality was assured by first-rate materials and high standards of manufacture. The emphasis on 'the luxury of taste' rather than 'the luxury of costliness', first set out in the firm's prospectus of 1861, remained a characteristic theme of its publicity in the 1880s and 1890s.

Another feature of the firm's marketing strategy in this period was the expansion of its range to include goods of varying grades and prices. Handmade Hammersmith carpets were extremely costly (£113 for a 16 x 13 ft. example), but by the late 1870s Morris designs were available for Wilton, Axminster, Brussels and Kidderminster carpets at a range of prices. This placed more of the firm's products within the reach of the middle classes. Most customers had relatively modest incomes and bought wallpapers, fabrics and carpets for inclusion in their own decorative schemes. Likewise, throughout the 1880s and 1890s, Morris & Co. sold a limited number of large, high-quality pieces of embroidery at high prices; but such small items as cushion covers, work bags and fire-screens were increasingly important, most being sold for 15s. to £1 10s. Embroidery was a popular and respectable occupation for middle-class women and many of the firm's designs were available as kits, with the pattern ready-traced on silk, or as a transfer.

In 1877, Morris & Co. opened an elegant showroom at 264 Oxford Street. After the establishment of the Merton workshops it was extended to provide more display space, and Morris took steps to reach a wider clientele beyond the metropolis. In January 1883 he opened a showroom in Manchester; a wealthy city with a reputation for patronage of the applied arts. Agents were appointed in the United States and continental Europe. Morris was exasperated by the generally high level of import duties, often complaining of 'almost prohibitory' tariffs, but was not put off, recognising that wealthy Germans and Americans were willing to pay premium prices for goods of the highest quality and originality.

Morris often looked to past ages for technology and artistic inspiration, yet the commercial side of his business was very much of the present. Morris knew his markets, and he knew how to attract those who could afford his goods. The shop in Oxford Street, not the Merton Abbey factory, was the strategic hub of his operations. It was here that his creations were displayed in a tastefully fashionable setting. The business, moreover, was managed in a prudent and professional manner. Due attention was paid to costs, prices and profit margins. If an estimate exceeded £500, advances were required as the work progressed to ease the problem of cash flow. Additional charges were made 'for attendance to view such buildings or rooms as are proposed for us to decorate'. Morris & Co.

Fig. 17 The exterior of the shop in Oxford Street. Originally 264, this was renumbered 449 in February 1882.

Fig. 18 An exterior view of part of the Merton Abbey Works looking across the bridge spanning the River Wandle.

Fig.19 The carpet weaving section at Merton Abbey.

never sold at discount prices, and prompt payment was demanded of all customers, whatever their rank or social standing. Prices were 'for ready-money payments', and the warning was issued that 'all sums unpaid after one month from the delivery of the account will be charged with interest at the rate of 5 per cent per annum'. This was a distinctly modern feature; the better-off were accustomed to long periods of credit. Another break with convention was that names, dimensions and prices were marked on all items. It was still the normal practice in high-class shops to avoid labelling, although the Morris approach was shared by newer types of retailers such as department stores.

Costs were carefully controlled. Subcontractors' charges were monitored, and, although Morris had the reputation of being a good employer who paid somewhat above the market rate, he always ensured that the wage bills did not drive up the price of goods to unsaleable levels. This was important, for whilst its leadership of the market may have allowed Morris & Co. some flexibility in setting prices, it could not completely ignore those of its rivals.

Morris & Co. demonstrated considerable shrewdness in combatting the competition. This was manifested in the way it exploited the reputation of its principal designers, Burne-Jones and Morris. To establish the identity of the firm, the partners had originally agreed to keep the names of individual designers secret. This policy was reversed in the 1880s and early 1890s when Burne-Jones's reputation was at its peak and his work commanded high prices. It was with some pride that Morris & Co. announced in 1882 that 'Mr Burne Jones entrusts us alone with the execution of his cartoons for stained glass'. Even more important was the reputation of Morris himself. He was by now a famous figure and his very name drew fashionable people to take an interest in his art, whether or not they agreed with his political ideas. His conversion to socialism appears to have done little to deter customers. Nor did his lofty attitude and forthright opinions. The firm was not slow to exploit the celebrity of its owner, announcing that he would 'personally advise Customers as to the best method and style of Decoration to be used in each case'. By the late 1880s, indeed, as Morris's personal reputation soared, he felt obliged to ration his time by charging fees for visiting clients – five guineas in London, and £20 elsewhere. He made it clear to his managers, however, that the

charges did not apply to 'well known and useful customers...but only to stop fools and impertinents'.

Morris was quick to recognise the firm's methods of design and manufacturing as a source of competitive advantage. Merton Abbey in particular attracted a steady stream of visitors who, directly or indirectly, helped spread the reputation of the firm. Yet, while many of his admirers believed him to combine high principles with business acumen, Morris himself was becoming more and more critical of his achievements. His disillusionment is summed up in the oft-quoted statement that 'art cannot have real life and growth under the present system of commercialism and profit-mongering'.

Morris's commitment to socialism, deep and passionate though it was, did not release him from the need to earn his living. He continued during the 1880s to visit Merton two or three times a week, and his enthusiasm for work continued unabated. However, his role in the business was now less intensive, and he delegated day-to-day responsibility to others. Throughout his career, Morris had the knack of getting the best out of senior colleagues and workpeople. He appointed managers who combined enthusiasm, shrewdness and integrity, and allowed them considerable freedom of action. George Wardle, general manager from 1870 to 1890, took overall control of operations at Merton. He fully concurred with Morris's views on design and manufacture, and his contribution to the success of the firm has not received due recognition. J.H.Dearle supervised the tapestry, weaving and fabric-printing departments. His best designs are often mistaken for those of Morris, and he became the firm's principal designer after the death of Morris in 1896. Frank and Robert Smith also made a major contribution to the mature firm. This was recognised in the late 1880s when Morris made them partners. His aim was to maintain his income while progressively withdrawing from active participation in the business. The deed of partnership (now at the PRO; IR59/173) signed by Morris and the Smiths on 19 March 1890 allowed the brothers to buy into the business on very favourable terms, and the firm continued to develop in the 1890s under their leadership, despite Morris's almost complete withdrawal from active management.

The overall picture revealed by our research into Morris & Co. is of a financially healthy and well managed-business with considerable scope to charge premium prices. But there were always limits; Morris operated in a highly competitive environment, and succeeded because he understood it very well. The truth is that William Morris was a practical, hard-working, hard-headed, imaginative and original man of affairs. The success of Morris & Co. owed much less to good fortune than it did to Morris himself.

Fig.20 An exterior view, from the garden, of 1 Holland Park.

Fig.21 A corner of the drawing room at 1 Holland Park, showing part of the Morris & Co. furnishings, including *Vine* wallpaper and the *Forest* tapestry.

D.1 Minute book for Morris, Marshall, Faulkner & Co.

10 December 1862 to 23 October 1874
Quarter bound in black leather with marbled boards,
containing ninety sheets of ruled paper with hand-written
entries; 17.75 x 11.5 cm
Sanford and Helen Berger Collection

Morris, Marshall, Faulkner & Co. was formed in April 1861.
The first recorded minutes in this, the only known record of
business meetings, is 10 December 1862. Weekly meetings, held
at the firm's earliest premises, 8 Red Lion Square, are recorded
until 18 February 1864.

Early commissions are itemised and the work apportioned out
to partners although at the first meeting recorded it was agreed
to withhold the names of the designers from the public. Those
present on 14 January 1863 (wrongly dated 1862) agreed that a
prospectus and circular letter be printed and be sent, thus
attempting to boost publicity of their work. The end-of-year
balance sheets provide lists of objects made and names of
patrons and employees.

In the first meeting noted at Queen Square on 16 May 1867 it
was agreed that £1 be paid to each member as capital returned
and Philip Webb be offered '£80 per annum as consulting
manager'. A more business-like tone continues until 23 October
1874, when it was 'resolved unanimously that it is desirable that
the firm be dissolved'. Disputes were noted and assessors
appointed to evaluate shares. The last meeting recorded is 4
November 1874. Solicitors were present and it was decided to
hold a general meeting of the firm 'to endeavour if possible to
come to an amicable adjustment of the process of dissolution'.
This took place in March 1875.   LP

D.2 *Scenes from Clerical Life:*
'The Labourer is Worthy of his Hire'

Peter Paul Marshall, *c.*1862
Oil on canvas, 50.8 x 38.2 cm
Signed: 'P. P. Marshall'
Private Collection

One of the only known pair of paintings by Marshall. The
subject is based on a quotation from Pope's *Epistle to Bathhurst*.
The paintings were exhibited in the Liverpool Academy of 1862
(237) and a label on the back of this canvas reads 'Paul
Marshall. 8 Red Lion Square' with the quotation 'The Labourer
is worthy of his hire'. It is significant that Marshall gave the
firm's first headquarters as his professional address.

Peter Paul Marshall (1830–1900) was a Scottish surveyor and
sanitary engineer by trade. He was introduced to Morris
through Madox Brown who was a friend of his father-in-law,
John Miller, a Liverpool patron. He became the seventh partner
in the firm of Morris, Marshall, Faulkner & Co. The pair of paintings was at one time owned by W.S. Caine, a Liverpool iron
merchant and radical politician, and was sold at his sale in 1873.

The conventional interior depicted in the painting has interesting artistic details, including a screen with a print of Raphael's
cartoon *Charge to Peter* and Holman Hunt's *Light of the World*.
This is a reference to Ruskin's comparison of the two paintings
in 'The False Religious Idea' in volume III of *Modern Painters*
(1856), where Ruskin describes the earlier work as 'that infinite
monstrosity and hypocrisy' and the Hunt 'a real vision of real
things'. Burne-Jones praised the passage in a review of this
work in the April 1856 edition of the *Oxford and Cambridge
Magazine*. The table cover depicted in Marshall's painting is,
almost certainly, a copy of one of the firm's earliest commercial
embroideries.   LP

D.1

D.2

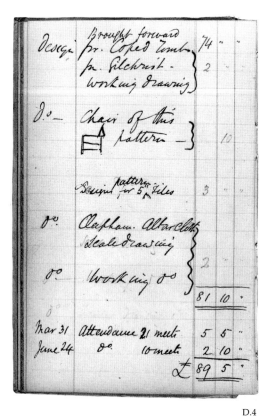

D.3 Notebook

William Morris, Edward Burne-Jones and possibly others, from *c.*1859
Bound book with drawings in pencil; 20.0 x 26.0 cm (open)
British Library (Add. MS 45,336)

A book with drawings, plans and notes in a number of different hands, almost certainly dating from before the foundation of Morris, Marshall, Faulkner & Co. in April 1861, but also including details of the firm's work. Sketches show details taken from medieval manuscripts and other historic sources including a page of drawings of knights in armour, probably by Morris.

Plans show the layout for hangings in the bedroom and drawing room of Red House plus a large tile scheme with a list of chosen subjects for 'Court of Love' in Burne-Jones's hand. A draft for a letter to a prospective client, in Morris's hand, listing services available from Morris, Marshall, Faulkner & Co. is the 'circular letter' that the partners agreed to have printed with a prospectus at their meeting at 62 Great Russell Street on 14 January 1863, noted in the firm's minute book (cat.no.D.1).   LP

D.3

D.4

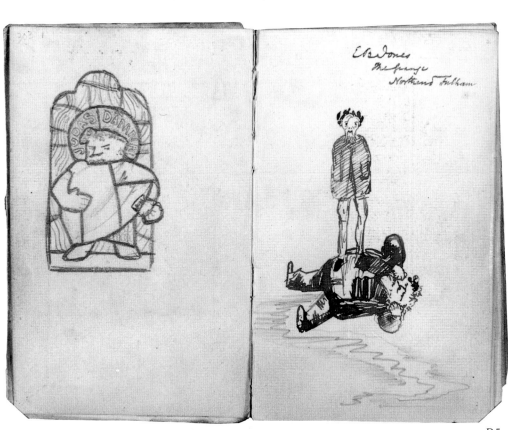

D.5

D.6

D.7

D.4 Account Book

Philip Webb, 1861–78
Vellum bound with brass clasp, pencil and ink notes
on blue ruled paper; 15.24 x 10.16 cm
Inscribed: 'P. Webb'
Private Collection
SEE ALSO FIG 16, PAGE 50)

Philip Webb's passbook for Morris, Marshall, Faulkner
& Co. and the early years of Morris & Co. It lists work
undertaken, attendances at business meetings and payments. The accounts also include goods that Webb
bought from or through the firm, including furniture,
household wares and wine.

Together with Burne-Jones's accounts (cat. no. D.5) this
provides one of the main sources of information concerning the firm's early work.
Exhib. 1934 (351); 1961 (21)   LP

D.5 Account Book

Edward Burne-Jones, from 1861
Bound in vellum with metal clasp, 15.5 x 10.0 cm
Fitzwilliam Museum, Cambridge   Given by
Sir Philip Burne-Jones and Mrs Margaret Mackail

One of two passbooks listing Burne-Jones's work for
Morris, Marshall, Faulkner & Co., and Morris & Co.
and payments made for these. As with Webb's records
(cat. no. D.4) these also list goods bought from the firm.
The books provide invaluable information on the firm
including 'inspecting premises at Queen's Square' in
August 1865 as well as evidence of the authorship of
designs and the dating of schemes associated with

them. They also hint at the tastes of the Burne-Jones
family and how they furnished their homes.

A number of amusing entries and caricatures illustrate
the camaraderie between partners and especially the
designer's close relationship with Morris.
Exhib. 1934 (351)   LP

D.6 *Rupes Topseia*

Dante Gabriel Rossetti, *c.*1874
Pen and brown ink, 17.9 x 11.2 cm
Inscribed with title and other notes
British Museum (1939-5-13-7)
Given by Dr Robert Steele

Rossetti's savage comment on the break up of the firm
of Morris, Marshall, Faulkner & Co. He depicts Morris
as Topsy thrown from the Tarpeian Rock in Rome as a
condemned criminal. Jane looks down on the scene and
in the top left corner six small figures, the other partners – Burne-Jones, Madox Brown, Philip Webb,
Charles Faulkner, P. P. Marshall and Rossetti himself –
are shown holding a banner inscribed 'We are Starving'
in front of the ruined building '...& Co.'

Morris had started to become disillusioned with the
partnership in the late 1860s. Whereas the firm was now
his main business, the other partners had other interests. He increasingly felt that he was taking the lion's
share of responsibility without proper recognition and
in August 1874 announced his intention to wind up the
firm and set up another under his sole ownership. The
resulting split between Morris, Burne-Jones, Faulkner
and Webb on one side and Rossetti, Madox Brown and

Marshall on the other became acrimonious and bitter.
The wrangle continued until March 1875, when Morris
agreed to pay the three protagonists £1,000 each in
compensation. The dissolution of the firm led to a
permanent estrangement between Morris and Rossetti
although they continued to meet socially.   LP

D.7 *The Pond at William Morris's Works at Merton*

Lexden Lewis Pocock (1850–1919), after 1881
Watercolour, 13.9 x 23.1 cm
V&A (P.34-1924)
Given by A. Lyndhurst Pocock

An idealised painting of the site of Morris's factory at
Merton Abbey.

The factory, erected in the early eighteenth century by
Huguenots for silk throwing, was transferred to a
printworks in the nineteenth century and had been used
by Welch Brothers, who were tablecloth printers, until a
few years before Morris took over. The buildings stood
in seven acres with a large meadow, an orchard and a
vegetable garden. There was a manager's house, a care-
taker's lodge and offices, and the old buildings already
included a dye-house and croft room. The site was first
spotted by William De Morgan and Morris first visited it
in March 1881. He wrote at the time 'The River Wandle...
runs through them, turning a water wheel and supplying water of a special quality...we brought away bottles
for analysis – to make sure that it was fit to dye with'.

The move from Queen Square to Merton Abbey took
place in June 1881 and the adaptation of the buildings
for stained glass, dyeing, textile printing, carpet and
fabric weaving followed almost immediately.   LP

THE POLITICAL
ACTIVIST

Nicholas Salmon

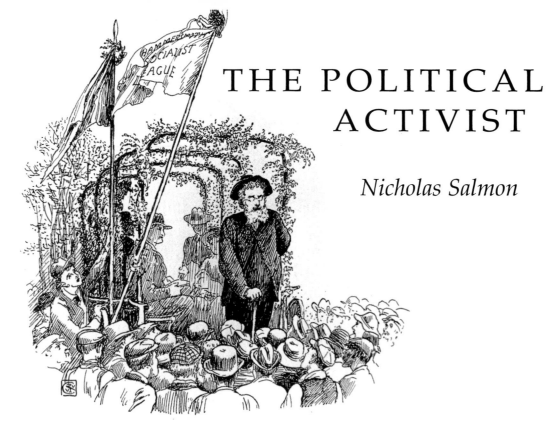

William Morris's early life gave little indication of the important role he was to play in the British socialist movement. The son of a wealthy city businessman, he entered Exeter College, Oxford, in 1853 with the intention of taking holy orders. At that time his views were High Church and he spent his first few terms immersed in such religious works as Henry Hart Milman's *Latin Christianity* and Kenelm Digby's *Mores Catholici*. At one point he and Edward Burne-Jones even considered founding a monastic order and becoming Roman Catholics.

This phase of Anglo-Catholicism was short-lived. Burne-Jones soon introduced him to a group of his friends at Pembroke College which included William Fulford, Richard Watson Dixon and Charles Faulkner. Their interests extended beyond religion to the discussion of secularism, modern literature and social reform. It was through this group of free-thinking students that Morris became acquainted with the criticisms of nineteenth-century capitalism made by Carlyle, Kingsley and Ruskin. Their arguments greatly impressed him, and, along with his reading of French and German philosophy, led him to renounce religion and devote his life to art. Morris's subsequent friendship with Rossetti, whose family were revolutionary refugees from Italy, also played a part in his political development. Rossetti introduced him to a number of continental radicals and encouraged him to support the nationalistic aspirations of the occupied states in Europe.

It was appropriate, therefore, that it was the Turkish suppression of a series of uprisings in its Balkan states that led Morris to enter national politics. In 1875 revolts against Turkish rule had broken out in Bosnia, Montenegro and Serbia. The following year these spread to Bulgaria where the rebellion was supported by Russia. During the suppression of this uprising Turkish mercenaries committed a number of atrocities, details of which were published in the *Daily News* on 23 June 1876. This report led to a wave of opposition to Disraeli's pro-Turkish foreign policy.

At first this protest was orchestrated by radical clubs and working-class organisations. It only became a national issue when Gladstone, seizing the opportunity of attacking the Conservative government, published his famous pamphlet *The Bulgarian Horrors and the Question of the East* in September 1876. In this he demanded an immediate Turkish withdrawal from Bulgaria. Morris, enraged by the 'Bulgarian Atrocities', pledged his support to the campaign the following month in a letter published in the *Daily News* under the title 'England and the Turks'. Following Gladstone's intervention, a conference was held at St James's Hall on 8 November 1876 at which the Eastern Question Association was formed with J. A. Mundella as chairman and Morris as treasurer.

Morris became one of the most active of the Association's campaigners. On 11 May 1877 he issued his manifesto 'To the Working-men of England', in which he bitterly condemned the Tories

Fig. 22 Walter Crane's sketch of Morris speaking at a May Day Rally in Hyde Park, in the 1890s.

Fig. 23 The first page of Morris's manuscript for *Unjust War* addressed to The Working Men of England (cat.no.E.1).

for defending their own class interests and urged the workers to speak out against Disraeli's 'unjust war'. Thereafter he devoted all his energy to the cause – making speeches, organising petitions and attending committee meetings.

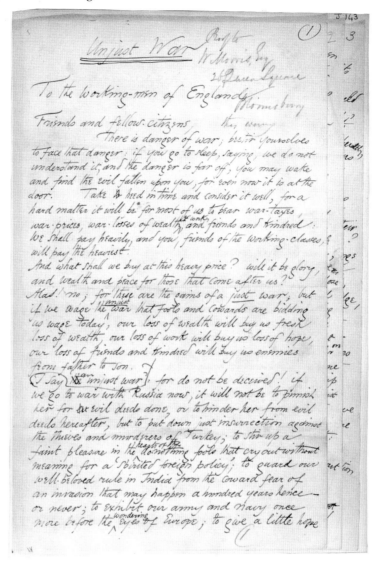

The agitation reached its climax when Russia declared war on Turkey and began to advance on Constantinople in early January 1878. For a time British intervention on the Turkish side appeared imminent. The Association responded by calling a large anti-war meeting at Exeter Hall for 16 January 1878. This was opened by a lusty rendition of 'Wake, London Lads!', a song specially written for the occasion by Morris, led by a choir from John Broadhurst's Stonemasons' Union. In his own speech Morris condemned the 'war-at-any-price' party and annoyed some of the audience by criticising Queen Victoria for her support of Disraeli.

This was to be the Association's last success, as the country was soon gripped by anti-Russian jingoism. Morris, along with friends such as Burne-Jones, desperately tried to keep the agitation going by attempting to organise another huge meeting at the Agricultural Hall for 25 February 1878. However, this never materialised as Gladstone, who had originally agreed to speak, decided it was politically expedient to withdraw from the agitation. Without the support of the parliamentary Liberals the Eastern Question Association effectively collapsed.

Despite the failure of the Association, Morris did not withdraw from politics. In 1879 he was elected treasurer of the National Liberal League, a largely working-class organisation formed from the groups who had opposed Disraeli's pro-Turkish foreign policy. Its initial aim was to help Gladstone win the general election of 1880. In this it was successful. However, its subsequent attempt to persuade the new government to implement a programme of radical reform proved a complete failure. The government instead pursued imperialistic policies in Africa and went on to pass the notorious Irish Coercion Bill, which gave it sweeping powers to enforce order in the province. Completely disillusioned with the Liberals, Morris resigned from the League early in 1882. He was now convinced 'that Radicalism is on the wrong line…and will never develope [*sic*] into anything more than Radicalism: in fact that it is made for and by the middle classes and will always be under the control of rich capitalists'.

Having rejected parliamentary politics, Morris was now ready to consider socialism. During 1882 he read a great deal of proto-socialist literature, including Henry George's *Progress and Poverty*, Henry Wallace's *Land Nationalisation* and Sergius Stepniak's *Underground Russia*. However, he was to claim later that the crucial event in his conversion to socialism was his reading of John Stuart Mill's critique of François Fourier's utopian socialism. Paradoxically, Mill's fairness in presenting Fourier's arguments convinced Morris 'that Socialism was a necessary change, and that it was possible to bring it about in our own days'. By the summer of 1882 he declared himself ready 'to join any body who distinctly called themselves Socialists'.

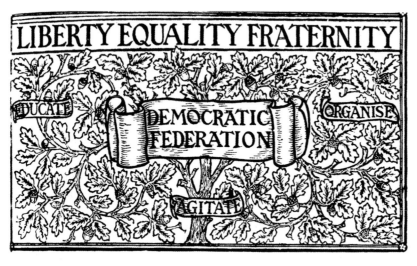

The only socialist organisation in England at this time was the Democratic Federation. This had been formed in 1881 as an amalgamation of radical clubs. However, it soon came under the leadership of the socialist H.M.Hyndman, who abandoned its original reformist programme in the summer of 1882. During the winter of 1882–3 Hyndman held a number of meetings, which Morris attended, to discuss a series of provisional reforms to be pursued on the way to the ultimate goal of social revolution. These included free education, public health improvements and land nationalisation. Impressed by the earnestness of these discussions, Morris joined the Federation in January 1883.

Hyndman was delighted to have secured the services of the famous author of *The Earthly Paradise*, and Morris was duly elected to the executive of the Federation in May 1883. His position as treasurer was especially appropriate as he was soon subsidising the campaign liberally from his own pocket. As part of his education in theoretical socialism Morris read Karl Marx's *Das Kapital* in French during the early months of 1883. He thoroughly enjoyed the 'great work' and his copy of the book became a treasured possession which he later had specially bound by T.J.Cobden-Sanderson (cat.no.E.3).

Morris threw himself wholeheartedly into the propaganda work. He gave many lectures, regularly attended the weekly meetings of the executive and even composed a series of 'chants' to be sung at meetings. He also contributed articles to *Justice*, the Federation's journal, and often sold the paper on street corners in the West End. The vigour of the Federation's early propaganda attracted such valuable recruits as Edward Aveling, H.H.Champion and John Burns, and Morris was to write enthusiastically that 'the *hope* is spreading, and even far more speedily than some of us would have thought possible a little time ago; and it is clear that when the hope is once received into the hearts of the mass of our people, the beginning of the new day is at hand'.

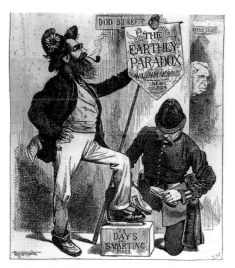

Fig. 25 'The Attitude of the Police'
J. P. Stafford's caricature from the
magazine *Funny Folks* for the week
ending 10 October 1885. Dod Street was
the scene of many meetings by the
Social Democratic Federation.

Fig. 26 The original cast-list for
The Tables Turned: or Nupkins Awakened,
with Morris as the Archbishop of
Canterbury.

THE TABLES TURNED; or NUPKINS
AWAKENED

ORIGINAL CAST
DRAMATIS PERSONÆ. PART I

Mr. La-di-da (*found guilty of swindling*)   H. Bartlett
Mr. Justice Nupkins   W. Blundell
Mr. Hungary, Q.C. (*Counsel for Prosecution*)
                                                    W. H. Utley
Sergeant Sticktoit (*Witness for Prosecution*) James Allman
Constable Potlegoff (*Witness for Prosecution*)
                                                    H. B. Tarleton
Constable Strongithoath (*Witness for Prosecution*)
                                                    J. Flockton
Mary Pinch (*a labourer's wife, accused of theft*) May Morris
Foreman of Jury   T. Cantwell
Jack Freeman (*a Socialist, accused of conspiracy, sedition, and
obstruction of the highway*)   H. H. Sparling
Archbishop of Canterbury (*Witness for Defence*)
                                                    W. Morris
Lord Tennyson (*Witness for Defence*)   A. Brookes
Professor Tyndall (*Witness for Defence*)   H. Bartlett
William Joyce (*a Socialist Ensign*)   H. A. Barker
Usher   J. Lane
Clerk of the Court   J. Turner
    Jurymen, Interrupters, Revolutionists, etc., etc.

DRAMATIS PERSONÆ. PART II

Citizen Nupkins (*late Justice*)   W. Blundell
Mary Pinch   May Morris
William Joyce (*late Socialist Ensign*)   H. A. Barker
Jack Freeman   H. H. Sparling
1st Neighbour   H. B. Tarleton
2nd Neighbour   J. Lane
3rd Neighbour   H. Graham
    Robert Pinch, and other Neighbours, Men and Women
528

However, it was not long before disagreements began to arise over aims and tactics. The central issue was whether the Federation should continue to support ameliorative reform or reject parliamentary methods in favour of educating the workers in socialism. A split appeared in the executive between those such as Hyndman, Champion and Aveling, who believed that legislative reforms should serve as the basis of the agitation, and those, like Morris, Joseph Lane and Andreas Scheu (the Viennese anarchist and furniture designer), who saw them as deflecting attention away from the real aim of social revolution. This dissent was accompanied by growing suspicion of Hyndman's autocratic role on the executive and his editorial control of *Justice*.

These differences emerged at the Federation's annual conference in 1884, when the opposition group succeeded in having Hyndman replaced as president by a rotating chairman elected by the executive. Despite this defeat, Hyndman refused to relinquish power and continued to present his own case through the editorship of *Justice*. When the executive attempted to gain control of the paper he refused to co-operate. Morris, who found Hyndman's intransigence increasingly frustrating, soon assumed the leadership of the opposition on the executive.

Things came to a head when Morris was on a lecture tour of Scotland. While he was visiting the Glasgow branch on 14 December 1884 a letter was read out from Hyndman denouncing Scheu as an anarchist. Morris was then heckled for his alleged ignorance of Marxist economics. Infuriated by this attempt to undermine his credibility, Morris returned to London determined to bring the dispute with Hyndman out into the open. Two weeks later, on 27 December 1884, a vote was forced on Hyndman's leadership. This was won by Morris and his supporters by ten votes to eight. They immediately resigned *en masse* to found the Socialist League on 30 December 1884.

The rebels had won a hollow victory. Hyndman retained the majority of the four hundred members of the Federation, which had been renamed the Social Democratic Federation at the annual conference in 1884, and had the benefit of an established organisation with branches throughout the country. More serious was the lack of unity among the rebels themselves; while there had been a common distrust of Hyndman's autocratic leadership, some of them still broadly agreed with his aims. Among this group were Eleanor Marx and Edward Aveling who were both in close contact with Friedrich Engels.

These differences were apparent from the start. Morris was determined that the League should adopt an anti-parliamentary stance and confine itself to educating and organising the workers. The *Manifesto* he wrote for the League was based on Marxist theory and committed the League to extra-parliamentary propaganda (cat. no. E.5). However, Aveling drafted a constitution that was pro-parliamentary and recommended that the League should work towards the formation of a Socialist Labour Party. Although this was rejected, at Morris's insistence, at the first annual conference in 1885, it marked the beginning of a serious difference of opinion in the council of the League.

At first these divisions were hidden by the enthusiasm with which the League set about its task. Nobody worked harder than Morris, who conscientiously attended committee meetings, spoke regularly at the open-air stands the League set up in the East End of London and travelled the country on extended lecture tours. He also almost single-handedly created a body of creative socialist literature, which included a long narrative poem based on the events of the Paris Commune called *The Pilgrims of Hope*, a topical play entitled *The Tables Turned; or, Nupkins Awakened* and two socialist prose romances: *A Dream of John Ball* and *News from Nowhere* (cat. no. E.12). The latter is an inspired vision of a decentralised communist society following the revolution.

Some of these works were published in the League's paper, *Commonweal*, which first appeared in February 1885 (cat. no. E.7). Morris's work for the paper, which quickly established itself as the foremost socialist journal in Britain, is probably his most underestimated achievement. Between 1885 and 1890 he made more than four hundred contributions to the paper, including reviews, numerous essays and a remarkable series of articles on contemporary events entitled 'Notes on News'. He also published essays by the most influential socialist thinkers of the age, including Engels and George Bernard Shaw. To advertise and sell the paper Morris was often seen walking the streets of London wearing sandwich boards.

At first the propaganda work of the League was helped by the prevailing economic conditions. A recession during the early 1880s had led to many unemployed men sleeping rough in London. In 1885 the Social Democratic Federation succeeded in organising these discontented workers and

Fig. 27 The Hammersmith Branch of the Socialist League. May and Jenny Morris sit in the front row third and fifth from the left. William stands in the row behind to the right (cat. no. E.4).

Fig. 28 The room in the boat house, Kelmscott House , used for socialist meetings in the 1890s. Before the move to Merton Abbey it was used for carpet weaving.

Fig. 29 Police summons for wilful obstruction issued to Morris on 20 July 1886.

began to hold weekly marches of the unemployed. This campaign culminated in a riot on 8 February 1886, when a large crowd ran amok looting and smashing windows along Pall Mall and Piccadilly. *The Times* described London as gripped by 'something little short of panic'.

The authorities responded by attempting to curb the activities of the socialists. What became known as the 'free speech' campaign began when the police broke up a meeting of the Social Democratic Federation and arrested two of its speakers. Thereafter, frequent attacks were made on the outdoor meetings of both the Federation and the League and a number of speakers sentenced to imprisonment for 'obstruction'. Morris, aware that his presence on the streets greatly embarrassed the police, made a point of speaking at the meetings they most frequently disrupted. He was even arrested and fined a shilling for addressing a crowd in Bell Street in July 1886. In persecuting the

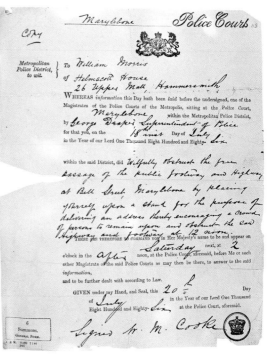

Fig.30 Engraving of the police dispersing the Clerkenwell contingent of the marchers on 'Bloody Sunday', from *The Graphic* 19 November 1887.

THE RIOT IN TRAFALGAR SQUARE

socialists in this way the authorities made a tactical mistake. Both the League and the Federation gained valuable publicity from the heavy-handed actions of the police and the harsh sentences of the courts.

By 1886 the League had succeeded in establishing a solid base for its agitation. Of its twenty branches, eleven were in provincial towns outside London. It had a particularly strong presence in the north with active branches in Leeds, Bradford, Glasgow and Edinburgh. Morris's own Hammersmith branch had over a hundred members and held regular outdoor meetings which attracted audiences in excess of two hundred people. In 1887 membership of the League peaked at about a thousand. It was during the most successful period of agitation that Morris began his short-lived *Socialist Diary*, which he hoped would give future generations some idea of his day-to-day propaganda activities.

However, there were already indications that the tactics of the League were failing. While it gained some radical recruits from its support of the agitation over Irish coercion, it failed to exploit the rise in trade unionism and the associated industrial unrest. This was because Morris refused to allow the League to become involved with issues that interfered with its main task of educating the workers in revolutionary socialism.

Two events contributed to the subsequent disintegration of the League. The first was what became known as 'Bloody Sunday'. As part of its programme of unemployment agitation the Federation had continued to hold meetings in Trafalgar Square. During October and early November 1887 these meetings were regularly dispersed by the police. On 8 November Sir Charles Warren, the Metropolitan Commissioner of Police, took the provocative step of banning any further meetings in the Square on the dubious grounds that it was Crown property. To protest against this attack on 'free speech' – and the government's policy of coercion in Ireland – a combined radical, Irish and socialist demonstration was called for Sunday, 13 November 1887. The plan was that several columns of marchers would converge on Trafalgar Square where a massive meeting would be held in defiance of the authorities.

Morris's experiences on 'Bloody Sunday' were similar to those of the other marchers. The Hammersmith branch of the League formed part of a contingent of 5,000 demonstrators who assembled on Clerkenwell Green. Here Morris and Annie Besant addressed the crowd, urging them to march to the Square in a dignified and orderly fashion. However, shortly after the marchers crossed Shaftesbury Avenue they were charged by the police and dispersed in complete disarray. 'It was all over in a few minutes,' Morris was to write later in *Commonweal*, 'our comrades fought valiantly, but they had not learned how to stand and turn their column into a line, or to march on to the front.' Morris managed to reach Trafalgar Square in time to see the Riot Act read and the Square cleared by a regiment of Guardsmen with fixed bayonets.

'Bloody Sunday' had a significant psychological affect on the British socialist movement. The ease with which the police achieved their victory destroyed many activists' faith in direct action and encouraged the movement towards Fabianism and parliamentary methods. Within the League this tendency had already been apparent at the third annual conference, when a resolution proposed by John Lincoln Mahon in favour of supporting parliamentary candidates was only defeated by seventeen votes to eleven. Following 'Bloody Sunday' Mahon withdrew from the League taking with him much of the support he had built up in the north. He was followed by E. Belfort Bax and the Bloomsbury branch after another pro-parliamentary resolution was defeated at the fourth annual conference in May 1888.

The divisions within the League were deepened by the case of the Chicago Anarchists. In May 1886 a fight had broken out between strikers and strike breakers at the McCormick Harvester Works in Chicago. When the police arrived they fired at a group of strikers running away from the scene, causing numerous injuries and four deaths. The American anarchists subsequently arranged a meeting in Haymarket Square in Chicago to protest at the police action. During this meeting a bomb was thrown at the police which wounded sixty-six officers of whom seven later died. The police then opened fire on the crowd wounding over two hundred and causing a number of fatalities. Unable to identify the bomb-thrower the authorities arrested eight Chicago anarchist leaders, only one of whom had actually been present at the Haymarket meeting. Despite this all of the men were found guilty. Long sentences were passed on three of them, while four were hanged in October 1887. Another, Louis Lingg, cheated the gallows by committing suicide in his cell.

Many socialists were impressed by the way the Chicago Anarchists conducted their defence and faced the prospect of death. Such influential figures within the League as Joseph Lane, Frank Kitz and Charles Mowbray began to listen with respect to the anarchists' case. By the early months of 1888 this group, along with James Tochatti and Henry Charles, had assumed a prominent position in the leadership of the League. Morris inadvertently strengthened their position at the fourth annual conference when he relied on their support in order to maintain the anti-parliamentary stance of the League.

In fact the fourth annual conference marked the end of the League as an effective organisation. The membership soon fell into decline and the remaining provincial branches became isolated and outside the control of the leadership in London. The end came at the annual conference in 1890 when the anarchists succeeded in gaining control of the council and ousted Morris from the editorship of *Commonweal*. Disheartened by this defeat, Morris and the Hammersmith branch withdrew from the League in November 1890. Without Morris's financial support and mediative influence the League subsequently disintegrated into a series of uncoordinated revolutionary groups and *Commonweal* ceased publication.

Nevertheless, Morris continued to play an active role in the socialist movement. In November 1890 the Hammersmith branch of the League was renamed the Hammersmith Socialist Society. Although its *Statement of Principles* reaffirmed Morris's purist views, it was never to pursue a fixed policy. Its weekly lectures and monthly discussions at Kelmscott House instead became a forum for debates within the wider socialist movement. This reflected Morris's growing conviction that the internal squabbles within the movement had been detrimental to the wider propaganda campaign. In 1894 he was to write that 'our business at present seems to me to preach Socialism to non-Socialists, and to preach unity of action to Socialists'.

In an attempt to foster unity within the movement the Hammersmith Socialist Society held a debate in December 1892 on the subject: 'Is it now desirable to form a Socialist Federation?' The question was answered in the affirmative and a sub-committee, including Morris, was formed 'to promote the alliance of Socialist organisations in Great Britain'. This sub-committee then approached the Fabians and the Social Democratic Federation and a joint committee of the three organisations was formed in January 1893, with Morris as chairman. There appeared to be real signs that the joint committee might succeed in May 1893 when it issued *The Manifesto of the English Socialists*: a collaborative work written by Morris, Hyndman and Shaw.

Fig. 31 Flyleaf satirising Morris and the anti-Parliamentary branches distributed by Socialist League Parliamentarists.

However, this initiative was to be overtaken by events. During 1892 a number of northern socialist and radical organisations had amalgamated to form the Independent Labour Party. This had immediate success in the general election of 1892, when three of its candidates were elected to Parliament. At its first conference, held in Bradford in January 1893, some of the ex-Leaguers, including J. L. Mahon and A. K. Donald played a prominent role. Such was Morris's standing in the movement that Robert Blatchford, in the *Clarion*, urged him to take his rightful place amongst the leadership of the new organisation.

For a few months it appeared that the Independent Labour Party might join the joint committee. In February 1893 the Hammersmith Socialist Society invited two prominent figures in the ILP, Keir Hardie and Shaw Maxwell, to lecture at Kelmscott House (fig. 28). Indeed, Shaw Maxwell returned the following month to lecture on the 'Aims and Objects of the Labour Party'. Morris wanted to call a united conference to include the Party but he once more came into conflict with Hyndman who considered the new organisation not to be a truly socialistic body. Faced with Hyndman's intransigence – and the withdrawal of the Fabians in July 1893 – the joint committee collapsed.

During his last few years in the movement a subtle change can be detected in Morris's views. Although he was never to lose his belief in the need for revolutionary change, he began to view industrial action and specific reform – like the eight-hour day and the minimum wage – more favourably. He came to the conclusion that the working classes could learn valuable lessons in organisation in pursuing such aims and that a transitional stage of state socialism might be inevitable before the revolution itself could be achieved. This change in attitude caused him to reconcile himself with the Social Democratic Federation in 1894, although he never rejoined the organisation, preferring to retain his independence while there was still a chance of uniting the various socialist bodies.

Some idea of the immense impact that Morris had on the socialist movement can be gained from the tributes paid to him after his death in October 1896. Robert Blatchford summed up the sorrow of his comrades when he wrote: 'I cannot help thinking that it does not matter what goes into the *Clarion* this week, because William Morris is dead...he was our best man, and he is dead.' Another moving tribute came from a Lancashire branch of the Federation: 'Comrade Morris is not dead there is not a Socialist living would believe him dead for he lives in the heart of all true men and women still and will do so to the end of time.' Such was the affection in which he was held that his name soon adorned socialist halls and Labour churches. His portrait was even hung alongside that of Marx in the clubrooms of the Federation. These were fitting tributes to a man who was one of the pivotal figures in the history of modern socialism.

Fig. 31 Flyleaf satirising Morris and the anti-Parliamentary branches distributed by Socialist League Parliamentarists.

E.1 Manuscript for Morris's political manifesto, *Unjust War*, 1877

Hand-written on unlined paper,
20.2 x 12.5 cm (paper size)
William Morris Gallery
(London Borough of Waltham Forest) (J143)
FOR ILLUSTRATION SEE FIG 23, PAGE 59

Morris's three-page handwritten manuscript for his first political manifesto, *Unjust War*, addressed 'To the working-men of England' and signed 'A Lover of Justice'. The manuscript was written during Morris's involvement with the Eastern Question Association shortly after Russia had declared war on Turkey on 24 April 1877. It is significant, as its anti-war message is presented in straightforward class terms: 'Who are they that are leading us into war?…Greedy gamblers on the Stock Exchange, idle officers of the army and navy (poor fellows!), worn-out mockers of the clubs, desperate purveyors of exciting war-news for the comfortable breakfast tables of those who have nothing to lose by war…' The manuscript was subsequently printed as a pamphlet, which appeared on 11 May 1877 and was distributed at meetings of the Association.

E.2 Membership card of the Democratic Federation, 1883

Designed by William Morris
Printed on card, 9.5 x 16.0 cm
Marx Memorial Library, Clerkenwell, London
FOR ILLUSTRATION SEE FIG 24, PAGE 60

The Democratic Federation's distinctive membership card was designed by Morris in 1883 shortly after he joined the organisation. The card bears the French revolutionary epithet 'Liberty, Equality and Fraternity' along with the Federation's propaganda slogan 'Educate, Agitate, Organise'. As Morris wrote in his lecture 'Art and the People' (1883): 'Educate, Agitate, Organise, these words, the motto of our Federation do most completely express what is necessary to be done by those who have any hope in the future of the people.' The central design of a spreading oak tree, with a pattern of stylised acorns and leaves, symbolises the aspirations of the Democratic Federation.

E.3 Morris's copy of *Le Capital* by Karl Marx

Translated from the original by M.J.Roy
Published by Maurice Lachatre et Cie, Paris, 1872–5
Binding, green leather tooled in gold by Thomas Cobden-Sanderson, completed 9 October 1884;
29.0 x 21.6 cm
J.Paul Getty, KBE, Wormsley Library

Morris's annotated copy of the French translation of Karl Marx's *Das Kapital* was one of his most treasured possessions. He probably purchased the book during the early months of 1883, shortly after he joined the Democratic Federation. Cormell Price noted in his unpublished Diary, on 13 April 1883, that he had visited the Burne-Joneses and found Morris 'full of Karl Marx whom he had begun to read in tr.' The book was so frequently handled and re-read that Morris sent it to be rebound by his fellow artist and socialist, Thomas Cobden-Sanderson, in 1884. On receiving the book Cobden-Sanderson noted that it 'had been worn to loose sections by his own constant study of it'. Cobden-Sanderson rebound the book in green leather decorated with gilt lettering. On the back of the book is an inscription which reads 'William Morris and Friends 1884'.

This, Cobden-Sanderson's second binding, was completed on 9 October 1884. It was forwarded by him to De Coverley's bindery and finished in his own workshop at Maiden Lane. Cobden-Sanderson later went on to establish the Doves Bindery at 15 Upper Mall opposite the Kelmscott Press. There is a long inscription in the book by Cobden-Sanderson describing the project and dated 24 February 1897.

The book was purchased from Morris's sale on 8 December 1898 by F.G. Bain and presented to Mrs Cobden-Sanderson. It was subsequently in the Estelle Doheny Collection.

E.4 William, May and Jenny Morris, and the Hammersmith Branch of the Socialist League, *c*.1885

Albumen print, 20.7 x 26.3 cm image
V&A (Ph.1817-1939) Given by Dr Robert Steele
FOR ILLUSTRATION SEE FIG 27, PAGE 62

The Hammersmith Branch of the Social Democratic Federation was reconstituted as a branch of the Socialist League on 7 January 1885. It adopted a folding membership card designed by Walter Crane, which depicted Morris in the character of a blacksmith. This photograph, probably dating from the mid-1880s, shows the bearded Morris standing in the centre row just to the right of the League's banner. His daughters are seated in the front row: May second from the left and Jenny centre. Another version of this photograph – obviously taken at the same time – has Jenny facing the camera and Morris standing with his arm across his chest. It is probable that both pictures were taken in the garden of Kelmscott House where the Hammersmith Branch of the Socialist League had its headquarters.

E.5 *Manifesto of the Socialist League*, 1885

Annotated by William Morris and E. Belfort Bax; cover designed by Walter Crane
Printed pamphlet, 19.0 x 12.6 cm
William Morris Gallery
(London Borough of Waltham Forest) (K604)

Morris and E. Belfort Bax co-wrote the *Manifesto of the Socialist League* shortly after they withdrew from the Social Democratic Federation at the end of 1884. Cormell Price found the two men hard at work on the manuscript when he arrived for dinner at Kelmscott House on New Year's Day 1885. The *Manifesto* was originally published as a pamphlet in January 1885 and later reprinted in the first edition of *Commonweal* a month later. It was formally adopted by the Socialist League at its first annual conference held on 5 July 1885. The second edition – illustrated here – was printed by Arthur Bonner and sported a cover designed by Walter Crane. It was published in October 1885. In this second edition the original *Manifesto* was reprinted along with a number of annotations made by the authors to 'clear up any possible ambiguities in the text'. The *Manifesto* was based closely on Marx's *Das Kapital* and described the Socialist League 'as a body advocating the principles of Revolutionary International Socialism'.

THE MANIFESTO

OF

9

SIGNED BY THE PROVISIONAL COUNCIL AT THE FOUNDATION OF THE LEAGUE ON 30th DEC. 1884, AND ADOPTED AT

THE GENERAL CONFERENCE

Held at FARRINGDON HALL, LONDON, on JULY 5th, 1885.

A New Edition, Annotated by

WILLIAM MORRIS AND E. BELFORT BAX.

LONDON:
Socialist League Office,
13 FARRINGDON ROAD, HOLBORN VIADUCT, E.C

1885.

PRICE ONE PENNY.

E.5

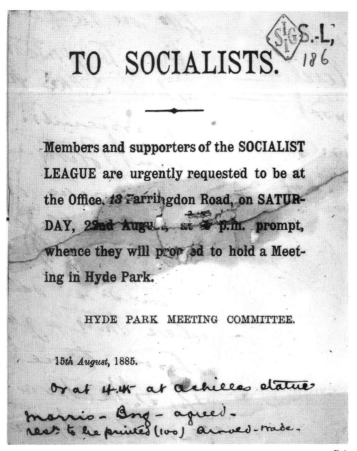

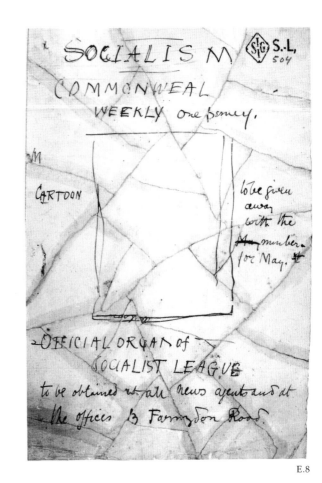

E.6

E.8

E.6 Handbill, 1885

Printed on paper with hand-written notes
20.5 x 12.5 cm
International Institute of Social History,
Amsterdam (F.V.186)

The various meetings and events sponsored by the
Socialist League were announced in *Commonweal* or
through the distribution of leaflets at open-air meetings
and lectures. This handbill, dated 15 August 1885,
requested members to meet at the League's headquarters at 13 Farringdon Road in order to form a
contingent at a mass demonstration to protest at the
exploitation of young girls and women in London to be
held on 22 August 1885. This meeting was called in
response to a series of articles W. T. Stead had published
in the *Pall Mall Gazette* exposing the extent of child
prostitution in the capital. The League's own protest
was opened by the singing of one of Morris's 'Chants
for Socialists'. Morris later addressed the crowd from a
brake. The Hyde Park rally is of interest as it was one of
the few political events that Jane Morris also attended.
She marched to Hyde Park in the procession organised
by the Ladies' National Society.

E.7 First edition of *Commonweal*, February 1885

Printed newspaper, 38.0 x 25.0 cm
British Library of Political and Economic Science,
London School of Economics
NOT ILLUSTRATED

The first edition of *Commonweal* was published in
February 1885. Subtitled 'The Official Organ of the
Socialist League', the eight-page paper was originally
published monthly priced 1d. However, in April 1885 a
four-page supplement was added, increasing its size to
twelve pages. It eventually became an eight-page weekly on 1 May 1886. Morris served as editor of the paper
from its inception until the summer of 1890 when the
anarchists on the League's Council succeeded in having
him replaced by D. J. Nicholl. Under Morris's editorship
the paper was soon established as one of the foremost
socialist journals in the country and Morris was able to
publish contributions by prominent socialists like
Friedrich Engels, George Bernard Shaw and Eleanor
Marx Aveling. Morris, himself, published hundreds of
articles in *Commonweal*, which included the serialisation
of A *Dream of John Ball* (1886–7) and *News from Nowhere*
(1890), numerous socialist essays and his regular 'Notes
on News' column in which he discussed contemporary
political events.

E8 Design for a leaflet to promote *Commonweal*, c.1886

Ink on paper, 14.0 x 21.0 cm
International Institute of Social History,
Amsterdam (H.VII)

This crude manuscript design, which has obviously
been screwed up and discarded, was for one of a number of leaflets produced by the Socialist League to
promote the sales of *Commonweal*. It probably dates
from the early months of 1886 and was intended to
advertise the relaunch of the paper as a weekly on
1 May. The sales of *Commonweal* were a continued

source of anxiety for Morris. Although the first edition
of the paper had sold 5,000 copies, sales soon stabilised
at around 2,000–3,000 a week. At this level of sales the
paper made a loss and its publication was only possible
because Morris subsidised its weekly deficit of £4 and
guaranteed the wages of the staff who printed it at the
League's offices at 13 Farringdon Road. Morris did
everything he could to promote *Commonweal*: advertising it on the streets of London wearing sandwich-boards,
selling it at open-air meetings and encouraging provincial branches of the League to urge local newsagents to
stock it in their shops.

E.9 Morris's Socialist Diary, January–April 1887

Handwritten manuscript, 25.0 x 46.0 cm open
British Library (Add. MS 45,335)

Morris began his Socialist Diary on 25 January 1887
during the period of his greatest activity on behalf of
the socialist cause. His original intention was that the
Diary should be 'published as a kind of view of the
Socialist movement seen from the inside, Jonah's view
of the Whale, you know'. In the event, the sheer volume of his lecture engagements, correspondence and
political journalism forced him to abandon the project
after just three months. The last entry, for 27 April 1887,
began with the apology that 'I have been busy about
many things and so unable to fill up this book'. The
entry for 16 February 1887 – shown here – begins 'I
spoke on a very cold windy (NE) morning at the
Walham Green station', and describes the scene at one
of the regular Sunday morning open-air meetings
Morris addressed in London.

On Wednesday I went to lecture at a schoolroom
in Peckham High St for some goody-goody literary society
or other: it was pretty different from my Tuesday's experience: the people were Christians & began the meeting
with prayer & finished with a blessing. However it is
worth noting that a good part of the audience (not a
large one about 100 I should think, there being counter-
attractions in the neighbourhood) was quite enthusiastic
though I suspect the presence of some of our people or the
S.D.F there: also I should not forget that they gave
me 30/5 towards our printing-fund.
Thursday I went to the Ways and Means Committee at
the League: found them cheerful there on the prospects
of Commonweal: I didn't quite feel as cheerful as the
others, but hope it may go on.
Friday I went in the evening to finish the debate begun
last week: the room full Sparling made a good speech;
I didn't; the meeting having got very conversational by
that time.]
(13 Feb)
Feb. 16th. Sunday I spoke on a very cold windy (NE)
morning at the Walham Green station: the people listened
well though the audience was not large about 60 at
the most. [I was busy all the afternoon enter-
taining Walker Scheu and his daughter Tarleton
& Tochatti; and Cunninghame Graham at last]

E.10

E.10 Banner for the Hammersmith Socialist Society

Probably designed and made by May Morris, *c*.1890

Felted woollen ground with painted inscription, 143.0 x 129.5 cm

Marx Memorial Library, Clerkenwell, London

On 21 November 1890 the Hammersmith Branch of the Socialist League was renamed the Hammersmith Socialist Society. Its Rules and Statement of Principles being ratified on 2 January 1891. The Society's banner was, almost certainly made around this time. It is probably the work of May Morris who, apart from sharing her father's socialist beliefs, had made banners for a number of other political organisations. Surprisingly, it is not embroidered, the technique in which she had, by this time, developed considerable expertise. It is likely that Morris had some part in deciding how it should be made. The use of painted decoration on political banners is traditional and the simple, not to say naïve style of this example must have been thought to be more appropriate for its purpose.   LP

E.11 *Hammersmith Socialist Record*, October 1891

Printed newspaper, 8.5 x 13.5 cm
Hammersmith and Fulham Archive and Local History Centre

The first edition of the *Hammersmith Socialist Record* was published in October 1891, the year after William Morris and his followers had withdrawn from the Socialist League. The four-page paper was issued monthly during the early 1890s and recorded the activities of the Hammersmith Socialist Society, the name adopted by the Hammersmith Branch of the Socialist League after it was reconstituted in November 1890. Morris was an occasional contributor to the paper and used it to record his views on the general progress of the socialist movement. Pages 2–3, illustrated here, give details of the books and pamphlets available at Kelmscott House, Hammersmith. These publications were kept on a bookstall situated at the end of the coach house where the society held its regular Sunday evening lectures (fig. 28).

E.11

E.12 *News from Nowhere* by William Morris

Kelmscott Press, issued 24 March 1893
Paper, 20.5 x 14.0 cm leaf
V&A (NAL L.883-1893)

News from Nowhere, the best-known of Morris's published books, first appeared as a serial of thirty-nine instalments in *Commonweal* between 11 January and 4 October 1890. Later in the same year this *Commonweal* text was appropriated by Messrs Robert Brothers of Boston – apparently without Morris's permission – and issued as an *editio princeps* in the United States. Morris revised the book in the autumn of 1890 and made a number of significant additions and alterations to the text. The revised edition of *News from Nowhere* was published by Reeves & Turner in the spring of 1891. Illustrated here is the Kelmscott Press edition of the book of which three hundred paper and ten vellum copies were printed bearing the date 22 November 1892. The book was bound in limp vellum with silk ties and sold for two guineas (paper copies) and ten guineas (vellum copies). The frontispiece is a wood engraving of the entrance to Kelmscott Manor by W.H. Hooper made from a drawing by C.M. Gere. The scroll leaf border in which the engraving is framed was designed by Morris. The book was printed using Morris's Golden type with decorated initials and red shoulder-notes.

This book was purchased from J. & J. Leighton for £2 10s.

THE CONSERVATIONIST

Chris Miele

My eye just now caught the word 'restoration' in the morning paper, and on looking
closer, I saw that this time it is nothing less than the Minster of Tewkesbury that is to be
destroyed by Sir Gilbert Scott.

So begins the letter of 5 March 1877 which Morris sent to *The Athenaeum* as a protest against the
widespread practice of church restoration. It is justly famous for leading to the founding of the first
pressure group dedicated to architectural conservation, the Society for the Protection of Ancient
Buildings, formally constituted with Morris as secretary on 22 March 1877. At this meeting held at
Morris and Co.'s Queen Square workshops (see cat.no.F.1), a subcommittee of Morris, George
Wardle and Philip Webb was appointed 'to draw up a statement to serve as a programme of the
Society's aims'. Their manifesto was ready in draft form by early April and, though the circum-
stances that gave rise to it have changed, it is still widely regarded as the purest statement of
conservation principles.

As defined in this document, 'protection' consists in doing no more to an ancient building than
is necessary to keep it in sound order. Where new work must be added for structural stability, it
must be frankly utilitarian. Morris and his colleagues placed the highest premium on genuine
ancient materials, arguing that antiquity was a finite resource that could only be managed. These
ideas had been debated since the early 1840s by J.L.Petit, E.A.Freeman and Ruskin among many
others, but what Morris, Wardle and Webb did with their manifesto was different in two very
significant ways. For the most part earlier writers had taken it for granted that modern liturgical
requirements could justify substantial alterations to medieval fabrics, even total demolition. The
manifesto took a hard line on this issue, arguing that the importance of ancient buildings as historical documents was too great to allow them to be altered merely to suit modern liturgy. Ancient
remains were 'sacred', and modern religious fashion, as Morris was fond of calling it, had to be
completely divorced from conservation. And whereas the debate over restoration had previously
been conducted from within the dominant practice of the Gothic Revival, Morris and his colleagues used protection as a platform from which to attack historicism in all its forms. Historicism
had, by its precise methods of stylistic analysis and its quasi-scientific theories of mimesis, tricked
Gothic Revival architects and their clients into thinking it was possible to give back to a building
something of its former greatness by rebuilding it in facsimile or making conjectural restorations
based on archaeological evidence. To claim, as architects and churchmen had, that restoration
made a church more ancient was contrary to common sense. The Revival was a mania, restoration
the most dramatic symptom of a larger cultural disease. Protection was, by implication, part of the
cure. Far from being reactionary and fogeyish, Morris hoped his Society's ideals would promote
modernity. A truly contemporary architect would never think to reproduce an old style exactly in
a new building or carry out conjectural restorations. Morris would have had very little time for
those in the late twentieth century who, fenced in by rigid ideologies, see conservation as the
enemy of progress in the arts. Respect for the past and belief in the future, he was certain, could
live together in harmony.

The facts of Morris's involvement with conservation are hard to untangle from the legends. One
of the most persistent is the claim that he first developed a hatred of restoration as an Oxford
undergraduate after reading Ruskin's *Seven Lamps of Architecture* (1849), with its celebrated attack
on the growing practice of restoration. However, had Morris taken this passage to heart, he would
not have signed articles with George Edmund Street, one of the century's foremost restorers. Street
believed that the experience a young architect gained reworking ancient buildings was an essential

Fig.32 Interior view of
Inglesham Church.

aspect of professional training. Furthermore, if Morris had really had a strong revulsion for restoration as a young man, then the significant early successes of Morris, Marshall, Faulkner and Co. would not have been achieved through commissions for the decoration of both new and lavishly restored ancient churches.

Morris's conversion came in the mid-1870s, when many progressive architects were beginning to doubt whether the Revival really had succeeded in updating ancient style and whether, in view of this perceived failure, restoration had been promoted with excessive zeal. In 1874 Ruskin rejected the Royal Institute of British Architects' prestigious Gold Medal on the grounds that architects had not adopted special charges for restoration work. He alleged they advised large-scale rebuilding to increase their commissions, which were rated at roughly five per cent of the total cost of a job. This charge was given substance by a parliamentary paper, the *Survey of Church Building and Restoration since 1840*. Its findings, first made public in March 1874, showed that spending on church restoration had outstripped that on new church construction since 1855. The *Survey* prompted F.G.Stephens, art editor and critic for *The Athenaeum* and an original member of the Pre-Raphaelite Brotherhood, to mount a campaign against church architects whom he accused of pillaging ancient buildings to line their pockets.

Fig.33 Hampstead Parish Church from the south-west corner of the churchyard.

In the summer of 1874, Morris signed his first organised protest against a restoration, adding his name to a petition which appeared in the *The Times* for 8 August. This document was written by Basil Champneys on behalf of the Committee for the Preservation of the Tower of Hampstead Parish Church. It was very likely composed with the help of George Gilbert Scott Jr., who was, as will be seen, very keen to support the fledgling Society despite its public opposition to his father. The church's trustees were proposing to replace an ailing Georgian tower with a larger one in the Gothic style. Champneys argued that as an important townscape feature the tower was in a sense public property, a state of affairs which meant that its owners were morally obliged to consult with local residents and interested parties before proposing any changes. No statute or common law principle supported this assertion. However, in Hampstead, thickly populated with architects and artists, it had the necessary effect, drying up public subscriptions to the restoration. The scheme was abandoned in July 1876.

This triumph furnished Morris with the practical example he needed and at exactly the right moment. May Morris later accurately observed that the idea for a society to oppose restoration first occured to her father in the summer of 1876. The efforts of the Commons Preservation Society to preserve for public use and enjoyment the remnants of the once vast Royal Forest of Epping must also have exerted a decisive influence on Morris's thinking. The enclosure of the forest was successfully opposed in the courts in March 1874, a decision confirmed by Royal Commission in 1875. Morris would have been aware of this widely publicised case, as his childhood home in Walthamstow stood on the verge of this area. Certainly in later years he would argue that the conservation of landscapes and buildings were complementary activities. In the mid-1880s the SPAB would itself collaborate with the Commons Preservation Society and the Metropolitan Public Gardens Association to conserve the settings of ancient buildings on village greens. Significantly, in 1895 the SPAB would be instrumental in persuading the newly founded National Trust to purchase its first property, the Clergy House at Alfriston in Sussex. Correspondence held in the Society's archives shows that the Trust was more concerned with the conservation of architecture in its early days than is commonly realised and, furthermore, that the two groups mounted many joint campaigns to save buildings and landscapes.

The obstacles facing the SPAB were far higher than those facing any landscape conservation group and fundamentally of a different kind. Through diligent legal research the solicitor of the Commons Preservation Society, Robert Hunter, discovered principles in common law which made it possible for local residents to sue landlords for the abrogation of rights of common. There was no corresponding principle in respect of ancient buildings, nor was the British Parliament of 1877 likely to pass any law limiting the rights of private property to satisfy a handful of aesthetes, archaeologists and artists, for this is precisely how the SPAB appeared to the public at large. The legal guardians of the country's finest and most extensive medieval remains were the Anglican clergy and diocesan hierarchy, and few of them sympathised with the Society's attempt to place aesthetic and historical values on the same footing as liturgical requirements.

It can hardly be surprising, then, with so many legal and institutional impediments standing in their way, that no one on the society's first committee had a clear idea of the best way forward. Several members were convinced that the only chance for success lay in using controversy to stimulate far-reaching public debate on restoration. The architect J.J.Stevenson delivered the first blow against the profession with a paper read at the 28 May 1877 meeting of the Royal Institute of British Architects. There followed W.J.Loftie's article 'Thorough Restoration' in the June number of *Macmillan's Magazine*, George Aitchison's 'The Principles of Restoration', read before the National Association for the Promotion of Social Sciences at Aberdeen in September (later published as a pamphlet), and Sydney Colvin's 'Restoration and Anti-Restoration' in the October number of *The Nineteenth Century*. Aitchison's lecture is perhaps the most interesting from a twentieth-century perspective since it considered the political ramifications of protection, declaring that 'most ancient buildings are common property'. The possibility that a Liberal government might assume control if not outright ownership of archaeological sites and medieval monuments was discussed at several annual general meetings of the Society during the 1880s, but the membership was not of one political mind and the official voice of the Society never endorsed any limitation of property rights.

Morris tried to make Scott's proposed restoration of Tewkesbury Abbey the Society's first case, and Stephens obliged by publishing correspondence between Morris and Sir Edmund Lechmere, chairman of the Tewkesbury Restoration Committee, in the pages of *The Athenaeum*. The SPAB had to drop the matter when it emerged that Morris did not know what exactly Scott was proposing, nor does he seem to have appreciated that the whole abbey had been gone over several years before by a little-known local architect. However Scott, an acknowledged leader of the profession and a prolific restorer, was too good a publicity target for Morris to let out of his sights, so when the chance to bring him down presented itself again in May 1877 Morris jumped at it. This time the building was Canterbury Cathedral, where Scott was proposing a schedule of works that included the removal of choir stalls said to be the work of Grinling Gibbons. Private protests had been made to the Dean and Bishop in February of the previous year. In 1877 W.J.Loftie wrote critically of the scheme in *The Times* but did not admit his connection with the SPAB. Alexander Beresford Hope, the Tory MP for Maidstone and an outspoken champion of the Gothic Revival, rose to Scott's defence, leaving the way clear for Morris to write in on behalf of the Society (cat.no.F.2). His letter, published in *The Times* for 4 June, is one of the best he ever wrote on behalf of the Society. It concludes with the prediction that the best intentions of Scott and the Cathedral Dean would result only in the 'usual mass of ecclesiastical trumpery and coarse daubing'. Classic Morris and fine words for those already converted to protection but not likely to lead to compromise.

To judge from the evidence of early casework files and agendas, Morris did little else that first summer. When the SPAB committee reconvened at the end of August it began to consider a more comprehensive strategy. Henry Brewer, an architectural draughtsman who was involved in virtually every one of the SPAB's early cases, persuaded the committee to sponsor the compiling of a national schedule of unrestored churches. Local vigilance committees would be formed to watch these buildings and report any proposed restorations to the London committee (see cat.no. F.7). A similar project to catalogue ancient buildings in the City of London was discussed and then scaled back to include only the churches of Wren and the Wren school. Morris took a dim view of the national schedule. Perhaps he realised that the Society would never have the resources to complete it, or perhaps, as seems more likely, he was just unable to join forces with anyone outside his closely knit circle of conspirators. In these early days SPAB business was conducted largely by his friends, clients and business associates. How could they trust provincial deputies to apply the principles set down in the manifesto intelligently? In the event Morris directed the Society to follow the path that was being set by its grass roots, the increasingly numerous people who, in return for their 10s.6d., not unreasonably expected the Society to help conserve the countless, humble village churches that preside over the countryside.

In September 1877 it was a 'gentleman' writing in to ask the Society to stop the destruction of two churches near Duxford. Later that month four members demanded the Society object to four different church restorations. Before the year's end members in the shires had notified roughly three dozen cases to the London committee. Within five years the annual figure had reached 150 and by the early 1890s had almost doubled. The overwhelming number of cases were to do with

Fig.34 St Andrew's Church, Cherry Hinton, from the south west.

medieval churches but gradually the number of secular buildings increased, so that by the turn of the century some ten to fifteen per cent of the Society's casework focused on small private houses, bridges and farm buildings. The volume of work generated by the Society's membership was soon too much even for a William Morris. Late in 1877 George Wardle suggested that the Society retain Newman Marks as part-time secretary at a monthly salary of £10. The bulk of his time would be spent investigating the details of cases by personal inspection or correspondence. Without first-hand knowledge the Society's chances for success were small.

The usefulness of knowing exactly the right people to contact was demonstrated in the first year of the Society's activities. In October 1877 Eustace Balfour, who was then serving his articles with Basil Champneys, alerted the SPAB to the proposed restoration of the church at Cherry Hinton, a village just outside Cambridge. Morris called at the office of the architect in charge, George Gilbert Scott Jr., who assured him that although earlier works by his father had been somewhat harsh, only routine maintenance was at present contemplated. The church was in the patronage of Peterhouse where a few years before Morris, Marshall, Faulkner and Co. had decorated the Old Hall after its rebuilding by the younger Scott. In 1883, when works at Cherry Hinton were contemplated in earnest, a carefully worded letter from the Society to the College Chancellor led to the appointment of J.T. Micklethwaite, the SPAB's preferred architect. It was all very chummy, and most of the Society's early successes came about in precisely this way.

Unfortunately, most of the Society's casework concerned churches in remote rural parishes where it had little or no influence. At about the same time that Morris was having a friendly chat with Scott about the fate of Cherry Hinton church, the Society received a fundraising circular for the church at North Frodingham in Yorkshire. This little pamphlet featured thumbnail-sized sketches of the building before and after the proposed restoration. On the basis of this evidence alone Morris sent off a hot-headed letter to the vicar, calling the plans an 'act of vandalism'. The vicar duly passed this communication to his architect, H.R. Gough, who was not impressed by Morris or his manifesto, and sent back a long testy letter in which he reminded Morris that by intervening in the professional relationship between architect and client he had left his Society open to the charge of libel. The Society, full of artists not lawyers, had not anticipated this possibility and it is likely that on this occasion, as he would several times during the Society's early years, Morris took legal

Fig. 35 Page from a fund-raising circular for North Frodingham Church, Yorkshire, 1879.

advice from Vernon Lushington, a barrister and Cambridge man who had consorted with Morris's Oxford set in the 1850s. Morris wrote to Gough pointing out that the Society's objections could not be construed as libel because they referred to common professional practice and not specifically to his proposals. Gough yielded but reminded Morris that not all architects would take such a tolerant view of what was essentially a theoretical issue. In future the SPAB committee would take great care to get its facts right before levelling charges, although from time to time, as with the campaign to save the west front of St Albans Abbey, the speed of events and the complexity of the archaeological evidence led to the Society getting its facts wrong (figs. 36–7).

Morris realised that the best way to meet the challenge of casework was to have a strict protocol. In October 1878 he, the ever-faithful Wardle and John Hebb (a draughtsman in the Metropolitan Board of Works and an early unsung hero of the SPAB) formed a subcommittee to report on the best means of transacting the Society's business. Their recommendations established the SPAB working methods for the next forty years, and beyond. Above all else they stressed the need to get a reliable eyewitness account of the building at issue. The Secretary or a member of the committee generally visited those in London and the Home Counties, producing a detailed fabric report. For more distant places a network of local reporters or correspondents was established. These men had to promise to follow the committee's instructions to the letter. All cases began with an informal letter of inquiry accompanied by a copy of the manifesto to the person in charge of the fabric. When negotiations reached a deadlock the Society threatened to bring the matter before the public.

These arrangements worked well and in November 1879 Morris handed over the job of casework secretary to Newman Marks. He conducted virtually all correspondence on instruction from a committee dominated by Morris, Wardle, Webb, Hebb, Brewer, G. P. Boyce and Stevenson. Thomas Wise, previously the Society's treasurer, took over from Marks (who appears to have mismanaged Society funds) in 1882, but Wise lacked the requisite technical expertise and was too busy with other things. In January 1883 he resigned in favour of a young architect, Hugh Thackeray Turner, who had trained in the elder Scott's office and then worked under his sons before forming a partner-

Fig.36 St Albans Abbey from the west before restoration.

Fig.37 St Albans Abbey from the west after restoration.

ship with Eustace Balfour. To make the poorly paid post more attractive the Society allowed Turner to conduct a portion of his private practice from its offices at 9 Buckingham Street, the Strand. He ran the Society expertly for the rest of Morris's life and into this century, resigning only in 1911. The appointment of a paid professional secretary came just in time, for in the middle 1880s Morris, now caught up in radical politics, became less active in the SPAB, with his attendance at committee meetings falling off dramatically between 1885 and 1890.

During these years Morris would occasionally trade on his celebrity to further important SPAB campaigns, but he retreated so far from the Society's day-to-day operations that he always needed Turner or Webb to brief him on the essentials of the case before putting it to the public. And there is considerable evidence to suggest that he merely signed his name to letters drafted in committee. For their part the committee could usually rely on Morris not to scandalise the Society by linking

Fig.38 Entrance to Westminster Hall,
Palace of Westminster, 1860s, before
demolition of the adjoining buildings
(see cat.no.F.15).

his politics to its agenda, even though in his own writings Morris was absolutely clear that unrestored ancient buildings were models for art in a socialist society. Morris understood that in the eyes of the public protection was an esoteric practice, and that, therefore, it would be folly to alienate such support as it had come to enjoy by engaging in socialist propaganda. The picture that emerges from the Society's archives shows a William Morris content to hold his tongue, perhaps because he understood that protection necessarily curtailed the rights of private property. Whether this was done for good socialist reasons or in the interests of art mattered little. The possibility that the ideals of the SPAB might serve a Tory ideology seems not to have occurred to him

When Morris's regular attendance at committee meetings resumed in 1890 he deferred to his old friend Philip Webb, who in Morris's absence had assumed control of SPAB policy, and to the younger men who were now attracted to the Society's ideas. Chief among these was W.R. Lethaby, who would develop and spread the Society's message into the 1930s. Morris sometimes volunteered to report on buildings he had known as a young man or those near to places he loved, like Kelmscott. Generally he left contentious cases to others. He would act, if asked, but he volunteered his services very rarely. He was content to sit sagelike by the committee table, a grey eminence, and then retire afterwards with friends and colleagues to eat and drink at Gatti's, the best known of many Italian restaurants then established in the Strand. Lethaby and Cockerell had fond memories of these evenings in later life, and one gets the impression that Morris, with his energy ebbing and slightly disillusioned, returned to the Society primarily for nostalgic and social reasons. His death made absolutely no difference to the workings of the Society for he had put those on a firm footing nearly twenty years before, but, as anyone who has ever attended an SPAB training course can attest, his contribution to the movement has barely flagged.

F.1 Minutes of the Inaugural Meeting of the
Society for the Protection of Ancient Buildings

Dated 22 March 1877
25.5 x 21.1 cm
The Society for the Protection of Ancient Buildings
NOT ILLUSTRATED

In a now famous letter to *The Athenaeum*, written on
5 March 1877, Morris called on those opposed to the
restoration of ancient buildings to establish an 'association for the purpose of watching over and protecting
these relics' (Kelvin 382). There was strong support for
such an association among friends, collaborators and
clients. On 22 March ten of them met at the firm's
Queen Square show-room to set up a pressure group
under the title of the Society for the Protection of
Ancient Buildings. Several of those present would form
the core of the SPAB's regular 'Restoration Committee':
George Wardle, Philip Webb, George Price Boyce and,
of course, Morris himself. Although the Society would
concern itself chiefly with medieval churches, there was
only one cleric present, the Reverend T.W. Norwood of
Nantwich, later its principal local correspondent in the
north west. Also present was F.G. Stephens, an original
member of the Pre-Raphaelite Brotherhood who as art
critic and editor at *The Athenaeum* had been airing the
views of the anti-restoration lobby since the early 1870s.
That journal stayed friendly to the Society even after
Stephens resigned from the executive committee in 1885,
one of several to leave in response to Morris's socialist
activities. The most important outcome of the inaugural
meeting was the creation of a subcommittee composed
of Morris, Wardle and Webb to draw up a 'statement to
serve as a programme of the Society's aims'. A draft of
the manifesto was ready by 3 April, 1877.

The committee of the SPAB usually met in the evening
and Thursdays were preferred, although at Webb's
insistence Fridays were tried so that members of the
press could attend. From September 1877 to January
1879 it met twice a month; thereafter meetings were
weekly. The committee met only in extraordinary circumstances during the summer months.

F.2 Letter draft, with corrections, of
William Morris's letter to *The Times* about Gilbert
Scott's restorations at Canterbury Cathedral

Dated May/June 1877
19.0 x 25.0 cm
The Society for the Protection of Ancient Buildings
NOT ILLUSTRATED

Scott's plans to reorder the choir of Canterbury
Cathedral called for the removal of late seventeenth-century woodwork and the restoration of a partly destroyed
medieval stone screen behind. Heated letters for and
against appeared in *The Times* of 4 May 1877, prompting
Morris to enter the fray on behalf of the Society.

The last paragraph of his draft shows amendments in
another hand (possibly Webb's or Henry Brewer's) and
reads: 'Sir, I think that our ancient historical monuments are *national* [sic] property, and ought no longer to
be left to the mercy of this that [or] the other sect, to be
dealt with as their variable ideas of ecclesiastical pro-
priety may dictate to them.' The emphasis on 'national'
was dropped in committee as was the reference to the
Church of England as a sect, but these changes hardly

offset the letter's disrespectful tone. It is an excellent
example of the combative style Morris cultivated in his
brief tenure as corresponding secretary. Within a year
his letters on behalf of the Society would show every
sign of having been edited or even drafted in committee
(Kelvin 521 and 537).

Morris resigned as casework secretary in the winter of
1878–9, possibly because he simply was too busy to
deal with the mounting caseload. Newman Marks took
on the job, then Thomas Wise, but a really effective
`official voice' only emerged with the appointment of
Thackeray Turner in January 1883.

F.3 Agenda Paper of the Society for the Protection
of Ancient Buildings for 27 September 1877

31.5 x 20.6 cm
The Society for the Protection of Ancient Buildings
NOT ILLUSTRATED

The Society's manifesto contained no concrete proposals
on the best way to realise its ideals. Morris was content
to fight the battle one step at a time, mounting protests
over particular restorations brought to the attention of

the committee, but other members argued that this
purely reactive way of working meant that by the time
the Society got involved plans were often too far
advanced for any protest to succeed. So in September
1877 the committee discussed the compilation of a
national register of unrestored churches to be watched
over by local vigilance committees.

Henry Brewer agreed to carry out a sample survey in
Norfolk which the Society eventually hoped to publish
using money from a special fund provided by Coventry
Patmore. Not surprisingly the resources of a small volun-
tary society were not up to such an ambitious scheme,
and the project foundered. A watch scheme for historic
buildings in the City of London was also discussed that
first year, but it too was abandoned as unworkable. The
committee then wisely set their sights a little lower and
closer to home, and in February 1878 established a special subcommittee to monitor threats to Wren's City
churches, which were being sold under the terms of the
1860 Union of Benefices Act and its 1873 amendment. To
this end the SPAB formed close ties with the recently
founded City Church and Churchyard Protection Society.

Society for the Protection
of Ancient Buildings.

FIRST ANNUAL REPORT
OF
THE COMMITTEE.

21st *JUNE*, 1878.

WILLIAM MORRIS,
Hon. Sec.

F.4

F.4 First Annual Report of the Committee, Society for the Protection of Ancient Buildings

Dated 21 June, 1878

18.0 x 12.3 cm

The Society for the Protection of Ancient Buildings

It was Morris's idea that the Society should publish a record of its proceedings. On 3 January 1878 he proposed an annual report 'be circulated with [the] subscription renewal request'. This survives in at least two editions, the most common being, in effect, a record of the proceedings of its first annual general meeting which was held on 21 June 1878 at Willis's Rooms, St James's. In his address Morris tried to explain why the Society had met with so little success in its first year of activity. With uncharacteristic gloom he concluded that it might have to focus resources on influencing public opinion, abandoning casework for good.

The Hon. Percy Wyndham MP was more hopeful. By asking wealthy members to exploit their contacts among the landowning set, the Society could, he was certain, exercise a decisive influence. Undemocratic means, to be sure, but nonetheless effective as it turned out, for Wyndham used his position in the House of Commons to further the Society's causes, most notably by inserting a clause in the Metropolitan District Railway Companies Bill of 1879 which stipulated the preservation of the Church of St Mary-at-Hill in the City of London. His county connections led directly to several important Society victories in the West Country, including East Knoyle (near his country house Clouds) and Edington churches, St Peter's Shaftesbury, and Tisbury church. Wyndham's work for the Society demonstrates that its architecturally radical aims could appeal to people from opposite ends of the political spectrum. An aristocrat and leading Conservative MP and enthusiastic customer of Morris & Co., he vehemently opposed Gladstone's 1884 Reform Bill which gave the franchise to working men in the shires.

F.5 Two documents concerning the work of the Society for the Protection of Ancient Buildings' Foreign Committee

a Minute book open to page showing formation of Foreign Subcommittee, 28 March 1879

21.0 x 34.5 cm

The Society for the Protection of Ancient Buildings

NOT ILLUSTRATED

b French translation of the Manifesto of the Society for the Protection of Ancient Buildings, by John Hebb or F.A. White

April to July 1879

25.0 x 16.6 cm

The Society for the Protection of Ancient Buildings

The possibility that the SPAB might work outside England was first raised by Morris in a committee meeting of 11 April 1878. The suggestion was almost certainly the product of his impending journey to Italy, where Janey and the girls had been wintering. The committee named Charles Fairfax Murray its first foreign corresponding secretary, charging him to 'arouse the Italians who regard this destruction of old buildings with disfavour (and there are some who do)

Société pour la Protection des Monuments Anciens.

BUREAUX—9, BUCKINGHAM STREET, STRAND, LONDRES, W.C.

SOUSCRIPTION ANNUELLE, TREIZE FRANCS.

COMITÉ.

G. AITCHISON.
W. C. ALEXANDER.
T. ARMSTRONG.
EUSTACE BALFOUR.
J. W. BARNES. [M.P.
Rt. Hon. EARL OF BECTIVE,
Rt. Hon. G. C. BENTINCK,
J. F. BENTLEY. [M.P.
G. P. BOYCE.
H. W. BREWER.
Rev. STOPFORD A. BROOKE.
JAMES BRYCE.
F. W. BURTON, F.S.A.
INGRAM BYWATER.
Rt. Hon. LORD CARLINGFORD.
THOMAS CARLYLE.
J. COMYNS CARR.
J. H. CHAMBERLAIN.
Mons. C. G. CLÉMENT.
Professor S. COLVIN.
LEONARD COURTNEY, M.P.
Rt. Hon. Earl COWPER, K.G.
Sir GEO. WEBB DASENT.
W. DE MORGAN.
RICHARD DOYLE.
EDWIN EDWARDS.
F. S ELLIS.
Rev. WHITWELL ELWIN.
C. J. FAULKNER.
WICKHAM FLOWER.

Miss R. GARRETT.
Rev. Canon GREENWELL.
Hon. N. GROSVENOR.
Hon. R. C. GROSVENOR.
JOHN HEBB.
J. P. HESELTINE.
J. E. HODGSON, A.R.A.
J. R. HOLLIDAY.
Rt. Hon. LORD HOUGHTON.
Geo. HOWARD, M.P.
SAMUEL HUGGINS.
A. W. HUNT.
W. HOLMAN HUNT.
E. BURNE JONES.
CHARLES KEENE.
WM. KENRICK.
S. WAYLAND KERSHAW, M.A.
CHARLES G. LELAND.
Rev. W. J. LOFTIE.
Sir JOHN LUBBOCK, Bart.,
NORMAN MACCOLL. [M.P.
F. MACMILLAN.
H. STACY MARKS, R.A.
A. B. MITFORD.
F. W. MOODY.
A. J. MUNDELLA, M.P.
Rev. T. W. NORWOOD, F.G.S.
J. W. OAKES, A.R.A.
W. W. OULESS, A.R.A.
COVENTRY PATMORE.

Rev. MARK PATTISON.
E. J. POYNTER, R.A.
G. W. REID.
Professor W. B. RICHMOND.
Mrs. R. THACKERAY RITCHIE.
E. R. ROBSON.
G. F. ROLPH.
JOHN RUSKIN.
W. B. SCOTT.
TEMPLE SOANES.
L. STEPHEN.
F. G. STEPHENS.
J. J. STEVENSON.
Rev. D. F. STEWART.
L. ALMA TADEMA, A.R.A.
Lord TALBOT DE MALAHIDE.
H. VIRTUE TEBBS.
S. TUCKER, Rouge Croix.
H. F. TURLE.
Rev. Canon VENABLES.
G. C. VINALL.
GEO. Y. WARDLE.
T. WARDLE.
P. WEBB.
Rt. Hon. Earl of WHARNCLIFFE.
F. A. WHITE.
T. J. WILLSON.
A. STUART WORTLEY.
W. ALDIS WRIGHT.
Hon. PERCY WYNDHAM, M.P.

(Le Comité peut s'augmenter.)

SECRÉTAIRE HONORAIRE.
WILLIAM MORRIS, 26, Queen Square, Bloomsbury, Londres, W.C.

TRÉSORIER HONORAIRE.
ALFRED MARKS, 52, Cornhill, Londres, E.C.

CORRESPONDANT POUR L'ITALIE.
C. FAIRFAX MURRAY, 108, Via Serragli, Florence.

SECRÉTAIRE.
NEWMAN MARKS, 9, Buckingham Street, Strand, Londres, W.C.

Une Société qui se présente au public sous un semblable titre, doit expliquer comment et pourquoi elle se propose de protéger les édifices anciens auxquels au premier abord, ni sous le rapport du nombre ni sous celui du zèle, les protecteurs ne paraissent point manquer.

F.5b

to band together as a body like this Society for Preservation'. It was agreed that French and Italian versions of the manifesto were required, but no translations were made, nor does Murray appear to have taken his duties seriously. The whole matter lapsed until March 1879, when once again Morris led the way, this time proposing the SPAB establish a permanent subcommittee to promote its ideals outside the United Kingdom. In April there were fresh calls for the manifesto to be translated, this time into Dutch, French, German, Italian, and Spanish. Versions in French and Italian were produced.

The Society's first campaign abroad was to oppose the restoration of San Marco in Venice (see cat. nos. F.8–9).

In 1880 it entered into correspondence with a sister organisation it had helped to found, the Societé des Amis des Monuments Parisiens. In 1881 the Society went further afield, to Egypt, working to good effect with the Comité de Conservation des Monuments de l'Art Arabe. Soon correspondents were reporting regularly on harsh restorations in Germany, Holland, Spain and Switzerland. In Belgium the journal L'Emulation promoted the SPAB's ideals and a group modelled on them was established. In 1885, using contacts in the Foreign Office, the Society persuaded state authorities in India to make a photographic record of monuments in the splendid walled city of Bijapur.

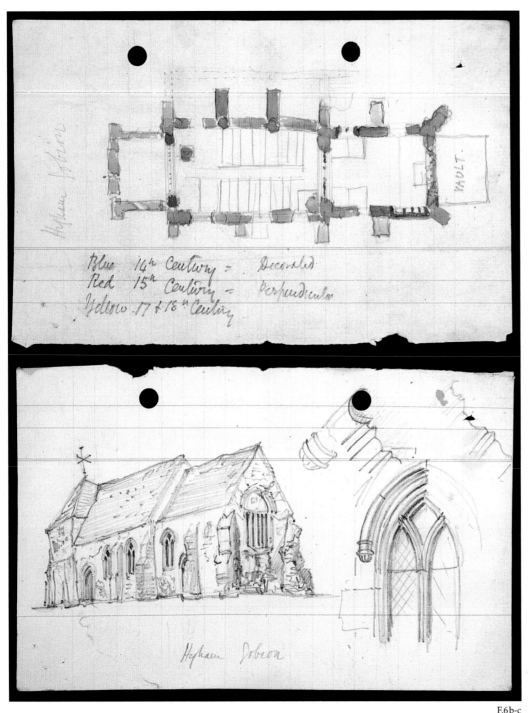

In September 1878 the rector of this small parish church asked the Earl Cowper, a local landowner, to contribute to its restoration. In return the Earl wrote: 'I cannot help suggesting that it would be a good idea if you were to consult the Society for the Protection of Ancient Buildings. The Secretary is Mr. Morris and the address is 26 Queen Square, Bloomsbury, London, WC.' He hinted that a contribution might be contingent on the rector obtaining the Society's advice, and this may explain why the Reverend W.H.Marvin responded positively to the Society's prospectus.

Henry Brewer was sent to report on the fabric of the church. His drawings and notes, dated 29 October 1878, persuaded the committee that the church, as Morris put it in a letter to Marvin, 'may be saved, without restoration, by the exercise of engineering skill: but that any works carried on for its preservation would have to be conducted with the greatest care and under constant and patient supervision'. Marvin began repairs according to the committee's instructions but within a year things began to go badly wrong. On 17 December 1879 he demanded the committee make a donation to the project 'as it was partly through the representation of your agent Mr. Brewer and partly in conformity with the wishes of Earl Cowper that my church was restored at a higher cost instead of rebuilt at a smaller'. The Society's initial estimate of £500 was already exceeded by £300, and the tower still needed urgent repairs. The Society took no further action in the matter, and Marvin retained a firm of architects, Benton and Wood, 14 York Buildings, Adelphi. Much of the exterior was rebuilt over the following year.

F.6b-c

F.7 Reporting forms of the Society for the Protection of Ancient Buildings

a Completed reporting form, Mells Church, Somerset
Dated 3 May 1879
26.0 x 40.6 cm
The Society for the Protection of Ancient Buildings

b Completed reporting form,
Grasmere Church, Westmorland
Completed spring 1879
26.0 x 20.7 cm
The Society for the Protection of Ancient Buildings
NOT ILLUSTRATED

Reporting forms, such as those printed by the SPAB in the late 1870s, had been used by English and Welsh antiquarians as aids to historical research and for recording as early as the seventeenth century, and enjoyed something of a revival in the 1840s when they were promoted by the Cambridge Camden Society. The SPAB hoped these forms would enable members to carry out a national survey of unrestored churches. Henry Brewer was asked to draft a sample, and this was approved for printing in spring 1878. A year later Morris told the audience asssembled for the Society's annual meeting that more than 700 had been completed. Even after the

F.6 Documents concerning the conservation of St Margaret's Church, Higham Gobion, Bedfordshire

a Report on St Margaret's by Henry Brewer
Dated 29 October 1878
31.8 x 20.0 cm
The Society for the Protection of Ancient Buildings
NOT ILLUSTRATED

b, c Two drawings of St Margaret's
by Henry Brewer
10.0 x 16.0 cm each
The Society for the Protection of Ancient Buildings

d Letter from Morris to Revd W.H.Marvin
Dated November 1878
19.3 x 24.7 cm open
The Society for the Protection of Ancient Buildings
NOT ILLUSTRATED

e Printed appeal for funds for restoration of
St Margaret's Church
23.6 x 20.0 cm
The Society for the Protection of Ancient Buildings
NOT ILLUSTRATED

Society had abandoned its plans for a survey, the committee remained convinced that the blank reporting forms had some role to play, and on a few occasions the forms did indeed prove useful years after they had been completed. Eventually photographs and detailed written reports took their place.

F.8 Letter from William Butterfield to the Society for the Protection of Ancient Buildings in support of its campaign to oppose the restoration of the principal front of San Marco in Venice

Dated 21 November 1879
18.0 x 11.3 cm
The Society for the Protection of Ancient Buildings
NOT ILLUSTRATED

Morris initiated the campaign to oppose the restoration of the west front of San Marco with a letter published in the *Daily News* on 1 November 1879 (Kelvin 585). A special meeting to consider the best course of action was held on 6 November at the Society's offices in Buckingham Street, and public protest meetings were organised for later that month in Birmingham, Cambridge and Oxford. At the same meeting Morris's memorial on the subject to various Italian newspapers was approved and translated (Kelvin 597). This was circulated in the form of a petition and by the end of November more than 1,500 people had signed, making this the most successful publicity campaign run by the Society in its first decade of activity. Even Gothic Revival architects normally hostile to the SPAB, such as William Butterfield, Ewan Christian and G.E.Street, lent their support. The latter actually visited Venice on behalf of the Society with J.J.Stevenson.

The swift mobilisation against an initiative of the Italian government outraged public opinion in Rome and Venice. Why, it was asked, had there been no objection to the restoration of the south front carried out by the Austrian government several years earlier? The Society was sensitive to this criticism and adopted a more deferential tone in later correspondence. In August 1880, to everyone's amazement, the Italian Ministry of Public Instruction's plans were laid aside and the work curtailed. Morris was quick to claim this as a victory for the Society, but letters (now in the British Library) written by the Society's Italian correspondent Henry Wallis, suggest that the plans were dropped for a lack of funds.

F.9 *The West Front of St Mark's, Venice*

John Wharlton Bunney, 1877–82
Oil on canvas, 161.5 x 242.3 cm
Ruskin Gallery,
Collection of the Guild of St George, Sheffield

This painting shows St Mark's under restoration with shored up columns, marble being removed and new, incorrectly cut marbling being added. It is part of the restoration work that Morris and the SPAB fought against in the campaign of November 1879 (cat. no. F.8) and managed to curtail. Ruskin commissioned a number of contemporary artists to chronicle the monuments of Venice. Bunney (1827–82), one of the senior employees of the Guild of St George, spent five years completing this painting. LP

F.7a

F.9

F.10

F.10 Letter from William Morris to Thomas Wise, Secretary of the Society for the Protection of Ancient Buildings, concerning Deopham Church, Norfolk

Dated 10 May 1882
19.9 x 12.8 cm
The Society for the Protection for Ancient Buildings

The vicar of Deopham wrote to the Society in October 1881 requesting a donation to the restoration of his church. Sensing an opportunity, the committee sent him a copy of the manifesto with a letter stating that although it would be glad to offer expert advice on fabric repairs, it was not not in the habit of making grants.

The vicar suggested the committee arrange a site meeting with Ewan Christian, architect to the Ecclesiastical Commission, which shared the patronage of this church with a local family. The Society had had a fairly hostile exchange of letters with him two years earlier over the reordering of Southwell Cathedral, so the committee cannot have expected much to come of any conference. Nevertheless a polite letter was sent, and when this went unanswered several equally polite reminders followed. After four months the Society decided Christian was not willing to meet them. In May 1882 George Wardle and John Henry Middleton were sent out to compile a fabric survey and schedule of repairs. Copies were posted to Christian, who, sensing the Society was questioning his professional competence, sent a stern letter in which he questioned the technical knowledge of the Society. Morris was livid and dictated a rude reply, leaving it for Thomas Wise, then corresponding secretary, to copy out and send. Wise, who had not attended the committee meeting at which the letter had been drafted, pointed out that it might be construed as libel, and asked Morris to reconsider, but Morris would not budge. On 10 May 1882 he wrote to Wise: 'As to Mr. Christian I don't see how I can alter the letter; he is a great criminal…' Works at Deopham continued under Christian's supervision until 1891.

F.11 Report by Philip Webb on the Church of Holy Trinity, Blythburgh, Suffolk

Dated 9 August 1882
32.0 x 19.8 cm
The Society for the Protection of Ancient Buildings
NOT ILLUSTRATED

A large proportion of early SPAB casework focused on East Anglian churches, renowned for their splendid medieval woodwork and painted decoration. Morris's knowledge of these buildings had been developing since at least 1865–6 when he first met George Wardle, the Norfolk-born draughtsman who had made splendid coloured studies of the area's finest churches for Morris, Marshall, Faulkner & Co. (cat.no.H.20b), including Blythburgh, between 1863 and 1865. Plans to restore Blythburgh church, a largely fifteenth-century building with a fine timber roof, were discussed by the vestry in December 1881, when the church was closed for fear its roof was near to collapse. The Society at once asked for permission to inspect plans for its restoration drawn up by A. E. Street and A. W. Blomfield. These were discussed at committee meetings in July 1882. Wardle felt strongly that the structural faults of the building were being exaggerated and dictated a letter of protest which was passed along to a barrister, Vernon Lushington, a long-standing acquaintance of Morris's who periodically did legal work for the Society, to see whether it might be construed as libel. It was decided that a professional opinion was needed if the Society were to take the matter further, so in early August Philip Webb visited Blythburgh, drawing up his first detailed fabric survey for the Society. Street and Blomfield's plans were scaled back for financial reasons and finally abandoned in February 1883.

In 1894 a new vicar at Blythburgh, who was sympathetic to the Society's principles, invited Thackeray Turner to report on the building. Morris asked if he could accompany him. More pressing Society business intervened and they did not get to Blythburgh until 17 July 1895, when they spent several hours at the church. The vicar was so thrilled by the prospect of actually meeting Morris that he proposed they stay the night as his guests, but Turner declined on the grounds of other pressing engagements. This visit proved to be one of Morris's last for the Society.

F.12 Documents concerning the proposed restorations at St Mary, St Catherine and All Saints, Edington, Wiltshire

a Postcard to the Society for the Protection of Ancient Buildings from Walter Crane
31 March 188[7]. (Misdated by Crane 31 March 1888)
7.4 x 12.0 cm
The Society for the Protection of Ancient Buildings

b Letter from Morris to Turner reporting on Edington Church, 15 May 1889
20.4 x 25.3 cm
The Society for the Protection of Ancient Buildings
NOT ILLUSTRATED

c Printed report on the repairs under way at Edington Church, and fund-raising circular, c.1887
24.5 x 18.7 cm
The Society for the Protection of Ancient Buildings

Edington was one of the Society's early successes. Its involvement with this splendid fourteenth-century church began in 1880, when the painter George Price Boyce reported rumours of an impending restoration. Percy Wyndham was asked to use his influence to find out more and Charles Vinall, a surveyor whom Webb frequently used, inspected the fabric on behalf of the Society. As it turned out the lay rector of the church was too poor to finance even the most rudimentary repairs, but the committee resolved to keep a close watch on the building.

In March 1887 Walter Crane (who misdated his post-card) wrote that plans were now being contemplated in earnest. Fortunately the architect in charge was Charles E. Ponting, the Diocesan Surveyor to Sarum, who sympathised with the Society's ideals but was never an official member. He agreed to consider the Society's advice carefully but pointedly refused to draw up a schedule of works based on their instructions, claiming that to do so would erode his professional status. The Society respected his request and asked merely to be sent regular reports of the work. All went well until April 1889 when there was some disagreement over whether or not the south transept roof could be strengthened. Morris offered to assess the situation and in the second week of May 1889 visited Kelmscott, Edington and Inglesham churches (see cat. no. F.13) on behalf of the Society. He gave a detailed account of this tour in a letter to Georgiana Burne-Jones dated 13 May, which Mackail published. Morris's report to the Society, written two days later, gave cause for concern, as he believed Ponting had done more than merely stabilise the fabric. He also asked the Society to condemn the removal of a row of very fine lime trees in the churchyard. Turner went to judge matters for himself but found that Morris had rather exaggerated the extent of Ponting's works. The case ended on a positive note in November.

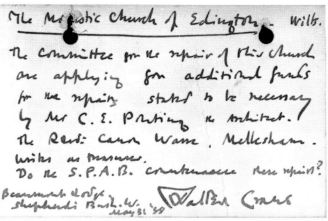

F.12 a

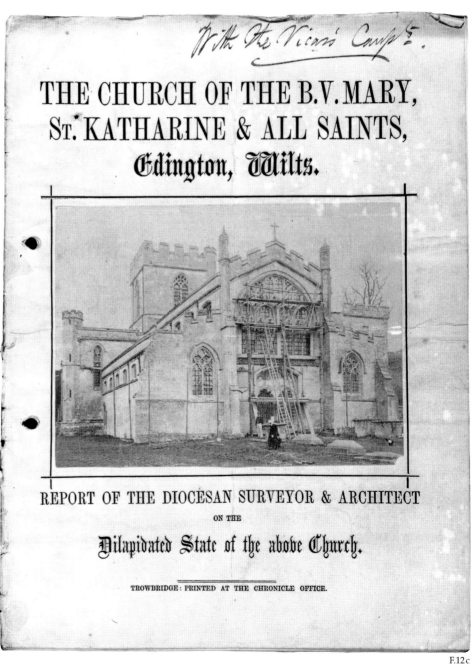

F.12 c

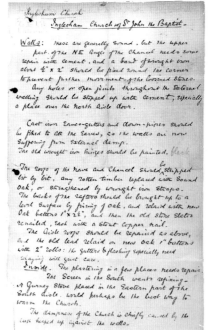
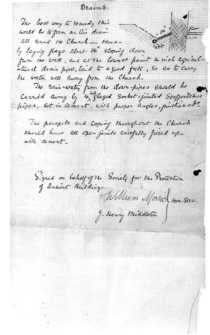

F.13a

F.14b

F.13 Documents concerning the church of St John the Baptist, Inglesham, Wiltshire

a Report by William Morris and J.H. Middleton
Undated [April–May 1885]
32.0 x 20.0 cm
The Society for the Protection of Ancient Buildings

b Minute Book open for 21 March 1889 to entry recording Morris's promised donation of fees earned for an article on Westminster Abbey to be donated to the Inglesham Church fund
24.0 x 40.5 cm
The Society for the Protection of Ancient Buildings
NOT ILLUSTRATED

Morris and John Henry Middleton, the architect and historian whom Morris had met during his second trip to Iceland, drew up a brief report on the largely thirteenth-century church at Inglesham in late April or May 1885. The village stands close by the headwaters of the Thames, an area that Morris knew very well. The rector of the church, the Reverend Oswald Birchall, lived at Buscot in Lechlade and was in correspondence with Morris over political matters during the mid-1880s. Birchall wrote that he was unable to pay for the rudimentary repairs and he doubted whether the farmers in the parish would be willing to contribute any money. If anything, they wanted a new building closer to the centre of the village. In June 1886, in a departure from normal practice, the Society undertook to raise the money needed for repairs.

The patron of the living, the Bishop of Gloucester and Bristol, agreed to the Society assuming control of the work so long as the church vestry approved. The vestry, composed largely of farmers, were happy to have the care of the church taken from them, expecting that the Society wanted to carry out a 'restoration'. J.T. Micklethwaite, an architect who had worked with the Society before, estimated that the first phase of necessary works would cost £430. To raise this Birchall

suggested the Society publish Mickelthwaite's report as a fundraising pamphlet with a preface by Morris 'so as to interest more people' in the project. By now, the church vestry realised that the Society was hoping to leave the building looking much as it had for decades, unimproved and ramshackle. Turner asked the Archdeacon, who was known to sympathise with the Society's aims, to intervene and the vestry reluctantly accepted the Society's proposals.

Works began in the winter of 1887–8. The first course of action was to lay new drains. Then came the repair of the aisle roofs and some exterior stonework. Three times over the next five years Morris made anonymous donations and loans to keep the builder on site and the works on course. In March 1889 he promised money he was to receive for an article on Westminster Abbey to the project's coffers. The first phase of the works was completed in November 1893. In this century the building has been cared for by architects trained in SPAB principles and is now vested in the Redundant Churches Fund.

F.14 Items concerning Morris's concern for the conservation of the countryside

a *Under the Elm Tree or Thoughts on the Countryside* by William Morris
Published by James Leatham, Aberdeen, 1891
14.5 x 11.0 cm
British Library (8289.A.B)
NOT ILLUSTRATED

b Morris's printed desk diary for 1895
Open on page for Tuesday 7 May
32.5 x 42.0 cm open
British Library (Add. MS 45,410)

In *Under the Elm Tree* Morris argued that the social inequalities that derived from capitalism were likely to bring about the destruction of traditional buildings and the countryside:

The architecture of the Crafts-guildsman will tumble down or be 'restored', for the benefit of the hunters of the picturesque, who, hopeless themselves, are incapable of understanding the hopes of past days, or the expression of them. The beauty of the landscape will be exploited and artificialized for the sake of the villa-dweller's purse, where it is striking enough to touch their jaded apetites; but in [some] quiet places…it will vanish year by year (as indeed it is now doing) under the attacks of the most grovelling commercialism.

Saving architecture and landscape were complementary activities for Morris. He did not object to new development, only to the speculative building which had overwhelmed the delicate landscape fringe of London in the wake of the commuter railway boom of the 1860s and 1870s. There was hardly any architectural beauty in these acres of new development to compensate Londoners for the loss of countryside.

For its part the SPAB extended the concept of 'protection' to the green settings of buildings it was trying to conserve. In its early days the Society worked with the City Church and Churchyard Protection Society. The SPAB's engagement with the open spaces movement intensified in the 1880s. In a letter published in *The Times* for 8 August 1885, Turner argued that proposals to sell and redevelop the Charterhouse in London would limit the already precious light and air provided by its gardens. 'It will be a great step towards sweetening and purifying the aspect of modern London if we succeed in making the existing open spaces inviolable.' The Society invited two landscape conservation societies to take part in their campaign, the Kyrle Society (of which Morris was a member) and the Commons Preservation Society. In 1886, the well-orchestrated lobbying efforts of this coalition resulted in the Charterhouse Bill failing on its second reading. That year saw the formation of a coalition with the Metropolitan Public Gardens Association to persuade the Prudential Assurance Company to keep the gardens at Staple Inn in Holborn open for public enjoyment.

In the last years of his life Morris was eager to extend

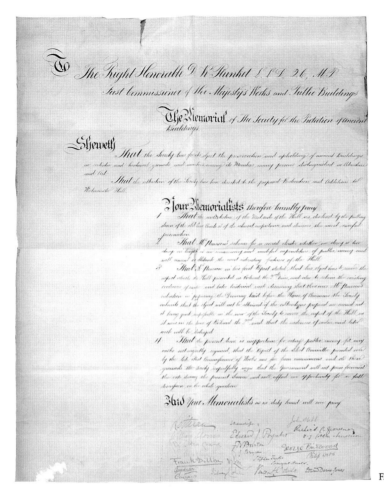

F.15

whom used this forum to express their mistrust of the 'antiquarian' school. Shaw-Lefevre stuck by Pearson and as Committee chairman his view carried the day. In the summer of 1886 the Society, hoping to take advantage of the change in government, made one last effort to put the case before a new First Commissioner, D.R. Plunkett. Their undated memorial was probably delivered to him in July or August 1886 but by this point the builder's contract was agreed.

F.16 Sheet of doodles by William Morris on Society for the Protection of Ancient Buildings notepaper

Dated 31 March 1892
Inscribed by Hugh Thackeray Turner,
SPAB Secretary
24.5 x 19.0 cm
Sanford and Helen Berger Collection

These doodles, which Morris made at an SPAB committee meeting, bear an obvious resemblance to the border designs of the Kelmscott Chaucer, a project that would take up much of Morris's time for the next year.

This sheet is an excellent illustration of Morris's legendary energy, of his remarkable ability to carry out several projects simultaneously, and the very fact of its survival is a measure of his reputation. Turner understood that Morris was an eminent Victorian, and sensing the importance of his book designs, indeed of everything such a 'great man' turned his hand to, he took the opportunity to transform Morris's doodles, presumably left behind after a committee meeting, into a memorial by inscribing them.

The Society had used Morris's stature as a public figure to further its causes as early as 1885, notably in its campaigns to oppose the sale of churches at York and the restoration of Westminster Hall. Afterwards the committee would hold him in reserve for special cases, because his name at the end of a letter to a newspaper was more likely to catch the public eye than one signed by Turner, an architect of modest reputation, on behalf of an anonymous committee.

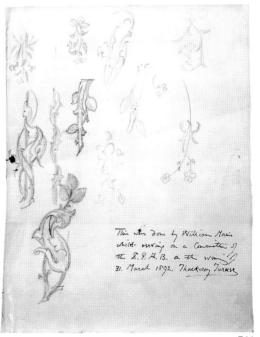

F.16

the Society's activities in this direction. In 1895 he wrote a letter to the *Daily Chronicle* (published on 23 April) in which he strongly objected to proposals to reduce the number of native hornbeams in Epping Forest. On 7 May he led a deputation of SPAB committee members on a site visit in order to judge the effect of the proposed changes. His diary entry for this day reads: 'to Epping Forest with Webb Lethaby Walker Ellis Cockerell. Nothing else.' After his death the Society continued its involvement in landscape conservation by forging strong ties with the National Trust which had been established in 1895. The two groups collaborated on projects in the first decades of this century.

F.15 Petition against additions to Westminster Hall, c.1886

Signed by William Morris, Philip Webb, Walter Crane, Edward Burne-Jones, Lawrence Alma-Tadema, and others
55.0 x 44.0 cm
Public Record Office, London, UK (Works 11/69)

In June 1881 Henry Brewer sent an anxious warning to the committee of the SPAB. The removal of the law courts from the Palaces of Westminster to G.E. Street's new Royal Courts of Justice in the Strand would result in the demolition of Kent and Soane's ranges along the western flank of Westminster Hall (fig. 38). He had no interest in saving their works, but he was concerned that the demolition would expose large sections of previously undisturbed medieval fabric, and that the Office of Works, under the agressive leadership of the Liberal Shaw-Lefevre, was bound to try to smarten up these remains.

When the site was eventually cleared, massive late fourteenth-century flying buttresses were revealed, as were the fragmentary remains of the earlier hall built around 1100. Shaw-Lefevre was committed to exposing as much of the old hall as possible but he also had to satisfy Parliament's ever-increasing need for space. In April 1883 he persuaded the Treasury to appoint an architect expert in the care of old buildings, J.L. Pearson. His plans of July 1884 incorporated the buttresses and Romanesque fragments within a two-storey 'restored' cloister range; he also proposed overlaying the elevation to Whitehall with a new skin of Puginian ornament to harmonise the new and old. 'The whole business,' Webb wrote Turner, 'is 100 times worse than we could have expected.'

By lobbying its members in the Commons – Charles Dilke, James Bryce, Leonard Courtney and George Howard – the SPAB was instrumental in setting up the Select Committee to consider the merits of Pearson's plans. It met eight times between 19 November and 19 March 1885, with Brewer, Micklethwaite, Morris, Stevenson and Somers Clarke appearing to argue for exposing these remains to public view, protecting them from London's harmful atmosphere by a covered walkway. Not surprisingly the profession came down firmly in favour of Pearson – Ewan Christian, James Brooks, Arthur Blomfield, Alfred Waterhouse, William White, J.O. Scott and the younger Charles Barry – several of

THE ART

PAINTING

Ray Watkinson

In 1854, Morris first saw in Bruges and Ghent the paintings of Memling and van Eyck, which fixed in his mind ideas of the painter's art: from Van Eyck he took that self-critical motto 'Als ik kan', meaning not 'If I can' but 'As well as I can'.

He shared with Burne-Jones the enthusiasm for Ruskin he had brought to Oxford – not only the verbal brilliance but the Pre-Raphaelite experience to which Ruskin directed them, and must often have admired the studies which Burne-Jones brought back from solitary hours in Wytham Woods. But on their French tour of 1855 he saw something which must have stirred new awareness. In Abbeville Burne-Jones stopped to draw. Here were buildings translated not into words but into an image, seen to grow under his fingers – not only record but a critique of things seen, a new creation, analysis and transformation in one, as is the nature of the work of art. Morris did not draw; he bought photographs.

Fig.39 Studio photograph of Morris, *c*.1855.

In Rouen they found Thackeray's new novel *The Newcomes,* which spoke to their condition as Kingsley's *Yeast* had done – but most in the matter of art.

At Le Havre, Burne-Jones knew and said he could not be a priest but must be a painter. Morris too rejected ordination: for him, not painting but architecture would give creative vent to all his passionate learning. When, back in England, the Pembroke Set came together the *Oxford and Cambridge Magazine* project filled their minds. Morris would write articles on the churches of north France, Burne-Jones a review of *The Newcomes*. It was the unillustrated Tauchnitz edition that had precipitated their decisions. They now saw the illustrated London edition.

Extolling Thackeray's tale for its moral sensibility, Burne-Jones criticised Richard Doyle's excess of illustration, unworthy of the author's theme, yet more the labour of the engravers. If we are to have illustrations, he said, we must have the best; best of all for such books as this. Just before they went to press, they encountered William Allingham's *Day and Night Songs* with Rossetti's 'Maids of Elfenmere' illustration. Jones went back to that first number of *The Germ* where they had seen, and he now praised, Holman Hunt's illustration to Woolner's 'My Beautiful Lady'. The depression induced by Doyle's drawings lifted; he wrote with joy of these deeply different works. Of *Elfenmere* – 'It is I think the most beautiful drawing for an illustration I have ever seen' – and of Hunt's etching – 'Something like this we cry for, is it not like a cry for food?'

No doubt the first number of the *Oxford and Cambridge Magazine* was sent to G.E. Street. Three weeks later, on 21 January 1856, Morris was put under Webb's care to learn the business of an architect. Morris would pay a fee: but Street would no less expect a portfolio of perspective drawings. There is no indication that Morris had yet made such drawings, even if he had fed since boyhood on brass rubbings and two-dimensional studies of traceries, doorways and buttresses. But of drawing in the artist's sense there is no evidence, no hint that he ever went on Burne-Jones's expeditions to draw Godstow ruins.

Such drawings now became part of his training, the more urgent since Morris was so much a beginner. He began to draw at weekends with Webb, as we learn from Lethaby. Not until late May did he begin 'running up to London' as Mackail puts it. Until then he drew with Webb and not just at weekends. Lethaby records one occasion when they went on successive working days (25 and 26 February) to draw churches at Bloxham, near Banbury; at nearby Adderbury; and three miles east, at King's Sutton in Northamptonshire. This location was Webb's choice. The remarkable frieze of animal musicians carved round Bloxham may have been in Morris's mind in *News From Nowhere* in his account of the Obstinate Refusers.

ON PREVIOUS PAGE 89
William Morris, *La Belle Iseult*, 1858
(cat.no.G.10).

This is the first evidence of his rendering real appearances, as distinct from what he may have copied from manuals or prints. Not until Rossetti provoked him six months later did Morris attempt another sort of drawing; but this *was* his beginning. Self-doubt and pressure of the firm's business led him too often to choose static figures when later he designed for glass. There was a frequent call for single-light windows of saints, to which he gravitated, leaving more active figures to Madox Brown and Burne-Jones – the former's expressive drawing pushing the medium to extremes of drama. Yet there are later drawings by Morris in which a freer vision asserts itself.

It is unlikely that either Morris or Burne-Jones had ever seen a naked woman before Rossetti took them in hand, although they had often seen naked men bathing, as they did, in the Isis. When Rossetti took them to draw from the model, they would have found themselves in a large room with men standing or seated around the 'throne' – a dais six feet square, twenty inches high – and on it, as directed by whoever set the pose, the model. If the model lay or sat, differences in sight levels might not be too marked, but if standing, the eyes of the draughtsman would level with the knees; torso, arms and head would tower above, compelling a vertical perspective not understood by beginners. Anatomy and perspective enabled the experienced draughtsman to make adjustments; but of such aids these two knew nothing – nor was Rossetti the man to help them. This distortion of vision makes the lower half of the figure too large, the upper too small: something seen in Morris's drawings.

This reinforced, or was reinforced by, his acquired medieval vision, in which the figures of women were always shown as a swaying line – hips and belly forward, upper body leaning back, small head forward to balance on the long neck. It would have taken more rigorous training than Morris ever had time for to free him – had he wished it. These conventions rule van Eyck's Arnolfini Wedding portrait (National Gallery), well known to Morris, and underlie the structure of *La Belle Iseult* (cat.no.G.10), though Jane's posture is more upright than that of the Arnolfini bride. Tristram banished, she stands with hands bringing together the ends of her girdle, as she looks, unfocused, at her mirror. Much as Morris owed to Rossetti's ruthless pressure, this vision preceded it. In all of his paintings, from *La Belle Iseult* onwards, the Gothic persists. In none are there any of the liberating spirals and diagonals so necessary to Madox Brown and Burne-Jones.

Fig. 40 Self-portrait by Morris 1856 (cat.no.G.4).

Street was as anxious to promote mural painting as embroidered hangings – but it was linear drawing only that Morris learned from Webb, valuable in presenting buildings to clients: Webb's instruments were pencil and pen, not brush and colour. But when Morris was pressed by Rossetti to paint (not to give up architecture) he had to embark on a freer kind of drawing, and by July 1856 had begun with fear and trembling to try. Morris cannot have met Rossetti until late May, when Burne-Jones settled in Sloane Terrace. A letter of 13 July from Burne-Jones to Crom Price, 'Topsy is here – he has come up to see me again and will stop till Tuesday – the dear little fellow is drawing away in the next room…', implies not only that Rossetti's persuasion has told but that, as Morris was 'drawing away' on weekdays, his summer vacation had begun: the next time he went to the office was mid-August, and in London.

The Summer Term over, a letter from Morris to Price, dated only 'July 1856' says:

> I have seen Rossetti twice since I saw the last of you… spent almost the whole day with
> him last time, last Monday that was. Hunt came in while we were there…Rossetti says I
> ought to paint, he says I shall be able…I am going to try, not giving up the architecture, but
> trying if it is possible to get six hours a day for drawing besides office work…

This is confirmed by another letter from Burne-Jones to Price '…whilst I was painting and Topsy was making drawings in Rossetti's studio, there entered the greatest genius that is on earth alive, William Holman Hunt'.

Now we encounter the first surviving fruits of Rossetti's urging: two self-portraits by Morris, one dated simply '29 July', which must have been made within days of the letter to Price and must be close to the first ever attempt (cat.no.G.3). It shows him awkwardly drawn but very recognisable: the hand that holds his drawing block stiffly done; the other, moving as he draws, has baffled him. The second (cat.no.G.4) is of the same year, as a comparison with the unique early photograph shows neither the neat moustache, fringe of beard nor thick dark hair would have been allowed an undergraduate. This is the young man who will meet Jane Burden a little over a year later.

After his vacation, Morris took rooms in London for himself and Burne-Jones, and in mid-August 1856 Street's office re-opened in Montagu Place. The accommodation soon proved too small for both to work in. In November Rossetti found his old rooms empty and took them to their first life-drawing class. He had no wish to nurse them needlessly, and wrote to Lowes Dickinson who organised these studies:

> Two friends of mine have already accompanied me [to Langham Chambers] and might often like to go when it might not be convenient to me to fetch them; and as they are both stunners as artists go and bricks as coves, I venture to make this request: viz: that you will bestow tickets of leave on Edward Jones and William Morris Esq., both of Red Lion Square…

Morris ceased to work in Street's office, the last number of the *Oxford and Cambridge Magazine* appeared on 1 December, and he now had no impediment to his development as a painter but the limits of technical skill.

In the following March the Leeds collector T.E.Plint was brought to the studio, to give the commission that launched Burne-Jones's career: when he came again, seeing Morris also painting, he commissioned him too. As Rossetti wrote to Bell Scott, 'Morris has as yet done nothing in art, but is now busily painting his first picture, Sir Tristram after his illness in the garden of King Mark's Palace, recognised by the dog he had given to Iseult. It is all being done from Nature of course'. But it was not finished that summer, or perhaps ever. First the Oxford murals, then the courtship of Jane Burden; Red House and the formation of the firm all conspired against it, though we know that it was worked on in Madox Brown's studio as late as 1861. A drawing for the Harden Grange window developed from it, in which Morris manoeuvred cut-out details from an earlier drawing to position them in the most satisfactory way, is now in the Victoria and Albert Museum.

Fig.41 *Sir Tristram Recognised by the Dog he has Given to Iseult,* a drawing developed from a stained-glass design for Harden Grange, Bradford.

At this stage both young men were painting a good deal out of doors; not only Rossetti but Ruskin influencing them. In May and June Burne-Jones was much in Birmingham where Georgiana Macdonald was staying, and where he painted apple-blossom for his *Blessed Damosel* (Private Collection) as earlier he had painted cherry-blossom in Morris's mother's garden. When in June Burne-Jones, Georgiana and her sister returned to London it was by way of the MacLaren's home near Oxford (Archibald MacLaren, whose gynmnasium Morris and Burne-Jones attended, had commissioned the latter to illustrate his *Fairy Family*). Here they found Morris painting a tree for the background of his Tristram picture with furious energy.

In June Rossetti wrote demanding that Morris should go with him to persuade the Building Committee of the University Union to have murals in their new Debating Hall, just built by Woodward, whom Rossetti had been cultivating. Burne-Jones had not taken his degree, but Morris was now a BA and so forever a member of the University as well as (now) a painter and friend of Ruskin – all of which strengthened argument when they met the Committee, which did commission Rossetti, and such others as he might engage, to paint the upper walls of the Hall with ten scenes from the *Morte d'Arthur*, and pattern the open timber roof, all in tempera. It was mid-July; Rossetti had already made studies. Now he set about recruiting – Val Prinsep; Watts's assistant, Spencer Stanhope; Hungerford Pollen, newly back from Dublin; Arthur Hughes, and Alexander Munro for a sculpture.

Morris, using trade connections from his time in Street's office, erected scaffolding, ordered materials, hired labour and set to work on his own allotted space – *How Sir Palomydes loved la Belle Iseult with exceeding great love*. Even if he found time to finish and scale up a design to the fourteen by ten foot area, squaring up and transferring it to the raw brick wall from which it was hard to step back far enough to see figures in proportion presented enormous problems. The final appearance suggests that he simply worked directly on it, hiding the figures behind roses, sunflowers and an apple tree. But with whatever difficulty, it was largely finished by August when Rossetti and Burne-Jones began.

For male figures they could rely on each other as models: for female figures they must rely on portfolio drawings unless they could find local girls to pose. Helmet, sword and gowns of Morris's design for these murals are in the William Morris Gallery in Walthamstow, though some costumes must have been made earlier in Red Lion Square for his Tristram painting. In Oxford he worked as both painter and designer: having finished his *Palomydes* he set to work on the open roof, with Faulkner, 'having always clever hands for drawing', to help in the afternoons.

By now, at the fit-up theatre in the old Music Room they had seen two sisters, and Rossetti wasted no time in asking the elder to pose for them. After one false start she did, and soon became more than just a model. Rossetti made a first portrait drawing of her in October (cat. no. A.6) but Morris's less skilful, less formal drawing (cat. no. G.8) may well have been made in late September just before he went to Manchester to see the Art Treasures Exhibition which ended on 7 October. While there, he made a watercolour, *The Soldan's Daughter in the Palace of Glass* (now lost), and wrote the poem *Praise of my Lady*. His portrait of Jane Burden has been folded, and in my view may well have gone in his pocket book to Manchester, the poem written with the drawing before him. More intimate than Rossetti's more skilled drawing, it is a love portrait, not a study for the new painting which he began in the New Year while working on proofs of his *Defence of Guenevere*. That published, they became engaged: the painting, a portrait of Jane as *Iseult*, was begun in Red Lion Square; but the figure must have been painted in Oxford: there is no evidence that Jane was ever in London before her marriage.

Between April 1858 and April 1859 all was bent towards their new life in the house at Bexleyheath in Kent, into which they moved in June 1860. Hangings, designed and embroidered in their first Great Ormond Street lodgings, went with them; did *La Belle Iseult* also first hang in Red House? What more likely? In 1874 it was in Madox Brown's studio, mysteriously belonging to his son Oliver, from whom for £20 and a measure of blackmail Rossetti then bought it, and it only returned to Jane's possession long after his death, from William Rossetti.

From July 1860, first Edward and Georgiana Burne-Jones, then Faulkner, sometimes Crom Price, the Madox Browns, Lizzie Siddal, least often Rossetti, came to help adorn the house and make it, as Morris meant, a splendid example of all its owner proposed to make and do. Rossetti was disquieted

Fig. 42 Right-hand panel of
St George Cabinet (cat. no. J.18)

Fig. 43 A preparatory drawing for the
press in the hall at Red House.

Fig. 44 A detail of the remaining painted
detail on the press in the hall at Red
House.

to see that one, and eventually both, of his acolytes might thus move out of orbit. By April 1861 all were brought back into one enterprise. The prospectus of Morris, Marshall, Faulkner & Co. announced 'the firm' to the world: premises were taken at 8 Red Lion Square and work focused for the next year on the International Exhibition of 1862 – under Morris's management. But he was equally active in designing and making embroideries, tiles, stained glass, furniture – painted furniture.

Though this must have halted Morris's easel painting, the furniture gave an alternative. Rossetti and he had painted chairs and possibly a cupboard, which he had had made for 17 Red Lion Square. Now, new furniture was designed by Webb, of which one piece surviving is the St George Cabinet (cat. no. J.18). Had its three doors been removed and framed – as were Rossetti's Dante paintings from Morris's great settle (cat. no. G.14) – we should have been familiar with Morris's triptych of 'Saint George and the Princess Sabra'. It remains as made, and decorated – seen only as a cabinet. Yet it is also a narrative painting, so ingeniously developed across the doors that it is clear that Webb and Morris must have set it out together – as surely they had designed Red House. Webb separated the three not quite square doors by strong narrow patterned strips: each door is subtly subdivided into a narrow left-hand half and a broader right, giving a rhythmic structure to the incidents, though little stress is laid on action.

Later, in Red House, Morris began another painting, also on a cupboard: not narrative, but full of animated, celebratory figures. It runs across the broad doors of the built-in hall cupboard – but is in no way articulated by them. It is one painting that runs from left to right, halted by a final, inward-facing figure at extreme right. Nothing is finished, though all is set out. The left-hand section has been drawn in pencil, the figures linked in gesture and movement, and colour has been laid in. The right half has no trace of preparatory drawing: all is laid in freely and directly with the brush, though we still have a single detached study of the group of three from the extreme right. Sketch though it remains, we see here what the St George promised – a mastery of composition which found expression in the great textile patterns.

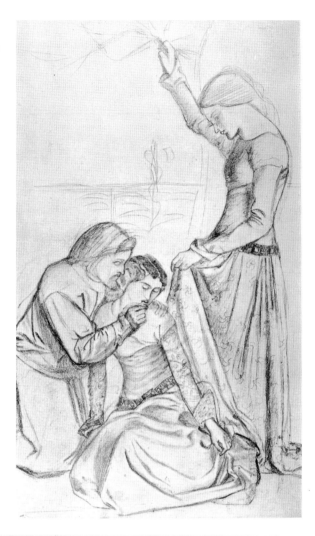

No story is told here, but linked rhythms, figure to figure, expressing the Garden of Delights Red House was to be. While no legendary characters are identified, in more than one figure we can see who posed for it: it is Burne-Jones who offers fruit to the woman seated on the ground, it is Lizzie Siddal who leans against the tree above. In this Earthly Paradise they make music, sing, dance in an enclosed garden – the house beyond a veil of trees. The theme is suggested by two sentences from Malory (book 10, chapter 52): 'And so Sir Lancelot brought Sir Tristram and La Belle Iseult unto Joyous Gard, that was his own castle that he had won with his own hands. And there Sir Lancelot put them in to weld [rule] for their own.' It had always been meant that Edward and Georgiana Burne-Jones should come to live in Bexley: a life of fellowship is what this painting projects. It is unlikely that it was begun until all the turmoil of the Exhibition was behind: and by November 1864 the scheme had fallen through. It looks as if Morris had made a hopeful beginning, let it lie awhile, then made a second forlorn urgent attempt. The design records the intention: its incompleteness, the abandonment of Red House for Queen Square, London.

In earliest days at Queen Square, Morris was able to resume some old and begin some new activities – calligraphy not least, including the never-finished 'Cupid and Psyche' with wood-engraved illustrations by Burne-Jones forecasting the Kelmscott Press of his last years. Between 1867 and 1870 he wrote *The Earthly Paradise*. In 1868 Eiríkr Magnússon was introduced; soon Morris was taking thrice-weekly lessons in Icelandic from him, out of which came the 'Story of Gudrun', best of all the *Earthly Paradise* poems. By 1870, George Wardle was effectively the firm's manager; his range of sympathies and skills no less than being freed from daily travel enabled Morris to experiment outside the firm's production, and in the summer of 1870 much time was given to the 'A Book of Verse' made for Georgiana Burne-Jones's thirtieth birthday, in which Wardle played a practical part as did Fairfax Murray. Its newly confident calligraphy was supported by large patterned margins and punctuated by miniature illustrations, reduced from drawings chosen from Morris's ten-year accumulation, painted by Murray.

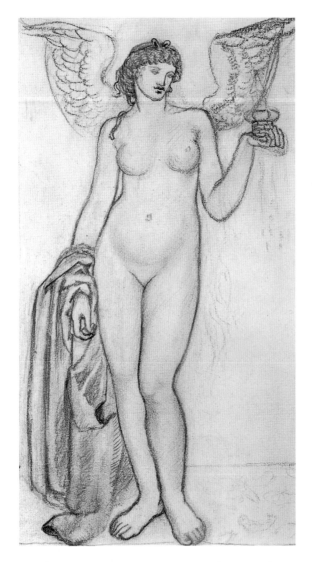
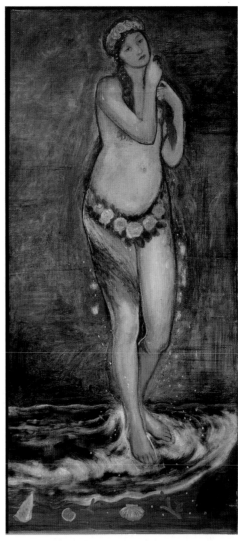

Fig.45 A drawing by Morris of a naked winged figure (cat.no.G.16).

Fig.46 A painting by Morris of Aphrodite rising out of the sea.

These, I believe, offer clues to the strange, unregarded painting, the *Aphrodite* – housed at Kelmscott Manor. It may well be the picture of which Morris's publisher, Ellis, spoke to Mackail: '…after the Earthly Paradise was finished Morris felt himself at a loose end, and thought of beginning to paint again…he worked for some time in Murray's studio (May Morris confirms this)…Murray has a figure he did then…' A note from Morris to Murray (probably written *c.*June 1870) says:

> I have got the writing all ready for you and have looked out the cartoons of the seasons: but don't know anything about the Spring baring her breast: it must have been some other drawing but would suit my verses very well, so I'll find it: will you come over here soon…to talk about these other illuminations: I shall be so glad to get them done this month if possible. p.s. Please don't show the little pictures to anyone before they are done.

Another note says 'Obliged to go out. Please leave the Venus with Wardle'.

The last poem in 'A Book of Verse' spills four lines from page fifty to rose-patterned fifty-one, across which lie three panels, in each a Venus. The inch-tall figures Murray reduced from Morris's drawings, under his eye, we may believe authentic expressions of his meaning. First, the goddess walks the greenwood in spring, heralded by a pair of doves: in summer she lies on the flowery bank of a stream: in the centre panel she stands at the edge of a luminous sea, which ripples towards a strand strewn with weeds and shells; the shore curves away to the right against a sky, with ragged stacks blue as any Flemish landscape, through which a golden sun streams and doves fly skimming over the waves. She takes weight on her right foot, left knee slack, left hand raised to her bosom, right lost in the cascade of golden hair. The pose reverses that of the *Aphrodite* – and both derive from one original, in Morris's portfolio. Such a painting Morris deeply needed to make in 1870. Did he make other attempts on the larger scale of the *Aphrodite*? Were they among the paintings that Webb told Lethaby were 'knocking about'?

The *Aphrodite* is painted, like the right half of the Red House cupboard, without any preliminary drawing, but developed much further, with much more fluent paint. She towers above the horizon, floating towards us on the waves, a girdle of flowers round her hips, rose wreath on her head, flecks of shining foam falling from the hair she braids. Grotesque as is her proportion, this is so different from any other work we have seen from Morris that I think it must be seen as part of a serious attempt to free himself from his unconfident beginnings, let paint dominate line, expression master description. May it be that in spite of, even because of the loss of Red House and of Jane, Morris was in the late 1860s moving to a new freedom? At the end of 1870 Magnússon, who had to go home to Iceland, persuaded Morris, now passionately immersed in the Icelandic stories, to go with him, to see for himself where the men and women of the sagas had lived and died; above all the place of Gudrun's story which had so moved him as he took it from the Laxdaela Saga.

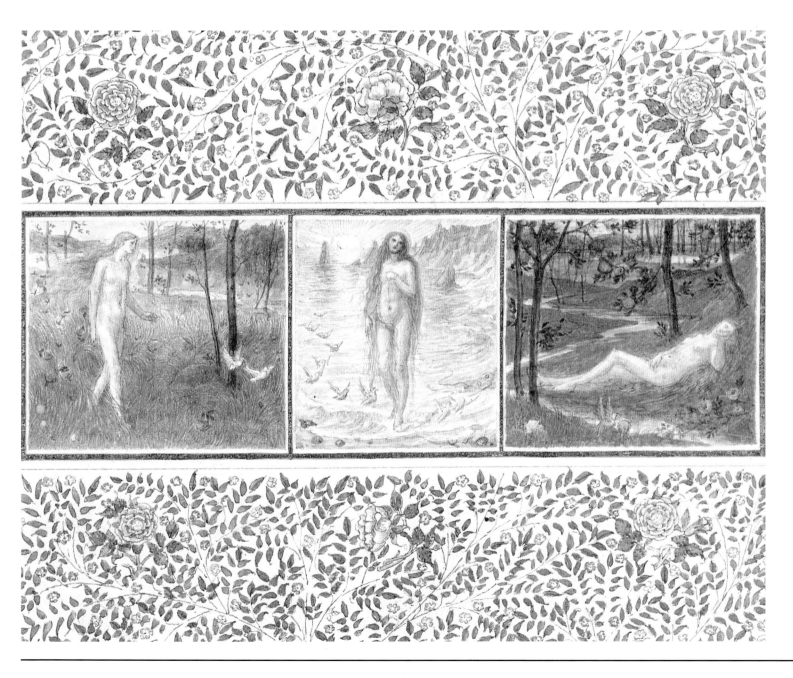

On the hillside above Hvammfirth he made one forlorn attempt to capture the home setting of Gudrun at Bathstead, of Bolli and Kjartan at Herdholt: but he hardly used the sketching materials he had with him. Though his journal gives vivid accounts of what he has seen, his lifelong habit of word painting stands in his way, enabling him to record in a few minutes what he could only draw with self-disgust in a long time. Only three times does he speak of his drawing materials – once of losing the haversack containing them – 'if they were any use', he comments, as if glad of any excuse not to attempt what he seems to have tried only twice, first near Thorshavn in the Faroes, before Iceland was reached. He ends a lively description with 'I am sorry to say though that I spoilt it for myself somewhat by making an imbecile sketch of the stead and its surroundings'. The second time, at Herdholt, he describes how 'I did at first make a last stand about the sketching, and sitting down on a hummock above the house began to try to draw it and the hill of Hauskuldstead on the other side of the valley; but I got so miserable over it that I gave it up'. Detailed as the journals are with fishing, cooking, games of whist, the hospitality of the Icelanders, the awesome landscapes, these are the only mention of attempts to draw. But the landscapes were fixed forever in his mind, to work their beauty and terror into *Sigurd the Volsung* and the late romances.

On his second Icelandic journey in 1873 he took no drawing gear, but had not given up his hope of new paintings, frustrated though he was by the heavy demands of the firm. He came to a resolve (with whatever doubts) to go back to beginnings and try if the brush would do what the pen had not. Though the firm's demands had effectively put an end to his painting, he had not given up drawing in the instrumental sense needed for design. Now he was impelled to go back to beginnings, with whatever self-doubt.

On his return to London, he spoke to intimate friends about this. He wrote to Aglaia Coronio excusing himself from an invitation, as he had engaged a model, meaning to resume painting – if he could. He wrote to Georgiana Burne-Jones's sister, Louisa Baldwin, to the same effect, and to Fairfax Murray in Rome. To Louisa he said it must be six years since he had drawn from a model and he was making the attempt with misgiving, not having, as he put it, 'the painter's memory' that enables him to imagine the appearances he meant to paint. This was October. By February 1874, he confessed to Murray that although he had many times engaged Colarossi (doyen of professional models) he had not been pleased with the results; and as often as not – shrinking from another failed drawing – had paid him and sent him off undrawn.

As with Iceland, Morris had begun in the wrong place. To free himself to paint, he needed to abandon himself to the brush, not labour over pencil drawings. He engaged the best of models, but men, never women. This itself was an evasion, and he knew it. It was not a heroic Michelangelesque picture Morris had in mind, such as Burne-Jones was making in his *Car of Love* (V&A). His hope was to take up a lost endeavour, he needed to paint a love scene and not a sad one. Had he joined Burne-Jones in his studio, he would have found there a variety of models, including the graceful girls who inhabit so many of Burne-Jones's pictures and all of Morris's late romances. But this was too close to the source of his problems. In 1874 he threw this forlorn hope over to set about reconstructing the firm. The romances took over what the paintings should have said.

G.1 *A Window at the Palazzo Foscari, Venice*

John Ruskin, 1845
Pencil, pen and ink and watercolour on paper watermarked
'J Whatman Turkey Mill 1844', 37.2 x 19.9 cm
Inscribed in ink in Ruskin's hand: 'CA' FOSCARI No 4
September 1845'. On the back in pencil a list of measure-
ments of various parts of the columns
V&A (D.1726-1908)

'A foul ruin' and 'the noblest example in Venice of the fifteenth
century Gothic' were Ruskin's descriptions of the Palazzo Foscari
in his book *The Stones of Venice* (1853). The rotting shutters and
hanging weeds are clearly depicted in this watercolour. Ruskin
used another window from this building in his book *The Seven
Lamps of Architecture* (1849), where it illustrates the Lamp of
Power. Both these books argue, in beautiful and eloquent prose,
the absolute primacy of Gothic and the necessity for honesty in
construction and ornament.

Morris had already read the first two volumes of Ruskin's
Modern Painters by the time he went up to Oxford, and from then
Ruskin's views on art and society became the basis for much of
his own thinking. While at Oxford he frequently read out loud to
friends extracts from *The Seven Lamps of Architecture* and *The
Stones of Venice*. In later life, when publishing a Kelmscott Press
edition of Ruskin's chapter 'On the Nature of Gothic' from *The
Stones of Venice*, he claimed it to be 'One of the very few necessary and inevitable utterances of the century'.

Bought at the collection of drawings and sketches by John
Ruskin on exhibition and sale at Ruskin House, 156 Charing
Cross Road, London, May – June 1908; no.35 in catalogue. Cost
£13 13s.   SA

G.2 Two drawings for illustration of St James's church,
Eastbury, Berkshire

George Edmund Street, 1851

a Pencil and pen and ink on blue paper, 22.6 x 36.8 cm
Initialled and dated in ink: 'G.E.S. March 1851' and
inscribed in ink 'Design for Church at Eastbury. Parish of
Lambourne. Berks', and other notes
V&A (E.292-1966)

b Pen and ink on Whatman watermarked paper
dated 1849, 23.1 x 35.6 cm
Signed in ink: 'George Edmund Street Architect. Wantage'
and inscribed in ink 'S.E. View' and
'Eastbury Church. Parish of Lambourne'
V&A (E.293-1966)
NOT ILLUSTRATED

George Gilbert Scott encouraged G.E.Street (1824–81) to start
his own practice before completing his pupillage in 1849. Street
established an office in Wantage in 1848 before moving to
Beaumont Street, Oxford, in May 1852. Shortly after this he took
two pupils of his own, Edmund Sedding and Philip Webb. Both
must have been involved in the supervision of this church, which
was consecrated in 1853, and the associated school. These drawings are not designs: they are drawings for illustration and show
the importance of publication in the architectural press to a
young architect working to establish a practice. The design of the
church reflects the influence of Street's 1850 and 1851 study tours
of French and German churches. Details like the massive buttress
show his admiration for simple rural structures such as barns, an
enthusiasm shared by Morris.   SA

G.1

G.2a

G.3

G.5

G.3 *Self-portrait*

William Morris, 1856
Pencil, 28.5 x 22.1 cm
Dated: 'July 29th'
V&A (E.376-1946)
Given by Dr R. Campbell-Thompson

This is the earliest known drawing by Morris. This self-portrait shows him with thick unshorn hair, faint moustache and beard, and working smock, all indicating it was undertaken by Morris in his early days in Street's office. The spiky monogram shows him resolved, under Rossetti's urging, to become a painter.　RW

G.4 *Self-portrait*

William Morris, 1856
Pencil, 18.0 x 18.5 cm
V&A (E.377-1946) Given by
Dr R. Campbell-Thompson
FOR ILLUSTRATION SEE FIG 40, PAGE 91

Morris's second self-portrait, which is likely to have closely followed his first (cat.no.G.3), and was probably made in Burne-Jones's Sloane Terrace rooms, which Morris visited each weekend returning to Oxford on the first train every Monday morning. It is close in appearance to the photograph of Morris reproduced in both Mackail and Georgiana Burne-Jones's *Memorials* as 'aet 23' and might almost have been stimulated by receiving prints from the photographer. The photograph shows a three-quarter view of the sitter, the drawing is full face with the hair parting to his right as he would have seen it in a mirror.　RW

G.5 *The Maids of Elfenmere*

The Dalziel brothers after Dante Gabriel Rossetti, 1855
Wood engraving, 15.1 x 10.8 cm
V&A (E.2923-1904) Given by Mr E. Dalziel

This illustration, first designed in 1854 for William Allingham's *Day and Night Songs* (1855), was singled out as an exemplar in Burne-Jones's review of *The Newcomes* in the *Oxford and Cambridge Magazine*. In the *Memorials*, Georgiana Burne-Jones quotes her husband as writing 'It is I think the most beautiful drawing for an illustration that I have ever seen, the musical timed movement of their arms together as they sing, the face of the man, above all, are such as only a great artist could achieve'. From this time Georgiana wrote of Burne-Jones's work 'This was done before and this after he had seen "The Maids of Elfenmere"'. It fired his determination to know Rossetti and deeply influenced his fine pen drawings of 1856 to 1859. It had an equally dynamic effect on Morris who, according to Mackail, '...at once set to work at drawing on wood and cutting the designs himself'.　RW/LP

G.6 Going To Battle

Edward Burne-Jones, 1858
Pen and ink and grey wash on vellum, 22.3 x 19.5 cm
Fitzwilliam Museum, Cambridge (1223)
Bequeathed by J.R.Holliday

One of the brilliant, tender ink drawings on vellum made between 1856 and 1859, stimulated by the vivid watercolours, the Tennyson illustrations and the elaborate pen drawings being produced by Rossetti when Burne-Jones worked in his studio.

Going to Battle must have some common origin with the similarly named watercolour *Before the Battle* made by Rossetti between November 1857 and May 1858, now in the Museum of Fine Arts, Boston. Both drawings may well have been inspired by Morris's poem 'The Sailing of the Sword' from *The Defence of Guenevere* (published in March 1858), which concerns three ladies seeing their knights off to battle. The poems were dedicated 'To My Friend, Dante Gabriel Rossetti, Painter'.

The drawing shows Burne-Jones's decorative early style and is enriched with minute textile patterns, pointing to the influence of the embroideries Morris had begun making for their rooms at Red Lion Square.

Originally owned by Richard Mills and then J.R.Holliday.   RW/LP

G.7 Four drapery sketches

William Morris, 1857–65
Pencil and ink; **a** 27.8 x 42.5 cm, **b** 39.0 x 27.75 cm,
NOT ILLUSTRATED 47.75 x 35.4 cm, 31.75 x 26.25 cm,
Sanford and Helen Berger Collection (109,121,124,135)

Surviving life studies made by Morris in the late 1850s and 1860s show his developing skills as a draughtsman. These examples are from a large group now in the Sanford and Helen Berger Collection which probably constitute Morris's portfolio. A few examples were dispersed, given to friends, and are now in British public collections (the Tate Gallery and Victoria and Albert Museum, amongst others). However, most were kept together and provided a constant source of reference for later work, including painted furniture, embroidery, stained glass and book illumination.

None of the four examples chosen is dated, although one (Berger 135, **b**) is suggested in Crom Price's diary for 18 October 1857 (Mackail, I, p. 130), although the true identity of the model is unclear: 'To Rossetti's…Prinsep there; six feet one, 15 stone, not fat, well-built, hair like fine wire, short, curly and seamless – aged only 19. Stood for Top for two hours in a dalmatic.' This drawing may be the first idea for the stained-glass design for *St Peter* (see cat.no.H.34). Sanford Berger has identified the drawing of a kneeling figure (Berger 124, **a**) as for the sleeping soldier in the stained-glass window *The Resurrection,* used in Dedworth (1863) and Pool-in-Wharfedale (1866).   RW/LP

G.6

G.7a

G.7b

G.8 *Jane Burden*

William Morris, 1857
Pen and black ink and grey wash,
10.4 x 7.6 cm
British Museum (1939-6-2-1)
Given by Dr Robert Steele

The only surviving drawing of Jane by Morris, this must have been made at much the same time as that by Rossetti, inscribed 'JB Aet XVII' (cat.no.A.6) – in late September or the first days of October 1857 when she had just began to model for them. It can be related to the head of *La Belle Iseult* which Morris began the following year, but it is not a study for it: it is simply the likeness of a young girl newly met, with whom Morris was already in love. It has been folded across and was possibly carried by Morris in a pocket book or purse when he went to the Manchester Art Treasures Exhibition at the end of September and, therefore, was in front of him as he wrote there the vivid word portrait 'Praise of my Lady.'

Originally owned by Jane Morris, this drawing was passed to her daughter May and then to May's executor. RW

G.9 Drawing for a wall painting, *Iseult Boarding the Ship*

William Morris, 1857–60
Pencil and ink, 51.0 x 41.0 cm
William Morris Gallery (London Borough of Waltham Forest) (D223)

A study of Jane for an unknown project. As the drawing lacks experience and skills, especially in the ill-drawn hands, it is possible that it was completed in Oxford while Morris was finishing *La Belle Iseult* and projecting subjects for other paintings on a similar theme. The subject may depict Iseult leaving Ireland, escorted by Tristram on the fatal voyage to Cornwall. Another possible theme is that of a Chaucerian Helen boarding the ship bearing the Greek heroes, a preparatory drawing for the projected Hall scheme for Red House that was never begun. Morris was, at that time, writing his *Scenes from the Fall of Troy*.
Exhib. 1931 (313) RW

G.10 *La Belle Iseult*

William Morris, 1858
Oil on canvas, 71.8 x 50.2 cm
Tate Gallery, London (4999)
Bequeathed by May Morris
FOR ILLUSTRATION SEE PAGE 89

Morris's one acknowledged easel picture, showing Jane Burden as Iseult. Some records have identified the subject in the past as Guenevere, but the scene, confirmed by May Morris, shows Iseult's mourning of Tristram's exile from King Mark's court. She stands wistful in her chamber, the little love-gift dog lying in Tristram's place in her bed. Down the side of her mirror is inscribed the word 'DOLOURS' – grief – and her crown has sprigs of rosemary for remembrance.

Morris worked on the painting in Red Lion Square and Oxford, and it presented him with

G.8

G.9

G.11

G.12

enormous difficulties. Philip Webb recalls that 'after struggling over his picture for months "hating the brute" [he] threw it up…yet Morris learnt all about painting in doing it' (Lethaby, 1935, p.34).

The painting relies heavily on artistic props, many of which must have been owned by Morris. The textiles are particularly interesting and an invaluable source of information on Morris's early collection. They include linen damask, a Turkish rug, a Persian embroidered cover and whitework hangings on the bed. The background shows a panel close in style to the heavy 'tapestries' designed by Morris for Red Lion Square. The table cover is a late *opus anglicanum* altar-frontal of the type admired and copied by Street and subsequently taken as a model by Morris and Webb for the firm's church furnishings.

It is likely that the painting hung in Red House though not in Queen Square. In 1874 it was claimed as his own by Madox Brown's son Oliver and in that year Rossetti offered him £20 for it as 'an early portrait of its original, of whom I have made so many studies myself'. The painting then came into the hands of William Michael Rossetti who, on the death of his wife Lucy (Oliver Madox Brown's half sister), 'found it in a cupboard in her room'. It was returned to Jane Morris in exchange for three Kelmscott Press books.

Exhib. 1934 (311)   RW/LP

G.11 Study for a wall painting for Red House, *The Wedding Procession of Sir Degrevaunt*
___

Edward Burne-Jones, 1860
Pen and ink on card, 26.5 x 26.5 cm
Fitzwilliam Museum, Cambridge (869)
Given by Charles Fairfax Murray

While staying at Red House in July 1860 Burne-Jones planned a series of wall paintings based on the romance of Sir Degrevaunt for the walls of the drawing room to flank the great settle. He painted *The Wedding Procession*, for which this is a study, during the summer of that year.

Burne-Jones had spent September and October 1859 in Italy visiting Pisa, Florence, Siena and Milan. In this scheme the larger broader forms of Southern Gothic and less brilliant colour show how much Italy had taken a hold. John Christian has pointed out that Burne-Jones's inspiration for this may have been Giotto's *The Wedding Procession of the Virgin* in the Arena Chapel, Padua, which he would have known from illustrations published by the Arundel Society in 1853–60 with notes by Ruskin.

A squared up study for the final composition is in Birmingham Museum and Art Gallery (452'27) and a third drawing of the subject belongs to the Royal Institute of British Architects.   RW/LP

G.12 Study for a wall painting for Red House, *The Wedding Feast of Sir Devrevaunt*
___

Edward Burne-Jones, 1860
Watercolour and bodycolour, 30.0 x 47.0 cm
Inscribed: 'E. Jones 1860'
Fitzwilliam Museum, Cambridge (677)
Given by Charles Fairfax Murray

This sheet of studies was made by Burne-Jones in preparation for his composition *The Wedding Feast of Sir Degrevaunt*, one of the wall paintings for the drawing room at Red House. The painting symbolically depicts Morris and Jane as Sir Degrevaunt and his bride.

In this study it is likely that Georgiana Burne-Jones posed for the back view of the seated woman. The brass vessel in the foreground is the same as appears in the foreground of Morris's painting *La Belle Iseult*, which may have hung in Red House.

The influence of Venetian painting is strongly marked in this drawing.   RW/LP

G.13

G.15

G.16a

G.13 The *Salutation of Beatrice*

Dante Gabriel Rossetti, 1859
Pencil, pen and Indian ink on card, 25.0 x 25.4 cm
Fitzwilliam Museum, Cambridge (2154)
Bequeathed by Charles Shannon

This study was made for the left-hand door of the
Red Lion Square settle painted by Rossetti in June
1859, soon after the Morrises returned from their six-
week honeymoon, and possibly as a wedding present
to them. The plain panels were detached for painting
and in a letter to the picture dealer Ernest Gambart on
10 August 1863 Rossetti wrote 'The first subject is the
early meeting of Dante with Beatrice in Florence…
The incident is described in Dante's *Vita Nuova*…'

The painted panels were taken from the settle by
early August 1863. The two outer paintings, showing
The Salutation of Beatrice on Earth and *The Salutation of
Beatrice in Eden* were then mounted together in an
ornate painted and gilded frame. This is now in the
National Gallery of Canada in Ottawa (6750)
(Toronto, 1993, pp. 104–7).

This drawing shows Jane Morris as Beatrice, and Red
Lion Mary is the handmaid in the foreground. In the
painting Mary's likeness was changed for that of
Fanny Cornforth.

The drawing was owned by Fanny Cornforth, Sir
William Rothenstein and then passed into the
Ricketts and Shannon Collection.   RW/LP

G.14 *Dantis Amor*

Dante Gabriel Rossetti, 1860
Oil on panel, 74.9 x 81.3 cm
Inscribed: 'QUI EST PER OMNIA SAECULA
BENEDICTUS'
Tate Gallery, London (3532)

This panel formed the central door to the settle
removed from Red Lion Square to Red House and
painted by Rossetti. In mid-October 1860 Rossetti
wrote to William Bell Scott that he was about to join
Lizzie Siddal there, '…I have a panel to paint there'.

The two outer doors, depicting *The Salutation of
Beatrice on Earth and in Eden*, were finished in 1859
(cat.no.G.13). This panel symbolises Beatrice's death
between the two events. In a preparatory design the
central figure of Love holds a dial marked with the
hour and day of her death with the inscription from
the last line of the *Divine Comedy*, 'Love that moves
the sun and the stars'. In the crescent moon cradling
Beatrice's face is the beginning of the closing passage
of the *Vita Nuova*.

Although it is likely that these panels were painted
by Rossetti as a wedding present for William and
Jane Morris, they were removed from the settle by
early August 1863 and returned to Rossetti, who then
sold them to Gambart the London dealer.   RW/LP

G.14

G.15 Drawing of a seated female figure holding an embroidery frame

William Morris, *c.*1861
Pencil, paper watermarked for 1861, 42.5 x 26.75 cm
Sanford and Helen Berger Collection (123)

This drawing would appear to be an impromptu sketch rather than a posed studio study and may well depict Jane Morris, her sister Bessie Burden or one of a number of friends embroidering at Red House. Morris's vow in 1856 '…to get six hours a day for drawing besides office work…' may well have come true. This drawing, made at least four years later, shows he has become more relaxed and confident with the material and subject.

Both Jane and Bessie would have learned how to sew as children and must have already been experienced needleworkers when they first embarked on the hangings for Red House. The legend suggesting Morris

taught them to embroider cannot be true, but he is likely to have instructed them in the unorthodox techniques needed to produce the desired effect.   LP

G.16 Five drawings

William Morris, *c.*1857–70
Pencil, brown ink;
a 38.75 x 24.0 cm, 36.0 x 26.0 cm,
37.0 x 22.0 cm, 38.5 x 24.5 cm, 26.6 x 15.2 cm
Sanford and Helen Berger Collection (10,15, 20,71)
V&A (E.2805-1927)
FOR ILLUSTRATION OF E.2805-1927 SEE FIG 45,
PAGE 96

It is unlikely that Morris drew from a female model before attending the Langham Chambers classes in London at the end of 1856. These drawings from his portfolio show an increasing interest in the curves of the body and the sexuality of the female form, and are

likely to date from the time of Morris's meeting with Jane in Oxford in the late summer of 1857.

His preoccupations for a number of years following his marriage in April 1859 – in the design and decoration of Red House, the setting up of the firm, the production of artefacts and completion of early commissions – meant that he did not have the time to return to the exercises of figure and drapery drawings until the move to Queen Square in 1865. It was then that calligraphy and the planning of the 'Cupid and Psyche' project demanded a resumption of such work.

The drawings selected show ideas for a variety of purposes which Sanford Berger has identified. These are book illumination (Berger 10; 'The Book of Verse': Berger 15; 'The Rubaiyat of Omar Khayyam'): church decoration (Berger 15; Jesus College, Cambridge) : tiles (Berger 20; *Spring* for Peterhouse, Cambridge) and stained glass (Berger 71; *Mary Magdalen* for Bradford Cathedral).   LP

CHURCH DECORATION AND STAINED GLASS

Martin Harrison

William Morris's first rapturous encounter with the cathedrals of Rouen, Chartres, Amiens and Beauvais in 1854 confirmed his belief that architecture was 'the foundation of all the arts'. Morris's essay 'Shadows of Amiens' romantically evokes 'the belt of the apse windows, rich with sweet mellowed stained glass', acknowledging the integral role of stained glass in an architectural context. At the end of their tour of northern France in 1855, he and Edward Burne-Jones abandoned their plans to take holy orders; Morris was to be an architect and Burne-Jones a painter. Burne-Jones's career as an easel artist had scarcely begun when he was pitched into the arena of public art. Early in 1857 he was recommended as a stained-glass designer to James Powell & Sons by Dante Gabriel Rossetti who, soon after, gathered both Morris and Burne-Jones into the team he was organising to paint the *Morte d'Arthur* murals around the Debating Hall of the Oxford Union. Burne-Jones had designed at least five sets of windows for the Powells by 1861, including three prestigious commissions. Morris, who spent most of 1856 in the office of G.E.Street, may have helped him. They shared lodgings from November 1856 until Morris's marriage in April 1859, during which time one of Morris's occupations was 'drawing and colouring designs for stained-glass windows'.

When the firm of Morris, Marshall, Faulkner & Co. was founded in April 1861, Burne-Jones's visible achievements reinforced their claims to be stained-glass manufacturers. Premises were leased at 8 Red Lion Square and a kiln for firing glass and tiles set up in the basement. Two experienced craftsmen were recruited, a glass painter, George Campfield, and a fret glazier, Charles Holloway, together with three apprentices from the nearby Industrial Home for Destitute Boys. By 1862 twelve men and boys were employed in the workshop. In keeping with the firm's somewhat experimental origins Morris first had to familiarise himself with the craft processes, and practised by painting glass quarries. Design and manufacture were distinctly separated; liaison was through Morris, who supervised all the stages of execution. He was not a technical innovator – the nineteenth-century revival of medieval stained-glass techniques was accomplished by Willement, Pugin and others long before 1861. Neither, though according to George Wardle it was something Morris 'often regretted', did he manufacture his own coloured or 'pot metal' glass; his suppliers, James Powell & Sons, had made glass equal to the medieval material since 1852. But stained glass was the first of the arts in which the firm excelled, and it became the mainstay of its business.

All of the partners except Charles Faulkner provided designs, but Philip Webb's contribution was crucial. As W.R.Lethaby remarked, 'the early work of Webb and Morris was so interwoven that we cannot tell in some instances where the work of one man began and the work of another finished'. The unimpeachable Webb was senior to Morris in practical experience of both architecture and stained glass – it fell to Webb, for example, to test George Campfield's abilities as a glass painter. He planned the architectural arrangements of many of the early windows and also designed most of their subsidiary elements – symbols of the evangelists, quarries, animals, heraldry, lettering and canopy-work. Rossetti and Peter Paul Marshall provided a limited number of designs until 1863, but subsequently figure cartoons were divided between Burne-Jones, Morris and Ford Madox Brown. Their disparate styles were synthesised by Webb and Morris into what was invariably an imaginative response to a given architectural situation.

In addition to his separate architectural practice, Webb also designed furniture and elegant tableware for the firm. His central role in the 1860s does not, however, diminish Morris's importance. As well as being the firm's largest financial investor, Morris was its guiding force. His facility for flat-pattern design, fundamental for wallpaper and textiles, enriched the vocabulary of background and drapery motifs in their stained glass. Above all, Morris addressed the spirit – rather than the letter – of medieval glass. He and his partners grasped that the essence of a medieval window was its simplicity. Morris's concern with process – with craftsmanship – enabled him to translate this understanding into practice. Compared to the firm's earliest stained glass, the work of most of their neo-Gothic counterparts appears both over-elaborate and religiose. Even their most distinguished contemporaries were compromised by archaeology and eclecticism. By 1861 Clayton & Bell, for example, were re-working medieval styles with some originality, but, lacking Morris's regenerative depth, they were unable to build further on their achievements. Morris was inspired by the Middle Ages but avoided pastiches. As Burne-Jones explained, 'All his life he hated the copying of ancient work as unfair to the old and stupid for the new'. Moreover, Morris reformed the taste for harsh, kaleidoscopic colours. Having assimilated the palette of muted blues, rubies, yellows and particularly greens of English fourteenth-century stained glass he reinterpreted it in an original and distinctive manner, using white as a foil for a palette of subtle earth colours comparable to those he obtained with vegetable dyes for fabrics. His firm initiated a transformation in the design and colouring of stained glass without which the developments of later Gothic revivalists, such as C. E. Kempe and Burlison & Grylls, or 'Aesthetic' designers such as Henry Holiday and Daniel Cottier, are inconceivable.

Morris and Burne-Jones's secularism – partly a consequence of their disenchantment with the Oxford Movement – was expressed in their anti-pietistic treatments of religious themes. The iconography of the firm's stained glass would repay detailed investigation, and would doubtless reveal much about contemporary cultural attitudes. The subjects they depicted that departed from the standard mid-Victorian repertory were clearly selected on the basis of their humanistic or visual appeal, rather than their liturgical relevance. For Burne-Jones especially, the principal attraction of such subjects as St Nicholas or St Ursula lay in the existence of established treatments of such themes within the history of art.

In 1869 Clement Heaton, founder of a rival firm, Heaton, Butler & Bayne, noted the public relations value to Morris's company of the Green Dining Room at the South Kensington Museum; he added, 'Their works are not always appreciated by the multitude, but their merit is fully seen and acknowledged by art-critics'. The taste for the firm's glass (evidenced by the demand for privately donated memorial windows – Morris called them 'grave stones') did not markedly increase until the 1870s, and few of their earlier commissions originated outside a limited coterie of friends and architect patrons. John Hungerford Pollen, Myles Birket Foster and Colonel Gillum all had artistic connections with members of the firm, and John Aldam Heaton introduced several clients in the Bradford district, which resulted in important windows for Bradford Cathedral and the *Tristram and Isolde* series for Harden Grange. But the bulk of their work was for Gothic Revival architects, the first and the most significant of whom was George Frederick Bodley.

On completing his pupillage with George Gilbert Scott in 1852, Bodley occasionally helped in the office of his friend G. E. Street in Oxford, where he would have met Webb, Street's assistant from 1854–8. Bodley knew Morris, Rossetti and Madox Brown by 1857, when they (along with Ruskin, William Burges, Street, Holman Hunt, J. P. Seddon, J. R. Clayton and William White, among others) were founder members of a short-lived group of enthusiasts for the arts of the early Middle Ages, the Medieval Society. Then, early in 1860 he commissioned Burne-Jones to paint an altarpiece for St Paul's, Brighton. In December 1860 the other partners asked Madox Brown if Bodley should be invited to join the firm. If the invitation was extended to Bodley he must have declined. But he became in effect the eighth partner, responsible for the firm's first three large church schemes – vital in establishing the new venture – and at least eleven further jobs in the 1860s.

The first Morris, Marshall, Faulkner & Co. windows, begun in 1861, were for Bodley's new church of All Saints, Selsley, Gloucestershire. The nave and apse windows follow the arrangement of the chancel windows (*c*.1294) of Merton College Chapel, Oxford, in which rectangular bands of richly coloured figure panels are set in pale geometric *grisailles*. Merton had been a favourite haunt of Morris and his friends at Oxford and he described its glass, with its 'singular elegance and richness', as 'the highest point reached by the art'. Philip Webb drew the Merton windows in 1861, doubtless on account of the Selsley job; he made preliminary sketches of the complete scheme at Selsley and designed all of the borders, quarries, canopy-work and lettering. Together with Morris

Fig. 48 Chancel roof, the church of St Martin-on-the-Hill, Scarborough.

Fig. 49 West windows, St Michael and All Angels, Brighton. Rose window of *Angels playing Bells* and *The Virgin and Child* (Burne-Jones) above, with lancets depicting Archangels. Morris provided the designs for St Raphael and St Gabriel; Madox Brown St Michael and St Uriel. The six-foil Annunciation is by Morris; St George by P. P. Marshall.

he integrated the individual styles of the figure cartoonists – Rossetti's vigour, Madox Brown's expressiveness, Burne-Jones's fluent elegance and modernity, Morris's own simple narrative directness – into a coherent entity.

Two more Bodley churches, St Michael and All Angels, Brighton, and St Martin's, Scarborough, were in progress in 1862. At Brighton, influenced by the theories of Ruskin and of Street, Bodley produced one of his most vigorous buildings, its unrelieved French Gothic forms and Italian brick and stone polychromy thrust audaciously into polite stuccoed terraces. His Scarborough church is tough and gaunt, of Whitby stone. Still in a High Victorian idiom, one senses in it the seeds of Bodley's reaction against his own assertiveness; the interior foreshadows the signature of his mature style – restrained forms and detailing as a foundation for richness in decoration. The painted chancel ceiling at Scarborough was designed by Morris and Webb, and beneath the high sill of the chancel east window the blank arcading contains Burne-Jones's painting of the *Adoration of the Magi*, flanked by angels designed by Morris; the pulpit is a *tour-de-force*, painted by George Campfield after designs by Madox Brown, Rossetti and Morris.

The firm's extensive series of windows at Scarborough was another unified scheme. Madox Brown's languid *Adam and Eve* in the west window are particularly effective, in spite of the intrusion of the stanchions. His confident handling of large-scale figures causes regret that so many of his designs were for small panels whose detail sometimes proved difficult to translate into glass. The glazing at Brighton was already begun, by Clayton & Bell, by the time Morris was brought in. The chancel roof (fig. 55), the firm's sole contribution to the painted decoration, was applied *in situ* by Morris, Webb and Faulkner: Webb's account book records that he spent five days at the task. Of the four windows placed by the firm in 1862, Morris's *Three Maries at the Sepulchre* was the first of his relatively few multi-figure compositions; set in light, square quarries, it combines the charm and the idiosyncratic spatial relationships associated with his early multi-figure compositions (fig. 50). The imposing Archangels in the lower part of the west window, designed by Morris and Madox Brown, are hieratic but subtly animated, recalling the *déhanchement* poses of thirteenth-century Gothic sculpture. Softened blues, greens and chestnut-ruby are introduced sparingly into a composition which, with Morris deftly exploiting the use of yellow stains on white glass, is predominantly a harmony in silver and gold. The frontality of the figures allowed Morris to arrange the lead-work in a regular, geometrical pattern – the 'mosaic system' he advocated but rarely achieved so convincingly before the 1880s.

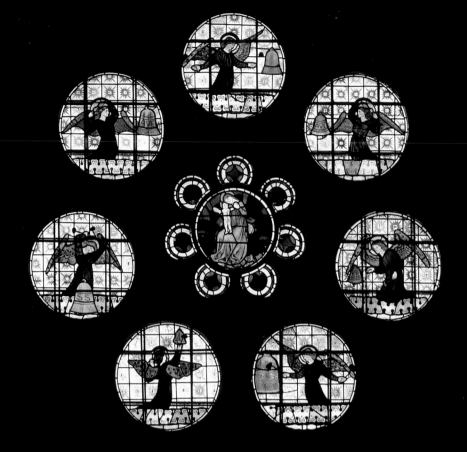

S·MICHAEL·ARCHANGELVS·
✠ IN MEMORY OF JANE BARBER ✠

S·RAPHAEL·ARCHANGELVS·
✠ DECEASED JAN·15 1880· 154 MERCY

S·VRIEL·ARCHANGELVS·
✠ IN MEMORY OF THOMAS BARBER

S·GABRIEL·ARCHANGELVS·
✠ DECEASED JAN·1·1885 154 MERCI

Fig. 50 East windows, south aisle of St Michael and All Angels Brighton, installed in 1862. These depict *Angel seated upon the Empty Tomb of Christ* and *Three Marys at the empty Sepulchre*, with *Pelican on Nest* above.

In the 1860s the firm's ecclesiastical (and most of its secular) stained glass was placed in Gothic Revival buildings, where its 'Anglo-aestheticism' was not entirely in keeping with the architectural context. Within Bodley's polychrome walls at Brighton, for example, Clayton & Bell's Franco-Italianate east window is arguably more appropriate than the Morris window facing it. After Bodley, Morris's principal clients in this period were all Goths – G. E. Street, George Gilbert Scott, E. R. Robson and Thomas Garner. Morris and his colleagues emerged from within the Gothic Revival, but quickly attempted to distance themselves from it. Their modernity was not widely apprehended – as George Wardle observed of Morris, 'so few recognized the real originality and modernness of his art'. The firm's display at the 1862 International Exhibition was, as Morris claimed, 'much ridiculed', and even the generally sympathetic *Building News* noted their 'strict adherence to mediaeval types'. Eight years later Webb was still at pains to explain to Charles Eastlake that he did not believe his buildings qualified for inclusion in his survey *A History of the Gothic Revival*.

The reaction against the Gothic Revival was partly a rejection of its Continental sources. This is a complicated subject – it was, after all, the cathedrals of Northern France that had persuaded Morris and Burne-Jones of their future paths. There was a political factor. When the firm began, Morris, Burne-Jones, Rossetti and Madox Brown were still drilling with the Corps of Artist

Volunteers, formed in 1859 when invasion by Napoleon III was considered a serious threat. The correspondence of Warington Taylor, with its Francophobic overtones, elucidates further. Taylor was Morris's business manager from 1865 until his early death in 1870, but had been close to the circle since about 1860; he was probably introduced by his Eton contemporary, Swinburne, though Mackail states that he had 'introduced himself' to Morris at Red House. The unofficial intellectual spokesman and conscience for the group, Taylor, as Georgiana Burne-Jones recalled, 'knew and cared a great deal about the arts'. In 1862 he wrote to E.R.Robson attacking the 'progressive' Goths Burges and Seddon for their 'huge coarse' French Gothic. He advocated instead English Gothic: 'small as our landscape is small, it is sweet picturesque homely farmyardish, Japanese, social, domestic.' Robson, about to build a heavy, thirteenth-century French Gothic fountain in Durham, may have been startled at such candour. In the *Building News* in 1865 Taylor cited the three architects, Butterfield, Webb and Bodley, who could be relied upon not to foist 'a small French cathedral' on to an English village. Webb believed in 'honest building' as the way out of the syncretic eclecticism that had failed to produce a modern architecture: 'You don't want any style', agreed Taylor, 'you want something English in character.' He suggested a specific model to Webb, the Old Grammar School at Rye, Sussex; a red-brick building of 1636, with dormers, Dutch gables and giant pilasters, it anticipates many of the vernacular elements of the Domestic Revival of Norman Shaw and J.J.Stevenson. Fundamentally, what Taylor and Webb were proposing – and the firm's stained glass is directly analogous – was an English vernacular.

Webb, however, built only one church and this was not completed until 1878 (St Martin's, Brampton, Cumberland; it has a full set of middle-period Morris glass, including a particularly beautiful east window). Robson used Morris glass in the early 1860s, at St Oswald's, Durham, and Shotley Hall, near Gateshead, Durham, and as Architect and Surveyor to Liverpool Corporation commissioned a design for the vast lunette window in St George's Hall; but he remained faithful to Gothic until taking up the Queen Anne style for his London School Board buildings in the 1870s.

George Gilbert Scott was nominally a client, though his son, George Gilbert Scott Junior, was more plausibly responsible for the Morris glass in his father's churches. Scott Junior was a frequent

visitor to 'the shop' in Red Lion Square and an admirer of the firm; his father, who thought their windows 'still more strange than those of any of their predecessors', evidently was not. Some of the earliest windows for Scott (at Christ Church, Southgate, Middlesex; All Saints, Langton Green, Kent) are in a figure-and-canopy idiom close to medieval prototypes, which may indicate Scott Junior's influence. The restoration of the church of St Edward the Confessor, Cheddleton, Staffordshire, is documented as the son's work; Webb's canopy designs for the chancel windows (1864) were modelled on surviving fourteenth-century fragments, an antiquarian conception which anticipates Scott Junior's supervision of Burlison & Grylls in the 1870s. In two further Scott commissions, Morris's figures of *St Paul* and *St John Baptist* at St Giles, Camberwell, London (1865), and *Ruth* and *Boaz* at Cheddleton (1868), are framed by canopies designed by Webb; he later repudiated them as having been done when he was a 'Gothic man', but his delicately translucent foliated arches effectively develop a traditional formula. The most outstanding result of the Scott–Morris collaboration, the east window of All Saints, Middleton Cheney, Northamptonshire (1865), incorporates figures by Madox Brown, Burne-Jones, Morris and Simeon Solomon; Solomon's *Tribes of Israel* hold aloft banners, designed by Webb, which carry the design up into the cusps and link with the traceries. The subdivision of the lights into a series of rectangular panels recalls the simple arrangement of the firm's earlier window at Darley Dale, but is particularly redolent of the layout of the fifteenth-century windows at East Harling, Norfolk, and St Peter Mancroft, Norwich.

Morris was less dogmatic with certain clients than his reputation perhaps suggests. He was, for example, not inflexible regarding iconography, and in his work for Bodley the prominence given to Annunciation scenes clearly reflects the architect's own predilection. Neither can his eminent architect-patrons be supposed to have entirely relinquished control over certain aspects of design. Some of the firm's most beautiful early glass was made for G.E.Street, the former employer of Webb and Morris; the rich foliage backgrounds to the *Crucifixion* lights at Amington, Staffordshire, Catton, Yorkshire, and Penkevil, Cornwall, are characteristic – and notably absent in contemporary windows for other architects. Again, Webb's chamfered rectangular quarries in Street's church of St Peter, Bournemouth (1864), were probably suggested by Street, who experimented with idiosyncratic quarry forms. Webb never tried the design again but later that year Street used a slight variant in a window he designed (made by James Powell & Sons) for his church of St James-the-Less, Pimlico, London.

Webb's involvement continued beyond 1869, but his Holy City canopy, designed in that year for a window at St Mary's, Bloxham, Oxfordshire, was his last major contribution of its kind and signals the closing of a phase. Now Morris, stimulated by his interest in flat-pattern design in other media, again turned his attention to the backgrounds for windows, many of which – the south aisle east window of St Michael's, Tilehurst, Berkshire (1869), is a striking example – were without precedent in the stained-glass canon. The firm's stained glass was in a period of transition. In another window at Cheddleton, dating from 1869, Burne-Jones's elegant *Trumpeting Angels* are undeniably impressive, but Scott Junior, who believed 'we make a great deal too much of stained glass [which is] essentially an architectural decoration', may have been concerned that their scale and restless energy undermined the stonework mullions that separate them. The contemporary east window of St Mary's, King's Walden, Hertfordshire, on the other hand, was entirely designed by Morris, whose figures are calmer than Burne-Jones's and less inclined to strain against their architectural framework. By 1870 though, Burne-Jones was supplying nearly all of the firm's new figure cartoons, and Scott Junior, together with most other leading architects, turned to more conservative stained-glass makers. The firm's windows of the later 1870s (e.g. Nun Monkton, Tadcaster, Easthampstead) have generally found most favour with recent critics, but they were rarely ordered by leading architects nor do they have the integral relationship with their architectural setting of the firm's earlier work.

Soon after the Scarborough church, Bodley forsook his attachment to Continental Gothic and, harking back to Pugin, reverted to English fourteenth-century models. Morris, Webb and Warington Taylor may have been catalysts for Bodley's conversion. Street, too, relaxed from High Victorian intensity into the graceful style of his maturity. In 1869, filling the apse windows of St Mary Magdalene's, Paddington, was one of the most prestigious commissions he ever assigned. It was awarded not to Morris but to Henry Holiday, the first stained-glass artist overtly influenced by Burne-Jones, Rossetti and Morris. Since they were arguably Holiday's finest windows, it is unlikely Street was disappointed. Neither had Street completely abandoned his earlier favourites, Clayton & Bell, and it was they, rather than Morris, who received the bulk of his patronage in the 1870s. In 1861, Morris had loftily dismissed Clayton & Bell as 'only glass painters in point of fact', but later conceded that they 'do very fair glass now we have taught them how to colour'. The hint of sarcasm may indicate Morris's awareness of his loss of business to those who had learned by his example; the veracity of his remark, however, is confirmed by the evidence of Clayton & Bell's windows, which, after 1862, became discernibly more subdued in colouring. Lewis F.Day's comment, that in technique 'he had something to learn from men like Mr John Clayton, who were before him in the field', suggests an alternative motive for Morris's attitude towards his rivals. The larger established workshops maintained other competitive advantages, as W.Eden Nesfield, the architect responsible for Morris's King's Walden window recognised when he warned a client that Morris's glass was liable to be both extremely costly and up to fifteen months late in delivery.

Of the 'progressive' Goths neither Burges nor E.W.Godwin commissioned glass from Morris. The firm's superb windows for St Michael's, Lyndhurst, Hampshire (1862–3), failed to persuade William White to try them again, and J.P.Seddon tired of what he felt was the lack of translucency of the firm's windows. In 1867, after Morris had completed the decoration of the nave roof at Jesus

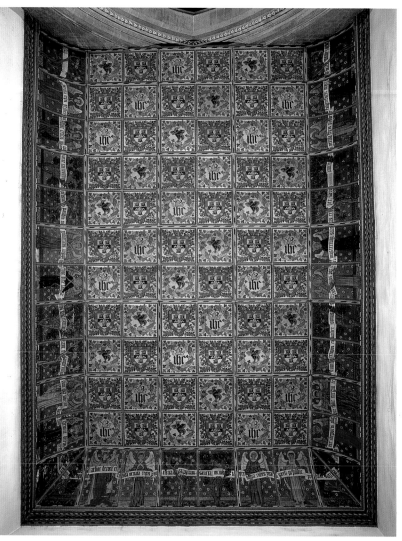

College Chapel, Cambridge, Bodley began to lobby the Dean to commence the glazing of the nave windows. By the time the Dean opted for Morris, in 1872, the architect had already suggested trying Burlison & Grylls, from whom, 'I have been getting some very good stained glass'. Bodley added, significantly, that with Burlison & Grylls 'I find I get my own way more than I can with Morris'. Nevertheless, the first Morris windows were in place early in 1873. At the same time Burlison & Grylls had begun the glazing and decoration of Bodley's church of St Augustine, Pendlebury, Lancashire. The contrast between the two schemes was clear. Apart from advising on the iconography, Bodley did not, at Jesus College, 'get his own way'. The sculptural vigour of many of the figures reveals that Burne-Jones had recently returned from the tour of Italy which confirmed his admiration for Michelangelo, an artist whose 'dark carnality' had appalled Ruskin. Nikolaus Pevsner found in them 'a touch of self-display which may get tiresome after a while'; Bodley, who preached 'the avoidance of extravagance of manner', might have concurred. But more than Burne-Jones's figures, Morris's breathtaking colour-scheme surely unsettled the architect. Very beautiful in its own right – Morris emphasised to the Dean that colour, particularly 'rich blues in the draperies' was his priority – the ensemble dominates the architecture. Bodley characterised medieval glass as 'the story of progress in refinement', and henceforth, like Scott Junior, found the stained glass of Burlison & Grylls, with its less strident draughtsmanship, adherence to late-medieval models and restrained colouring, more congenial.

Morris's warning that stained-glass artists 'should not attempt to design pictures but rather pieces of ornamental glazing…decorating the building of which they form a part', indicates his awareness of the dilemma. The art in architecture debate is no nearer resolution today, but in the

Fig. 53 Design for an angel for the nave ceiling for Jesus College Chapel (cat. no. H.35).

Fig. 54 Nave ceiling, Jesus College Chapel, Cambridge.

Fig.55 Chancel roof, St Michael and All Angels, Brighton, (detail).

last century it was an architect, J.J.Stevenson, pioneer of the Queen Anne revival, who left one of the more extreme views in favour of the artist's autonomy: 'Dante Rossetti, when designing a for a stained glass window in a church, once asked me if I thought the architect would be offended if he asked him to cut away the cusps, as he could make a better design for his picture if they were away. As Rossetti's picture was a more interesting work of art than the architect's regulation cusps, I said the architect would do well to remove them.'

The chief attraction in more than a few routine late nineteenth-century churches is the stained glass designed by Burne-Jones. His growing assurance at handling large-scale compositions in his paintings was paralleled in the power and fluency of his stained-glass designs. Although Morris sometimes received cartoons which he may have considered were 'wandering from their true purpose of decoration', he deeply respected Burne-Jones's abilities and produced some compelling performances in responding to his mastery. In the 1870s he evolved innovative tapestry-like backgrounds in attempting to reconcile Burne-Jones's Italianate pictorialism, and developed a more mosaic-like system of leading in response to the artist's Byzantine manner around 1885. The move to Merton Abbey in 1881 revitalised Morris's interest in glass and to some extent he retrieved the 'glow and glitter' which Ruskin said he missed. Nevertheless, Morris remained concerned about the compatibility of his stained glass with medieval architecture and in 1877, consistent with his founding of the Society for the Protection of Ancient Buildings, he announced that he was ceasing to install windows in medieval buildings. Over the next twenty years only the windows designed by Burne-Jones for specific locations, for instance the late masterpieces in Birmingham Cathedral (1885–97), generally uphold the firm's reputation, and the increasing tendency to re-use and adapt old cartoons resulted in some lacklustre windows. More damaging still were the pallid imitations perpetrated in the name of Morris & Co. long after the deaths of Morris and Burne-Jones – a depressing coda to an inspired venture.

Of the many craftsmen who passed through the Morris workshops a few achieved minor renown in stained glass, including John W. Brown (who became chief designer for James Powell & Sons) and James Egan (who had partnered another Morris protégé, Fletcher, and made interesting windows on his own account from the 1880s). More eminent figures, such as Frank Brangwyn, stayed only briefly. The firm's wider influence was by example. Though Webb doubted that the devolved workshop system had been compatible with 'right good craftsmen's glass', the legacy of the firm's early stained glass remained an inspiration to the Arts and Crafts Movement he and Morris helped to initiate. Conversely, their work was anathema to the more traditionalist architects of the later Gothic Revival, many of whom, ironically, had trained under G.F.Bodley. But in the 1860s, before these alternative schools of thought diverged, Morris and his circle had been at the centre of a debate that transformed both architecture and the role of the artist-craftsman. Their stained glass amply demonstrated the feasibilty of building on a tradition ineluctably associated with the Middle Ages.

H.1a

H.1b

H.1 Window, *The Good Shepherd* for the United Reformed Church, Maidstone

a Stained glass panel
Edward Burne-Jones for James Powell & Sons, Whitefriars, 1857, installed 1861
Stained and painted glass, 132.0 x 51.0 cm
Trustees of the United Reformed Church in Maidstone
(The window is normally to be seen at Maidstone Museum)

b Cartoon for above, 1857
Watercolour and ink, 128.0 x 47.7 cm
V&A (E.1317-1970)

Approached by James Powell & Sons as a designer for stained glass in 1856 or 1857, Rossetti declined, and instead suggested his friends Madox Brown and Burne-Jones. Madox Brown, so far as is known, made only one design, a *Transfiguration* (whereabouts unknown). *The Good Shepherd*, dated 1857, was probably the first stained-glass cartoon Burne-Jones produced. According to Rossetti it had 'driven Ruskin wild with joy' and the young, untrained artist did indeed exhibit a precocious grasp of the requirements of the medium.

It is uncertain whether the design was immediately translated into glass. This was the first version known to have been ordered, which was not until 1861, when it was fitted into the centre of the five-light east window of the Congregational Church, King Street, Maidstone. The order was placed by Reverend Henry Hamlet Dobney (1809–83), who, if in fact he specifically selected this design at the Powells' glass works, may well have been attracted by its spontaneity and directness. As a young man Dobney was prominent in a group of dissenting churchmen who were considered heretical for preaching the hope of Universal Restoration; he was the first editor of the *Christian Spectator* and an obituary described him as 'an artist of no mean order'. In 1858 Burne-Jones was staying with Arthur Hughes in Maidstone. Hughes was based at the house of his wife's parents, the Foords, in Marsham Street; it may not be coincidental that Dobney lived in the same street. The window was removed from the church prior to demolition in 1974. The cartoon was re-used by James Powell & Sons on at least one further occasion, at St Patrick's, Trim, Co. Meath, Eire, in 1869.

H.2 Three cartoons for stained glass for the Dining Hall, St Andrew's College, Bradfield, Berkshire

Edward Burne-Jones for James Powell & Sons, Whitefriars, 1857

a *Adam and Eve after the Fall*
Watercolour and Indian ink, 214.4 x 47.8 cm
Inscribed: 'EBJ 1857', 'No.510'
V&A (E.1319-1970)

b *Building of the Tower of Babel*
Watercolour and Indian ink, 220.4 x 52.0 cm
Inscribed: 'EBJ 1857', 'No.508'
V&A (E.1318-1970)

c *Solomon and the Queen of Sheba*
Watercolour and Indian ink, 213.0 x 49.5 cm
Inscribed: 'No.509'
V&A (E.1320-1970)

The archives of James Powell & Sons (Victoria & Albert Museum collection) record that two lights of the Bradfield window were fitted in July 1857. Since Burne-Jones's 1857 *Good Shepherd* was not installed into any building until four years later, the Bradfield window was presumably the first of his stained-glass commissions to be seen by a wider public. The cartoons were almost certainly among those which Burne-Jones exhibited at the Hogarth Club in 1858. The artist G.P.Boyce, who visited Bradfield in 1858, found the glass, though 'powerful and glowing', 'a little glaring and coarse'. In common with all of the Powell–Burne-Jones windows, but in contrast with the rest of James Powell & Sons' contemporary windows, which are generally rather dull, the glass is indeed intense in colour. It is made from the best 'pot metal' or 'muff' glass, which A.C. Sewter misrepresented as 'poor and thin' in quality. At Bradfield, Burne-Jones introduced a device to which he frequently returned, building up the composition in vertical 'layers' as a means of unfolding a narrative with minimal spatial recession. The disparity in scale between the densely packed central *Tower of* and the outer lights of *Adam and Eve* and *Solomon and Sheba* is perhaps a sign that he was still experimenting with the medium.

The founders' letters at the college furnish no evidence to suggest how the commission came about. There are several intriguing possibilities. The order for the window was placed by Reverend Thomas Stevens, Warden of the College and a close friend of G.G.Scott, the architect responsible for the Hall, which was built in 1856. Scott's second son, John Oldrid, who was a pupil at the College when Burne-Jones's window was installed, married Stevens's daughter. Arthur Powell, of the glass firm, was a trustee. The Reverend F.B.Guy, headmaster of the College from 1850–52, was Morris's private tutor in 1853; Stevens kept in touch with Guy, however, and made several attempts to entice him back to the College. A tradition at the college says that Morris helped Burne-Jones with the windows (he was certainly the model for Adam); did Guy, through Morris, introduce Burne-Jones? Finally, Thomas Acland was a prominent member of the College Council; in 1857 his son Henry Acland and John Ruskin were building the Oxford Museum. In 1859 their architect, Benjamin Woodward, was responsible for the design of the stonework containing Burne-Jones's *St Frideswide* window at Christ Church Cathedral, Oxford, and his sculptors, the O'Shea brothers, carved the window's surrounds. Ruskin often regretted not having become more directly involved in stained glass. He may have had to give up his ambitions for Edmund Oldfield and later for Millais, but was driven 'wild with joy' by Burne-Jones's first design; was he influencing others on his young protégé's behalf in all of these early commissions?

H.2a   H.2b   H.2c

H.3a

H.3b

H.4

H.3 Two cartoons for stained glass for Holy Cross and St Lawrence church, Waltham Abbey, Essex

Edward Burne-Jones for James Powell & Son, Whitefriars, 1860
Gouache

a *Christin Majesty*   **b** *The Third Day of Creation*
131.0 cm diameter   96.0 cm diameter
V&A (E.1321-1970)   V&A (E.1322-1970)

The designs for the chancel east wall windows at Waltham Abbey were the last which Burne-Jones made before he became a founding partner in Morris, Marshall, Faulkner & Co. These cartoons, for the centre and one of the lobes of the upper rose, are the only two that have survived, although a preliminary sketch for the three-light *Tree of Jesse* below belongs to the City of Birmingham Museum and Art Gallery. David O'Connor has identified the early fourteenth-century Gorleston Psalter (fol. 8, British Library Add. MS 49622) as the probable source for the inclusion of events in the life of Christ in the 'extended-Jesse' design, and another manuscript, the Queen Mary Psalter (British Library, MS Royal 2 B. viii), probably provided the concept of the circular Creation scenes.

Notwithstanding both Morris's and Burne-Jones's familiarity with illuminated manuscripts, the architect of the restoration at Waltham, William Burges, is more likely to have suggested these sources. Among the designs exhibited by Lavers & Barraud at a meeting of the Ecclesiological Society in May 1860 were cartoons by their new young designer, Nathaniel H.J.Westlake, for Waltham Abbey. Westlake was a protégé of Burges, and in 1860 published a volume of drawings based on the Queen Mary Psalter, containing, significantly, the *Creation* scenes referred to above. Westlake's own *Death of King Harold* designs for Waltham Abbey were, however, rejected and the commission was given instead to Burne-Jones. Burges was a close friend of Charles Winston, an antiquarian of stained glass who had initiated the research that resulted in James Powell and Sons' revived manufacture of 'pot metal' glass in 1852. This glass was used in all of the windows they made to designs by Burne-Jones. In *The Builder*, August 1861, Burges stated that the defects of modern stained glass were due to poor quality raw material and the 'lack of adequately coloured cartoon from the artist to guide the workman'. Aware that a conspicuous exception to these criticisms was the Burne-Jones–Powell *Legend of St Frideswide* window recently placed at Christ Church Cathedral, Oxford, he settled on the same combination for Waltham Abbey.

H.4 Triptych of the *Adoration of the Kings and Shepherds* and the *Annunciation* for St Paul's, Brighton

Edward Burne-Jones, 1860
Oil on canvas, centre 109.0 x 156.0 cm, wings 109.0 x 73.0 cm each
Tate Gallery, London (N04743)

The architect of St Paul, Brighton (1846–8), was R.C.Carpenter, but even before Carpenter's

H.5   H.6   H.7

death in 1855, G.F. Bodley had begun his long association with the church. He was its churchwarden and organist and had built the adjacent school-room in 1854. About 1860 he was asked to design a reredos, but instead commissioned a painted altarpiece from Burne-Jones. The artist's first substantial work in oils, it reflects the studies – instigated by Ruskin – made on his first Italian tour in autumn 1859. His previous experience of working on a large scale was limited to designs for stained glass, his Oxford Union mural of *Merlin and Nimue*, and his painting of the *Prioress's Tale* on the Webb-designed wardrobe which was their wedding gift to Morris in 1859. Burne-Jones's murals for Morris's Red House were also in progress in 1860. Hitherto dated 1861, the triptych, too, must have been substantially completed in 1860, for it was recommended by the architect J.P. Seddon to a meeting of the Ecclesiological Society on 11 June 1860. In the context of the Gothic revival, its fusion of eclectic Renaissance sources represents a remarkable break from medievalism.

When it was installed above the high altar the composition was deemed too elaborate to be intelligible from a distance, and a second version, in which the shepherds and attendant women were eliminated from the central *Adoration*, was substituted in 1861. The original was then offered by Burne-Jones in settlement of his debts to the estate of his patron T.E. Plint, who had recently died. In 1867 a dealer sold it to G.F. Bodley for £50. Following the death of his son, G.H. Bodley, in 1934, it was presented to the Tate Gallery. The church sold the second version in 1993.

Several of the models can be identified. The king presenting his gift to Christ is recognisable as Morris, Swinburne is the shepherd playing bagpipes and Burne-Jones himself is behind him. The king in armour in the foreground was painted from an Italian model, Ciamelli; studies for the Virgin were made from Georgiana Burne-Jones, but H.C. Marillier claimed that the finished version in oils showed Jane Morris.

H.5   Stained glass panel, possibly from the Nursery at Red House

Designed by Philip Webb, possibly produced by James Powell & Sons, Whitefriars, *c*.1859–60

Nine individual panels, painted and leaded glass with metal leading, 50.0 x 50.0 cm
V&A (C.63-1979)

Red House was completed – and presumably glazed – before the firm was set up to make stained glass, and it is possible these quarries were executed by other hands. Webb's lively, stylized birds, relieved with silver stain, are closely based on a common fifteenth-century type.

H.6   Cartoon for stained glass from the series *The Song of Solomon* for St Helen's, Darley Dale, Derbyshire.

Edward Burne-Jones for Morris, Marshall, Faulkner & Co., 1862
Pencil and sepia, 101.5 x 48.2 cm
Inscribed
Birmingham Museums and Art Gallery (176'00)
Presented by Charles Fairfax Murray

The Darley Dale window was ordered as a memorial to Raphael Gillum MD by his great-nephew and principal beneficiary, Colonel William James Gillum. Raphael Gillum had had lead, mining interests in the district and is buried in the churchyard alongside his wife, who predeceased him. Colonel Gillum was an important friend and patron of the firm. He was an amateur artist, a pupil of Madox Brown and member of the Hogarth Club; he sat on the management committee of the Home for Boys which provided the firm's early apprentices, ordered numerous items of furniture designed by Philip Webb, and bought paintings from Rossetti and Burne-Jones. In 1861 Webb built a row of houses and workshops for him (on land bequeathed by Raphael Gillum) in Worship Street, Finsbury, London. Gillum seems the most likely candidate for having suggested the Song of Solomon theme, a paean to earthly love which was unprecedented in stained glass and never repeated by the firm.

Unusually, the Darley Dale commission is not documented in any of the partners' account books; a list compiled by Warington Taylor confirms the date as 1862. In its colour, simplicity and direct expressiveness, the window exemplifies the gulf between the firm's stained glass and that of their competitors. The cartoons for all eleven of the principal subjects (one is repeated)

have traditionally been assigned to Burne-Jones. *As the lily among the thorns…* was drawn by Burne-Jones, but the conception appears to be Morris's. The angle of the woman's head and the position of her left hand, tentatively raising her skirt, are characteristics which recur frequently in Morris's work – for example in his paintings of *La Belle Iseult*, and of *Princess Sabra* on the St George Cabinet, in his cartoons of *Isoude* and of *Ruth*, and in several drawings. In one of the firm's photographic albums an almost identical design is catalogued under Morris; significantly, the alternative version is bordered with Morris's 'Si je puis' motto. The date of Morris's *Trellis* wallpaper, 1862, corresponds exactly with the trellis background in this design.

H.7   Design for stained glass, *Feast of the Vintage* from the series *The Parable of the Vineyard*, for St Martin's Church, Scarborough, Yorkshire.

Dante Gabriel Rossetti for Morris, Marshall, Faulkner & Co., 1861–2
Charcoal, black and grey wash; 61.6 x 60.3 cm
William Morris Gallery (London Borough of Waltham Forest) (A267)

Designed in 1861, the seven scenes which make up Rossetti's depiction of the *Parable of the Vineyard* are uncomfortably disposed around Madox Brown's central *Crucifixion* in the east window of Bodley's Church of St Martin, Scarborough. Some, or all of the series was displayed in the 1862 International Exhibition; *The Builder*, 22 November 1862, records that the window had been taken down from the exhibition and set up in the church.

Where the suggestion for this unprecedented treatment of the subject-matter originated is unknown; the dense, sometimes ribald and even sinister scenes are more likely to have appealed to Rossetti's sensibilities than Bodley's, and it certainly never recurred in the architect's iconographical schemes. The alcoholic abandon in the *Feast of the Vintage* might conceivably have provoked controversy, had the panels been in a more accessible position. Rossetti wrote to Madox Brown on 2 December 1861 asking if he had a number of the *Pictorial History of England* which contained an illustration of a Saxon wine-press for use in this series, though the idea was evidently discarded.

H.8

H.8 Cartoon for stained glass, *Adam Naming the Animals*, for the west window, All Saints Church, Selsley, Gloucestershire

---

Philip Webb for Morris, Marshall, Faulkner & Co., *c.*1862
Watercolour, 64.5 cm diameter;
68.8 x 67.0 cm sheet
V&A (E.1289-1931)
Bequeathed by J.R.Holliday

One of the eight outer lobes of the *Creation* rose window at Selsley, designed by Morris and Webb. In this panel, Adam is a rare instance of Webb drawing a figure cartoon for the firm. In some respects the conception for this window borrows from Burne-Jones's 1860 *Creation* design for Waltham Abbey (cat.no.H.3), but the indebtedness is more marked in Morris's cartoons than in Webb's. William Burges, like Bodley a friend of Revd John Gibson who commissioned the church, designed the altar-plate at Selsley, and may well have suggested repeating the Creation theme here.
Exhib. 1934 (8)

H.9 Cartoon for stained glass, *The Sermon on the Mount* for All Saints Church, Selsley, Gloucestershire

---

Dante Gabriel Rossetti for Morris, Marshall, Faulkner & Co., 1862

Pencil and wash, 88.3 x 63.3 cm
Inscribed
V&A (E.2916-1927)
Bequeathed by J.R. Holliday

There are two other versions of this design (William Morris Gallery, Walthamstow, and Leeds City Art Gallery), neither of which indicates the lead-lines; it was the firm's usual practice for Morris to add the lead-lines to a tracing of the full-sized designs submitted by the various artists. According to Madox Brown, Rossetti had said 'Anything will do for glass', and his comments on the Leeds version of this cartoon – 'Dear Top…It strikes now it's done there's no space left for lead lines is there ?…Note signs that I've added a little bit at bottom to get Christ in…' – appear to confirm his cavalier attitude. There are no grounds for concluding from these remarks, however, that his work was unfitted for stained glass.

This version is the working cartoon, on which Morris has indicated the pattern of leads. Christina Rossetti is said to have sat for the Virgin, George Meredith for Christ, Swinburne and Simeon Solomon for St John and St James; St Peter is readily indentifiable as Morris and the art-dealer Gambart is cast as Judas.

H.9

H.10a

H.10 Two designs for stained glass, from the series *The Story of Dives and Lazarus*

Charles Faulkner, *c*.1860
Watercolour
Inscribed

a *Lazarus at the Rich Man'sDoor*
52.8 x 56.4 cm
V&A (E.1162-1940)

b *The Death of Lazarus*
55.4 x 46.5 cm
V&A (E.1163-1940)
NOT ILLUSTRATED

Charles Faulkner, who kept the firm's books until the arrival of Warington Taylor, is not recorded as having designed stained glass, though he painted glass and tiles and operated the kiln in the early years. A sketch he made of stained glass in Amiens Cathedral while touring Northern France with Morris and Webb in August 1858 is in the collection of the William Morris Gallery, Walthamstow.

Two of a set of four subjects illustrating the story of *Dives and Lazarus*, the location of the window for which these cartoons were made is unknown. The Burges-ian architecture in the backgrounds suggests a connection with the architect; if this is correct, a potential destination for the windows was a privy or dog kennel (the documentation is ambiguous) at Gayhurst, Buckinghamshire. Designed by Burges in 1859–60 for the eccentric Lord Carrington, the building has four circular dormer windows of exactly the right size; if they ever contained stained glass, however, it is no longer *in situ*. The stone (erberus at the apex of the roof provides a canine link with the Lazarus story. The sculptor at Gayhurst was to have been John Lucas Tupper, a friend of Rossetti. Another link, which may be relevant, is that the Faulkners owned two Burges-designed chairs (now at the William Morris Gallery, Walthamstow).

H.11 Cartoon for stained glass, *Angel of the Resurrection*, for the church of St Michael and All Angels, Brighton

William Morris for Morris, Marshall, Faulkner & Co., 1862
Watercolour, 47.0 x 68.9 cm
Tate Gallery, London (N5223)
East window of south chancel aisle (now Lady Chapel). Left-hand of two lights (see fig. 50).

This was the first complex multi-figure design that Morris undertook for stained glass. Unlike its neighbour, Burne-Jones's *Flight into Egypt* (cat.no. H.12), the window was arranged in the 'banded' idiom established at Selsley, with Webb's quarries above and below the subject (and Webb's *Pelican in her Piety* in the circle above).

H.12

H.11

H.13

H.12 Design for stained glass, *Flight into Egypt*, for the church of St Michael and All Angels, Brighton

Edward Burne-Jones for Morris, Marshall, Faulkner & Co., 1862
Watercolour and ink over pencil, gold surround to mount; 15.5 x 13.2 cm
Inscribed in ink, verso: 'Sketches for window at Brighton Flight into Egypt by Edward Burne-Jones July 1862 the cartoons which I also possess were finished in the following August. See acct. book with the firm of Morris & Co. CFM'
Fitzwilliam Museum, Cambridge (720)

Right-hand light of a window for the south wall of south chancel aisle (now Lady Chapel) (see fig.12).

Burne-Jones's account book with Morris records this design in July 1862; the full-sized cartoons were prepared two months later. The window shows Burne-Jones's already consummate grasp of design. It is unusual in the firm's work for Bodley in that it entirely eschews any Gothic accessories such as borders or canopy-work. Intended to be read from close quarters, the narrative is intimately and gracefully drawn. The composition skilfully accommodates the arched tops of the lights, as exemplified by the slightly stooping angels in the left-hand light.

H.13 Cartoon for stained glass, *St Michael and the Dragon*, for the church of St Michael and All Angels, Brighton

Peter Paul Marshall for Morris, Marshall, Faulkner & Co., 1862
Wash, 81.5 x 86.8 cm
V&A (E.1166-1940)

Peter Paul Marshall provided at least ten cartoons for the firm's windows in 1862–3. These were mostly of single saints, more than competently drawn in a style close to Rossetti's; but as A.C.Sewter noted there is 'tremendous dramatic energy' in *St Michael and the Dragon*, which was designed for a sexfoil tracery light in the west window of Bodley's church of St Michael and All Angels, Brighton (see fig.49). After 1863 Marshall continued his career as a surveyor and sanitary engineer. When Morris was attempting to dissolve the original firm in 1874 Marshall set up in opposition, trading under the name Morris, Marshall & Co. He, together with Madox Brown and Rossetti, eventually accepted £1,000 in compensation from Morris in 1875. Little is known of his subsequent career, but in 1897 he supplied cartoons for a window in the English Church, Le Havre, to the Exeter glazier, Frederick Drake; the window was destroyed by bombing in 1943.

H.14

H.15a

H.15b

H.14 Stained-glass panel,
The Baptism of Christ in Jordan

Edward Burne-Jones for Morris,
Marshall, Faulkner & Co., 1862
Stained and painted glass,
106.0 x 53.3 cm
V&A (C.440-1940)

The full window of which this
panel is a portion was of two lights
and was made in 1862 for the
baptistery of St Michael and All
Angels, Brighton. The window was
presented by the architect, Bodley,
in memory of his father. The present panel was probably part of the
firm's display in the 1862
International Exhibition. Before
easy and widespread travel, or the
reproduction of half-tone
photographs in periodicals, the
dissemination of the firm's stained
glass outside their immediate circle
depended largely on public exhibitions. Their glass was awarded a
medal by the jury of the 1862 exhibition and Burne-Jones received a
separate medal for his designs.
Exhib. 1961 (12)

H.15 Stained-glass series,
The Legend of St George

Dante Gabriel Rossetti for
Morris, Marshall, Faulkner
& Co., *c*.1862
Six stained and painted glass
panels; 82.5 x 58.5 cm,
a 83.0 x 59.0 cm, 58.5 x 67.3 cm,
58.5 x 67.0 cm, **b** 59.0 x 66.8 cm,
58.3 x 67.2 cm
V&A (C.315 to 320-1927)
Bequeathed by J.R.Holliday

Vigorously dramatic and spatially
compressed, this impressive series
is typical of many of Rossetti's
designs for stained glass. Their history is still far from complete.
According to Rossetti's biographer,
H.C.Marillier, they were made for
Harden Grange, Bradford,
Yorkshire, and while this is quite
feasible, no confirmation has been
found. Even their dating is uncertain. They may have been shown,
as A.C.Sewter suggested, at the
1862 International Exhibition, but it
is perhaps significant that the
Wedding of St George panel was
included in the 1864 Exhibition of
Stained Glass, Mosaics, Etc.
J.R.Holliday bequeathed them to
the Museum in 1927, with no
provenance.
Exhib. 1934 (1)

H.16 Design for stained glass, *Music* from *King René's Honeymoon* series

Dante Gabriel Rossetti for Morris, Marshall, Faulkner & Co., 1862
Brush and ink with wash, 43.2 x 33.7 cm
Williamson Art Gallery and Museum, Birkenhead, Wirral (BIKGM2075)

For this stained-glass version of his Seddon cabinet design, Rossetti has omitted the arched top and simplified the background. In 1864, J. Hamilton Trist, who had already bought an oil painting of *Architecture* from Ford Madox Brown, commissioned Rossetti to paint a pendant picture of *Music*.

H.17 Four stained-glass panels depicting scenes from *King René's Honeymoon*

Morris, Marshall, Faulkner & Co., c.1863
Stained and painted glass
a *Architecture*
Ford Madox Brown
63.7 x 54.3 cm
V&A (Circ.516-1953)
b *Painting*
Edward Burne-Jones
63.7 x 54.3 cm
V&A (Circ.517-1953)
NOT ILLUSTRATED

c *Sculpture*
Edward Burne-Jones
63.5 x 54.0 cm
V&A (Circ.518-1953)
NOT ILLUSTRATED

d *Music*
Dante Gabriel Rossetti
63.5 x 54.0 cm
V&A (Circ.519-1953)

The four designs were originally made in 1861–2 for the King René's Honeymoon cabinet designed by J.P. Seddon and shown in the Medieval Court of the International Exhibition in 1862. Seddon intended the heavy oak cabinet for his own use (see cat.no.J.13). The panels depict incidents during the honeymoon of King René of Anjou, as related by Sir Walter Scott in *Anne of Geierstein*, who was 'endowed with a love of fine arts'.

The stained-glass versions of the subjects were made about 1863 as part of the firm's extensive interior decoration of the house of the painter Myles Birket Foster, The Hill, Witley, Surrey. Morris's adroit exploitation of variegated depths of flashed ruby glass in the tiled-floor foregrounds is noteworthy.

Exhib. Music 1934 (2); 1961 (14)

H.16

H.17a

H.17d

III.

H.18b

H.18 Three record drawings and two photographs of the church of St Edmund, Southwold, Suffolk

Purchased from the artist 1864

a Record drawing of two bays of the screen, plan, elevation and section, to scale, 1½ in. to 1 ft.
George Wardle, 1862–3
Pencil, pen and ink and watercolour on paper laid on to board; paper: 33.2 x 23.5 cm, board: 38.6 x 27.7 cm
Numbered in ink 'II' and on backing board numbered in pencil '3'
V&A (3489)
NOT ILLUSTRATED

b Record drawing of a part of the rail and a profile of the moulding
George Wardle, 1862–3
Pencil and watercolour on paper laid onto board; paper: 22.5 x 19.5 cm, board: 27.5 x 24.2 cm
Numbered in ink 'III'
V&A (3490)

c Record drawing of foliate decoration
George Wardle, 1862–3
Pen and ink on tracing paper laid on to board; paper: 11.2 x 13.1 cm, board: 15.3 x 17.5 cm

Inscribed in pencil on backing board: 'Southwold' and '2'
V&A (3490a)
NOT ILLUSTRATED

d Photograph of the interior looking towards the altar through the screen
Albumen print laid on to backing card; photograph: 8.4 x 6.0 cm, card: 10.1 x 6.6 cm
Printed on back of backing card: 'J. Court Photographic Artist Southwold'
V&A (42.858)
NOT ILLUSTRATED

e Photograph of the exterior
Possibly J. Court
Albumen print laid on to card; photograph: 6.1 x 9.9 cm; card: 6.4 x 10.4 cm
V&A (42.859)
NOT ILLUSTRATED

In 1862–3 George Wardle, artist and draughtsman, toured East Anglian churches making record drawings of the fittings and decorations, especially painted decoration. These are highly accomplished measured drawings that provide, together with his copious and painstaking notes, a very accurate record. Any restora-

tion of the paintwork was carefully noted. Wardle's hand-written description, 'An Account of the Rood Screen in Southwold Church, Suffolk by George Wardle', was marked 'Appd R.D.Redgrave 26/2/64 to be registered in Library' when it was bought by the Museum. St Edmund's is one of the finest of the great perpendicular churches built in Suffolk although of a type more common in Norfolk. The woman in the photograph of the interior may be Wardle's wife Madeleine. Before her marriage to Wardle she had, as Madeleine Smith, been the defendant in one of the most sensational trials of the period. Accused of murdering her lover with poison, she stood trial in Scotland, where the case was found Not Proven.   SA

H.19 Letter from George Wardle to Morris, Marshall, Faulkner & Co., 1865

Pen and ink on blue writing paper; 18.1 x 11.3 cm folded, 18.1 x 22.6 cm open
V&A (NAL Box I 86 DD)
NOT ILLUSTRATED

This is one of a series of letters that Wardle sent to Morris, Marshall, Faulkner & Co. between April and October 1865. Most accompanied parcels of drawings and copies of painted decoration from East Anglian churches. In them he explains what the sketches are, the problems he encountered – '…I have had an accident with the Ranworth sketch…' – and in almost all expresses regret that he '…had not time to do all I saw, or to see all I intended…' One thanks the firm for forwarding a parcel of drawings to the architect G.F.Bodley. Most contain an invoice. A parcel of drawings might be sold for £4 10s. and expenses charged at 28s. 6d. (including 14s. for lodging). The letter of 8 July 1865 says of the drawings of one roof 'They are not quite accurate in some points but you will not be misled in anything essential'. SA

H.20 Record drawings of East Anglian church roofs and their decoration

George Wardle, 1865 or 1866

a Pencil, watercolour and gold pigment on tracing paper laid on to board; paper: 23.3 x 28.5 cm, board: 27.7 x 37.8 cm
Inscribed: in ink 'about A.D. 1503', and in pencil 'looking west', and in ink on the backing board 'Knapton Church, Norfolk'
V&A (4982)

b Pencil, pen and ink, watercolour and chinese white on tracing paper laid on to board; paper 21.8 x 32.4 cm, board 27.8 x 38.1 cm
Inscribed: in ink 'Blythburgh Ch. Suffolk', and 'Aylmerton Ch. Norfolk', and 'The soffits of arches & purlins, with masks at their intersections, are the only parts painted' and with notes on the drawings
V&A (4611)

Possibly on the strength of his drawings of the rood screen at Southwold that had been purchased in 1864 by the South Kensington Museum, Wardle was commissioned by the firm to tour East Anglian churches recording their decoration. These drawings, bound into a volume were used by the firm as a source for decorative motifs. They were bequeathed to the Museum in 1939 by May Morris (Museum nos. E.317–404-1939). Wardle made copies of the drawings and sold them to the Museum in 1866 and 1867. The drawings shown here are part of these groups. The perspective of Knapton is untypical, being both a documentary record and yet managing to capture the stillness of the interior. The other sheet is more typical in that it is essentially fulfilling a documentary role. St Peter and St Paul, Knapton, has one of the best roofs in Norfolk, decorated with 138 carved and painted angels with outstretched wings. Holy Trinity, Blythburgh, was of interest because much of the original paintwork survives, having proved too high for the seventeenth-century iconoclast William Dowsing to destroy. SA

H.20a

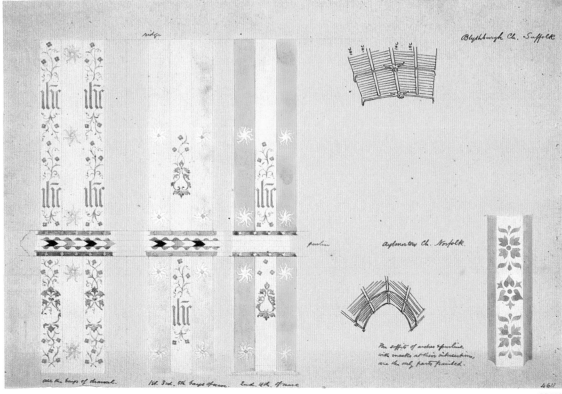

H.20b

Ecce virgo concipiet et pariet filium et vocabitur nomen eius Emmanuel | Spiritus Sanctus superveniet in te et virtus Altissimi obumbrabit tibi

H.21

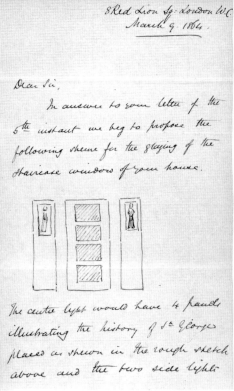

8 Red Lion Sq: London W.C.
March 9. 1864.

Dear Sir,

In answer to your letter of the 5th instant we beg to propose the following scheme for the glazing of the Staircase windows of your house.

The centre light would have 4 panels illustrating the history of St George placed as shown in the rough sketch above and the two side lights

H.25

H.22

H.21 Two-light window, *The Annunciation* for All Saints Church, Dedworth

Edward Burne-Jones for Morris, Marshall, Faulkner & Co., 1863
Stained and painted glass, each 45.5 x 31.5 cm
All Saints Church, Dedworth, Windsor

The architect of Dedworth Church, opened in 1863, was G.F.Bodley. A small, unpretentious brick building, it was demolished in 1973. According to Nikolaus Pevsner it was its series of Morris windows that 'makes a visit imperative for anyone walking around Windsor'. The *Annunciation*, which Pevsner thought 'specially lovely', was in the west window of the south aisle, set in Webb's square quarries. A.C. Sewter noted damage to the window in 1956, and further minor breakages occurred subsequently. The line of half-quarries at the top of the panels in their present condition is a modern replacement. The design was first made in 1862 for painted tiles, and its translation into stained glass is an early example of the firm's re-use of designs in different media. Burne-Jones, as the firm's minute book for 18 February 1863 records, was paid 15s. to superintend the necessary alterations.

Burne-Jones had already painted an *Annunciation* for Bodley – in the wings of the Brighton triptych (cat.no.H.4) – before the firm was set up. The architect's fondness for the subject is indicated by its presence, before Dedworth, in the firm's glazing schemes at Selsley, Brighton and Scarborough; by 1865 it was placed even more prominently in the chancel east windows at Malling Abbey, Kent; All Saints, Coddington, Nottinghamshire; and St Stephen, Guernsey, Channel Islands.

H.22 One-inch scale drawing for the west window of Holy Trinity Church, Ossett, Yorkshire

Philip Webb for Morris, Marshall, Faulkner & Co., 1863
Watercolour, 70.0 x 42.5 cm
Brian Clarke

This important early sketch design by Webb was drawn on the unusually large scale of one inch to one foot. Webb's account book for October 1862 records designs for the east and west windows at Ossett, charged at £4 10s. and £3 10s. respectively. The firm's minute book for 25 February 1863 adds, however, that both designs were to be 'considerably simplified', and it is probably one of these simplified versions that survives. The architect of Holy Trinity, W.H.Crossland, had sought tenders from at least two other London firms, James Powell & Sons (E.J.Poynter drew their sketch for the east window) and A. & W.H. O'Connor, and it was the O'Connors who eventually glazed both east and west windows when the church was completed in 1865. Since Morris was intending to charge the high price of £400 for each window, cost may have been the principal factor in Crossland's decision to look elsewhere.

H.23 Scale sketch for stained glass

Painted in the workshop of Morris, Marshall, Faulkner & Co.
Ink and watercolour, 38.5 x 56.25 cm
Inscribed: 'Mr Hastings, 1863'
Sanford and Helen Berger Collection

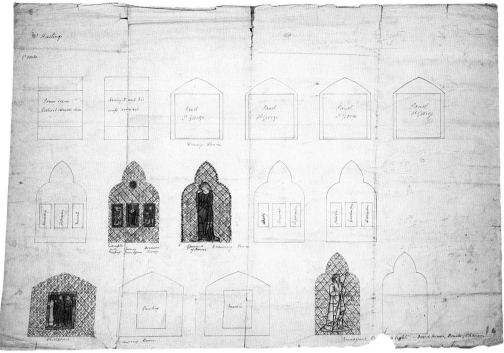

These designs, including a number of different subjects, were for windows in a house that Norman Shaw was to have built for Charles Hastings, a Bradford manufacturer associated with J. Aldam Heaton.

Minutes for the meeting of 15 February 1863 (in the firm's minute book) lists the scheme:

Agreed that the design for Hastings window be allotted as follows. 2 windows in dining room 'Prison Scene, Richard I' and 'Henry V and his queen crowned' to Marshall at 3£ each. 4 other lights (history of St George) in dining room to Rossetti at 5£ a piece. Centre light of the 5-light bay window of drawing room (genius of house) Rossetti's old design. 4 other lights of – do – the calender. In 3 light window of drawing room 'Sculpture' 'Painting' and 'Music'. For lights in breakfast-room single figures 'David' 'Homer' 'Dante' 'Chaucer'. Each to be done by Morris for 1£.

Unfortunately the windows were, almost certainly, never executed; they would have been one of the most extensive and interesting of the firm's domestic glazing schemes.

H.24 Stained glass, *Parable of the Labourers in the Vineyard* and *Solomon Building the Temple*

Edward Burne-Jones and Philip Webb for Morris, Marshall, Faulkner & Co., 1863
Stained and painted glass, 200.0 x 60.0 cm
Parish of Kentish Town

Burne-Jones designed a two-light window for Kentish Town Parish Church in 1862, but the cartoons for the subject medallions in this, the right-hand light, date from 1863. The background was designed by Philip Webb. The window was commissioned by Alfred Burges, marine engineer, partner in the highly successful firm Walker & Burges, and father of the architect William Burges. *Solomon Building the Temple* was presumably chosen on account of the profession of the deceased, James Cooper, who was a civil engineer.

H.25 Letter from Morris, Marshall, Faulkner & Co. to an Irish client

Dated 9 March 1864
20.2 x 12.5 cm folded
William Morris Gallery (London Borough of Waltham Forest) (J892)

This is the second of two surviving letters from Morris, Marshall, Faulkner & Co. to a potential client, Finlay Chester, concerning a staircase window for his home, Williamstown House, Castlebellingham, Co. Louth, Eire. The house (now a hotel) apparently contains no Morris glass, and indeed there is no evidence that the commission was carried out. The letter maintains the principle of anonymity that was agreed among the firm's designers; a reference to 'designs made by an eminent artist' conceals Rossetti (and perhaps also Burne-Jones) as the source of the proposed 'History of St George' subjects.

H.26

H.28

H.27

H.26 Design for stained glass, *Banners of the Tribes of Israel*, for All Saints Church, Middleton Cheney, Northamptonshire

Philip Webb, 1864
Indian ink and watercolour,
47.5 x 56.5 cm
V&A (E.2940-1927) Bequeathed by J.R.Holliday

Three of Webb's twelve banners carried by the *Tribes of Israel* (designed by Simeon Solomon), which process across the uppermost tiers of the four lights in the east window at Middleton Cheney.

H.27 Design for roof decoration, All Saints Church, Middleton Cheney, Northamptonshire

William Morris, 1864–5
Watercolour and pencil,
57.0 x 21.7 cm
Inscribed
William Morris Gallery (London Borough of Waltham Forest) (A27)

The stained glass which Morris, Marshall, Faulkner & Co. supplied to Middleton Cheney church made it, in Pevsner's words, 'a place of unforgettable enjoyment'; the firm's painted decoration of the nave and chancel roofs, however, completed in 1865, has previously been overlooked. Webb's *Lion's Head*, for which Sewter sought in vain in the glass, is gilded on the east and west faces of the nave tie-beams. One of two designs by Morris for the scheme to have survived, the single pomegranate is repeated on each of the king-posts of the chancel roof (fig.52). The pomegranate was one of the first designs Morris made for wallpaper, in 1862, and it also features in the backgrounds to the main lights of the east window at Middleton Cheney.

Morris has appended precise instructions on the roof designs since the work was to be carried out not by his own workmen but by a local contractor, George Cottam of Banbury, who ran an established business as a painter, plumber, glazier and gilder. As the firm's business increased in the 1860s it was not practicable for a team of painters to be away from the London workshops for a considerable length of time. In engaging a competent local firm Morris anticipated what became a standard Arts and Crafts practice at the end of the century.

H.29a

H.30

H.28 Design for stained glass, *Tree of Jesse*, for west window, St Stephen's Church, Guernsey

Philip Webb for Morris, Marshall, Faulkner & Co., 1864
Watercolour, 31.25 x 20.75 cm
Inscribed
Sanford and Helen Berger Collection

Apart from the single-light *Tree of Jesse* which Burne-Jones designed for St Margaret's, Rottingdean, Sussex, after Morris's death, in 1897, this was the only version of the subject the firm ever made. The Burne-Jones–James Powell & Sons *Tree of Jesse* for Waltham Abbey, Essex, was designed before the firm was founded.

The architect of St Stephen's was G. F. Bodley, and the firm also supplied the east window and three windows in the north aisle. Webb's account book confirms that he was responsible for this sketch. In Morris's fine colour scheme, richly draped figures are set against white quarries picked out with yellow stain, while the tree is in a pale, translucent purple. The twenty principal figures are incompletely documented; seven had previously been used elsewhere and most of the new figures appear to be designed by Morris.

H.29 Three stained-glass panels from the series *Chaucer's Goode Wimmen*

Edward Burne-Jones for Morris, Marshall, Faulkner & Co., c.1864
Stained and painted glass
a *Chaucer Asleep*
46.2 x 47.2 cm
V&A (774-1864)

b *Dido and Cleopatra*
46.0 x 49.5 cm

V&A (775-1864)
NOT ILLUSTRATED

c *The God of Love and Alceste*
46.2 x 49.5 cm
V&A (776-1864)
NOT ILLUSTRATED

In 1863 Ruskin was threatening to leave England and build a house in his beloved Swiss Alps, so Burne-Jones set about persuading him to reconsider. Part of his plan was to encourage Ruskin to settle in the Wye Valley, in a house for which Burne-Jones would design a series of tapestry embroideries of Chaucer's *Legend of Goode Wimmen* that could be worked by the girls of Winnington Hall School, Cheshire, in whom Ruskin took a close interest. Some of the designing was done *in situ*, and Burne-Jones wrote to Ruskin describing how 'damozels such as these at Winnington can't see how Cleopatra and Medea can be good women'. He had designed an earlier set of *Goode Wimmen* tiles, made in 1862 for Sandroyd, the house at Cobham, Surrey, built by Philip Webb for R. Spencer-Stanhope; these designs were substantially modified for the embroidery series, and it was the embroidery designs that became the basis for a set of stained-glass cartoons.

The relevant entry for the stained-glass versions of the *Goode Wimmen* is probably that for seven designs in Burne-Jones's account book under January 1864. The full series was intended for Birket Foster's house, The Hill, Witley, Surrey, where it formed part of a large collection of both Burne-Jones's paintings and the firm's products (now dispersed). Duplicate versions of three of the seven were included in the 1864 exhibition and were acquired directly by the Museum at that time. They must have been the panels the critic for *The Ecclesiologist* had in mind when he described Morris's glass as 'more nearly a reminiscence of late Dutch or

Flemish domestic glass than anything else'. The same writer admired 'their dabs and blots of strong colour in the midst of silvery or creamy white', and their use of flesh tints, which 'applied by them perfectly flat, are in delightful contrast to the treatment of flesh by most other artists'.

The *Goode Wimmen* series proved poular and was repeated in many different versions. The most complete surviving set (it lacks *Chaucer's Dream*) is in the Combination Room at Peterhouse College, Cambridge; dating from 1869 it is part of an extensive scheme of tiles, stained glass and painted decoration which the firm carried out there for G. G. Scott Jnr. A further set of six of the subjects (again without *Chaucer's Dream*) belongs to the Victoria and Albert Museum; it was made by Morris & Co. after the deaths of the principals in 1909, and the glass was painted by William Glasby, who had been a pupil of Henry Holiday and later made stained glass independently.

Exhib. 1934; *Chaucer Asleep* (3), *Dido and Cleopatra* (5), *The God of Love and Alceste* (4)

H.30 Stained-glass panel, *Penelope*

Edward Burne-Jones for Morris, Marshall, Faulkner & Co., 1864.
Stained and painted glass, 57.0 x 51.5 cm
V&A (773-1864)

This panel was acquired by the Museum directly from the 1864 Exhibition of Stained Glass, Mosaics Etc. An adaptation in roundel form of the head of *Phyllis* from the *Goode Wimmen* series it proved a popular design for the firm's domestic stained glass commissions.

Exhib. 1934 (6)

H.31a

H.31b

H.31 Two stained-glass panels

Edward Burne-Jones for Morris, Marshall, Faulkner & Co., *c.*1864
Stained and painted glass
Bequeathed by J.R. Holliday

a *The Prince*
33.6 x 18.5 cm
V&A (C.323-1927)

b *Merchant's Daughter*
33.6 x 18.5 cm
V&A (C.323A-1927)

These panels were made specifically to be shown at the 1864 Exhibition of Stained Glass, Mosaics Etc. at the South Kensington Museum. The cartoons, as the size of the glass indicates, were adapted from painted tile designs, in this case two of the series designed by Burne-Jones for the fireplace in the house of the painter Myles Birket Foster and dating from 1863. No doubt the firm considered the highly attractive panels an effective advertisement for their small-scale domestic glass; no further versions were ever made.

Exhib. 1934 (9) and (8)

H.32 Cartoon for a stained-glass window, *St Oswald Crowned King of Bernicia*, from *Scenes from the Life of St Oswald*, for St Oswald's Church, Durham

Designed by Ford Madox Brown for Morris, Marshall, Faulkner & Co., 1864–5
Chalk and wash, 49.6 x 50.8 cm
Inscribed: 'FMB Sep. '64'
V&A (E.1853-1910)

One of six cartoons for a three-light window set high at the west end of the medieval church of St Oswald at Durham, executed at intervals during 1864–5 (Hueffer, 1896; Sewter, I, 1974, figs. 209–15; II, 1975, p. 65). The panels are positioned between shield and decorative work by Webb and roundels of angels by Morris on a field of light quarries.

Full of vigorous line and detail within a limited depth, they characterise the artist's approach to stained-glass design. He considered that 'invention, expression and good dramatic action' should be combined with the imperative requirement of fine colour (1865 statement). He made nearly 130 subject and single figure designs for the firm up to 1874. He retained the copyright, considering them, as a history painter, basic material for his paintings. The *Baptism* in this series was long after developed for part of his first wall painting in Manchester Town Hall, 1878.   MB

H.33 Two tracery designs for stained glass from *Signs of the Zodiac* series

Philip Webb, 1865
Pencil, Indian ink and watercolour
Inscribed
Bequeathed by J.R. Holliday

a *Flaming Star*
20.3 x 41.0 cm
V&A (E.2937-1927)
NOT ILLUSTRATED

b *Dog Barking at Moon*
18.7 x 55.2 cm
V&A (E.2938-1927)

If Webb's designs for tracery lights are under-appreciated, it is probably because they are normally situated in the less accessible parts of windows. These attractive examples can be found in the *Signs of the Zodiac* tracery of the east window in the chapel of the Royal Agricultural College, Cirencester, Gloucestershire. The 'Flaming Star', was a favourite motif of Webb's, and he repeated it in many different forms. It is a common medieval device and Pugin and others had used it in the nineteenth century. In 1863 Webb drew a detail of a flaming star in the fifteenth-century window depicting St Enoch at New College Chapel, Oxford, and another possible source was the fourteenth-century glass in the tracery lights of the east window in the chapel of St Lucy, Christ Church Cathedral, Oxford.

H.34 Two-light window, *SS Peter and Paul* for the south nave window, St Nicholas's Church, Beaudesert, Henley-in-Arden, Warwickshire

William Morris (*St Peter*),
Ford Madox Brown (*St Paul*), 1865
Stained and painted glass, 198.1 x 43.2 cm each
St Nicholas, Beaudesert, Parish Church,
Henley-in-Arden, Warwickshire

Beaudesert was one of several churches in Warwickshire restored in the 1860s by the architect Thomas Garner, most of which contain important early Morris windows. Garner, who had left the office of G.G.Scott in 1861, continued to work as his 'sub-architect' on certain Warwickshire commissions, as well as on his own account. He also worked for G.F.Bodley from 1866, and became his partner in 1869. The pattern of diagonal bands that runs through the background of this window was designed by Philip Webb, and was a device first used by the firm in 1863 at Bradford Cathedral. It is based on the secular heraldic glazing in the great hall of Ockwells, Berkshire, about 1460.

The tracery shield in the original setting is by Philip Webb.

H.35 Design for nave ceiling for Jesus College Chapel, Cambridge

William Morris, 1866
Watercolour over chalk, 122.8 x 78.8 cm
The Master and Fellows of Jesus College, Cambridge
FOR ILLUSTRATION SEE FIG 53, PAGE 114

Morris's decoration of the nave ceiling in Jesus College Chapel was commissioned by G.F.Bodley in 1866. The scheme was entirely designed by Webb, with the exception of the angels around the coving. It was not

H.32

H.33b

H.34

practicable for Morris to employ a permanent team of craftsmen to execute painted decoration and – as at Middleton Cheney – he elected to have the work carried out by a local firm, F.R.Leach of Cambridge; Morris's scroll-bearing angels were, however, painted by his own men, superintended by Campfield.

Stephen Wildman (*Morris & Company in Cambridge*, 1980) has described the Dean's disappointment that Morris used a sub-contractor. Frederick Richard Leach was in fact a highly competent craftsman. He worked extensively for Bodley & Garner and G.G.Scott Junior, as well as for Morris in the 1870s, and his practical knowledge was invaluable in enabling C.E.Kempe to set up his workshops for stained glass and church decoration in 1868. The north transept ceiling at Jesus College was painted by Leach between July and November 1869; its commencement was delayed while Leach completed C.E.Kempe's scheme of decoration in Bodley's Church of St John, Tuebrook, Liverpool. George Wardle paid several visits to oversee Leach's work, and indeed Wardle's drawings of medieval painted decoration in East Anglian churches possibly had a direct bearing on the Jesus College scheme – the chevroned ribs and the alternating green and red backgrounds of Morris's angels, for example, follow familiar medieval prototypes.

Exhib. 1934 (43)

MORS ET VITA DVELLO CONFLIXERE MIRANDO

H.36

H.36 Triptych, *Lamentation for The Dead Christ* and *The Annunciation*

Side panels designed by William Morris, painted by Charles Napier Hemy; central panel relief sculpture Franconian, second half of the fifteenth century
Morris, Marshall, Faulkner & Co., 1866
Side panels: oils on oak panels; centre: polychrome gesso on oak panels; 152.4 x 193.0 cm
Private Collection

Even in its present condition – it was partly restored following fire damage in 1957 – this triptych for Cheddleton Church, Leek, Staffordshire, is an instructive example of the firm's church decoration in the 1860s and of their attitudes towards late-medieval art. It was made 'under the immediate superintendence' of the architect G.G. Scott Junior, who wrote to one of the churchwardens that 'I am greatly pleased with it. It is a great thing to have a good work of art, combining new and old work, and both of them good'. 'The work of these men', he added, 'will have a constantly increasing value, for it is such good work that it cannot be duly appreciated at first'.

Among several conflicting accounts of the provenance of the central *Lamentation of Christ*, the most convincing version is that reported in the *Building News*, 13 April 1866, when the triptych was nearing completion, which stated that the reredos was a gift of Edward Wood, of Newbold Revell Hall, Warwickshire. Thomas Wardle, in a paper written in consultation with Morris in 1876,

noted that it had been bought 'at an old furniture mart, at the request of the architect'. The Wood family – well-known Staffordshire potters – had Cheddleton ancestors. The *Lamentation* had been painted a 'dark oak colour' but the polychromy found under this coating was restored under Morris's direction and augmented with his own drapery patterns. The brocade design on the tunic of Joseph of Arimathaea is closely related to the pattern on the Southwold rood screen, copied by George Wardle (see cat. no. H.18). The triptych's new oak casing was designed by G.G. Scott Junior and made by Rattee and Kett of Cambridge. The wings depicting the *Annunciation* were designed by Morris and painted by Charles Napier Hemy, who left soon after to pursue a successful career as a marine painter, had been introduced to the firm by William Bell Scott, with whom he had studied at the Government School of Design, Newcastle upon Tyne. Until 1862 Hemy had been attached to the Dominican Order, and executed painted decoration for their chapels at Newcastle upon Tyne and Lyons.

H.37 Two-light window, *The Annunciation* for Chapel of St James, Lord Leycester Hospital, Warwick

William Morris for Morris, Marshall, Faulkner & Co., 1866
Stained and painted glass, 78.0 x 17.5 cm each panel
The Patron and Governors of the Lord Leycester Hospital, Warwick

The delightful Warwick *Annunciation* is an interesting example of the firm's re-use of designs in different media. Gabriel and the Virgin Mary were adapted from the figures designed for the painted wings of the Cheddleton altarpiece in the same year (cat. no. H.36), with which they can be directly compared. The architect who restored the chapel of St James in 1864–6 was Thomas Garner. According to Mr Donald J.R. Green the figures were repeated on at least five more occasions in stained glass.

H.38 Scale sketch for stained glass, east window, St Wilfrid's Church, Cuckfield, Sussex

Unattributed design for Morris, Marshall, Faulkner & Co., 14 June 1867
Watercolour, 31.25 x 15.2 cm
Inscribed and dated
Sanford and Helen Berger Collection

Dated 14 June 1867 and inscribed as destined for Cuckfield Church, this drawing clearly refers in fact to the east window of St Wilfrid's, Hayward's Heath, Sussex. Cuckfield church is in any case dedicated to the Holy Trinity. The architect of Hayward's Heath church was G.F. Bodley, and again the presence of an *Annunciation* across the base of the window should be noticed. Set against the pale quarries that Bodley preferred in the mid-1860s, the *Crucifixion* in the upper half of the window has the appearance of a rood, an allusion that would seem to have been consciously intended. It is unknown who was responsible for the firm's sketch drawings by 1867. Regrettably, the window itself was destroyed in 1962, shortly before the revival of interest in Morris began to gather pace.

H.39 Scale sketch for stained glass

Painted in the workshops of Morris, Marshall, Faulkner & Co.
Ink and watercolour, 19.0 x 14.7 cm
Inscribed: 'No 3' and dated '14 Nov '67'
Sanford and Helen Berger Collection

Morris, Marshall, Faulkner & Co. supplied a window for the Lady Chapel of Dalkeith church in 1868, for which this is, almost certainly the preliminary sketch design. A different design for the tracery light – Morris's *Angel Playing a Lute* – was sub-stitued in the finished window. The commission may have been due to J. Hungerford Pollen, who was responsible for the statue of St Aloysius in the church.

H.40 Stained-glass panel, *Elaine*

Edward Burne-Jones for Morris & Co., 1870
Painted and stained glass, 86.3 x 51.4 cm
V&A (C.321-1927)
Bequeathed by J. R. Holliday

Figures of *Lancelot* and *Elaine* were designed by Burne-Jones in 1870 as part of an extensive stained-glass scheme for Hill Place, Upminster, Essex. The designs were repeated in 1882 for Lunefield, Kirkby Lonsdale, Lancashire. Lunefield was built for Alfred Harris, a Bradford banker; he and John Aldam Heaton were at the centre of the group of industrialists, based around Bradford and Bingley, who were important patrons of the Pre-Raphaelites in the 1860s. Harris's architect was Alfred Waterhouse, whose work Morris detested. The house is now demolished.

The companion figure of *Lancelot* is now lost (although the whole of the series at Upminster survives; the building there is now the Convent of the Sacred Heart of Mary). *Elaine* is an early example of what became a standard pattern for Morris's windows in the 1870s and later, in which the figure was placed on a plain quarry background. Appropriate and functional in the case of this secular commission, it was an idiom that did not meet with universal approval. In *Modern Parish Churches*, (1874), the architect J. T. Micklethwaite condemned Morris's practice of 'the placing of a single figure, without any preparation, in the middle of a light, otherwise made up of uniform quarry-glazing. The two never seem properly to belong to one another, a defect which may be corrected by a very little modification of the groundwork as it approaches the figure'.

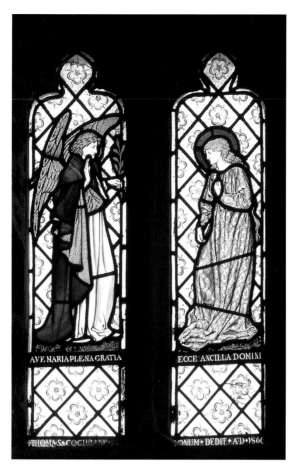

H.37

H.40

H.38

H.39

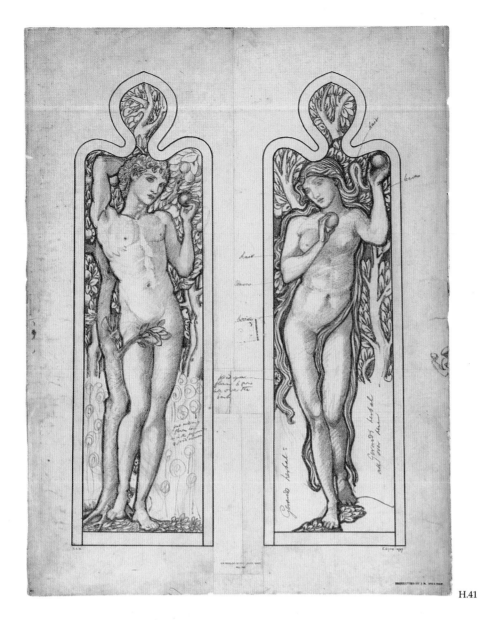

H.41

H.42

H.41 Design for tracery light, *Adam and Eve*, west window, All Saints, Middleton Cheney, Northamptonshire

Edward Burne-Jones, for Morris, Marshall, Faulkner & Co., 1870
Pencil, pen and ink, 83.4 x 64.4 cm
Inscribed
V&A (E.2908-1927). Bequeathed by J.R.Holliday

The notes which Burne-Jones appended to this full-sized design offer an insight into the nature of his collaboration with Morris. By Adam's knee he wrote 'put millions of flowers here as in the foregrounds of good women', and alongside Eve, 'Gerard's herbal all over here' – indicating an important source-document for such details.

H.42 Cartoon for stained glass, background design with blank figure, for St Martin's Church, Marple, Cheshire

Unattributed designer for Morris & Co., 1873
Pencil and wash, 99.0 x 36.8 cm

V&A (E.2791-1927) Bequeathed by J.R.Holliday

Cartoon for the background of the upper left-hand light of a two-light window in the south wall of the chancel. The blank space in this cartoon has been left to accommodate a figure of the Virgin Mary designed by Burne-Jones some ten years earlier for the east window of Bradford Cathedral. Adapting the backgrounds enabled figures to be re-used on numerous occasions in windows of different shapes. By this time the backgrounds were generally drawn not by Morris but by William Emile Pozzi, so windows could be designed with Morris merely supervising and without necessitating the direct involvement of Burne-Jones. This streamlining of the company's methods facilitated increased productivity but perhaps also accounts for those windows in which the firm's original inspiration appears diluted.

The restoration of Marple church was completed under the architect J.D.Sedding in 1870, when the firm supplied the east window of the chancel. Sedding does not appear to have used Morris glass again – the large and disappointing east window of his church of Holy Trinity, Sloane Street, London, was not fixed until four years after his death.

H.43 Two decorative domestic panels of stained glass

a *Homer*
Edward Burne-Jones for Morris & Co. *c*.1874
Stained and painted glass, 73.0 x 44.0 cm
V&A (C.681-1923) Bequeathed by May Morris
NOT ILLUSTRATED

b *Minstrel (Woman Playing Lute)*
William Morris for Morris & Co., *c*.1874
Stained and painted glass, 75.0 x 46.5 cm
V&A (C.678-1923) Bequeathed by May Morris

These domestic panels examplify the streamlining of Morris's workshop practices to facilitate the re-use of cartoons. *Homer* was originally designed by Burne-Jones for the *Poets* window (1871–4) in the Combination Room at Peterhouse, Cambridge. Morris's *Minstrel* was one of a series of figures frequently used for secular commissions (both painted tiles and stained glass) and which, with the addition of wings, became minstrel angels for church windows. The backgrounds of simple quarries allowed flexibility in terms of accommodating different window shapes, and brought homogeneity to sometimes disparate figure styles.

Exhib. 1934 (10, 11)

H.44 Three designs for stained-glass quarries

Unattributed designer for Morris & Co., 1890s
a Pen and ink, watercolour and wash on paper, 19.5 x 19.3 cm
Inscribed: 'Q.P No.9' called 'Mater'
Sanford and Helen Berger Collection
NOT ILLUSTRATED

b Pen and ink, watercolour and wash on paper, 45.0 x 28.0 cm
Inscribed: 'Q.P 34' 'Meole Brace 1893'
Sanford and Helen Berger Collection

c Pen and ink, watercolour and wash on paper, 35.5 x 27.6 cm
Inscribed: 'Q.P.100' 'Top'
Sanford and Helen Berger Collection
NOT ILLUSTRATED

These designs indicate that Morris's firm kept a systematic inventory of quarry patterns, which, like figure cartoons, could be recycled where appropriate. It is unlikely that Morris designed any of these examples himself, though they all conform to his established treatments of stylised natural plant forms. The identified example (H.44b) can be found in the background of the window depicting Enoch, Faith and Elijah, in the south aisle of Holy Trinity Church, Meole Brace, Shropshire (1894).

H.44b

H.43b

DOMESTIC DECORATION

Linda Parry

> If I were asked to say what is at once the most important
> production of Art and the thing most to be longed for I should answer,
> A beautiful House...

This statement by Morris illustrates his modest aims as designer and retailer. His success in achieving this intent can be judged by his obituaries, many of which remembered him not as a designer, poet, writer or radical socialist, but as a decorator. This was not meant to downgrade his work in other spheres, but simply reflected his popularity in what was then, in 1896, an admired and reputable trade without any of its modern connotations of self-indulgence, materialism and privilege.

All of the decorative patterns and objects that Morris designed or helped to make were purposefully conceived to fit together in room settings, and although beauty was the aim all were made to be appropriate for their use. This pragmatism is the most overriding characteristic of his work and is a quality that has been seldom recognised in the past, despite it being one of the main reasons why his furnishings are so popular today. It is, therefore, appropriate that a survey of his achievements in various artistic spheres should include a study of his views on the decoration and furnishing of houses and how he actually carried this out in his own commercial practice. As soon as Morris was first able to choose his own surroundings he felt a strong need to decorate and furnish them to his own taste, and he continued to do this for himself and his family and for friends and clients for the rest of his life.

The rooms he rented with Burne-Jones at 17 Red Lion Square, London, from the late summer of 1856 presented him with his first opportunity for such self-expression. The sheer anticipation of a bohemian life, and the freedom from constraints of home, school, university and Street's office provided Morris with the opportunity and confidence, and he begin to amass objects and ideas that would later develop into his own personal style of domestic decoration. He had already had some furniture made to his design before moving in and these pieces were now painted especially for the rooms by Morris, Burne-Jones and their frequent visitor, Rossetti. Once installed, Morris designed and embroidered a set of hangings for the walls with the help, volunteered or otherwise, of their servant, Red Lion Mary (see cat.no.A.11). The grouping of these new furnishings (cat.nos. J.3, 4, 6, 7, M.4) with the mass of collected items – easels, lay figures, armour, prints and brass-rubbings – that Morris and Burne-Jones acquired for artistic reference or effect, provided a general jumble about which Burne-Jones declared 'all domestic arrangements are of the most limited description'; a fact illustrated by the only existing illustration of the rooms (fig. 67).

The first official project that Morris took part in was the decoration of the Debating Hall of Benjamin Woodward's new Oxford Union building (fig. 6), a commission organised initially by Rossetti. After the exuberance of Red Lion Square, this scheme was important to Morris in introducing him to the organisation and economics of business life. With his knowledge of Oxford building trades, learned in Street's office, he became responsible for the purchase of materials and the hire and organisation of labour. As the Union was only willing to pay for equipment and materials and the food and lodgings of the participants, this must have been an onerous duty. Morris designed a repeating pattern for the roof which, despite being re-painted some years later, was generally approved of, whereas his contribution to the Arthurian themes around the walls, *How Sir Palomydes loved la Belle Iseult with exceeding great love*, has proved to be of more historic than artistic interest.

While painting at the Oxford Union in 1857 Morris first met Jane Burden. They were engaged in

the spring of 1858 and married in April 1859, by which time Morris was well advanced with plans for his next decorative project – the biggest so far – the building and decoration of a house for them to live in. He had first broached the subject with Philip Webb while on a boat trip on the Seine in Paris in August 1858. Webb was to design the house and Morris to organise the decoration and furnishing of it; a working partnership that lasted for over thirty years.

As Webb's first building as an independent architect, Morris's commission presented him with an unprecedented opportunity, that of designing a home for a close friend with comparable tastes. His notebooks and delicate, meticulous drawings (cat. nos. A.9, I.4) show the care with which he undertook the challenge. Morris's intended that most of the walls and ceilings of the house should be decorated; either painted with repeating patterns and narrative compositions or covered with embroidered hangings. Some ceiling patterns have survived and others been repainted, and where-as the arrangements planned for each room can be traced through preparatory drawings, and notes made by Burne-Jones and recorded by Mackail and Georgiana Burne-Jones, only fragments now exist. For the hall and staircase with its specially designed and painted press, Morris and Burne-Jones planned a series of wall paintings based on the story of Troy (cat. no. G.9). These were never attempted, although the painted roof of the stairway (fig. 57), one of Morris's earliest attempts at pattern-making which looks both medieval and modern in its use of simple motifs, can still be seen. To hang around the walls of the dining room on the ground floor, Morris conceived a set of embroidered hangings depicting heroines, and for the principal bedroom he chose a simpler design of embroidered daisies on a dark blue ground (cat. nos. M.6–9). The most adventurous plans were left for the drawing room on the first floor, a room that extends into the roof and is flooded by light from windows on the north and the south west. A large settle was installed on one wall. Originally part of Morris's furnishings for Red Lion Square, it had been included in Webb's detailed drawings of the architectural fittings of the house. This was now re-painted by Rossetti (cat. nos. G.13–14). For the walls a series of seven tempera paintings depicting the fifteenth-century romance of Sir Degrevaunt, a favourite of Morris's, was planned by Burne-Jones (cat. nos. G.11, 12). Only three

Fig.57 Ceiling decoration above the main staircase at Red House.

were completed and survive in the house. These show The Procession, The Wedding Ceremony and The Wedding Feast, in which William and Jane appear, appropriately, as Sir Degrevaunt and his bride. Morris intended the walls below the paintings to be decorated, although there is some confusion as to whether this originally showed a painted rendition of the earlier *If I Can* embroidered hangings or the embroideries themselves.

It is now generally accepted that the decoration of Red House, both in terms of original artistic endeavour and the comradeship experienced by Morris and his friends, convinced them to exploit the situation commercially and led to the foundation of the firm of Morris, Marshall, Faulkner & Co. in 1861. Their intentions were not solely mercenary for, however the others may have felt about the project, Morris saw it as a crusade; '...all the minor arts were in a state of complete degradation especially in England, and accordingly in 1861 with the conceited courage of a young man I set myself to reforming all that...', was how he described it 'in a long-winded sketch of my very uneventful life' in a letter of 1883.

It is clear that Morris and Webb saw house decoration as one of the main functions of the new company, and at the top of the list of services offered in its initial circular was 'Mural Decoration either in Pictures or in Pattern Work, or merely in the arrangement of Colours, as applied to dwelling-houses, churches, or public buildings'. The 1862 exhibition established the firm in the minds of a section of the fashionable London buying public and a steady flow of work followed over the next few years. By 1865 they were recognised as one of the most exciting new firms, even though the business, now moved to Queen Square, was still small and additional financial backing was needed to keep going.

Many more commissions for the decoration of houses were carried out by the firm in their first decade than is now realised. Few of these houses still exist, and the difficulty in identifying which of the clients or locations mentioned in the firm's minute book represent schemes or simply orders for individual objects has added to the confusion. It is likely that a number of commissions were arranged through contacts within the partners' various artistic circles and those that are known rep-

Fig. 58 *Sir Degrevaunt's Wedding Feast*, one of three wall paintings by Burne-Jones in the drawing room at Red House. William and Jane Morris were the models for the bride and groom.

resent a varied and interesting group. These include the decoration of houses for the painters Spencer Stanhope (Sandroyd, Cobham), Myles Birket Foster (The Hill, Whitley), both in Surrey, and G. P. Boyce (Glebe Place, Chelsea); Woodbank and Harden Grange in Bingley, Yorkshire, the homes of the decorator J. Aldam Heaton and his neighbour Walter Dunlop, and Wensum Lodge in Park Hill, Carshalton, Surrey, for the civil servant and writer William Hale White.

These private commissions can only be evaluated now through a few photographs and from dispersed furnishings such as tiles, stained-glass panels and furniture, so there has been a misleading tendency to judge the firm's early decorative style through existing public commissions in Cambridge (Queen's College and Peterhouse) and in London (the South Kensington Museum and St James's Palace).

The two prestigious London commissions, conceived and completed between 1866 and 1869, were exceedingly important in establishing the firm. Rossetti had been instrumental in organising these and one can only marvel at his success in convincing a royal court not known for its love of avant-garde design and a museum that had only moved from temporary headquarters at Marlborough House a few years before, that a new, inexperienced firm of decorators was capable of carrying out work of the quality and standard demanded. Morris and Webb worked on both schemes together, although Webb produced most of the individual designs required and supervised

the firm's staff and the work of their sub-contractors, S. & S. Dunn of 31 Brewer Street, Golden Square. Work at South Kensington started a little earlier than the Palace, although the latter took precedence over the next three years. Webb's diaries and account books, and letters between him and the firm's manager Warington Taylor, provide a near blow-by-blow account of the schemes' developments including visits, measurements, designs, estimates, progress on the work itself and the behaviour of workers. The final costs are not known although S. & S. Dunn charged the firm £602 1s. 4d. for three years' work at St James's Palace, the largest bill (£465 13s. 4d.) being for 1866, the first year of their accounts. Warington Taylor humorously referred to MMF&Co. 'robbing' the public (a reference to being paid from public funds), but this was far from the truth. Webb, as always, charged the firm little if anything for his designs, so final invoices are unlikely to have reflected the real cost of the work.

The overall schemes in both the Armoury and Tapestry Room at St James's Palace, are eye-catching. Ceilings and cornices, panelled dados, architraves, windows and doors are all painted with repeating patterns of stylised floral decoration intended to complement rather than compete with the existing displays of early tapestries and armour. The unifying colour of the woodwork, gold and brightly coloured highlights on a black ground, is regal in effect yet uncharacteristically dark. However, Webb had already designed a range of ebonised furniture with gilded decoration (cat.nos. J.16, 21), and existing photographs of Birket Foster's house, The Hill, decorated from 1865, show a rich, dark interior far more in line with contemporary Aesthetic tastes than is now associated with the firm's work.

Fig. 59 A painted doorway in the Armoury at St James's Palace.

The Green Dining Room (as it later became known) at the South Kensington Museum, looks quite different and, apart from panelled walls (this time plain) and the use of stylised sunflower motifs, there is little else to connect the two contemporary commissions. By choosing a blue-green for the predominating woodwork and plasterwork, it is likely that Morris and Webb intended to provide a restful effect suitable for the domestic purpose of the room. Surface pattern was provided with Webb's repeating design in the plaster filling of the wall and a brightly coloured cornice frieze of a dog chasing a hare (cat.no. I.6). At eye level a series of painted panels of tree and fruit branches is interspersed with Burne-Jones's figurative panels representing the Zodiac or the Months. The three stained-glass windows show garlanded figures surrounded by quarries of animals and flowers. Estimates for the work included £272 for the stained glass, £277 14s. for 'colouring and gilding the plaster ceiling and painting the panelled dado' and £291 6s. for the seventy panels 'with figures and patterns' of which Burne-Jones mentions the sum of £35 for '7 SK cartoons' in his accounts.

It is possible to trace the progress of the ceiling and plaster decoration quite closely. Webb drew the wall design of repeating olive branches on 26 October 1866, for which he charged the firm £7 plus £1 3s. for one of his many visits (on 15 November) to check on the plaster modelling. Once complete, the painting of the plaster took one man one and a half days to finish 'one square of boughs' (one plaster-cast repeat) according to Warington Taylor's notes. The preparation of the ceiling was equally laborious, with one man taking two and a half days to trace, prick and prepare 'two copies of ceiling pattern' (cat.no. I.7), followed by four men working for two days 'To set out pattern on ceiling'. The final painting was completed at a rate of four and a half square feet a day. Taylor adds that it was always necessary to have a man employed full time mixing colours, and he estimated that 'The whole work above dado' would take one man 243 days at a cost of £86 16s.

The scheme at South Kensington and its efficient completion became a guide for future practice. It taught three important lessons; accurate estimating, efficient organisation and the need for a versatile workforce. Before this commission Morris had tended to underprice work, charging an unrealistic five per cent profit. Furthermore, Taylor believed 'Morris is very nervous about work; and he consequently often suddenly takes men off one job and puts them to another'. The partners' lack of experience in handling their workforce presented a number of problems. While work on Jesus College Chapel, Cambridge, was in progress Morris had written to the foreman, George Campfield, complaining that 'The escapades of our men have enraged the dons, and they want to get rid of you…' The aftermath of the London commissions was equally worrying; 'What guarantee is there that the men will keep good time when they return to the shop', Warington Taylor wrote to

Fig. 60 The Green Dining Room, South Kensington Museum.

Webb in January 1869, 'because after 3 months at the Palace their habits will be loose – I know 'em – because about every five weeks they require touching up under ordinary circumstances.'

The project, 'a lesson at being Jack of all trades…' according to Taylor, emphasised the need for the firm's workers to extend the range and versatility of skills, and this was greatly helped with the assistance of successful and efficient subcontractors. The Cambridge decorator Frederick Leach was used on a number of commissions, mostly churches, and the records of the firm of S. & S. Dunn show that not only did they work on a great many London and home counties decorative schemes for the Morris firm between 1866 and 1884, but were also responsible for supplying many of the necessary accessories of home furnishings including curtain poles, bronze rings and brackets, canvas and bell balls that the firm needed to carry on this side of their business. Their charges to the firm for four years from 1876 to 1879 (£2,637 5s., £2,460 7s. 11d., £4,520 9s. 7d. and £2,003 5s. 7d. respectively) not only show the extent of their work, but actually provide the only record of the firm's activities as decorators in one of their most popular periods.

Morris's partners, particularly Webb and Burne-Jones, also became dependent on the firm's products for decorating their homes. Burne-Jones's account books and existing photographs of his house The Grange, North End Road, Fulham, show how extensive this was (figs. 75, 86). In the autumn of 1867, the year he moved in, he ordered fifty-three pieces of Morris wallpaper in five different patterns as well as plain textiles, furniture and tableware (including numerous drinking glasses and crates of wine). This was not unusual, for his accounts for the years from 1866 to 1870

show a debit account with the firm, despite this being one of his busiest periods for supplying designs.

In 1865 the Morris family moved from Red House to live on the first floor of the firm's head-quarters at Queen Square. William and Jane did their best to provide attractive quarters, and various carpentry and painting works listed by Dunn's for the address may refer to these rooms. George Wardle, the firm's manager, remembered them as 'extremely simple, very beautiful'. This seems to define Morris's own preference in domestic decoration and both Kelmscott Manor, the family's country retreat found in 1871 (fig. 85) and Kelmscott House, Hammersmith, where they moved in 1878 (cat. no. I.9, figs. 61, 96) displayed a comfort and simplicity of style absent from many of the firm's commercial schemes.

The difference between countryside and town living became more marked in the firm's interior decoration of the 1870s and 1880s. Dunn's records of work completed for Morris & Co. in 1875 lists an extraordinary range of fashionable London addresses – Grosvenor Street, Carlton House Terrace, Belgrave Square, Palace Gate, Stanhope Gardens, Curzon Street, Bryanston Square, Jermyn Street, Princes Gardens and Kensington Palace – to name a few. But the firm was also engaged on work outside London from Dorset to Cumbria and Yorkshire. The Howard and Bell families were important clients and work produced for both in the north of England helped the firm become known further afield. George Howard, Earl of Carlisle, and his wife Rosalind were close family friends of the Morrises, and Rosalind Howard records her first visit to 'Morris and Webb's furniture place' at Queen Square in November 1866. The decoration of their London home at 1 Palace Green, built for them by Philip Webb, was started soon after the house was finished in 1872. Using a similar decorative style to the Green Dining Room, this showed elaborately patterned ceilings and wall panelling with, in the dining room, Burne-Jones's early *tour de force*, a series of paintings of *Cupid and Psyche* from Morris's longer poem *The Earthly Paradise*. Morris also designed a carpet for the Howards' Cumbrian home, Naworth Castle (cat. no. M.106), and advised on furnishings for Castle Howard in Yorkshire for which a large quantity of wallpapers and fabrics was bought, with no less than fifty-four Sussex chairs ordered in 1882 for the dining room.

Philip Webb was responsible for introducing Morris & Co.'s work to the Bell family. Isaac Lowthian Bell, the northern ironmaster and chemist, first employed him in 1868 for alterations to Washington Hall, County Durham, and Webb was subsequently commissioned to build his second home, Rounton Grange, as well as Red Barns in Redcar for Bell's son, Hugh (cat. nos. M.104–5) and Smeaton Manor (cat. no. M.21) for his daughter Ada Godman.

The decoration of Rounton Grange from about 1874 provided an extensive and varied commission, and despite poor Bell being subject to Morris's confrontational remark that he was sick of 'ministering to the swinish luxury of the rich', photographs show how lucrative this must have been to the firm. For the dining room, painted wooden wainscoting followed the style of earlier work, but instead of a painted frieze, as in South Kensington and Palace Green, Morris and Burne-Jones designed a set of embroideries to be worked by Margaret Bell and her daughters (cat. no. M.15). A large carpet was designed for the house (cat. no. M.107), ceilings were painted and the walls of most rooms (which were filled with Morris furniture) were either wallpapered or covered in fabric. The overall effect of the furnishings provided an elegant yet comfortable interior.

By the late 1870s Morris's increasing political awareness began to affect his views on house decoration. Whereas he believed his own duty as a manufacturer and retailer was 'to revive a sense of beauty in home life, to restore the dignity of art to ordinary household decoration', he realised that the high prices charged by Morris & Co. meant his work was not available to all. In 1879, through his membership of the Kyrle Society ('formed to supply charity in the form of artistic adornment for those who cannot possibly afford to indulge themselves in such taste, and perhaps partly in the hope of forming artistic taste and sympathy where it did not already exist'), he contributed designs for the decoration by volunteers of two wards in Westminster Hospital, London. These comprised ceiling and wall friezes of fruit and flowers and, in one room, the Bouverie Ward, a tiled fireplace. *The Builder* magazine approved the use of bright colours in this usually colourless environment, but criticised the stylised patterns in one ward, believing that naturalistic ornament was more appropriate 'in rooms used by poor and uneducated people'.

Fig. 63 The model sitting room of a 'Workman's Small House' devised by Morris and shown at the newly opened Art Gallery, in Queen's Park, Manchester, 1884.

Morris's second attempt to provide inexpensive ideas for furnishings came with the design of 'a model workman's small house' displayed in the newly opened Art Gallery in Queen's Park, Manchester, in 1884. This was commission by Thomas Coglan Horsfall, a Manchester philanthropist for whom Morris had visited Manchester in February 1879 to speak on 'Working Folk and the Future of Art', a lecture in which he expounded his now famous advice '…do not have anything in your house that you do not know to be useful or believe to be beautiful'. At first Morris was very unhappy about Horsfall's proposals for displays in the newly opened museum, believing that 'what furniture a workman can buy should be exactly the same (if his room be large enough) as a lord buys'. However, he was persuaded and the rooms he designed included chairs from the Sussex range, a Madox Brown designed wash-stand (cat. no. J.8) and numerous wallpapers and chintzes. Altruism was not Morris's only reason for becoming involved with the scheme. He had been keen to establish a footing in markets outside London for some years and this provided a means of advertising the work of the firm through its northern agents and newly opened premises at 34 John Dalton Street, Manchester.

The 1880s saw Morris & Co. complete a number of extensive London commissions, the most important of which was a return to St James's Palace for the decoration of the Throne Room, Blue Room and reception staircases (fig. 88). S. & S. Dunn's charges of £1,110 indicate extensive work, all of which was closely monitored by the parsimonious Office of Works. As well as new ceiling, cove and cornice decorations Morris specially designed a new wallpaper, two silk damasks and embroidered pelmets for the rooms (cat. nos. I.10–16, L.18–19, M.26). It is possible that Morris's first designs for the rooms were far less conventional than appears from photographs of the finished work. All of the original estimates were cut, and the firm expressed distress that a curtailing of detail would result in a loss of originality. They need not have worried about the effect on the public, however, as this second royal appointment finally established Morris & Co. as one of the most fashionable firms of London decorators, and, as their appeal widened, their bohemian reputation diminished.

The grandest private commission of the period came from Aleco Ionides for the decoration and partial furnishing of 1 Holland Park. The firm was employed between March 1880 and October 1888 (figs. 21, 87), and documentation concerning the work which has survived the house, in the form of Morris & Co.'s invoices and bills (cat. no. I.17) and photographs (cat. no. I.18), provides a unique source of information on the firm's products and costings over this long period. Morris closely supervised the work which, as well as a wealth of decorative painting and furnishings, included two

Hammersmith carpets (cat.nos. M.108–9), *The Forest* tapestry (cat.no. M.120) and Burne-Jones's extraordinarily ornate piano (cat.no. J.31). The rooms were extravagantly decorated with ostentatious use of heavy silk furnishings on walls, windows, across doors and for furniture upholstery. This suggests the client's choice rather than Morris's, but each detail of the work complied with Morris's own views on the rights and wrongs of house decoration.

Comparing the work at St James's Palace and Holland Park with the model room at Manchester and Morris's own homes, one is immediately struck by how versatile Morris could be within the boundaries of his own strongly held views, the details of which were explained by George Wardle in the introduction to the Morris exhibit at the 1883 Boston Fair. Morris worked hard to destroy the fashionable mid-nineteenth-century habit of splitting walls into layers with skirting, dado, chair-rail, filling, cornice and ceiling all receiving different treatment. Instead, he advocated a much simpler and harmonious effect with skirtings ignored, dado and filling treated as one and cornice and ceiling united, the look adopted generally from the end of the nineteenth century. Decoration of the walls should be simple, either painted with plain colours or covered with wallpapers, draped printed cotton or stretched woven damasks for a more decorative effect. The choice of pattern should depend on the character of the room or the colour of woodwork and furniture rather than the popularity of the design. More specific recommendations include the use of metallic papers with walnut or dark-stained ash and textile wallcovering for well-designed (this tended to mean plain) and finished timber.

The environmental setting of houses also played a major role in Morris's attitude towards interior decoration. Whereas it is known that Kelmscott Manor, the country home he visited for rest and recreation, had little done to it in the form of repair or decoration during his occupancy, his London home, Kelmscott House, was decorated and furnished to suit the family's metropolitan lifestyle. Country living, in which gardens and the countryside played an important part, involved quite different requirements from the town and Morris's decorations reflect his own experience. The firm was employed to decorate a number of country houses and Morris developed a much plainer style for such masterpieces as Clouds, a house outside Salisbury built by Philip Webb between 1881 and 1885, which became famous for fashionable weekend house parties of 'The Souls', a group of aristocratic politicians led by the owners, the Hon. Percy and Madeline Wyndham. The difference between Morris's town and country styles is further emphasised by comparing the decoration of Wickham Flowers' two homes, Old Swan House, Chelsea Embankment, and Great Tangley Manor, near Guildford in Surrey, a sixteenth-century country house extended by Philip Webb from 1884. The London house, which featured existing extensive architectural detailing, was decorated with an abundance of specially designed ceiling and wall decoration, furniture and carpets, the overall effect of which was luxurious yet conventionally fashionable. In contrast, the Flowers' country home, though elegant, was decorated very simply, to provide an aura of relaxation and easy living with light coloured woods, plain colours and mass-produced, practical Morris furniture, printed cottons and machine-woven carpeting. Described by Herman Muthesius in his influential work *Das Englische Haus* (Berlin, 1904) as 'simply a house in which one wants to live…it is without pomp or decoration, and has the natural decency which…is so rare in our present culture', this scheme anticipated a style of light, open, airy interiors exemplified in the work of a number of British, European and American architects working at the beginning of the twentieth century.

Morris & Co.'s decoration of Bullerswood, a house in Chislehurst, Kent, built by Ernest Newton for the Sanderson family, combined both of Morris's town and country styles. The ground-floor rooms had plain white walls with pattern-work on cornices and ceilings (fig. 97). The bedrooms were equally unfussy, with plain or wallpapered walls and white paintwork. The commission is likely to have been the last Morris took an active part in, and it exemplifies his most sophisticated style of decoration. Similar detailing was adopted in a number of later projects by the firm, including Compton Hall in Wolverhampton, and Standen near East Grinstead in Sussex. In these there is a suggestion of Georgian revivalism, first seen in the spaciousness of furniture arrangement and ceiling plaster patterns at Bullerswood, a style that was to be exploited a great deal in the firm's later work.

Fig.64 A photograph of the drawing room at Old Swan House, Chelsea Embankment, taken by Bedford Lemere in 1884.

Fig.65 A bedroom at Great Tangley Manor near Guildford in Surrey.

Stanmore Hall in Middlesex was the most extensive decoration scheme that Morris & Co. completed and it was also the last commission before Morris's death. The baronial proportions of the house were only eclipsed by the extravagance of the internal decorations. Although Morris visited the wealthy owner of the house, William Knox D'Arcy, at Christmas 1887 to discuss the forthcoming work, it is unlikely that he took any further part in the general decoration, his time being spent on the preparation of a spectacular series of tapestries based on the legend of the Holy Grail

Fig.66 One of the drawing rooms at
Stanmore Hall, Middlesex.

for the dining room (cat.no. M.130). All of Morris's rules concerning the application of decoration on walls, ceiling and floors so succinctly delineated in the Boston Fair catalogue were followed in the house, yet the effect is unoriginal and typically Victorian. Much of this is due to the intervention of Morris's assistant, Henry Dearle, whose new designs for the house – mosaic floors, wallpaintings, woven silks and carpets – compete in scale and style with the overpowering Gothicised architecture of the mid-nineteenth-century building. Through inexperience Dearle included everything he found admirable in Morris's work, neither selecting nor truly understanding the basic principles on which such ideas were based.

This mattered little to the prosperity and popularity of Morris & Co.'s work after Morris's death in 1896. Interior design continued to be an important side of business, shown by the firm's change of name to Morris & Company Decorators Ltd in 1905. Yet the style adopted in most interiors continued to diversify away from Morris styles into reproduction design in an attempt to maintain a place in the fashionable London market. Instead it was left to followers outside Britain – in America, Canada and across Europe and Scandinavia – to develop Morris's ideas within a modern, forward-looking world.

I.1

I.2

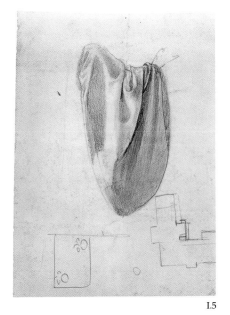

I.3

I.5

I.2 Study for *How Sir Galahad, Sir Bors and Sir Percival received the Sanc Grael: but Sir Percival's Sister died by the Way*

Dante Gabriel Rossetti, 1857
Pen and brown ink, 24.9 x 35.1 cm
Inscribed with the names of the figures
British Museum (1885-6-13-81)

A study for the second of Rossetti's proposed contributions for the mural painting of the Old Debating Hall of the Oxford Union. This was never executed.

In 1864 Rossetti painted a watercolour of the same subject and a very similar composition. This is now in the British Museum (PD 1910-12-10-3).   RW

I.3 *Topsy and Ned Jones Settled on the Settle in Red Lion Square*

Max Beerbohm, *c*.1922
Watercolour, 31.1 x 38.7 cm
Tate Gallery, London (AO1049)

A fanciful composition drawn by Beerbohm for his volume of caricatures *Rossetti and His Circle*, first published in 1922. The artist based his drawing on J. W. Mackail's description of the sparse furnishings of Morris and Burne-Jones's lodgings at 17 Red Lion Square. Beerbohm has concentrated on the large painted settle made at the time (and subsequently moved to Red House) and although this is quite unlike the actual piece, his imaginary furniture has an uncanny similarity to existing panels painted with female figures about the same time and possibly intended for furniture (cat.no.J.6).

Beerbohm had little regard for Morris or his work, which he felt was overrated. In a letter to Holbrook Jackson of 1913 he wrote 'He is splendid, certainly, by reason of the bulk and variety of his work, but when it comes to the quality...I leave a wide margin...for my necessary injustice' (see N.J.Hall's introduction to a new edition of *Rossetti and His Circle*, 1897).

Exhib. 1931 (334)

I.1 Study for the Angel in
Sir Lancelot's Dream of the Sanc Grael

Dante Gabriel Rossetti, 1857
Pencil, pen and ink, 22.7 x 13.6 cm
Signed bottom left with monogram
Fitzwilliam Museum, Cambridge (2150)
Bequeathed by Charles Shannon

Having missed a commission for a mural in the Museum being built in Oxford to Benjamin Woodward's design, Rossetti was determined not to miss the second chance offered by the Union Debating Hall, also designed by Woodward, whom he had been cultivating a friendship with since 1854. At the end of June 1857 he had made designs for a scheme of murals on themes from the *Morte d'Arthur* for its ten fourteen-foot wall-bays, and went with Morris to meet the Building Committee who consented that it should be carried out by Rossetti and friends, for no fees but their costs of material and maintenance. Seven friends were involved in the scheme: Rossetti, Morris, Burne-Jones, Arthur Hughes, John Hungerford Pollen, Roddam Spencer Stanhope and Val Prinsep.

This is one of several studies that Rossetti made of Lizzie Siddal for the first of his own proposed two bays and the only one finished. This shows the *Dream of Sir Lancelot*, in which Guenevere leans from the apple tree to tempt him, barring his hope of a vision of the Grail. This drawing shows the angel of the Grail. A cut out circle shows the position of one of the two windows in this bay.   RW

I.4 Five architectural drawings for Red House, Bexleyheath, Kent

Philip Webb, 1859
Pencil, pen and ink and watercolour
Inscribed with title, dimensions, specifications, contract details and each signed 'Philip Webb Archt
7 Gt Ormond St. London' and dated
Given by Lady Burne-Jones

a Ground- and first-floor plans
53.3 x 66.0 cm
V&A (E.59-1916)
NOT ILLUSTRATED

b North and south elevations and details
52.1 × 63.5 cm
V&A (E.60-1916)

c East and west elevations
52.9 × 63.5 cm
V&A (E.61-1916)
NOT ILLUSTRATED

d Entrance gates. On the reverse plans, elevations and sections of the stables
52.1 × 65.4 cm
V&A (E.63-1916)
NOT ILLUSTRATED

e Details of the roof over the well
53.0 × 65.8 cm
V&A (E.64-1916)

These drawings form part of the contract with the builder for the construction of Red House. They are signed by the contractor, William Kent. Unusually, Webb acted as witness. Again unusually for contract drawings they contain many alterations in pencil, suggesting Webb's desire to ensure the best possible house for his friend and perhaps something of his relationship with a demanding client. Although apparently simple in style, plan and construction, Webb specified every detail as the drawings for the gates and well-head show. The plan shows how the house radiates from the staircase and also that the kitchen faces west. This means that it receives full sun while dinner is being prepared. It was defects such as this that prompted Webb, years later, to reflect that houses should only be designed by architects who were over forty years of age.

Exhib. 1934, 2 drawings (345), Well House (346)
SA

I.5 Drapery sketch overdrawn with details of Red House

William Morris, *c.*1856–9
Pencil and ink, 31.5 × 22.6 cm
Sanford and Helen Berger Collection

In July 1856 Morris wrote 'Rossetti says I ought to paint, he says I shall be able…I must try'. A large number of sketches by Morris still exist and probably date from this time, showing his eagerness to improve his draughtsmanship. This sketch, one of a number that concentrate on the drapery of cloth, has been used as a piece of scrap paper, indicating that a number of these must have littered Morris's home and studio at this time.

In the lower right-hand corner of the drawing is a rough sketch of the south wing of Red House. This shows the outline as designed by Philip Webb and shown in his architectural plan dated 16 May 1859 (cat. no. I.4). To the side of this, and on the reverse of the paper, there are a number of repeating patterns arranged on rectangular grids. These may well be trials or suggestions for the very characteristic ceiling designs used in the house.

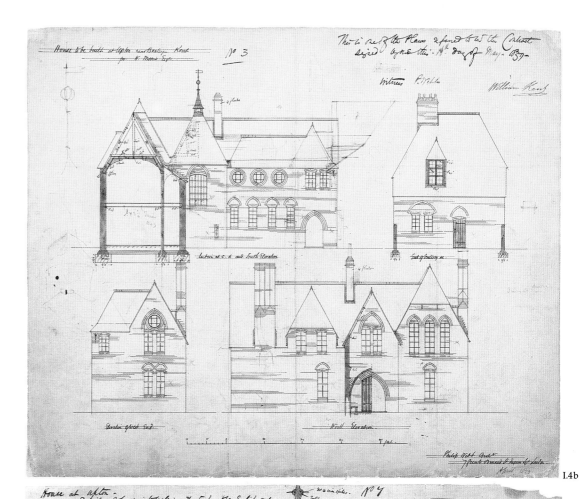

I.4b

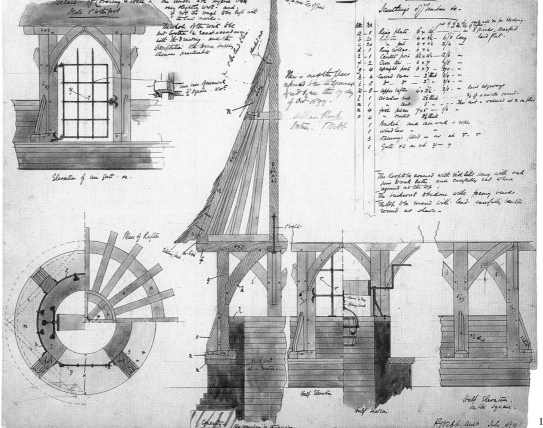

I.4e

I.6 Design for the decoration of the wall and cornice of the Green Dining Room, South Kensington Museum, London

Philip Webb, 1866
Pencil, pen and ink, watercolour, body colour and gold pigment, 47.5 x 28.0 cm
Inscribed in ink: 'The blue panelling comes up to this line'
V&A (E.5096-1960)
Given by H.B. Johnson

This highly finished drawing was presumably intended to be shown to the client, either the Government Department or the South Kensington Museum authorities. It shows a section of the decorations as executed except for changes to the colour scheme. These include the egg and dart cornice, shown here as red but gilded, and the background to the dog which was made much darker in tone. The panels showing the running hound, which alternates with trees and running hares, was derived from the decorations on the font in Newcastle Cathedral. Below the frieze the wall is covered with moulded plaster panels. Olive branches are depicted in low relief. The effect of distributing the pattern evenly over the whole wall is similar to the effect of some of Morris's earlier wallpapers.   SA

I.6

I.7a

I.7b

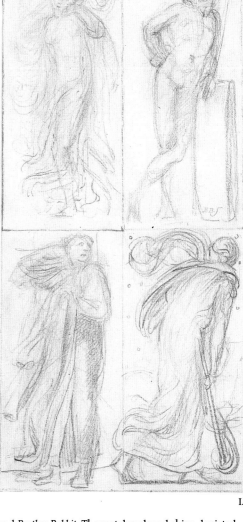

I.8

I.7 Two designs for the decoration of the ceiling, the Green Dining Room, South Kensington Museum, London

Philip Webb and William Morris, 1866 or 1867 for Morris, Marshall, Faulkner & Co., 1867
a Pencil, charcoal and watercolour on a sheet collaged from two pieces of paper, 131.0 x 101.5 cm
V&A (E.1169-1940)
b Pencil, charcoal and watercolour on a sheet collaged from four pieces of paper, 139.8 x 102.5 cm
Inscribed in pencil with some dimensions
V&A (E.1170-1940)

These two designs show the ceiling to be a collaboration between Morris and Webb. The looser, more organic, and largely ignored charcoal under-drawing (I.7a) is by Morris. This contrasts with the more carefully drawn and painted arabesques by Webb (I.7b) which are more akin to the decorative styles being executed in the rest of the growing museum. Both designs mix stylised foliage with a geometric structure and more organic motifs. The designs show some difficulties in setting out to full scale, especially Morris's, which has two attempts at diagonals. Both are splashed with a pigment-rich paint, suggesting that they were used when the actual ceiling was being painted using water-based paints on lining paper.

Purchased from the Receiver of Morris & Co. SA

I.8 Eight designs for painted panels for the Green Dining Room, South Kensington Museum, London

Edward Burne-Jones, 1866 or 1867
Pencil and chalk, various sizes
Some inscribed in ink in Charles Fairfax Murray's hand: 'EBJ'
V&A (E.2897 to 2904-1927).
Bequeathed by J.R. Holliday
(E.2899-1927 ILLUSTRATED)

These are preliminary designs for the painted panels to be set into the upper part of the panelling that covered the lower part of the walls in the Green Dining Room. The figures represent the twelve months of the year or their zodiacal symbols. They were interspersed with other panels representing fruits, flowers and foliage. Although designed by Burne-Jones the panels were executed in oil paint by several different painters from the company. Morris felt the result insufficiently uniform in style to give a harmonious decorative scheme, and remedied this by having them repainted by Charles Fairfax Murray, who had been Rossetti's assistant and acted as a copyist for Ruskin. He also worked for the firm scrupulously transferring cartoons to stained glass and drawings to wood blocks. SA

I.9 Two interior photographs of Kelmscott House

Probably by Emery Walker, 1896
Gelatin-silver prints
Given by Wilfrid Blunt
a The Dining Room
29.5 x 24.2 cm
V&A (Ph.1-1973)
SEE FIG 61, PAGE 142
b The Drawing Room
23.3 x 29.0 cm
V&A (Ph.2-1973)
SEE FIG 73, PAGE 159

Photographs of the dining room and the drawing room at Kelmscott House, Hammersmith, probably taken by Emery Walker soon after Morris's death.

The dining room photograph shows the massive seventeenth-century Persian carpet which was sold to the Museum in 1897 for £200. The wallpaper is *Pimpernel*, and other Morris & Co. products include a Sussex chair and daybed designed by Philip Webb, an embroidered cover and loose cotton chair covers of *Rose and Thistle*

and *Brother Rabbit*. The metalwork and china depicted show Morris's eclectic taste, with blue and white and traditional pottery, Grès de Flandres ware, and oriental metalwork, including two Persian peacocks later described by May Morris as looking 'like guardians of a secret treasure'.

The second photograph is taken from one end of the drawing room showing the fireplace with the Red House settle (cat. no. J.9) to one side. The Prioress's Tale Wardrobe, and Webb's candlesticks (cat. no. K.27) were other Red House furnishings used in this room with more modern Morris items such as adjustable chairs and *Bird* woollen curtains.

I.10 Sketch elevation of the window wall, the Throne Room, St James's Palace, London

William Morris, 1881
Pencil and pen and ink, 25.5 x 55.6 cm
Inscribed in pencil: 'Throne room Buckram.'
Inscribed in ink with notes, dimensions and calculations, and on the back in ink: 'Mr Wardle St James Palace Buckram.'
V&A (E.53-1940)
Bequeathed by May Morris
NOT ILLUSTRATED

The drawing shows details of the windows and pier glass in the Throne Room with measurements for the shaped buckram valances which were part of the decoration of the room (cat.no.M.26). It is inscribed:'I see nothing for it but making each repeat of the pattern of the exact length required. The lengths or widths of the pattern are marked above, the adjustment must be made when the point of the leaves intersect. Make the leaves in the smallest spaces a little smaller. In ink, but crossed out: 'These are the most accurate measurements I can make from the buckram'.

This sketch shows the difficulties of actually executing a commission. Above is a valance. There are several attempts at measuring and calculating for the valance which was decorated with fleur-de-lis and pomegranate motifs. Notes show how problematic matching the pattern was and, by implication, how important it was to ensure a perfect result. A note suggests making the buckram one inch longer on an overall width of 44 ft. 9 in. This drawing represents the real and obviously difficult business of translating an idea into reality. George Wardle would have been responsible for producing working drawings of the pelmets for the firm's embroiderers and this accounts for the note on the reverse.

On 13 March 1882 the firm estimated that the curtains for the Throne Room would cost £750 with £360 for the valances. The parsimonious Office of Works asked for a less costly proposal and a revised estimate of £530 for the curtains offered woollen linings instead of satin with a reduction of silk lace trimming. Initially the firm was unhappy to reduce the cost of the valances as this could only affect the embroidery, but eventually they agreed to a revised scheme costing £200.

By 1947 the curtains and valances had been transferred to Queen Anne's Bedroom (Mitchell, 1947), but the scheme remained intact in the Ante Room although it no longer now exists in this form.   SA/LP

I.11 Elevation sketch of windows in the Blue Room at St James's Palace

Probably Philip Webb for Morris & Co., 1881
Pencil, pen and ink on Morris & Co. notepaper, 12.6 x 19.4 cm
Inscribed: 'Blue Room', with measurements
V&A (E.54-1940)
Bequeathed by May Morris

This drawing shows measurements for a shaped window valance divided into three sections. The disposition of the pomegranates and fleur-de-lis design motifs is marked and is the same as that designed for the Throne Room (cat.no.I.10) and the existing sample (cat.no.M.26).

On 13 March 1882 the Blue Room curtains were estimated at £375, with £180 for the valance but, like the furnishings for the Throne Room were reduced on request.

The curtains still remained intact in the room in 1947. Recent redecoration at the palace uses modern reproduction weavings of the *St James* silk damask.

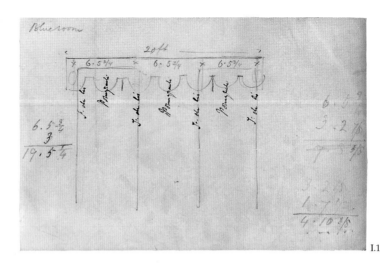

I.11

I.12 Design for painted decoration, Blue Room, St James's Palace, London

William Morris, 1881
Pencil, pen and ink and watercolour, 66.6 x 100.3 cm
Inscribed in watercolour: 'ST. JAMES'S PALACE BLUE ROOM COVE OF CORNICE', and 'Scale 3" = 1'.'
On the back in Charles Fairfax Murray's hand in ink 'Original design by William Morris'
V&A (E.289-1939)
Bequeathed by May Morris

This design is for decoration to be painted on to the plaster cove of the cornice and shows the richness of effect that Morris was to achieve. Having drawn the cove to scale Morris then drew in soft pencil the scrolling, swirling pattern of vegetal decoration. Over this is the final design of acanthus, branches and leaves which in form and density bears a strong relationship to his wallpaper designs from that time. Only a small part of the decoration is shown, the painter presumably being left to extrapolate the pattern to the length of the room.

The Blue Room or Council Room was painted in yellow as was the adjoining Queen Anne's Room (aptly called the Yellow Room). Walls of the Blue Room were covered with *St James* silk damask in dark red with matching curtains and embroidered valances (cat.no.M.26)   SA/LP

I.13 Three drawings for ceiling decoration in the Ambassadors' Entrance and Ambassadors' Room, St James's Palace

William Morris or Philip Webb for Morris & Co., 1880–81
Pencil and watercolour,
68 x 73.2 cm, 66.9 x 67.1 cm, **a** 60.5 x 61.5 cm
Various inscriptions
William Morris Society, Kelmscott House, London
(D14, D15, D21) (D 15 illus)

Morris & Co.'s estimate for the painting and redecoration of the entrances to St James's Palace is dated 20 August 1880. This included £657 for the Ambassador's Entrance. A new fireplace 'in the recess of oak with panelling all round and seats on either side' was suggested, with a painted ceiling similar in style to that on the Grand Staircase and the Queen's Staircase.

The entire scheme was approved by Queen Victoria, and on 2 November Morris & Co. were instructed to

proceed with the scheme as submitted.

Two drawings (Morris Society, D14 and D15) are a monochrome and a full-colour design (shown) for the cornice of the ceiling. The third design (D21) is for the cornice of the Ambassadors' Room.

I.14 Design for painted decoration for the Queen's Staircase, St James's Palace

William Morris or Philip Webb for Morris & Co., 1880–81
Pencil and watercolour, 47.1 x 49.2 cm
With various inscriptions
William Morris Society, Kelmscott House, London (D18)

The decoration of the Queen's Staircase, which is at the Garden Entrance of St James's Palace, was similar to that of the Grand Staircase and Ambassador's Entrance (cat. no. I.13) with gilded ceilings. It was part of Morris & Co.'s estimate of 20 August 1880 for £4,779 for the redecoration of all entrances at the Palace, which was finally approved in November of the same year. Morris's diary notes that he went to the Palace on 21 March 1881 '…to get our work passed'.

This drawing is inscribed 'the yellow for soffit of stairs same colouring as Carbrook…' refers to an earlier Morris & Co. decorative commission (see cat.no.M.109).

I.15 Design for painted decoration for a clock case for St James's Palace

William Morris for Morris & Co., 1881
Pencil and watercolour, 43.9 x 68 cm
Inscribed
William Morris Society, Kelmscott House, London (D9)

Presumably, from the wording of the inscription, this is the drawing Morris was working on 10 January 1881, 'sketched ornament for clock-case' (Morris's diary, BL Add. MS 45,407). Two days later he notes a visit to the Palace '…to St James…clockcase'. The decoration is very similar to another design for the same project, illustrated in Day, 1899, described as 'Painted Decoration of soffits of arches on staircases in St James's Palace'.

I.12

I.13a

I.14

I.15

I.16

I.16 Design for the drawing room ceiling of 1 Holland Park

William Morris or Philip Webb for Morris & Co., *c*.1880
Pencil and watercolour, 53.0 x 50.8 cm
William Morris Society, Kelmscott House, London (D29)

The commission from A. A. Ionides for Morris & Co. to redecorate 1 Holland Park, a house he acquired from his father, Alexander Constantine Ionides, in 1875, lasted from 1881 to 1888. Discussions with the firm began in 1879. Major work in the drawing room and Antiquities Room was estimated by Morris & Co. on 2 May 1883, and included 'Drawing Room – The decoration of the ceiling might cost about £160. 0. 0d'. Following the completion of the rooms a bill for £1330 8s. 9d. was sent on 26 May 1884.

The completed drawing room was colourful and highly decorative; as well as the painted repeating ceiling design, *Flower Garden* woven fabric was used stretched on the walls and also for curtains with embroidered valances. The specially designed *Holland Park* carpet (cat. no. M.108) and piano (cat. no. J.31) also provided part of the furniture for the room.

I.17

I.18

I.17 Estimates and bills for the decoration and furnishing of 1 Holland Park, London

Morris & Co., 1880–88
Hand-written on headed notepaper; estimate: 25.0 x 42.0 cm; bill: 32.3 x 22 cm
V&A (NAL MS. L.885-1954)
Given by Miss Aglaia Ionides

Part of a set of estimates and bills for the redecoration and partial furnishing of 1 Holland Park, the home of A.A. Ionides (1840–98). The collection of documentation covers work completed in three stages; in 1880, 1884 and 1888, and includes two estimates and three bills. The firm's first bill (illus.) is dated March 1880. The last, 23 October 1888, followed Morris's announcement that he must '...make a call on our decoration at Holland Park' in a letter of 14 September the same year (Kelvin, 1537).

The estimates and bills (which total £2360 2s. 10d.) are not compatible so must reflect changes, nor do they include a number of items known to have been bought for the house. (see Harvey and Press, 1994).

The estimate dated 2 May 1883 includes extensive work on the Antiquities Room (fig.89) and the drawing room including new woodwork, fireplace and window screen, ceiling painting and various items of furnishing, including two Hammersmith carpets (cat.nos.M.108, 109).

The following bill of 26 May 1884 (for £1330 8s. 9d.) includes much of the estimated work, plus additional decoration and furnishing for the billiard and breakfast rooms.

I.18 Album of photographs of 1 Holland Park, London

Bedford Lemere, 1890s
Albumen prints set into boxed and bound album,
Album 31.8 x 40.6 cm closed;
photographs 21.7 x 27.5 cm
Private Collection
SEE ALSO FIGS 20, 21, PAGE 54, FIG 87, PAGE 201, AND FIG 89, PAGE 205

Nineteen photographs showing exterior and interior views of 1 Holland Park, the home of A.A.(Aleco) Ionides. These show the Morris & Co. furnishings completed in 1888.

This presentation album, is inscribed 'Bedford Lemere & Co: 147 Strand: London WC: Architectural Photographers to Her Majesty The Queen'.

Interior views of the house appeared in a number of magazine articles including *The Art Journal* ('A Kensington Interior', May 1893) for which the Bedford Lemere photographs were used, *Architectural Review* ('On Mr Philip Webb's Town Work', 1897) and *The Studio* ('An Epoch-Making House', 1898).

Harry Bedford Lemere joined his father's photographic business in 1881 working there until his death in 1944. The firm specialised exclusively in architectural photography, producing many thousands of negatives showing the most luxurious and artistic houses, castles and palaces of the period. Many of these were destroyed in the early twentieth century, according to correspondence in the 1950s between the Victoria and Albert Museum and the firm, which was then based in Croydon. Extant negatives and prints (now owned by the Royal Commission on Historic Monuments) provide an invaluable source of information on British interior decoration in the last quarter of the nineteenth century.

FURNITURE

Frances Collard

Fig. 67 The young Ned Jones among the debris and new furniture at Red Lion Square.

Morris summarised his theories on the design and construction of furniture in a lecture, 'The Lesser Arts of Life', in 1878. These principles epitomised the furniture associated with Morris and produced by his firm. He advocated 'good citizen's furniture, solid and well made in workmanship, and in design [it] should have nothing about it that is not easily defensible, no monstrosities or extravagances'. Whilst he recognised the practical necessity for certain pieces, such as chairs, to be moveable, he preferred furniture 'made of timber rather than walking-sticks'.

For Morris furniture was divided into two categories, 'necessary work-a-day furniture' and 'state-furniture', the latter being elegant and elaborate with carving, inlaying and painting, all of which were 'blossoms of the art of furniture'. These grander pieces, which should be readily available, were recommended for the more prominent positions in important rooms. Furniture for everyday use was to be well made and well proportioned but simple and even crude in execution.

His brief apprenticeship in G. E. Street's office had stimulated him in various ways, including his learning to carve in wood. Meeting Webb was the opportunity to share ideas about architecture, both ecclesiastical and domestic, and design with a friend who had professional skills as a designer. Although Philip Webb became chiefly responsible for the firm's furniture, he clearly always valued Morris's artistic judgement, even asking him in 1891 to look at a design before sending it to the carver.

In 1856 Morris, stimulated by compatible companions, and by his studies of medieval architecture and literature, designed his first furniture for the rooms in Red Lion Square. These pieces were enthusiastically described by Burne-Jones and quoted in the *Memorials*, 'Topsy has had some furniture (chairs and table) made after his own design; they are as beautiful as mediaeval work, and when we have painted designs of knights and ladies upon them they will be perfect marvels'.

The furniture was probably made by Henry Price, a local cabinet maker employed by Tommy Baker of Christopher Street, Hatton Garden. Price's diary, published by Pat Kirkham, records that he was asked to make some 'old-fashioned Furniture in the Mideavel Style', including a 'large Cabinet about 7 ft high and as long, a seat forming a bunk, with arms each end Carv to represent Fishes. Three Cupboards the Doors with fantastic ironwork hinges, representing Birds, fishes and Flowers Bolted on, and giltcoloured. The hinges cost 14 pounds'.

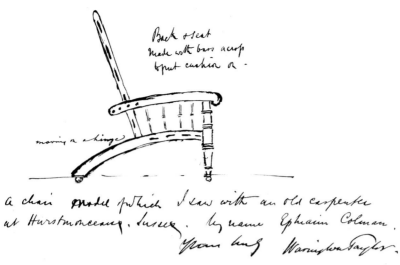

Back & seat made with bars across & put cushion on –

moving a hinge

a chair model of which I saw with an old carpenter at Hurstmonceaux, Sussex, by name Ephraim Coleman. Yours truly Warington Taylor.

Price's ambiguous remark that 'He spent a lot of his Leisure in carving the arms and panels' may refer to Morris himself working on the settle with the tools he kept in the folds of a white evening tie nailed to the wall at Red Lion Square. However, Morris's enthusiasm was not matched by practical skills and when the settle was delivered it had clearly been made too large for the available space. Max Beerbohm's cartoon, *Topsy and Ned Jones settled on the settle in Red Lion Square* (cat.no.I.3), is probably based on Burne-Jones's description of this large piece rather than a record of another settle made for the relatively small rooms in Red Lion Square.

Other pieces of furniture mentioned by Price included 'tables and High backed chairs like what I have seen in Abyes and Cathedrals. A large Oak Table on tressels with a Iron Stretcher twisted and partly burnished'. Whilst the chairs were probably those described by Burne-Jones, the table does not match the description of one thought to be from Red Lion Square (cat.no.J.3), which suggests that Morris may have designed a second table. Another chair is described in the *Memorials* as a 'large one with a box overhead in which Gabriel suggested owls might be kept with advantage'. Reminiscent of a large canopied chair shown in Rossetti's *The Tune of Seven Towers* (cat.no.A.5) of 1857, such designs were probaby inspired by illuminated manuscripts of the fourteenth and fifteenth centuries.

The small painted chair (cat.no.J.4) may also have been part of Morris's early furniture, made in this spirit of enthusiasm for the Middle Ages. Certainly the overall impression of the painted furniture at Red Lion Square was sufficiently gorgeous for G.P.Boyce to comment on it, in his diary for 4 May 1858, when attending a meeting of the Hogarth Club there in 1860. Another painted piece, the Prioress's Wardrobe (Ashmolean Museum, Oxford; fig. 70), was hurriedly finished for exhibition at the Club in 1858, when Burne-Jones wrote to Cormell Price, 'Is Topsy in Oxford? love to him and everyone – tell him not to come up yet till I've done more to the wardrobe'.

Described by Janey Morris as a wedding present from Burne-Jones and placed in her bedroom at Red House and subsequently in the Kelmscott House drawing room, the wardrobe's exterior depicts episodes from Chaucer's 'Prioress's Tale', with Janey as the Virgin Mary. On the interior Morris's unfinished scheme (on the theme of a dressing room) includes figures against decorative backgrounds, very similar to those on the four painted panels (cat.no.J.6). This intriguing discovery suggests that Morris might have painted the panels as part of a larger scheme, possibly a piece of furniture.

This burgeoning of interest in painted furniture in the late 1850s was not peculiar to Morris and his circle but clearly reflected interest among contemporary artists, architects and designers. The influence of William Burges and his furniture, particularly the iconographic and carefully structured cabinets shown in the 1859 Architectural Exhibition and at the International Exhibition of 1862, must be acknowledged. Burges's use of a medieval technique for painting furniture, taken from the twelfth-century manuscript of a monk, Theophilus, was to be copied by Morris on furniture exhibited in 1862.

His early experience in designing and overseeing the making of furniture proved helpful for Morris when planning the furnishing of Red House, designed by Philip Webb. Webb made various changes to the settle from Red Lion Square when it was installed in the drawing room, including the addition of a minstrel's gallery. Rossetti's painted doors of 1859–60 were removed when the Morris family left Red House in 1865 and the settle now has plain doors. The house also contains another large piece, a cupboard or press designed by Webb, in the hall which combines drawers and cupboards with a seat. This retains remnants of its original painted decoration which has been attributed to Morris. The same dark red was used on the interiors of this settle and of the minstrel's gallery, and on the dresser in the dining room, a piece that illustrates Webb's early mastery of Gothic details in its relatively simple design.

Early examples of Webb's work also included two oak trestle tables designed in 1859, one for the dining room and the other for the hall, which could be put together for parties. He described them in a letter to Sydney Cockerell of 28 May 1898, 'Both tables were bound round the edge with scoured iron fixed with clout-headed nails, to keep the impatient from whittling away the edge if victuals lingered on the road'. The smaller table was given to Wilfrid Blunt by Janey Morris in 1897. Both tables were probably made at the Euston Road Boy's Club with the dining table designed by Webb for Edward and Georgiana Burne-Jones in 1860. The design, with chamfered edges to the legs and small Gothic arches at the bottom, was to become part of the firm's range (fig.72).

Another example of Webb's early crude furniture from Red House is Janey's oak work table, and also at Kelmscott Manor is her jewel casket, made in the form of a Gothic reliquary and decorated by Rossetti and Elizabeth Siddal with painted panels of figures in fifteenth-century dress. Red House was furnished with plain black or red chairs with rush seats, possibly early examples of the Sussex range and probably also made at the Boy's Club, as similar chairs were made there in 1860 for the Burne-Jones family.

Painted chairs, presumably those from Red Lion Square, and other chairs of elegant design by Webb, which have not yet been identified, are also recorded at Red House by May Morris. It is likely

Fig.71 A photograph by William Downey of Rossetti, Ruskin and William Bell Scott in Rossetti's garden at Cheyne Row, 29 July 1863.

that most of the Red House furniture was made at the Boy's Club under the auspices of Colonel W.J. Gillum, introduced by Robert and Elizabeth Browning to Rossetti and an important early patron of the firm.

The essentially collaborative nature of the Red House furniture was to prove a valuable training for the establishment of the firm in 1861. Rossetti's comment, made in a letter to William Allingham in January 1861, that they did not intend to compete with the expensive products of Messrs. Crace but wished to 'give real good taste at the price as far as possible of ordinary furniture', gives a flavour of their idealistic wish to improve the standards of furniture design. The opportunity to display their work at the International Exhibition of 1862 was taken with speed and energy.

Exhibits included the St George Cabinet, King René's Honeymoon Cabinet, Rossetti's sofa, Webb's painted chest and black and gold chair (cat. nos. J.18, 13, 14, 19, 16), the Backgammon Players cabinet (fig. 69) as well as a black and gold lacquer bookcase, depicting scenes from English life 1810–60, a red lacquer music stand and two more chairs. Not all the exhibits can be definitely identified since the official catalogue did not give details and critical reviews in contemporary periodicals are not specific. Although the firm sold £150 worth of goods at the exhibition some exhibits (such as the St George Cabinet) did not sell, and Morris himself kept the black and gold chair. Rossetti's couch may have remained with the artist (see cat.no. J.14).

Fig.72 Trestle table designed by Philip Webb.

Fig.73 Photograph of the drawing room at Kelmscott House furnished with the Prioress's Tale Wardrobe, Webb's early settle and various other items, including Morris & Co. adjustable chairs (cat.no.I.9).

Also produced by the firm in 1861–2 and possibly shown in 1862 was an iron bedstead designed by Webb, but too heavy to carry according to Rossetti, which Webb subsequently gave to Sydney Cockerell. Other pieces listed in Webb's account book with the 1862 exhibits included a screen, two tables, a sideboard with painted and lacquered panels and more domestic pieces such as a wash stand, dressing table, and towel horse. Colonel Gillum ordered a hall table and Val Prinsep a wardrobe. The range of furniture was surprisingly varied, indicating the talent and imagination of Morris and his friends.

In his draft letter to accompany the firm's prospectus, Morris specifically mentioned 'the great beauty that can be produced by the ornamentation of cabinets with both gilded and lacquered patterns and figures combined with the use of stained glass and polished woods', and mentioned the firm's medal awarded for this class at 1862. He also suggested stamped leather panels, coloured and varnished, as suitable for screens, furniture, panelling and for use in ecclesiastical woodwork, as the firm had 'several patterns of great beauty for inspection and are ready to submit designs and prices for any amount' (cat.no.D.3). This is confirmed by various entries of the early 1860s in Webb's account book.

Such impressive statements were tempered by modest entries in the firm's minute book in 1863 (cat.no.D.1). Webb, Burne-Jones and Morris all provided designs for the decoration of stereoscopic boxes, while Webb supplied a carpenter's drawing of a four-poster bed and Morris discussed a potential commission for furniture with Rossetti. By May 1867 Webb's responsibility for furniture designs was formally acknowledged when he was appointed manager, although Morris retained overall control, commissioning Charles Fairfax Murray, for example, in 1875, to provide painted panels for a sideboard.

The structure and actual location of the furniture workshops is unclear, although premises in Great Ormond Yard were apparently used. A local cabinet maker, Mr Curwen, was responsible for some of the early furniture, but few details are known about the individual craftsmen. One cabinet maker employed by the firm was called Stennett, listed in Webb's address book at 23 Wilmot Street, Brunswick Square, who was working on furniture for Burne-Jones in 1865 and 1866. Warington Taylor issued a warning about his prices to Webb, mentioning an estimate for a sideboard, in 1867 or 1868 (NAL 86.SS.57).

Before joining the firm in 1865 Taylor recorded his impressions of their furniture in a series of letters to E.R.Robson in 1862–3. He mentions Seddon's desk and Rossetti's responsibility for its colouring as well as two other pieces. One, 'a jolly little round table at Morris' on six legs with trays

Fig. 75 Georgiana Burne-Jones's sitting room on the first floor of The Grange, North End Road, Fulham, showing Morris & Co. furniture.

underneath', may be an early example of Webb's circular table (cat. no. J.22). He enthusiastically described the other piece, 'Anything more beautiful than the turned pillars and mouldings in their new sideboard I have never seen' (Burne-Jones Papers, XXIII –11, 24). This could be Webb's sideboard (fig. 77), several examples of which survive, including one at Kelmscott Manor. Supplied by the firm for the dining room at The Hill, Witley, probably during their work at the house in 1864 and 1866, and praised by Robert Edis in *Decoration and Furniture of Town Houses* (1880), the design remained available until at least the early twentieth century.

Webb's modest yet subtle use of mouldings in this sideboard, inspired by seventeenth-century architectural woodwork and furniture, was echoed in other pieces produced by the firm in the early 1860s which also became part of the standard range. Both architectural and vernacular sources may have provided such details as the use of turned details, as in Webb's round table (cat. no. J.22) or on the music stand or whatnot (cat. no. J.23). Ebonised finishes, often combined with gilded decoration, as in Webb's 1862 chair or the cheval mirror (cat. no. J.21), were inspired by seventeenth-century furniture but also indicate an awareness of oriental art, the spatial quality of whose woodwork became increasingly influential among contemporary furniture designers, including Godwin and Christopher Dresser. An oak table, based on an oriental altar table, is strikingly abstract and pared down in form and may be one of the pieces commissioned from the firm by Colonel Gillum, which is now in the Musée d'Orsay, Paris.

This introduction of smaller and lighter furniture, in complete contrast to the earlier massive medieval painted pieces, was noticed by Taylor: 'Are not the Red Lion people in the right direction in this matter they get gradually lighter, and Rossetti keeps them up to the point' (Burne-Jones Papers, XXIII–7). Certainly Rossetti's documented enthusiasm for antique furniture may have influenced the development of such designs, but he was less involved with the direction of the firm than Morris and Webb.

Ford Madox Brown was influential, having decorated the bookcase shown at the exhibition, and designed various pieces, including the firm's Egyptian chair and a range of bedroom furniture. He is credited with introducing the Sussex chair with the round seat (cat. no. J.25). However, versions of a simple, rush-seated chair with turned uprights existed, particularltly in vernacular furniture. The appeal of the Sussex range was, as Taylor said, because it was 'essentially gentlemanly with a total absence of ex-tallow chandler vulgarity – it possesses poetry of simplicity' (Burne-Jones Papers, XXIII–13).

The introduction of alternative designs was an astute commercial move, as by this means the firm considerably widened their range of furniture and offered items at a lower price. The longevity and popularity of such designs, which became standard products of the firm and were to be copied by other firms, may be explained by Taylor, in another enthusiastic outburst, 'Red Lion Sq. furniture has no style, modern work must only be founded on nature, severity, and true construction. There must be no notion of precedent, fashion, century… The beauty of Red Lion woodwork I think is that you cannot say it has any style – it is original, it has its own style, it is in fact Victorian' (Burne-Jones Papers, XXIII–13).

Following his principles Morris furnished his own homes with such pieces, including chairs from the Sussex range, the adjustable armchair, Webb's sideboard, and the settle. Known to have been used at Kelmscott House was Webb's oak table (*c*.1870), with strong architectural mouldings (fig.72), which was also offered in the firm's catalogue. Two very interesting versions of a trestle table with ringed legs, probably attributable to Webb, survive at Kelmscott Manor, recorded in E.H. New's drawings of the Tapestry Room and of Morris's study at Kelmscott House.

Morris reduced his involvement in the furniture side of the business as part of the significant changes following the appointment of George Jack as Webb's assistant in 1880 and as his successor in 1890. Jack introduced new designs, clearly inspired by eighteenth-century styles rather than vernacular sources, and techniques, particularly marquetry, and preferred timbers such as walnut and mahogany. Typical of his sophisticated work was the mahogany sideboard with marquetry (fig.78), a version of which was shown at the Manchester 1887 Jubilee Exhibition, although he was also praised for his carving. Designs were also supplied by W.A.S. Benson who advised Burne-Jones over a grand piano and designed plain oak furniture for the Burne-Jones family home in Rottingdean.

It is clear when comparing surviving examples of furniture, contemporary photographs, the firm's catalogue and other information that pieces were made to order from designs kept in the

Fig.76 Watercolour by May Morris of the drawing room, Kelmscott House, early 1880s. Jane Morris is depicted at the piano.

Fig.77 Sideboard designed by Philip Webb in the 1860s.

Fig.78 Sideboard designed by George Jack and made by Morris & Co. in 1887.

shop, sometimes involving variations on the original (see *The Cabinet Maker*, no. 29, 1 Nov. 1882, p. 83). Later examples of Webb's designs included two cabinets with painted panels by William De Morgan made for Mrs Horatio Lucas (*c.*1870–80; William Morris Gallery and Cardiff Castle). Jack's dining table with herringbone inlay and stylised floral sprays, supplied with eight legs for 1 Holland Park in 1880 (Fitzwilliam Museum, Cambridge), was also made for Melsetter (Orkneys) with four legs, and in a six-legged version (William Morris Gallery).

Commercial success and the expansion of the firm in the 1880s included the opening of a shop in Manchester in 1883 with premises nearby for cabinet making and upholstery. Their display at the Manchester Fine Art and Industrial Exhibition of 1882 received critical praise in the *Cabinet Maker and Art Furnisher* and Jack's furniture was further praised at the Arts and Crafts Exhibition in 1889. Other developments included the acquisition of cabinet-making workshops in Pimlico, formerly owned by the fashionable firm of Holland & Sons, and the introduction of a system of stamping pieces with the firm's name and a batch number.

Involvement in furniture manufacture taught Morris that his principles of providing good design at a reasonable cost could not necessarily be sustained. In February 1881 he acknowledged this when asked for advice by Thomas Coglan Horsfall, Morris wrote

> The furniture for a workman's cottage? What can be done? If it be well made instead of ill made it will cost not twice as much, but twenty times as much: crede mihi experte.

> I have made rough furniture, oftenest of the type of what would have been found in a yeoman's stead of old, and I have been aghast at the cost of it.

This compromise of his earlier principles cannot, however, spoil Morris's achievement in encouraging a radical change in contemporary attitudes to furniture design although he does not appear to have designed many pieces himself. The originality and longevity of the furniture designed and produced under his supervision and by his firm are clear evidence of his influence not only over his contemporaries but also over his successors.

J.1

J.5

J.2

J.3

J.1 Armchair

Early nineteenth century
Painted wood with rush seat, 85.0 x 58.0 x 50.0 cm
Society of Antiquaries of London
(Kelmscott Manor)

This simple country chair with the remnants of painted decoration is typical of the type of design that inspired the Sussex range of rush-seated chairs. Contemporary interest in such furniture, particularly in the early nineteenth-century fashion for rusticity and *cottages ornées*, resulted in a wide range of such chairs, rush seated,

with turned sections imitating bamboo, or shaped uprights. The structural detail of the straight arm and its support, which continues through the seat rail down to the stretcher, was a feature particularly taken up in the Sussex range.

The chair comes from Kelmscott Manor, but it is impossible to know whether it was originally owned by Morris or by a later occupant.

J.2 Table

Designed by George Edmund Street
Manufactured by George Myers, *c*.1854
Oak, 66.0 x 98.0 cm diameter
V&A (W.88-1975)

Street designed little domestic furniture because his practice was predominately involved in ecclesiastical commissions. His furniture for Cuddesdon College, Oxford, built to his designs between 1852 and 1854, included both large dining tables and these smaller versions which were intended for use in the students'

J.4

rooms. Street's influence on his pupils, Webb and Morris, is illustrated in the very similar table made for Red Lion Square (cat.no.J.3)

This table, with its revealed construction and structural honesty, clearly reflects the influence of A.W.N. Pugin, and one design in the Victoria and Albert Museum shows a table with three legs of similar form to the Street version (see fig.111). George Myers, Pugin's builder, who also worked for Street at Cuddesdon College, is known to have made domestic and ecclesiastical furniture and woodwork, notably the cabinet designed by Pugin for his own dining room at The Grange, Ramsgate, now on loan to the Museum.

The table was purchased from Cuddesdon College, Oxford.

J.3 Table

Designed by William Morris
Manufactured by, ?Tommy Baker of Christopher Street, Hatton Garden, *c*.1856
Painted oak, 71.1 x 141.0 x 138.4 cm
Cheltenham Art Gallery and Museums (1982 1114)
Bought with the assistance of MGC/V&A
Purchase Grant Fund

Morris's earliest furniture designs were for the unfur-nished rooms he shared with Burne-Jones at 17 Red Lion Square in 1856, and this table may be a rare sur-viving example (Carruthers, 1989, pp. 55–61). The furniture was apparently made by a local joiner follow-ing Morris's rough drawings and included a round table, memorably described by Rossetti as 'firm, and as heavy, as a rock' (Mackail, p.113) and illustrated in Burne-Jones's cluttered interior of 1856 (fig.64.)

Clearly influenced by Street's Cuddesdon table, of

about 1854 (cat.no.J.2), the design could represent a collaboration between Webb and Morris. Morris's knowledge of medieval illuminated manuscripts prob-ably prompted his 'having some intensely medieval furniture made – tables and chairs like incubi and suc-cubi' (Rossetti to William Allingham, 18 Dec. 1856, *Letters*, ed. Doughty and Wahl, 1965, p. 312)

The plank-like construction and Gothic detail of the legs is similar to Webb's trestle tables of 1859 for Red House and for the Burne-Joneses in 1860. Under the green paint, added on May Morris's instructions, is a red-brown layer, suggesting an original finish similar to that on the stand for the St George Cabinet (cat.no.J.18).

The table was purchased from the Trustees of Kelmscott Village Hall.

J.4 Chair

Designed by William Morris, *c*.1856
Painted wood, 61.5 x 76.3 x 53.5 cm
William Morris Gallery (London Borough of Waltham Forest) (H26) Given by Dr C.E.Newman

Although this has been described as the chair used by Morris for weaving at the Queen's Square workshops and at Merton Abbey, it is unlikely that it was originally intended for this purpose as the arms would hamper weaving. The medieval form, simple construction and distinctive painted decoration suggest that it may have been part of the furniture designed originally by Morris for the rooms he shared with Burne-Jones in Red Lion Square.

Burne-Jones depicted similar tub-shaped chairs in his *Holy Grail* tapestry, and these are probably inspired by that shown in the panel of *St Jerome in his Study* by

Antonello da Messina (National Gallery). A carpenter friend made up actual round- and square-backed chairs to assist Burne-Jones in his drawing of the tapestry car-toon and these, although uncomfortable, were used by the Burne-Jones grandchildren in the summer house at North End House, Rottingdean (Angela Thirkell, *Three Houses*, London, 1932, pp. 80–81).

The chair was given by H.C.Marillier to C.A.Newman when the Morris & Co. shop closed and was donated by his son.

J.5 Egyptian chair

Designed by Ford Madox Brown, 1857–8
Satinised wood, part ebonised with incised decoration, 84.5 x 55.0 x 54.5 cm
V&A (W.13-1985)

One of a pair, inspired by an elaborately worked pair of chairs designed by William Holman Hunt in 1856–7, which had been based on an ancient Egyptian stool in the British Museum (see Ormond, 1965, pp. 55–68). Hunt invited Madox Brown to view them in December 1857 and long after commented that he had 'idolised' them and had 'set a carpenter to work to make some of similar proportions' (Hunt, 1905, II, pp. 134–7). Madox Brown, who had already had a massive table made in 1857, probably inspired by Morris (and in turn copied by Hunt), noted in January 1858 amongst work done since November, 'also 4 designs for chairs' (Surtees, 1981). The entry may refer both to this chair and to another pair with ladder-backs and rush seats (see *Furnisher*, 1900–1). The simple construction and finish, compared with Hunt's, shows a kinship with tradition-al English ladder-backs. The incised circles on sides and back replacing Hunt's seven lotuses, seem to anticipate some of Madox Brown's frame designs.   MB

J.6a/J.6b

J.6c/J.6d

J.6 Four painted panels

William Morris, Dante Gabriel Rossetti or Edward Burne-Jones, *c*.1857
Oil on panel, 61.0 x 41.0 x 3.2 cm each
V&A (Circ.128, 129-1953)
Given by Mrs Christabel Marillier
V&A (Circ.310, 311-1960)

G.P.Boyce's diary for 4 May 1858 records a 'Meeting of the (just forming) Hogarth Club at Jones and Morris's rooms. In the room some interesting drawings, tapestries, and furniture, the latter gorgeously painted in subjects by Jones and Morris and Gabriel Rossetti'. These panels are likely to have been part of the furniture Boyce saw that day and could have come from a bookcase or a settle of the type caricatured by Max Beerbohm in his cartoon of 1922 (cat.no.I.3). The subject suggests the Seasons. The compositions and background patterns are very similar to Morris's painted figures on the insides of the doors of the Prioress's Tale Cabinet (fig.70). When given to the Museum by

Christabel, wife of H.C.Marillier, Rossetti's biographer, the first two panels (J.6a, b) were said to have been painted by Rossetti. However, they have a closer stylistic resemblance to contemporary work by Burne-Jones including the cabinet depicting ladies and animals (cat.no.J.7) and the more sophisticated painting *Fair Rosamund* (Fogg Art Museum, Cambridge, Mass.) of 1863. The second two panels (J.6c, d) from the set were found in Romford market before being sold to the Museum. It was suggested on acquisition that they were the work of William Morris.

Exhib. 1961 (3)   RW/LP

J.7 Ladies and Animals Sideboard

Designed by Edward Burne-Jones and painted *c*.1860
Deal with oil paint and gold and silver leaf,
116.8 x 152.4 x 73.7 cm
V&A (W.10-1953)
Given by Mrs J.W. Mackail

Burne-Jones's first interest in painting furniture was mentioned in a letter of 1856 (*Memorials*, I, p.147). He painted this sideboard, which was in his possession, in the week before his marriage in June 1860. The theme he chose was that of 'Ladies and animals'. The three panels on the front show ladies feeding pigs, parrots and fishes, while the two panels on each end depict the cruel treatment of an owl and some fish, counterbalanced by an attack of angry bees and a frightening newt.

The arrangement of the painted decoration is quite carefully contained within the structure of the sideboard and the red-brown finish on the top and bottom shelf is similar to that used on the stand of the St George Cabinet. After the Burne-Joneses moved to Kensington in 1865 the sideboard was varnished and it is shown with a long, low mirror hung above in a T.M. Rooke 1898 watercolour of the dining room of their last home, The Grange, in Fulham (private collection).

Exhib. 1952 (I4)

J.7

J.8

J.10

J.9

J.11

J.8 Washstand

Designed by Ford Madox Brown, *c*.1860
Manufactured by Morris, Marshall,
Faulkner & Co.
Painted wood, originally stained,
88.0 x 93.0 x 63.0 cm
Society of Antiquaries of London
(Kelmscott Manor)

Part of a group of unpretentiously simple and massive bedroom furniture, appropriate for execution by a joiner rather than a cabinetmaker, formerly apparently at Red House and now at Kelmscott Manor. The series is traditionally ascribed to Madox Brown, who himself had some examples, including a double version of this washstand. His household account book lists three 'Firm by Furniture' receipts in 1862, 1864 and 1865, but his passbook with the firm is missing. *The Artist* (May 1898), probably quoting it, states that he designed 'eight different chairs, four tables, a piano, bookshelves, couches, wall-papers, embroideries, stamped velvets, tiles, wineglasses and decanters, and silk and "two sets of worsted bell ropes". The firm also executed for him a number of washstands, towel horses and toilet tables which he had designed for his own use.' The toilet table (examples are also at Kelmscott Manor), was still in the firm's catalogue about 1910. To Madox Brown is also

ascribed the green stain used in the early days on the plain woods of this type.

Exhib. 1934 (212)   MB

J.9 Settle

Designed by Philip Webb, *c*.1860
Ebonised oak with panels of embossed leather, painted and gilded,
209.0 x 194.0 x 56.5 cm
Society of Antiquaries of London
(Kelmscott Manor)

Made for Red House, where it stood by the fire-place in the dining room (Vallance, 1897, p. 35), this settle was subsequently moved to the drawing room at Kelmscott House. The design, with its canopied top, like Webb's sideboard (cat. no. J.20), was probably based both on medieval ceremonial chairs with canopies and on 'quaint old-fashioned settles' appreciated by Morris (Theodore Watts-Dutton, *The Atheneum*, 10 Oct. 1896, p. 487). Webb's account book for 1862–3 includes designs for painted and lac-quered leather panels, indicating a demand for such decoration, and the ebonised finish was also subsequently used on the firm's furniture.

Several other versions of this settle were made by the firm, some with gilt gesso deco-ration by Kate Faulkner and others with painted decoration by J.H.Dearle. The firm's catalogue offered settles with embossed leather panels at £35 or undecorated at £30.

A plain oak version, with gilt gesso panels of flowers in vases on the back, was supplied for Wickham Flowers' drawing room at Old Swan House, Chelsea (*The Studio*, I, 1893, p. 218), an unidentified photograph of which was used by the firm for publicity purposes.

Exhib. 1934 (206)

J.10 Round table

Designed by Philip Webb, *c*.1860
Oak, 72.0 x 142.5 cm
Society of Antiquaries, London
(Kelmscott Manor)

May Morris described a table in the Memorandum attached to her Will (*The Antiquaries Journal*, XLIII, 1, 1963, p.112) as 'Red House the first made', which may be this one. Although its exact location at Red House is now not clear the table fits into that environment of youthful enthusiasm for the thirteenth and fourteenth centuries that Morris, Webb and their friends embraced. The combination of boarded sides pierced with openings, massive column-like legs with their crenallated bases and the solid top result in a truly medieval-looking piece.

It illustrates Webb's interest in medieval details, probably taken from architectural sources, particularly church woodwork and stonework, rather than a dependence on Puginian principles of revealed construction. The crenallated bases on the legs were also used by Webb on a side table for the Burne-Jones family, probably supplied about 1865 (cat.no.J.28).

Exhib. 1952 (I2)

J.11 Armchair from the Sussex range

Possibly designed by Philip Webb, *c*.1860
Manufactured by Morris, Marshall, Faulkner & Co.
Ebonised beech with rush seat, 85.6 x 52.4 x 43.0 cm
V&A (Circ.288-1960)

One of the most recognisable pieces of furniture associated with Morris and the firm, the Sussex armchair in its quirky angularity became an icon of artistic taste and was much copied, notably by Liberty and Heals. It is based on a Regency prototype, a painted chair or armchair, with turned uprights and imitation bamboo frame. Mackail's comment that the chair was adapted from a country chair found in Sussex suggests the origin of the name, not necessarily that the design was typical for chairs made in that region.

Black or red Sussex chairs, probably armchairs, were used at Red House and by Edward and Georgiana Burne-Jones who ordered black chairs with rush seats from the Euston Road Boys' Home in 1860 (*Memorials*, I, p. 205). Chosen by Birket Foster for The Hill, they were recommended by Edis (*Decoration and Furniture of Town Houses*, 1881, pp. 27–7) as excellent, comfortable and artistic, at 9s. 9d., although 'somewhat rough in make'. Sussex armchairs furnished the studios of Burne-Jones and Alfred Gilbert, and one appears in Picasso's 1922 drawing of Bertie Landsberg (Fitzwilliam Museum, Cambridge).

J.12 Cabinet

Designed by Richard Norman Shaw
Made by James Forsyth, 1861
Oak inlaid with various woods and painted, 280.8 x 142.0 x 78.7 cm
V&A (Circ.96-1963)

Shaw, another of Street's pupils, designed this cabinet, incorporating a bookcase and writing table, for himself and it was made by his friend, the ecclesiastical sculptor and carver, James Forsyth. Shown at the Architectural Exhibition in 1861, it was praised by *The Builder* (20 April 1861, p.269) who stated that 'Mr.Shaw is thoroughly embued with the Mediaeval spirit'. Also shown in the Medieval Court at the 1862 Exhibition, it received critical recognition from *Cassell's Illustrated Family Paper Exhibitor* (28 June, 1862, p.44) as a fine example of a thirteenth-century bookcase.

The cabinet embodies all the features of the Reformed Gothic style, including stumpy columns and geometric inlays, which Shaw and his fellow architects, including Street and Butterfield, developed as a result of their ecclesiastical work. The architectural appearance of the upper section, and the use of tin foil, subsequently painted and varnished, on the roof indicate the influence of Burges's Yatman Cabinet of 1858. This medieval decorative technique was also used on at least two pieces shown by the Morris firm at the 1862 Exhibition (see cat.nos.J.18–19).

Acquired from the Sisters of Bethany to whom it was given by Shaw's daughter.

J.12

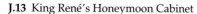

J.13

J.13 King René's Honeymoon Cabinet

Designed by John Pollard Seddon, 1861
Manufactured by Thomas Seddon, 1861–2
Oak inlaid with various woods, painted metal-
work, painted panels; 133.3 x 279.5 x 94.0 cm
V&A (W.10-1927)

This cabinet, designed in 1861 by Seddon for his architectural office, was made by his father's cabinet making
firm. J.P.Seddon also designed the metalwork and inlay
but commissioned ten panels depicting the Fine and
Applied Arts from the Morris firm (J.P.Seddon, *King
René's Honeymoon Cabinet*, 1898, pp. 4–5).

The theme, imaginary incidents in the life of King René
of Anjou, a noted artistic patron, was suggested by
Ford Madox Brown who designed the left-hand panel,
representing Architecture. Painting and Sculpture were
by Burne-Jones, while Rossetti was responsible for
Music and also for the smaller panel, Gardening. The
other small panels were Embroidery by Prinsep,
Pottery, Weaving, Ironwork (showing Morris as a
smith) and Glass Blowing. Morris designed the decorative background for each panel.

Displayed at the 1862 Exhibition by Seddon, the cabinet
received mixed reviews for its overall design, the inlaid
woodwork and the painted panels. However the South
Kensington Museum, recognising its importance,
attempted, unsuccessfully, to purchase it from the
Exhibition and finally acquired it from Seddon's
daughter, Mrs Walter de Hoghton Birch, in 1927.
Exhib. 1952 (I6)

J.14 Design for a sofa

Dante Gabriel Rossetti for Morris, Marshall,
Faulkner & Co., 1861–2,
Pencil, pen and black ink, 25.1 x 35.2 cm
Inscribed; the lower left-hand annotations on the
design are by Morris
Birmingham Museums and Art Gallery (471'04)
Presented by Subscribers

This Egyptian design for a sofa was made of ebonised
and white wood for the firm's display at the 1862
Exhibition. It had covers of red serge decorated with
lines and crotchets in imitation of bars of music and

was priced at £30. Ridiculed by various critics including Charles Dickens in *All the Year Round* (30 Aug. 1862,
p. 585) for its uncomfortable rectangular construction,
the sofa was praised by *The Atheneum* (27 Sept. 1862,
p. 407) for the ingenious upholstery and for the
admirable colour scheme which apparently constrasted
with the firm's embroidered green serge hangings nearby.

Rossetti's 1860 drawing of *Joseph before Potiphar* (also in
Birmingham Museum and Art Gallery) shows a similar
sofa and may be the design source for the piece of furniture. An illustration of Rossetti's Chelsea dining room
(Gere, 1989, p. 15) shows a dresser with the same pal-
mette finials and possibly the sofa remained in his
possession after 1862. Although its present whereabouts are unknown, in 1900 it belonged to Harold
Rathbone who may have acquired it either from
Rossetti's collection or from Ford Madox Brown. It was
illustrated in *The Furnisher* (III, no.13, Nov. 1900, see
illustration top right).

The drawing was owned by Philip Webb, Sydney
Cockerell and Charles Fairfax Murray.

J.15 Seven designs for the decorative panels of a bookcase, depicting the life of an English family from 1810 to 1860

Ford Madox Brown, c.1861

a *The Proposal*
Pencil, pen and ink, with ink wash borders
Inscribed: upper right 'AD 1809' and verso 'FMB No.1'
15.0 x 15.0 cm
Fitzwilliam Museum, Cambridge (776/1–7)

b *The Departure for the Peninsula*
Pencil, pen and ink
Inscribed: upper right 'AD 1812'
13.7 x 14.0 cm

c *The Charge*
Pencil, pen and ink
Inscribed: upper left 'AD 1815' and verso,'Ford Madox Brown No.5'
14.0 x 23.0 cm

d *The Gazette*
Pencil, pen and ink
Inscribed: verso 'F. Madox Brown' and a faint pencil study of a head
21.4 x 20.6 cm

e *Wounded*
Pencil, pen and ink
Inscribed: upper right 'AD 1815' and verso 'F. Madox Brown No.2'
13.9 x 23.0 cm

f *The Return*
Pencil, pen and ink
Inscribed: upper right 'AD 1816'
14.0 x 14.8 cm

g *The Story of the Battle*
Pencil, pen and ink
Inscribed: upper right 'AD 1862'
14.0 x 16.3 cm.

The bookcase, now lost, was shown by Morris, Marshall, Faulkner & Co. at the International Exhibition of 1862. *The Building News* (8 Aug. 1862, p. 99) commented: 'A set of blacked bookshelves with amber curtains, are really very beautiful in their simple outline and in the fidelity to old art with which every line is traced.' However the panels, 'outlines on gilt grounds', were found incongruous and their subjects, from the Peninsular War to 1860 may well have looked out of place in the setting of the Medieval Court. The artist no doubt intended, in this new type of project, to be up-to-date in the ultimate effect. He may have been inspired by the career of Colonel Gillum, or as a result of joining the Volunteers, to which Peter Paul Marshall, the subsequent owner of the bookcase, also belonged.

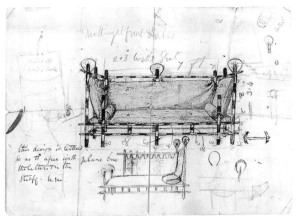

J.14   The sofa as illustrated in *The Furnisher*, 1900

J.15

An extant sketch shows a side elevation for the bookcase is inscribed 'designed and decorated by me' (*Ford Madox Brown* exhibition catalogue, Piccadillly, 1865), a narrow plank cut back from a broader base, with lines of incised decoration crossed diagonally by floral motifs and with three of the panels set at intervals.   MB

J.16

J.17a

J.16 Armchair

Designed by Philip Webb
Manufactured by Morris, Marshall, Faulkner
& Co., 1861–2
Ebonised wood with gilded bands,
99.0 x 41.0 x 43.0 cm
Society of Antiquaries of London
(Kelmscott Manor)

This distinctive design by Webb was one of two different 'stained and gilded drawing-room chairs' shown at the 1862 Exhibition noted by Christopher Dresser (*Development of Ornamental Art in the International Exhibition*, London, 1862, p. 85). He commented approvingly on the structural design, achieved by the unusual combination of extended side rails on the seat joining diagonal struts from the back, a feature found in his own furniture. Although it was also praised by the *Illustrated London News* (Oct. 18 1862, p. 424) the chair was clearly too unconventional for general approval and remained unsold in Morris's possession (fig. 76).

Webb's account book (cat. no. D.4) includes a simple sketch, possibly the same chair, in 1861–2, at 10s., and in one of his sketch books, annotated 'February 1851 No.1' (private collection) is an undated measured drawing, possibly a preliminary idea for this chair. The combination of an ebonised finish and gilded bands is reminiscent of Egyptian design and of Rossetti's 1862 couch (cat. no. J.14). However, this could also be an example of the firm's interest in eighteenth-century sources as mentioned by Warington Taylor.

J.17 Four preliminary drawings for the painted doors of the St George Cabinet

William Morris, 1861
a Pencil, pen and ink and brush and ink on paper, watermarked 'J Whatman 185[illegible]';
44.2 x 51.0 cm

V&A (E.2787-1927)
b Pencil, pen and ink and brush and ink on blue paper, 44.7 x 15.8 cm
V&A (E.2788-1927)

c Pencil, pen and ink and brush and ink,
43.7 x 35.4 cm
V&A (E.2789-1927)

d Pencil, pen and ink, brush and ink and coloured chalk, 43.9 x 50.4 cm
V&A (E.2790-1927)
Bequeathed by J. R. Holliday, formerly in the collection of Charles Fairfax Murray

These sketches, stylistically much influenced by Burne-Jones, and of very uneven degrees of finish, form a narrative sequence. They include much detail that must have been based on observation, such as the architecture and the soldiers' uniform.

The panels tell the story of a town which appeased the dragon living in the local swamp with human victims chosen by lot. The first drawing shows the distraught king, his daughter having been chosen. She is led away by soldiers before being seen tied to a post awaiting her fate. The next panel shows St George having slain the dragon rescuing the swooning princess before leading the triumphant procession back to the town. The princess was modelled from Jane Morris; the dragon may have been inspired by early German prints but looks suspiciously like a stuffed crocodile.

Exhib. 1934 (200); 1961 (2) one design   SA

J.18 Cabinet on stand, depicting the Legend of St George

Designed by Philip Webb and painted by William Morris
Manufactured by Morris, Marshall, Faulkner
& Co., 1861–2
Mahogany, oak and pine, painted and gilded, copper handles; 95.9 x 177.7 x 43.2 cm
V&A (341-1906)

This cabinet was painted by Morris himself for the 1862 Exhibition, although Webb was responsible for the design, charging the firm £1 10s. Rossetti enthusiastically described it in January 1862, 'I wish you could see a painted cabinet, with the history of St. George, and other furniture of great beauty which we have in hand. We have bespoke space at the Great Exhibition…' (*Letters*, II, 1965, p. 436). It was shown at the Exhibition with some of Webb's glasses on top and priced at fifty guineas.

The cabinet was criticised for lack of co-ordination between structure and painted panels by *The Building News* (9 Aug. 1862, p. 99): 'This studied affectation of truthfulness, in placing ironwork in the middle of a picture, is one of the many sins which have to be purged from the Mediaevalists.' Although Morris used Burges's revived medieval method of layers of tinted varnishes on silver leaf to create the decoration inside the cabinet, he did not follow Burges's lead in integrating painted decoration into the overall structure.

The cabinet apparently remained part of the firm's stock until 1863. It subsequently belonged to Laurence Hodson, of Compton Hall, near Wolverhampton, an enthusiatic client of the firm and was acquired from his sale (Christies, 6 July 1906, lot 96).

Exhib. 1934 (199); 1952 (I5); 1961 (1)

J.17b

J.17c

J.17d

J.18

J.19 Chest

Designed by Philip Webb
Manufactured by Morris, Marshall, Faulkner & Co., 1862
Probably pine, covered with silver leaf, glazed and painted with tinted varnishes, iron mounts; 53.3 x 132.0 x 51.2 cm
V&A (W.35-1978)

Although this chest has no provenance, its Gothic form, the painted design and the decorative technique suggest that it was the chest shown by the firm in the Medieval Court at the 1862 exhibition. Webb's 1862 accounts for this first public display of the firm's work included a chest with ironwork, at £1 10s. *The Parthenon*, (no. 23, 4 Oct. 1862, p. 724), in reviewing the firm's furniture, mentioned 'a lacquered chest', described as having 'diaper flower-decorations'. Patterns of formalised daisies were used by Morris in many of his earliest designs and the pattern on this chest may well have been inspired by similar themes in the decoration and furnishings at Red House.

The design on the painted panels was created using silver leaf, glazes and tinted varnishes, an unusual medieval technique revived by Burges for his Yatman cabinet of 1858 and also found on the interior of the St George Cabinet, shown at the 1862 Exhibition. Indian red, a popular paint colour for medieval enthusiasts, was used on the inside of the chest, and also on the stand for the St George Cabinet and on Burne-Jones's sideboard of 1860 (cat.no.J.7).

J.20 Sideboard

Designed by Philip Webb
Manufactured by Morris, Marshall, Faulkner & Co., c.1862
Ebonised wood with painted decoration and panels of stamped leather, 195.7 x 198.2 x 66.0 cm
V&A, (Circ.540-1963) Given by Ben Weinreb

Webb's 1862–3 account book records designs for three sideboards, and work on painted and lacquered leather panels, some of which were intended for a sideboard. This may represent one of these early commissions. The base was originally open but has been altered and is now filled with drawers. The leather panels, with birds and flowers in roundels and stiff, meandering floral trails, are quite distinctive and very similar to those on a sideboard illustrated in the firm's late catalogue where it was described as being made 'in the earliest days of the firm at Red Lion Square (c.1862)'.

Frederick Leyland, an important patron of both Rossetti and Whistler and a client of the firm, owned a similar sideboard, photographed in his dining room at 49 Princes Gate, London, in 1892. He may have acquired it either for this house, which he bought in 1874, or for his earlier house in Queen's Gate furnished from 1867. Both this and another example, now in the Musée d'Orsay, are of similar form to the Museum's example, but their leather panels have a large-scale scrolling pattern, more reminiscent of seventeenth-century Dutch or Spanish leather.

J.21 Mirror on stand

Designed by Philip Webb
Manufactured by Morris, Marshall, Faulkner & Co., c.1862
Ebonised wood with gilt decoration, 90.0 x 49.0 x 33.0 cm
Society of Antiquaries of London (Kelmscott Manor)

There are two mirrors of this design at Kelmscott Manor, either of which could be the one May Morris listed as from Red House in her Memorandum attached to her Will (*The Antiquaries Journal*, XLIII, pt 1, 1963). The ebonised finish and gilded decoration relate to other pieces of furniture made in the 1860s, particularly for the 1862 exhibition, and Rossetti apparently ordered an ebony chimney

glass and shelf from the firm in 1868 (*Dante Gabriel Rossetti and Jane Morris: Their Correspondence,* ed. John Bryson, Oxford 1976, pp. 4–5).

The design, which indicates Webb's awareness of Puginian principles of revealed construction, is an interesting reminder of the firm's more practical furniture. Originally the mirror incorporated a pin which could be adjusted at different points in the curved arm (a feature also used by Ford Madox Brown for a similar mirror), and at least one oak version survives (Gere and Whiteway, 1993, pl. 107). Another example, with candle holders, was supplied for Red Barns, Coatham, Redcar, the house designed by Webb in 1868 for Hugh Bell.

Exhib. 1934 (210)

J.22 Circular table

Designed by Philip Webb
Manufactured by Morris, Marshall, Faulkner & Co., *c.*1865
Walnut, stained; 74.0 x 122.0 cm diameter
Ivor Braka Limited–London

Several pieces of furniture designed by Webb in the 1860s combine turned stretchers and abstract structures, probably derived from a mixture of vernacular and oriental sources. This table, typical of his work, is one of several examples in walnut and mahogany, indicating the success of the design. Part of the firm's standard range, it was supplied for Wickham Flowers' London house, Old Swan House, Chelsea, and one survives in the Morning Room at Standen.

Webb also designed a round table with flat, circular stretchers and turned legs which was made by the boys of the Euston Road Home for Edward and Georgiana Burne-Jones in 1860 and remains in the collection of their descendants. Other versions include one with six legs described by Warington Taylor in a letter to E. R. Robson in the early 1860s (Fitzwilliam Museum, Cambridge, Burne-Jones Papers), and one supplied for the sitting room at Great Tangley Manor, probably in 1885.

By 1889, George Jack had designed another small round table, with shaped stretchers attached to a central fitting, which was shown at the Arts and Crafts Exhibition that year. This table, also produced with straight, radiating stretchers, was made for several of the firm's later clients, including William Knox D'Arcy of Stanmore Hall.

J.23 Music stand

Designed by Philip Webb
Manufactured by Morris, Marshall, Faulkner & Co., *c.*1864
Ebonised and turned wood, 142.5 x 46.2 x 32.0 cm
Francesca and Massimo Valsecchi

This music stand, which could also be described as a whatnot, is an example of more conventional and domestic furniture developed by Webb for the firm in the 1860s. The combination of plain panels and intricate turned uprights is typical of his absorption with details derived from both oriental and vernacular sources. An early version of the design may have been the red lacquer music stand with floral decoration included in the firm's display at the 1862 Exhibition.

Entries in Webb's account book include a painted music stand in 1863 for £9 and another for £2, perhaps less elaborate, in 1866. Several examples can be seen in photographs of Birket Foster's house, The Hill, Witley, which was furnished by the firm from 1864. These included both this simpler version and a more elaborate one, with painted floral decoration on the shelf supports. Later versions can be seen in photographs of the drawing room at Old Swan House, Chelsea, and of the Morris window display at 449 Oxford Street (fig. 17).

Exhib. 1934 (209)

J.21

J.23

J.22

J.24

J.25

J.26

J.24 The 'Rossetti' Armchair

Possibly designed by Dante Gabriel Rossetti
Manufactured by Morris, Marshall, Faulkner &
Co., in production from *c.*1863
Ebonised beech with red painted decoration and
rush seat, 88.9 x 49.5 x 47.0 cm
V&A (Circ.304-1961)

This chair, based on early nineteenth-century French
country chairs, was traditionally known as the Rossetti
armchair although no actual evidence identifying him
as the designer has yet been found. He was clearly
involved with the firm's furniture and wrote to Webb in
1866, 'If there is anything besides rush-bottoms and
ascetic glutaei on which I should be glad to offer a
fundamental remark as regards the principles of the
firm…' (V&A NAL).

William Downey's 1863 photograph of Rossetti with
John Ruskin and W.B. Scott in his Chelsea garden
shows an almost identical chair (see fig.7). This may be
one of the firm's early products or one of Rossetti's sec-
ondhand pieces. His interest in antique furniture,
particularly Sheraton and Regency pieces, and his
patronage of Minster of Buckingham Street and other
dealers, is recorded in his letters and by William
Allingham and H.Treffry Dunn. A satinwood
pembroke table, acquired by Rossetti from Murray
Marks (*Letters*, III, 1967, pp. 955–8) for use at Kelmscott
Manor in 1871, and a number of other items from his
collection are still in the house.

Acquired from Mrs Barbara Morris.

J.25 Chair with round seat from the Sussex range

Possibly designed by Ford Madox Brown
Manufactured by Morris, Marshall, Faulkner &
Co., in production from *c.*1865
Ebonised wood with rush seat, 83.0 x 41.9 x 43.0 cm
Society of Antiquaries of London
(Kelmscott Manor)

The design of this chair was attributed to F.M.Brown
by E.M.Tait in *The Furnisher* (III, 1900–1, pp. 61–3).
Amongst a number of items of furniture designed by
Brown were two picture stands for Rossetti, which
were made by Stennett in 1865 and he could have
provided the firm with the original design for this chair.
Burne-Jones purchased a number of Sussex chairs in
1865 for his new home in Kensington which might have
included this version. He certainly ordered four round-
seated chairs at a cost of £2 in 1878 and had two in the
dining room and two in the upstairs sitting room at The
Grange in Fulham.

Described by Edis as a bedroom chair and recommended for its cheapness and serviceability (*Decoration and
Furniture of Town Houses*, 1881, p.29), this model was
available for 10s. 6d. according to the Morris & Co.
catalogue about 1910.

J.26 Single chair from the Sussex range

Manufactured by Morris & Co., in production from
*c.*1865
Ebonised wood with rush seat, 83.8 x 42.0 x 35.6 cm
William Morris Gallery (London Borough of
Waltham Forest) (3/1961)
Given by Miss A.Rigby

Burne-Jones noted in his account book that in May 1865
he paid the firm £3 4s. for eight plain Sussex chairs and
in February 1868 he paid another £2 16s. for twelve
Sussex chairs. Either of these entries could refer to this
inexpensive chair from the Sussex range whose design
was probably an adaptation by Webb of a standard side
chair with turned back sections and legs.

This design was priced at 7s. in the Morris & Co. catalogue (*c.*1910), and Morris referred to its production in
a letter to James Mavor, 'The cheapest chair that we can
sell costs about 7s/0 (and they are made 4 or 5 dozen at
a time too)…' (Kelvin, 1343). It was certainly very popular and was supplied to numerous clients for many
different locations including the Hall, Common Room
and students' rooms at Newnham College, Cambridge,
in the 1890s. When Sydney Cockerell became Director
of the Fitzwilliam Museum he acquired examples for
use there in the galleries and offices, where they still
remain.

J.27 Settle from the Sussex range

Manufactured by Morris & Co., in
production from *c*.1865
Ebonised wood with rush seat,
85.1 x 137.2 x 41.0 cm
William Morris Gallery
(London Borough of Waltham Forest)
(187/1963). Given in 1963 by Lady
Richmond, sister of Lady Trevelyan

Traditionally settles were made with high
or low backs. This variation was obviously
a useful addition to the popular Sussex
range. Recommended by Robert Edis
(*Decoration and Furniture of Town Houses*,
1881, pp. 156–7) for use in halls, at a price
of 35s., it was still available at that price
when featured in the firm's catalogue some
years later.

Lady Richmond was a sister of Lady
Trevelyan, an enthusiastic client of the firm.

J.28 Table

Designed by Philip Webb
Manufactured by Morris, Marshall,
Faulkner & Co., *c*.1865
Oak, 73.7 x 165.0 x 59.8 cm
V&A (W.45-1926)
Given by Mrs J.W.Mackail

The design of this table epitomises Webb's
subtle use of medieval details and is one of
the most successful pieces of Reformed
Gothic furniture.

Some of Webb's most interesting furniture
was designed for the Burne-Jones family,
including a trestle dining table, a round
one with flat circular stretcher, and this
side table. A photograph of their first-floor
sitting room, at The Grange, Fulham, about
1898, (fig.75) shows both round and side
tables, together with the piano painted by
Burne-Jones (now in the V&A) and some of
the round-seated Sussex chairs.

According to Margaret Mackail, the side
table was acquired later than the 1860 dining table and may have been the example,
costing £6 6s., ordered by Burne-Jones from
the firm in 1865 for his new home in
Kensington Square. Originally plain oak,
the table was apparently stained green by
Burne-Jones in the 1880s. Webb certainly
designed tables for Burne-Jones and for
Vernon Lushington in 1865, and another
version of this design, with ebonised finish
and gilt details, was sold by the Lushington
family at Sothebys in 1983.

Exhib. 1934 (203); 1961 (7)

J.27

J.28

J.29

J.30

J.32

J.34

Although originally supplied with *Utrecht Velvet* covers at £10s. 10d., chintz covers were also available at £8. *Utrecht Velvet*, a embossed mohair plush, recommended by Christopher Dresser in *Principles of Decorative Design*, 1873, and probably supplied by Heaton and Co. of Manchester, was sold by Morris & Co. in a number of colourways for seat upholstery and wall coverings (see cat.no.M.39).

J.G. Carruthers was the son of John Carruthers, a friend of Morris (see cat.no.J.34).

Exhib. 1952 (I9)

J.30 Corner chair from the Sussex range

Manufactured by Morris & Co., c.1870
Ebonised wood with rush seat, 70.0 x 70.0 x 70.0 cm
National Trust, Wightwick Manor
Acquired by Lady Mander in 1937

Corner or smoking chairs were a popular established type with strong provincial roots before these were made by the firm (Gerry Cotton, "Common" Chairs from the Norwich Chair Makers' Price Book of 1801', *Regional Furniture*, II, 1988, pp. 88–9). Clearly inspired by the same vernacular traditions as the Sussex range single chair and armchair, the corner chair may have been taken from an actual model or might have been a variation on the basic design in order to expand the range.

Priced at 10s. 6d. in the Morris & Co. catalogue, the corner chair was chosen by W.A.S.Benson for the drawing room in his house, Windleshaw, in Sussex.

J.31 Grand piano

Designed by Edward Burne-Jones, decoration by Kate Faulkner
Manufactured by John Broadwood, 1884–5
Oak, stained and decorated with gold and silver gesso on dark ground, 96.5 x 259.0 x 141.0 cm
V&A (W.23-1927)
Given by Mrs A.C.Ionides

This piano was commissioned from Morris & Co. by Alexander Ionides for the second drawing room of 1 Holland Park. The design and green stain were innovations suggested by Burne-Jones. The completion of the delicate gesso clearly caused difficulties for Kate Faulkner (W.R.Lethaby, *Philip Webb and His Work*, reprint, London 1979, pp. 177, 181–2, 184–6).

Lent by Ionides to the first exhibition organised by the Arts and Crafts' Society in 1888, full details were given in the catalogue of the ten craftsmen involved in making the case and movement. According to *The British Architect*, (23 Nov. 1888, p.362), who admired the design and execution of the gesso, Kate Faulkner had other commissions for similar piano cases. Webb and Morris discussed her difficulties over another piano case with gesso in 1892–3 (V&A, NAL 86.TT.13, nos.30–32, 36, 39).

The Builder (LV, 2, 1888, pp. 242–3), also admired the rich and striking effect of the gesso, although considering it 'rather overdone; at all events, it would certainly require the whole apartment to be designed up to it'. That such a setting was provided is confirmed in contemporary photographs of the interiors at 1 Holland Park.

The donor was a daughter-in-law of A.A.Ionides.

Exhib. 1952 (I12)

J.29 Adjustable-back chair

Designed by Philip Webb
Manufactured by Morris, Marshall, Faulkner & Co., in production from c.1866
Ebonised wood with *Utrecht Velvet* upholstery, 99.0 x 63.0 x 79.0 cm
V&A (Circ.250-1961)
Given by J.G. Carruthers

Warington Taylor sketched the model for this chair in a letter to Philip Webb in 1866, (V&A NAL 86.ss.57) (see fig.68) having seen it in the workshop of Ephraim Colman, a carpenter in Herstmonceux, Sussex. Webb clearly altered the original conventional reclining chair, retaining the bars in the seat but substituted bobbin turning. This traditional technique and the ebonised finish were used on other seat furniture produced by the firm, including a day bed from the dining room at Kelmscott House, which is now at Kelmscott Manor. Used in the Kelmscott House drawing room and by Burne-Jones, this popular design which was also available in mahogany, was widely copied by British and American firms, including Liberty and Gustav Stickley's worshops in America.

J.31

J.32 Saville armchair

Designed by George Jack
Manufactured by Morris & Co., *c*.1890
Mahogany upholstered in *Utrecht Velvet*,
96.5 x 60.9 x 76.2 cm
V&A (Circ. 401-1960)
Given by Miss F. J. Lefroy

George Jack probably designed this armchair, although no definite evidence has yet been found. The wavy outlines of the vertical rails under the arms are reminiscent of details on Jack's sideboard shown by the firm at the Manchester Jubilee Exhibition in 1887 (*The Cabinet Maker and Art Furnisher*, VIII, 1 July 1887, p. 11).

The *Utrecht Velvet* on this chair has faded from its original olive-green, the same colourway as on the adjustable chair (cat. no. J.29), although in the Morris & Co. catalogue (*c*.1910) the chair was offered with *Cherwell* velvet at £7 5s. or in chintz for £6 5s.

Miss. F. J. Lefroy, the donor, was the niece of Wickham Flower, whose country house, Great Tangley Manor, was furnished with Saville armchairs in the sitting room and a bedroom. Alternative versions, with arm supports and legs in the shape of balusters, survive at Standen, West Sussex. That in the hall is covered in *Acorn* stamped plush while the arm chair in the drawing room has *Utrecht Velvet* covers.
Exhib. 1952 (I13)

J.33 Secretaire

Designed by George Jack
Manufactured by Morris & Co., *c*.1893
Sycamore with marquetry of various woods,
130.8 x 140.9 x 68.5 cm
V&A (Circ.40-1953)

This secretaire reflects Jack's knowledge of eighteenth-century furniture in its singular appearance and revival of marquetry. Inside the shaped top is a velvet lined compartment, and the central panel opens to reveal a writing desk and pigeon holes. First shown at the 1889 Arts and Crafts Exhibition, the secretaire was generally praised for the design of the marquetry, choice of materials and quality of workmanship, although *The Cabinet Maker and Art Furnisher* (1 Nov. 1889, pp. 114–15), described it as 'an exaggerated inlaid tea-caddy on a clumsy stand'.

Used by the Middlemore family at Melsetter, other examples with variations in the design of the marquetry were used as furnishings at Stanmore Hall, Compton Hall, Tapeley Park (two still *in situ*) and Ickworth (private collection). One was acquired by Ralph Radcliffe-Whitehead for his American Arts and Crafts community (now Philadelphia Museum of Art) and three others, with unknown provenances, also survive. Normally the firm's stamp on the fall front included a number, suggesting a production sequence. Marquetry versions cost 98 guineas with plain alternatives at 60 guineas.

Acquired from the Trustees of the Middlemore Estates.
Exhib. 1952 (I15)

J.34 Bergère armchair

Designed by George Jack
Manufactured by Morris & Co., *c*.1893
Mahogany with cane sides and loose cushions
covered with *Tulip* chintz,
102.0 approx. x 62.0 x 68.0 cm
V&A (Circ.249to B-1961)
Bequeathed by Mrs Amy Tozer

J.33

Closely based on a Regency model, this armchair is typical of the type of furniture the firm was producing in the 1890s, and such designs were still available in the early twentieth century according to their published catalogue. By this date Morris and Co. were using the Pimlico cabinet-working workshops of Holland and Co. for furniture which reflected contemporary fashions with the revival of Sheraton, Empire and Regency designs.

This chair was apparently bought from Morris & Co. by John Carruthers, a friend of Morris's, a fellow member of the Hammersmith Socialist Society and his companion on the final journey to Norway. It was bequeathed to the Museum by his daughter.

TILES AND TABLEWARE

Jennifer Hawkins Opie

In May 1862 Morris, Marshall, Faulkner & Co. was confident enough to advertise itself by purchasing space in the Medieval Court of the International Exhibition, held on the South Kensington site. In effect the exhibition extended the company from being a 'design studio', responding solely to commissions, to retailing. Potential customers could now visit the showroom on the first floor at Red Lion Square and by the end of the year the company's accounts record the importance of the sale of tiles and table glass.

For the decoration of much of the firm's early production, Morris and his colleagues drew inspiration from the 'medieval' period of many different countries. In Britain, from the thirteenth century onwards, sturdy, practical tiles were made for floors in red and white clays with honey-coloured lead glazing. Morris firmly rejected these, perhaps because from the 1830s reproductions had been made by the hugely successful Staffordshire and Shropshire industries. This overwhelming commerce combined with the stiffly formal, gothic patterns was doubly unappealing – heraldry without chivalry. Instead, Morris's tiles were developed either as decorative panels for furniture or – in much the same spirit as were the embroidered hangings and the papers – as wall decoration. Patterns or images were often derived from the same sources. Soon after 1862 Morris himself, in a letter to prospective clients claimed to have been 'particularly successful in the revival (as we think we may call it) of the art of painting on china tiles for walls similar in manner to the ancient maiolica…', and called 'attention to the suitability of these tiles for the decoration both internal and

Fig.79 A detail of the *Si Je Puis* tiles in the porch at Red House.

Fig.80 Fireplace tiles in the dining room at Red House.

external of churches and public buildings…' By this date the collections in the South Kensington Museum, a favourite haunt of both Morris and Philip Webb, were already rich in Renaissance Italian ceramics. Clearly Morris was well aware of the technique as well as attracted by the appearance of this colourful, attractive ware.

Morris was a decorator. He never made his own tiles. He turned to an outside source for the production of the tile blank and for several reasons he went to the Netherlands, for which he had a well-developed affection. He probably had a ready-made contact with tileries through the London-based Dutch dealer Murray Marks. Until at least the 1880s tile production there still used traditional methods, in a hand-based but streamlined technique which allowed mass-production and inexpensive prices. Hand-made and hand-cut blanks were covered with a tin-based lead glaze (which when fired turned to a warm, softly glossy white) and then painted. Glaze and decoration were fired in one operation so that the colour was 'absorbed', giving the typically soft-edged appearance of 'in-glaze' decoration.

Nineteenth-century Dutch patterns too were a continuing tradition, developed from the seventeenth and eighteenth centuries on tiles as well as dishes and other wares. Hand-painted decoration was of simple scenes and patterns, often flowers, reduced to stylised folk elements, sometimes in bright colours but most particularly in a distinctive blue on the white tin-glazed background. These are the type known as 'Dutch Delft'. Similar ceramics were also made in the mid-eighteenth century in Britain as Lambeth, Bristol or Liverpool 'Delft'. For Morris these, together with early illustrated manuscripts, herbals and 'millefleur' tapestries, spoke more than anything of a simple medieval domesticity which he loved.

Although documentary evidence is lacking, it is accepted that white, undecorated tiles ordered from Dutch manufacturers arrived at the Morris works in London ready glazed and fired. These were then decorated by the painters of stained glass already employed by Morris. Of necessity this was done in enamel colours and this 'on-glaze' decoration was fired (a second firing for the tin-glaze) alongside the enamel-decorated stained glass in the firm's own kilns in the basement of Red Lion Square. Aymer Vallance records that in 1862 'Morris, Faulkner and others set about experimenting with various glazes, enamels, etc., until the desired results were obtained. An iron muffle with iron shelves carried the glass in the middle part while the tiles were so placed as to be exposed to the greatest heat, at the top and bottom. A small wind-furnace was employed for slips and for colour-testing experiments.' Such 'on-glaze' decoration is not as sturdy as the 'in-glaze' type (cat.no. K.5). Combined with the attendant complications of firing in a kiln shared with, and built for stained glass, the tiles were often less than successful. A second and sometimes a third firing risked dull, bubbled or even lost colours.

Vallance remarks in his narrative that in about 1870,

> Some early Morris tiles having suffered through the excess of borax in the ordinary enamels of commerce, the only colours available at the time that the industry was revived, it was decided to abandon them, and latterly the only colours used by Morris & Co. for the purpose have been those prepared and supplied by Mr de [*sic*] Morgan.

However, De Morgan was not in a position regularly to supply reliable colours before 1870. Perhaps Powell's Whitefriars glassworks, with which members of the firm had previously been associated, also supplied glass enamels to be used on the tiles, with an extra flux. Vallance's somewhat mysterious statement is at odds with the evidence of many of the tiles themselves and his earlier remarks, but certainly production was a recognised problem. Warington Taylor, joining the firm as business manager in 1865, wrote in the following year as part of one of his fearsome letter-memos to Philip Webb, 'About this Findon tile reredos – we cannot do it – *see this settled at once*. must write Lady Bath saying circumstances have compelled us to discontinue their manufacture. Bournemouth was a disgrace – & only half done now. *see this letter written to Lady Bath*'. The Findon reredos, in the church of St John the Baptist, was completed in 1867 (see fig.82).

At first, designs for the tiles were made by Morris himself, Burne-Jones, Ford Madox Brown and Rossetti as well as, occasionally, Albert Moore and Simeon Solomon. Painters other than the firm's regular employees were, again, Morris himself, Georgiana Burne-Jones and Charles Faulkner, all very occasionally. More regularly, Faulkner's sisters Lucy and Kate and George Campfield the chief stained-glass painter were employed. Lucy Faulkner specialised particularly in the figure tiles until around 1870, after her marriage.

Patterns relate to embroidery and wallpaper motifs, in some cases foreshadowing printed or woven textiles. Panels of two or more tiles were in the form of 'easel' paintings on ceramic. Where these paintings are of figures in an interior this often includes a tiled background, a flat-pattern device frequently used in both interior and exterior scenes in medieval manuscripts. Sometimes, the firm's own tile patterns are identifiable. Otherwise, figures are placed against a foliate background or sylvan landscape, as in the firm's stained glass. The most elaborate are composite designs such as *The Judgement of Paris*, which includes figures in a landscape and a lengthy text. It was probably by Edward Burne-Jones and is now at Kelmscott Manor.

William De Morgan occasionally designed for the firm from 1863, the year in which he met Morris, and the intermeshing of Morris and De Morgan tile design, production and sales is immensely complicated. Both designed for each other; both imported blanks from the Netherlands, and production of the same design by both companies overlapped. The firm sold both its own production and, increasingly, that of De Morgan; by the 1880s De Morgan was the main supplier to the Morris shop. Both the firm and De Morgan's tiles were sold by other dealers and by manufacturers of cast-iron fireplaces such as Barnard, Bishop & Barnard, or Thomas Elsley of the Portland Metal Works. In addition, De Morgan produced designs that are variations on those of Morris, as did many manufacturers, including the Dutch companies (cat.nos.13–14).

Perhaps because of the technical difficulties, production of the most popular repeating patterns was transferred by Morris to the Netherlands from some time in the mid-1870s and entrusted to those makers who had hitherto supplied the blanks for London decoration. These same manufacturers, the best known of which appears to be the Utrecht company, Ravesteijn, shrewdly assessed the British taste and advertised their own designs on tiles made to the British six-inch size.

It seems that Morris was willing to sell and use these entirely Dutch-made tiles, both to his own and their designs. Aymer Vallance, writing in 1897, states that 'It was at the beginning of 1862, [that] some tiles were required for use at the Red House'. The porch tiles, which included his adopted motto 'Si je puis', were designed by Morris himself (see fig.79), and were decorated by the firm. But the fireplaces (see figs.80–81) are tiled with an eclectic mix of Dutch picture and pattern tiles. These were almost certainly bought from the dealer Murray Marks. The son of an immigrant Dutch Jew, Murray Marks was working at his father's furniture and decorative-goods shop in Oxford Street in the early 1860s. Aymer Vallance records in the Easter *Art Annual* of 1900 that in about 1868 Burne-Jones made two designs for tiles for Marks who 'intended to have them made in Holland; but they were never executed'. Some of the tiles which are now in the Red House fireplaces appear in the 1880s in the catalogues of Thomas Elsley who took over Murray Marks's own business, Marks & Durlacher, around 1879. Unfortunately there are no photographs of the house and fireplaces during Morris's short tenancy and there is therefore no way of telling if these tiles were there in his time. This same problem arises with the tiles now in Kelmscott Manor. These are all Dutch-made and many have been re-sited or changed since 1921, when they were illustrated in an article in *Country Life*. The tiles at Kelmscott House, which the Morris family rented from 1878, appear to be Dutch-designed and made, where they are visible in contemporary photographs of 1896. There is no record of their business connections either in the firm's accounts or those of the Dutch potteries. Only the tiles, the Dutch pattern-books and some advertisements survive.

All of these inter-related permutations and the enormous number of variations between glowing success (see cat.no.K.15a) and outright failure (see cat.no.K.7) of the firm's own production make the precise identification of tiles often difficult.

Murray Marks took a particular interest in ceramics. He supplied the painters J.M.Whistler and Rossetti with Chinese seventeenth- and eighteenth-century blue-and-white porcelain, fanning their competitive and obsessive collecting. Rossetti was himself an arbiter of taste, and in the 1860s still had influence over the youthful Morris. Morris too had a collection of such porcelain, although in general his choice of ceramics was rather wider and less obsessive. Probably he too was supplied by Marks. Over fifty items of porcelain (mostly Chinese but including some Dutch) are held at Kelmscott Manor, although there is no evidence to show how much of this collection was actually Morris's own or one assembled later. It is displayed on shelving said to have been designed by

Fig.81 Bedroom fireplace tiles at Red House (detail).

Fig.82 Panel of tiles, St John the Baptist Church, Findon, Sussex.

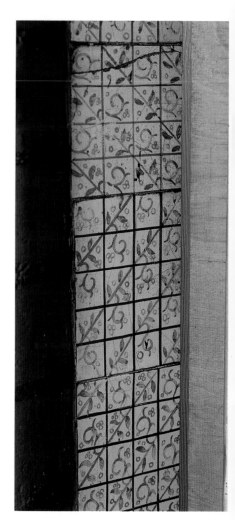

Philip Webb especially for Morris's blue-and-white-porcelain. At the same time Marks was a major international trader. The South Kensington Museum itself had dealings with him, most notably in the acquisition in 1871 of one of the largest Museum objects, the seventeenth-century rood-loft from the cathedral of St John in 's-Hertogenbosch. He also advised on the Salting Collection, perhaps the Museum's single largest and most important acquisition, with George Durlacher, a business connection of Marks's. Morris, after the Green Dining Room commission for the South Kensington Museum, was himself advising the Museum on textile purchases from around 1870. Both men therefore moved within similar social circles of influence and interest. Morris is recorded in Treffry Dunn's biography of Rossetti, as having been present – with Whistler, Rossetti, George Howard, Burne-Jones, two of the Ionides brothers and others – at a famous dinner party given by the shady Charles Augustus Howell to show off 'a magnificent piece of choice Nankin, a "dish of Imperial ware" as fine as had ever been seen', with which Howell wanted to excite Rossetti's envy. It seems an unexpected setting for the distinctly unrarified Morris.

Morris was famously a bon viveur. Surely he chose his tablewares with as much pleasure and care as he chose and enjoyed his food and wine. His preference in ceramics, as far as can be deduced from chance comments, the evidence of contemporary photographs showing rows of dishes displayed on shelves and surviving Morris-related wares, seems to have been more inclined towards earthenwares and stonewares, more colourfully decorated and less sophisticated than the precious 'Nankin' porcelain. Ceramics at Kelmscott Manor other than the blue-and-white porcelains, are 'Isnik' wares – that is Turkish earthenwares of the sixteenth and seventeenth centuries, with painted decoration in blues, reds and greens – blue-decorated Persian ceramics, sixteenth- and seventeenth-century Hispano-Moresque lustred wares, nineteenth-century Swiss and Italian painted wares and what Morris and his contemporaries called 'Grès de Flandres'. All of these are distinctive for their wealth of rich patterning. The most restrained is perhaps the Grès de Flandres, a grey-blue stoneware with scratched flat patterns decorated in dark cobalt blue and manganese purple made in the Westerwald area of Germany. It was erroneously given a Franco-Flemish name in the mid-nineteenth century, presumably because it was more fashionable and thought more subtle than a Germanic one, but Morris himself was probably not confused by this. He travelled to Germany and, if the Burne-Jones family's taste was in any way similar, the fact of Margaret Burne-Jones's donation to the Victoria and Albert Museum of slip-decorated pots brought back from the Mannheim area by her father shows an interest in, or at least no prejudice against German ceramics by one of Morris's closest friends. This disparate evidence suggests that Morris's own tableware was colourful, not too precious and collected on his travels as well as from dealers in London.

Glasswares too were investigated wherever he travelled, as is recounted by May Morris about the family's visit to a glasshouse in Murano when the glassmaker quickly produced – 'a simple little glass of slightly coloured, bubbly metal...' – Morris failed to convince him that he wanted to place a serious order. Perhaps he was less than convinced himself. After all, the Whitefriars glasshouse was in London and reliable.

He certainly had views on the design and some knowledge of glassmaking. In 'The Lesser Arts of Life' he said 'in the hands of a good workman the metal is positively alive and is, you may say, coaxing him to make something pretty. Nothing but commercial enterprise capturing the unlucky man and setting him down in the glass-maker's chair with his pattern book beside him...could turn out ugly glasses'.

The glass intended for his own use was that designed by Philip Webb specifically for Red House (see cat.no.K.24). This range was largely Germanic in taste, with overtones of Venice in its forms and its enamel decoration. It is unmistakably identifiable with the beginnings of emerging mid-nineteenth-century glass historicism. Webb was a regular visitor to the South Kensington Museum from the later 1850s, where he could have studied such Venetian and Northern European glass.

This personal tableware was to be made by James Powell & Sons' Whitefriars glassworks. Webb, as an architect, very likely had well-established contacts with the stained-glass department. Rossetti, Burne-Jones and Ford Madox Brown had all designed for Powell's stained glass during the late 1850s. The fact that only one example of this Red House range is known – and that is one of the unpainted goblets – suggests that little if any was made. The degree of time-consuming skill and the multiple processes necessary for enamelling and gilding glass and consequent expense

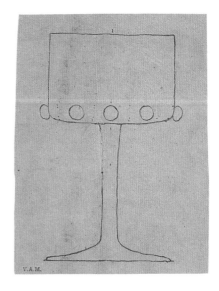

Fig. 83 Design for a claret glass, Philip Webb for Powell & Sons.

Fig. 84 Claret glass, designed by Philip Webb for Powell & Sons.

may be one reason. It may also be that Morris himself preferred unpainted glass as more in keeping with Ruskinian principles. Within a year Webb had produced designs for a much larger, plainer range for sale through the shop (cat.no.K.25). Its deceptively simple undecorated shapes formed by highly skilled hand-blowing are now seen as pioneeringly uncluttered and modernistic, although it too has its design roots in seventeenth- and eighteenth-century Venetian and Northern European glass. This sold well at first but, curiously, from 1873 to some time after 1900 there is no record of table glass made to Webb's design and supplied by Powells to the firm. A brochure produced in the 1880s makes no mention of table glass in an otherwise detailed list of stock. The firm was in financial difficulties in the mid-1870s and was reconstituted as Morris & Co. in 1875; this may be part of the explanation.

As the designs developed and moved further away from Webb's originals, his name and that of Morris were both embedded in the increasingly mythic association. Powells themselves capitalised on this. After initial caution, as the Webb glass began to be sold successfully through Morris, Marshall, Faulkner & Co. in the early years, Powell's commissioned further designs in similar taste from the architect T. G. Jackson and also evolved 'in-house' a range for standard glasshouse production, of both Webb- and Jackson-style glass. After 1900 parts of the 1862 range were re-introduced into production by Powells.

Like much to do with Morris, even glassware legends grow. There is no firm evidence that Morris either designed or made any glass. Sir Arthur Richmond, son of the painter William Blake Richmond, left an account of 'Morris in a blue blouse, untidy trousers and disordered hair and beard…in each hand he carried a large glass goblet he had just made…and pointing out their noble proportions each capable of containing nearly a bottle of champagne, goblets fit for a Viking to drink from'. As a boy, Sir Arthur remembered the occasion, probably in the 1880s, and Morris presenting the glasses to his mother. The two glasses (in a private collection) survive but are surely the work of a skilled glassmaker. They are in the form of a Dutch or German *berkemeyer* (beaker) of around 1600 – generous but not over-sized. Were they made at Powell's perhaps? There James Crofts Powell was responsible for designs inspired by paintings seen in Dutch museums in the 1880s, ten or fifteen years after Webb's first venture into such historicism. If so, it is possible that Morris, who may well have been one of the many visitors to the glassworks, had some say in the detail and size of glasses presented to him on such an occasion.

In 1866 Warington Taylor was writing to Webb of Morris: 'how is he looking – I trust well and rosy with good wine'. A year or two later, censorious of the expense of Morris's good living and the state of the firm's finances he wrote to Morris direct: 'You must reduce your wine consumption down to 2½ bottles a day – this at 1/6 is somewhere around £68 a year.'

Webb's notebooks also record substantial wine orders and it seems possible that the sizeable consumption also resulted in the need for regular replacements of the glassware. In both Webb and Burne-Jones's notebooks there are references to Morris tiles and glassware apparently being purchased or taken in payment from stock at regular intervals, presumably for their own use. In the 1860s and early 1870s, the circle of Morris's own family, friends and followers all used Powell's glass tableware. In the twentieth century a second generation of devotees continued to do so.

K.1

K.2

V&A (Circ.530-1962)
Given by the Crown Estate Commissioners

From a series of tiles based on Chaucer's *Legend of Goode Wimmen*. This panel is one of two acquired by the Museum from 1 Palace Green, the London house of George Howard, the Earl of Carlisle. As tiles, Chaucer's *Legend of Goode Wimmen* first appeared on a fireplace in Sandroyd, the house designed by Philip Webb for the painter J.R.Spencer Stanhope in 1860 and furnished thereafter. This figure was designed for windows at Birket Foster's house The Hill. Burne-Jones noted in his passbook now in the Fitzwilliam Museum in 1869: 'To touching up some Good Women and I would rather have been boiled ten times over £1.1.0.' In the Museum's panel, the figure has suffered some of the technical problems that Morris encountered in the firing of his tiles. The skilfully decorated framing *Scroll*-pattern tiles with special border painted for the Palace Green commission (see also cat.no.K.3) are the only known examples painted at MMF&Co. All other examples of the pattern, and many variations, are Dutch-made.

K.3 *Scroll* tile

Designed by William Morris or Philip Webb, *c.*1870
Morris, Marshall, Faulkner & Co.
Hand-painted in blue on a tin-glazed earthenware
Dutch blank, 15.5 x 14.0 cm
V&A (C.25-1995)

This *Scroll* tile is a relatively successfully fired example of the pattern. Under the microscope the successive layers of earthenware (the tile body), the lead glaze with added tin, both Dutch and then the MMF&Co.-applied blue enamel and the final clear glaze are all visible. The final glaze covering, which is clear but of a distinct grey-blue colour, has protected and preserved the blue underneath. This partly cut-down tile is from the same batch as that surrounding the panel of *Imago Phyllidis Martyris* (cat. no. K.2) and is therefore from the only group known of MMF&Co. decorated *Scroll*. Because they were mounted as fireplace decoration, many of the tiles in this group are seriously smoke-stained.

K.4 *Swan* tile

Originally designed by William Morris, 1862
Possibly made by Ravesteijn tileworks, Utrecht,
*c.*1880s
Tin-glazed earthenware, hand-painted with
in-glaze blue, 15.3 x 15.3 cm
British Museum (1994-5-12-1)

This tile is entirely Dutch-made. The *Swan* decoration is a version of the original pattern (see cat. no. K.10). Tiles like this example are to be found, irregularly applied, in the Green Drawing Room fireplace in Kelmscott Manor. Unfortunately there is no firm evidence as to when they were put into the fireplace, but they were certainly there during May's tenancy and possibly while Jane Morris was still alive, before 1912. They were photographed in 1921 for *Country Life* but, although the same tiles – as far as can be seen in the photograph – they have been reduced in number and re-affixed, probably when building work was done in the 1960s.

K.1 Panel of two tiles,
Imago Philomela de Atheni Martyris

Designed by Edward Burne-Jones, 1862
Morris, Marshall, Faulkner & Co. until 1868 or the early 1870s
Hand-painted in various colours on tin-glazed earthenware Dutch blanks, 30.5 x 15.3 cm
V&A (C.55-1931)
Bequeathed by J.R.Holliday

One of a series of designs based on Chaucer's *Legend of Goode Wimmen*. *Philomela* was first used at Sandroyd (see cat.no.K.2). The painted tile background includes an approximation of the *Swan* pattern (cat.no.K.4) and a fleur-de-lis.

For the brightest result, different colours can be fired at different temperatures, depending on the metallic oxides and fluxes composing them. This is a time-consuming and expensive practice and here Morris followed the more usual route of applying and firing all the colours in a single process, which can present a number of problems. On this panel, the blue has been painted on to the tin-glaze first, followed by the brown details. Although cobalt blue is a colour that can survive very high temperatures (hence its use in blue-and-white porcelain) here much of it is lost. Some is visible underneath the brown which otherwise, remarkably, survives where the blue under or around it does not. The tin-glaze is drastically discoloured on the 'tiled' background. Vallance states that 'after a first firing a soft glaze of the firm's own composition was applied to the surface of the tiles'. All the surviving painting is glossy, which may indicate the presence of the 'soft' glaze.

K.2 Panel of tiles, *Imago Phyllidis Martyris* with *Scroll* border

Designed by Edward Burne-Jones and William Morris, 1864 and *c.*1870 respectively
Morris, Marshall, Faulkner & Co.,
1868 to early 1870s
Hand-painted in various colours (the figure) and blue (*Scroll*) on tin-glazed earthenware Dutch blanks, 77.2 x 30.2 cm

K.5 Three *Daisy* tiles

Designed by William Morris, *c.*1862
a Morris, Marshall, Faulkner & Co., 1870s
Hand painted in blue and yellow on a tin-glazed earthenware Dutch blank, 13.0 x 13.0 cm
Mark: '108' painted and remains of paper label
V&A (C.58-1931) Bequeathed by J.R.Holliday
NOT ILLUSTRATED

b Morris, Marshall, Faulkner & Co., 1870s
Hand-painted in blue and yellow on a tin-glazed earthenware Dutch blank, 15.0 x 15.0 cm
Hans van Lemmen

c Made by unidentified Dutch tileworks, 1890–1914
Tin-glazed earthenware hand-painted with in-glaze colours, 15.0 x 15.0 cm
Hans van Lemmen

Both of the MMF&Co. tiles were painted on Dutch blanks. They were made by rolling out the damp clay and hand-cutting it to size by means of a template and a cutter. The lead glaze contains tin, giving it an opaque white appearance when fired. They were then decorated by Morris, Marshall, Faulkner & Co. painters at either 8 Red Lion Square (1861–5) or 26 Queen Square (1865–81). The blue and yellow was then painted on top of the already-fired Dutch glaze. The tile was then fired again at a lower temperature, 700–800°C. The glaze therefore has barely softened and consequently the colour sits on top of the background and is not fully fused into it.

Daisy was a very popular pattern and versions were also produced by the 1880s by the Dutch tile companies: Ravesteijn made this design as their pattern 438; it was made by Tjallingi of Harlingen (their number 428), in 5 and 6 inch sizes for both Dutch and English markets. The Dutch tile was decorated before any glaze firing. The glaze and decoration were fired in one operation and consequently the colours have been fully fused into the glaze and become part of it.

Birket Foster had a washstand with *Daisy* tiles which, it is thought, was bought from the 1862 exhibition, and possibly another with *Swan*-pattern tiles.

K.6 *Primrose* tile

Designed by William Morris, 1862–5
Morris, Marshall, Faulkner & Co, 1862 to early 1870s
Hand-painted in blue on tin-glazed earthenware Dutch blank, 13.0 x 13.0 cm
Mark: '102' painted
V&A (C.59-1931) Bequeathed by J.R. Holliday

Morris's inspiration for such simple flower patterns as these, used on both tiles and embroideries, came from medieval herbals as well as the eighteenth-century Dutch and English tradition of flower-painted tin-glazed tiles. No title has been identified for this pattern but it relates closely to Red House embroidery designs.

K.3

K.4

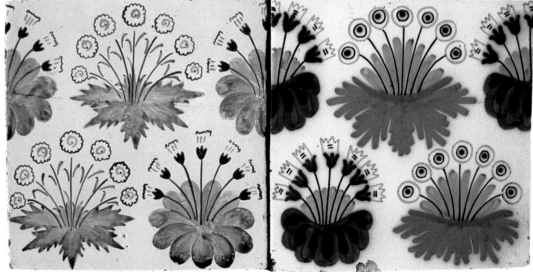

K.5b,c

K.6

K.7

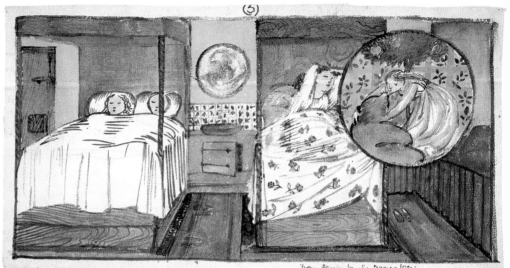

K.8a

K.9

K.7 *Summer* tile

Designed by Edward Burne-Jones, 1863–4
Morris, Marshall, Faulkner & Co., 1870s
Hand-painted in blue on tin-glazed earthenware
Dutch blanks, 15.0 x 15.0 cm
Mark: 'H C Marillier' painted in black
British Museum (1980-10-10-9)

One from a set of *The Four Seasons*. This example
formerly belonged to H.C. Marillier, who lent it to the
centenary exhibition of 1934, held in the Victoria and
Albert Museum. The design was used in the house of
the painter Myles Birket Foster (see cat.no.K.10) where
a set was mounted in panels interspersed with *Swan*
pattern. A complete set of four is in the William Morris
Gallery, Walthamstow. In this single example (as in the
Walthamstow set) the blue seems to have been painted
over the Dutch tin-glaze, without any further glazing.
The blue has flaked off leaving behind only the residual
effects of the colour on the glaze. Perhaps this problem
was caused by an inappropriate kiln (the tiles were
fired with stained glass in the enamelling kilns) and

insufficient control over temperature, atmosphere and
rates of heating. Such flaking could occur during firing
or very soon afterwards. The well-documented problems
of firing enamels on to the stained glass for which an
excess of borax was blamed may also have affected the
tiles. Insufficiently glazed tiles fixed where they were
subjected to daily wear or to extreme temperatures or
smoke would quickly deteriorate.

Exhib. 1934 (189)

K.8 Three drawings for *Beauty and the Beast* tiles

Edward Burne-Jones and Charles Fairfax Murray,
c.1863
Watercolour, pen and ink, crayon;
a 15.8 x 32.0 cm, 16.0 x 30.8 cm, 22.5 x 36.0 cm
Inscribed
V&A (E.1293,1297,1298-1931)
Bequeathed by J.R. Holliday

These tracings and others in the Museum's collections
were made probably by Charles Fairfax Murray from

now lost originals. Sketches for three of the subjects are
in the Tate Gallery collection.

Part of the Holliday bequest and, like the tiles (see
cat.no.K.9), perhaps acquired through Morris & Co.
These are Scene 3 and two versions of Scene 5, in which
Beauty appears to be having an agitated dream about
kissing the Beast whom she meets in a trellis-enclosed
bower. Philip Burne-Jones, the artist's son, added a
signed and dated note to the reverse of the coloured
scene in 1921: 'Note. These and accompanying designs
are *not* wholly – & some *not at all* – original work by
Edward Burne-Jones. They appear, here & there, to have
been touched by him, noticeably where *colour* is
employed, but in the main they seem to be tracings by an
employee of Morris & Co. – from original designs – the
date would seem to be about 1861.'

K.9 Panel of two tiles, *Beauty and the Beast*

Designed by Edward Burne-Jones, 1863
Morris, Marshall, Faulkner & Co.,
1863 to early 1870s
Hand-painted in various colours on tin-glazed
earthenware Dutch blanks, 30.5 x 15.3 cm
Mark: 'RI Tiles G/L7/1 From I/S £5.10.0'
paper label
V&A (C.54-1931) Bequeathed by J.R. Holliday.

This is the third scene in Beauty and the Beast, the full
title of which is: 'How a Prince who by enchantment
was under the form of a beast became a man again by
the love of a certain maiden.' Here Beauty is comforted
by her father before she is led in to meet the Beast. From
one of three designs for narrative panels ordered in 1862
by the painter Myles Birket Foster for his house, The
Hill (see also cat.no.K.10). The original panel of six
scenes from The Hill is now at the William Morris
Gallery, Walthamstow. Burne-Jones noted in his passbook, now in the Fitzwilliam Museum, payment of £6
and £2 for 'sets of subjects for tiles "Beauty & Beast"' in
July, August and November 1863. Orders were taken
later for panels in which the scenes, borders and title
differed from the original. It seems probable that J.R.
Holliday acquired this framed single scene and the tracings (see cat.no.K.8) direct from Morris & Co.

Curiously, it is described as 'Lear & His Daughters' in the 1931 Museum cataloguing. No reference is made to this on the acquisition papers, however.

K.10 Panel of tiles, *Sleeping Beauty* with *Swan* border tiles

Designed by Edward Burne-Jones and William Morris, 1862–5
Morris, Marshall, Faulkner & Co., 1864–5; possibly painted by Lucy Faulkner
Hand-painted in various colours on tin-glazed earthenware Dutch blanks, 76.2 x 120.6 cm
V&A (Circ.520-1953)

Entitled 'of a certain prince who delivered a King's daughter from a sleep of a hundred years, wherein she & all hers had been cast by enchantment'. One of three narrative panels, overmantels for bedrooms, ordered, with stained glass and other tiles and furnishings, in 1862 by the painter Myles Birket Foster for his new house, The Hill, at Witley, Surrey. There he was a neighbour to Henry Cole, first Director of the South Kensington Museum. Burne-Jones noted in his passbook of 1864, now in the Fitzwilliam Museum, 'To 10 designs of Sleeping Beauty at the mean and unremunerative price of 30/- each'. This panel was purchased by the Museum following their loan to the exhibition of Victorian and Edwardian Arts held in the Museum in 1952. Birket Foster left The Hill in 1893 and the lender bought this panel and *Beauty and the Beast*, which is now in the William Morris Gallery, Walthamstow, and stained glass from the last owner of the house. The third panel, *Cinderella*, is now in the Walker Art Gallery, Liverpool. As the other two are signed by Lucy Faulkner it seems likely that she also painted the Museum's panel.

The *Swan* pattern (possibly included in the 1862 exhibition, see cat.nos.K.4–5) was almost certainly designed by William Morris himself. Aymer Vallance attributed it to him as did May Morris in the catalogue, no.176, of the 1934 centenary exhibition held in the Museum.

Exhib. 1952 (I18); 1961 (6)

K.10

K.10 detail

K.11

K.12b

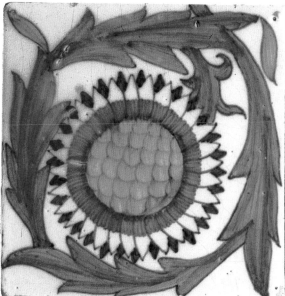

K.13

K.12 Two *Bough* tiles

Designed by William Morris, *c*.1870
Morris, Marshall Faulkner & Co., early 1870s

a Hand-painted in blue on a tin-glazed earthenware Dutch blank, 13.0 x 13.0 cm
Mark: '100'
V&A (C.57-1931)
Bequeathed by J.R. Holliday
NOT ILLUSTRATED

b Hand-painted in yellow on a tin-glazed earthenware Dutch blank,
15.3 x 14.0 cm
Private Collection

This is a recorded Morris, Marshall, Faulkner & Co. tile design, here shown in two colourways. Versions were also produced by the Dutch tile companies Ravesteijn of Utrecht (probably with Morris's approval) and Tjallingi of Harlingen by the 1880s, in 5-inch and 6-inch sizes for both Dutch and English markets, as are these Dutch blanks. William De Morgan made his own version of *Bough* known as 'Small B' or 'Small Bough'.

K.13 Two *Sunflower* tiles

Designed by William Morris, *c*.1870
a William De Morgan, *c*.1870–80
Stencilled, red lustre on an earthenware English blank, 15.3 x 15.3 cm
Hans van Lemmen

b Made by unidentified Dutch tileworks, *c*.1890
Tin-glazed earthenware hand-painted with in-glaze blue, 15.3 x 15.3 cm
Hans van Lemmen

The design for *Sunflower* was lent by Morris & Co. to the centenary exhibition held in the Victoria and Albert Museum in 1934 and was credited to Morris in the catalogue (no.196) by his daughter, May Morris.

William De Morgan set up his own works for tiles and pottery in 1869. He made tiles using several designs by William Morris, adopting them more or less unchanged. He also adapted some Morris patterns to suit his style (see cat.no.K.12). He made *Sunflower* in both coloured and, as here, in lustre glazes. The English tile is a dust-pressed glazed blank. The Dutch tile was tin-glazed and decorated and then fired in one operation. The blue decoration has therefore fused into the glaze. On the Dutch tile, possibly by Ravesteijn, Utrecht, the pattern was transferred from a paper tracing probably by 'pouncing': minute holes delineate the outline of the pattern and this outline is transferred to the tile by dabbing powdered colour through the holes on to the tile. The ruby lustre De Morgan tile had its decoration stencilled onto the already fired glaze. The metallic

K.11 *Geoffrey Chaucer* tile

Designed by Edward Burne-Jones, 1863,
said to be painted by William Morris
Morris, Marshall, Faulkner & Co.
Hand-painted in various colours on a tin-glazed earthenware Dutch blank, 15.3 x 15.3 cm
Mark: see below
V&A (C.61-1979)

The frame has a hand-written inscription on the reverse: 'Enamelled by W Morris, 1864. Very few of the tiles subsequently issued by Morris & Co. appear to have been painted by Morris himself but rather by draughtsmen employed in his works. Mr Morris told me with respect to this tile that he painted it himself. Arthur Church.'

The model for Chaucer is believed to have been Rossetti. The subject was designed for a stained-glass roundel at Birket Foster's house The Hill, which MMF&Co. decorated from 1862–4. The lettering, although typical for its period, is also similar to that on a visiting card for the dealer Murray Marks, and said to be 'the work of young William Morris'.

Professor Arthur Church (1834–1915) wrote the handbooks on *English Pottery* (1884), and *English Porcelain* (1885), for the South Kensington Museum, the forerunner of the Victoria and Albert Museum. Morris was adviser to the Museum and, possibly, the two men met through this, if no other connection.

The frame, although clearly dating from before 1915, is not contemporaneous with the tile. Despite the relevance to the Museum of the Arthur Church inscription, the tile was acquired from an untraced source via the Fine Art Society.

finish is created by introducing smoke into the kiln during the lustre firing.

K.14 *Tulip and Trellis* tile

Designed by William Morris, 1870
William De Morgan
Hand-painted in blue and green on a tin-glazed earthenware Dutch blank, 15.5 x 15.5 cm
V&A (C.220-1976)

William De Morgan set up his own tile and pottery works in 1869, after working at Morris's own Red Lion Square works providing designs for tiles and stained glass. De Morgan's sister-in-law, Mrs Stirling, recalled that he said 'Morris never made but three designs for my execution, the Tulip and Trellis, the Poppy and another – I forget the name. I never could work except by myself and in my own manner'. Although this suggests that the designs were exclusive to De Morgan, for some years *Tulip and Trellis* was made by both De Morgan (in colours) and the firm (in blue), simultaneously.

K.15 Three tiles, probably *Longden* design

Probably designed by Philip Webb
Morris, Marshall, Faulkner & Co., *c*.1870
a Hand-painted in blue on a tin-glazed Dutch earthenware blank, 15.5 x 14.0 cm
V&A (C.219-1976)
NOT ILLUSTRATED

b Two tiles, hand-painted in blue on a tin-glazed earthenware Dutch blank, 15.3 x 15.3 cm each
Mark on one: '449 Oxford Street Morris London W', after 1877
Private Collection

The *Longden* tile (15a) demonstrates how very successful the firm could be with ceramic firing. Much depends on temperature and this example was presumably fired in a reasonably hot part of the kiln. Under a microscope, the blue clearly sits on top of the tin glaze. This dispels any doubt that this is a Dutch-made tile decorated in London. Interestingly, no further glaze layer over the painting is visible. The pits or holes are probably stilt-marks. Tiles are normally fired in stacks of about six, each supported one on top of the other by tiny unglazed clay props known as 'stilts'. The confidently painted cobalt blue includes a form of gum to help it to adhere and has been thinned, possibly with water, to make possible the washed, shaded areas.

Philip Webb was paid 10s. for the *Longden* design, he noted in his account book for 1 January 1870, a year in which he records designing at least five other tile patterns. *Longden*, thought to be this oak, bayleaf and sunflower pattern, was one of the firm's most popular designs and was produced in yellow as well as blue. It was sold by Barnard, Bishop & Barnard as side panels to their cast-iron fireplace surrounds. Once the Dutch blanks were imported and decorated by the firm, they were, on occasions, marked with a printed stamp. The tile on the right, reversed to show the stamp, is decorated in the same way, with the same pattern as that on the left. Almost certainly, Morris's chief suppliers of tin-glazed blanks were Ravesteijn of Utrecht. They also made their own versions of this pattern.

K.14

K.15b

K.16

K.16 Panel of four tiles:
Two figures of medieval minstrels

Possibly designed by Edward Burne-Jones or Charles
Fairfax Murray after William Morris for Morris,
Marshall, Faulkner & Co., designed and made c.1872
Hand-painted in blue-green on tin-glazed earthen-
ware Dutch blanks, frame size 41.9 x 44.5 cm
V&A (Circ.104-1965)
Given by Novello & Co.

Possibly in its original frame, this panel of four tiles was
supplied as part of a decorative scheme to the music
publishers Novello & Co. between 1868 and 1872. Vallance
says that very few figure tiles were painted after 1870,
following Lucy Faulkner's marriage, and it is therefore
often assumed that the numbers of such subjects dwindled
after that date. However, this panel was not painted by her
and obviously other painters were employed on figure-
painting.

The earliest minstrels were designed for church tiles and
stained glass by William Morris himself, but the figures of
medieval minstrels, like the *Legend of Goode Wimmen*, were
a much-repeated and re-worked series, appearing on tiles,
stained glass and in tapestries. The Ashmolean Museum,
Oxford, owns a drawing for the *St Cecilia* design, used in
stained-glass windows at Christ Church, Oxford, attributed to Burne-Jones. This is the model for the female
player here. Another tile, a later-made version of the male
figure, is also in the Museum's collections (C.325-1927).

K.17 Four tiles

Probably designed by William Morris for Morris &
Co.; designed and made about 1875
Hand-painted in blue on tin-glazed earthenware
Dutch blanks, 15.2 x 60.8 cm
V&A (C.62&A to C-1979)

This design has not been identified so far, nor are any
other examples of the tiles known. No commission or interior has been identified with the pattern. Technically the
tiles are typical of Morris, Marshall, Faulkner & Co. and
there is no doubt that they are by the firm. They are well-
painted and stylistically compare with those for the
Membland Hall commission (see cat. no. K.19) of 1876,
which were painted at William De Morgan's pottery.

Presumably dating from about 1875, they appear to be
among the earliest of Morris & Co.'s production, following
the reorganisation of the company in that year.

K.17

K.18 Tile

Possibly designed by Kate Faulkner or John
Henry Dearle for Morris & Co.; designed
and made about 1875–80
Hand-painted in green, brown and yellow
on a tin-glazed earthenware Dutch blank,
15.3 x 15.3 cm
Marks: '5A' on edge, '711' or '144 :' on back,
painted
V&A (C.56-1931)
Bequeathed by J.R. Holliday
FOR ILLUSTRATION SEE OVERPAGE

Morris & Co.'s tiles of this pattern were used in
Stanmore Hall, Middlesex. Morris left the management of this commission and many of the
new designs required to Henry Dearle. Despite
the wealth of the commission, this tile design,
used in a fireplace, is not extravagant.
Stylistically it appears to date from some years
earlier and it was therefore apparently chosen
from 'stock'. This pattern, using brown in place
of yellow, was also made by the Dutch pottery,
Tjallingi of Harlingen, who marketed it as their
pattern 537 in the 1890s.

K.19 Panel of tiles

Designed by William Morris
William De Morgan, 1876
Slip-covered and hand-painted in various
colours and glazed, on earthenware blanks
made by the Architectural Pottery, Poole,
Dorset; 160.0 x 91.5 cm
V&A (C.36-1972)
Given by Charles and Lavinia Handley-Read

This panel is one of six surviving from
Membland Hall which was demolished in 1928.
Morris & Co. were commissioned to decorate
Membland Hall in Devon, by George Devey,
architect to the banker E.C. Baring, Baron
Revelstoke. The squared-up pattern and one
other panel is at the William Morris Gallery,
Walthamstow, with a note indicating that the
design was intended for the bathroom. It is the
only floral pattern for a tile panel on this scale by
Morris. Presumably its ambitious size (of sixty-
six individual tiles) and the need to produce a
matching set suggested to Morris that he should
turn to the better equipped De Morgan for its
production. The design remained on Morris &
Co.'s stocklists until 1912–13 and a number of
panels, other than the Membland six, are known
to have been made. At least one uses De
Morgan's own Fulham Pottery tiles. Far less
particular than Morris, De Morgan supplement-
ed his own production by using the Hamworthy
tileworks (and other commercial manufacturers
in Staffordshire and Shropshire) and the Carter
& Co. pottery, also at Poole, to supply blanks for
his own lustre- and coloured-glaze wares.

K.19

K.18

K.20

K.21

K.20 *Peony* tile

Designed by Kate Faulkner, *c*.1877
Morris & Co., *c*.1880
Hand-painted in greens and yellow on a tin-glazed earthenware Dutch
blank, 15.3 x 15.3 cm
V&A (Circ.614-1954)
Given by Miss E. Wilkinson

The *Peony* pattern for printed cotton was registered on 22 June 1877. In the textile
pattern the flowers are open to reveal their stamens and the leafy background is
more formal. However, while not identical, the similarities are close enough to suggest that the design for the tile was probably made at around the same time. Very
few tiles of this design survive. One showing the matching repeat is in the William
Morris Gallery, Walthamstow.

K.21 *Star flower* dish

Designed and decorated by Kate Faulkner for Morris & Co., 1880
Hand-painted on-glaze in blue on an earthenware blank made by Pinder,
Bourne & Co., Burslem, Stoke-on-Trent; diameter 45.0 cm
Marks: see below
V&A (C.324-1930)

Purchased from Morris & Co. in 1930, no further information came with the dish at
the time of its acquisition. Possibly 'in stock' from the 1880s it was described as
being 'painted by the late Miss Kate Faulkner'. The blank was made by Pinder,
Bourne & Co. of Nile Street, Burslem, a company founded in 1849 which had under-
gone several changes of name and which was finally purchased by Doulton in 1878.
The name was retained until 1882. The rimless form was made by many commercial
factories and was thought especially suitable as an uninterrupted surface for painted decoration. No other versions of this pattern are known on either tiles or textiles.
Painted over a commercial lead-glaze and re-fired without further glazing, the decoration has consequently been subject to some colour loss.

The plate is impressed 'KF 1880' painted; 'Morris & Co, 17 George St. Hanover Sq.,
W1' printed paper label; 'R 1297 Star flower plate Faulkner .6.6Y.Y' (or '.L.LY.Y') '£5'
handwritten in ink; 'Pinder, Bourne & Co'.

K.22 Four *Pink and Hawthorn* tiles

Possibly designed by 1887 by William Morris
William De Morgan
Slip-covered, hand-painted in colours and glazed on
earthenware blanks made by the Architectural Pottery,
Poole, Dorset; 15.5 x 15.0 cm each
Mark: Architectural Pottery Poole Dorset
V&A (C.39&A-C-1975)

Mrs Evelyn De Morgan, William De Morgan's widow,
bequeathed a large collection of De Morgan's designs and
other papers including stock lists to the Museum in 1917. Three
of these mention Morris's name:

Midsummer 1885
Stock at Morris's, Neills etc [£]100 say

Midsummer 1887
Morris patterns 35.9.1 [£] 5.12.6
5 x 5 Morris Elcho 60 @ 2/- [£] 6.0.0.

[*undated but in the same hand as that dated 1887*]
Prices of 6" Tiles
D M Tulip
Morris Tulip
"   Pink & Hawthorn

Not a typical Morris design, these tiles nevertheless appear to
be the ones described as '*Pink & Hawthorn*'. It is not clear from
De Morgan's list if the design is by Morris himself or simply a
pattern done for Morris & Co. Like others (cat.no.K.19), they
are painted on blanks made by the Architectural Pottery. The
firm is known to have produced tiles to this pattern also.

K.23 Four *Persian Flower No.77* tiles

Design copied from sixteenth-century pattern
Made by unidentified Dutch tileworks, 1880s–1930s
Tin-glazed and hand-painted on earthenware through a
stencil in colours; each 15.2 x 15.2 cm
V&A (C.205&A-C-1976)

This design is copied from a sixteenth-century Turkish (Iznik)
pattern. From the 1880s (at 12s. per dozen) until possibly as late
as the 1930s it was sold in Britain by the London retailer,
Thomas Elsley, Portland Metal Works, as suitable for fireplace
surrounds. It was made in at least two colourways, and examples in blue and yellow (pattern No.77A) surround a fireplace
in the room at Kelmscott Manor. The date of their appearance
at Kelmscott is unknown, but they were certainly there during
May Morris's tenancy and possibly as early as the turn of the
century, during Jane Morris's lifetime.

K.22

K.23

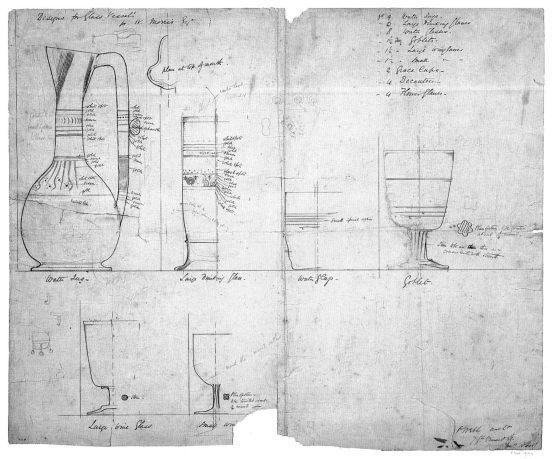

K.24

K.24 Sheet of designs for table glass for Red House

Philip Webb for James Powell & Sons, dated January 1860
Pencil, pen and wash, 53.0 x 66.0 cm
Inscribed: 'Designs for Glass Vessels for W. Morris Esq' and other notes
V&A (E.340-1944)
Given by Miss Dorothy Walker

By January 1860 Philip Webb had designed a set of table glass intended for William Morris's personal use at Red House. These were to be made by James Powell & Sons, Whitefriars Glassworks.

The historicism of these designs was relatively avant-garde for its time. Fully developed historicism appeared in glass some two or three years later and then was largely Italian-based. Historic influences here range from Roman, in the use of thinly trailed lines of hot glass, to seventeenth-century German and eighteenth-century English in the shapes. Painted enamel decoration makes an unexpected appearance and may have been derived from either Venetian or German examples which Webb – and Morris – could have seen in the South Kensington Museum. Webb was a regular visitor from 1859 and by that date the Museum had over 350 glass vessels – many of them as part of the Bernal and Soulages collections – of which the majority were Venetian and North European. Enamelled decoration may have appealed to Morris for its affinity with medieval illustrations in its minutely jewel-like gilding and preciousness, although it was in direct confrontation with Ruskin's influential principle of allowing undecorated glass to speak for itself.

Only one example of table glass is known that precisely matches the Red House designs; this is a goblet in Birmingham Museum, bequeathed by May Morris.

K.25 Five items of table glass

Designed by Philip Webb for James Powell & Sons, Whitefriars
Hand-blown and part mould-blown
a Tumbler, possibly 1862–3
9.3 x 7.8 cm
V&A (C.261-1926)
Given by Mrs J.Mackail
b Goblet, 1860
12.8 x 7.5 cm
V&A (C.263-1926)
Given by Mrs J. Mackail
c Finger bowl, possibly 1862–3
9.0 x 14.0 cm
V&A (C.79-1939)
Bequeathed by May Morris
d Champagne glass, 1862–3
15.5 x 8.2 cm
V&A (C.80A-1939)
Bequeathed by May Morris
e White-wine glass, possibly 1862–3
13.0 x 7.0 cm
V&A (C.81-1939)
Bequeathed by May Morris

K.25

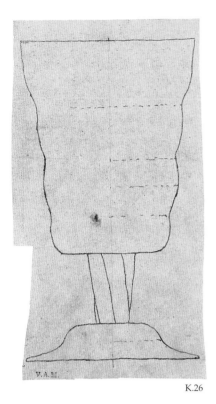

K.26   K.27   K.28

By December 1862, when glassware features significantly in MMF&Co. balance sheets, Webb had extended and amended the 'Red House designs' (see cat.no.K.24) to form a much plainer range for sale by MMF&Co., for whom they were made exclusively by Powells. Curiously, despite its importance in the firm's accounts, very little of this range has survived.

Among these designs (see cat.no.K.26) only the goblet in this group appears. The goblet, in six different sizes, was exhibited by Powells in their Wigmore Street showroom in 1927 and illustrated in an article in *The Studio*.

The champagne glass corresponds to a sketch, part of a list of entries in Philip Webb's passbook, probably of 1862.

The tumbler, finger bowl and white-wine glass are all distantly related to the known Webb designs.

All of this glass forms part of the gift from Mrs Mackail (Burne-Jones's daughter) and the bequest from May Morris, Morris's daughter. May's continued occupation of Kelmscott Manor after her parents' death until her own lends considerable weight to their provenance, suggesting the possibility that some of the items may have been chosen by Jane or William.

Exhib. 1934 (226,227,228); 1952 (184); 1961 (18)

K.26 Two designs for table glass

Philip Webb for James Powell & Sons, *c.*1862
Pen; 14.0 x 10.2 cm, 14.8 x 8.1 cm
V&A (E.330 and 333-1944)
Given by Miss Dorothy Walker
SEE ALSO FIG.83, PAGE 184

By 1862, Webb was converting the more elaborate, enamelled designs for Morris's own use (see cat.no.K.24) into a plainer range, which relied for its

decorative effect on hot-worked glass. These two line drawings are from a group of seven in the Museum's collections. Glasses to these two designs are in the Museum – the goblet (see cat.no.K.25b) – and Birmingham Museum and Art Gallery – the 'claret' glass. Both also appear among sketches in Philip Webb's passbook where the 'claret' glass is described as having 'green spots'. The drawings for the rummer-style goblets are marked '3/2d' which could be the fee paid to Webb for the design or the cost of the glass when made; the 'claret' glass with applied prunts or spots (see figs.83–4) is marked '2/3d'.

K.27 Pair of Candlesticks

Designed by Philip Webb, 1861–3
Made by Morris, Marshall, Faulkner & Co.
Copper, 26.7 x 17.8 cm diameter
V&A (M.1130 & A-1926)
Purchased from J.W. Mackail

Although 'Metal work in all its branches including Jewellery' was one of the five categories advertised by Morris, Marshall, Faulkner & Co. in their 1861 prospectus, these candlesticks are a rarity. Problems with technique or in finding a suitable manufacturer willing to undertake small-scale production may have been the cause. However, these candlesticks were popular with the partners. Designed originally for William and Jane Morris for Red House (and both copper and brass examples survive at Kelmscott Manor) this pair was purchased from the firm by Burne-Jones. Webb's account book lists a design for candlesticks on 28 June 1863, for which he charged £1 10s.

Jewellery was designed by Rossetti and Burne-Jones, whose grandfather Benjamin Coley was a Birmingham jeweller, but none made under the firm's name. The

Victoria and Albert Museum has a collection of items designed by May Morris and by Rossetti for Jane Morris.

Exhib. 1961 (19)   ET/LP

K.28 Table Lamp

Designed and manufactured by William Arthur Smith Benson, *c.*1890
Originally supplied through Morris & Co.'s shop
Brass and copper, height 68.5 cm
V&A (Circ.21 to C-1961) Given by Miss H.M. Beale

W.A.S.Benson (1854–1924) initially trained as an architect in the office of Basil Champneys. It was through his friendship with Burne-Jones that he met Morris, who persuaded him to set up a workshop for the manufacture of turned metalwork in 1880. The firm prospered and survived until his retirement in 1920. Benson designed his goods almost exclusively for mechanical production and had been interested in engineering since boyhood. Benson became chairman of Morris & Co. on Morris's death and remained a member of the board for some time. Through him H.C. Marillier, a previous partner, became Managing Director.

Benson's fittings became an integral part of many Morris & Co. interiors – either bought directly from the Morris & Co. shop or simply seen as a congenial accessory. Many important houses owned such fittings and this example was part of the 1890s decorations of Standen, East Grinstead.   ET

WALLPAPER

Lesley Hoskins

'The poet and paper-maker' was how Henry James described Morris in 1881 and it was in wallpaper that Morris first achieved his mastery of flat, repeating pattern. This was in spite of Morris's often-stated belief that the medium was a mere 'makeshift' and that 'printing patterns on paper for wall hangings' was only a 'quite modern and very humble, but, as things go, useful art' ('The Lesser Arts of Life', 1882).

Wallpapers were not offered in the first prospectus produced by Morris, Marshall, Faulkner & Co., but by 1862 plans were under way for their introduction, making them the second item of serial production after glass tableware. Morris, helped by Philip Webb, worked the first design in November. The intention was to print at Red Lion Square using etched zinc plates and oil-based inks; early accounts show that paper and plates were to hand by Christmas (cat.no.D.1). This was not an established method of printing wallpaper and it is hard to visualise the technique and its results. Morris was perhaps aiming at producing transparent washes of colour (later successfully achieved with the use of watercolour). However, this attempt proved tedious and unsatisfactory and the decision was taken to print by the traditional wood-block process (see cat.no.L.27) widely used for the production of high-quality papers.

The blocks were cut by Barrett's in the Bethnal Green Road, an old-established family business specialising in this work. Transferring a design to a set of blocks (called 'putting on') requires skill and sensitivity if the intention of the original is to be kept, and it appears that MMF&Co. dealt directly with Barrett's rather than allowing the printer to supervise. A letter from Warington Taylor states that the cost of cutting the twelve blocks for the *Pomegranate* pattern was £15, plus £1 10s. for trial proofs.

Printing was contracted out to Jeffrey & Co., one of about fifteen English paperhanging manu-facturers showing at the International Exhibition of 1862. Jeffrey's had been printing Owen Jones's own patterns since the beginning of the 1860s and therefore already had experience of dealing with this type of 'private' work. They managed MMF&Co.'s papers separately and maintained special logbooks recording all the published patterns and colourways, each with their own number. (The logs, now held in the Sanderson Archive, are a valuable source of information, but it is not wise to rely on them too heavily for dating the earliest papers, as the books were probably not instigated until the late 1860s or early 1870s.) Details of the arrangement between the two companies are not known, but it seems from Taylor's correspondence that, in the late 1860s, MMF& Co. would take an initial one hundred rolls of a new pattern or colourway for stock. This was a sizeable amount and, as Taylor pointed out, expensive. With the exception of certain special effects (wash, flock, mica and lacquer) the printing medium was distemper, that is pigment carried in a water-based medium of size or whiting, giving a somewhat thick and chalky result. Many of the colours were manufac-tured chemically but a huge number of shades was achievable and there is no evidence for the kind of problems that arose with textile printing.

The reported smoothness of the relationship between the two firms owed much to Metford Warner, who joined Jeffrey's as a junior partner in 1866 and was sole proprietor by 1871. Warner was an enthusiast for good new design and saw its commercial potential, making his company the most highly regarded wallpaper manufacturer of the last quarter of the nineteenth century. He later recalled Morris as characteristically forceful: 'tell them "not to improve my colourings" was a message I had to convey to the factory from the master in blue blouse – bare feet in slippers and hands blue from the dye vat.' (V&A, NAL 86.HH.13) He testified elsewhere that Morris took the greatest personal interest in production and allowed nothing to pass until he was quite satisfied that it was right both in colour and design (*Journal of the Society of Arts*, XLVI, May 1898, pp.629–30); he remembered a case where Morris had an entire set of expensive blocks put aside because he was not satisfied with the design. Some of the artwork (e.g. cat.no.L.9) bears very detailed colour notes for the printer. But there are indications of collaboration too; in the early 1870s Jeffrey's did experimental wash printing on Morris's behalf, with some success, while in the late 1870s Morris adopted the imitation leathers that Jeffrey's had perfected. Jeffrey & Co. continued to print the firm's papers until 1927 when it went out of business and its work was taken over by Arthur Sanderson & Sons Ltd.

By 1862 the wallpaper industry was booming. National production rose from 1,222,753 rolls in 1834 to 32,000,000 in 1874 and paperhangings were a standard decorative item at all levels of the market. Morris, Marshall, Faulkner & Co. entered at the upper end, which was dominated by two stylistic types: 'French' and 'reformed'. The former included realistic (almost super-realistic) floral bunches or trails and imitation textiles – moirés, watered silks, ribbon trellises and upholstery

trimming borders. They were pretty, sugary confections on pale satin grounds. Many were French imports but some very creditable attempts at the genre were made by such English companies as William Woollams. The designs were produced anonymously by the block cutter/designer or were bought in France. In economic, aesthetic and moral opposition to these were the English patterns issuing from the Design Reform movement. With their abhorrence of realism, their insistence on the conventionalisation of natural forms and their respect for the flatness of the wall, they are exemplified by the work of Owen Jones, who had been designing wallpapers since about 1840, both for decorative commissions and for general sale.

It has been said that between 1855 and 1873 'informed taste' abandoned naturalism in favour of 'reform'. But a glimpse at the order books of the decorating firm Cowtan & Sons (held in the V&A) shows that 'French' patterns were favoured by its aristocratic and upper-class clientele. The printing records of Jeffrey & Co. for 1862 also show a preponderance of pretty florals and pale trellis or diaper patterns.

Morris's first three papers, *Trellis*, *Daisy* and *Pomegranate* (also known as *Fruit*), issued between 1864 and 1866/7 (cat.nos.L.1–3), were closely associated with the informal medievalism of the early firm. Although, in their use of fruit and flowers, they had something in common with the 'naturalistic' type and, in their strong colouring and conventionalisation of nature, they were akin to 'reformed' patterns, they were sufficiently different from both kinds that it is difficult to know just where they fitted into the market. An anecdote related by Lady Mount Temple in her *Memorials* (1890, pp. 64–5) gives a clue. Referring to the time around 1865, she describes the 'French' decoration of her London house – 'watered papers on the walls, garlands of roses tied with blue bows! Glazed chintzes with bunches of roses…' Rossetti came to dinner and was asked his opinion. '"Well," he said frankly, "I should begin by burning everything you have got".' Shortly afterwards, she wrote, when the staircase needed renovation, the firm did it up with a Morris paper on the walls and a Burne-Jones stained glass in the window. In addition, in September 1865, Morris's grey

Fig.86 A room at The Grange, showing *Jasmine* wallpaper and Morris & Co. furnishings. The photograph was part of a set taken of the house by Frederick Hollyer in 1887.

Fig.87 The stairs at 1 Holland Park showing *Pink and Poppy* wallpaper from a photograph by Harry Bedford Lemere (see cat.no.I.18).

Daisy pattern was installed in one of the attic rooms by Cowtan & Sons, whose order books reveal this to be a completely isolated example at the time. Lady Mount Temple goes on to say: 'Now our taste was attacked on the other side, and all our candid relations and friends intimated that they thought we had made our pretty little house hideous.'

A more likely milieu for Morris papers in the early days was the sort offered by Frederick Leyland, the Liverpool shipping magnate and patron of the arts, who had close connections with Rossetti. *Daisy*, *Trellis* and *Pomegranate* were used at Speke Hall, his house near Liverpool, in about 1867. Morris papers were also used for his famously decorated London houses in the late 1860s and 1870s. Similarly, E.W. Godwin's designs for a wall decoration for Dromore Castle, County Limerick, of about 1869, which use the *Trellis* pattern, also locate the patterns in artistic circles. The clientele at this stage certainly seems to have been very small (Warington Taylor wrote to Webb about the 'limited sale of our papers') and the marketing personal; Mackail describes 'visits made to Queen Square in its first days by purchasers who had accidently [*sic*] seen some of his [Morris's] wall-papers'. Rossetti's contacts were most useful.

The first three patterns were followed in the late 1860s by a small group of a very different type. *Diaper* (cat. no. L.5), designed by Morris, is a straightforward, two-colour, non-directional, tile pattern, useful as a companion paper or on its own. *Venetian*, *Indian* (cat. no. L.4), *Spray* and *Queen Anne* are adaptations of eighteenth-century examples, at least some of which were provided by a group of architects associated with G.F. Bodley. These papers, using only one or two light fresh colours each, were cheaper than the earlier designs and less challenging to use. W.R. Lethaby later said, in *Philip Webb and his Work* (1935), that they were an early manifestation of the 'Queen Anne' decorative style, which was also much influenced by Morris's use of white paint in his drawing room at Queen Square.

It was in the 1870s, however, that Morris definitively mastered designing for wallpaper and that the firm widened its range to attract a variety of customers. *Scroll and Branch* (*c*.1870), is the first pattern based on a structure that was used a great deal for the next ten years and from time to time thereafter. The design is built up in two layers, in this case an all-over background of foliage over-laid with vertically scrolling stems whose curling offshoots bear flowers. In *Scroll and Branch* the two layers remain rather separate (indeed, the backprint could be had as a pattern in its own right) but at its most successful, as in *Jasmine* (cat. no. L.7), 1872, or *Vine* (cat. no. L.8), designed about 1873, the background and foreground are sufficiently interwoven to provide a complex all-over pattern with a shallow depth. Morris also used this structure for printed textiles (e.g. *Tulip and Willow*, 1873), but it is particularly suited for wallpaper, a flat and unforgiving medium.

At the same time, some simpler or cheaper patterns were introduced. *Lily* and *Powdered*, both 1874, return to the sprightly freshness of *Daisy*. *Willow*, 1874, is a stylised all-over foliage pattern, very similar to the back-print of *Vine*. Less susceptible to the layered approach were the mono-chrome designs *Larkspur* (cat. no. L.6), 1872, and *Marigold*, of about 1875. Writing to Morris about the break up of the firm, Rossetti adds a postcript – 'I have been making a pattern for a new colouring of the marigold paper and will send it with remarks' – which shows that he still had some involve-ment in the firm's activities (Hammersmith and Fulham Archives Department, DD/235/2). The mid-1870s also saw the introduction of a new palette, less colourful and more 'aesthetic' – pale terracottas and greeny-blues for example – both for new patterns and for additional versions of old ones. Some designs were issued in transparent watercolour wash.

Acanthus, designed 1874 (cat. no. L.11), marks the start of a period of rich effects. Here and in *Pimpernel*, *Wreath*, *Rose* and *Chrysanthemum* (1876–7) are vigorous curves and scrolls of foliage and flowers; the colours are deep and sombre; hatching and veining gives some three-dimensionality. Techniques of embossing, metalling and lacquering were then developed and were used for *Vine* and *Chrysanthemum* (cat. nos. L.8, 22). *Sunflower* (cat. no. L.15) and *Acorn*, two new, rather rigid, single-colour designs of 1879, were issued from the very beginning as gold-ground papers as well as distemper prints. Although they show traces of the firm's early medievalism, they probably owed more to the growing fashion for papers imitating embossed and gilded leather. Excellent examples had been available from a French company, Balin, since the mid-1860s but by the later 1870s they were also produced by several English firms, not least Jeffrey & Co. The firm used gold-ground versions of *Sunflower* and *Acorn* in its work for the Howards at 1 Palace Green and Castle Howard

Fig.88 The Grand Staircase at St James's Palace.

though there were problems with the colours on both occasions. It is not known whether the gold-ground versions were specially developed for the Howards and then put into the range or *vice versa*, but the *St James's* pattern (cat.no.L.18) designed for the entrances and banqueting room at St James's Palace, 1880–81, subsequently entered the standard range and is known to have been used elsewhere, for example in H.F.Makins's house in Queen's Gate. Perhaps the proliferation of rich effects at the end of the 1870s and beginning of the 1880s was influenced by the several lavish commissions that the firm was undertaking at the time.

In the late 1870s Morris was willing to relax his hold a little and, of the nine new patterns between *Chrysanthemum* and *St James's*, four were designed by Kate Faulkner. One of them, *Carnation* of 1880 (cat.no.L.16), was a machine-print. Morris himself seems to have been contemplating designing for machine at about this time, but in the end only one other roller-print, *Merton* (1888), also designed by Faulkner, was issued during his lifetime. The cheaper papers that fleshed out the range at the Oxford Street showroom were the work of other manufacturers.

At the end of the decade the firm had 32 patterns (125 ways) on offer, costing from 2s. 6d. for a machine-print to 40s. per roll for a gold-ground paper. The ordinary hand-prints ran from 3s. to 16s. (prices are taken from a catalogue of *c*.1915, but are the same as amounts quoted in a bill of 1888 for decoration of 1 Holland Park). It has been suggested that Morris & Co.'s goods were expensive, but their papers, while certainly at the upper end of the market, were in the same sort of range as Sanderson's which, in the 1870s, was distributing French hand-printed papers for between 4s. 6d. and 16s. a piece and which around 1880 was selling its own single-colour block-prints for 3s. or 3s. 6d. Morris & Co. papers were distributed by their London (and after 1883, Manchester) showrooms and, from 1873, by J.F.Bumstead & Co. and, later, by A.H.Davenport & Co. in North America. They showed in exhibitions at home and abroad. The patterns were recommended in numbers of books on decorating, such as *The Drawing Room* (1878), by Mrs Orrinsmith (Kate Faulkner's sister), and *The Decoration of Town Houses* (1881), by Colonel R.Edis.

The papers were commercially successful but, perhaps more importantly, they played a significant part in raising the status of English wallpaper to a position of international pre-eminence in the last quarter of the nineteenth century. Morris had been one of the first to take wallpaper design out of anonymity and it was possibly his example that encouraged Metford Warner to commission patterns from important architects and designers. From 1871 onwards the Jeffrey & Co. logbooks show a fast increasing number of 'art' patterns (Arts and Crafts, Gothic, Japanesque) which, by about 1875, had completely ousted the previously dominant 'French' styles. Some of them were clearly influenced by Morris's designs (especially the first three); good examples are Bruce Talbert's *Fruit* frieze, 1877, and Walter Crane's *Margarete*, which won a prize at the Philadelphia Centennial Exhibition in 1876. Other companies followed suit; mass manufacturers took up the Arts and Crafts style – by 1884 'Morrisonian' had become a recognisable term throughout the trade; press coverage increased and paperhangings had a heyday.

Although Morris contributed to the spate of 'art' wallpapers he remained unconvinced by the rampant 'artistic' fashion of using different patterns for dado, filling, frieze, ceiling and borders. His views on the appropriate use of paper are given in his lecture of about 1879, 'Making the Best of It', and, in great detail, in Wardle's brochure for the firm's display at the Foreign Fair, Boston, in 1883. He suggested that, unless a room was very high, the division of the wall into two – either with a dado of about 4 ft. 6 in. or with a narrow frieze – was quite enough. 'Never stoop to the ignominy of the paper dado'; 'Our wallpapers…are simple fillings: they imitate no architectural features, neither dados, friezes, nor angles'; 'I have seen a good deal of the practice of putting pattern over pattern in paperhanging, and it seems to me a very unsatisfactory one.' Only one pattern should be used in a room. A second one was just permissible if it merely broke the surface colour. He disliked papered ceilings – 'a room papered all over would be like a box to live in'. But, in the face of fashionable usage, the firm compromised to an extent, offering several special ceiling papers and suggesting the use of some of the single-colour patterns, such as *Diaper*, *Venetian*, *Mallow*, and *Bird and Anemone*. The yellow and pale-green ways were said to be the most suitable. Similarly, although during Morris's lifetime the firm never issued any frieze designs, it was proposed that *Daisy*, *Fruit*, *Larkspur*, *Apple* and *Sunflower* could be adapted for this purpose. The Boston brochure also made suggestions for complementary paint colours.

In his own rooms, Morris used paper very simply, sometimes merely running it from skirting to ceiling (see fig.85). Linda Parry's discussion of the commissioned schemes shows some richer effects, while in the houses of ordinary customers there was nothing to prevent the papers being used in complex and cluttered 'artistic' schemes. A fine example can still be seen at 18 Stafford Terrace, London.

Between 1882 and 1896 the firm issued a further thirty-five new patterns in a variety of types and prices. But by this time the papers were no longer Morris's main concern and tend to reflect his other aesthetic interests. *Bird and Anemone* (cat.no.L.20), for example, was a pattern of the same name and design as the first textile to be printed at Merton Abbey. From 1884 onwards many (but not all) of the papers, like the printed textiles, showed a structure based on diagonally meandering stems; layering was reduced in favour of backgrounds dotted or covered with tiny stylised flowers and trails.

A curious development of 1887–8 was the introduction of flocking, a technique originated in about 1700 to simulate wall hangings of cut velvet or silk damask. Morris & Co. used it only for the textile-based patterns, *Indian*, *Venetian* and *Bruges* (cat.no.L.25), and for two particularly rigid, non-naturalistic designs, *Autumn Flowers* (1888), and *Ceiling*. Powdered mica grounds were also introduced at this point, in some cases combined with flocking. It is hard to imagine these innovations as Morris's own. He was at this time actively involved in politics, and a letter of February 1887 to his wife suggests that his heart was far from the day-to-day development of the range: 'Smith is insisting on paper-hangings so I must do one at least, besides those I have in hand'. Dearle was increasingly in charge of the production side. Faulkner produced one more pattern, *Blossom*, in 1885; May Morris made two or three designs – *Arcadia*, of about 1886, and *Horn Poppy*, of 1885, both use her father's diagonal structure, the latter being very similar to his *Fritillary* of the same year. Dearle's first known pattern is *Iris*, 1887–8; thereafter his contribution increased considerably, although his emulation of Morris's style makes some attributions difficult. Morris's diary, however,

Fig.89 The Antiquities Room in
1 Holland Park (see cat.no.I.18).

shows that he was still designing wallpaper in 1895. By the time of his death he had been responsible for approximately seventy patterns, of which about fifty were his own work. This is a tiny output compared with the major manufacturers who regularly issued hundreds a year, but Morris never believed in fashion. (His work was, willy-nilly, fashionable.) Even after his death, the firm continued to offer the old patterns, going to great lengths to standardise colourings to the original versions. Initially, additional designs and ways were much in Morris's own style but, within a few years, current taste began to have an effect. The last pattern of all, though, *Bird and Pomegranate*, issued in 1927, was, as the name suggests, a return to the very earliest imagery.

L.1 *Trellis* wallpaper

a Original design William Morris, birds drawn by
Philip Webb, November 1862
Pencil and watercolour, 66.0 x 61.0 cm
William Morris Gallery
(London Borough of Waltham Forest) (BLA472)

b Wallpaper sample, *Trellis, 9*
Designed by William Morris, birds by Philip Webb,
registered 1 February 1864
Printed by Jeffrey & Co. for Morris, Marshall,
Faulkner & Co.
Block-printed in distemper colours, 68.6 x 50.0 cm
V&A (E.452-1919)
Given by Morris & Co.

The precise date of this, Morris's first wallpaper design,
is given by Mackail (p.156). The layout is complete but
additional detailing would have been necessary for
etching or block cutting. As in the other early patterns,
there is some depth in the drawing but no integration
between the motifs and the ground.

Flower trellises also appear elsewhere in the work of
Morris and his associates, for example in 1862 stained
glass for St Helen's, Darley Dale (cat.no.H.6) and All
Saints, Selsley, and in Burne-Jones's 1863 sketch design
for an embroidery for Ruskin illustrating Chaucer's
Legend of Goode Wimmen. Mackail (p. 143) describes the
'wattled rose-trellises inclosing richly-flowered square
garden plots' at Red House. This is a typical medieval
garden plan, illustrated in numerous manuscripts.

The delay between design and registration was a result
of the firm's attempt to print using oil colours and
etched zinc plates. After the failure of this previously
untried method, production was handed over to Jeffrey
& Co., a reputable wallpaper manufacturer, who used
the standard woodblock process and distemper colours.

Morris remained fond of the early, simple patterns and
hung a blue-ground version of *Trellis* in his bedroom at
Kelmscott House.

L.1a

L.2 Wallpaper sample, *Daisy, 2*

Designed by William Morris, registered 1 February
1864
Printed by Jeffrey & Co. for Morris, Marshall,
Faulkner & Co.
Block-printed in distemper colours, 68.6 x 50.0 cm
V&A (E.442-1919)
Given by Morris & Co.

According to Mackail (p.156), *Daisy* was designed after
Trellis but published first. There is no attempt to dress
up the repeat of the simple pattern with its free-stand-
ing clumps of meadow flowers on a grass-like ground.
Nevertheless, *Daisy* was one of the most consistently
popular of the firm's papers, still selling well nearly
fifty years after it was issued.

The first three wallpapers - *Trellis, Daisy* and *Fruit* –
were all, from an early date, offered on a light, a
medium and a dark ground. Further colourings were
added later. This colourway was called *Light Daisy*.

The source of the pattern can be seen in a wall hanging
illustrated in a fifteenth-century version of Froissart's
Chronicles (BL Ms 4380, fol.1). The hangings embroidered for the bedroom at Red House, 1860, used similar
flower groups though on a larger scale (cat.no.M.6).

L.3 Wallpaper sample, *Fruit*
(also known as *Pomegranate*), 5

Designed by William Morris; designed and first
issued c.1866
Printed by Jeffrey & Co. for Morris, Marshall,
Faulkner & Co.
Block-printed in distemper colours, 68.6 x 50.0 cm
V&A (E.446-1919)
Given by Morris & Co.

This pattern is usually given an earlier date because the
serial numbering in the printing log places it between
Daisy and *Trellis*. Mackail, however, states (p.176) that
Morris was seen at Queen Square working on the
design for *Pomegranate* in 1866. Mackail's notes also
show that Campfield, the firm's foreman, recollected
the design being made at Queen Square (i.e. no earlier

than 1865). There are strong resemblances between *Fruit*
and the painted panels that form part of the decoration
of the Green Dining Room at the South Kensington
Museum, 1866. A letter from Warington Taylor, probably
of 1867 (NAL 86.SS.57) calls it 'our last new paper'.

The design is built up of the repetition of four rectangular elements. It appears more complex than *Daisy* because
of the diagonally thrusting branches and because leaves
from each rectangle creep into the adjoining spaces.
Two versions for the design are recorded (see The Arts
Council, *Morris and Company Centenary*, 1961) but their
current whereabouts are unknown.

L.1b

L.2

L.3

L.4 Wallpaper sample, *Indian, Red Indian*

Possibly designed by George Gilbert Scott,
first issued 1868–70
Printed by Jeffrey & Co. for Morris, Marshall,
Faulkner & Co.
Block-printed in distemper colour (also available
as a two-colour print), 68.6 x 50.0 cm
V&A (E.3706-1927)
Given by Morris & Co.

'Mural Decoration' in *The Encyclopaedia Britannica*,
XVII, 1884, by Morris and Professor Middleton, illustrates the source of this pattern, describing it as an
'Early 18th-century wall-paper'. It is one of a group of
four designs (the others are *Queen Anne*, *Spray* and
Venetian), adapted from earlier examples, which were
possibly designed by G. F. Bodley and his associates.

Similarities between the firm's group of adapted
patterns and the early papers of Watts & Co., founded
in 1874 by Bodley, George Gilbert Scott Jnr. and
Thomas Garner, tend to support the connection and a
generally accurate account of Bodley's career (E.
Warren, 'The Life and Work of George Frederick
Bodley', *Journal of the RIBA*, 3rd ser., 17, 1910,
pp. 305–36) states that he had designed one or two of
William Morris's early wallpapers.

Warington Taylor refers (V&A NAL) to a wallpaper
as 'Scott's "Indian"', which perhaps suggests that
George Gilbert Scott Jnr. was the designer.

Spray and *Queen Anne* were based on samples found
by Chambrey Corker Townshend (see V&A NAL and
Townshend Nominal File), who had been a pupil in
the office of G. E. Street, also an associate of Bodley
and Scott.

L.4

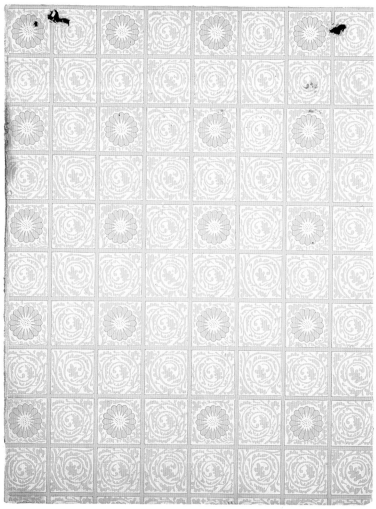

L.5

L.6b

L.5 Wallpaper sample, *Diaper, 18*

Designed by William Morris, first issued 1868–70
Printed by Jeffrey & Co. for Morris, Marshall,
Faulkner & Co.
Block-printed in distemper colours, 68.6 x 50.0 cm
V&A (E.458-1919) Given by Morris & Co.

Although an original design, *Diaper* sits happily with
the group of adapted patterns of similar date. One of
Warington Taylor's letters shows that it was issued
before *Indian* and *Queen Anne*.

Initially produced in two colourways, yellow and olive,
another seven were added in the 1870s. In most cases
the printed colours were only slightly deeper than the
ground. Morris disapproved of using more than one
paper in a room but, if a second was required, he
recommended using a pattern like this. A non-directional design, it was also suitable for use as a ceiling paper.

L.6 *Larkspur* wallpaper

a Sample, *Larkspur, 28*
Designed by William Morris, first issued *c*.1872
Printed by Jeffrey & Co. for Morris, Marshall,
Faulkner & Co.
Block-printed in one distemper colour, 68.0 x 52.5 cm
V&A (E.468-1919)
Given by Morris & Co.
NOT ILLUSTRATED

b Sample, *(Light) Larkspur, 46*
Designed by William Morris. First issued *c*.1875
Printed by Jeffrey & Co. for Morris, Marshall,
Faulkner & Co.
Block-printed in distemper colours, 67.8 x 52.6
V&A (E.472-1919)
Given by Morris & Co.

A lightly meandering vertical stem carries curving
sprays of foilage; the individual repeating unit is disguised. A similar format appears in *Scroll, c*.1871, and
Marigold, c.1875.

Larkspur was first issued as a monochrome paper. A
single-colour version was registered as a printed textile
in April 1875. Similarly, *Marigold*, another monochrome
design, was registered as a wallpaper in 1875 (its
design was well under way by late 1874) and as a fabric
later in the same year (cat.no.M.46).

Although the detailing helps to break up monotony, the
later multi-coloured version is more successful. The
veining on the flowers, variations in the green and a
dotted background gives a pretty pattern with depth
and variety.

L.7b

L.7 *Jasmine* wallpaper

a Original design
William Morris, *c*.1872
Pencil and watercolour, 90.3 x 64.1 cm
William Morris Society, Kelmscott House, London
(D3)

b Wallpaper sample, *Jasmine*, 31
Designed by William Morris, first issued 1872
Printed by Jeffrey & Co. for Morris, Marshall,
Faulkner & Co.
Block-printed in distemper colours, 68.6 x 50.0 cm
V&A (E.475-1919) Given by Morris & Co.

This is a fine example of the design structure perfected
by Morris in the early 1870s. The background is an all-
over pattern of hawthorn leaves, blossoms and
branches on a disguised vertical meander. A scrolling
tracery of jasmine, delicately but clearly defined, provides the foreground. The two layers are so well
integrated that, from a distance, the paper gives an
effect of subtle broken colour. One of the firm's earliest
printed textiles was *Jasmine Trail* and Morris's first
known fabric design was *Jasmine Trellis* (cat.no.M.38).
Both are, however, much less complex designs than the
paper.

There are three other known drawings for this wallpaper: one is at Birmingham Museum and Art Gallery and
two are in the Berger Collection.

The many deletions and substitutions in the printing
record indicate initial difficulties with the pattern and it
appears that the the number of blocks used for its production was reduced from twenty to eleven. Attempts
made in 1874 to print it in wash colours seem to have
been unsuccessful.

The Burne-Jones's used *Jasmine*, probably in this colourway, in the drawing-room at The Grange, their house in
Fulham (see fig.86).

L.7a

L.8c

L.8a

L.8 *Vine* wallpaper

a Original design
William Morris, *c*.1873
Pencil and watercolour, 81.5 x 65.2 cm
Inscribed with instructions
V&A (E.1074-1988)

b Wallpaper sample, *Vine, 50*
Designed by William Morris, first issued 1874
Printed by Jeffrey & Co. for Morris, Marshall, Faulkner & Co.
Block-printed in distemper colours, 81.5 x 65.2 cm
V&A (E.485-1919) Given by Morris & Co.
NOT ILLUSTRATED

c Wallpaper sample, *Vine, 80*
Designed by William Morris, this colourway first issued 1875
Printed by Jeffrey & Co. for Morris & Co.
Block-printed in distemper and oil colours on foiled and lacquered crape-embossed paper, 94.0 x 48.5 cm
William Morris Society, Kelmscott House, London (WMS/WP/1/138)

Like *Jasmine* this too uses the 'layered' format. The background of stylised willow leaves is overlaid and interwoven with a vertically meandering slender vine stem bearing, in almost circular scrolls, bunches of grapes and groups of leaves. The central portion of the design, a complete repeat, is fully worked and coloured

and the beginnings of the adjoining repeats are clearly traced in. Notes, in Morris's hand, give instructions on the order of printing from the blocks.

After publication as an ordinary distemper print, *Vine* was very soon brought out on a gold crape-embossed ground, a material which had earlier appeared in Jeffrey's own range, but which the firm was now using for the first time. The gold, glimpsed through the deep greens, is reminiscent of the firm's early painted furniture. It demonstrates the move into richer wallpaper effects and, at 40s. a roll, was extremely expensive; the ordinary distemper print cost 12s.

Willow, issued in the same year, is a simple pattern derived from the backprint of *Vine.*

L.9 Wallpaper sample, *Lily*

Designed by William Morris, *c*.1874
Printed, partially painted in watercolour, attached
working notes for printer; 40.0 x 55.0 cm
Arthur Sanderson & Sons Ltd.

This example gives a valuable insight into the design
and production process. Worked on a wash ground, it
is at an intermediate stage. Some of the colours are
printed but others have been painted on as a guide.
The accompanying note with its very precise colour
details includes an instruction to get a new block cut.
There appear to have been considerable problems
with printing *Lily* as the logbook shows several deleted
versions.

Morris must have considered *Lily* particularly suitable
for bedrooms; it was used at Kelmscott Manor (fig.85)
and in Margaret Burne-Jones's room at The Grange.

L.10 Wallpaper Logbook

Maintained by Jeffrey & Co. for Morris & Co.,
c.1865–93
Wallpaper samples, pasted into an old account
book, with pattern names, numbers and annotations in the margins; 39.7 x 41.0 x 6.0 cm
Arthur Sanderson & Sons Ltd. (Logbook 1a)

Jeffrey & Co. kept a log of the firm's papers. A sample
of each published colouring of a pattern (known as a
'way') annotated with name and number, was entered
as a permanent record. The book is open to show
Venetian, Diaper, both first issued in the late 1860s, and
Willow, first issued 1874. New colourings were often
added some time after a pattern had been brought
out. When *Venetian* first appeared it was in soft bright
colours on a white ground; the ways shown here are
more 'aesthetic'. A similar palette was frequently used
for different patterns.

Number 59 in the book is an unsatisfactory attempt at
a wash effect. Morris's original intent in 1862 was to
make papers with transparent colours, and the printing log for 1874 and 1875 shows a return to this aim.
Although success was eventually achieved there were
problems in perfecting the process; Rosalind Howard
had obviously found such a paper unsatisfactory for,
in July 1875, Morris wrote to her, 'I am very vexed but
not at all surprised, knowing, as I told you, what a
risky thing that transparent colour was: I don't believe
it to be the paperhanger's fault' (Kelvin, 283). The
wash patterns were made on Morris & Co.'s own
paper and the logs often record the colours required.

L.9

L.10

L.11b

L.12

L.11 *Acanthus* wallpaper

a Original design
William Morris, 1874
Pencil, watercolour and bodycolour, 81.5 x 65.2 cm
Inscribed
V&A (Circ.297-1955)

b Wallpaper sample, *Acanthus, 79*
Designed by William Morris, registered 22 July 1875
Printed by Jeffrey & Co. for Morris & Co.
Block-printed in distemper colours, 68.6 x 50.0 cm
V&A (E.494-1919) Given by Morris & Co.

The two layers in this design are given equal weight. Veining and the use of fifteen subtly different colours (more than in any previous design) emphasise the vigour of the acanthus scrolls. A very similar conjunction of tiny background motif and scrolling leaves also appear in Morris's calligraphic and illuminated manuscripts.

The design is largely worked in watercolour and the printer would have had to interpret this in distemper – hence the colour notes on the front – including 'get Mr. Morris to paint in front leaves.' Notes on the back include 'The property of Mr. Morris 15/12/74.' Another version of the design is in Birmingham Museum and Art Gallery.

Acanthus was the first of a group of large-scale, heavily patterned and deep coloured papers: the others were *Pimpernel* (1876), *Wreath* (1876), *Rose* (1877) and *Chrysanthemum* (1877). The large size of this design requires thirty blocks to complete the pattern, making it an expensive paper costing 16s. a roll.

L.12 Wallpaper sample, *Pimpernel, 82*

Designed by William Morris, registered 29 February 1876
Printed by Jeffrey & Co. for Morris & Co.
Block-printed in distemper colours, 68.0 x 52.5 cm
V&A (E.497-1919). Given by Morris & Co.

In general effect and colouring, *Pimpernel* is similar to *Acanthus*. However, the pattern is more like the mirror repeat of the *African Marigold* printed textile, registered in October 1876.

This pattern was hung in the dining room at Kelmscott House.

L.13

L.14

L.13 Wallpaper sample, *Loop Trail, 169*

Designed by Kate Faulkner, registered 12 May 1877
Printed by Jeffrey & Co. for Morris & Co.
Block-printed in distemper colours, 84.5 x 47.5 cm
William Morris Society, Kelmscott House, London
(WMS/WP/2/56)

Loop Trail is the first of the firm's papers, apart from the
adaptions of the late 1860s, by a designer other than
Morris. He had by now mastered the medium, production was running smoothly and, absorbed in textile
printing and dyeing, he was able to delegate. As well as
working for Morris & Co. in other media, Faulkner
designed wallpapers on her own account. Several of
her patterns were issued by Jeffrey & Co. in the early
1880s.

With its small floral trails, the paper is not in the immediately recognisable 'Morris & Co.' style. This was
perhaps an advantage in widening the range.

L.14 Wallpaper sample, *Ceiling, 101*

Designed by William Morris, registered
22 November 1877
Printed by Jeffrey & Co. for Morris & Co.
Block-printed in distemper colour, 68.0 x 49.3 cm
V&A (E.510-1919) Given by Morris & Co.

Morris disliked papered ceilings, preferring the design
to be painted. This reticent monochrome pattern – with
a flat treatment of the leaf, fruit and flower forms –
repeats vertically and horizontally on a rectangular
scheme. The initial colourway, this was followed by
several others, all employing pale colours and light
grounds. It was issued as a flock in 1887.

L.15 *Sunflower* wallpaper

a Original design
William Morris, 1877–8
Pen and watercolour, 101.0 x 68.7 cm
William Morris Society, Kelmscott House, London
(D4)

b Wallpaper sample, *Sunflower, 110*
Designed by William Morris, registered
7 January 1879
Printed by Jeffrey & Co. for Morris & Co.
Block-printed in distemper colour, 67.9 x 52.6 cm
V&A (E.513-1919) Given by Morris & Co.
NOT ILLUSTRATED

c Wallpaper, partial roll, *Sunflower, 132*
Designed by William Morris, this version first
issued *c*.1881
Printed by Jeffrey & Co. for Morris & Co.

L.15a

L.15c

Block-printed in oil colour on a crape-embossed, foiled and lacquered ground; width 57.1 cm
Maltwood Art Museum and Gallery, University of Victoria, Victoria, British Columbia

This is a very straightforward design compared with many of the earlier patterns of the 1870s. It uses the turn-over structure associated with woven fabrics and hand-knotted carpets. There is no attempt to mask the obvious horizontal and vertical repeats and there is no backprint to draw attention from the main pattern. The use of line on the flowers, leaves and fruit gives only the slightest sense of depth. *Acorn*, of the same date, is very similar.

According to George Wardle, original drawings showed two repeats vertically and more than one horizontally:

In preparing the design…constant watch had to be kept for the effect produced by the necessary repetitions of the pattern on wall or curtain and curious experiences were sometimes had when the repeats of a pattern came to be joined round the original unit. In order to see that all went well therefore it was necessary to have at least parts of eight repeats of the design and sometimes entire repeats carefully drawn round the central 'model'.

Sunflower, *Acorn* and *Mallow* (the last designed by Kate Faulkner) were registered as a group. They are all simple, single-colour patterns, issued, for the most part, in soft and pale tones with blues and yellows predominating. The cheapness of these patterns (4s. 6d. to 5s. 6d. per piece) was intended to balance the range against papers such as *Chrysanthemum* and *Bower* (1877), which cost 11s. and 9s.

However, also in 1879, an extremely expensive version was published. *Sunflower, 108*, was printed in greenish-black oil colour on a gold crape-embossed ground and cost 30s. a roll. Morris wrote in December of the same year to the Howards (Kelvin 601, 604) about a gold *Sunflower* paper which upon inspection 'to our grief…would not do…'

The version shown here, printed in red on a gold ground, is entered in the printing log about 1881. In November that year Morris was writing to Rosalind Howard (see Kelvin, 742, 749, 750, 753): 'The gold and red sunflower is on my board at Queen Square and I will do my best to hit the due colour.' Obviously, the gold-ground papers tended to look too bright on the wall. It is not clear whether these variants were designed first for the Howards or for the stock range.

L.17a

L.17b

L.16

L.16 Wallpaper sample, *Carnation, 125*

Designed by Kate Faulkner, first issued 1880
Printed by Jeffrey & Co. for Morris & Co.
Machine-printed by surface roller in distemper
colours, 84.5 x 47.5 cm
William Morris Society, Kelmscott House,
London (WMS/WP/2/172)

The firm issued only two machine-printed papers
during Morris's lifetime. This and *Merton*, of 1888,
were designed by Kate Faulkner. *Carnation* is a
respectable example of a roller-print and, at only 2s.
6d. for a four-colour pattern, it was considerably
cheaper than even a single-colour hand-print; but
the thin, smeary colours show why Morris preferred
block-prints. Although this pattern was available,
Morris and W.A.S. Benson used the more expensive
Daisy (costing 6s. 6d. a roll) in their design for an
Artisan's Model Kitchen, shown at the opening of
the Queen's Park Museum, Manchester, in 1884.

L.17 *Pink and Poppy* wallpaper

a Original design
William Morris, April 1880
Pen, pencil and watercolour, 94.0 x 48.2 cm

Inscribed at top: '21"', 'April 1880
Machine Wall Paper'
William Morris Society, Kelmscott House,
London (D.6)

b Wallpaper sample, *Poppy*
(also known as *Pink and Poppy*), *123*
Designed by William Morris, 1880
Printed by Jeffrey & Co. for Morris & Co.
Block-printed in silver paint and lacquer,
67.8 x 52.5 cm
V&A (E.521-1919) Given by Morris & Co.

Veining and dotting (printed by pins hammered into
the blocks) give movement to wallpaper patterns.
Speaking about designing paperhangings in his 1882
lecture 'The Lesser Arts of Life', Morris said 'Here is
the place, if anywhere, for dots and lines and hatch-
ings: mechanical enrichment is the first necessity in it'.

There is another version of this design, also held at
the William Morris Society. Both are inscribed
'April 1880' and both are marked 'Machine
Wallpaper'. In the event, however, the published
paper was block-printed and the ways that used
gold or silver were both expensive (21s. a roll) and
rich looking. Ten colourways were issued between

L.18a

L.18b

1880 and 1882. A Morris & Co. bill of October 1888 for 1, Holland Park (cat. no. I.17) refers to 'providing and hanging Gold Poppy Paper' (fig. 87).

L.18 *St James's* wallpaper

a Original design
William Morris, 23 July 1880
Monochrome version, pencil and sepia,
190.5 x 69.0 cm
Inscribed
William Morris Gallery
(London Borough of Waltham Forest) (A40a)

b Wallpaper sample, *St James's, 126*
Designed by William Morris, first issued 1881
Printed by Jeffrey & Co. for Morris & Co.
Block-printed in distemper colours and silver and gold, 68.0 x 52.0 cm
V&A (E.528-1919)
Given by Morris & Co.

On 16 July 1880, Morris met representatives of the Board of Works concerning the redecoration of the Visitors' Entrance, the Grand Staircase, the Garden Entrance and the Ambassadors' Entrance at

St James's Palace (see also cat. no. I.13).

The firm's proposal for the Grand Staircase (PRO Work 19/20) was that 'The lower stage...would have the walls covered with embossed and gilded paper, very thick, the upper stage and gallery would have the walls also covered with paper of different design and flat varnished...' The latter was the specially designed *St James's* pattern on which Morris immediately started work. A scheme for the decorations, including a fully worked and coloured design for the paper (held at the William Morris Gallery, Walthamstow) was submitted to the Board of Works on 24 October 1880 and approved by the Queen on 2 November.

This design shows a great deal of working, particularly on the central motif; the upright stem meander. In his *c.*1879 lecture 'Making the Best Of It', Morris said '...no amount of delicacy is too great in drawing the curves of a pattern, no amount of care in getting the leading lines right from the first, can be thrown away, for beauty of detail cannot afterwards cure any shortcomings in this'.

As befitting the grandeur and size of the space, the *St James's* is very large. The formality of the treatment of the acanthus leaves and flowerheads in the foreground is, however, relieved by the more domestic handling of the roses, leaves and small flowers in the underlay. Two

widths of paper are needed to complete the pattern horizontally, while the vertical repeat of 119.4 cm requires two blocks to print each colour. Sixty-eight blocks are needed to complete the pattern. The cutting and printing must have been a gigantic task, carried out at speed. Only four months separated the approval of the plan and its completion. The blocks were destroyed in a fire at Jeffrey's on 22 November 1881. The printing for the Palace was complete by this time but the blocks were recut for future use.

This colouring was used for the Queen's Staircase, the Grand Staircase (fig. 88) – where it was used in conjunction with an imitation leather paper, *Peacocks and Amorini*, designed by Walter Crane and issued by Jeffrey & Co. – and the Ambassadors' Staircase where it was teamed with another Jeffrey's 'leather', the *Cupid*, designed by Bruce Talbert.

The successful completion of the decoration of the entrances was followed by a commission for the main suite of State Apartments, including the Banqueting or Waterloo Room. This was hung with a red re-colouring of the *St James's*, varnished, as on the staircases.

Both colourings were included in Morris & Co.'s stock range, priced at 32s. 6d. a roll.

L.19

L.20

L.21

L.19 Wallpaper sample, *St James's Ceiling, 293*

Designed by William Morris, 1881
Printed by Jeffrey & Co. for Morris & Co.
Block-printed in distemper colours,
68.3 x 52.7 cm
V&A (E.594-1919)
Given by Morris & Co.

A large ceiling paper, designed to be hung with the red *St James's* in the Banqueting Room at the Palace. The pattern is very similar to Philip Webb's design for the painted ceiling of the Green Dining Room at the South Kensington Museum, 1866–8. (cat. no. I.7).

Morris's diary (BL Add. Ms 45407B) records that he was working on the design in late August and early September 1881.

Like the *St James's* wallpaper, this too entered the standard range.

L.20 Wallpaper sample, *Bird and Anemone, 143*

Designed by William Morris, first issued 1882
Printed by Jeffrey & Co. for Morris & Co.
Block-printed in distemper colours,
67.7 x 52.2 cm
V&A (E.530-1919)
Given by Morris & Co.

Morris is perhaps referring to this design in his diary for 17 May 1881: 'Working on paper hanging tulip and anemone' (BL Add. MS 45,407B).

According to the wallpaper logbook the first set was sent out on 15 June 1882. A printed fabric of the same name and design was registered on 17 June. A comparison of paper and textile reveals differences which are partly due to technique but which also indicate that straight matching was not intended. The wallpaper pattern is larger

L.22

than that of the fabric; the crispness, solidity and distinctness of the colours in the paper is far removed from the unevenness and slight blurring seen in the cottons, especially those initially printed by the discharge process. The paper version has the same colour balance as the fabric (i.e. the pattern shows light on a darker ground). Although not always used, this was Morris's preferred method of dealing with one-colour prints.

L.21 Wallpaper sample, *Wild Tulip, 162*

Designed by William Morris, registered 21 November 1884
Printed by Jeffrey & Co. for Morris & Co.
Block-printed in distemper colours, 68.3 x 53.0 cm
V&A (E.538-1919)
Given by Morris & Co.

May Morris wrote (1936, p.36): 'The character of this design is all Kelmscott to me: the peony and wild tulip are two of the richest blossomings of the spring garden at the Manor…'

Wild Tulip is similar to the *Cray* printed textile of the same date and was the first wallpaper to show the diagonal meander that characterises many of Morris's designs thereafter. Although, with its mass of pin-dotting, it appears to be a simple design, it uses many subtly different colours and eighteen blocks were needed to complete the pattern. It was issued initially in eight ways; some expensive variants employed gold or silver spot grounds.

The original design is at Birmingham Museum and Art Gallery.

L.22 Wallpaper sample, *Chrysanthemum*

Designed by William Morris, this version issued 1886
Printed by Jeffrey & Co. for Morris & Co.
Foiled paper, lacquered, stamped and stencilled in oil colour, 53.3 x 57.0 cm
Arthur Sanderson & Sons Ltd.

Paper imitations of embossed and gilded leather hangings were very fashionable from the 1870s to the 1890s. Jeffrey & Co. was one of the English manufacturers to perfect a technique for their production, winning a medal at the Paris International Exhibition of 1878 for a 'leather' version of *Peacocks and Amorini*, designed by Walter Crane. (For descriptions relating to the process see *The Building and Engineering Times*, 6 Sept. 1884, and NAL 86.HH.13.)

Morris, Marshall, Faulkner & Co. had, from about 1862, patterns of real embossed leather and first adopted imitations in 1878. (Unlike the earlier gold-ground papers, the patterns were stamped rather than printed.) This example probably dates from about 1886. Another version (described in the *Art Journal*, 1893, pp. 139–141) was used in the Antiquities Room at 1 Holland Park (see cat.no.I.18).

Morris commended imitation leathers in his and Professor Middleton's entry 'Mural Decoration', in the *Encyclopaedia Britannica*, XVII, 1884.

L.23

L.23 Wallpaper logbook, open to show ways *201–8, c.*1886

Maintained by Jeffrey & Co. for Morris & Co., *c.*1865–93
Wallpaper samples pasted into an old account book with pattern names, numbers and annotations in the margins; 39.6 x 41.0 x 5.5 cm
Arthur Sandersons & Sons Ltd. (Logbook 1b)

The opening shows three imitation leather variants of *Sunflower*, two 'leather' and one distemper-printed version of *Lily and Pomegranate* (1886); *Scroll* and a flocked *Ceiling*. *Lily and Pomegranate* is the only new design. The others are additional versions of existing patterns.

L.24 Wallpaper sample, *Willow Bough, 210*

Designed by William Morris, first issued 1887
Printed by Jeffrey & Co. for Morris & Co.
Block-printed in distemper colours, 68.5 x 53.0 cm
V&A (E.557-1919) Given by Morris & Co.

A naturalistic treatment of one of Morris's favourite themes. May Morris wrote (1936, p. 36): 'We were walking one day by our little stream that runs into the Thames, and my Father pointed out the detail and variety in the leaf forms, and soon afterwards this paper was done, a keenly-observed rendering of our willows that has embowered many a London living-room.'

The original design is at the Whitworth Art Gallery, University of Manchester.

L.25 Wallpaper sample, *Bruges, 237*

Designed by William Morris, first issued 1888
Printed by Jeffrey & Co. for Morris & Co.
Block-printed in distemper colour on mica ground, 68.3 x 53.0 cm
V&A (E.561-1919)
Given by Morris & Co.

A large, formal textile-based pattern.

The logbook shows that *Bruges* was issued in ten ways at this time. Some were distemper printed, some flocked, some (as in this example) on a mica ground to give a sparkling effect, and examples were also in a combination of these techniques. It was available in either one or two colours. The mica-ground version was more expensive than the ordinary distemper print.

L.26 Design for *Grafton* wallpaper

William Morris, *c.*1883
Pencil, watercolour and bodycolour, 68.8 x 43.5 cm
Inscribed
William Morris Society, Kelmscott House, London (D5)

A fully worked and coloured design ready for the cutter and printer. It is marked 'leave out pins' – and the paper was issued without the dotted ground. The pattern has been traced out in pencil, and horizontal and vertical guidelines are visible. The repeating element is small, appearing twice within the 21-inch inch square format. The central portion has been coloured, somewhat roughly, and a list of blocks is given: 'Pale Green 1; Yellow 2; 2nd green 3'.

Without dotting, hatching, veining, outline or underprint, this is a very two dimensional, non-naturalistic pattern. The use of the ground to separate individual elements in the flowers and stems is reminiscent of stencilling, where the natural qualities of the process result in such an effect.

L.24

L.25

L.26

L.27 a

L.27 b

L.27 c

L.28

L.27 Three wallpaper printing blocks for *Grafton* pattern

Probably cut by Barrett's, *c*.1883
Carved deal and fruit wood,
approx. 56.0 x 51.0 x 5.0 cm each
Arthur Sandersons & Sons Ltd.

The blocks are composed of a triple sandwich of wood: the bottom two layers are deal; the topmost is a hard and fine-grained fruit wood. Those areas that are not required to print have been cut away. *Grafton* is built up of flat fields of colour, without lines or dots, and the blocks do not feature any of the metal strips or pins that would be necessary for fine detail.

During the course of normal use, blocks sometimes have to be repaired or recut. These examples, however, are the original set and still bear the 1883 registration mark at the edge. They were produced by Barrett's of Bethnal Green, a specialist firm which cut blocks and rollers for other companies as well, including Jeffrey's. At least four generations of Barretts were employed in this very skilled work; Morris dealt with Joseph (1812–76) and Alfred (1847–1918). Much depends on the cutter's skill in tracing the original design, transferring the outlines of each colour to a separate block and then accurately routing out the unwanted portions. George Wardle recalled that the cutter's tracing was always submitted to Morris before it could be 'rubbed off'.

L.28 Wallpaper matchpiece, *Grafton, 235*

Designed by William Morris, pattern registered 29 June 1883, matchpiece made *c*.1950
Printed by Arthur Sanderson & Sons Ltd.
Block-printed in distemper colours,
1000.00 x 56.0 cm
Arthur Sanderson & Sons Ltd.

A matchpiece is the printer's template. It shows the colours to be used and the order of printing.

In the printing process a block is dipped, face down, onto a 'blanket' furnished with pigment, charging the raised surfaces with colour. Still face down, it is pressed onto a waiting roll of paper, transferring a portion of the pattern. This is repeated all along the roll, taking care that each impression is placed correctly alongside its predecessor. When the pigment is dry, the next colour is printed in the same manner, until the pattern is complete. Accurately fitting the impressions together ('registration') is essential.

Three blocks were used to print *Grafton* (cat. no. L.27), which was available as both a two- and three colour pattern. In this example two blocks print the same shade of yellow.

L.29 Wallpaper stand-book

Morris & Co. from 449 Oxford Street, *c*.1905
Wooden easel stand, wallpaper samples,
leatherette cover; 89.0 x 53.0 x 9.0 cm
V&A (E.2734 to 2866-1980)
Given by Shand Kydd Ltd

A display book from the Oxford Street showroom
containing 132 specimens, each marked on the
back with pattern name, way number and price.
(No machine-prints are included.) It is big enough
to show a full repeat of all but the very largest
patterns. Similar 'table books' were also available,
probably for loan to customers.

It is pointed out on the cover that the papers are
'free from arsenic'.

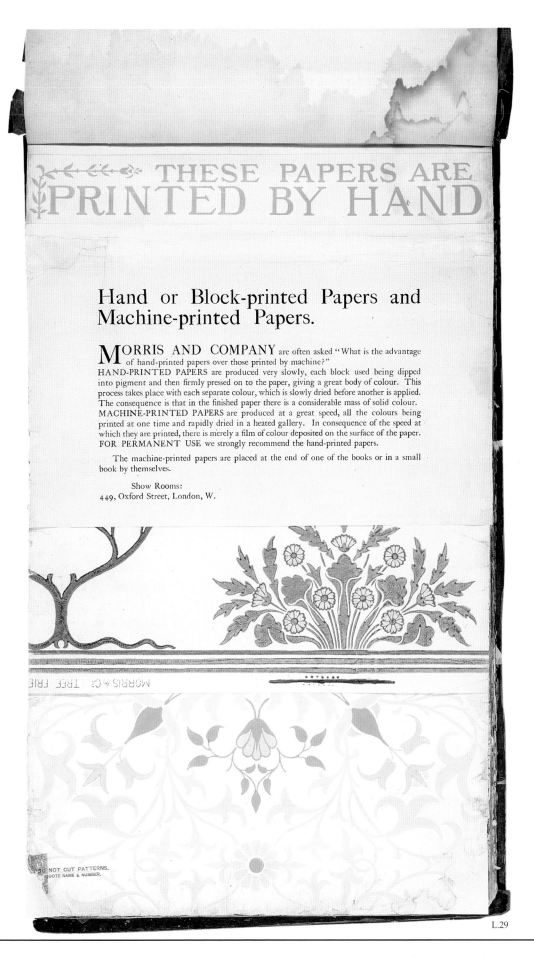

THESE PAPERS ARE PRINTED BY HAND

Hand or Block-printed Papers and Machine-printed Papers.

MORRIS AND COMPANY are often asked "What is the advantage of hand-printed papers over those printed by machine?"
HAND-PRINTED PAPERS are produced very slowly, each block used being dipped into pigment and then firmly pressed on to the paper, giving a great body of colour. This process takes place with each separate colour, which is slowly dried before another is applied. The consequence is that in the finished paper there is a considerable mass of solid colour.
MACHINE-PRINTED PAPERS are produced at a great speed, all the colours being printed at one time and rapidly dried in a heated gallery. In consequence of the speed at which they are printed, there is merely a film of colour deposited on the surface of the paper.
FOR PERMANENT USE we strongly recommend the hand-printed papers.

The machine-printed papers are placed at the end of one of the books or in a small book by themselves.

Show Rooms:
449, Oxford Street, London, W.

TEXTILES

Linda Parry

Morris remained fascinated with textiles throughout his life. His first interests were purely aesthetic, developed through a natural love of pattern and texture. In an attempt to produce the effects he most admired this was followed by a preoccupation with the complexities of technique. Visual and practical aspects became equally important to him, and his ability to balance and harmonise these two vital elements in his own work, a rare quality for a textile designer of any age, is the single most important reason for his success.

Designing and making textiles helped Morris to solve a number of problems. Having failed as a painter, they provided the means of creating figurative art on a grand scale. More modestly, they improved the appearance of his own homes and those he furnished and decorated for others. Furthermore, by undertaking the often hard physical labour involved in manufacture his intellectual and manual needs were exercised and frequently fulfilled.

His career as a designer both began and ended with the design and production of textiles, and this catalogue shows how this preoccupation outpaced his involvement with any other form of the visual arts. His earliest crudely worked panels, embroidered from about 1856, were attempts to reproduce medieval-looking hangings. His last examples, tapestries woven shortly before he died, finally achieved this dream. What developed between was a long and complex search for perfect patterns, colours, textures and effects for the home. Because such interests tend to be associated with women rather than men and, furthermore, as Morris is seen to have succeeded in these activities with apparent ease, this side of his achievements is frequently underestimated, depreciated or simply misunderstood. This is unfortunate, as a study of his textile career, because of the length of time and consistency of his interest, provides a fascinating analogy for his life as a whole.

Morris's childhood brought him into contact with good quality yet conventional textile furnishings. Whereas his family lived in considerable middle-class comfort, original art and avant-garde design was, apparently, absent from the home. As an adult he remembered only one textile item, a crewel-work embroidered picture of *Abraham and Isaac*. In describing the subject and technique he added nothing of its history. For someone who was to become one of the great textile historians of his generation this is strange but shows how, in his formative years, aesthetic judgements preceded intellectual curiosity.

History and romance soon took a firm hold, nurtured by childhood wanderings and through the family's library at Woodford Hall. As well as popular adventure novels, he introduced himself to Gerard's *Herball* (1597) with plant drawings and recipes, which was to remain a favourite reference book throughout his life. His first sight of historic textiles used as decorative furnishings was tapestry hangings, of leaf and plant design, hung in the upper room at a hunting lodge, built originally for Henry VIII, that survived in neighbouring Epping Forest. The impression of the 'faded greenery and the impression of romance it always made…' was, no doubt, heightened by entering the house itself, his first tangible experience of early British domestic life and one he spent his first years as a decorator attempting to recreate.

From such early experiences Morris realised that textiles were an essential part of the decoration and comfort of a home, so it is not surprising that they were included in his first attempts at house furnishing; the rooms rented with Burne-Jones from August 1856 in Upper Gordon Street and soon afterwards at 17 Red Lion Square in Bloomsbury. Morris's first hangings were attempts to reproduce the effect of medieval tapestries, but the results were unconventional and must have looked incongruous in the Georgian architecture of the rented rooms (cat.no.M.4). With neither experience

Fig. 90 *The Dance of the Wodehouses*, from Froissart's Chronicles.

nor skills he used the only means available, stitching in a haphazard way with darning needles and thick wools on to a coarse linen ground. For the design of the embroideries Morris chose as his source wall hangings depicting a repeating design of trees, bird and animals shown in court scenes from Froissart's Chronicles, a fifteenth-century illuminated manuscript that he had studied either in the British Museum or through H. N. Humphreys' 1844 edited volume. Morris's design was similar but included what was to be the first use of his boyish motto 'If I Can'. The form of these wall hangings remained at the back of Morris's mind for some time. He included a similar panel in the decorative detailing in his 1858 textile-strewn painting of Jane as *La Belle Iseult* (cat. no. G.10) and other examples were made in the first years of commercial production by Morris, Marshall, Faulkner & Co. (cat. no. M.5).

The naive appearance and structure of this early work is surprising when it is realised that Morris had, by the time he settled in London, already spent nine months apprenticed to the notable neo-Gothic architect George Edmund Street. One of the most influential and experienced church textile designers of the nineteenth century, Street's embroidery (cat. no. M.3) had already attracted 'widespread notice and imitation' when shown at the Great Exhibition of 1851, five years before Morris entered his office. Whereas Morris's first amateur attempts can be seen as the results of his own naive experiments, they may also suggest a reaction against the socially acceptable, very high standards of Street's professional church embroidery.

However, although Morris continued to develop his own quite individual style for domestic textiles and particularly those made for his own use, Street's work did provide the inspiration for Morris, Marshall, Faulkner & Co.'s early ecclesiastical textile furnishings. Morris and Philip Webb shared these projects and it is difficult to separate their work. They had met in Street's office and were aware of daily practice and procedure there; Webb more so than Morris, being chief assistant at the time. The first documented textile produced by the firm, and now the only known example from the first three important decorative schemes, commissioned by G. F. Bodley for churches in Brighton, Selsley and Scarborough, is an embroidered frontal for St Martin's church, Scarborough. This shows a 'powdered' design of floral sprigs worked in silks and then cut out and applied to a velvet ground (cat. no. M.12), echoing the late medieval *opus anglicanum* technique used by Street in his own work and advocated by him in lectures. In one of Webb's existing notebooks, used during his early years in Street's office, he authoritatively describes a technical variation in the gold embroidery of a thirteenth-century cloth. The notebook also lists Street's thread suppliers, and, alongside a note 'wd give info', the name and address of Agnes Blencowe, one of the most competent and celebrated professional embroiderers of her day and an expert on medieval work. Webb, like Morris, had begun to build up historic references for later use.

Embroidery continued to provide the only practical means of decorating textiles for the first years of the firm's existence. Work was sewn domestically by Jane Morris, her sister Bessie Burden and friends. Mackail claims that several women worked under the supervision of Jane and Bessie, including Mrs Campfield, the wife of the foreman of the stained-glass painters. However, no payments to embroiderers appear in the accounts for the firm's first years of production (which include wages for George Campfield, amongst others) and few embroidery orders are mentioned in the discussion of business at each meeting (cat.no.D.1). This suggests that most of the work undertaken was for personal use and that of friends. This lack of a professional framework may account for only a brief mention of textiles in the firm's first prospectus sent out in 1861, as quoted by Mackail. However, following success at the 1862 International Exhibition, the partners decided, at their meeting on 14 January 1863, to circulate prospective clients with an updated list of the firm's work. An accompanying letter was drafted which included the information that they were '…ready to supply all kinds of embroidered hangings both for domestic and ecclesiastical purposes in linen, cotton, wool[len] silk or velvet from the simplest line embroidery to elaborate needlework tapestry of figures and subjects…' (cat.no.D.3).

Morris, Marshall, Faulkner & Co. had occupied two stands at the 1862 exhibition for which they were awarded two medals with the judges' commendation that 'the general form of the furniture, the arrangement of the tapestry, and the character of the details are satisfying to the archaeologist for the exactness of the imitation, at the same time that the general effect is excellent'. With no details in the official exhibition catalogue (it is probable that the firm refused to pay), it is difficult to discover what they exhibited. It is likely that all embroideries produced to date were shown, although only the Scarborough frontal can be identified positively. Contemporary newspaper and magazine accounts hint tantalisingly at the rest. Both *The Ecclesiologist*'s reference to 'most antique looking tapestry-hangings which are effective in colour but of rude manufacture' and *The Clerical Journal*'s description of items unsuitable for church use because of their 'homliness', are likely to refer to examples of the *If I Can* design.

The unusual nature of the firm's exhibits was further emphasised by Christopher Dresser, himself one of the most inventive designers of the period, who wrote of 'a series of quaint fabrics that have the pattern wrought upon them in thick worsted threads of many colours which is sewn to the surface'. The hangings that caught his attention were, almost certainly, those made for use in the Morris's first home, Red House (cat.no.M.6). For these Morris, yet again, derived the design, of brightly coloured daisy clumps, from Froissart. Morris was to use this pattern continuously throughout his career and it appears on painted furniture, stained glass, tiles, wallpaper, calligraphy, machine-woven carpeting and tapestry weaving. The Red House hangings were embroidered in outline with couched wools on a dark blue woollen ground, a technique characteristically belittled by Rossetti with the comment 'Top has taken to worsted work'. It is likely that this simple yet effective stitching was actually suggested by Jane Morris, a skilful practitioner who by then had become the busy mother of two babies with little time to devote to the firm's work. It proved to be the most practical and successful to date and was also used for another contemporary hanging of sunflower design, which is now housed at Kelmscott Manor.

Not nearly so successful were Morris's plans for a set of figurative panels to be hung around the walls of the drawing room at Red House. Despite careful planning and design the scheme, loosely based on one of Morris's favourite medieval romances, Chaucer's *Legend of Goode Wimmen*, and depicting a number of Classical and Arthurian heroines, was over ambitious. He had underestimated the enthusiasm and expertise of his resident workforce. Choosing the complex appliqué technique first used for the Scarborough altar-frontal, the design of draped figures proved far more testing, requiring a level of skills that only Jane and her sister Bessie possessed. With Jane preoccupied, the scheme was never realised, although a number of panels in various stages of completion survive. The most finished is the figure of *St Catherine* worked by Jane, which shows one of the decorative trees that were part of the intended composition. Three figures embroidered by Bessie Burden were retained by her following the move from Red House and later incorporated into a screen for George Howard (cat.no.M.7).

The firm's range of commercial textile goods was expanded following the move of headquarters in 1865 from 8 Red Lion Square to 26 Queen Square. The Morris family now also occupied these

Fig.91 St Catherine, one of Jane Morris's embroideries for Red House.

Fig.92 William Morris's embroidery design for the figure of Guenevere, one of the heroines of the Red House scheme.

premises and, while living over the shop, William became engrossed in the dyeing of embroidery threads and plain fabrics. By using natural dyestuffs he hoped to reproduce the colours and tones that he most admired in historic textiles, which he had modestly begun to collect and to study in the South Kensington Museum. Despite using historic sources for reference, Morris was surprisingly scientific in application, combining ancient recipes (often requiring translation) with modern technology (cat.no.M.45).

Morris remained responsible for the firm's production of textiles but other partners also contributed designs. Both Philip Webb and Burne-Jones's account books dealing with the firm list embroideries. Madox Brown's household accounts mention designs for two worsted bell-ropes (see cat.no.M.13) and he is also said to have contributed designs for embroideries, stamped velvets and silks although, sadly, none of these is identifiable today. Though exaggerated, the opinion that 'As a designer for tiles and textiles Ford Madox Brown was probably unequalled' (Tait, 1900) suggests he was a more significant contributor than has been recognised. From the late 1860s, a hard-wearing woollen velvet with an impressed design (cat.no.M.39) provided an alternative furnishing to the plain blue and green woollen serges that the firm had sold from their beginnings and this was used as upholstery on a number of early chairs (cat.no.J.29). Probably supplied by the Manchester decorating firm of Aldam Heaton and based on a Flemish seventeenth-century type, this is possibly one of the stamped velvets said to have been designed by Madox Brown. At least one other *Utrecht Velvet* was sold by the firm.

Morris's next textile furnishings were a series of reproduction designs, block-printed on to fine woollen grounds at his request by a leading Lancashire firm (cat.no.M.37). These copies of 1830s patterns were very popular throughout the life of the firm and, ironically, contributed to Morris's reputation as the major British designer of naturalistic floral 'chintz' patterns.

By 1870 Morris finally accepted that his talents lay not with the figurative forms of the artist but as a practical designer of applied repeating pattern. This had been demonstrated by the popularity of his commercial work so far, his wallpapers and painted decoration for interiors in particular, and by the increasingly decorative quality of his book illumination, the only form of narrative painting that he still occasionally practised. Following what proved a lifetime's habit of studying and perfecting one technique at a time, Morris devoted the next decade to becoming a successful designer, manufacturer and retailer of printed and woven textiles, machine-made and hand-knotted carpets and tapestries.

Initial dyeing, block-printing and weaving experiments took place at the firm's headquarters in Queen Square and the adjacent Great Ormond Yard. This complex and time-consuming procedure, and Morris's subsequent search for suitable outside firms capable of manufacturing his designs in the form he desired, is documented through specific examples in the following catalogue section. What is not evident simply by studying individual designs is the vital part played by others in helping Morris achieve his aims. Reading the extensive correspondence between Morris and Thomas Wardle of Leek in Staffordshire (cat.no.M.43), for instance, gives insight into the tortuous path this frequently took. Not only is Wardle's enormous contribution as Morris's main early printer and dyer evident, but the letters also demonstrate how this was often completed under the most difficult and demanding of conditions. Why Wardle should have continued to co-operate in an undertaking with such a difficult client and for which he suffered personal financial loss is debatable. Morris's forceful yet charismatic personality can only have been part of the reason. More likely was Wardle's realisation that Morris's work was of considerable aesthetic and technical significance.

While emphasising the importance of Morris's strong management to the success of early textile production, it must not be forgotten that he too contributed considerable physical and mental effort. He believed, rightly, that successful design could not be achieved without a sound understanding of 'all about the ware…and its relation to similar wares', as he described it in his lecture 'Making the Best of It' in 1879. Yet this did not always come easily to him despite his considerable natural abilities as a designer, a talent referred to by his daughter May as his 'heaven sent gift'. This is demonstrated by his first heavy-handed attempts at embroidery, the months spent in the dye vats at Leek (when his blue hands often providing the most successful results) and the 517 hours spent weaving one tapestry in his bedroom at Kelmscott House (cat. nos. M.113–16). Such tenacity proved of major importance to his eventual success and added to the enjoyment of his participation. Writing to his friend Aglaia Coronio from Leek in 1875 he excused his shaky handwriting caused '…with doing journeyman's work the last few days: delightful work, hard for the body and easy for the mind'.

It is understandable that, of all the textile techniques Morris used, he left weaving to the last. Not only did mastering the working of the various looms for furnishings, carpet weaving and tapestry present the greatest number of technical difficulties, but he also demanded a great deal of the craft. His appreciation of texture, and particularly the natural qualities of wool, silk, cotton and linen, was of paramount importance to him as a designer and manufacturer. Not only did he wish to weave traditional structures – damasks, brocatelles, double cloths, for instance – but also new cloths derived from mixing fibres to achieve new effects that would satisfy himself and the firm's clients. Morris never underestimated the intricacies of the loom and, despite the great commercial success of this side of production, preparation did not always go well. The time spent building a loom for gold brocading (cat.no.M.87) was commercially unsound, yet Morris had to prove it was possible. Even as late as 1888, the year he drew his last designs for repeating textile patterns, he was still struggling to overcome weaving problems which, in a letter to his daughter Jenny he describes as '…not so simple as the world in general seems to think'.

Morris had taught himself the various textile techniques he wished to use in cramped and unsuitable conditions and for a number of years he relied, frustratingly, on outside contractors to produce the commercial quantities of his textiles needed for the shop. His search, in 1881, for a factory in which he could undertake this work for himself was conditioned by the need to find the facilities necessary for textile production, even though other forms of the firm's manufacture were also to be moved there. Merton Abbey, an old textile-printing works near Wimbledon, was chosen because the River Wandle which ran alongside the workshops provided limitless supplies of soft water and this, and the acres of grounds surrounding the site, allowed for the necessary washing and drying of cloth before and after production. The existing, many-windowed buildings provided

Fig. 93 Washing cotton in the River Wandle at Merton Abbey. This process was undertaken before printing. It removed impurities and prepared the cloth for printing.

Fig. 94 Indigo-discharge printing at Merton Abbey. Once dyed in these deep vats, the cloth was printed with a bleaching agent which drew dye out of the patterned areas.

Fig. 95 The fabric-weaving sheds at Merton Abbey showing hand-activated jacquard looms in use.

both light and space for the printing and weaving of furnishings (figs. 8, 95) and the large-scale manufacture of tapestries and carpets (fig. 19). Within a short time of moving there Morris had also built indigo vats (fig. 94) in order to produce the blue dye so important to his work which had eluded him throughout his career. At last he was able to establish himself as a comprehensive manufacturer of textiles and no other London decorator or retailer could boast of producing such a wide and varied range of fabrics under one roof.

The sale of printed and woven textiles, machine-woven carpets and embroideries had become an important side of the business from the time the firm's shop moved from Queen Square to Oxford Street in 1877. Embroidery was then worked by a small band of professionals under the direction of Bessie Burden and later, from 1885, by May Morris who had inherited skills from both parents. Whereas important commissions such as the Rounton Grange or Smeaton Manor schemes (cat. nos. M.15, 21) occasionally enticed Morris back to his drawing board, an endless stream of designs for cushion covers, screens, portières and bedcovers was needed to provide the shop with the staple commercial stock demanded by clients. Initially these items were designed by Morris and later by May and Henry Dearle, Morris's assistant. Although 'Morris' embroideries (as they all became known, irrespective of who had designed them) were one of the popular forms of 'art needlework', competition was rife. Morris's work was not exclusive to Morris & Co., and a series of designs produced by Morris and Burne-Jones for the Royal School of Art Needlework in the 1870s (cat. nos. M.17, 18) continued to be sold as finished embroideries and kits throughout the rest of the century. Examples were shown in important international exhibitions such as the Philadelphia Centennial Exhibition of 1876 and this greatly helped in advertising Morris's work outside Britain before he had even considered this himself.

Fig. 96 One end of the drawing room at Kelmscott House, Hammersmith, showing *Bird* woven fabric on the walls and *Peacock and Dragon* curtains.

Fig.97 The drawing room at
Bullerswood, Chislehurst, a house
decorated by Morris & Co. from 1889.

Despite some early reluctance to sell abroad on their own account, Morris & Co. produced a stand of six compartments for the Boston Foreign Fair of 1883. The catalogue to this section, written by the firm's manager George Wardle, is important not only in listing the range of goods available during their most commercially successful period but also in its recommendations concerning house decoration and how Morris products should be used in the home. As the only existing account of the firm's practice this is vital study for anyone attempting to assess Morris's role as a designer, as for him appropriateness of use was as vital a component in controlling the way he drew his patterns as choosing the correct technique for manufacture. Wardle's introduction recommends, amongst other items, printed wools for bed and window curtains and unlined cotton damasks 'for portières in summer cottages, or for window-curtains'. He also gives specific details of the firm's most original use of fabrics; draped or stretched on walls around the room. This method was first used by Morris in the drawing room of his London home, Kelmscott House, where it hung 'to within two feet of the ceiling'. 'The cloth is hooked up, to the top rail,' Wardle continues, 'and is but slightly plaited – only enough modulation of the surface being allowed to just break the pattern here and there.' The second method involves attaching fabrics to 'thin laths or batons first nailed to the margins of the wall – that is, above the dado, under the cornice or frieze, and around doors and windows'. From these instructions a very clear picture evolves of the importance, and occasional dominance, of textiles in the ideal 'Morris' interior.

Despite Wardle's very specific advice in the 1883 catalogue, the firm's use of textiles in their own decorative design schemes was very varied, controlled as much by the client and architecture of the building as by the firm itself. A comparison of the interiors of two houses, 1 Holland Park and Bullerswood, both decorated by Morris & Co., shows how different these could look. The decoration of Holland Park is opulent and cluttered, designed to show to advantage the Ionides family's own possessions, whereas the decoration of the drawing room in Bullerswood, a house

near Chislehurst in Kent (fig. 97), centres on the specially designed hand-knotted carpets made for the house.

Original furnishings such as the *Rounton Grange*, *Redcar*, *Carbrook*, *Holland Park* and *Bullerswood* carpets provided additional individuality in the furnishing of many houses. More pragmatically, such commissions allowed Morris to explore new sources of design and manufacture at the expense of the wealthy client. He had begun his career designing special embroideries for his own use at Red House, his last years were devoted to designing individual carpets and tapestries for the homes of others. These late labours represent many of his most original designs and are now judged as his most prized artefacts.

Since 1879 Morris had been responsible for producing a number of tapestry panels of various subjects designed chiefly by Burne-Jones but also by himself and others. However, it was not until 1890 with the decoration of Stanmore Hall, Middlesex, the last commission he worked on, that Morris was able to achieve his most important ambition, the production of a set of narrative tapestries in the medieval manner (cat. no. M.130), the 'bright dream' he had nurtured since childhood. Even the choice of subject for the tapestries, the Search for the Holy Grail, provided an appropriately romantic ending to his career. By accomplishing this scheme shortly before his death, Morris finally completed a full circle as designer, manufacturer and retailer of textiles. Whereas his initial ambitions to produce cloth which was attractive and useful, were modest, his final achievements in the scale and range of activities went far beyond this, unequalled in his own or any other age.

Fig. 98 *The Summons*, tapestry from the Holy Grail series.

Fig.99 Philip Webb's drawing of a hare for the tapestry *The Forest*.

M.1

M.2

M.3

EMBROIDERY

M.1 Bedcover

Icelandic, seventeenth century
Linen canvas embroidered in wools in
cross-stitch, 172.7 x 134.6 cm
V&A (8-1884)

William Morris recommended the acquisition of
this hanging to the South Kensington Museum
in 1884. It is part of a small group of textiles
bought for £120 from Sigridur, the wife of Eiríkr
Magnússon, from whom Morris learned
Icelandic and with whom he translated the
sagas. The Magnússons travelled with Morris on
his first trip to Iceland in 1871 and their common
interest in the country led to a long friendship. In
1882 Mrs Magnússon recruited Morris to her
Mansion House Relief Committee set up to help
relieve famine in her native land. The proceeds
of the sale of these textiles were to be used for
this purpose. It is strange, therefore, that Morris
suggested the Museum pay £40 less than the
asking price.

The hanging shows a traditional Northern
European composition based, Morris believed,
on a thirteenth-century design which showed,
'the abiding influence of Byzantine Art in
Iceland…' The subject is religious and the hanging is said to have hung formerly in a church.
However, its original use was domestic, part of
the inscription translating 'This coverlet is
owned by þorbjorg…' The work has recently
been identified as the work of Þorbjorg
Magnusdottir (1667–1716), a noted Icelandic
embroiderer.

Morris was as fascinated by traditional European
craft textiles as those from the commercial manufacturing centres of Italy and the Near East. This
is reflected in his own collection, which he used
chiefly for technique identification.

In his Kelmscott Chaucer illustration of
Philomena in *The Legend of Goode Wimmen*,
Burne-Jones depicts a warp-weighted loom from
the Faroe Islands. It is likely that Morris selected
this image and provided an illustration for
Burne-Jones to copy.

M.2 Fragment of embroidery

Greek Islands, seventeenth or eighteenth
century
Linen embroidered in silks in satin, darning
and herringbone stitches, 36.8 x 19.0 cm
V&A (T.121-1939)
Bequeathed by May Morris

This fragment belonged to William Morris.

Apart from a number of fine oriental carpets and
rugs and the *Samson* tapestries housed at
Kelmscott Manor, Morris collected textiles mostly for practical purposes. Jane Morris referred to
this collection when she described how occasionally embroideries were unravelled to see how
they were made.

Morris's interest in, and knowledge of, historic

textiles was second to none; while acting as an
adviser to the South Kensington Museums some
of its finest early textile exhibits were acquired,
including a seventeenth-century embroidered
Bengali cover (then thought to have been made
in Goa) bought from him in 1886 for the not
inconsiderable sum of £120 (No. 616-1886).

This small embroidered band, from the hem or
sleeve of a garment, may have been acquired at
the same time as two faded pieces of Cretan
embroidery 'brought back by the English
Consul' which Morris sent to Thomas Wardle in
April 1876 stating 'Mrs Wardle will find some
stitches in them worth looking at'. The patterns
were also worth noting as '…there are strong
marks of Italian influence in many of the
designs…' (Kelvin, I, 323, 324)

M.3 Sedilia hanging

Designed by George Edmund Street
Worked by Miss Hutchinson of Checkley,
1850
Felted woollen ground with silk surface
embroidery and applied motifs, couched
metal thread and spangles in long and short
stem and couching stitched with braid and
fringing; 84.0 x 111.0 cm
Vicar and Church Wardens of the Church of
St John, Hollington

'The first altar-cloth I ever designed was for the
first church I ever restored…' was how Street
described the commission which included this
hanging to the Durham Architectural Society,
later published in *The Ecclesiologist*, XXI, 1863.

Designed shortly before Morris entered Street's
office, this curtain shows 'powdered' floral motifs
influenced by late fifteenth-century British *opus
anglicanum*, a style much favoured by the architect. Having seen such designs in Street's office,
some of Morris's earliest patterns take this form,
including the dresser cover in his painting *La Belle
Iseult* (cat. no. G.10), and decorative detailing on
the St George Cabinet (cat. no. J.18). A similar
dispersed design was used on the firm's earliest
church embroidery, a frontal made for the church
of St Martin-on-the-Hill, Scarborough
(cat. no. M.12). From 1854 many of Street's designs
were carried out by the Ladies Ecclesiastical
Embroidery Society set up by his sister and Miss
Agnes Blencowe. One of Webb's earliest notebooks gives technical details of medieval
embroidery with Miss Blencowe's name and
address and a note, 'wd give info[rmation]'.

M.4 *If I Can* hanging

Designed by William Morris, 1856–7
Worked by Morris possibly assisted by Mary
Nicholson
Linen ground embroidered with natural
dyed wools in unorthodox flat and padded
stitches, 168.5 x 187.0 cm
Society of Antiquaries of London
(Kelmscott Manor)

The remaining example of Morris's first textile

scheme made for his rooms at Upper Gordon Street or 17 Red Lion Square. '…He started his experiments (in embroidery) before he knew me,' wrote Jane, 'got frames made, had worsted dyed to his taste by an old French couple, and began a piece of work with his own hands.' The pattern of repeating fruit trees with birds in flight is taken from the Froissart's Chronicle 'Dance of the Wodehouses' (BL, MS. 4380, fol. 1). Morris adopted and anglicised Jan van Eyck's motto 'Als ich kanne' following his trip to the Low Countries in the summer of 1856.

Despite the naivety of technique, there is a suggestion, in the rendition of leaves and fruit, of a more experienced hand, possibly Mary Nicholson (see cat. no. A.11). In the *Memorials,* Georgiana Burne-Jones quotes from her husband's notes that Morris produced wall paintings of identical design to these embroideries under the *Degrevaunt* pictures in Red House. Whether this is a mistake and the actual hangings were used or whether these influenced this later rendition is debatable.

A hanging of a similar design appears in the background of the painting *La Belle Iseult* (cat. no. G.10).

Exhib. 1934 (69)

M.5 *Qui bien aime tard oublie* hanging

Probably designed by William Morris, early 1860s
Worked by more than one hand
Linen ground embroidered with wools in random embroidery stitches; 180.0 x 136.5 cm
Private Collection

One of four existing embroidered hangings from Penkhill Castle, Ayrshire, the home of Alice Boyd, mistress of William Bell Scott. Rossetti's association with the house, which Morris also visited, and the various technical and stylistic similarities of these embroideries to the *If I Can* hanging suggest the same provenance (Jan Marsh and Liz Woods, *The Order of the Owl,* Autumn 1991). However, these examples are later in date as dye analysis has detected a synthetic violet dye not available until the early 1860s (information from G. W. Taylor).

When and how the embroideries arrived in Scotland is unknown, although Rossetti refers to 'the Topsaic tapestries' in the house in a letter to Alice Boyd dated 17 November 1868. The panels show the work of at least three embroiderers, one far more competent than the others.

These are likely to be the type of hangings exhibited at the 1862 International Exhibition described by Christopher Dresser as 'a series of quaint fabrics' and in *The Ecclesiologist* (XX, 1862) as 'antique looking tapestry-hangings….effective in colour, but of rude manufacture and (we fancy) not at all economical'. Such 'tapestries' were priced at £3 per square yard on the firm's stand.

M.4

M.5

M.6

M.6 Curtain

Designed by William Morris, early 1860s
Worked by Jane Morris, Bessie Burden and others
Woollen ground embroidered with wools in couched
stitches; 167.0 x 299.0 cm
Society of Antiquaries of London (Kelmscott Manor)

Five curtains survive from this scheme made for the
master bedroom at Red House. The design is from 'Dance
of the Wodehouses', a favourite late fifteenth-century manuscript, Froissart's Chronicles. The daisy, one of Morris's
most enduring designs, features in Chaucer's prologue to
The Legend of Goode Wimmen, so there is a literary link
between the two schemes worked for Red House (see
cat.nos.M.7–10).

Jane noted that 'The first stuff I got to embroider on was a
piece of indigo dyed blue serge I found by chance in a
London shop…I took it home and he was delighted with
it, and set to work at once designing flowers – these were
worked in bright colours in a simple rough way – the
work went quickly'.

Jane's discovery was significant and wool soon became the
favoured ground for embroidery. 'Serge hangings' exhibited by the firm at the 1862 exhibition cost 12s. per square
yard. This blue cloth, dyed with indigo and sulphuric acid,
was very popular in the nineteenth century despite being
prone to fading (information from G.W. Taylor). The red
embroidery threads are produced with synthetic dyes.
Following the move from Red House, the embroidered
curtains hung for many years in the dining room of The
Grange, Fulham (Angela Thirkell, *Three Houses,* 1931).

Exhib. 1934 (73)

M.7

M.7 Three-fold screen with embroidered panels depicting Heroines

Designed by William Morris, *c.*1860
Worked by Elizabeth (Bessie) Burden, completed
1888
Wooden surround; woollen ground embroidered
with wools and silks in chain, long and short, brick
and darning stitches with gold couched threads; each
panel: 171.5 x 73.6 cm
From the Castle Howard Collection

These panels were part of an ambitious decorative scheme
planned to hang around the walls of the drawing room at
Red House. An existing notebook (cat.no.D.3) includes
preliminary sketches for the composition. In his design,
Morris followed the theme of Chaucer's late fourteenth-
century poem *Legend of Goode Wimmen* by choosing a
group of heroines. However, his selection differs from the
original and derives from classical, religious and
medieval sources.

Mackail notes that twelve figures were selected 'with trees
between and above them, and a belt of flowers, running
below their feet'. Ten characters are recorded either as
designs, finished embroideries or both. The figures in the
screen have been identified as Lucretia (with a sword),
Hyppolyte (sword and lance) and Helen. Other subjects
used were St Catherine, Penelope, Iseult, Aphrodite,
Artemis, Ariadne and Phyllis (see cat.no.M.10). Three of
these, Ariadne, Artemis and Aphrodite are now lost, the
latter surviving only as a painting (fig.46). Designs and
corresponding embroideries exist for Helen (cat.no.M.8),
Guenevere and Penelope.

M.8

M.9

M.10

It was intended that the panels would be embroidered in a traditional late medieval technique with each figure worked on linen, cut out and applied to a more sumptuous ground, in this case woollen serge. This scheme was never finished and when the Morris family moved out of Red House in 1865 the panels were dispersed among the various embroiderers, who included Jane Morris, Bessie Burden, Kate Faulkner, Georgiana Burne-Jones and possibly her sister Alice Macdonald (see cat.no.M.9). Bessie Burden exhibited three panels at the 1888 Arts and Crafts Exhibition. Catalogued as Penelope, Hyppolyte and Helen these may well have been the three panels of the screen. On 8 February 1889 George Howard sent a cheque for £80 to Bessie 'in payment for the three needlework figures which you have sent to Messrs Morris to be framed'.

The scheme is often confused with two Burne-Jones projects of the same subject; a set of stained-glass panels (cat.no.H.29) first used in 1862 and another embroidery scheme designed for Ruskin in 1863 (see cat.no.M.10).
Exhib. 1952 (I 20).

M.8 Design for an embroidered panel depicting *Helen (Flamme Troiae)*

William Morris, *c*.1860
Pencil and watercolour, 124.7 x 62.45 cm
Inscribed: 'FP 374' and 'Flamma'

V&A (E.571-1940) Bequeathed by May Morris

Original design for one of the figures in the Red House drawing-room scheme (see cat.no.M.7).
Exhib. 1934 (81).

M.9 Unfinished panel depicting a pomegranate tree

Designed by William Morris, *c*.1860
Linen ground embroidered with wools in brick, stem, satin and long and short and couching stitches, 160.5 x 69.8 cm
V&A (T.124-1985)

Part of the Red House drawing-room scheme (see cat.no.M.7).

Two other embroidered trees from this scheme survive. One, an orange tree which was later made into a curtain, is at Bateman's, Rudyard Kipling's house in Sussex. This may have been embroidered by Kipling's mother, Alice, one of Georgiana Burne-Jones's sisters. The other, depicting lemons, is used with the figure of St Catherine in a panel now at Kelmscott Manor, which was for many years in the Burne-Jones household.

The similarity between these stylised trees and images in early Coptic tapestry-weaving is proof of Morris's early interest in historic textiles.

M.10 Unfinished panel, *Phyllis*

Designed by William Morris or Edward Burne-Jones, 1860–63
Probably worked by Georgiana Burne-Jones
Linen ground, partially painted, embroidered with wools in brick, stem and long and short stitches, 129.0 x 81.2 cm
V&A (T.122-1985)

Possibly part of the drawing-room scheme at Red House. It has also been suggested (see A.R.Dufty, 1985) that this panel was part of a second heroines scheme designed by Edward Burne-Jones to be embroidered for John Ruskin by the girls of Winnington Hall School in Cheshire.

The figure is similar to the existing sketch plan for the Winnington scheme and identical to the Burne-Jones stained-glass design for the Phyllis subjects, both of which are in Birmingham Museums and Art Gallery. However, the style, dimensions and technique of the embroidery strongly compares with the earlier Red House scheme, although not of such good workmanship as examples worked by Jane Morris and Bessie Burden. Furthermore, Georgiana Burne-Jones in the *Memorials*, the only source of information for the Winnington scheme apart from the sketch plan, and the person in charge of the work, states that only 'one…[Hypsipyle] was actually begun'.

M.11

M.11 Two embroidered figures of *King Arthur* and *Merlin*

Designed by Edward Burne-Jones, 1863
Worked by Georgiana Burne-Jones
Watercolour, linen ground embroidered with wools and couched gold thread in stem and long and short stitches; irregular 106.0 x 50.0 cm; height of figures: 72.3 cm
V&A (T.118,121-1985)

Two figures from an embroidery scheme designed for the Burne-Jones's first home at 62 Great Russell Street. The *King Arthur* panel has a label attached stating '…drawn in 1863 by Edward Burne-Jones, upon the holland and embroidered by G.B-J. It was intended for one of a set from the Morte d'Arthur, with which we hoped to decorate a room of our own. Note made by G. Burne-Jones Feb 27 '09'. The scheme was not finished. Two other panels, *Morgan le Fay* and *Lancelot*, are also in the Museum collection.

Clearly influenced by the Red House heroine scheme, this was intended to be approximately half the size. A preliminary sketch for the scheme, in the Whitworth Art Gallery (verso D.73.1927), shows a two-tier composition with thirteen figures. An existing similar design for *King Arthur* (V&A E.449-1949) is inscribed 'Charlemagne by Wm Morris sketch at side by E.B.J'.

The rather naive preparation, of painting the design directly on to the ground, can be clearly seen in these examples, one of which is unfinished. *Merlin* has been cut out ready to apply to a finished ground for display. The embroidery technique shows a lack of both knowledge and skills, and compares unfavourably with contemporary examples worked for Red House.

M.12 Altar-frontal

Probably designed by William Morris
Embroidered by Morris, Marshall, Faulkner & Co. for the church of St Martin-on-the-Hill, Scarborough, 1862
Velvet ground laid and couched with silks and gold threads, 96.5 x 246.4 cm
(superfrontal 25.4 cm deep)
The Vicar and Church Wardens of the Parish of St Martin-on-the-Hill, Scarborough

Produced as part of the Bodley commission to decorate St Martin's which was consecrated in July 1862.

Although Webb was heavily involved in the decoration at St Martin's there is no mention of the frontal in his account book with Morris, Marshall, Faulkner & Co. which lists similar work for the same year (working drawings for 'Clapham Altar cloth'). It is likely, therefore, that Morris was responsible for the design which is strongly influenced by both English late medieval embroideries and G.E. Street's commercial church textiles (see cat. no. M.3).

The frontal appears listed under 'Stock' in the end-of-year statement minuted at the firm's meeting on 11 February 1863 at Red Lion Square. By 20 May 1863 the debt of £28 had increased to £42 9s. for 'Scarborough altar cloth and hangings'.

It is likely that the frontal was finished specifically to be exhibited in the 1862 International Exhibition.

M.12

M.13 Bell-pull

Designed by William Morris or, possibly, Ford Madox Brown, *c*.1865
Manufactured by Morris, Marshall, Faulkner & Co.
Brass fastenings and ring: velvet embroidered with silks in stem, satin stitches and couching;
257.3 cm x 10.7 cm
V&A (T.5-1919) Given by Mrs Edward Wormald

An early example of a practical domestic object purchased from the firm. The design and shape resembles an ecclesiastical stole. In an article in *The Artist* for May 1898, a list of Madox Brown's work for the firm includes 'embroideries, stamped velvets and silks'. His household account book mentions 'two sets of worsted bell ropes' designed for the firm. No examples have been identified.

The donor, said to be a friend of Jane Morris's, lived in Woodcote, a house in Carshalton in Surrey. According to the S. & S. Dunn's records Morris & Co. undertook some work on the house in 1876. Another version of this object survives and was bought from the Oxford Street shop in the 1920s.

M.14 Design for an embroidery

William Morris, 1865–70
Pencil and ink, 36.2 x 23.5 cm
Inscribed: 'Lines for the directions of the stitches'
Sanford and Helen Berger Collection

It is likely that this drawing dates from the early period of the firm, when Morris personally instructed the embroiderers. The paper has been folded to fit an envelope so is likely to have been sent to one of the firm's freelance workers. Morris's directions are interesting for two reasons. The lines suggested conventionally emphasise the growth of the plant by following the veins of the leaves but also show a sophisticated laying of stitches across leaves, a much more difficult result to achieve. A border may be suggested as the design is intended to repeat, but no sideways matching has been attempted.

The sunflower was a favourite early Morris motif, as it was for many contemporary designers. It can be seen in other 1860s work, including the inside of the St George Cabinet and an embroidered hanging made for Red House and now at Kelmscott Manor. It was also used for a later embroidery, worked by Catherine Holiday in 1875 (see cat.no.M.19).

M.13

M.14

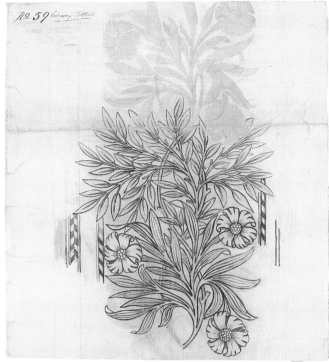

M.15b

M.16

M.15 Two scenes from the *The Romance of the Rose* embroidered frieze

Designed by Edward Burne-Jones and William Morris, 1874–6
Embroidered by Margaret Bell and her daughter Florence, 1874–82
Linen embroidered with coloured silks, wools and couched gold thread in long and short, split, stem, satin and other stitches
William Morris Gallery (London Borough of Waltham Forest) Gift of Sir Hugh Bell

a *The Pilgrim in the Garden of Idleness*
86.3 x 628.7 cm
(F140/C)
DETAIL ILLUSTRATED

b *The Pilgrim at the Heart of the Rose*
92.7 x 115.5 cm
(F140/E)

A series of wall hangings made for the dining room of Rounton Grange, Northallerton, a house built by Philip Webb in 1872 for the Northern ironmaster and metallurgist, Sir Isaac Lowthian Bell and his wife Margaret. The first of a number of collaborative embroidery designs with Burne-Jones supplying the general figurative composition and Morris adding decorative details (see cat.no.M.17).

The literary source for this scheme is *Romaunt of the Rose*, a poem by Chaucer based on an early medieval French original. The design was devised in three sections, for the north, south and west walls of the room. Emblematic figures representing the Miseries and Beauties of Life hung opposite each other with the Pilgrim dreaming among the roses in the Garden of Idleness; seeing himself led on one side by Love and on the other by Danger. The subject was later used for other Morris & Co. projects, including a series of tapestries worked at Merton Abbey in the 1890s. *The Pilgrim at the Heart of the Rose* is one of two designs common to both embroidered and woven versions.

The frieze featured early in plans for the furnishing of the house and a note in Webb's account book with Morris & Co., dated between 16 November and 17 December 1873, mentions 'Arrangement for Mr Bell's Tapestry…Not charged'. An 1874 entry in Burne-Jones's accounts lists £40 for '1st panel of the Romance of the Rose for tapestry'. Four further entries from November 1874 until 1876 give a total cost of £340 for designs. Whether additional charges were made by the firm for transcribing Burne-Jones's designs into working drawings is not recorded. A letter from Burne-Jones to Bessie Burden (Sanford and Helen Berger Collection) urging her to hurry George Wardle with some drawings for the project, suggests this process occasionally held up work.

Margaret Bell and her two daughters, Florence and Ada (see cat.nos.M.21, 23) were very experienced and accomplished embroiderers. Margaret and Florence took eight years to complete this frieze. Their efforts were admired by Morris who must have mentioned the work to his mother, Emma. She expressed a desire to see part of the completed work when it was in London. In a letter to her of 13 July 1877 (Kelvin, 419) he welcomes a visit 'but I am afraid that Mrs Bell's work will be gone in two or three days'.

Working drawings for two of the panels of the frieze are in the Museum (E.63,64-1940).

Exhib. 1952 (I 21); 1961 (one panel:26).

M.16 Embroidery design

William Morris, *c.*1875
Pencil, pen and ink and watercolour, 71.7 x 67.3 cm
Inscribed in ink: 'No 59 Embroidery Portfolio' and with some technical notes, partly erased
V&A (E.41-1940) Bequeathed by May Morris

Very similar to the *Marigold* wallpaper and fabric design registered in April 1875 (cat.no.M.46), this is part of a small series of designs made for the Royal School of Art Needlework soon after it was founded in 1872. Morris was probably introduced to the school through his sister-in-law, Bessie Burden, who taught there in the 1870s and organised its highly influential stand at the Philadelphia Centennial Exhibition of 1876.

A fuller repeating version of this described as 'Design for a Sofa-Back Cover' is illustrated in a publication devoted to the school's work, *Handbook of Embroidery* by L. Higgin (1880). Linen chair-back covers are listed in the book as costing between 7s. 1d. and one guinea for 'prepared work and materials'.

M.17

M.18

M.17 *The Musicians* hanging

Designed by Edward Burne-Jones and William Morris, *c*.1875
Worked at the Royal School of Art Needlework
Linen ground embroidered with wools in outline, chain, stem, satin stitches and
French knots; 107.4 x 140.3 cm
V&A (T.121-1953)   Given by P. J. Schryver Esq.

Burne-Jones and Morris supplied a number of designs for the Royal School of Art
Needlework in the 1870s.

It is not known whether these designs, which combine Burne-Jones figures and Morris's decorative details, were supplied privately or as part of the firm's output. However, as the
school held copyright on all their designs, a business arrangement was likely. This panel, like
the two other most popular figurative designs *Musica* and *Poesea*, was available either in
complex multicoloured silk versions or worked in monochrome wools in outline. The school
also produced embroidered versions of other works, including a vast copy of Burne-Jones's
painting *The Mill*, (V&A loan to Wightwick Manor) and the Morris & Co. tapestry *Pomona*.

The Royal School frequently exhibited abroad and it is likely that Morris embroideries featured on the stand at Philadelphia in 1876. The exhibit proved very popular and may be the
reason Morris considered, but finally decided against, shipping examples to the USA for sale
in December 1879 (Kelvin, 599).

M.18 *Honeysuckle* curtain or hanging

Designed by William Morris, 1876
Worked by Jane and Jenny Morris
Block-printed linen embroidered with silks in long and short, stem and satin stitches;
266.7 x 144.7 cm
Private Collection

This design was sold through the Royal School of Art Needlework in the 1870s (see
L. Higgin, *Handbook of Embroidery*, 1880). Worked over an outline version of the printed
fabric, this technique was also adopted by the Leek Embroidery Society, an organisation
founded by Elizabeth, the wife of Thomas Wardle (Morris's early printer), about 1879. The
group used both Morris and Wardle fabrics printed at Leek as the ground design and guide
for their work.

One of the few existing embroideries known to have been worked by Jane and her daughter
Jenny, both experienced and talented embroiderers. May described this as 'one of the finest of
all Morris embroideries' (V&A correspondence). It was exhibited at the first Arts and Crafts
Exhibition in 1888 and sent by May to the Louvre exhibition of British and Irish Decorative
Work in 1914. The panel was purchased from the Kelmscott Manor sale in 1939 (lot 180).
Exhib. 1934 (68); 1952 (I 22)

M.19 *Sunflower* coverlet or hanging

Designed by William Morris, *c.*1876
Worked by Catherine Holiday
Linen embroidered with silks in various stitches including long and short, stem and satin; 190.5 x 166.4 cm
V&A (Circ.196-1961)

The only identifiable Morris design by his favourite embroiderer, Catherine Holiday. A very experienced professional worker with a strong, individual style, she is now best known for work embroidered from designs by her artist husband, Henry Holiday.

Mrs Holiday worked for Morris & Co. on a freelance basis. The firm supplied her with all materials and kept ten per cent of any work sold through the shop. Mrs Holiday was very ambitious for her work. She wished to export before Morris was ready and he was also worried that she would price herself out of the market by overcharging. Sending a cheque for £60 on 6 December 1877 'on account of the coverlit [sic]...', he explained 'I must ask you to wait to see what I can sell it for...I am afraid we are hardly likely to get £120 for it...this opens up the difficulty in a commercial way of the whole industry'.

A series of letters from Morris to her concerning specific orders (Sanford and Helen Berger Collection) emphasises not only his vast experience and knowledge of embroidery technique but also his great admiration for her work. Henry Holiday claimed that Morris thought her 'the only person he had ever met whose work is as good as the old'.

M.20 Unworked embroidery silks used by Catherine Holiday

Morris & Co., *c.*1870s–80s
Silk skeins of various ply (thickness) and colour wound around cards, various sizes
V&A (T.123-1985)
NOT ILLUSTRATED

Part of a collection of nineteen different pastel coloured silks contained within a package labelled 'Portiere. Darning silks'. The silks are wound around cards, including one from the Hampstead Liberal Club addressed to Henry Holiday. Others have technical notes in pencil.

Morris was fussy not only how silk was used in his work but also about the type of yarn employed. In a letter to Catherine Holiday he stated that 'nothing will do but floss' for fine stitchery with broader areas worked in the coarser, less glossy, filoselle yarns. (Kelvin, 452).

M.19

M.21

M.22

M.21 *Artichoke* hanging

Designed by William Morris, August 1877
Worked by Ada Phoebe Godman, 1877–1900
Linen embroidered with wools, 213.0 x 150.0 cm
V&A (T.166-1978)

Repeating patterns of large traditional motifs are a characteristic of Morris's embroidery designs in the late 1870s and 1880s (see cat.no.M.22). These indicate a pre-occupation with Near Eastern and Italian woven silks and velvets, a number of which he studied at the South Kensington Museum.

The design was delivered to Smeaton Manor, Northallerton on Friday 31 August 1877. The client, Mrs Godman, a daughter of Margaret and Lowthian Bell (see cat.no.M.15), spent many years embroidering the design on to a number of panels for the drawing-room walls of her Philip Webb designed house.

This design did not remain exclusive to the client. A pair of hangings of the same pattern were worked by Mrs Margaret Beale and her daughters for their home, Standen, Sussex. The original design which is inscribed 'Mrs Godman. Design for embroidered hanging (artichoke design)' was acquired by the Victoria and Albert Museum (65-1898) before the Smeaton panels were finished.

A drawing by Paul Bramley, showing Mrs Godman working on the embroideries in 1900, was sold with three of the panels in 1978. A smaller, fourth piece was sold in 1981.

Exhib. 1952 (I 23)

M.22 *Lotus* hanging

Designed by William Morris, 1875–80
Worked by Mrs Margaret Beale and her daughters
Canvas embroidered with silks in various techniques including long and short, brick, satin and darning stitches with woven braid trimming; 241.4 x 187.9 cm
V&A (T.192-1953)
Given by Mr G. Beale from the estate of the late Mrs Kate Beale

Stylistically this repeating design dates from the 1870s, before Morris's large designs show quartered mirror-images, a direct influence of his interest in hand-knotted carpets manufacture. The hanging was embroidered by the Beale family when living in Holland Park, London, before their move to Standen in 1894. It is likely that the Beales were introduced to the

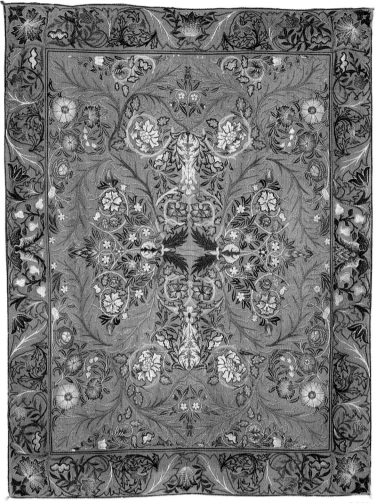

M.23

M.24

work of Morris & Co. by their near neighbours in Holland Park, the Ionides family.

The work is extremely accomplished, both in technique and rendition of the design, and it is possible that it was partially worked in the Morris & Co. workshops.

A working drawing is in the Museum (E.32-1940).

Exhib. 1961 (41)

M.23 *Acanthus* coverlet or hanging

Designed by William Morris, *c.*1880
Worked by May Morris and others
Felted woollen cloth embroidered with silks in stem, satin and darning stitches with laid and couched work and speckling; edged with silk cord;
248.8 x 200.6 cm
V&A (T.66-1939)

Bequeathed by May Morris

This quartered design reflects the form of hand-knotted carpets, a subject that preoccupied Morris from the late 1870s.

One of Morris & Co.'s most popular embroidery compositions, the Museum owns three examples (see cat. no. M.24) including one worked in wools on linen about 1880 by Florence Bell and her daughters for Rounton Grange, Northallerton (Circ. 524-1953). This example shows May Morris's great skills as a colourist and an interpreter of her father's designs.

A working drawing is in the Museum (E.55-1940).

M.24 *Acanthus* sample hanging

Designed by William Morris, *c.*1880
Worked in the Morris & Co. workshops
Cotton embroidered with silks in vertical flame, long and short and satin stitches with laid and couched work and French knots;
129.5 x 108.0 cm
V&A (T.153-1979)

A sample hanging of the *Acanthus* design (see also cat. no. M.23). This shows a truncated version of the upper half of the design with part of the original side border and other geometric alternatives. Probably used in the Oxford Street shop of Morris & Co. to show to potential clients.

M.25

M.27

M.26

M.25 *Flowerpot* firescreen panel or cushion cover

Designed by William Morris, *c*.1878–80
Worked by May Morris and others
Wool embroidered with silks in chain, satin and stem stitches and
French knots; 54.6 x 54.6 cm
V&A (T.68-1939) Bequeathed by May Morris

One of a number of small square designs produced for cushions or mounted
firescreens. Many of these were sold throughout the 1880s and 1890s
(see cat.nos.M.27–9) and provided an inexpensive means of acquiring
an example of Morris design. They could be purchased as completed
embroideries or in kit form to be completed at home.

This design is likely to be one of Morris's last patterns for embroidery and is
based on two Italian seventeenth-century lacis-work panels acquired by the
South Kensington Museums in 1875. A number of amateur and professional
versions survive. This example and one at the William Morris Gallery,
Walthamstow, are both said to have been worked by Morris's daughter, May,
and show different interpretations of the design.
Exhib. 1934 (65).

M.26 Trial sample for an embroidered pelmet

Designed by William Morris, 1881–2
Ground of *St James* silk damask with padded and appliqué motifs in
silk and couched silk braid, 95.8 x 130.8 cm
V&A (T.87-1946)

Morris's diary for 21 December 1881 notes a meeting with Algernon Freeman-
Mitford, Secretary to the Board of Works, from whom he '…got orders to give
estimates for curtains'. These were for the Throne Room and Blue Room in
St James's Palace, part of a larger commission for decoration at the palace.

M.28

M.29a

Existing drawings (cat.nos.I.10–11) show the intended position of the curtains and the buckram pelmets for these rooms. Both were made from the specially designed *St James* silk damask. In their estimate of 13 March 1882, Morris & Co. quoted £375 for valances for the Throne Room and £180 for the Blue Room, 'The valances will be made in two parts, the lower portion shaped and made of the same silk as the curtains, embroidered, with fringe on edge. The upper part will also be of the same silk, but draped in swags and tail ornamented with fringe and rosettes'. When asked to reduce the estimate the firm replied, 'we will endeavour by some economies to bring the work within the limits you have fixed with the understanding that we will do our best to carry out the design submitted to you within these limits'. It is impossible to know whether this trial was made before or after this saving was made.

The original watercolour design for the pelmet is in the William Morris Gallery, Walthamstow (A41).
Exhib. 1934 (70); 1961 (62)

M.27 Firescreen panel

Possibly designed by Philip Webb or May Morris, 1885–90
Worked by May Morris
Linen canvas embroidered with silks in cross, tent and mosaic diamond filling stitches; 65.4 x 65.4 cm
V&A (T.69-1939)
Bequeathed by May Morris

Worked to the same format as the commercial cushion cover and firescreen panels sold through Morris & Co. Only two embroidered versions of this design are known. The symbolic motifs of tree, vine and flame-shaped leaves suggest that the original may have been intended for church use.

May Morris was manager of the embroidery department of Morris & Co. from 1885 until 1896. As well as embroidering and supervising the work of the firm during this time she also completed and exhibited embroideries of her own design and by other leading artists. (see cat.nos.M.34–6).

This is a delicately worked example of canvas embroidery, a technique disliked by William Morris who believed that its popular use throughout the nineteenth century had resulted in a loss of general skills. All of the firm's own commercial kits were intended to be worked in surface embroidery (see cat.no.M.25).

M.28 *Rose and Olive* firescreen

Designed by William Morris, *c.*1880
Worked by Mrs Laurence Hodson of Compton Hall, Wolverhampton, *c.*1900
Glazed mahogany frame: cotton panel embroidered in silks in long and short, stem, out-line and satin stitches; approx. 110.0 x 70.0 cm (panel 55.8 x 55.8 cm)
Private Collection

A commercially popular Morris & Co. design sold as a firescreen or cushion cover. This example was worked from a kit bought from the Oxford Street shop. An unfinished version of this design is in the Victoria and Albert Museum (Circ.300-1960).

The design is illustrated in Morris & Co.'s undated catalogue *Embroidery Work* (*c.*1912) both as a panel and a firescreen where it is priced at £4 10s. This included 'stretching and mounting customers' own embroidery under glass'.

A number of variations of this design survive, including examples in monochrome and outline stitches as well as ones in which the ground is embroidered in darning stitches (Whitworth Art Gallery, Manchester). Another example was worked by Mary, Lady Trevelyan, of Wallington, Northumberland.

M.29 Two unfinished embroidery kits

Designed by May Morris
Morris & Co., *c.*1890s
Cotton ground with ink tracing, partially worked with silks; a 38.1 x 49.5 cm, 62.2 x 66 cm
V&A (Circ. 301, 302-1960)
Given by Miss Vere Roberts

Two unworked kits bought from Morris & Co. in the late nineteenth century. The firm sold embroideries in various levels of completion, as finished work, as kits complete with marked ground and silks and, more popularly, in this form with a small corner of the ground completed so that the recommended technique could be seen and followed at home.

M.30

M.30 Design for *Anemone* screen panel

John Henry Dearle, *c.*1885–90
Pencil, ink and watercolour,
31.75 x 34.25 cm
Inscribed:
'A' 'Embroidery Screen panel Ox. St.'
Sanford and Helen Berger Collection

Although May Morris designed most of Morris & Co.'s embroidery from the mid-1880s, Henry Dearle (1860–1932) also produced a number of single panels for wallhangings (see cat. no. M.33) and screens (cat. nos. M.31–2). As with the smaller screen panels and cushion covers sold by Morris & Co. these panels were sold as completed works or in kit form.

May was responsible for the completion of all embroideries sold by the firm and her spirited interpretation of Dearle's designs has led to confusion over design author-ship. However, Dearle's style is quite different, often using designs centred on single meandering trees and leaves, where-as May Morris's work is more brightly coloured and complex in detail.

These panel designs, usually based on one particular plant, were very popular and occasionally the same subject is used for more than one design. On the reverse of this drawing is a *Peony* panel marked 'B' with May Morris's comments 'This is likely to be most suited as 'A' is rather too like 'Anemone' panel already worked'. Embroidered versions of these two design are illustrated in the firm's catalogue *Embroidery Work*. They also appear, identi-fied as Dearle's work, in Lewis F. Day's article 'A Disciple of William Morris' (*The Art Journal*, 1905), one of the few articles on Morris's vastly underrated assistant who became Artistic Director of Morris & Co. on Morris's death.

M.31 Three-fold screen with *Parrot Tulip, Large Horned Poppy* and *Anemone* panels

Designed by John Henry Dearle
*c.*1885–90
Glazed mahogany frame; panels of can-vas embroidered with silks in darning, stem and satin stitches; each panel 155.1 x 49.5 cm
V&A (Circ.848-1956)

This shows three of Dearle's panel designs, including the first version of the *Anemone* (see cat. no. M.30).

An identical three-fold screen with reversible hinges and with panels of *Large Horned Poppy* and *Anemone* is illustrated in Morris & Co.'s *Embroidery Work*, where it is priced at £17 10s.

Contemporary photographs of later Morris & Co. interiors, show that a number of clients, including the Sanderson, D'Arcy and Barr Smith families, all found these screens essential furnishing for the drawing room.
Exhib. 1961 (64)

M.32 Design for four panels, *Apple Tree, Vine, Pomegranate* and *Plum*

John Henry Dearle *c.*1895
Pencil and wash, 52.4 x 78.6 cm
Sanford and Helen Berger Collection

Four designs from a series based on fruit trees, a variation of the bird panels designed a few years earlier (cat. no. M.33). May Morris also produced designs based on similar subjects.

Many of these tree panels were sold sepa-rately as wall hangings rather than mounted into wooden screens, and a number sur-vived. A set of six, worked between 1919 and 1923 by Helen, Lady Lucas-Tooth, now at the William Morris Gallery, Walthamstow, includes the *Apple Tree*. However, in this, the strongly characteristic Morris motif of a trailing acanthus leaf is omitted, an indication how fashion had changed in the quarter century between the drawing of the design and this version of the embroidery.

M.32

M.33a

M.33b

M.33 *Owl* and *Pigeon* wall hangings or portières

Designed by John Henry Dearle, *c*.1895
Worked by Mrs Battye, from 1898
Embroidered in silks in satin, stem and darning
stitches on *Oak* silk damask, approx. 189.0 x 161.0 cm
V&A (T.369&A-1982)
Given by Mr Christopher Brasier-Creagh in the
names of the Misses Audrey and Norah Battye

Bought from Morris & Co. as kits, these panels were
very ambitious projects. The finely worked results show
the high standard of amateur needlework among
middle-class women at the time. Mrs Battye was a good
client. A panel incorporating the arms of the Battye
family, drawn in the Morris workshops and worked by
her, is now at the William Morris Gallery, Walthamstow.

Dearle designed three bird hangings, all larger and more
complex than the tree screen panels. *Owl* is a variation of
the third design, *Partridge,* which is illustrated in the *Art
Journal* for 1905. A number of versions survive. One,
bought in 1904 by Mrs Cuncliffe of Eaton Square, is
now in a private collection in Canada, another, with an
embroidered inscription was sold at Christies in 1991.

M.34 Tablecloth

Probably designed by May Morris, *c*.1890
Worked by Mrs Laurence Hodson or in the Morris
& Co. workshops, 1895
Linen embroidered in silks with stem, satin and
darning stitches; 108.0 x 108.0 cm
V&A (T.426-1993)

Given by Mr and Mrs L.G.Hodson

May Morris's embroidery designs for Morris & Co.
comprise many practical domestic items including
cushion covers, firescreens, tablecloths, table runners,
bedspreads, card cases and sachets. Although many
examples were sold in the Oxford Street shop, the firm
is now best known for large, showy hangings. Because
of this May Morris's work is under-appreciated today.
This tablecloth is one of her finest designs for the purpose and shows her ability to produce an interesting
and complex design for a mundane purpose.

This tablecover was bought for Compton Hall, a house
near Wolverhampton which Morris & Co. decorated for
Laurence Hodson, a Midlands brewer.

Tablecloths were also sold by Morris & Co. as kits, and

six, including one of this design, have recently come to light in Australia. All were embroidered by the Barr Smith family of Adelaide (Adelaide, 1994).

M.35 Design for a super-frontal for an altar

Philip Webb, 1898–9
Pencil, ink and watercolour,
51.4 x 76.3 cm
Signed and dated with extensive technical notes
V&A (E.58-1940)
Bequeathed by May Morris

This piece is likely to have been ordered by Isabella Gilmore, William Morris's third sister, who was Deaconess at Rochester and Southwark House.

Webb's design shows half of the finished frontal (cat.no.M.36) and it is suggested in the inscriptions that it was destined to hang on a recently constructed wooden altar, probably designed by him. The drawing is full of meticulous detail; however, he does not underestimate the talents and abilities of the embroiderer, May Morris, and whereas some effects he hopes to achieve, such as jewels, are suggested, much is left for her interpretation.

M.36 Super-frontal

Designed by Philip Webb, 1898–9
Embroidered by May Morris
Linen embroidered with silks and gold thread in stem, long and short, satin and split stitches with French knots and laid and couched work;
34.9 x 145.4 cm
V&A (T.379-1970)
Given by the Rochester and Southwark Deaconess's House

From 1896, when she gave up management of the embroidery department of Morris & Co., May Morris concentrated more and more on private embroidery commissions. This work, which is quite different from her commercial production, shows her very great abilities, both in the sensitivity of her interpretation of Webb's design and in her superb craftsmanship. Like her father before her, she advocated the revival of traditional techniques to regain the skills of the past. As a well-known practitioner, teacher and writer on the subject, she has probably been of far greater influence that her father over following generations of British embroiderers.

M.34

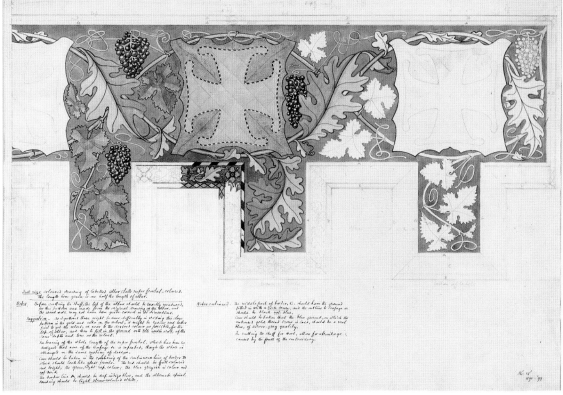

M.35

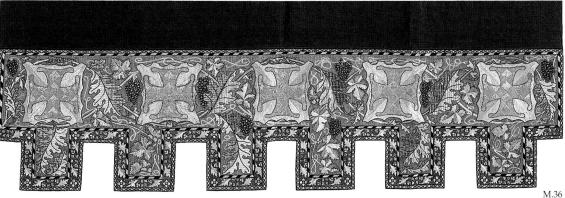

M.36

PRINTED TEXTILES

M.37 *Small Stem* curtain of printed wool

Adapted from an 1830s British design
Sold by Morris, Marshall, Faulkner & Co. from *c*.1868
Block-printed wool; 254.0 x 175.0 cm, pattern repeat 89.5 x 91.5 cm
V&A (T.37-1979)
Given by Mr and Mrs M. Woodall

After organising the firm's production of wallpapers, Morris next turned his attention to furnishing textiles by approaching Thomas Clarkson of Bannister Hall, the leading Lancashire cotton printer. As Clarkson's production centred on roller-printing, the results of which Morris disliked, a compromise was found and his first textiles printed by Clarkson's were from 1830s blocks selected from the store at the Lancashire factory. This woollen example was one of the first and bears the early Queen Square selvedge mark. Three other designs printed at that time were *Large Stem, Jasmine Trail* and *Coiling Trail*.

George Wardle remembered that '…the best of these patterns were reproduced in the original colourings and they took their place as novelties when exhibited "in the shop".' May Morris's description is more succinct: 'These were on a white ground and several of them were copied from the pleasant old-fashioned shiny chintzes. I remember two Chinese rose patterns, large and small and a pretty open "Coiling Trail" pattern.' (*William Morris, Artist, Writer, Socialist*, 1936.)

A revival of interest in these designs in the early twentieth century followed the fashion for white-ground chintzes.

M.38 *Jasmine Trellis* furnishing textile

Designed by William Morris, 1868–70
Manufactured for Morris, Marshall, Faulkner & Co. by Thomas Clarkson and later by Thomas Wardle
Block-printed cotton, 22.9 x 94.0 cm, pattern repeat 45.0 x 45.5 cm
V&A (T.70-1953)
Given by Mrs Winifred Nicholson

Satisfied with the early results from Clarkson, Morris then commissioned the firm to print this, his first design for furnishing textiles. Drawn during the early period when Morris was designing both wallpapers and textiles, there is ambiguity in this design. It is not as original as the earlier *Trellis* wallpaper (cat.no.L.1), and the simplification of pattern and colouring, which suited Clarkson's commercial, mostly chemical, palette of dyes may be the result of Morris attempting to design a pattern that he knew could be produced successfully. Because of this the pattern is the closest Morris ever came to attempting an 'Aesthetic' design, the style most fashionable in London at that time. This pattern is very similar to commercial patterns by G.F.Bodley and Bruce Talbert, and Morris may have been influenced by their work. However, the firm's products did not go unnoticed in these circles and E.W.Godwin, one of the most original Aesthetic architects and designers, used *Trellis* wallpaper in one of his most influential interior schemes.

M.37

M.38

M.39

M.39 *Utrecht Velvet* furnishing textile

Sold by Morris, Marshall Faulkner & Co from about 1871
Stamped woollen plush; 46.4 x 62.2 cm, pattern repeat 66.0 x 61.0 cm
V&A (T.210-1953)
Given by Mrs Gubbins

This fabric was not produced by the firm but was selected as a suitable furnishing textile and sold under its name, initially from the Queen Square shop. George Wardle claims that a Manchester firm, Heaton & Co., supplied woollen serges, so it is possible that they also provided woollen plushes. A practical and hard-wearing fabric, it imitates and takes its name from stamped velvets first produced in the Low Countries in the seventeenth and eighteenth centuries.

Morris refers to the dyeing of 'woollen velvet… done…in any colours that are possible…' in a letter to Thomas Wardle dated 10 September 1875, so it is likely that he tried to manufacture similar cloth himself or had these dyed at Leek. The fabric, which continued to be commercially successful throughout the nineteenth century, was used by the firm for upholstery on a number of Morris chairs (cat. nos. J.29, 32) and was sold in a wide range of colours. A second design, *Acorn*, was also sold by the firm after Morris's death.

M.40

254   WILLIAM MORRIS, 1834–1896

M.41

M.42

M.40 Design for *Tulip and Willow* printed textile

William Morris, 1873
Pencil, watercolour and bodycolour,
114.3 x 94.0 cm
Inscribed in pencil: 'Top'
Birmingham Museums and Art Gallery (393'41)
Presented by the Friends of Birmingham Museum and Art Gallery

Morris's second textile design, printed initially by Clarkson's and later at Merton Abbey. This is the first of a number of patterns with a dense background of willow leaves, a form seen in his textile designs throughout the 1870s and 1880s.

The design was purchased from Morris & Co.

Exhib. 1934 (97)

M.41 Registered sample of *Tulip and Willow* printed textile

Designed by William Morris, 1873
Printed by Thomas Clarkson, December 1973
Block-printed cotton, 54.5 x 91.5 cm
Public Record Office, London, UK (BT 43/370)

This sample of *Tulip and Willow* was submitted to the Design Registry and registered in Thomas Clarkson's name on 30 December 1873.

This sample clearly shows the crude effect of Prussian blue dye, which caused Morris to abandon the pattern until 1883, when he was finally able to gain the effect he required with indigo-discharge printing.

M.42 *Tulip and Willow* furnishing textile

Designed by William Morris, 1873
Printed at the Merton Abbey Works, 1883
Block-printed and indigo-discharged cotton,
137.16 x 88.9 cm
V&A (Circ.91-1933)
Given by the London County Council

This, the final version of this textile, was printed successfully ten years after it was designed. After moving to Merton Abbey in 1881 Morris set about constructing an indigo vat. His first discharge prints were monochrome patterns (*Brer Rabbit, Bird and Anemone* and *Rose and Thistle*). This pattern, which used only two colours, blue (indigo) and yellow (weld) and mixtures of these, is likely to have followed these into production.

The original printing blocks are at the William Morris Gallery, Walthamstow.

M.43 Typescript copies of three letters from William Morris to Thomas Wardle, 1875–6

Typewritten on copy paper,
each sheet 25.5 x 20.0 cm
V&A (NAL L.2877-1956)   Given by Mr Fred Wardle
NOT ILLUSTRATED

Unhappy with Clarkson's printing of *Tulip and Willow* (cat.no. M.41), Morris approached Thomas Wardle, the brother-in-law of George Wardle, the firm's manager, who had recently set up his own dyeing and printworks in Leek in Staffordshire. Keen to re-establish the use of natural dyestuffs, Morris and Wardle worked in Leek throughout July 1875 combining old recipes with new techniques, including steam setting and chemical mordants. When Morris returned to London their work continued in the form of correspondence. Through this collection of letters it is possible to trace Morris's views and preferences not only for the dyeing and manufacture of printed textiles and the samples sent to him, but on a range of subjects.

Morris's first letter, of 3 August, shows his dissatisfaction with Wardle's Prussian blues: 'They wash worse that than Clarkson's blues; in fact worse than any I have ever seen and it would be useless for us to sell them in their present state.' Morris knew the only solution was the successful use of indigo, a subject he returned to time and time again. By 17 November 1876 the process is still under discussion. This letter, describing the use of twigs found on the river bank at Kelmscott, shows Morris's preoccupation with dyeing, even when in the countryside.

The originals of these letters are now part of the Sir Thomas Wardle Papers, Perkins Library, Duke University, Durham, North Carolina, USA.

M.44

M.44 Pattern book of printed fabrics

Thomas Wardle, 1875
Block-printed cottons stuck to paper, printed labels, pencil and ink notes; 33.0 x 21.0 x 5.0 cm closed, 33.0 x 43.0 x 3.0 cm open
Whitworth Art Gallery,
The University of Manchester (14003)

A record book of printed textiles manufactured at Thomas Wardle's Hencroft Printworks in Leek, Staffordshire. All of Morris's printed textiles designed between 1875 and 1878 were printed here and this, the first volume, shows only Morris & Co. patterns. Included are samples of all colour trials attempted by Wardle and Morris, a number of which were not put into commercial production. From February 1878 Wardle was printing fourteen designs for Morris & Co. This collaboration lasted throughout the nineteenth century and these patterns continued to be produced at Leek despite the move to Merton Abbey in 1881–2.

M.45 *Printer's Notes*

Morris & Co., 1880–5
With notes in ink and pencil, 26.6 x 18.2 cm closed
Private Collection

A unique yet unfinished record of the firm's early printing practices. Although the only discernible date is 1883, it is possible that the book was started by Morris (early entries are in his hand) before the move to Merton Abbey in to attempt to record details he wished to follow when he became a manufacturer in his own right. The book also included details of practices at Merton Abbey after the move in 1881.

Early information includes a reference list of dyeing manuals, covering volumes published between 1760 and 1876–7, and a comparison of recipes for indigo dyeing from such publications as Persoz's *L'Impression des Tissus* (Paris, 1846) and Napier's *A manual of the art of dyeing* (London, 1853). Morris's ability to read and select from these publications shows an extraordinary comprehension of the technological and chemical components of the craft.

Other entries include hints on how to keep the printing shed warm and moist 'some boil a kettle in the shop to keep the air moist; some hang up damp clothes; this last is best'.

M.46 *Marigold* furnishing textile

Designed by William Morris, registered as a wallpaper, February 1875, and as a textile on 15 April 1875
Manufactured for Morris & Co. by Thomas Wardle, Leek

Block-printed silk, 97.5 x 55.0 cm
V&A (Circ.496-1965)

This is likely to have been the first of Morris's patterns to be printed by Wardle at Leek, although the first colour experiments for this design are dated 25 November 1875 (cat.no.M.44).

One of a small group of Morris designs on printed silk exhibited by Thomas Wardle at the Paris Exposition Universelle of 1878. Included in the Indian Section (presumably because of their imported ground) they were acquired by the Victoria and Albert Museum soon afterwards and lay undiscovered as British work until the 1960s.

Morris refers to an earlier display of silk examples when writing to Wardle on 23 November 1875. 'You are quite welcome to send the prints to the India House…As to our using them the only drawback seems to be that they are made awkward widths for our present blocks…By the way I think the Carnation would look well on the Tussore.'

Wardle was particularly interested in silk. He spent a number of years experimenting with sericulture and perfecting the dyeing and printing of tussah, the ground for this example. He was a founder member and President of the influential Silk Association and published books and articles on the subject.

M.47 *Tulip* furnishing textile

Designed by William Morris,
registered 15 April 1875
Manufactured for Morris & Co.
by Thomas Wardle, Leek
Block-printed cotton, 167.0 x 92.0 cm
V&A (Circ.410-1953)
Given by Mrs Gubbins

Morris drew five textile designs in 1875, this is one of three (with *Marigold* and *Larkspur*) registered on the same day. All three are densely floriated with a repeating zigzag of wavy leaves, and show Morris's preoccupation with wallpaper design at this time. Despite the simplicity of the pattern, many colour trials were undertaken and a letter as early as 3 September 1875 refers to the 'dark outline of the tulip…' (Kelvin, 288).

This example is a late nineteenth– or early twentieth-century printing of the design and was bought from Morris & Co.'s Oxford Street shop by a good client, Mrs Gubbins of Blackwater Road, Eastbourne. This unused length shows the full width of the fabric.

The original design and twelve original printing blocks are owned by the William Morris Gallery, Walthamstow.

M.46

M.45

M.47

M.48

M.49

M.51

M.48 *Carnation* furnishing textile

Probably designed by Kate Faulkner, registered 15 October 1875
Manufactured for Morris & Co. by Thomas Wardle, Leek
Block-printed cotton, 16.6 x 93.0 cm
V&A (T.248-1984)
Given by Sue Tarran

One of the few existing early examples of Morris printed textiles in pristine condition. This shows Wardle's use of Prussian blue dye, which Morris believed 'a terrible disappointment'. The pattern is first mentioned in a letter from Morris and Wardle in September 1875.

This sample, which has a selvedge mark for 26 Queen Square, was printed before April 1877.

Although always previously recorded as a William Morris design, it was claimed not to be by him when a sample of the cotton was acquired by the Museum from Morris & Co. in the 1930s. On stylistic grounds it is possible that this pattern was drawn by Kate Faulkner, who (with her brother Charles and sister Lucy were all involved with the firm) was a friend and neighbour of the Morrises in Queen Square. Kate worked as a designer and as a tile and gesso painter for the firm as well as producing wallpaper patterns for Jeffrey & Co.

This sample was taken from inside the lining of curtains used at Belton House, Lincolnshire.

M.49 Trial printing of *Iris* furnishing textile

Designed by William Morris, registered 25 April 1876
Manufactured for Morris & Co. by Thomas Wardle, Leek
Block-printed cotton, 59.0 x 45.0 cm
V&A (T.45-1919) Given by Morris & Co.

The printed diamond registration mark on this sample is incorrect and gives the date when *Tulip*, *Marigold* and *Larkspur* were registered.

Morris called the pattern 'Flower de luce' and referred to an example printed in madder red (no. 1106) in a letter to Wardle as early as 24 December 1875. This colouring (no.1063) may well have preceded the red printing mentioned above.

The original design, now in the Berger Collection, is inscribed by Morris, 'The block must have square ends. This is it must not follow the shape of the pattern'. This trial shows that the blocks were cut to Morris's instructions.

M.50 Design for *Bluebell* or *Columbine* printed textile

William Morris, 1876
Pencil and watercolour, 72.4 x 45.7 cm
Inscribed: 'Blue Bell Chintz' [crossed out], 'Columbine', 'The property of Morris & Company, 26 Queen Square, Bloomsbury, London W.C' and 'half worth'
V&A (E.44-1940) Bequeathed by May Morris
FOR ILLUSTRATION SEE FIG 10, PAGE 39

Designed early in 1876, the first trial printing of this design was on 4 May 1876.

Peter Floud (1959) has claimed that the design is based on a Rhenish linen, one of a small group said to have been printed in the fifteenth century when acquired by the South Kensington Museum soon after opening. Morris knew and admired these examples, unaware that they were to be exposed as fakes in 1962.

M.51 Trial printing for *Bluebell* or *Columbine* furnishing textile

Designed by William Morris, 1876
Manufactured for Morris & Co. by Thomas Wardle, Leek
Block-printed cotton, 99.0 x 88.9 cm
V&A (Circ.44-1956) Given by B.Wardle & Co.

Wardle's first printing trials for this design are dated 4 May 1876. This later printer's trial shows the initials of the block-printer plus 'No.1', suggesting that this may be the first trial of this particular colouring. Other printed references include 'Registered', (although no registration has been found), and the name and address of the firm. According to Philip Webb's address book the number of the Oxford Street shop was changed from 264 to 449 in 1881, so this dates later.

Morris was very critical of Wardle's dyers and printers. He referred to a number of them by name in various letters, demanding from them efficiency and economy for his work. On 23 November 1875 he suggested that rather than needing more staff to undertake the new technique of pencilling indigo blue, children could be used, 'Our boys at 5/6d would be quite up to it'.

M.52 *Honeysuckle* furnishing textile

Designed by William Morris, registered 11 October 1876
Manufactured for Morris & Co. by Thomas Wardle, Leek
Block-printed silk, 49.5 x 99.0 cm
V&A (Circ.491-1965)

One of Morris's most complex patterns, showing a large-scale (76 x 91.5 cm) turn-over repeat. This shows his increasing interest in designing for the loom, where this type of design is best suited. Trial printing of the pattern started about June 1876 (Kelvin, 332) and continued to be vetted by Morris until 29 November, when Morris claimed the sample sent '…is not right yet, but is hopeful'(Kelvin, 361).

This experimental silk shows only half of the width of the pattern but the translucency of colouring is very effective. It was acquired by the South Kensington Museum directly from the 1878 Paris Exposition, where it was exhibited by Wardle in the Indian Section under his name.

The original design, which is owned by Birmingham Museum and Art Gallery (401'41), is inscribed 'No. 15'.

The pattern was also used for embroidery (cat.no.M.18).

M.52

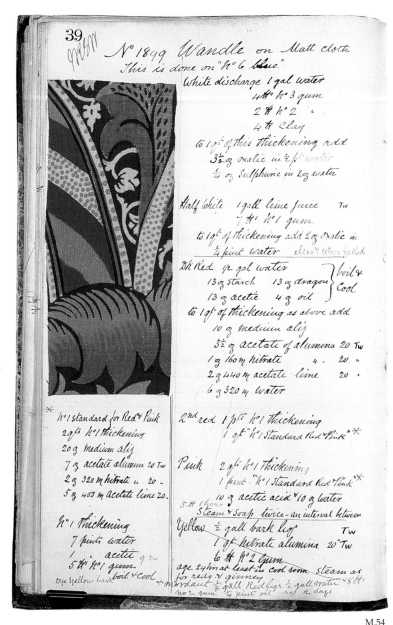

M.53

M.54

M.53 *Snakeshead* furnishing textile

Designed by William Morris, 1876
Manufactured for Morris & Co. by Thomas Wardle, Leek
Block-printed cotton, 123.0 x 93.0 cm
V&A (T.37-1919) Given by Morris & Co.

Between late 1875 and 1877 Morris produced a small group of patterns influenced by the colouring and patterns of Indian textiles. Wardle was, at this time importing silks and dyeing and overprinting these for Liberty's. Morris may well have seen examples during his visits to Leek.

This pattern first appears in the Wardle pattern books for January 1877. Printed onto a pre-dyed dark ground, it shows Morris's increasing interest in gaining depth of pattern through the overprinting of primary colours. He was finally to achieve this effect with indigo-discharge printing.

Wardle did not produce the most satisfactory printing of the pattern, according to Morris, until 27 March 1877 (Kelvin, 390). The original design is owned by Birmingham Museum and Art Gallery (397′41) and four printing blocks by the William Morris Gallery, Walthamstow.

M.54 Pattern book of dye recipes for printed textiles

Morris & Co., Merton Abbey, 1882–91
Printed fabrics glued to paper, notes in ink;
34.0 x 22.75 x 6.5 cm
Sanford and Helen Berger Collection

This hand-written ledger is a working record of printed-cotton manufactured at Merton Abbey between 1882 and 1891. Each page lists recipes used for printing identified and numbered patterns, many of which are illustrated with samples of cloth. Pages 1 to 72 are initialled 'JREW' and pages 73 to 111 'JHD' (for John Henry Dearle). Later amendments show changes in recipes and processing. As Morris's early printed fabric designs continued to be printed at Thomas Wardle's factory at Leek, this book itemises only patterns designed and printed after 1881. Only *Honeysuckle* (in red) and *Peony* (in brown) appear to have been printed in both places.

Recipes are arranged according to colour. Madder red examples are listed first (*Bird and Anemone*, *Brother Rabbit*, *Wey*, *Windrush*, *Florence* and *Mole*) then yellows and buffs from weld (*Rose and Thistle*, *Lea*, *Kennet*, *Corncockle*, *Cray* and *Cherwell*). These are followed by indigo-discharge blues (*Bird and Anemone*, *Brother Rabbit*, *Lea*, *Windrush*, *Wey*, *Tulip and Willow*, *Kennet*, *Lodden*, *Wandle*, *Evenlode* and *Cray*), greens (*Cherwell*,

Windrush and *Florence*) and samples of miscellaneous and mixed colours (*Strawberry Thief, Trent, Severn, Daffodil, Medway, Trail, Honeysuckle, Avon, Rose* and *Cray*). The last section of the book is unillustrated and repeats a number of recipes.

Exhib. 1961 (54)

M.55 Scrap of cotton, printer's end

Morris & Co., Merton Abbey, 1885–9
Printed and painted cotton, 21.5 x 96.5 cm
V&A (T.105-1985)
Given by S. Franses Ltd
NOT ILLUSTRATED

Discoloured printer's end from a length of block-printed cotton of William Morris's design, *Lea,* which was registered 2 February 1885.

This end is printed 'REGD MORRIS and COMPANY' with the printer's initials 'H.H.' These probably stand for Harry Hill, a block-printer with Morris & Co. from about 1883. He was listed as the printer of two fabrics designed by Morris that were exhibited in the 1889 Arts and Crafts Exhibition (426, 427).

This scrap of cotton was found stitched into the lining of a historic tapestry which had been restored by Morris & Co. at the beginning of this century.

M.56 Two samples of *Brother Rabbit* furnishing textile

Designed by William Morris, 1880–81
Manufactured at Merton Abbey
Indigo-discharged and block-printed cotton, 64.7 x 93.9 cm
V&A (T.647,648-1919)
FOR ILLUSTRATION SEE FIG 12, PAGE 42

In January 1878 Morris registered his last design to be printed at Leek. Unhappy with Wardle's general standard of printing and inability to undertake indigo dyeing successfully it was not until 1881, when he had found Merton Abbey and set up the indigo vat, that he returned to designing for this technique. This is one of three patterns drawn before April 1881 for this method.

However, its registration was delayed until May 1882 and printing not perfected until December 1882 (Kelvin, 833).

The pattern, also called *Brer Rabbit,* is named from J.C. Harris's children's stories *Uncle Remus, his Songs and Sayings,* published in 1881, which was being

read by the Morris family at this time. Philip Webb is credited with drawing the birds and animals for this design (John Brandon-Jones, Farnham, 1981). These samples show the pattern in full (dark blue and white) and half-discharged (pale and dark blue) indigo. It was also available in reds and yellows.

The printing blocks are owned by the William Morris Gallery, Walthamstow.

M.57 Design for *Rose and Thistle* printed textile

William Morris, 1881
Pencil, pen and ink, coloured chalk and watercolour; 103.0 x 68.2 cm
Inscribed: 'for chintz'
V&A (E.293-1939)
Bequeathed by May Morris

The design is marked '26 Queen Square', confirming that it was drawn before the move to Merton Abbey in June 1881, when Morris was experimenting with the indigo-discharge process at Queen Square. It is one of three patterns drawn by Morris especially for the technique, a fact emphasised by the dark blue colour used. This is the first of Morris's printed designs in which a meandering or, as he called it, 'branch' repeat is used, and marks a transition from the symmetrical 'net' patterns characterised in his printed fabrics before 1880.

M.58 *Rose and Thistle* furnishing textile

Designed by William Morris before April 1881
Manufactured at Merton Abbey
Madder-discharged and block-printed cotton, 64.7 x 97.1 cm
V&A (T.637-1919)
Given by Morris & Co.

Designed specially for the discharge technique, this example is printed with madder and shows a half discharge of the dye in the lighter areas.

It is one of Morris's first designs for indigo discharge, and the second printed by this method at Merton Abbey. The blocks were first tried in December 1882 (Kelvin, 833).

This is one of four examples of this design printed with madder and indigo discharge given to the Museum by Morris & Co. in 1919, although printed much earlier.

The four original printing blocks are owned by the William Morris Gallery, Walthamstow.

M.57

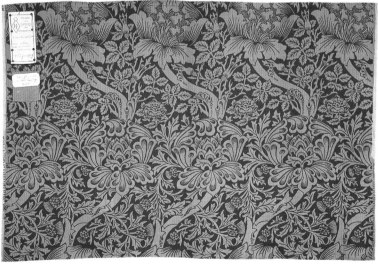

M.58

M.59

M.60

M.59 Set of printing blocks for *Strawberry Thief* textile

Made by Barrett's for Morris & Co., 1883
Pearwood with metal; felt inlay, various sizes
V&A (T.125 & A-1980)
Given by Stead McAlpin & Co.

Morris had personal experience of cutting blocks for printing having taught himself the craft while preparing illustrations for his aborted publication of *The Earthly Paradise* (fig.102). However, there is no evidence to suggest he cut any of his own fabric blocks. Examples used for printing early Morris textiles are likely to have been made at Bannister Hall (Thomas Clarkson) and at Leek (Thomas Wardle) and once the firm moved to Merton Abbey, instead of employing a block-cutter at the works, Morris sent his designs to Barrett's of Bethnal Green Road to be cut. Joseph

Barrett (1812–76) and his son Alfred (1847–1918) ran their business from 246 Bethnal Green Road. Morris is likely to have been introduced to their work through Metford Warner of Jeffrey and Co.

This design was originally printed by the indigo-discharge method and the main pattern-blocks cut in negative so that when printed with a bleaching agent on the solid indigo-dyed ground a white, or lightly coloured image was produced.

Some of these blocks were later re-cut for surface printing.

M.60 *Strawberry Thief* furnishing textile

Designed by William Morris, registered 11 May 1883
Manufactured at Merton Abbey
Indigo-discharge and block-printed cotton,
60.0 x 95.2 cm
V&A (T.586-1919) Given by Morris & Co.

On Whit Monday, only three days after registration of this design, Morris wrote to Jenny, 'I was a great deal at Merton last week…anxiously superintending the first printing of the Strawberry thief, which I think we shall manage this time' (Kelvin, 872). As this was his first indigo-discharged design also using red (in this case alizarin) and yellow (weld), Morris's anxiety is understandable. The Merton Abbey dye book (cat.no.M.54) states that the design '…comes three times on table' and lists the order that colour should be applied with blue, red and then yellow, each being dyed, printed and cleared in turn. This entire process would have taken a number of days to complete and, consequently, this is one of the firm's most expensive cottons. Clients were not put off by this and it proved to be one of Morris's most commercially popular patterns.

M.61

M.62

M.61 Brocaded velvet

Italian (Genoese), seventeenth century
163.0 x 53.3 cm
V&A (442A-1883)

In Peter Floud's seminal article 'Dating Morris Patterns' in *The Architectural Review* of July 1959, this velvet is cited as the single greatest influence on Morris's later pattern-making. The repeating devise of meandering stems with curving leaves and flower heads was used by Morris for a number of his designs drawn after 1883, when the Museum acquired this piece, in particular *Evenlode, Wey, Kennet, Windrush, Wandle, Cray* and *Medway*. However, the same structure is also seen in two earlier patterns, *Rose and Thistle* a printed fabric and the woven *Madras Muslin,* both designed in 1881. As if to emphasise the natural elements of these designs, all patterns of this type are named after tributaries of the Thames.

M.62 Design for *Evenlode* printed textile

William Morris, registered 2 September 1883
Pencil, pen and ink, black chalk, watercolour and bodycolour; 99.9 x 62.9 cm
Inscribed: 'Evenlode chintz', '5 blocks', 'No. 6848', with various technical notes
V&A (E.543-1939)

A complex pattern designed for the indigo-discharge technique originally printed with a dark green ground. One inscription refers to the number of colours needed to print the design not the actual blocks used. 'No. 6848' is the number of one particular colouring of this pattern and is likely to have been added at a later date.

This is the first of Morris's designs named after tributaries of the Thames. He drew the pattern at Kelmscott House while suffering from gout, and found some difficulty in naming it. In a letter to May on Saturday 3

March 1883 he wrote 'I have been at work pretty hard & have made a new pattern which in honour of the occasion I ought to call "Colchicum": only as Colchicum is nothing less than a crocus & I have stupidly omitted to put a crocus in, to avoid questions being asked I must fall back on a river and call it Evenlode' (Kelvin, 852).

In 1906 Morris & Co. produced the pattern on a white-discharged ground in line with current fashions.

The thirty-three blocks used to print this design are owned by the William Morris Gallery, Walthamstow.

Exhib. 1934 (102)

M.63

M.65

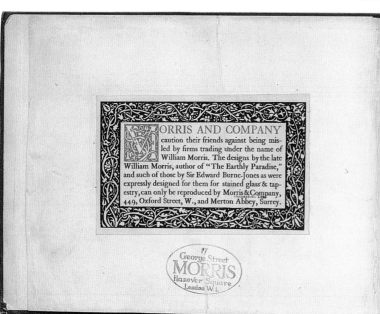

M.64

M.63 *Wey* velveteen curtain

Designed by William Morris, *c*.1883
Block-printed cotton velveteen, 231.0 x 396.0 cm
V&A (T.87a-1980)
Given by Forest Gate Unitarian Church

The pattern was originally designed to be printed as an indigo-discharged cotton but was also produced in this form, as a printed cotton velveteen.

This curtain is one of a pair, part of the Morris & Co. decoration of Forest Gate Unitarian Church, London. The estimate, dated 28 October 1901 quotes 'to make a curtain 14ft x 7ft 9ins if in cotton velvet £10.10.0d (ten guineas)', 'if in 3-ply tapestry without lining £10.15.0d'. The original design is owned by Birmingham Museum and Art Gallery (395'41).

M.64 Sample book of printed velveteens

Morris & Co., 1890s
Paper and board binding, printed velveteen samples; 21.0 x 31.0 x 2.0 cm closed, 21.0 x 54.5 x 2.0 cm open
V&A (T.660-1919) Given by Morris & Co.

Sample book of ten printed velveteens manufactured by Morris & Co. and sold through their shop. Designs represented are three different colourways of *Acanthus*, two of *Cherwell* and *Florence* and single samples of *Wey*, *Severn* and *Mole*.

Printed velveteens became very fashionable in the 1870s and provided one of the most recognisable artistic furnishings of the period. In February 1877 Morris wrote to Wardle, 'We could have a trade in velvets and serges if we could get the colours good and fast'

(Kelvin, 378). Examples were exhibited by Morris & Co. at the first Arts and Crafts Exhibition in 1888 and the patterns included in this book were designed by Morris and Henry Dearle over a wide period from 1876 (*Acanthus*, registered on 25 April) to *Mole*, designed after 1892. *Acanthus*, *Florence* and *Mole*, were only used as velveteens whereas *Cherwell* and *Wey* were also available on cotton.

The velveteen, which was printed on a narrow 27-inch (68.5 cm) ground, was used for curtaining and upholstery. It fell from popularity some years before this book was offered to the Museum in February 1919. H.C. Marillier wrote 'I have found you after a long hunt an ancient pattern book of Morris's printed cotton velvets, which had a great vogue in their day. They are beautiful materials and I can't imagine why they ever lost popularity but they did'.

M.66

M.67

M.65 Sample of *Kennet* furnishing textile

Designed by William Morris, registered
18 October 1883
Manufactured at Merton Abbey
Block-printed and indigo-discharged cotton,
68.0 x 96.5 cm
V&A (T.48-1912)
Given by Morris & Co.

A very strong diagonal pattern designed for indigo-discharge, the pattern is shown at its best when printed by this technique in full and half discharge with weld yellow in flower-heads and over-printed producing a part green leaf. The Merton Abbey dye book gives recipes for both indigo and Prussian blue versions of this design.

The design was also used at the end of the nineteenth century as a woven silk (cat.no.M.90) and a printed velveteen. Records for the firm of Alexander Morton show that the firm wove a muslin of a very similar design. Whether this was produced for Morris & Co. is not known.

A preparatory design is owned by Birmingham Museum and Art Gallery (404'41) and a working drawing for 'block No. 1' (BL A453) and the original printing blocks by the William Morris Gallery, Walthamstow.

M.66 Design for *Windrush* printed textile

William Morris, 1881–3
Pencil, pen and ink, and watercolour, on Whatman paper 1881; 131.5 x 99.6 cm
Inscribed: 'Windrush chintz',
'3 block white brown yellow'
William Morris Society, Kelmscott House, London
(D32)

Morris's designs became more and more impressionistic and although grid-lines are shown in this example, he has included only enough of the pattern to make it clear to the block-cutter how it works as a repeat. The design moves one stage further from the simple meandering stem seen before and here a second stem cuts across, providing complicated figures of eight. It also contains a formal motif of a pattern within a flower-head, which Morris described as 'the inhabited leaf'. His source for this was the Persian and Turkish carpets he was studying at this time.

The colours used on the design are surprisingly bright for Morris's natural dye palette and the pattern was usually produced as a surface print.

M.67 *Windrush* printed furnishing textile

Designed by William Morris, registered
18 October 1883
Manufactured at Merton Abbey
Block-printed cotton, 206.0 x 98.0 cm
V&A (Circ.424-1953)
Given by Mrs Lucius Gubbins

Printed on to cotton and linen, both discharged and surface-printing techniques were used for this design. It is, almost certainly, the discharged version that Morris promised Janey to hang in the drawing room at Kelmscott House 'as a summer change' in January 1884 (Kelvin, 948).

This example is not madder discharge, as expected from a design showing vast areas of the same colour, but is a late surface-print. Manufactured after 1917, it shows an attempt to neutralise Morris's multi-coloured design for the twentieth-century market.

The design is owned by the William Morris Society (cat.no.M.66) and seventeen printing blocks used to print the design are in the collection of the William Morris Gallery, Walthamstow.

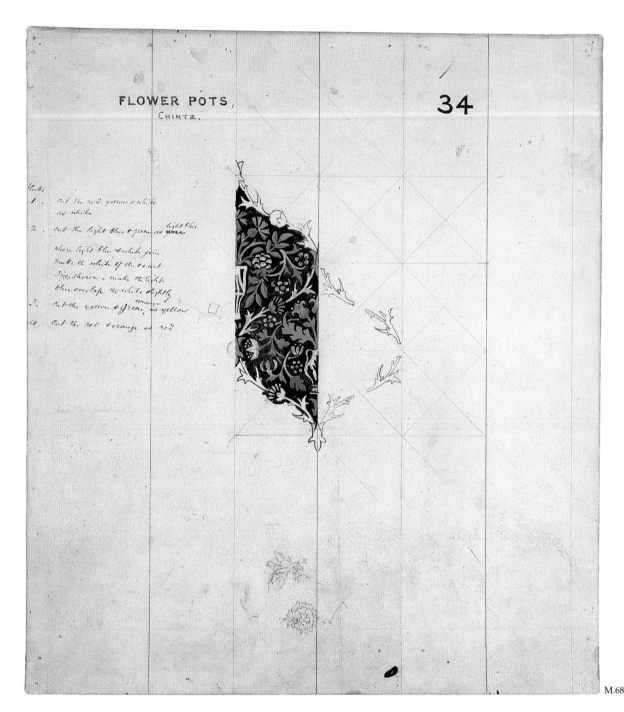

FLOWER POTS,
CHINTZ.
34

Blocks
1. Cut the red, yellow or white
as white

2. cut the light blue & green as green light blue

When light blue & white join
make it white of the exact
sizes shown - make the light
blue overlap the white slightly

3. cut the yellow & green as yellow orange

4. cut the red + orange as red

M.68

M.68 Design for *Flower Pots* printed textile

William Morris, 1882–3
Pencil, ink and watercolour, 43.0 x 39.0 cm
Inscribed: 'FLOWER POTS /CHINTZ 34' with
extensive notes
Birmingham Museums and Art Gallery (417'41)
Presented by the Association of Friends of
Birmingham Museum and Art Gallery

Registered on 18 October 1883, this is one of four small-scale designs drawn by Morris for curtain linings. These patterns were also used as dress fabrics. On 6 January 1883 Morris wrote to May referring to an earlier designed example, 'There is a new block come in for the printed dresses and we can dye piece cotton goods for such things so give your orders ladies as even the humble can indulge in these simple articles'.

Morris's design, which is very similar to contemporary embroidered panels, shows only half of the turn-over pattern. As it is one of the few discharged designs to use all of his primary palette of red, blue and yellow as well as overprinted greens and oranges his notes are very specific:

1. *Cut the red, yellow and white as white*
2. *Cut the light blue and green as light blue where light and white join*
   Make the white of the exact sizes shown and make the light blue overlap the white slightly
3. *Cut the yellow and green and orange as yellow*
4. *Cut the red and orange as red*

M.69 Design for *Rose* printed textile

William Morris, 1883
Pencil, pen and ink, watercolour, 90.6 x 66.3 cm
Inscribed: 'Chintz', 'Cherwell [crossed out]/Rose' and other notes
V&A (E.1075-1988)
Purchased with the aid of contributions from the National Heritage Memorial Fund, the Friends of the V&A and the Eugene Cremetti Fund of the National Art Collections Fund

Registered on 8 December 1883, this is only one of three printed textile patterns in which Morris depicted birds (see also *Strawberry Thief*, cat.no.M.60, and *Bird and Anemone*). As he claimed in a letter to Thomas Wardle of 25 March 1877 that he was studying birds to put in his next design it is probable that he alone was responsible for these.

Morris insisted on printing this complex design by the indigo-discharge process, despite this involving the bleaching and clearing of most of the white ground.

Once owned by Halcrow Verstage, the design was purchased by the Museum at Christies on 13 December 1988 (lot 165).

Exhib. 1934 (104)

M.70 Trial sample of *Wandle* printed textile

Designed by William Morris, registered
28 July 1884
Manufactured at Merton Abbey
Indigo-discharged and block-printed cotton,
160.0 x 96.5 cm
V&A (Circ.427-1953)
Given by Mrs Lucius Gubbins

This is a trial piece left at the indigo-discharge stage. The fabric has been dipped and dyed in the indigo vat, then soaped and washed until the dye was set. It was then block-printed with two sets of blocks, one having a strong bleaching agent to clear all of the blue from the ground leaving the white areas of the pattern, the other a weaker solution so that only part of the blue was discharged, resulting in a pale blue. The edge of the cloth shows the pin-marks made when securing the cotton in the vat.

M.71 *Wandle* furnishing textile

Designed by William Morris, registered 28 July
1884
Manufactured at Merton Abbey
Indigo-discharged and block-printed cotton,
165.0 x 92.0 cm
V&A (T.425-1934)
Given by the British Institute of Industrial Art

This large and splendid design took some time to develop. Drawing began in September 1883. Morris wrote to Jenny on the 4th saying '....if it succeeds I shall call it Wandle: the connection may not seem obvious to you as the wet Wandle is not big but small, but you see it will have to be very elaborate & splendid and so I want to honour our helpful stream...' (Kelvin, 908). Fents were not struck (trial printings made) until 18 March 1884, when Morris expressed his view that 'it will be very grand' in a letter to Jane (Kelvin, 959), and it was not registered for another four months.

The design repeat is the largest attempted by Morris (98.4 x 44.5 cm), and the striped barber's-pole effect his only attempt at geometric pattern. After *Cray* (cat.no. M.72) it was the most expensive cotton produced by Morris & Co.

A simplified version of this design was woven as a muslin by Alexander Morton.

The original printing blocks are owned by the William Morris Gallery, Walthamstow.

M.69

M.70

M.71

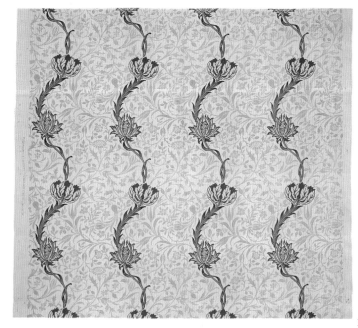

M.73

M.72

M.74

M.72 *Cray* furnishing textile

Designed by William Morris, 1884
Manufactured at Merton Abbey
Block-printed cotton, 96.5 x 107.9 cm
V&A (Circ. 82-1953)
Given by Mrs Winifred Nicholson

Thirty-four blocks were needed to print this complicat-ed large pattern (repeat: 92 x 45 cm), consequently this was the most expensive of all printed textiles produced by Morris & Co. Despite this it became very popular and was available in a number of different colourways on dark and light grounds in cotton or in linen. The pattern adapted to changing fashions and a number of early twentieth-century printings have survived show-ing pale colours on a white ground.

The last of Morris's grand designs for printed textiles. He was already preoccupied with complex weaving techniques at this time, and for the next four years con-centrated on designing for the loom. A few more printed patterns were drawn but none has the scale or breadth of design or depth of colouring of *Cray* or *Wandle*.

The printing blocks are owned by the William Morris Gallery, Walthamstow.

M.73 *Trail* furnishing textile

Designed by John Henry Dearle as a wallpaper (*Flora*), 1891
Manufactured at Merton Abbey
Block-printed cotton, 259.0 x 91.0 cm
V&A (Circ. 432-1953)
Given by Mrs Lucius Gubbins

By 1890 Morris had already stopped producing repeat-ing textile designs. He was now more interested in the successful development of the Kelmscott Press and overseeing his greatest commission, the *Holy Grail* tapestries for Stanmore Hall (cat.no.M.130). From the late 1880s Morris's assistant, Henry Dearle, had begun to produce patterns, and by 1890 was the firm's chief designer.

This pattern uses Morris's characteristic meandering stem on a multi-patterned background but the effect is altogether simpler. Originally designed for wallpaper, it is far more effective as fabric, the rather hard lines of the pattern being softened when seen in folds. Dearle was far less purist than Morris in his attitude to how his patterns were used and was responsible for adapt-ing a number of Morris wallpapers to textiles after the designer's death.

M.74 Sample book of printed cotton

Morris & Co., 1925–40
Manufactured at Merton Abbey
Printed cotton samples with printed labels;
21.0 x 29.0 x 5.5 cm closed
V&A (T.34 to E-1982)

A swatch sample book of fifty-eight printed cottons showing the range of patterns and colourways avail-able from Morris & Co. These swatches were used both in the George Street, Hanover Square, shop and sent out to customers in the country. Similar examples are in the collections of the Cooper Hewitt Museum, New York, and the Art Gallery of South Australia, Adelaide, both of which were sent to prospective clients abroad.

Included are some of the earliest designs recorded for the firm (*Small Stem*, *Large Stem* and *Coiling Trail*) plus seventeen well-known Morris patterns, six Dearle designs (*Daffodil*, *Yare*, *Compton*, *Bourne*, *Eden*, *Briar*) and two adapted Morris wallpaper patterns (*Willow* and *Powdered*). *Tangley*, *Haddon* and *Holkam* are early nine-teenth-century designs adapted for the early twentieth-century fashion for revival patterns.

Prices range from 3s. a yard for *Bird and Anemone* in madder-discharged cotton, to 10s. 6d. for a wider example (137 cm) of *Large Stem* on linen.

M.75

M.76

M.77

WOVEN TEXTILES

M.75 Woven band

Italian or German, first half of the seventeenth century
Silk and linen double cloth, 38.1 x 11.4 cm
V&A (T.123-1939) Bequeathed by May Morris

A small sample of Italian or Italian-influenced German weaving from Morris's own collection, retained by him for technical rather than pattern reference.

Morris designed a number of early woollen double cloths and one example, *Dove and Rose*, in silk and wool. His rare understanding and appreciation of the tactile quality of fibres and interest in how they react when woven together shows in many of his woven textiles. He was particularly fond of using linen, although the firm's first commercial silk and linen fabric, *Golden Bough* was one of Morris's last designs for the technique.

M.76 *Tulip and Rose* curtain with tie cord

Designed by William Morris, registered
20 January 1876
Manufactured for Morris & Co. by the
Heckmondwike Manufacturing Company,
Heckmondwike, Yorkshire
Woven woollen triple cloth, tie of twisted wools

with silk trim; curtain 297.0 x 171.0 cm
V&A (Circ.390A-1970) Given by Mrs G.M.Spear

Although this pattern is the first dateable design by Morris for woven furnishing textiles, he had been considering adding these to the firm's range for some time. In November 1875 reference was made, in Morris's letters, to the Macclesfield silk weaver J.O.Nicholson, so it is clear that, having no facilities to weave commercial quantities of cloth himself, he followed the practice he had adopted earlier with printed textile production by approaching outside contractors.

Morris had already had triple cloths of his design woven as Kidderminster-type carpeting by the Heckmondwike Manufacturing Company (cat.no.M.94). He then employed them to produce a series of fabrics of the same structure but showing designs intended to be seen in folds rather than flat on the floor.

Although registered specifically as a textile, it is probable that the design was also considered for carpeting. In the twentieth century it was also available as power-loom woven silk and linen, and silk and cotton mixed fabrics, and recommended for seat upholstery in wool.

M.77 *Vine and Pomegranate* furnishing length

Designed by William Morris or Kate Faulkner, *c*.1877
Manufactured for Morris & Co. by the

Heckmondwike Manufacturing
Company, Heckmondwike, Yorkshire
Woven woollen triple cloth, 221.0 x 183.0 cm
V&A (Circ.383-1962)
Given by Mr and Mrs W. Waterhouse

Morris & Co. often referred to two- and three-ply woven textiles as 'tapestries', to differentiate them from the Kidderminster carpeting of the same technique and to suggest the effect of the fabric's draping qualities. This technically incorrect term, which was never used by Morris, has led to considerable confusion with the firm's actual production of tapestry.

Designed at a period when Kate Faulkner was working for Morris & Co., it has been suggested that this may be one of a small group of her designs. A particularly bold pattern using the traditional repeating devise of intersecting ogees, the influence of early Italian and Near Eastern woven silks and velvets is plain to see, although the trailing grape and willow leaf would have given the pattern a modern appearance in its time.

This red version was admired by Morris and recommended by him to George Howard in January 1882 for Brampton Church, '…I fear there is nothing for it but the bright red: we have a woollen stuff very bright and telling (3 ply pomegranate)' (Kelvin, 765).

This textile was given to the Museum by the grandson of Alfred Waterhouse, the architect, and originally used in the furnishing of Yattendon Court, near Newbury.

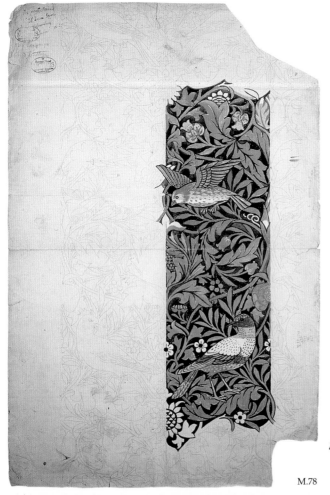

M.78

M.80

M.79

M.78 Design for *Bird* woven textile

William Morris, 1877–8
Pencil and watercolour, 101.6 x 68.2 cm
Inscribed with Queen Square address and
later address stamps
William Morris Society, Kelmscott House,
London (D31)

On 25 March 1877 Morris wrote to Thomas
Wardle, 'I am studying birds now to see if I can't
get some of them into my next design'. This is
the first of a group of designs showing pairs of
facing birds, perched and in flight. Morris's
inspiration for these patterns came from
sixteenth- and seventeenth-century Italian
woven silks from Lucca and Sicily seen in the
collections of the South Kensington Museum.
He was obviously well acquainted with this
type as, by 1882, he describes studying a set of
textiles offered to the Museum by Canon Bock
'…among them a noble piece of Sicilian woven
stuff of a pattern I havn't seen before…' (Kelvin,
831). In his lecture 'Textile Fabrics' given at the
International Health Exhibition of 1884, he
claimed these textiles provided the perfect balance between 'the wild fantasy and luxurious
intricacy of the East with the straight-forward
story-telling imagination…of medieval Europe'.

M.79 *Bird* curtain

Designed by William Morris, 1877–8
Manufactured at Queen Square and later
Merton Abbey
Hand-loom jacquard-woven woollen
double cloth, 304.0 x 182.0 cm
V&A (Circ.501a-1962)
Given by Mrs J.Laughton

By 1877 Morris decided to attempt weaving at
Queen Square. His initial preoccupation was
with brocade weaving, and Thomas Wardle
assisted Morris in finding a French silk
weaver, Bazin, who, with his loom, arrived in
June 1877. Major problems ensued, but these
were cleared up by October and from this
time most of Morris's woven textiles were
produced at Queen Square and then Merton
Abbey. Contractors were employed only if the
technique demanded equipment not owned
by the firm or if large quantities of cloth were
needed.

Morris leased Kelmscott House from April
1878 and this fabric was used draped around
the walls of the first-floor drawing room. May
Morris believed the pattern 'intimate and
friendly…the most adaptable to the needs of
everyday life. It suggests not the wealth of the
millionaire but the modest competence of a
middle-class merchant who lives…with the

few beautiful things he has collected slowly and carefully'.

This curtain is one of a pair from the house of Sir Sydney Cockerell, Morris's secretary and one of May Morris's executors. The Museum also owns *Bird* curtains given by May Morris which are almost certainly from Kelmscott House.

The design is owned by the William Morris Society.

M.80 *Peacock and Dragon* curtain

Designed by William Morris, 1878
Manufactured at Queen Square and later at Merton Abbey
Hand-loom jacquard-woven woollen twill, 396.0 x 353.0 cm
V&A (T.64-1933)

Morris's increasing study of early woven textiles, either through his duties as adviser to the South Kensington Museum or simply by attending exhibitions, is particularly noticeable in his woven textile patterns of the late 1870s and 1880s. A visit to Vincent Robinson's shop in March 1878 to see a complete room 'from Damascus....all vermillion and gold & ultramarine very beautiful and is just like going into the Arabian Nights', is likely to have influenced the colouring of this example and the alternative red colouring. Although based on Sicilian weavings of the fifteenth and sixteenth centuries Morris developed these ideas quite differently, producing a massive design (repeat: 109.0 x 90.0 cm) in wool and not silk; the perfect hanging for a pseudo-medieval interior.

Used in a number of houses, including the drawing room at Kelmscott House, this proved one of Morris's most popular textiles, particularly with clients from abroad. This curtain is part of a set of four from the Hall in Clouds, the Hon. Percy Wyndham's country house near Salisbury. Bought for eighteen guineas by Morris & Co. on behalf of the Museum they added a modest fee of three guineas, plus carriage, for the service.

M.81 *Flower Garden* curtain

Designed by William Morris, 1879
Manufactured at Queen Square and later Merton Abbey
Hand-loom jacquard-woven silk and wool, 231.6 x 271.0 cm
V&A (Circ.80a-1966) Given by Mrs John Webster and Mrs Claude Coombe

On 4 March 1879 Morris wrote to Georgiana Burne-Jones, 'I am writing in a whirlwind of dyeing and weaving, and even to the latter rather excited by a new piece just off the loom, which looks beautiful, like a flower garden' (Kelvin, 556).

Morris claims to have chosen the colours to 'suggest the beauties of inlaid metal' influenced, no doubt, by items from Damascus he had studied in Vincent Robinson's shop in March 1878.

The pattern type, of formal repeating flower-heads in cross-section was used by Morris in the

background of *Bird* and for large embroidered hangings being produced at this time, particularly the *Artichoke* designed for Phoebe Godman in 1877 (cat.no.M.21).

The design was used in a number of Morris & Co. decorative commissions, including Rounton Grange, 1 Holland Park and Stanmore Hall. This is one of a pair of curtains from Holland Park, given to the Museum by descendants of Aleco Ionides.

M.82 Preparatory design for *Bird and Vine* woven textile

William Morris, 1879
Pencil, pen and ink, coloured chalks, water-colour and bodycolour; 101.5 x 68.4 cm
V&A (E.40-1940)
Bequeathed by May Morris

Comparing this design with the finished woven textile (cat.no.M.83) a number of differences can be seen. Vine leaves not used in this design are substituted for the more complicated arrangements of flowers and leaves of the lower cartouche and the positioning of grapes around the repeating birds is different. The strong, rather crude colouring suggests that Morris intended this textile to be a multicoloured pattern and consequently a complex and costly woven fabric. The final woven version was produced in restrained colourways.

M.81

M.83 *Bird and Vine* furnishing sample

Designed by William Morris, registered 15 May 1879
Manufactured at Queen Square and later at Merton Abbey
Hand-loom jacquard-woven wool, 60.0 x 90.5 cm
V&A (T.14-1919) Given by Morris & Co.

M.82

M.83

One of a series of designs by Morris showing pairs of birds on a traditionally stylised pattern ground. This fabric proved very popular for church use because of the use of grapes and dove-like birds in its design.

The fabric was available in eleven different colourings, four of which were given to the Museum following the move of Morris & Co.'s shop from Oxford Street to George Street, Hanover Square.

A preparatory design is owned by the Museum (cat.no.M.82).

M.84 Three samples of *Dove and Rose* furnishing textile

Designed by William Morris, 1879
Manufactured for Morris & Co. by Alexander Morton & Co., Darvel, and later at Merton Abbey
Hand-loom jacquard-woven silk and wool double cloth, some metal thread; 27.3 x 88.2 cm, 29.2 x 44.4 cm, **a** 64.5 x 94.5 cm
V&A (T.25,26-1919, Circ.126-1953)
Given by Morris & Co. and by Mrs Christabel Marillier

A very similar pattern to *Bird and Vine* (cat. no. M.83), however, the choice of different weaving structures provides quite a different result.

A complex cloth, with two separate warps of wool and silk, the pattern is made by varying the lifting of threads in weaving and can produce areas of solid wool, silk and also mixtures of the two. It was first woven for Morris & Co. by Alexander Morton, the Scottish manufacturer, and it is likely that early samples of this fabric were woven by Scottish outworkers. The structure of the fabric made it suitable only for curtains and hangings and although Morris tried a piece on a chair at home, and found it had worked better than expected, he did not recommend it for upholstery.

Morris was pleased with the subtle colourings available, even though these were not always fast, a common problem with contractor's work. On recommending a red version of the fabric to Rosalind Howard on 24 November 1881 he declared, '…it will last as long as need be since the cloth is really very strong. I can't answer so decidedly as to the colour; but the colours in it when looked at by themselves you will find rather full…'tis the mixture that makes them look delicate' (Kelvin, 750).

The pattern was available in different sizes during Morris's lifetime and a number of different colourings. Two of these samples, one shot with gold thread, show trials not put into commercial production. The third shows the most popular version, in pinks and blues. This example was given to the Museum by the wife of H. C. Marillier, Managing Director of Morris & Co. from 1905.

The design is owned by Birmingham Museum and Art Gallery (399'41) and a point paper by the William Morris Gallery, Walthamstow (A451).

M.85 *Madras Muslin* furnishing textile

Designed by William Morris, 1880–81
Manufactured for Morris & Co. by Alexander Morton & Co., Darvel, Scotland
Woven cotton and silk leno (gauze), 60.9 x 173.9 cm
V&A (T.657-1919)
Given by Morris & Co.

This cloth provided the perfect alternative to roller-blinds or machine-made Nottingham lace curtains which Morris disliked. Morris's use of silk provides a contrasting sheen to the cotton. As specialised equipment was needed for the manufacture, it is probable that Alexander Morton and Co. was the sole manufacturer. Highly experienced in supplying such goods, the firm had been set up in the 1860s to take advantage of the impoverished local muslin industry in Darvel, Scotland.

Morris & Co. were supplying gauzes by March 1880, as the first bill for decorations at 1 Holland Park included muslin curtains for both the dining room and the Antiquities Room (eight in all) at a cost of £12 3s. Unfortunately, the designs used are not named on this bill nor are they identifiable from contemporary photographs.

This pattern, with its meandering repeat, is similar to a number of printed textile designs, *Kennet* in particular (cat. no. M.65). Other Morris designs were woven as muslins although few examples have been found. A second example appears in the firm's twentieth-century pattern book (cat. no. M.92) and later versions of *Cherwell* and *Cray* were produced under Morton's own name.

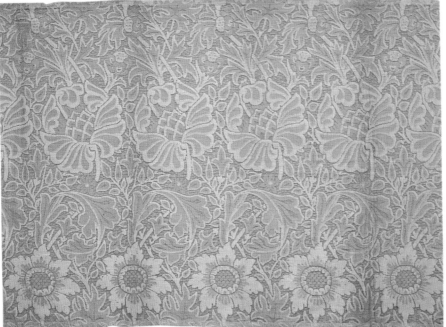

M.85

M.86

M.87

M.86 *Oak* furnishing textile

Designed by William Morris 1881
Manufactured by J.O. Nicholson, Macclesfield,
and at Merton Abbey
Hand- and power-loom jacquard-woven silk
damask, 270.5 x 53.3 cm sight
V&A (T.74-1919)
Given by May Morris

One of two designs for silk damasks made for the decorations of the Throne Room and Blue Room at St James's Palace. None of the existing photographs of the Morris & Co. decorations shows this pattern, so it may have been offered initially as an alternative to the *St James*, which was used stretched on the walls and for curtains and valances. Although the commission for curtains at the palace was not received until December 1881 (cat.no.M.26), Morris was busy designing the silks in September of that year (Kelvin, 727).

This design was very popular and used extensively by Morris & Co. for furnishings and as the background for embroidered hangings (cat.no.M.33). It was available in a large number of colourways, both as single shades or with two 'shot' colours, an effect Morris used to imitate nature. In writing about the *St James* silk to Rosalind Howard in November 1881 he declared, '…what would you say to dullish pink shot with amber; like some of those chrysanthemums we see just now?'

M.87 *Granada* furnishing textile

Designed by William Morris, 1884
Manufactured at Merton Abbey
Woven silk velvet brocaded with gilt thread
(gilt paper round a silk core), 194.9 x 67.3 cm
V&A (T.4-1919)

Morris's interest in the technical aspects of weaving increased, and some of his last designs attempt to reproduce complex historic structures. The Introduction to *Review of the Principal Acquisitions* (Victoria and Albert Museum, 1912), states 'It is not surprising that William Morris, whose appreciation of the beauty of mediaeval textiles finds expression in so much of his work, should have desired to produce a fabric on the lines of the sumptuous brocaded velvets of the fifteenth and sixteenth centuries'. The *Art Journal* for 1891 claimed it to be 'the only English velvet that bears any comparison to the old Flemish velvets'.

He began to weave this, his only velvet, in March 1884 (Kelvin, 959) on a specially constructed loom. Although he was successful, this was so time-consuming and expensive that the fabric was not put into commercial production. Only twenty yards were woven and the price was £10 a yard.

The Museum owns two examples, a small strip and this panel, which the Museum purchased for £35 (despite competition from a member of the Rothschild family), from Morris & Co.'s agent in Paris where it had been on exhibition.

M.88 Two samples of *Brocatel* furnishing textile

Designed by William Morris or J.H. Dearle, 1888
Manufactured at Merton Abbey
Hand-loom jacquard-woven silk and cotton,
63.0 x 135.0 cm, 76.0 x 68.0 cm
V&A (Circ.86-1953, Circ.125-1953)   Given by
Mr W.G.Howell and Mrs Christabel Marillier
FOR ILLUSTRATION, SEE FIG 115, PAGE 358

An attempt by Morris to reproduce the effect of a traditional brocatelle in which the raised pattern shows through a ribbed surface. Using the nineteenth-century invention of jacquard weaving and gold coloured silks he was able to suggest the sumptuous stiffness of the original.

A tightly woven fabric, this proved ideal for upholstery and, with its large repeat (72.5 x 45.5 cm), for hangings where the fabric was stretched and battened to the walls. Exhibited at the 1888 Arts and Crafts exhibition this could be one of the designs that Morris's partners, the Smith brothers, were pressing him to finish earlier in the year. If so, then it is one of his last repeating patterns. The design is simplistic and, in parts, naively drawn. This may simply point to Morris's preoccupation with technique or to the fact that Dearle was the designer. It is often confused with the later, similar Dearle design *Persian Brocatel*.

M.89

M.90 *Kennet* furnishing textile

Designed by William Morris as a printed cotton, 1883
Manufactured by Merton Abbey or by an outside contractor
Hand-loom jacquard-woven silk, 69.8 x 70.4 cm
V&A (T.69-1919)
Given by Morris & Co.

The only example of a Morris design used as both a printed (cat.no.M.65) and woven textile. It is not known when it was first woven, although the pattern is reversed suggesting that it was adapted for the loom after Morris's time. A sample was exhibited at the 1899 Arts and Crafts Exhibition, where the catalogue no. 278 is described as 'Design for "Kennet" silk hangings', suggesting that this form was more popular at the time. It also appears in the Morris & Co. catalogue *Printed Linens and Cottons* published about 1912, where it is advertised under the erroneous description of a 'figured silk brocade' at the high cost of 19s. 6d. per yard.

M.91 *Cross Twigs* sample weaving

Designed by John Henry Dearle, *c*.1898
Manufactured at Merton Abbey
Hand-loom jacquard-woven silk and linen, 88.9 x 139.7 cm
V&A (T.20-1919) Given by Morris & Co.

This trial sample, which shows two different colourings of this design, was probably kept for reference. An example of this fabric was exhibited at the 1899 Arts and Crafts Exhibition.

M.92 Working pattern book

Morris & Co., twentieth century
Board binding, linen and paper with woven and printed samples; 52.0 x 62.5 x 12.5 cm
V&A (T.30-1940)
Given by H.C. Marillier

This pattern book is a record of Morris & Co. textiles available in the twentieth century. It includes swatches of woven and printed fabrics with pattern numbers and prices, a few of these are prefaced with 'sell...' suggesting that this was a guide used for clients in the Morris shops (Oxford Street and George Street, Hanover Square) and for information when transferring orders to Merton Abbey or one of Morris & Co.'s contractors.

Pages 1–28 show a wide range of different woven fabrics (in wool, silk, cotton and linen), pages 29–55, printed cottons, and there are three pages of printed velveteens and embossed velvets.

Many of Morris's most popular designs are represented, often in new colourways and with altered pattern sizes. This book also provides the only means of identifying some late designs by Henry Dearle. It was given to the Museum in July 1940 by H.C. Marillier, the last Managing Director of Morris & Co., two months after the firm was placed in the hands of the Receiver.

M.89 *Tulip and Net* furnishing length

Designed by J.H. Dearle, 1888–9
Manufactured at Merton Abbey
Hand-loom jacquard-woven wool, 193.0 x 178.0 cm
V&A (T.57-1934)

Morris's last identifiable textile patterns were drawn in 1888. With his increasing interest in tapestry weaving, not to mention his plans for book production and role as lecturer, adviser, committee member and political activist, all textile designs produced after this time were by Henry Dearle. Having worked alongside Morris since he entered the firm as a young boy in 1878, Dearle was more than capable of providing what was suitable for production and popular with the firm's clients. Dearle's patterns are more stylised than Morris's, and although they often include such Morrisian devices as curling acanthus leaves these are often stiff and not as intuitively drawn. However, he produced many original patterns, a number of which, like this example, show the influence of Persian design. Existing drawings show that, like Morris, he frequently studied the collections at the South Kensington Museum.

M.90

M.91

M.92

M.93

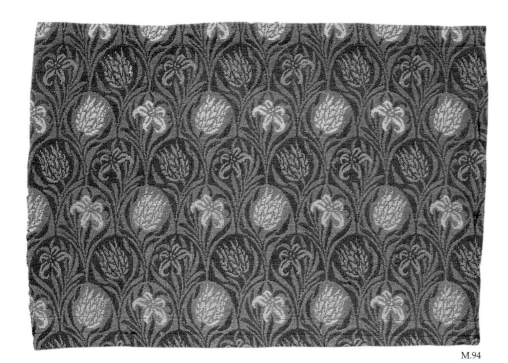

M.94

FLOOR COVERINGS

M.93 Sample of linoleum floor-covering

Designed by William Morris, and registered on 7 June 1875
Manufactured for Morris & Co. by an unknown contractor
Printed Corticine floor-covering, 40.6 x 60.9 cm
V&A (Circ.527-1953)

Morris's first design for floor-covering of any type. As a significant new manufacturing venture, this warranted registration
with the Patent Office. It is possible that this linoleum was manufactured by Nairn's of Kirkaldy in Scotland, the most prolific
manufacturers at this time, whose own designs show a marked
similarity to Morris's work.

Lino was as popular as woven carpeting in the mid-nineteenth
century, although only used selectively. Morris's pragmatic
advocacy of the use of both in the home, helped these cheaper
forms become more respectable.

Only one linoleum design has been traced. This was available in
72-inch widths (182.8 cm) and in two colourways at a cost of 3s.
10d. per square yard.

The design of marigolds against an arched trellis shows Morris's
preoccupation at this time with the manufacture of wallpapers
and tiles. It is similar to contemporary patterns for both
techniques.

M.94 Sample of *Tulip and Lily* machine-woven carpeting

Designed by William Morris about 1875
Manufactured for Morris & Co. by the Heckmondwike
Manufacturing Co., Heckmondwike, Yorkshire
Machine-woven three-ply woollen Kidderminster-type
carpeting; 58.4 x 85.2 cm, pattern repeat: 35.5 x 23.0 cm
V&A (T.101-1953) Given by Miss D. Walker

In May 1875 Morris was already designing carpets and 'trying to
get the manufacturers to do them' (Kelvin, 273).

It was probably Kidderminster (also known as 'Scotch' or
'Inlaid') carpet that he first attempted and the 'Heck-people', as
he referred to them later, was a newly incorporated company
when first approached by Morris. The initial process of transferring Morris's designs to point papers for the loom did not go
well. The manufacturer blamed this on the simplicity of the
design and Morris on the work of the Yorkshire draughtsmen.
From this time on all Morris & Co.'s point papers for woven
goods were supplied by them. Unhappy with the colours produced in early samples, from 1876 Morris supplied all the wools
needed for manufacture, having them dyed to his specification
by Thomas Wardle at Leek.

This design was originally available in various colourways with
a matching border. The Heckmondwike firm produced a number
of similar carpets and a *Daisy* pattern, close to Morris's own, was
registered by them in 1876.

This sample was given to the Museum by the daughter of Emery
Walker and was used in their house in Hammersmith Terrace.

M.95 Sample of *Artichoke* machine-woven carpeting

Designed by William Morris, 1875–80
Manufactured for Morris & Co. by the Heckmondwike
Manufacturing Co., Heckmondwike, Yorkshire
Machine-woven three-ply woollen Kidderminster-type
carpeting; 113.0 x 89.5 cm, pattern repeat: 27.3 x 21.9 cm
V&A (T.188-1984) Given by S. Franses Ltd

Kidderminster carpets were woven in two qualities of double
and triple thickness (two- and three-ply) and in three widths; 22

and 27 inches for stairs and corridors and 36 inches for rooms. The prices ranged from 4s. 5d. to 7s. per square yard. Plain colours with patterned borders were also available, as was fringing for which the firm charged 9d. per yard.

Morris & Co. catalogues mention seven separate Kidderminster designs. There is confusion over the identification of patterns, as a number of two-ply weaves were used for curtaining and it is impossible to know which designs were recommended for walls and which for floors.

Morris helped to popularise this type of cheaper carpeting which before his time tended to be used only for service corridors and secondary rooms. In the 1870s and 1880s Morris & Co. received a number of orders from clients living in large town and country houses, including Alexander Ionides who, in 1884, ordered a Kidderminster carpet for 1 Holland Park. Made of thirteen yards of carpeting with fringed borders it cost £4 18s. 2d. Morris & Co. charged 5s 6d. for 'making up'.

A design for this is at the William Morris Gallery, Walthamstow (BL A 449).

M.96 Sample of *Lily* machine-woven carpeting

Designed by William Morris about 1875
Manufactured for Morris & Co. by Yates & Co.
(later Wilton Royal Carpet Factory Ltd) of Wilton, Wiltshire
Machine-woven Wilton-type carpeting with woollen pile on jute; 66.0 x 43.2 cm, pattern repeat: 24.0 x 22.0 cm
V&A (Circ.65B-1959)

At Christmas 1875 Morris & Co. registered two carpet designs, both of which were woven at Wilton. Morris believed 'Wiltons must be classed as the best kind of machine-woven carpets...If well made the material is very durable, and by skilful treatment in the designing, the restrictions as to color are not noticeable' (Brochure for the Boston Foreign Fair, 1883).

The carpet has a soft velvety texture (woven at 50–150 tufts to the inch), and the pattern is formed on the surface of the carpet by different coloured warp thread loops (which are later cut) on a strong woven foundation.

Lily was one of twenty-four Wilton carpet designs available through Morris & Co. and this type of floor covering proved the most commercially popular of all those sold by the firm. Available in four widths, from 18 to 36 inches, they cost 10s. 6d. per yard. 'Saxony-Wilton' or 'velvet Carpet' a more luxurious pile carpet was available at 12s. 6d. per yard.

Patterned borders became popular, and complete Wilton bordered carpets were sold through the shop.

This sample was part of a larger carpet used in a house in Lowndes Square.

M.97 Fotaband

Icelandic, eighteenth or nineteenth century
Knotted woollen pile, 81.2 x 7.6 cm
V&A (T.122-1939)
Bequeathed by May Morris

From William Morris's own collection. Fotabands were used in Iceland for tying skirts below the knee when riding side-saddle.

A label attached to the band is inscribed 'Icelandic Fine Carpet pile – given by Mrs Magnússon 8/5/78'. The wording of the label emphasises its technical interest to Morris. Mrs Magnússon and her husband were in frequent contact with Morris throughout the 1870s so she probably gave Morris the band knowing of his preoccupation with hand-knotted carpeting at this time. It was acquired only a short time after his first experiments with the technique and the same year that he produced his first commercial hand-woven rug.

M.95

M.96

M.97

M.98

M.99

M.98 Miniature carpet loom

Made at Merton Abbey,
late nineteenth century
Wood with metal fittings,
68.0 x 56.0 x 29.5 cm
V&A (293-1893)
Given by William Morris

Used at the Merton Abbey Works for the
instruction of carpet weavers, the loom
holds a small sample of work in progress.
This is a simplified version of the full-sized
looms constructed by Morris, initially in the
coach house at Kelmscott House at later at
Merton Abbey.

It is likely that Morris undertook considerable research before finally deciding on the
equipment he would use when first
attempting carpet-knotting in 1877.

Unlike tapestry, carpets were knotted with
the weavers facing the front of the work (see
fig. 19). At Merton Abbey the looms faced
the windows for maximum light. The design
point paper, which indicates the colour of
each knot, was pinned as a guide to the front
of the loom above the area being woven.

All of the carpet weavers at Merton Abbey
were women, and catalogues of various
Arts and Crafts exhibitions, indicate that a
number of sisters were employed.

M.99 Sample of pile weaving

Woven at Merton Abbey, late nineteenth
or early twentieth century
Hand-knotted woollen pile on a cotton
warp, 11.4 x 26.6 cm
Sanford and Helen Berger Collection

Probably made by an apprentice carpet-
weaver at Merton Abbey, this miniature rug
shows a very stylised design but its
Morrisian origins are unmistakable.

Morris & Co. hand-knotted carpets were
woven at a thickness of twenty-five knots to
the square inch although when beaten down
these were closer to twenty-eight knots to
the square inch. At first carpets were woven
on a mohair warp, but this proved impractical and all later samples use cotton. Morris
chose the Turkish (Giordes) technique in
which the pile was produced by binding a
two-inch-long thread of wool around two
warp threads with the ends brought
through the middle to the front. This was
neither the finest nor his preferred form of
knotting, but he believed that it best suited
his own broad designs and the coarser work
produced at Merton Abbey.

M.100 Small rug

Designed by William Morris, c.1878–9
Made at Kelmscott House,
Hammersmith
Hand-knotted woollen pile on a worsted
warp, 95.0 x 110.0 cm

From the Castle Howard Collection

On 13 April 1877 Morris wrote to Wardle
that he was unwilling to undertake other
new work 'till I get my carpets going'
(Kelvin, 395). By 1 January 1878 he was
more confident 'I want my Iceland wool
tried on a rug: I will take the greatest pains
in designing one when the frame is ready'
(Kelvin, 475). The frame is likely to have
been a simple loom used for these small
early wall rugs and it was not until 1879
that the coach house and adjoining stable at
Kelmscott House were converted for large-
scale carpet manufacture.

A number of these small rugs, which were
hung on walls as well as laid on floors,
survive. These may well have been woven as
trials and novelties for clients and friends.
This, an early example, has a worsted warp, a
technique abandoned by Morris as impractical
within a short period of the start of production. It is one of a number of small examples
made for the Howard family for whom
Morris produced one of his first large-scale
Hammersmith carpets (see cat. no. M.106).

The rug has an early Hammersmith mark of
a hammer and the letter 'M', denoting that it
was made at Kelmscott House. The term
'Hammersmith' continued to be used for
Morris hand-knotted carpets after the move
of production to Merton Abbey. Later
carpets bear no identification marks.

M.101 Small rug

Designed and possibly made by William
Morris, 1878–81
Made at Kelmscott House,
Hammersmith
Hand-knotted woollen pile on a worsted
warp, 106.7 x 94.0 cm
Private Collection

Another small rug made by Morris at
Kelmscott House and acquired by George
Howard. The design is very close to a series
of embroidered cushion covers and firescreen panels designed by Morris
(cat. nos. M.25, 27, 28) and based on two
Italian seventeenth-century darned lacis
panels acquired by the South Kensington
Museum in 1875. This rug shows another
form of the early Hammersmith mark in
which stylised waves are added to the hammer and letter 'M', signifying that it was
woven in the coach house at Kelmscott
House, before the carpet looms were transferred to Merton Abbey.

It is not known whether these small format
rugs were put into regular commercial
production.

Between 1884 and 1888, Morris & Co.
produced a series of similar small rugs for
the Century Guild using designs by A.H.
Mackmurdo. These were sold through the
Morris shop and in turn the firm advertised
through the Guild's magazine *Hobby Horse*.

M.100

M.101

M.102

M.102 Rug

Designed by William Morris, *c*.1879–81
Hand-knotted wool on a cotton warp,
248.8 x 135.9 cm
V&A (T.104-1953)
Purchased from Margaret Mackail

This rug was a wedding present to Margaret, daughter of Edward and Georgiana Burne-Jones on her marriage to John William Mackail in 1888. On 21 August Morris wrote, 'I have bidden our Mr Smith to send you an "article" called a Hammermith Rug (made at Merton Abbey) which Janey and I ask you to take as a small and unimportant addition to your "hards"'.

Morris's letter, describing the piece as '...made at Merton Abbey...', is confusing as it shows an early Hammersmith mark, thought to signify that it was woven in the coach house at Kelmscott House. However, Morris does not suggest that he had seen it and Mr Smith may well have selected the rug from stock, choosing an old weaving rather than undertaking a new one. When acquired by the Museum, through Miss Clare Mackail, the rug was said to have been 'produced at *Hammersmith*'.

The design, with pale camel colouring, tightly curving leaves and profiled flower-heads shows Chinese influence, especially in the pastel colouring and peony motifs of the inner border.

This is one of Morris's most popular small rug designs and a number were woven. An example given by Morris to his sister Henrietta was displayed at the Museum in 1952 (Victorian and Edwardian Decorative Arts Exhibition (I 55)).

Exhib. 1961 (72)

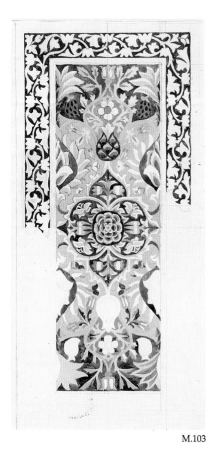

M.103

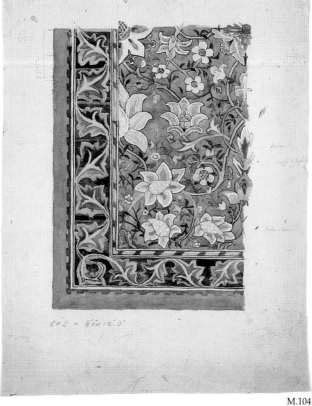

M.104

M.103 Design for a Hammersmith carpet

William Morris, *c.*1880
Pencil and bodycolour, 35.7 x 67.7 cm
V&A (E.298-1939)
Bequeathed by May Morris

The intended colouring of this design, almost certainly intended for a rug rather than a larger carpet, is the same as a set of small rugs first woven in the coach house at Kelmscott House, Hammersmith (see cat. nos. M.100–1). The combination of pale blues, pinks and camel colours comes directly from Chinese carpets and shows Morris's interest in this work at the time.

M.104 Design for *Redcar* carpet

William Morris, *c.*1881.
Pencil, watercolour, bodycolour and Chinese white; 44.8 x 34.9 cm
Inscribed in pencil: 'Redcar 4 x 4', with various notes including the intended size, 8 x 12 ft.
V&A (E.144-1919)
Given by Morris & Co.

The original carpet was designed for Sir Hugh Bell, the son of Margaret and Isaac Lowthian Bell, and brother of Florence and Ada, for his home Red Barns in

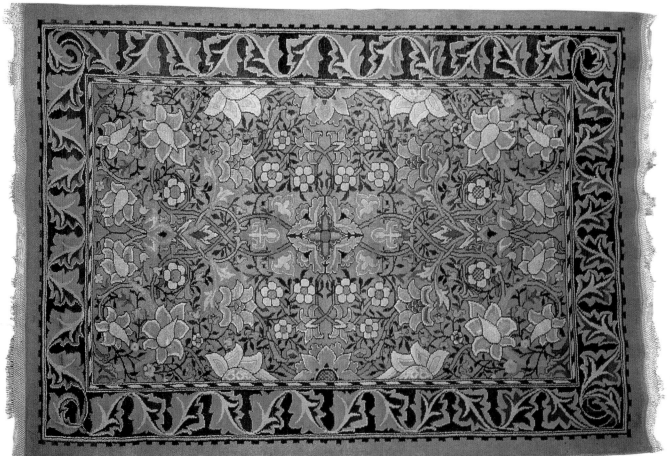

M.105

Coatham near Redcar, designed and built for him by Philip Webb between 1868 and 1870. An 1881–2 extension to the house included a drawing room (see Rosemary J. Curry and Sheila Kirk, *Philip Webb in The North*, 1984) and the carpet is likely to have been commissioned at this time.

The design, which shows one-sixth full size, was used by Morris & Co. to show to prospective clients and various inscribed notes such as 'softer and lighter', and 'softer and duller' suggest requests from clients rather than instructions from the designer. When it was given to the Museum, at the same time as the newly acquired carpet of the same design (see cat. no. M.105), the firm asked if it could be returned temporarily for use should they receive further orders.

Exhib. 1934 (86)

M.105 *Redcar* carpet

Designed by William Morris, 1881; originally made at Kelmscott House, Hammersmith, this version woven early twentieth century
Hand-knotted cotton warp with mohair, camel hair and woollen pile with jute binding wefts; twenty-eight knots to the square inch; 304.8 x 243.8 cm
V&A (T.3-1919)
Given by Thomas Glass

Originally designed and woven for Sir Hugh Bell for Red Barns in Coatham near Redcar, then in Yorkshire. Existing photographs (Newcastle University) show that the carpet was used in the drawing room of the new extension designed and built in 1881–2.

The original carpet (now on loan to Kelmscott Manor) has the early Hammersmith mark, denoting that it was woven in the coach house at Kelmscott House, Hammersmith. On 17 February 1881 Morris wrote to Janey, 'Bell's carpet is well on, and I believe if it were not really dark today it would look well'. A week later he wrote 'I am starting designing the long carpet for Naworth as Bell's gets on a pace'.

The pale colouring of this carpet with camel ground and pastel detailing is the same as some early wall rugs (see cat. no. M.100) and may have been Morris's first chosen colour scheme for carpets. Although this was repeated in a few later commissions, most of his mature work woven at Merton Abbey relied on his characteristic combination of indigo blue and madder red.

A number of versions of the carpet were made including this, woven in the twentieth century. It was bought from Morris & Co. and presented to the Museum by Thomas Glass, who was associated with the Glasgow carpet manufacturers, Templeton's. In a letter from Morris & Co. to the Museum, the carpet was described as showing 'the original colours rather better than a carpet which has had about twenty five years wear…' An article by C. E. Tattersall in the *Burlington Magazine* (XXXIV, Jan.–June 1919) celebrates the Museum's acquisition of this Morris carpet and drawing (see cat. no. M.104) describing the design as 'probably one of his earliest'.

Exhib. 1934 (85); 1952 (I 53)

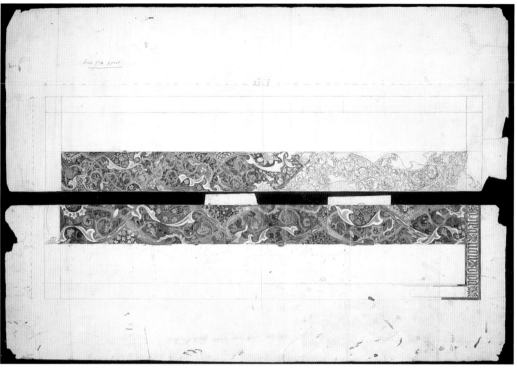

M.106

M.106 Three designs for a carpet for Naworth Castle

William Morris, 1881
Pencil, bodycolour and watercolour;
31.5 x 58.0 cm, 33.7 x 102.3 cm, 36.9 x 102.3 cm
Inscribed: '1" to 1 foot', '½ full size' and other measurements and technical notes
V&A (E.287-1939, E.47,48-1940 illustrated)
Bequeathed by May Morris

This commission was for a carpet for the library at Naworth Castle, Cumberland, the home of George Howard, Earl of Carlisle. Morris's diary for 20 February 1881 notes, 'Began a sketch of Howard's carpet'. Three days later in a letter to Janey he wrote, 'I am starting designing the long carpet for Naworth…'tis rather a difficult job, & I am puffing and blowing over it rather…' (Kelvin, 675). This letter is interesting as it suggests this may well have been Morris's first large, complicated commission, it also includes Morris's first mention of looking for new premises. The projects may well be linked, as the weaving of the *Naworth* carpet was delayed until the move to Merton Abbey, the finished size (31 ft. 3 in. x 15 ft. 2 in., or 952.5 x 462.2 cm), being too large for the fifteen-foot looms at Hammersmith.

These drawings, which include the Howard family motto 'volo non valeo quid negneo quad desidero', show two pattern samplers and the finished design. The variety of motifs seen in the preparatory trials, including seagulls and wading birds, palm trees and naturalistic fruit trees and flowers, was not attempted again until 1889 with the *Bullerswood* design (see cat. no. M.110). George and Rosalind Howard were conservative in their choice of patterns, and the finished design is quite dull in comparison with that offered. Although the painting of point papers for weaving took a month the weaving was speedy. The move to Merton took place in June 1881, yet on 3 November

Morris wrote to Howard 'your carpet has been finished for a week or two: I have been keeping it back to try for a fine day to spread it on our lawn; so that I may see it all at once…it looks very well I think & seems to be satisfactory as to manufacture…I shall have to send someone down to Naworth to get it into its place: it weighs about a ton I fancy'. It cost £200 (Hartley, 1995).

The purchase appears in the Howard's accounts for 1882 (at Castle Howard, ref. J23/105/14 p. 90). The carpet was sold in 1947 and was later used in the Hotel Ambassador, Bournemouth. Its present whereabouts are unknown.

M.107 *Rounton Grange* carpet

Designed by William Morris and woven at Merton Abbey, c.1881–2
Hand-knotted woollen pile on a cotton warp with jute binding threads, 678.1 x 441.0 cm
Private Collection
FOR ILLUSTRATION SEE OVERLEAF

Morris produced two hand-knotted carpets for the Bell family, *Redcar* (see cat. no. M.105), and this larger example, designed for Sir Isaac Lowthian Bell and Lady Bell for their home Rounton Grange in Northallerton, Yorkshire, a house designed for them by Philip Webb in 1872 and built between 1872 and 1876.

It is difficult to date the carpet precisely. Reference by Morris to 'Bell's carpet' in a letter of February 1881 is likely to refer to *Redcar* as this has the early Hammersmith mark. However, it is probable that this piece was woven soon afterwards and was one of three massive examples produced on the Merton Abbey looms soon after the move there in June 1881. The completion of these three pieces, for Bell, George Howard and Lord Portsmouth, may well have been delayed

M.107

M.108

until Morris had suitable equipment to deal with such technically difficult examples. *Hurstbourne*, woven for Lord Portsmouth, is curved, and the design for this and *Naworth* include inscriptions and heraldic devises. George Howard's carpet for Naworth Castle (see cat.no.M.106), is likely to have been the first made and the other two followed. This example, and *Hurstbourne*, show similar repeating designs of curving branches, filled with stylised branches of fruit and garden flowers.

May Morris remembers that following the completion of the embroidered frieze (cat.no.M.15) the dining room at Rounton Grange was 'further enriched with a painted ceiling and Hammersmith carpet'. The ceiling was admired by George Howard in January 1882 and the weaving of the carpet probably followed soon after. If May is correct is placing the carpet initially in the dining room then it was moved some years later, as existing photographs, taken after 1896, show it in the drawing room.

M.108 *Holland Park* carpet

Designed by William Morris and woven at Merton Abbey in 1883
Hand-knotted woollen pile on cotton warp with jute binding threads; 528.3 x 397.5 cm
Private Collection

This carpet was designed specially for the drawing room of the home of A.A. (Aleco) Ionides at 1 Holland Park and was one of four Hammersmith carpets made for the house (see also cat.no.109).

Detailed estimates and bills from Morris & Co. (cat.no.I.17) show that the carpet cost £113.

This is Morris's most popular carpet design, and at least six examples are traceable today. Four are in this, Morris's most widely used colour scheme, of an indigo-blue field with a madder-red border. Other known examples have cream and apricot coloured grounds.

This example is likely to be the original carpet, although when purchased from Morris & Co. in the 1920s it was said to have come from Clouds, Percy Wyndham's house near Salisbury. However, the 1889 weaving is likely to be that sold at Sotheby's in 1986 by a descendant of the Wyndham family (19 Dec., lot 381).

Gleeson White in his *Studio* magazine article on 1 Holland Park (XIV, 1898) described the carpet as displaying features that Morris had made his own, 'robust generous curves blossoming into flower-like patterns, and with a sense of space…' While it does retain these characteristic elements, this carpet presents a turning point in Morris's style. Its format is far more traditional than had been seen before and from this time all his designs tend to show quartered designs based around a central medallion. This change was affected by Morris's increasing interest in historic carpets. In February 1883 he was asked to advise the South Kensington Museum on the acquisition of a group of Persian carpets offered by a Bond Street dealer. Although Morris had collected oriental carpets for many years and knew a great deal about them, the coincidence of this visit and this new departure in pattern is significant.

Two versions of the carpet were exhibited at the Arts and Crafts Exhibitions for 1888 (399) and 1899 (398).

M.109 *Carbrook* carpet

Designed by William Morris, 1881–3; this version woven 1883–4
Hand-knotted woollen pile with cotton warp and jute binding threads, 541.0 x 292.0 cm
V&A (Circ.458-1965)
Bequeathed by Miss Aglaia Ionides

Because of its pattern name, it is probable that this carpet was designed for a earlier commission and that this example, made for the Antiquities Room of A.A.Ionides's house at 1 Holland Park, is a later version. The carpet was estimated in 1883 at £82 (see cat.no.I.17) and billed (and presumably woven), the following year.

Inscriptions on two 1880–81 drawings for St James's Palace (William Morris Society, see cat.no.I.14) suggest that work was being prepared for *Carbrook* at the same time. In C.E.C.Tattersall's *History of British Carpets*

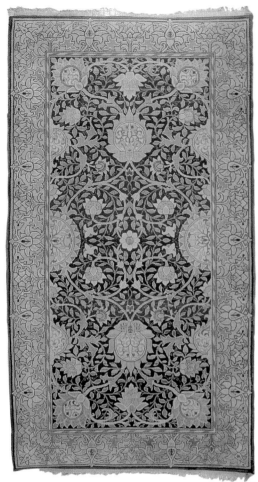

M.109

M.110

(1934) the carpet is described as having a blue field and red border which was probably the original colouring. This lighter version was probably chosen to match the exotic surroundings of the room, which had a Morris silver lacquer paper on the walls and displayed Ionides's collection of Tanagra statues.

The carpet design is uncharacteristically formal for this early date. The overall network of trailing leaves, Morris's most identifiable style, is subsidiary, the main interest of the pattern lying in the repeat of large traditional medallions and palmettes.

M.110 *Bullerswood* carpet

Designed by William Morris with John Henry Dearle and woven 1889
Hand-knotted with woollen pile on a cotton warp, 764.8 x 398.8 cm
V&A (T.31-1923) Given by J.Sanderson Esq.

In 1889 John Sanderson, a wool trader, commissioned Morris & Co. to decorate his house, Bullerswood in Chislehurst, Kent. Built in 1866 it had been subject to recent alterations by Ernest Newton, possibly to accommodate the nine Sanderson children. Two Hammersmith carpets were ordered for the house; one for the hall and another for the drawing room. Museum records dating from a visit to the house in 1921 state 'it appears that the drawing room was decorated by

William Morris under his personal supervision and nothing was allowed to be placed in it in addition to objects executed by himself'. If accurate then, clearly, the clients were very accommodating. This carpet is an extraordinarily exuberant amalgamation of almost every motif devised by Morris for carpets. It is reminiscent of the early sampler designs prepared for Naworth Castle (cat.no.M.106) but it also shows later, more formal, design elements characteristic of Henry Dearle's work.

There is a strong possibility, therefore, that the carpet was a collaborative project.

It was exhibited at the 1893 Arts and Crafts Exhibition.

Despite the size and complicated design three versions are known. One formed part of the Henderson bequest to Bath City Council in 1954 and is now on loan to Kelmscott Manor and the other is said to be in Australia.

Exhib. 1934 (87)

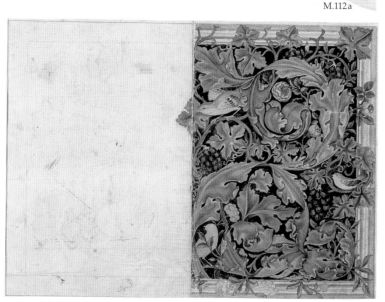

M.111 Design for a hand-knotted rug

John Henry Dearle, *c.*1898–1902
Pencil, ink and watercolour, 25.25 x 34.0 cm
Inscribed with measurements and notes
Sanford and Helen Berger Collection

A design made for George McCulloch a good client of Morris & Co. who ordered a partial set of *Holy Grail* tapestries in 1898 and a special Hammersmith carpet (known as *McCulloch*) a little later. McCulloch, who lived at 184 Queen's Gate in London, was probably introduced to the work of the firm, through his friend and fellow Australian, W.K.D'Arcy, of Stanmore Hall, Middlesex.

Dearle's design technique shows only one quarter of the design, painted with notes of the client's preferred colours, which are brighter than earlier, Morris examples.

The design is simple and disproportionately long at 8 ft. x 3 ft. 10 in. (243 x 116.8 cm). Dearle's suggestion that 'This can be made 6 x 4 if approved' would be more appropriate for the composition.

M.112 Three designs for hand-knotted rugs

Morris & Co., late nineteenth century
Pencil, bodycolour and Chinese white;
24.7 x 42.4 cm, 41.5 x 44.9 cm, **a** 50.3 x 37.7 cm
V&A (E.295, 296 and 301-1939)
Bequeathed by May Morris

These bold, colourful drawings are likely to have been painted in the Morris & Co. workshop to be used to show to potential clients. They show a range of patterns, from Morris's earliest square rugs (see cat.nos.M.100–1) to the late repeating patterns of Henry Dearle. The repeating bird border was used on a plain carpet now in the chapel of Peterhouse College, Cambridge. This has strong similarities with embroidery designs drawn by May Morris in the 1890s and may point to her involvement in this side of the firm's work.

TAPESTRY

M.113 Design for *Acanthus and Vine* tapestry

William Morris, 1879
Pencil, pen and ink, black chalk, watercolour and bodycolour; 49.8 x 68.6 cm
V&A (E.45-1940).
Bequeathed by May Morris

The original design for Morris's first woven tapestry. It shows half of the mirror-imaged composition with the remaining left-hand section faintly suggested. There are splashes of colour on one side and the drawing has a sharp fold down the centre.

The structure of the design, with plant growth emanating from the centre of the lower border, is one Morris used frequently when designing for a square or rectangular format in the late 1870s and early 1880s, especially wall rugs (cat.no.M.100) and embroidered cushion covers and screen panels (cat.nos.M.25,27,28).

M.114 Cartoon for *Acanthus and Vine* tapestry

Possibly drawn in the Morris & Co. studio after a design by William Morris, 1879
Pencil and watercolour, 181.0 x 136.2 cm
V&A (E.3472-1932)

Working cartoon for Morris's first tapestry. As with the original design (cat.no.M.113) only half of the composition has been worked in detail. Morris used this at the loom both as a guide to the composition as a whole and for marking sections of the warp.

The cartoon is life-size although Morris's inexperienced use of the techniques accounts for a slight discrepancy in size between this and the finished tapestry.

In later years the firm's tapestry (and stained-glass) cartoons were made from photographic enlargements of the original design (cat.no.M.128).

Whereas the original design and finished tapestry remained with the Morris family, the cartoon, which was probably drawn in the Morris & Co. studio, possibly by George Campfield, under Morris's supervision, remained the property of the firm until purchased by the Museum in 1932.

Exhib. 1934 (55)

M.114

M.115

M.115 *Acanthus and Vine* tapestry

Designed by William Morris and woven at
Kelmscott House, 1879
Tapestry woven wool, with some silk, on a cotton
warp, max. 191.0 x 234.0 cm
Society of Antiquaries of London
(Kelmscott Manor)

Morris's first attempt at tapestry weaving which May
Morris described as 'W.M's own piece'. He first set up a
tapestry loom in 1877 and it is likely that experimental
work preceded this. 'I used to get up at daylight to
puzzle out the tricks of the loom for myself', was how
he described this later (*Daily Chronicle,* 9 Oct. 1893).

Morris prepared the project in a traditional manner
with a design and cartoon (cat.nos.113–14). He began
weaving on 10 May 1879 in his bedroom at Kelmscott
House, snatching hours between other commercial
duties. The tapestry took 516 ½ hours (see cat.no.116)
and was finished on 17 September.

Coarsely woven at seven to ten warp threads to the
inch, distortion is due to this variation in weave and
uneven loom tension.

The choice of large curving leaves in the design and the
use of faded colours in the weaving is significant.
Morris's historic source is 'large-leaf' verdure tapestries

woven in France and Flanders in the sixteenth century.
It is probably examples of these that were the 'faded
greenery' that made a significant impression on Morris
as a young boy visiting Queen Elizabeth Lodge in
Epping Forest. The tapestry remained the property of
the Morris family and was always referred to as
Cabbage and Vine.

Exhib. 1934 (45)

M.116 Notebook

William Morris, notes for 1879
Handwritten in pencil, 18.0 x 23.0 cm
V&A (NAL L.2637-1939)
NOT ILLUSTRATED

Notebook in which Morris kept a personal record of the
time spent weaving the *Acanthus and Vine* tapestry. The
book is inscribed 'Diary of work on Cabbage & Vine
Tapestry at Kelmscott House, Hammersmith. Began
May 10th 1879 after Campfield about a week's work
vetting in also after weaving a blue list [sic]'.

The hours devoted each day are noted line by line and
the last entry, for three hours, is on Wednesday 17
September. For this four month period (131 days)
Morris spent 516 ½ hours working on the panel. How
he found the time for this non-commercial venture with

Morris & Co. going through one of its busiest
periods is difficult to comprehend.

M.117 Design for a tapestry depicting acanthus and peacocks

William Morris, 1879–81
Pencil, pen and ink, watercolour and bodycolour;
68.6 x 49.8 cm, inner design 43.8 x 30.9 cm
V&A (E.620-1939)
Bequeathed by May Morris

Because of the similarities in colouring, composition
and style this tapestry design is likely to have been
drawn either before or soon after the *Acanthus and Vine*
(cat.nos.M.113–15). It may have been Morris's first idea
which proved too complex for his initial attempts at
weaving. The motifs of a date palm and exotic birds are
also seen in Morris's preliminary designs for the
Naworth carpet begun in February 1881 (cat.no.M.106).

The drawing has been remounted and a monochrome
tree and scroll border added, probably in the latter
years of Morris & Co. when the firm were attempting to
adapt early designs for the modern market. It is
inscribed 'original design by William Morris' in the hand
of Sydney Cockerell, one of May Morris's executors.

Exhib. 1934 (56), catalogued as 'Peacock and Acanthus'.

M.118 Miniature tapestry loom

Merton Abbey, late nineteenth century
Wood with metal fittings, 71.5 x 55.2 x 38.7 cm
V&A (156-1893) Given by William Morris

This loom was used to instruct apprentice tapestry weavers at Merton Abbey. It still retains the original partially worked warp and bobbins.

Morris chose to use the *haute lisse* or upright tapestry loom in preference to the horizontally worked *basse lisse*. This was the technique used by medieval weavers and gave the effects that he most admired. Using this type of loom, weavers work from the back of the weaving tracing their progress by looking through the warp threads to a mirror that hangs in front of the work. Because of the limits of the widths of the loom, designs are usually worked sideways.

Morris visited the Gobelins factory in Paris in his Oxford vacation of 1854. This was the only commercial tapestry manufactory using the upright loom at that time and, whereas he claims not to have liked their work, in late years referring to it as an 'Upholsterer's toy', the visit provided an opportunity for him to see tapestry production on a large scale.

Morris's equipment was uncluttered and practical and did not follow the romantic, symbolic and decorative vision of weaving represented in a number of Pre-Raphaelite works of art.

M.119 Apprentice sample weavings

Woven by D. Griffiths at Merton Abbey, 1935–9
Tapestry woven wool and silk on a cotton warp,
max. 70.0 x 60.0 cm
William Morris Gallery
(London Borough of Waltham Forest) (F275)

A group of tapestry samplers showing exercises woven by an apprentice at Merton Abbey in the twentieth century. The method of training is likely to have changed little since Morris took J.H. Dearle from the glass-painter's shop at Queen Square to become his first tapestry apprentice in 1878. Morris believed that young boys were the best recruits as tapestry '…involves little muscular effort and is best carried out by small flexible fingers'. They were given 'a weekly stipend', board and lodgings and were looked after by a housekeeper in the works house at Merton Abbey.

Weaving exercises took a number of forms and both historic and contemporary patterns were copied. Geometric border designs were followed by more complex floral forms with hands, feet and finally heads being given to the more experienced weavers. These samples show a range of patterns and abilities. Another example in the William Morris Gallery, Walthamstow, shows a copy of the head of one of the principal figures in the Brussels sixteenth-century tapestry *Pity Restraining Justice*, which Morris had advised the South Kensington Museum to buy in 1890.

M.119

M.120

M.121

M.122 Design for *The Orchard*, or *The Seasons* tapestry

Morris & Co. after William Morris, *c.*1890
Pencil, pen and ink, watercolour heightened with Chinese white, bodycolour; 49.4 x 66.7 cm
Inscribed: 'Greenery' and 'The Seasons', with measurements '16'0" x 7'0"',
'Scale 1 ½' = 1"' and '⅛ full size'
V&A (E.544-1939)

Morris first used these figures in his design for the ceiling decoration for Jesus College Chapel, Cambridge, in 1866 (cat. no. H.35). In the original, the angels hold scrolls inscribed with the medieval hymn *Vexilla regis prodeunt*.

Whereas the idea to use the ceiling angels as allegorical female figures in a tapestry was Morris's, this scale design was drawn in the Morris & Co. workshop. The background of fruit trees and trellis fence is by Henry Dearle, although in the Morris tradition. The figures, copied from the originals in the firm's studio, are probably by George Wardle. Drawn on re-used paper, they are detachable and have been partially stuck over the top of the floral background.

Exhib. 1934 (51)

M.120 *The Forest* tapestry

Designed by William Morris, Philip Webb and John Henry Dearle
Woven at Merton Abbey by William Knight, John Martin and William Sleath, 1887
Tapestry woven wool and silk on a cotton warp, 121.9 x 452.0 cm
Embroidered inscription: 'the beast that be in woodland waste, now sit and see nor ride nor haste'
V&A (T.111-1926)

Morris's use of birds and animals in early tapestries is a direct development from his later carpet patterns. This design, one of his most successful compositions, uses a dense cover of trailing acanthus leaves, as seen in his first tapestry *Acanthus and Vine*, into which have been placed Philip Webb's five studies of animals and birds (fig. 99). It is possible that Henry Dearle supplied foreground floral details, although these are similar to Webb's preparatory drawings. The verse was later published under the title 'The Lion' in Morris's *Poems By The Way* (Reeves and Turner, 1891).

The tapestry was woven by Morris & Co.'s three most senior weavers 'under the superintendence of William Morris', according to the 1890 Arts and Crafts Exhibition catalogue (318).

Bought by Aleco Ionides for 1 Holland Park, it hung in the study together with an acanthus-leaf panel.

The Museum purchased the tapestry in 1926 for £500 (The National Art Collections Fund donating £100) from Morris & Co. acting on behalf of George Ionides.

Exhib. 1934 (49); 1952 (I 18); 1961 (43)

M.121 Tapestry of a scrolling acanthus leaf

Designed by William Morris or John Henry Dearle and woven at Merton Abbey, *c.*1890
Tapestry woven wool on a cotton warp, 54.6 x 156.2 cm
V&A (T.111-1986)

This panel is similar in design to a tapestry owned by Aleco Ionides, which hung above the study door, alongside *The Forest*, at 1 Holland Park. This example is unfinished and without a border and may have been woven at Merton Abbey as a pattern trial.

M.123 *The Orchard* or *The Seasons* tapestry

Designed by William Morris and John Henry Dearle and woven at Merton Abbey, 1890
Tapestry woven in wool, silk and mohair on a cotton warp, 221.0 x 472.0 cm
Inscribed with verse: 'Midst bitten mead…'
V&A (154-1898)

By 1890, with ten years' production behind the firm, Merton Abbey tapestries were becoming increasingly popular with rich clients who wished to own unique works of art by Morris. Figurative designs, in particular, were sought after and a number depicting Burne-Jones figures had already been woven (cat. no. M.126). This was Morris's first attempt to produce a figurative design for tapestry. It had been twenty years since he had last drawn from a model so it was to earlier studies that he referred. The Jesus College Chapel commission provided him not only with successful figures but also scrolls for inscriptions, an essential part of Morris's tapestry designs at the time. These he updated by using his own poem 'The Orchard', composed especially and

GREENERY
The Seasons

M.122

whilst bitten mead and are shorn / the world without is waste and worn / but here within our orchard close / the guerdon of our labour shows / o valiant earth o happy year / the altar of mine year / and hangs aloft from tree to tree / the banners of the spring to be

M.123

later published in 1891 in *Poems by the Way*.

The tapestry was woven by William Knight, William Sleath and John Martin under the close supervision of Henry Dearle who reported, when it was acquired, to the Museum that 'The colouring as well as the general design are by Mr Morris and parts of the figures have been woven by his own hand'. Sleath and Knight were the first tapestry apprentices taken on after Dearle and

were trained by him. John Martin eventually became the first tapestry restorer employed by the Victoria and Albert Museum.

The design was woven only once and the panel did not find a private buyer, indicating that Burne-Jones's figure designs (and by now he was a much sought-after artist) were far more popular. The tapestry was sent on approval to Clouds, Percy Wyndham's country house

near Salisbury, and an existing photograph shows it hanging in the hall. However, Dearle's *Greenery* tapestry was eventually purchased. The Museum bought the tapestry from Morris & Co. in 1898 for £405, on the recommendation of J.H. Pollen and the Earl of Carlisle. The original design (cat. no. M.122) and a working drawing (E.1173-1940) are also in the collections.

Exhib. 1934 (51); 1952 (I 19)

M.124a

M.124b

M.124 Two designs depicting angels

Edward Burne-Jones, 1877 or 1878
Coloured chalks on paper, stretched over a canvas-covered frame
Fitzwilliam Museum, Cambridge
Given by Charles Fairfax Murray

a *Angeli Laudantes*
212.8 x 154.3 cm
(699.1)

b *Angeli Ministrantes*
212.3 x 150.5 cm
(699.2)

Originally drawn by Burne-Jones for twin lancet stained-glass windows in the south choir of Salisbury Cathedral, these designs were later used for tapestries woven at Merton Abbey (cat.no.M.125). An entry between March and August 1878 in Burne-Jones's account book listed '4 colossal and sublime figures of angels £20 each'.

The figures are the same size as the original finished tapestries and these drawings may have been used at the loom, although it is likely that the cartoons took the form of photographic copies on to which foreground, background and border details were added by hand.

A label on the back of *Angeli Ministrantes* is inscribed in Georgiana Burne-Jones's hand 'Design made for a

window / in Salisbury Cathedral / by E. Burne-Jones / December 6th 1887 / Lent to the South London Free Li / brary for 3 months…'
Exhib. 1934 (57, 58)

M.125 Pair of tapestries depicting angels

Designed by Henry Dearle with figures by Edward Burne-Jones and woven at Merton Abbey, 1894
Tapestry woven wool, silk and mohair on a cotton warp

a *Angeli Laudantes*
237.5 x 202.0 cm
V&A (153-1898)

b *Angeli Ministrantes*
241.5 x 200.0 cm
V&A (T.459-1993)

Burne-Jones's angel figures were originally drawn in 1877 or 1878 for stained-glass in Salisbury Cathedral (cat.no.M.124). These were converted to tapestry with added millefleurs grounds and matching orange and pomegranate borders designed by Henry Dearle. Manufactured at Merton Abbey in 1894 by Merton Abbey's most experienced weavers at that time, John Martin, William Haines and William Elliman, they are woven at fifteen warp threads to the inch, the average pitch of the firm's tapestries throughout production.

In 1898 the South Kensington Museum purchased the *Laudantes* panel from Morris & Co. for £225 on the recommendation of J. H. Pollen and the Earl of Carlisle. The *Ministrantes* tapestry was bought by Edwin Waterhouse of Feldemore in Surrey. Since this time it formed part of the Handley-Read Collection and, in 1993, was purchased from an American buyer by the Museum with assistance from the National Art Collection Fund and the National Heritage Memorial Fund.

A number of later variations of these tapestries were woven, including *Laudantes* panels in 1898 (for Mr Goldman) and 1902 (Mr Jordan), and a single angel with a harp inscribed 'Allelulia' in 1904 (Harris Art Gallery, Preston). The designs proved particularly appropriate for church use, and in 1902 a pair of single angels was woven for All Saints, Brockhampton, Herefordshire. These were repeated in 1904 for a private memorial and in 1905 both panels were adapted for Eton College Chapel. These, woven as war memorials for the Boer War, have an inscription and a lower additional verdure border of shields. An embroidered copy of *Laudantes* with additional medieval figures worked by Lady Catherine Milnes Gaskell (1856–1935) is now in Much Wenlock parish church.
Exhib. Laudantes 1934 (54): 1952 (O11)

M.125a

M.125b

M.126 *Pomona* tapestry

Designed by Edward Burne-Jones and John Henry
Dearle and woven at Merton Abbey, *c.*1900
Tapestry woven wool and silk on a cotton warp,
168.0 x 109.0 cm
V&A (T.33-1981)

Burne-Jones's account book shows that he was paid £25
by Morris & Co. in December 1882 for the figure of
Pomona, his first design specifically for tapestry. A letter
from Morris to Jenny on 28 February 1883 (Kelvin, 851)
states, 'Uncle Ned has done me two lovely figures for
tapestry, but I have got to design a background for them.
I shall probably bring them down [to Kelmscott Manor]
next time I come for my holiday task'. The original
tapestry with Morris's background and border design
was woven with its pair, *Flora,* at Merton Abbey in 1885.
Both panels are now in the Whitworth Art Gallery,
Manchester.

This is one of seven later versions approximately half the
size of the original, with a background design by Henry
Dearle. Reducing the size and adding a millefleur
ground proved to be commercially expedient. In his 1927
publication, *History of the Merton Abbey Tapestry Works,*
H.C. Marillier records six examples woven between 1898
and 1920. Apart from this panel, which was purchased
from Sotheby's Belgravia on 4 March 1981 (lot 151),
others have been traced to Exeter College, Oxford, the

Harris Art Gallery, Preston, and the Art Institute of
Chicago. The 1920 version woven for Mr Fleming of
Aldwick Grange was sold at Sotheby's on 12 February
1965 (lot 45) and yet another version, with a slightly
altered ground, was woven in 1937 as part of the cele-
brations for the coronation of Edward VIII. This was
sold at Christies South Kensington on 3 October 1989
(lot 55).

Eleven small-scale *Flora* tapestries are recorded. Two
have the same border design as this panel. One, which
shows similar weaving interpretations to this example
and may be contemporary, was sold at Sotheby's,
4 December 1985 (lot 140), the other, a later version, is in
a private collection in Australia (see Adelaide, 1994,
no.199).

A watercolour design, probably painted in the Morris
workshops, is at Wightwick Manor, near
Wolverhampton.

M.126

M.127

M.127 Sketch Book

Edward Burne-Jones, 1880s
Bound book with sketches in pencil and
coloured crayons with various inscriptions in the artist's hand;
10.2 x 17.2 x 2 cm,
V&A (E.9-1955)
Given by Dr W. L. Hildburgh FSA

Burne-Jones sketch book 'No. 15'. This
includes various studies for paintings,
including *The Hill Fairies* and *The Passing of
Arthur*. It also shows a number of
preliminary drawings for *The Adoration*
tapestry, including one page inscribed:
'8 x 6 x 12.9 figures near life size'.

Burne-Jones's finished watercolour design
for this tapestry (Private Collection) was
exhibited at the Burlington Fine Arts Club in
1899 (83) and at the Fine Arts Society in 1979
(184).

M.128 Cartoon for *The Adoration* tapestry

After Edward Burne-Jones with details
added by the artist, 1888
Photographic paper heightened with
watercolour and bodycolour,
240.0 x 375.9 cm
V&A (E.5012-1919)

Photographic tapestry cartoon in four parts.

The process used by Morris & Co. for transferring tapestry designs to the loom is
described in E.B. Bence-Jones's unpublished
manuscript *The Holy Grail Tapestries*
(National Art Library). Burne-Jones's watercolour designs, which were usually small,
were photographed and then enlarged to
the desired finished size of the tapestry.
These were then worked on by Burne-Jones
for adjustments to his figures and general
composition and by Morris or Dearle for the
addition of background, foreground and
clothing patterns. These finished cartoons
were then placed in the tapestry studio close
to the weavers and the design marked on
the warp in sections before each was woven.
A partial set of cartoons for the *Holy Grail*
series is at the William Morris Gallery,
Walthamstow.

It is difficult to discover when Morris first
used photography in the production of
stained glass, tapestry and books, although
it is likely to have developed from the 1870s
when Burne-Jones first collaborated with
Frederick Hollyer, the noted photographer.

M.128

M.129 *The Adoration* tapestry

Designed by Edward Burne-Jones, William Morris and Henry Dearle, 1888, this version woven at Merton Abbey, 1906
Tapestry woven wool, silk and mohair on a cotton warp, 345.3 x 502.9 cm
Norfolk Museums Service
(Castle Museum, Norwich)

Morris first mentions this project in a letter to John Prideaux Lightfoot, Rector of Exeter College, Oxford, on 4 September 1886 (Kelvin, 1271). 'I do not think you need go further to look for a subject, since the one you suggest seems a good one…and especially would suit the genius of tapestry completely; I feel sure that Burne-Jones will agree with me in this. I shall be seeing him tomorrow & will talk over the matter.' By 7 September Morris had viewed the proposed site in the college chapel and suggested that the colour be 'both harmonious & powerful, so that it would not be overpowered by the stained glass…' (Kelvin, 1273).

The commission took four years to realise, including two years' work by three weavers. Morris applied his usual eye for detail including a visit to Hampton Court on 1 September 1888, 'to have a good look at the tapestries as we [are] about beginning the figure of the Virgin in our big tapestry' (Kelvin, 1531). It was finally finished in February 1890 and put on display in the Oxford Street shop for Easter from Saturday 14 April. With hyperbolic approval *The Queen* reported, 'The outlines of the design only are Mr Burne-Jones's, the colouring and the ornamentation being Mr Morris's, and very beautiful are all three – so perfect, indeed, in every detail, that there is nothing left to desire…' (26 April 1890).

Morris described the resulting tapestry as 'The most important piece I have yet done…' in a letter dated 5 April 1893. He was fortunate that a religious subject had been chosen for the commission as this design proved the firm's most popular tapestry for both church and domestic settings and ten versions were woven. The second, in 1890–94 was for Wilfrid Scawen Blunt. This cost £525, the same price as the original commission. Other weavings followed: in 1894 for Manchester Corporation; 1895 for Eton College; 1900 for the Museum für Kunst und Gewerbe, Hamburg; 1901 for Sir George Brookman, now in the Art Gallery of South Australia, Adelaide; 1902 for S.I.Shchukin, now in The Hermitage, St Petersburg; 1904 for Guillaume Mallet for his Lutyens house, Le Bois des Moutiers, near Dieppe; and in 1907 for Roker Church, Sunderland.

This larger version, which has a wider more ornate border than any other weaving, was produced in 1906 for the Colman family of Carrow Abbey, Norwich. Despite Morris having advised in 1887 that the design was 'purposely schemed out for a narrow border, the widening of it would throw out the proportion of the picture…' (Kelvin, 1423), this late variation is surprisingly successful.

The cartoon (cat.no.M.128) and a working drawing (E.224-1911) are in the Museum.

Following the first weaving of the tapestry, Birmingham Museum and Art Gallery commissioned from Burne-Jones a full-sized watercolour of the design, entitled *The Star of Bethlehem* (75'91).

M.129

M.130 Two tapestries from the *Holy Grail* series

Designed by Edward Burne-Jones, William Morris,
John Henry Dearle, from 1890
Woven at Merton Abbey by Martin, Taylor, Sleath,
Ellis, Knight and Keach, 1890–94
Cotton warp, wool and silk weft
Private Collection

a *The Arming and Departure of the Knights of the
Round Table on the Quest for the Holy Grail*
240.0 x 347.0 cm

b *The Attainment: The Vision of the Holy Grail to Sir
Galahad, Sir Bors and Sir Perceval*
239.0 x 749.0 cm

Morris's first visited Stanmore Hall, Middlesex, the
home of William Knox D'Arcy, on 22 December 1888, in
order to discuss a substantial commission comprising
the complete decoration of two floors of Stanmore Hall.
This included specially designed furnishings, the most
important of which was a set of tapestries for the
dining room. D'Arcy, whose considerable wealth was
earned from interests in mining and oil, seemed content
to finance Morris's dream commission, allowing him
considerable leeway in the design and arrangement of
the tapestries.

It is likely that tapestries were not part of the original
furnishing scheme, as early photographs of the dining
room show the walls papered with *Acanthus* wallpaper.
The first detailed mention of them is in a letter of 23
December 1890 from Burne-Jones to his friend Lady
Leighton of Tapley Hall in Knutsford, Cheshire, in
which he talks of his present work being designs '…for
tapestry to go round a big room…not in an ancient
room, such bliss isn't for me – in some newfangled
place but there, there. The subjects are five in number –
with life size figures…'

The tapestry commission was documented for D'Arcy
by A.B.Bence-Jones through interviews with Morris,
Burne-Jones and Dearle. This typewritten manuscript is
now in the National Art Library. The choice of subject
was simple for Morris and Burne-Jones,who had been
smitten with the Arthurian Romances since Oxford
days. Morris believed the Quest for the Holy Grail was
'the most beautiful and complete episode of the legends'
and 'in itself a series of pictures'. Whereas five separate
narrative scenes were eventually chosen, a narrow
panel depicting a ship was added to indicate travel and
the passage of time between incidents. The final
subjects chosen were: 'The Beckoning', 'The Knights
Departing', 'The Failure of Sir Gawaine', 'The Failure of
Sir Lancelot', 'The Ship' and 'The Attainment'. One
further scene dropped before weaving was 'The death
of Galahad amid the Host in the City of Sarras'.

To explain the narrative, six smaller verdure panels
with inscriptions were designed by Henry Dearle to
hang below five of the figurative tapestries (two under
the first and second panels, none under the last). These
showed woodland scenes of deer with shields of the
knights hung from trees.

The series took four years to weave and it is likely that

M.130b

designing and weaving, with Morris and Dearle supervising, occurred simultaneously. The final cost of the tapestries was a considerable £3,500, of which Burne-Jones was paid £1,000 for his designs.

The Attainment was exhibited at the 1893 Arts and Crafts Exhibition (89) and noted, with mixed feelings, in the artistic press. *The Artist* (4 Nov. 1893) believing that the panel 'is so befogged with detail, and overloaded with foreground that we envy not the mansion destined to receive it'. In sharp contrast, the *Daily News* noted that the scene was reproduced 'in a manner that would have been incredible in the most sanguine hopes for textiles a short time ago'.

The original tapestries were sold at Sotheby's on 16 July 1920 (lot 130) and bought by the Duke of Westminster for 3,400 guineas (£3,683). These two panels, together with *The Failure of Gawaine,* were sold again at Sotheby's in April 1978 to two separate buyers for a total price of £94,000.

Three further partial sets were woven from these designs. In 1895–6 the second, fourth and sixth panels were woven for Laurence Hodson of Compton Hall. These are now in Birmingham Museum and Art Gallery. In 1898–9 the full set of narrative scenes plus one verdure was woven for George McCulloch, an associate of D'Arcy's. These were exhibited at the Paris International Exhibition of 1900 (see fig. 124) and at the Wembley Exhibition of 1925. Briefly on loan to the Victoria and Albert Museum, they were sold in 1927 to Lord Lee of Fareham (880 guineas) and again in 1953 (370 guineas) after which they went abroad. The *Beckoning* tapestry was brought back to England and bought for £90,000 (Sotheby's Belgravia, 24 September 1980) by Birmingham Museum and Art Gallery. The remaining four McCulloch narrative panels (cut into six pieces) were sold on 16 November 1994 for a total of £760,000.

In 1929–32 *The Beckoning* and *The Attainment* designs were woven for Henry Beacham of Lympne Castle, Kent. For many years these were in the Stadtmuseum, Munich. *The Attainment* was sold at Sotheby's on 20 March 1987 for £60,500.

Single re-weavings included a *Ship* panel plus one verdure for the Middlemore family (now in the Birmingham Museum and Art Gallery) and a verdure panel without shields for Mr Ellis of Wrea Head, Scalby, Scarborough (now Wrea College).

Numerous Burne-Jones drawings for the series are known and the photographic cartoons for part of the series are at the William Morris Gallery, Walthamstow.

Tapestries from the series have been exhibited frequently and the subject of numerous articles over the past fifty years.

Exhib. 1934 (53b)

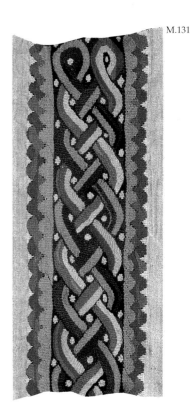

M.131

M.131 Four borders

Reproduction designs woven by Morris & Co., 1911–14
Tapestry woven linen, 46.9 x 17.7 cm;
others approx. 36.5 x 12.7 cm
V&A (Circ.423-1911; Circ.1914-1 (illustrated), 2 & 3)

H.C. Marillier, Managing Director of Morris & Co. from 1905 until 1940, wrote to the Victoria and Albert Museum in 1909 suggesting that they commission a new tapestry 'as the technical skills of the weavers has improved since the two examples in the Museum [cat.nos. M.123, 125 a] were made'. The advice from A.F. Kendrick, then Keeper of Textiles, to the Director, Cecil Harcourt-Smith, was, 'In my opinion this increased skill has led them astray'.

These borders, which are copies of fifth- to eighth-century Egyptian Coptic weavings in the Museum collection (1327-1888, 821 to B-1905), are likely to be the compromise suggested by the Museum, and they paid £13 5s. for the four examples. They also ordered from the firm copies of other small historic tapestries.

Probably woven on a demonstration tapestry loom set up in the Oxford Street shop. This equipment continued to be used throughout the First World War when the Merton Abbey Tapestry Works closed down. Jean Orage, the noted tapestry weaver, worked for the firm at this time and was responsible for training a number of young women, including one of Henry Marillier's daughters.

CALLIGRAPHY

John Nash

Between 1870 and 1875 William Morris planned, wrote out and (in whole or in part) illuminated some twenty-one manuscript books. Of these only two could be said to be complete, and of others only fragments and trial pages survive, but it says something for Morris' prodigious energy that these works, usually delicate and exacting to an excruciating degree, were carried out at the same time as running a thriving business, moving house, travelling to Iceland, studying Icelandic and translating Icelandic sagas, and (not least) coping with great emotional pain caused by the relationship between his wife Jane and the painter Rossetti.

Morris's energy, however, is well known and well documented. What is less well known is the extent of his achievement during this period, not only in the way he developed medieval and Renaissance illuminated page design to his own idiom (which was to manifest itself much later in the design of the Kelmscott Press books) but in his research into gilding techniques, and most particularly in his instinctive rediscovery of the basic principles underlying the beautiful, clear writing of the early manuscripts that he had so much admired as a student at Oxford, and later as a collector. Unlike Edward Johnston, some thirty-five years later, Morris's insights did not come about through careful research or application of theory, but the value of these intuitive experiments was to be gladly acknowledged by the younger man when, at the beginning of the twentieth century, he was to demonstrate in print and in the classroom that the beauty of the writing in Carolingian, medieval and Renaissance manuscripts was the direct product of an edged pen used (in most cases) at a consistent angle and with little manipulation, and that this writing, in the eyes of both makers and readers of these often heavily illuminated manuscripts, was fully as important as the illumination, and in most cases more so.

By the beginning of the Victorian period these notions had long been forgotten. From the early eighteenth century the pointed steel nib increasingly superseded the cut quill; the result was the dominance of copperplate scripts, with their thicks and thins entirely produced by varying pressure. In the nineteenth century palaeography developed rapidly as a historical discipline, but the scholars who dissected the great scripts had next to no idea of the practical disciplines that lay behind these, and (in general) no particular interest in finding out. The Gothic Revival brought a great upsurge of interest in illuminated manuscripts, especially those of the thirteenth and fourteenth centuries whose complicated historiated decoration offered glimpses of medieval life. Aided by the invention of chromolithography, popularisers such as Henry Shaw, Owen Jones and Noel Humphreys were able to produce a succession of books, some very elaborate, which brought the colourful details of Gothic ornament and illumination within reach of the general public. The steady stream of lesser handbooks that followed in their wake (bearing such titles as *The Art of Illuminating – What it was –What it should be – And how it may be practised*) resulted in a great vogue for 'illuminated gift books', both printed and hand-made, decorated to look as 'medieval' as possible, and setting forth texts that were usually biblical and inspiring, and always written in ornate 'textura' Gothic – or rather not written, as the letterforms tended to be drawn in minute outline and more or less neatly filled in.

According to Morris, the formative impression made on him as a boy by Canterbury Cathedral, and by his first sight of illuminated manuscripts, was crucial: 'These first pleasures which I discovered for myself were stronger than anything else I have had in life.' While at Oxford, from 1853 to 1855, he was a constant visitor to the Bodleian, as can be seen from the Visitors' Book (though which were his favourite manuscripts remains a matter of guesswork) and in later life he was to

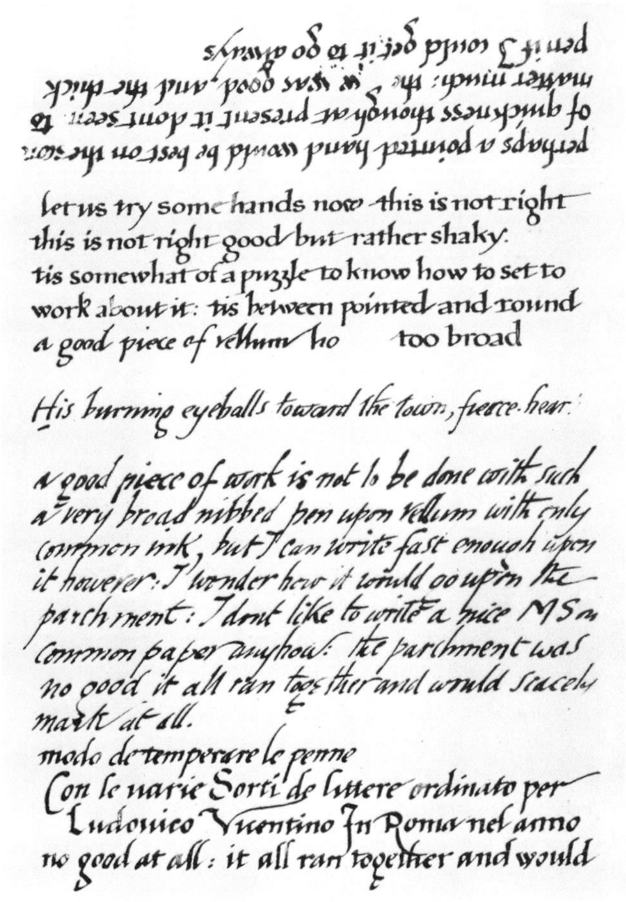

let us try some hands now this is not right
this is not right good but rather shaky:
tis somewhat of a puzzle to know how to set to
work about it: tis between pointed and round
a good piece of vellum ho too broad

His burning eyeballs toward the town, fierce hear:

a good piece of work is not to be done with such
a very broad nibbed pen upon vellum with only
common ink, but I can write fast enough upon
it however: I wonder how it would go upon the
parchment: I dont like to write a nice MS on
common paper anyhow: the parchment was
no good it all ran together and would scarcely
mark at all.
modo de temperare le penne
Con le uarie Sorti de littere ordinato per
Ludouico Vicentino In Roma nel anno
no good at all: it all ran together and would

Fig. 100 Page of writing trials by Morris.

become so familiar with the manuscripts in the British Museum that (as his daughter May remarked) he liked to consider them his. Given his absorption in things medieval as an antidote to the ugliness of the capitalist and industrialist world around him, it was only to be expected that by 1856 and 1857, when first sharing lodgings with Edward Burne-Jones in London and studying painting under Rossetti's influence, he had already been trying his own hand at illumination, Rossetti describing him at the time as 'unrivalled among moderns in all illumination and work of that kind'. Three examples from this period are known, of which his rendering of a tale from the Brothers Grimm, 'Der Eisenhans' (The Iron Man), is shown (cat. no. N.1).

Morris could not have been oblivious to the Victorian illumination fad which was then gaining momentum (Jones and Humphreys' *Illuminated Books of the Middle Ages* had been published seven years before) and the influence shows in his ornate and somewhat eccentric illumination scheme, and his heavy-footed Gothic. However, it is noticeable that in none of these early efforts does he imitate his contemporaries in going to the Bible for his texts, and the illumination, drawn probably from fourteenth-century sources, seems much too lively to have been copied from any pattern book. As Joseph Dunlap observes in his definitive study *The Road to Kelmscott*, 'All his life he hated the copying of ancient work as unfair to the old and stupid for the present, only good for inspiration and hope'. It may be significant that no Victorian manuals figure in a list of the books in his library drawn up in (or about) 1876; it is certainly significant that there does appear in this list a bound volume containing four sixteenth-century Italian Renaissance writing-books (cat. no. N.2): Ludovico Vicentino degli Arrighi's *La Operina* and *Il Modo de Temperare le Penne*, Giovannantonio Tagliente's *Lo presento libro* and Ugo da Carpi's *Thesauro de scrittori*. The date of purchase of these books remains uncertain, but in 1864 Morris became friends with F.S. Ellis, publisher and rare-book dealer, and it is more than possible that the writing-books were bought at around that time, as a natural result of the turning of Morris's interest from Gothic towards Renaissance. He certainly studied them and kept returning to them – a sheet of writing trials refers directly to Arrighi – and he may also have owned copies of the writing-books by Yciar and Palatino.

At this time he was working on his long poem sequence *The Earthly Paradise*, filling page after trial page with his rapid scrawl and doodling in the margins either as he did so or shortly thereafter. As 1870 approached, flower and vine designs began to give way to sketches for illuminated initials, and to trials of letters and sentence fragments. In a draft of *Bellerophon in Lycia* (cat.no.N.3) we see flowers in the margin of the verso page and, on the recto, the beginnings of the small flattened italic script, furnished with many extraneous hairlines, of which Morris was to make great use; this, along with a scattering of rather awkward capitals, is definitely written with an edged pen, producing natural thicks and thins.

In 1869 *The Earthly Paradise* was completed, and Morris had become intensely interested in the literature of the Icelandic sagas, which he began reading and translating with Eiríkr Magnússon in 1868. He naturally used these translations as texts for most of the manuscripts which he now began to work on, developing as he did so a repertoire of five scripts – two based on Renaissance humanist (now called 'roman') minuscule, three on humanist cursive, or 'italic'. In his first manuscript, 'The Story of the Dwellers at Eyr' (cat.no.N.4), three of these scripts are in use – rounded, rather laboured roman minuscule (perhaps influenced by 'antica tonda' models to be found in Arrighi and Tagliente), used for the running heads, descriptive chapter headings in the flattened italic already referred to, and (for much of the text) a larger, more cursive and lighter weight italic with connecting strokes and curved ascenders which are definitely Renaissance based. Capitals, both in the title at the top of the opening page (following the Renaissance model) and in the decorated initials which form almost the only illumination, are what one would expect from a beginner – amateurish in the extreme; those used in the text are laboriously formed and generally over-tall, one of the many mannerisms of which Morris was never to rid himself.

In Morris's second manuscript, 'The Story of the Volsungs and Niblungs' (cat.no.N.6), there is a marked improvement in written quality both of capitals and of the text hand: flattened italic with

Watching the weary spindle fly

diagonal hair-strokes to m, n and h, curved descenders to f and y, curved ascenders generally, straight descender to p, and earless g with a sharpened flourish. This is also the text hand of Morris's next effort, one of only two or three in which both writing and illumination were fully carried out – 'A Book of Verse' (cat. no. N.5), dated 1870. Like Morris's more ambitious calligraphic projects, it was a collaborative venture – Morris carried out the writing and involved himself heavily in the gilding and decoration, but he had little confidence in his abilities as draftsman or painter and brought in Burne-Jones and the painter and illustrator Charles Fairfax Murray to carry out illustrations and historiated initials. A second version of 'The Story of the Dwellers at Eyr' (Birmingham Museum and Art Gallery) bore a proud colophon, dated 9 April 1871, in which Morris noted that he carried out all the work, except for the gilding.

For his next project – 'The Rubaiyat of Omar Khayyam' (cat.no.N.8) – Morris thought at least fleetingly along italic lines, as trial versions show; but the completed version of 1872 is in tiny,

this Universe, and why not knowing

formal, almost monoline roman minuscule, with straight y, cut-off f, g with rounded flourish and sticking up ear, and tall ascenders with minute tick serifs. (As with other aspects of Morris's work, it is most engaging to imagine this burly, vastly impatient man, subject to famous rages, subjecting himself to the most minute and exacting tasks, such as writing microscopically with a crow quill.)

In this, as in his other four major manuscripts, he was able to discipline himself to remain consistent in his writing, but it must be stressed that this was usually far from the case. Warington Taylor, manager of Morris, Marshall, Faulkner & Co., wrote in 1868 of his work habits: 'Morris will start half a dozen jobs; he has designs for perhaps half of them, and therefore in a week or two they have to be given up. They are put away, bits get lost, have to be done over again; hence great loss of time and money.' It is highly likely that this was also the approach Morris took to his manuscript work. In the first version of 'The Dwellers at Eyr' the open, lightweight, rather tentative italic of the opening pages changes, after around page 40, to the flattened, blacker and more angular italic which characterises 'The Volsungs and Niblungs'. In other words, Morris either developed a different script as he wrote, or (as Dr Dunlap suggests) wrote the second part of 'The Dwellers', 'after he had succumbed to the diagonals', or the persistent hair-lines which plague that particular script. In the period 1873–4 at least ten or eleven of his Icelandic translations were produced calligraphically in the form of incomplete versions or trial pages; few of those which extended beyond four or five pages are written in the same script throughout. The italic of 'King Hafbur and King Siward' (cat. no. N.9) is fundamentally that of 'The Volsungs and Niblungs', but w has acquired a Gothic look, f has acquired a strange hairline flourish to its top, ascenders tend to end suddenly in a slashing

In swift words nowise light

diagonal stroke, and the ornate capitals are definitely Gothic inspired. 'The Story of the Banded Men' and 'The Story of Hen-Thorir' (cat. nos. N.11–12) were probably written at around the same time, and each employs basically the same script (small, rounded formal italic with flourished f and 'sharpened' g), but the former manuscript supplies this italic with the famous diagonal hair-strokes which then die out after page 10, and the latter changes script markedly after page 28, the rather

$$e \rightarrow \epsilon \qquad a \rightarrow \partial \qquad f \rightarrow f \qquad g \rightarrow g$$

squat g becoming narrower and more graceful, e and a taking on uncial forms and the descender of flourished f becoming straight. (The quality and sharpness of the writing also improves dramatically; what this probably means is that Morris's skill at quill-cutting was improving along with his skill as a penman.)

The contrast between a single page of 'Ogier the Dane', in minuscule which really *is* minuscule, and the black, angular Gothic italic of 'Haroon al Rasheed' (fig. 101) – a non-Icelandic tale – is dramatic evidence of Morris's versatility and his constant drive to experiment, to develop writing appropriate (in his eyes) to the text. And, in the manuscript of 'The Story of Gunnlaug Worm-Tongue' (cat. no. N.10), after thirty-two pages of neat 'Rubaiyat' roman, Morris breaks off at the bottom of the page with 'arma virumque cano' written in an excellent, straightforward emulation of humanist cursive. Whatever the reason (had he simply become fed up with 'Gunnlaug'?), this shows that he had studied and gained from original Renaissance humanist manuscripts, apart from the wood-engraved models in his Renaissance writing-books, and that the idea of writing out all or part of the *Aeneids* was already in his mind. His work throughout this period, finally, demonstrates more than simply his restless nature; it shows that his main preoccupation was with the writing. Where manuscripts remain unfinished, it is almost invariably the illumination which remains incomplete; and most of the manuscripts just named have either a minimum of gilding and illumination, or none at all.

The two manuscripts with which Morris ended his five years of concentrated calligraphic activity – the 'Odes of Horace' and the 'Virgil's Aeneids' (cat. nos. N.13–14), both in their original Latin – also represent, respectively, the culmination of his efforts at developing an italic and roman minuscule as formal book-hands, faithful as possible to the range of Renaissance models which he kept always in mind and attempting to reach a standard that might be worthy of those models. It is uncanny how far he succeeded. Consciously or unconsciously he expressed in practice what Johnston was later to express in words: that the secret of recreating the beauty and clarity of the best of ancient scripts lay not in simply copying *styles*, but in analysing and following the best scribal *methods*, in order to acquire deeper understanding. It must be admitted that the italic of the Horace and the roman of the Virgil are not entirely free from irritating mannerisms. The f's of the italic retain the little hairline flourish that Morris found so unaccountably delightful; in the roman, the tops of v and u are closed off by over long serifs (interfering with legibility) and straight descenders (as on p and q) sprout obtrusively long diagonal finishing strokes. But the consistency and quality of each is, in the end, most remarkable. Morris, though intensely self-critical at all times, was proud of himself ('I have much improved by the way in both my ornament and my writing', he wrote to Fairfax Murray in February of 1874), and he had reason to be. Working only on Sundays and at odd moments snatched from an overpoweringly busy life, he had not only reached a remarkably high personal standard, but had laid the groundwork for Johnston's discoveries and for a clearer understanding of the principles of Western writing which was to benefit scholars and teachers to come.

Morris was to produce no more extended calligraphic manuscripts. His involvement with the 'Aeneids' had led him, with his usual enthusiasm, to set himself the immense task of translating the work himself; this project, not unnaturally, began to occupy all his spare time. Also, he now reorganised both the firm and his private life by buying out his partners and removing Rossetti from Kelmscott Manor; and he began increasingly to involve himself in Socialism. In effect, a new period in his life was beginning. But his interest in calligraphy did not die. The doodlings in the margins of his rough drafts and socialist lecture notes continued to include letter forms; the last page of a large notebook containing his 1882 journal contains various letters and parts of sentences in upright and sloping roman, and (curiously) a carefully written roman minuscule alphabet similar in weight and characteristics not so much to the Aeneid hand as to the *antica tonda* shown in rather crude wood-engraved form in his copy of Arrighi's *Il modo*. Around 1890 (according to Sydney Cockerell's well-informed guess) – the same year as the appearance of the Golden type and the designing of the first Kelmscott Press book – he returned to his flattened italic to write out a short catalogue of manuscripts and books then owned by him, in a carefully planned, wholly Renaissance inspired layout on vellum. A letter written in 1894 to an enthusiastic amateur who had sent him an example of calligraphy for his opinion produced some pointed comments, including (ironically enough), 'There are too many "flicks" in it.' It is curious to note that, while he sends his correspondent to look at books written before the sixteenth century to find the best models for page layout, he cites only manuscripts 'written about 1120 or even earlier' as providing the best models for writing – no mention of the Renaissance scribes by whom he had once set such store. Two years later he was dead – as his doctor put it, simply from being William Morris and cramming into one life several lifetimes' achievements, of which his venture into calligraphy was by no means the least.

Fig.101 Opening from 'Ogier the Dane' (on the left) and 'The Story of Haroon al Rasheed'.

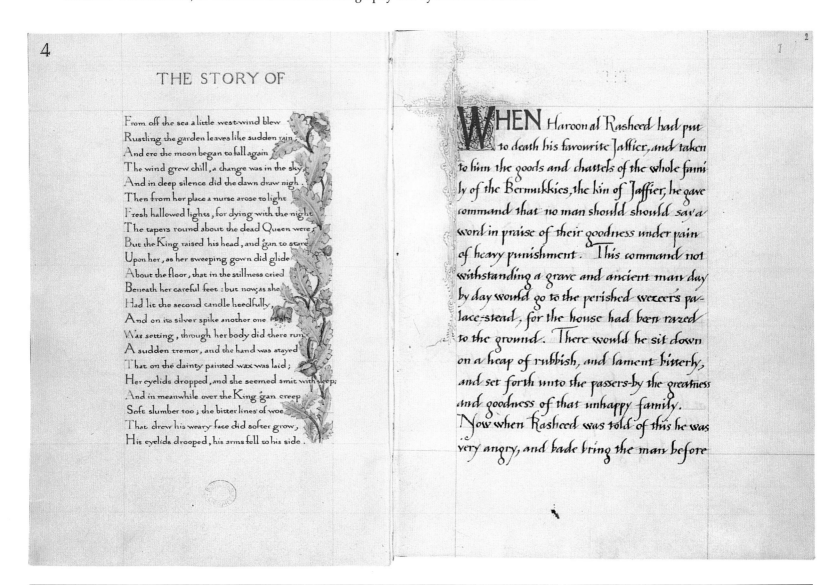

N.1 The Brothers Grimm, 'Der Eisenhans' (The Iron Man)

William Morris, 1857
One leaf, watercolour and gold paint on vellum, 23.5 x 37.0 cm sight
J. Paul Getty, KBE, Wormsley Library

By 1857 Morris was established with Burne-Jones in their rooms at Red Lion Square, and had already tried his hand at various pursuits, including (as was the Victorian fashion at the time) manuscript illumination. Three of his attempts from this period are known to have survived, of which this, an incomplete transcription of his own retelling of a Grimm Brothers tale, was given to Louisa, younger sister of Georgiana Macdonald (later Burne-Jones). Morris was later to dismiss this as his 'first attempt at illumination' (although this was almost certainly not the case); and it is not difficult to see why. Leaving the drawing, colour and decoration aside, the writing is so formless as to look brush-written, though it's most likely that a soft, badly-cut quill was to blame. Morris himself was undoubtedly conscious of the failings of the piece, as can be witnessed in the unfinished decorative elements, the badly smudged erasures down the right-hand margin and the perverse breaking off of the story at a particularly dramatic point. However, it remains valuable for two principal reasons: it demonstrates the heavy Gothic influence from which Morris's later manuscript work was to free itself, and it shows what a very long way he had to go.

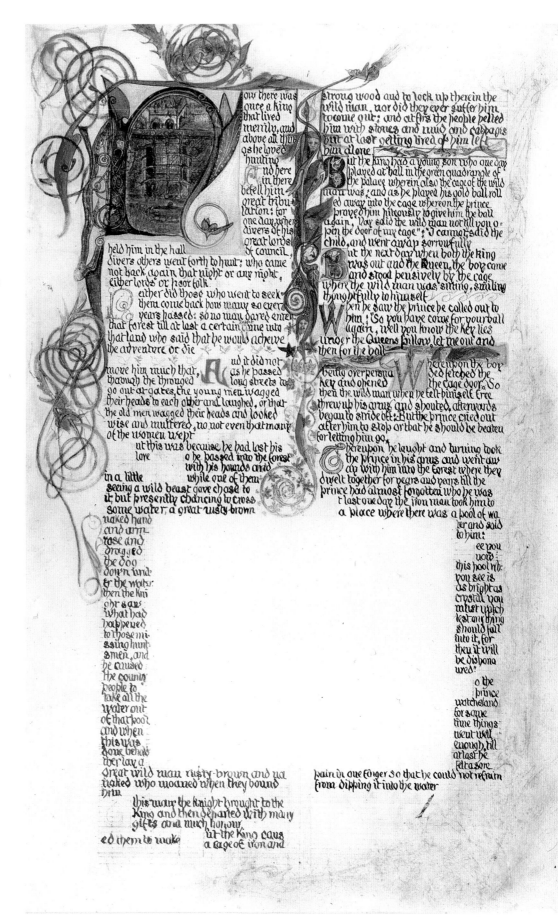

N.1

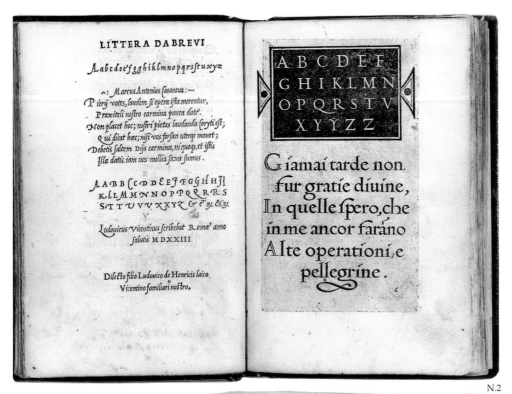

N.2

N.2 Bound copy of writing books by Ludovico Vicentino degli Arrighi, Giovannantonio Tagliente and Ugo da Carpi

Italian, sixteenth century
20.9 x 13.5 cm leaf
Society of Antiquaries of London
(Kelmscott Manor) (ref.:141.166.167.159)

By 1876, and probably considerably before that, Morris had acquired at least four Renaissance writing manuals: Arrighi's *La Operina* (in the edition printed by Ugo da Carpi in 1525 after his quarrel with Arrighi) and *Il Modo de temperare le Penne* (*c*.1526), Tagliente's *Lo presente libro* (third or fourth edition, 1525) and da Carpi's *Thesauro de Scrittori* (1525–6). Arrighi's *Operina* is concerned only with the *cancelleresca corsiva* but his *Il modo*, as well as illustrating different stages in quill-cutting, offers models of commercial hands, inscriptional capitals and decorative alphabets. The pages shown demonstrate, on the left, another version of italic ('litera da brevi'), and on the right, capitals in small size and a bold version of roman minuscule ('antica tonda') which undoubtedly had an influence on Morris (see A.S. Osley, 'The Kelmscott Manor Volume of Italian Writing-Books', *The Antiquaries Journal*, LXIV, pt 2, 1984).

N.3 Draft of 'Bellerophon in Lycia', from *The Earthly Paradise* by William Morris

Autograph copy by Morris with marginalia, 1869
Ink on paper, 33.5 x 45.0 cm open
British Library (Add. MS 45,301, fol. 43)
SEE ALSO FIG 15, PAGE 48

As he produced rough drafts of the poems that would go to make up *The Earthly Paradise*, mostly written in his everyday hand, Morris's customary marginal doodles, entirely flower and vine designs to begin with, demonstrate more and more that his mind was turning to lettering and calligraphy. Drafts of 'Orpheus and Eurydice' (1866–7) (BL Add. Ms 45307) and 'Rhodope' (1868) (BL Add. Ms 45304) show trials of capitals and designs for ornamented initials; the 1869 draft of 'Bellerophon' shows extensive trials of flourished ('swash') capitals and of the flattened italic with diagonal hair-strokes to *m*, *n*, and *h*, of which he was to make extensive use, already well developed. In the pages shown (see also fig. 15), Morris switches, from one page to the next, from sketches of floral designs to lettering trials in which his use of the edged pen is already clear.

N.4 'The Story of the Dwellers at Eyr', translated by William Morris

William Morris, 1869–70
Ink and watercolour on paper,
36.5 x 25.5 x 1.3 cm
Bodleian Library
(MS. Eng. misc. c. 265)

This is generally accepted as Morris's first manuscript. As such, the capitals of the title at the beginning and the italic of the text are both amateurish and tentative, and the illuminated initials, both in quality and design, are nothing short of dismal. In the pages shown, however, it can be seen that the roman minuscule of the running heads (somewhat reminiscent of the 'antica tonda' of Arrighi's *Il modo*) and the flattened, weightier italic of the chapter headings is already done with confidence.

N.5 'A Book of Verse'

William Morris,
Charles Fairfax Murray,
Edward Burne-Jones
and George Wardle
Date: 'August 26th 1870'
Ink, watercolour and gilding on paper, 27.9 x 21.6 cm leaf
V&A (NAL L.131-1953)
Purchased with assistance from the National Art Collections Fund and Friends of National Libraries

This, one of Morris's few completed manuscripts, was a collaborative effort, somewhat in the medieval tradition – Burne-Jones did one illustration at the beginning, Morris, the figures of Venus (pp. 50–51), Fairfax Murray did the rest of the illustration and painting as well as the famous portrait of Morris, done from a photograph. George Wardle helped with the ornamentation and did the coloured initials. Dunlap notes the relation of the ornament to Morris's *Powdered* fabric design, and goes on to describe it as 'crucial evidence of the great turning point in Morris's pattern design'
(*The Road to Kelmscott*, p. 174).

Given by Morris to Georgiana Burne-Jones; two of the poems are translations from the Icelandic.

Exhib. 1934 (229)

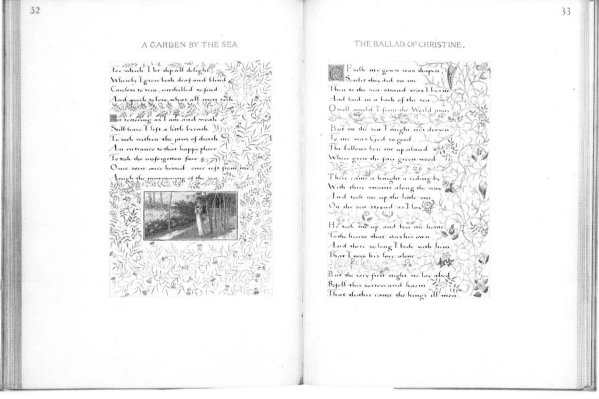

N.4

N.5

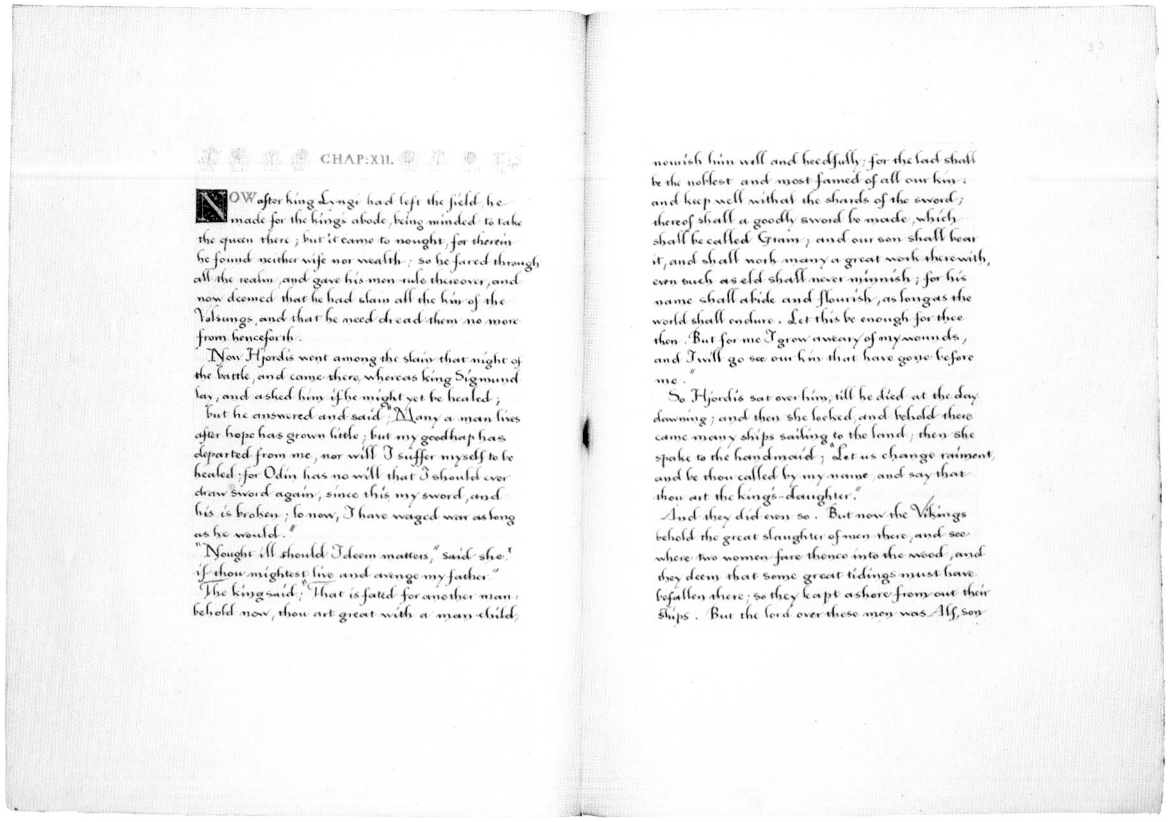

N.6

N.8

N.6 'The Story of the Volsungs and Niblungs', translated by William Morris

William Morris, 1871
Ink and watercolour on paper, 29.0 x 23.0 x 2.3 cm
Bodleian Library (MS. Eng. misc. d. 268, fols. 21v–22r)

This manuscript, of which seventy-three leaves were completed, is contemporary with the heavily illuminated 'A Book of Verse'. However, it is almost without illumination itself, except for a beautiful title-page with figures lightly sketched with pencil and an historiated initial, painted by Fairfax Murray, of Sigurd seated on the body of Fafnir. It is noticeable that the initial capitals of the beginnings of the chapters have improved greatly in quality. Assuming they are Morris's work, he must have been practising hard. In fact, it seems probable that the entire manuscript, done in the same flattened italic as 'A Book of Verse', may have been a preparation for it.

N.7 'The Story of Frithiof the Bold', translated by William Morris and Eiríkr Magnússon

William Morris, Charles Fairfax Murray, Louise Powell and Graily Hewitt, c.1873
Watercolour and gilding on paper, 40.1 x 27.0 cm closed, 40.1 x 53.0 cm open
J. Paul Getty, KBE, Wormsley Library

Although Morris completed little of the decoration and illumination of this twenty-two page manuscript himself, he worked the design out so carefully that Fairfax Murray (doing the two historical initials), Louise Powell (completing the floral decoration) and Graily Hewitt (completing the gilded running heads, chapter headings and initials) were eventually able to carry out his intentions very faithfully – even more so, perhaps, than in the *Aeneids*. Hewitt's trained hand is evident in the beautiful and precise gilded capitals of the initials – something Morris never quite mastered – and in the running heads, where, although he cannot help improving on Morris's capitals, he is careful to preserve the Master's somewhat haphazard spacing. Morris did, however, complete the writing – another indication that this was the facet of his manuscript work in which he was most involved. It is perhaps the single most consistent and beautifully sustained example of his compressed formal roman minuscule, which would seem to indicate that it was done towards the end of his 'manuscript period' (1873–4).

The book was given or sold by Morris to Fairfax Murray. The binding, by T. J. Cobden Sanderson, is in turquoise straight-grain morocco.

N.8 'Rubaiyat of Omar Khayyam', by Edward Fitzgerald

William Morris, finished
16 October 1872
Ink, watercolour and gilding on vellum, 13.5 x 23.5 cm open
British Library (Add. MS 37,832)

This, another gift for Georgiana Burne-Jones, was both written and illuminated by Morris, and is the only completed version of four. Here Morris opts for an entirely different script - a tiny roman minuscule, probably written with a crow-quill. The ending gives a good idea of the quality and profusion of the illumination. May Morris claimed that each flower used in the design was different and identifiable.

CHAP. XIII.

NOW weareth away the mid-win ter, and when spring cometh, the weather groweth fair, the wood bloom eth, the grass groweth, and ships may glide betwixt land and land.

So on a day the king says to his folk: "I will that ye come with us for our disport out into the woods, that we may look upon the fairness of the earth."

So did they, and went flock-meal with the king into the woods: but so it befell, that the king and Frith iof were gotten alone together afar from other men, and the king said he was heavy, and would fain sleep: then said Thief: "Get thee home, then, lord, for it better beseemeth men of high estate to lie at home than abroad."

"Nay" said the king "so will I not do." And he laid him down there with, and slept fast, snoring loud. Thief sat close by him, and present ly drew his sword from his sheath, & cast it far away from him.

A little while after the king woke up, and said "Was it not so, Frith iof, that a many things came into thy mind een now? but well hast thou dealt with them, and great hon our shalt thou have of me. Lo now, I knew thee straightway, that first evening thou camest into our hall: now nowise speedily shalt thou de part from us; and somewhat great abideth thee."

39

Said Frithiof: "Lord king, thou hast done to me well, and in friend ly wise; but yet must I get me gone soon, because my company cometh speedily to meet me, as I have given them charge to do."

So then they rode home from the wood, and the king's folk came flock ing to him, and home they fared to the hall and drank joyously: and it was made known to all folk that Fri thiof the Bold had been abiding there through the winter-tide.

CHAP. XIV.

EARLY of a morning-tide one smote on the door of that hall, wherein slept the king and queen, and many others: then the king ask ed who it was that called at the hall door; and so he who was without said: "Here am I, Frithiof; and I am arrayed for my departure."

Then was the door opened, and Frithiof came in, and sang a stave:

Have great thanks for the guesting
Thou gavest with all bounty;
Right fully for departure
Is the eagles' feeder now;
But Ingibiorg I mind thee
While yet on earth I dwell;
Live gloriously! I give thee
This gift for many kisses

40

N.7

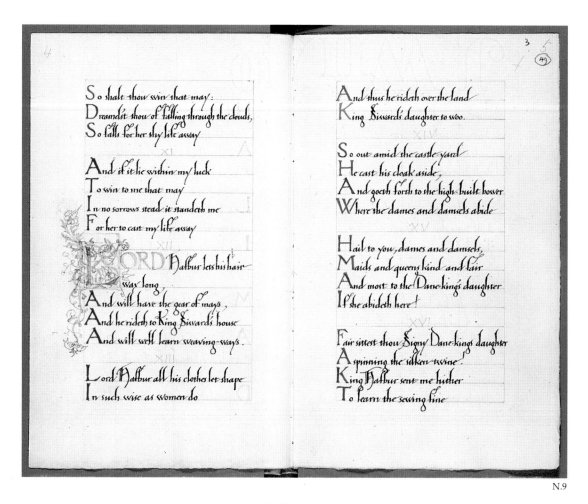

N.9

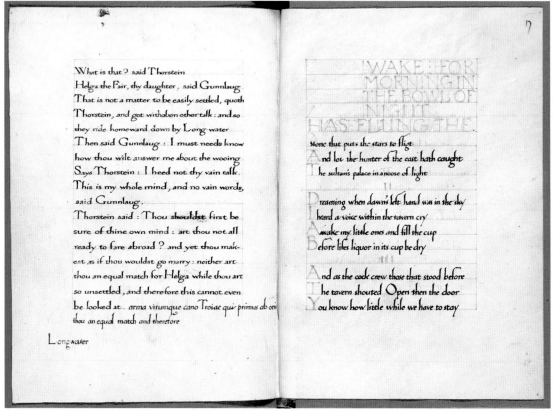

N.10

N.9 'King Hafbur and King Siward', translated by William Morris

William Morris, *c.*1873
Ink, watercolour and gilding on paper, 20.8 x 13.5 cm
Bodleian Library
(MS. Eng.misc.e. 233/2, fols. 2v–3r)

Of this translation Morris wrote fifty-six quatrains out of ninety before abandoning the work. It marks the appearance of a new, angular, more upright italic with a somewhat Gothic look (especially where *w* and capitals are concerned). As can be seen, the illumination is merely a pencilled design.

Exhib. 1934 (246)

N.10 'The Story of Gunnlaug Worm-Tongue', translated by William Morris

William Morris, *c.*1874
Ink on vellum, 16.0 x 12.0 cm
Bodleian Library
(MS. Eng. misc.e. 233/1, fols. 16v–17r)

After writing out more than thirty pages of his translation in the fine roman minuscule seen for example, in the 'Rubaiyat' (cat.no.N.8) and in the single leaf of 'Ogier the Dane' (fig.101), Morris's attention began to wander. On folio 16 he strayed at three points into a very competent emulation of humanist cursive, free of mannerisms; on the following page (seen here on the left) he abandons Gunnlaug altogether at the bottom with the opening words from the *Aeneids*, written in this same cursive – the script of the Horace. He therefore had both his final projects already firmly in mind. Note the isolated name 'Longwater' in the bottom left corner – half in roman, half in italic.

Exhib. 1934 (248)

N.11 'The Story of the Banded Men', translated by William Morris

William Morris, *c*.1874
Ink on paper, 29.0 x 22.5 cm
Bodleian Library (MS. Eng. misc. d. 267)

Close examination reveals a distinct improvement in sharpness, form and legibility of writing half-way down the page, changing from a stiff, monoline 'typographical' italic, which almost looks roman, to a more natural script which looks forward to the Horace. Note especially the change in *g*.

N.12 'The Story of Hen-Thorir', translated by William Morris

William Morris, *c*.1874
Ink and watercolour on paper, 29.0 x 22.5 x 1.3 cm
Bodleian Library (MS. Eng. misc. d. 266)

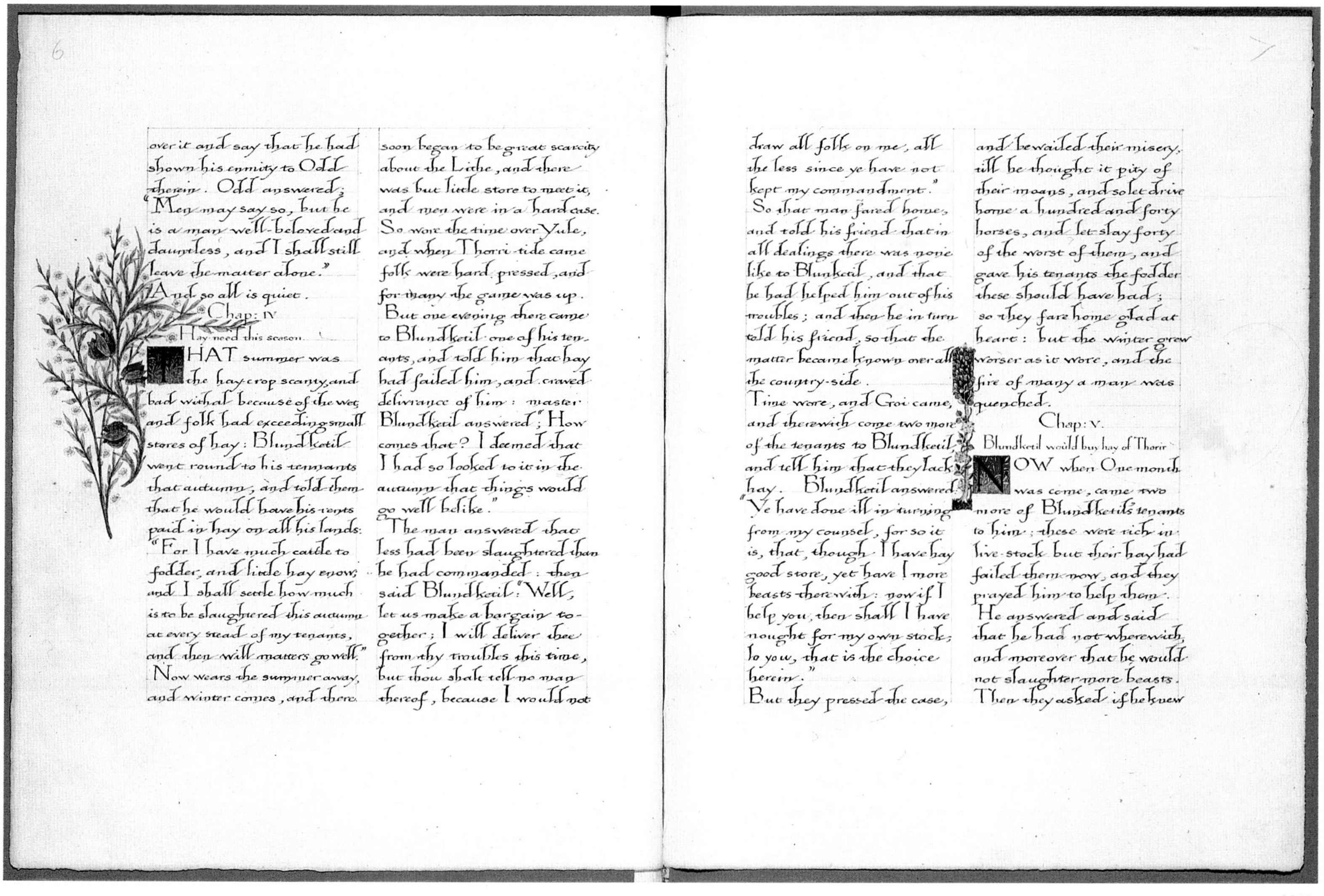

Morris's inventiveness seemed endless – no two of his designs were alike. The quality and colour of his decorated versal capitals had, by the time of this manuscript, improved enormously (compare with the 'The Dwellers at Eyr' (cat. no. N.4)).

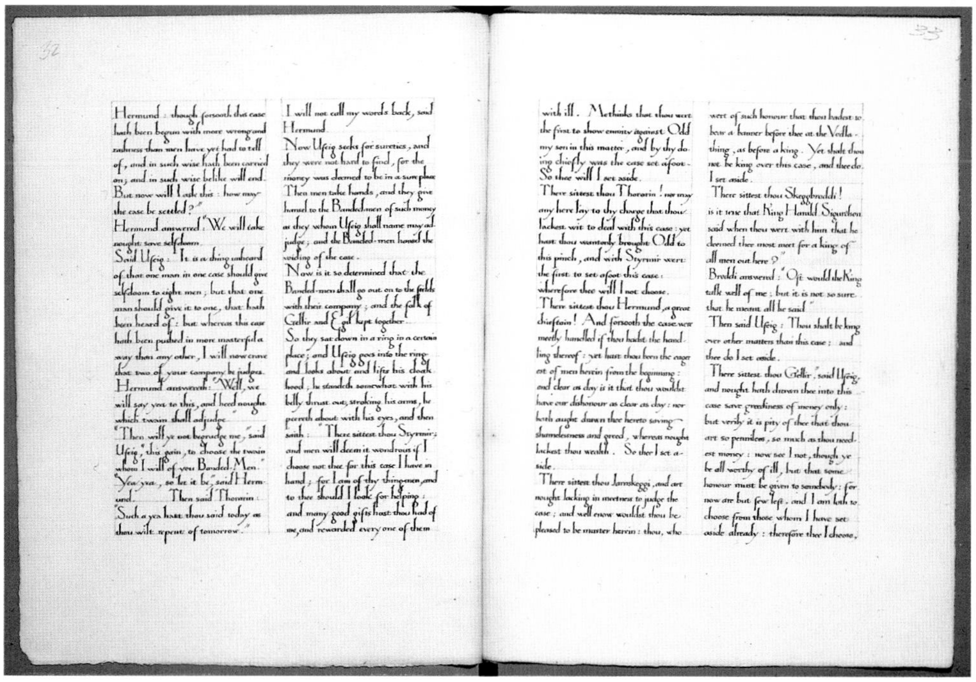

N.11

N.12

N.13 'Odes of Horace',

William Morris, Edward Burne-Jones and
Charles Fairfax Murray, 1874
Ink, watercolour and gilding on vellum,
17.5 x 13.0 x 2.0 cm
Bodleian Library (MS. Lat. class e. 38)

The culmination of Morris's italic, showing how far his study of Renaissance hands
had borne fruit – the only irritating mannerism remaining is the hairline curlicue on *f*.
Although he finished the writing of all four books, on 183 pages, he never completely
finished the decoration; this did not prevent a few of the pages (principally the openings of three of the books) from being, with Burne-Jones and Fairfax Murray's help,
among the most elaborate illumination schemes he ever carried out.

N.14 'The Aeneids of Virgil'

William Morris, Edward Burne-Jones and Charles Fairfax Murray, 1874–5;
completed later by Louise Powell and Graily Hewitt
Ink, watercolour and gilding on vellum, 35.0 x 22.3 cm
Private Collection, UK

The culmination of Morris's roman minuscule. Graily Hewitt identified the writing
as being modelled specifically on a fifteenth-century manuscript of the works of St
Jerome (BM Ms. Harley 45309), but Alfred Fairbank disagreed, and indeed it seems
much more likely that this beautiful clear script, marred by one or two strange traits,
was the result of Morris's study and experimentation over several years rather than
the conscious copying of one hand. Although Morris ended the writing at 177 pages
(the writing and illumination to be completed by Fairfax Murray, to whom he sold
the manuscript, Graily Hewitt and Louise Powell) it represents a magnificent sustained effort, and is, as he planned it to be, his calligraphic masterpiece.

UT BELLI SIGNUM LAUREN
TI TURNUS AB ARCE EXTU
LIT, ET RAUCO STREPUE
RUNT CORNUA CANTU;
UTQUE ACRES CONCUSSIT
EQUOS, UTQUE IMPULIT
ARMA: EXTEMPLO TUR
BATI ANIMI, SIMUL OM
NE TUMULTU CONIU
RAT TREPIDO LATIUM,
SAEVITQUE IUVENTUS

THE KELMSCOTT PRESS

John Dreyfus

All through his adult life, Morris persistently wrote, designed, collected and produced numerous books and manuscripts. Why then did he reach his mid-fifties before deciding to become a printer and publisher with his own private press?

Fig. 102 Burne-Jones's caricature of Morris cutting a woodblock.

In part it was because a host of other commitments left him too little time; but there was also a technical obstacle. To design his own type would have involved a great deal of intricate work on a very small scale which Morris found uncongenial. Then it suddenly struck him that he could in fact design his types on a conveniently large scale. The idea came to him in November 1888 when his Hammersmith friend and neighbour, Emery Walker, projected greatly enlarged photographic images of fifteenth-century types during a lecture on printing given to the Arts and Crafts Exhibition Society in London. Walker had wide experience of the printing trade and ran his own photo-engraving business. Some of Walker's slides had been made in his studio from books lent by Morris, who suddenly realised that if Walker were to supply enlarged photographic prints of the types projected during the lecture, he could study them in detail. Next he could draw his own types on the same enlarged scale, relying on Walker to reduce them to the size in which they would be needed.

More than once before the lecture, Morris had remarked casually to Walker that he would like 'to have a shot at type-designing'. As he left the lecture he said to Walker, 'Let's make a new fount of type'. At Walker's suggestion, all the punches for the Kelmscott Press types were made by Edward Prince, an extremely competent punchcutter who had previously done some work for Walker.

By 1888 Morris was well qualified to become a great producer of books. Much skill and invention had gone into the books written by hand in a variety of beautiful scripts which John Nash describes on pages 296–309. The experience of making these calligraphical masterpieces taught Morris a great deal about the shapes of letters as well as the decoration and illustration of text pages. Moreover, he had learnt the secrets of how to use space and how to control margins to enhance the effect of what was placed upon the pages of a book. His extensive library of books and manuscripts was another source from which he built up his typographic skill. He loved to spend hours examining and discussing works in his library with his close friends Emery Walker and Sydney Cockerell (who became Secretary of the Kelmscott Press). Morris had a particularly high regard for the books illustrated with woodcuts printed during the 1460s in Augsburg.

He had also acquired a practical knowledge of contemporary printing from his early twenties. Editing the first number of the *Oxford and Cambridge Magazine* in 1856 had brought him into contact with one of the best book printers of that time, Charles Whittingham of the Chiswick Press. Several of Morris's own books were later printed at the Chiswick Press, which had played a leading role in bringing back into favour Caslon's eighteenth-century types. It also owned some unique types and ornaments made for its own exclusive use. Nearer to the time when Morris decided to start his own press, he gained some managerial experience of printing when he became editor and publisher of *Commonweal*. This was the official journal of the Socialist League. Its foreman printer was Thomas

Binning, of whom Morris wrote to a fellow-socialist, 'He is to be my man you understand, and I am to be the capitalist printer'. A few years later, Binning became father of the chapel (and the workers' representative) at the Kelmscott Press.

The formation of the Arts and Crafts Exhibition Society in 1887 brought Morris into more frequent contact with bookish founder-members such as Emery Walker, Walter Crane and the book-binder T. J. Cobden-Sanderson who later worked in close association with the Kelmscott Press. The newly formed Society's first exhibition catalogue was printed at the Chiswick Press, whose books were well represented in the 1888 display. In the same year work started at the Chiswick Press on Morris's book *The House of the Wolfings*, his first long prose romance. While writing it, his daughter May recalled, 'his taste of younger days for early printed books had been developing into a practical interest in all the details of fine printing'. Proof of this can be found in *The Roots of the Mountains*, his next book printed at the Chiswick Press. Morris admitted he was 'so pleased with my book – typography, binding and must I say its literary matter – that I am any day to be seen huggling it up, and am become a spectacle to God and man because of it'. Even deeper pleasure was soon to follow from printing his own works in his own types and on his own presses.

By the late 1880s he had shed or reduced many of his commercial and political commitments. Aware that his health might deteriorate further, he relished the prospect of setting up his press within two minutes walk of Kelmscott House. There he could count on frequent visits and help from Walker, who lived and worked nearby. With such competent help, Morris was able to write and translate more than a third of the works printed at the Kelmscott Press. He also designed every Kelmscott edition published in his lifetime, and drew 644 initials, borders, ornaments, frames for illustrations, title-pages, large initial words and printer's marks.

Morris set out to print books hoping that some would, as he put it, 'have a definite claim to beauty'. Admitting that it was only natural for him to try to ornament his books suitably because he was a decorator by profession, he nevertheless tried to keep in mind the need for decoration to be made part of the page of type. He believed a book without ornament could look positively beautiful, not merely un-ugly, provided that it was architecturally good. By this he meant that pages needed to be clear and easy to read. This they could not be unless the type was well-designed, and therefore easy to read; never should it be troublesome to the mind because of any eccentricity in the letter forms. To present-day readers both the types Morris designed for his press may look rather eccentric, if only a few lines are seen in reproduction. Their effect is quite different when used in Kelmscott books, accompanied by woodcut ornament and illustration, and printed on fine hand-made paper or vellum with dense black ink, occasionally relieved by brightly coloured inks.

Morris sought to recreate the rich Gothic texture he admired in books printed in the third quarter of the fifteenth century. He began by designing a roman type named Golden because he meant it to be seen for the first time in the Kelmscott edition of *The Golden Legend*. Such difficulties arose in producing this lengthy text in three volumes that publication was delayed until 1892. So the Golden type's début was in his own work *The Story of the Glittering Plain*, when the first Kelmscott edition appeared on 8 May 1891. Designing this type proved to be the most troublesome task Morris ever undertook. Although we speak of designing a type in the singular, it actually involves making a set of drawings for upwards of eighty characters, merely to produce a fount which includes capitals, lower-case, numerals, punctuation marks, and tied letters such as Æ and ff. Trial proofs always show up a few awkward letter combinations which can be overcome only by altering the original designs. Morris brooded for hours over his punchcutter's proofs, which he carried around in matchboxes stuffed into his pockets.

It suited Morris to base his design for a roman type on enlarged photos of types used at Venice in 1476 by Nicolaus Jenson and Jacobus Rubeus; but he decided to make his own type much stronger in colour. In this way its weight would match the woodcut lines of the decorations and illustrations that he intended to make such a feature of Kelmscott books; moreover, these woodcuts could be placed alongside the type on the bed of the hand press used for printing his books. His type turned out to be a hybrid. Walter Crane reacted in a way that delighted Morris: 'Crane when he saw it beside Jenson thought it more Gothic-looking; this is a fact and a cheerful one to me.'

Morris was even happier with his second type, a Gothic letter named Troy because it was intended for setting his edition of the *Recuyell of the Historyes of Troye* (1892). In designing Troy he

Within the illustration:

THE DOVES
FULLERS SMITHS & TURNERS

26 24 UPPER MALL 16 14 12 15

RIVER THAMES

Hammersmith Bridge ➤

12 SUSSEX HOUSE · Emery Walker's Works Est.1886
14 SUSSEX COTTAGE · Kelmscott Press 1891-1898
15 Doves Bindery Est.1893
16 Kelmscott Press Jan-May 1891
24 RIVER HOUSE · Cobden-Sanderson 1903-1909
26 KELMSCOTT HOUSE · William Morris 1878-1896

Fig.103 Bird's-eye view of the Upper Mall, from a drawing by Leo Wyatt.

set himself the task of redeeming Gothic type from the charge of unreadableness commonly brought against it. He felt that charge could not be reasonably brought against the types used by Peter Schoeffer at Mainz for his Bible of 1462, nor against Gunther Zainer for his editions of *The Golden Legend* printed at Ausgburg between 1471 and 1475. Morris believed his Troy type to be 'as readable as a roman one, and to say the truth I prefer it to the roman'. He called his design a semi-Gothic, designed with a special regard to legibility. Two sizes of Troy were used in *The Recuyell*, an 18-point for the text and a 12-point for the table of contents and glossary. Later the smaller size was used in double column for the great folio Chaucer, and became known as the Chaucer type.

From his pre-Kelmscott experience of printing, Morris knew that type looked at its best only if it was most carefully spaced. Too much space between letters and between words tends to make a page harder to read. Morris disliked wide gaps between lines, although he sometimes added a little extra space between lines set in his own types. His experience of writing formal manuscripts had strengthened his conviction that words needed to be set close together to prevent vertical shafts of white from disrupting the solid texture he wanted to maintain in a page of type. He insisted that the unit to be considered in book design was the pair of facing pages which form an 'opening'. He followed the practice established in medieval times of having all four margins around the type area differ successively by twenty per cent; the inner margin narrowest, the top twenty per cent wider, the outer edge twenty per cent wider again, with the bottom margin widest of all by a further twenty per cent. (In his Kelmscott books, he did not precisely follow this advice.)

Morris had very clear ideas about the paper he wanted for his Kelmscott books. Realising that 'it would be a very false economy to stint in the quality of paper as to price', he opted for a paper with the same characteristics that he admired in books printed during the 1470s in Venice and Bologna. He owned a book printed in Venice by J. de Colonia and J. Manthen in 1475, with a text by Alexander de Ales, Super III *Sententiarum*. Inside this copy a note by Cockerell records that Morris took it to discuss with Joseph Batchelor, a hand papermaker at Little Chart in Kent. This mill had been recommended by Walker, who went down with Morris to place the order in October 1890. They obtained an excellent making of pure linen paper, well sized, very tough, and ideally suited for printing on a hand press. Like the early Italian paper which Morris admired, the paper made by Batchelor had narrowly spaced wire-lines, without unduly prominent chain-lines. Morris drew three watermarks – flower, perch and apple – for the different sizes in which his paper was supplied.

As he disapproved of large paper editions because of their badly proportioned margins, he decided to print copies on vellum for his richer customers, just as Gutenberg had done with the first printed book in 1456. Morris persuaded a dealer in vellum and parchment, Henry Band of Brentford in Middlesex, to experiment with skins chosen from calves less than six weeks old. Eventually Kelmscott vellum was made specially thin and its fine surface was untainted by white

Fig. 104 William and May Morris and the staff of the Kelmscott Press (cat. no. O.5). FRONT ROW, FROM THE LEFT: Stephen Mowlem (pressman), William H. Bowden (pressman), William Morris and his daughter May, W. Collins (pressman), W. L. Tasker (printer). BACK ROW FROM THE LEFT: H. Howes (printer), Carpenter (printer), F. Collins (printer), Emery Walker (friend and adviser), R. Eatley (printer), Henry Halliday Sparling (Secretary until July 1894), J. Tippet (printer), Thomas Binning (printer and father of the chapel), G. Heath (printer). (The word printer has been used where an individual is known to have worked at the Press, but where it is uncertain whether he worked as a compositor or pressman, or proof reader.)

lead. When larger quantities were needed than Band could deliver, vellum was also supplied by William J. Turney of Stourbridge in Worcestershire.

Morris realised that the full effect of his own types upon his specially made paper and vellum would depend to a great extent upon the quality of his ink. After many trials, samples were sent to him by inkmakers in England and America. Neither was perfect because of red or blue undertones; but neither maker was willing to meet Morris's criticisms. So once again Walker was consulted. He recommended an excellent ink made in Hanover by the firm of Jaenecke. Its colour was good, without any distracting undertone. It never clogged the type nor spoiled the impression. But it had one drawback. It was tremendously stiff, which made very hard work for the pressmen. It provoked something close to a strike when it was introduced at the Kelmscott Press, until Morris threatened to close it unless the German ink was used. As the pressmen received very good pay, they gave way. But as Walker added, 'they took it out of Morris another way and the number of sheets turned out per day was extraordinarily small'.

When the Press reached full production, about ten or twelve compositors and pressmen were employed. Printing began in January 1891 at its premises on Upper Mall, a few doors away from Kelmscott House. As output increased, rooms were taken in the adjacent building known as Sussex

House, where some of Walker's staff worked. In 1893, soon after T.J.Cobden-Sanderson set up his Doves Bindery opposite Sussex House, Morris was able to rent upstairs rooms for his proofreaders who stayed there until the summer of 1894. Additional premises were taken on 1 January 1895 to house a third Albion press, which had been specially reinforced to take the great pressure needed to do full justice to the woodcuts in the folio Chaucer, on which work had fallen seriously behind schedule. The new premises were next to the Doves Inn, even closer to Kelmscott House.

Walker declined to become a partner in the Press, but he constantly gave advice to Morris on typographical questions. For help in various matters, Morris turned to his son-in-law, Henry Halliday Sparling, and gave him the title Secretary of the Kelmscott Press (fig.104). Sparling was detested by his mother-in-law, and not much liked by Sydney Cockerell who later took over his post and referred to Sparling as 'a rather second-rate Socialist'. Morris and Sparling had been co-editors on *Commonweal*. Sparling edited three long Kelmscott editions published in 1892–3, but then resigned his position in July 1894 after his marriage to May Morris had collapsed.

Cockerell became a far more effective Secretary, and a much closer friend of Morris. He was a deft administrator whose sound judgement and devotion to detail brought great benefits to the Press. He also helped to improve the accuracy of its texts. Further help with proofreading and editing came from F.S.Ellis, a retired bookseller who had previously been Morris's publisher (*The Earthly Paradise*, 1868–70, had appeared over his imprint). Cockerell and Ellis gave invaluable help and attention to Morris in his final years; as trustees they ran the Press for about eighteen months after his death and completed several of his unfinished projects.

Apart from receiving administrative help in running the Press, Morris relied on other artists to design illustrations for Kelmscott books. The major contribution came from his old friend Edward Burne-Jones, who had sketched at least forty-four illustrations for *The Earthly Paradise* in the 1860s before the scheme was abandoned. The two friends collaborated again with dazzling success in the Kelmscott Chaucer, completed shortly before Morris died. His decorative designs for that work and Burne-Jones's drawings for illustrations were all photographed on to wood, and then cut by skilled trade engravers. Before Burne-Jones's delicate pencil drawings were cut on wood, every line and

Fig. 106 May Morris, Henry Halliday
Sparling, Emery Walker and George
Bernard Shaw.

dot was strengthened or adjusted by Robert Catterson-Smith. He developed a set of consistent linear abbreviations to provide marks which the trade engravers could follow and which were approved by Burne-Jones.

Other illustrators of Kelmscott books included Walter Crane and two artists from the Birmingham School, C.M. Gere and A.J. Gaskin. Of these three artists, Gaskin's work has attracted particular praise, partly because it brought 'a strictness of form and composition none of the others provided', as Colin Franklin remarked. However, the mass of decorations, ornaments, borders and lettering supplied by Morris have such strength and consistency that most readers are more impressed by his contribution to Kelmscott books than they are by the illustrations supplied by other artists. An exception must be made of the Kelmscott Chaucer for reasons given on pp.330–37.

Because that massive folio has been displayed and reproduced so often, it is often forgotten that Morris used seven different formats at his Press. His three translations from the French appeared in an elegant little 16mo format (14.3 x 10.4 cm) which was also used in 1893 with great success for his essay on *Gothic Architecture*. Various other formats were appropriately used to print his other texts.

His previous experience of manufacture and marketing led Morris to take a keen interest in the way his Kelmscott books were financed and sold. Profit earned him the freedom to work as he wished, both as an author and as a designer. Of the 66 titles published, 23 were by Morris, 22 were medieval works and 13 by contemporary poets; 21,401 copies were printed on paper and 677 on vellum. The total gross value of sales was £50,299. Throughout 1891–2 these books were sold either by Reeves & Turner who ran a bookshop on the Strand with a small publishing department, or by George Allan at Temple Bar, or by the antiquarian bookseller and publisher Bernard Quaritch. From May 1893 Morris published thirty-four of the forty works issued. These became so well known to collectors and librarians that most editions were subscribed in advance. By becoming his own publisher, Morris increased his profits. From October 1895 announcements of new Kelmscott books were only sent out if the edition was not almost sold out by the time that sheets were sent to the binder.

Two standard Kelmscott bindings were devised by Morris and both were carried out in London by the firm of J. & J. Leighton. Distrusting the quality of goat and calf skins available through leather suppliers, Morris decided to use limp vellum with coloured silk ties dyed by his own firm. His alternative was a quarter linen binding with a printed label on the spine, and with sides of blue-grey laid paper. The latter style was regarded by Morris as a satisfactory temporary binding; but most surviving Kelmscott books have never been rebound. Occasionally the Doves Bindery produced leather bindings for individual Kelmscott customers. While Douglas Cockerell (Sydney's younger brother) was working at the Doves Bindery, he carried out forty-eight special bindings in blind-stamped pigskin with silver clasps for the Kelmscott Chaucer, to a design devised by Morris.

Other private presses soon copied the two standard styles devised by Morris for his Kelmscott books. So powerful and inventive were his designs for every aspect of bookwork that it was hard to escape his influence. The outcome was sometimes sadly inept; a style so well suited to Morris's medieval taste was inappropriate for texts of an entirely different character. Far happier results came about when other designers paid attention to the principles which led to the development of his style. These principles were clearly set out in Morris's essays and lectures on the 'Ideal Book', under which title they were published in 1983 by the University of California Press, most capably edited and introduced by William S. Peterson.

Morris had a healthy influence on those who never mimicked his mannerisms but applied his principles to books produced by twentieth-century production methods. Brilliant artificers of the book such as Bruce Rogers in the United States and Francis Meynell in Britain placed as much importance as Morris on fine papers, carefully designed and spaced type with suitable ornament, and high standards of presswork. Unlike Morris they accepted modern methods for making paper by machine, as well as mechanical typesetting and power-driven presses. Rogers and Meynell found fresh ways of applying decoration to the printed page, and used new types (or good revivals of old types made for mechanical typesetting machines) which resulted in books that differed greatly in style from those printed at the Kelmscott Press. Nevertheless, Morris's insistence on matters such as tight spacing of words, decent margins, and the need to integrate illustrations with text, all had their effect on later typo- graphers who had looked closely at the way Morris's books reflected his clearly stated ideals. Kelmscott books were real eye-openers – and they opened minds.

Fig. 107 Original design by Morris for the binding for the Kelmscott *Chaucer*.

O.1 Illustration for *The Procession to the Hill: Psyche and the King*, from 'The Story of Cupid and Psyche' for *The Earthly Paradise*

a Drawing for the above
Edward Burne-Jones, 1866
Pencil, 16.7 x 23.4 cm
V&A (E.30-1955)

b Wood block for the above
Possibly cut by William Morris, 1866
10.3 x 15.7 x 2.4 cm
Society of Antiquaries of London

c Proof from the above
1866
15.0 x 19.7 cm
V&A (E.1814-1920)

O.2 Illustration for *Psyche and Ceres*, from
'The Story of Cupid and Psyche' for *The Earthly Paradise*

a Wood block for the above
Possibly cut by William Morris, 1866
10.5 x 8.1 x 2.4 cm
Society of Antiquaries of London
NOT ILLUSTRATED

b Proof from the above
Edward Burne-Jones, 1866
15.5 x 13.2 cm
V&A (E.1836-1920)
NOT ILLUSTRATED

'Cupid and Psyche' was written by Morris as one of the twenty-four tales in his longest work, *The Earthly Paradise*. This huge undertaking has been seen as his homage to Chaucer's *Canterbury Tales* and to the English tradition of ceremonial tale-telling. The work contained two narrative poems for each month of the year, and was set as a series of tales exchanged by Norse exiles and their Greek hosts. So successful was Morris's handling of the idea that it made him the most popular poet of his period for more than a decade, and eventually put him in line for consideration as Poet Laureate to succeed Tennyson.

Morris intended to publish the work at his own expense as a large folio with five hundred woodcut illustrations based on drawings by Burne-Jones. Work on these illustrations began in earnest during the summer of 1866. Burne-Jones sketched more than a hundred designs, including seventy illustrations for 'Cupid and Psyche'. Partly because Morris was dissatisfied with the quality of work produced by trade wood engravers, and partly to save money, he decided to share with his friends the task of rendering Burne-Jones's pencil drawings on wood.

Considerable sensitivity was needed to transpose on to wood the rather tenuous lines drawn in pencil by Burne-Jones. The artist's drawings were traced and transferred on to wood by George Wardle, a draughtsman who later became manager of Morris & Co. Wardle also cut two of the designs on wood; but he was surprised at not being asked to cut any more. He explained: 'The reason was a characteristic one, Mr Morris became obsessed by the idea of cutting the blocks himself. If I could do it, why not he? and he took them all in hand and carried them through, though not without some lively scenes in Queen Square. He cut with great ardour and with much knowledge of the forms certainly, but the work did not always go to his mind. It was necessarily slow and he was constitutionally quick: there were then quarrels between them.'

Burne-Jones's caricature (see fig. 102) reflects what Wardle observed and remarked. In his impatience Morris has sent nearly as many graving tools flying to the floor as remain on his work table. His daughter May recalled how her father 'would work with bright cutting tools on a little block of wood, which sat on a plump leather cushion', as can be plainly seen in this caricature. Despite his temperamental difficulties with such a slow process and such an exacting medium, Morris mastered the craft

O.1a

O.1b

O.1c

O.4b

and produced blocks of such artistic excellence that they won praise from his fastidious fellow-artist and collector, Charles Fairfax Murray.

Of the fifty blocks cut by Morris, forty-four were bequeathed by May Morris to the Society of Antiquaries. In addition to some pencil drawings by Burne-Jones for this project in the Victoria and Albert Museum, there are important collections of his drawings for 'Cupid and Psyche' in the Birmingham City Museums and Art Gallery, in the Ashmolean at Oxford, and in the Pierpont Morgan Library, New York.

Work on the illustrations for *The Earthly Paradise* went on until about 1867. Why the work was then abandoned is not entirely clear; but it may have been because Morris was unable to devise a satisfactory typographical setting to match the quality of the wood-engraved illustrations. Long after his death, the problem was overcome in 1974 when the original wood blocks for 'Cupid and Psyche' were printed with Morris's text composed in his own Troy type. First used for a Kelmscott book in 1892, the type was made available for the 1974 edition by Cambridge University Press which had custody of the Kelmscott Press types (see cat.no.O.12).

O.3 *A Tale of The House of the Wolfings* by William Morris

London, Reeves and Turner, 1889
20.0 x 14.0 cm approx. leaf
William Morris Society, Kelmscott House, London
NOT ILLUSTRATED

The first of two books written by Morris, both of them printed to his order at the Chiswick Press while he prepared to launch his own Press with his own types.

The same type was chosen by Morris for both books. It had been completed by 1852 for use exclusively at the Chiswick Press. The name 'Basle' was given to the type because its design had been influenced by types used by Johann Froben, a printer in that city from 1491. Morris had experimented with the Basle type in specimen pages for 'The Story of Cupid and Psyche' – a project he later abandoned (see cat.nos.O.1–2)

At first Morris was pleased with this book, calling it 'a pretty piece of typography for modern times'. Later he admitted that the printers had somehow 'managed to knock the guts' out of the type. He began to see 'what a lot of difference there is between the work of the conceited numskulls of today and that of the 15th and 16th century printers merely in the arrangement of the words, I mean the spacing out: it makes all the difference in the beauty of a page of print'.

O.4 a *The Roots of the Mountains* by William Morris

London, Reeves and Turner, 1890
19.5 x 16.0 cm approx. leaf
William Morris Society, Kelmscott House, London
NOT ILLUSTRATED

b *The Roots of the Mountains* by William Morris
London, Reeves and Turner, 1890
19.5 x 16.0 cm leaf
John Dreyfus

According to Sir Sydney Cockerell, Morris considered this to be the best-looking book issued since the seventeenth century. It was exhibited in the Arts and Crafts Exhibition of 1890.

Though similar in design to *The House of the Wolfings* issued in the previous year, Morris improved several features. Margins are better proportioned. Spacing between words is generally tighter. Instead of page headings, shoulder notes are set at the top of both outer margins. (Walker had remarked while lecturing in 1890 that many early books had no headlines, which he believed often destroyed the effect of unity in a page.) Morris worked out a better way to compose and display his chapter titles. The Basle type was also improved by replacing the 'e' with a new cutting in which the distracting oblique cross-bar was made horizontal. A superior edition of 250 copies was printed on slightly larger Whatman paper; these were bound in Merton Abbey block-printed linens, designed by Morris – either *Honeysuckle*, as here, or *Little Chintz*.

O.6

O.7

O.5 William and May Morris with staff and friends of the Kelmscott Press, c.1893.

Albumen print, 15.2 x 20.9 cm image
V&A (Ph.1819-1939) Given by Dr Robert Steele
FOR ILLUSTRATION, SEE FIG 104, PAGE 113

Other prints of photographs taken on the same occasion are in the British Library, the National Portrait Gallery and the Berger Collection.

O.6 Bound volume of photographic enlargements of fifteenth-century printing types

Made by Emery Walker, given by William Morris to his typefounder, Talbot Baines Reed, 1891
38.2 x 66.0 cm open
St Bride Printing Library

Morris was greatly excited in 1888 by seeing photographic enlargements of early printing types projected during Emery Walker's lecture on printing to the Arts and Crafts Exhibition Society. He realised that large-scale prints of Walker's slides would simplify his own detailed study of types he greatly admired, and would also allow him to draw his types on the same conveniently large scale, reduced afterwards to the sizes in which his types would be cast.

Walker made enlarged prints in the studio at his photo-engraving business. A duplicate set was made up into an album owned by Talbot Baines Reed, head of the family typefoundry where the Kelmscott types were cast. Reed noted that the album contained 'enlarged photos of early Roman and Gothic type collected and presented to me by William Morris, 1891', and that the prints included 'the models of the founts designed for use in the Kelmscott books'.

The album is opened at a page showing an edition of Pliny's *Historia naturalis* printed by Nicolaus Jenson at Venice in 1476, enlarged to five times the original size.

O.7 *Spiegel des menschlichen lebens*
[Speculum vitae humanae] by Rodericus Zamorensis

Published by Gunther Zainer of Augsburg, c.1475
Binding: sixteenth-century pigskin, blind stamped; spine blind stamped, spine hand-lettered, raised bands; leather ties; boxed; 31.0 x 22.2 x 4.5 cm
Fitzwilliam Museum, Cambridge (Sayle 274 6H4)

Morris bought a copy of this book on 1 August 1890 (it is now in the Pierpont Morgan Library, New York). He had a particularly high regard for the artistic qualities of woodcut books printed at Ulm and Augsburg in the fifteenth century. His essay on this subject published in 1895 asserted that the most distinguished of these woodcut books were those published by Gunther Zainer of Augsburg and by his kinsman Johann Zainer of Ulm.

An insertion in Morris's copy of this work describes his feelings for it: '…I should call this the best of the Augsburg picture books…These cuts together with the beautiful "Blooming-letters", and Gunter Zainer's bold and handsome second Gothic type make up as good ornamented pages as are to be found in all typography'.

The decorated initials and woodcut illustrations in this book clearly influenced the style of woodcuts that Morris commissioned for his Press, as well as the decorated initials he designed in tribute to Zainer's sturdy blooming-letters.

O.8 Early designs for Troy type

William Morris, 1891
Pencil and ink, 35.4 x 39.4 cm
Sanford and Helen Berger Collection

An insight into Morris's methods of type design can be gained from this sheet of early designs for his Troy type. At the left he has traced letters from a photographic enlargement supplied by Walker. Fragments of words in ten successive lines are inked-in tracings from an edition of St Augustine, *De civitate Dei*, printed at Subiaco near Rome by Sweynheym and Pannartz in 1467. Morris later abandoned the idea of basing his own type on this interesting pattern.

To the right of the Subiaco letters are four different versions of a lower-case alphabet (one incomplete), and a sketch for a set of capitals. None of these was based on a single specific model. The final design of Troy type differed greatly from many of the letters on this sheet, but there are nevertheless many similarities in the weight and proportions shown here.

See also cat.no.O.9, which shows how the final inked-in alphabet of lower-case was used for an experimental model of the Troy type.

O.9 Experimental model of Troy type for the Kelmscott Press, 1891

37.8 x 29.7 cm
Inscribed by Emery Walker: '⅕ Scale i.e redone 10in to 2in greatest care', 'model of "Troy"' type designed by William Morris for the Kelmscott Press' Cheltenham Art Gallery and Museums.
Bought with the assistance of generous grants from the Trustees of the National Heritage Memorial Fund, the MGC/V&A Purchase Grant Fund, The British Library (from the Wolfson Foundation and the Wolfson Family Charitable Trust), The Pilgrim Trust, The J. Paul Getty Jr. Charitable Trust and the National Art Collections Fund

This paste-up was made so that Morris could judge how one of his designs for an alphabet of type would look when its individual letters were combined to form words. By resorting to a paste-up, Morris was able to form a judgement without going to the expense, or through the delay, of cutting trial punches and casting an experimental fount.

The paste-up was made probably by draughtsmen employed by Emery Walker; his note at the foot of this sheet describes it as a 'model of "Troy" type designed by William Morris for the Kelmscott Press'. Another line in Walker's handwriting instructs that the paste-up is to be reduced with the greatest care to one fifth of its original size; the reduced print was then used to make a line-engraving, from which two or more proofs were printed, thus creating a realistic impression of how type might look if made from the experimental model. The complete alphabet of letters used in this paste-up is seen in the last full line of cat.no.O.8, on which other trial alphabets for Troy are also shown.

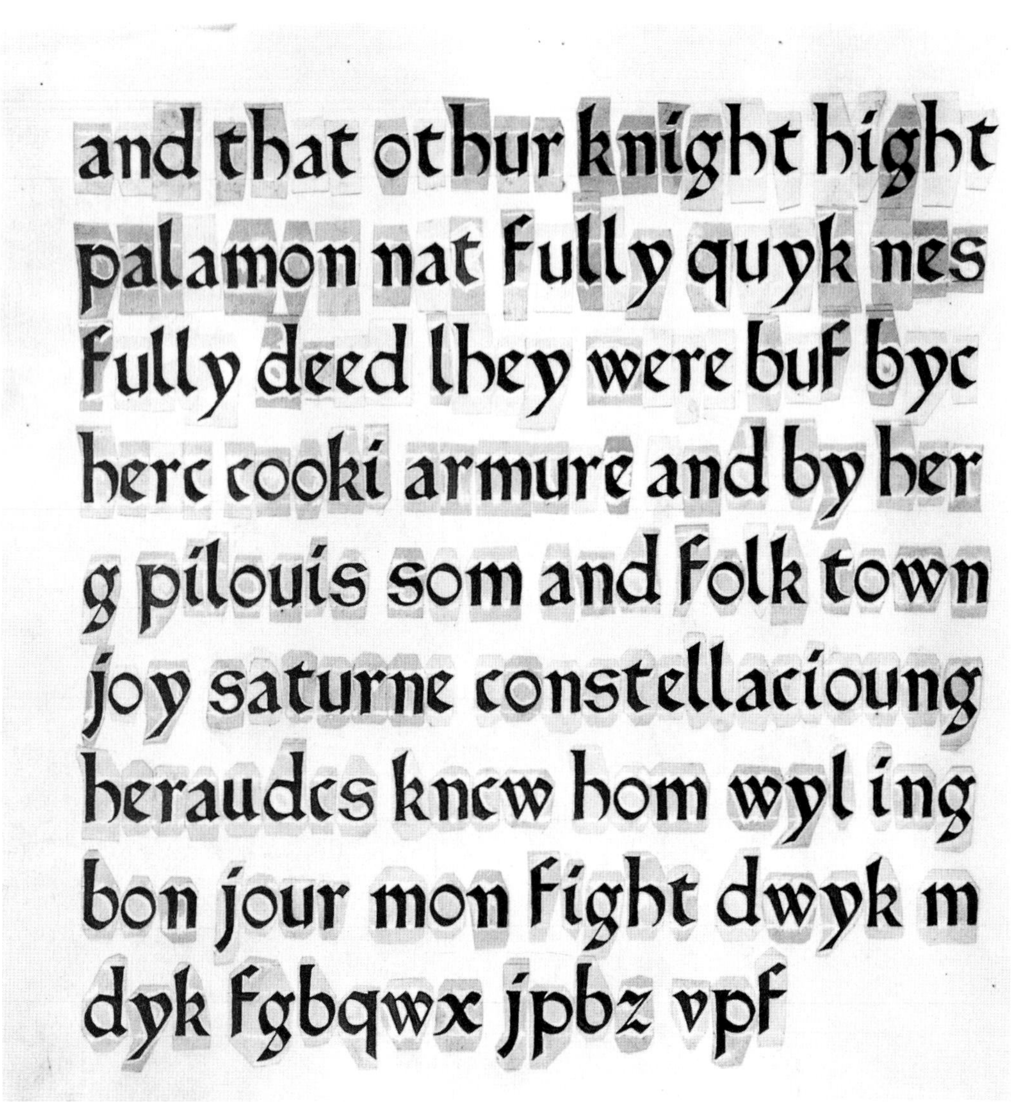

O.8

O.9

O.10 Final designs for lower-case Troy type

William Morris, 1891
Pencil and ink, 26.6 x 42.0 cm
Sanford and Helen Berger Collection

The letters inked-in on this sheet by Morris are very close to the shapes cut by Edward Prince for the Troy type. In a few cases Morris pencilled sketches next to an inked-in letter to indicate how it might look when adjacent to a letter of different structure.

Troy lower-case has a character of its own, even though several letters show similarities to letters found in books printed by Gunther Zainer (notably g and s), or in Peter Schoeffer's books where similar shapes are found of a, d, e, f, m, n, o, p, r and t.

Illness prevented Morris from handing over his designs until late in the summer of 1891. Punchcutting was completed by the end of the year and a full fount cast early in 1892. On balance, the small alterations introduced by Prince during punchcutting made Morris's designs work better as cast type; and Morris paid tribute to Prince's 'intelligence and skill'.

O.11 Specimen of Troy type

Designed by William Morris, 1891
Ink, 29.0 x 20.4 cm
Sanford and Helen Berger Collection

The text of this specimen is taken from 'The Franklin's Tale' by Chaucer. It is one of several specimens set in Troy type late in 1891, all using passages from the same tale by Chaucer. This indicates that as soon as he could, Morris began to test Troy's suitability for his ambitious plan to print Chaucer's works. For such a lengthy text it proved impractical to use a type as large as Troy. So a smaller 12-point size of the same design was cut between February and May 1892, and was named Chaucer. Production of the Chaucer type was preceded by trial photographic reductions; these were sensitively interpreted by Edward Prince when he cut the smaller version.

The capital I in this specimen looks as if it had crept in from a roman fount. Morris replaced it by a more Gothic form with swirling, asymmetrical serifs (final strokes at the top and bottom of the letter), taking further an idea that he had sketched in pencil (see cat. no. O.8).

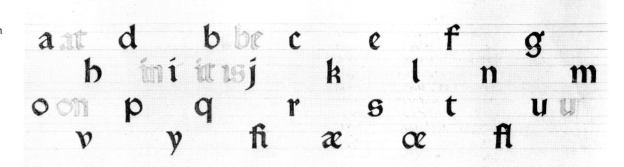

O.10

Wher he schal have his love or fare amys,
Awayteth night and day on this miracle;
And whan he knew that ther was noon obstacle,
That voyded were these rokkes everichoon,
Doun to his maistres feet he fel anoon,
And sayd; 'I wrecched woful Aurilius,
Thanke you, lord, and my lady Venus,
That me han holpe fro my cares colde.'
And to the temple his way forth he hath holde,
Wher as he knew he schold his lady se.
And whan he saugh his tyme, anoon right he
With dredful hert and with ful humble cheere
Salued hath his owne lady deere.
'My soverayn lady,' quod this woful man,
'Whom I most drede, and love, as I best can,
And lothest were of al this world displese,
Nere it that I for you have such desese,
That I most deye her at youre foot anoon,
Nought wold I telle how me is wo bygoon,
But certes outher most I dye or pleyne;
Ye sleen me gulteles for verrey peyne.
But of my deth though that ye have no routhe;
Avyseth yow, or that ye breke your trouthe;
Repenteth yow for thilke God above,
Or ye me sleen, bycause that I you love.
For, Madame, wel ye woot what ye han kigkt;

O.11

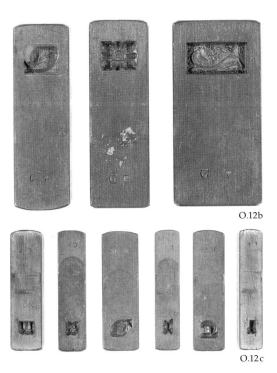

O.12b

O.12c

O.12a

O.12 Punches, matrices and type for the Kelmscott Press

Various sizes
Cambridge University Library

Morris's drawings for his types were reduced photographically to the sizes in which his types were needed. These reduced prints were then used by a highly skilled punchcutter, Edward Prince, as a model for the letters he cut on steel punches. Before steel is hardened (by exposure to great heat followed at once by immersion in cold water), it is relatively easy to file and cut; but the punchcutter's task requires exceptional co-ordination of eye and hand, and a deep understanding of the factors that make a set of types combine into evenly-spaced and perfectly aligned words.

Punches (O.12a) are needed for each letter and sign in order to strike a reverse impression into a matrix made of softer metal. Matrices (O.12b–c) are then attached to a casting machine. This produces founts of type in a mixture of lead, antimony and other ingredients, strong enough to withstand the pressure of a hand press.

After Prince cut the Kelmscott Press types, he was engaged to cut punches for other prominent private presses in England, Germany, the Netherlands and the USA – notably for the Doves, Vale, Ashendene, Essex House, Cranach, Zilverdistel and Merrymount presses.

O.13 The Story of the Glittering Plain by William Morris

Kelmscott Press, issued 8 May 1891
Paper, 19.9 x 14.0 cm leaf
V&A (NAL L.1620-1893)

In the autumn of 1890 Morris planned to issue this story with illustrations by Walter Crane. After serious problems delayed publication of *The Golden*

Legend (cat.no. O.15), which Morris had intended to be the first Kelmscott book and the first use of his Golden type, he decided to publish his story without waiting for Crane's illustrations; these were published later (cat.no.O.23).

Morris created an inviting and restful page with his Golden type. Ornamentation in this book was restricted to one border and some six- and ten-line initials designed by Morris. Six copies were printed on vellum which he had imported about twenty years earlier for his calligraphic experiments.

Purchased by the Museum for £6 10s. from J.& J.Leighton.

O.14 The Love Lyrics and Songs of Proteus by Wilfrid Scawen Blunt

Kelmscott Press, issued 27 February 1892
Paper, 20.5 x 14.2 cm leaf
V&A (NAL L.888-1893)

The poet Blunt was a friend of William and Jane Morris. It is not known whether Morris was aware that his wife was having an affair with Blunt when he agreed to print these poems at the Kelmscott Press. Normally Jane took little interest in her husband's Press, but she read and criticised both manuscript and proofs, and also conveyed messages between Blunt and Morris. Blunt had visited the Kelmscott Press while its second publication, Morris's *Poems by the Way*, was being printed in red and black; he remarked, 'most beautiful they are with their rubrics'.

On 18 November 1890, Morris informed Blunt, 'I shall of course be very pleased to print your book, if I may have my own way about the get up – which I take it is what you want'. In fact Blunt persuaded Morris against his better judgement to print the large initials in red. When Morris saw the finished book, he made a rueful comment that it looked very gay and pretty with its red letters, but he still preferred his own style, and never again used red in this way.

Purchased by the Museum for £2 12s. from J.& J.Leighton.

Top book (O.13):

CHAPTER XIII. HALLBLITHE BE-
HOLDETH THE WOMAN WHO
LOVETH HIM.

 UT on the morrow the men arose, and the Sea-eagle & his damsel came to Hallblithe; for the other two damsels were departed, and the Sea-eagle said to him: "Here am I well honoured and measurelessly happy; & I have a message for thee from the King." ¶ "What is it?" said Hallblithe; but he deemed that he knew what it would be, and he reddened for the joy of his assured hope. ¶ Said the Sea-eagle: "Joy to thee, O shipmate! I am to take thee to the place where thy beloved abideth, and there shalt thou see her, but not so as she can see thee; and thereafter shalt thou go to the King, that thou mayst tell him if she shall accomplish thy desire." ¶ Then was Hallblithe glad beyond measure, and his heart danced within him, and he deemed it but meet that the others should be so joyous and blithe with him, for they led him along without any delay, and were glad at his rejoicing; and words failed him to tell of his gladness. ¶ But as he went, the thoughts of his coming converse with his beloved curled sweetly

86

round his heart, so that scarce anything had seemed so sweet to him before; and he fell a-pondering what they twain, he & the Hostage, should do when they came together again; whe-ther they should abide on the Glittering Plain or go back again to Cleveland by the Sea and dwell in the House of the Kindred; and for his part he yearned to behold the roof of his fathers and to tread the meadow which his scythe had swept, and the acres where his hook had smitten the wheat. But he said to himself, "I will wait till I hear her desire hereon." ¶ Now they went into the wood at the back of the King's pavilion and through it and so over the hill, and beyond it came into a land of hills and dales exceeding fair and lovely; and a river wound about the dales, lapping in turn the feet of one hill-side or the other; and in each dale (for they passed through two) was a goodly house of men, and tillage about it, and vineyards and orchards. They went all day till the sun was near setting, and were not weary, for they turn-ed into the houses by the way when they would, and had good welcome, and meat & drink, and what they would of the folk that dwelt there. Thus anigh sunset they came into a dale fairer than either of the others, and nigh to the end where they had entered it was an exceeding goodly house. Then said the damsel: ¶ "We are nigh-hand to our journey's end; let us sit

87

O.13

Bottom book (O.14):

LXV.

TO ONE WHO SPOKE ILL OF HIM.

HAT is your quarrel with me, in Love's name, Fair queen of wrath? What evil have I done, What treason to the thought of our dear shame Subscribed or plotted?
Is my heart less one
In its obedience to your stern decrees
Than on the day when first you said, "I please,"
And with your lips ordained our union?
Am I not now, as then, upon my knees?
You bade me love you, and the deed was done,
And when you cried, "Enough," I stopped, and when
You bade me go I went, and when you said
"Forget me" I forgot. Alas, what wrong
Would you avenge upon a loyal head,
Which ever bowed to you in joy and pain,
That you thus scourge me with your pitiless tongue?

172

LXVI.

TO ONE WHO HAD LEFT HER
CONVENT TO MARRY.

YEAR ago you gave yourself to God. It was a noble gift and nobly given, And we who watched you as you fearless trod, Like one inspired, your pilgrimage to Heaven,
Rejoiced, poor sinners, there was still this leaven
For a bad world, this bud on Aaron's rod,
This virgin still at watch with the wise seven,
And envying you we almost envied God.
A year ago! Another service now
Moves your delight, another noble whim,
Another bride-groom and another vow.
Again we envy you and envy him,
First God's, then Man's! Your love all ranks would level.
Who knows? Next year may add a third, the Devil.

173

O.14

O.15a

O.15c

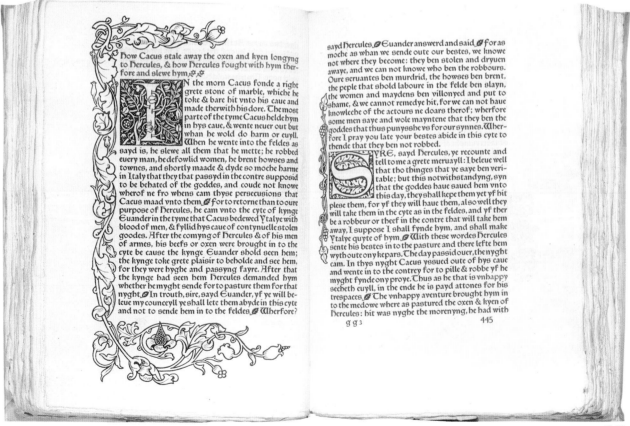

O.16

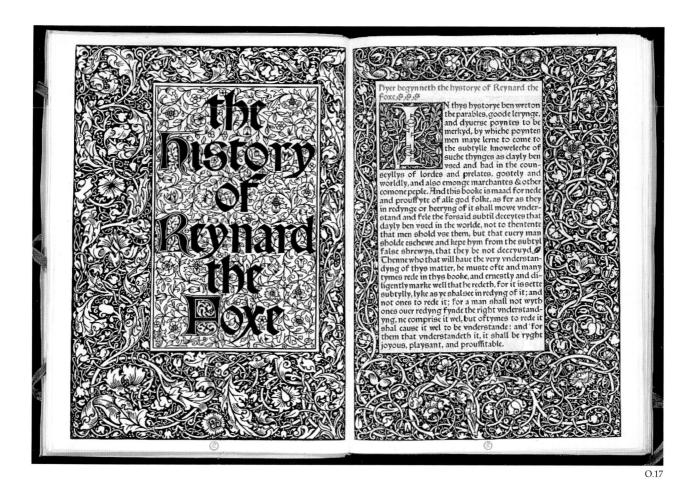

O.17

O.15 *The Golden Legend* by Jacobus de Voragine (translated by William Caxton), Volume I

a Kelmscott Press book, issued 3 November 1892
Paper, 28.7 x 20.5 cm leaf
Private Collection

b Trial proof sheet for *The Golden Legend*, Volume I, p.104, illustration by Edward Burne-Jones
Vellum, 28.1 x 21.2 cm
V&A (NAL L.2634c-1939)
NOT ILLUSTRATED

c Trial proof sheet for *The Golden Legend*, Volume I, p.244, illustration by Edward Burne-Jones
Paper, 31.0 x 24.8 cm
V&A (E.1784-1920)

'The most superbly beautiful book that ever, I should think, came from any press', was the opinion of A.C. Swinburne. It had been intended as the first publication of the Press, and was the reason why Morris named his first type Golden. But the immense task of transcribing the text from Caxton's 1483 edition, preparing it for publication and creating the decorations and illustrations could not be rushed.

Two illustrations by Burne-Jones were his first contributions to the Kelmscott Press. The edition also contained the first woodcut title designed by Morris.

This was the first Kelmscott edition to be sold by Bernard Quaritch. His contract made with Morris and F.S. Ellis (who edited the text) specified: 'Mr Morris to have absolute and sole control over choice of paper,

choice of type, size of the reprint and selection of the printer.' Unfortunately the publication of this work gave rise to several misunderstandings between Morris and Quaritch, which soured their dealings.

O.16 *The Recuyell of the Historyes of Troye* by Raoul Lefevre (translated by William Caxton), Volumes I and II

Kelmscott Press, issued 24 November 1892
Paper, both 28.7 x 20.5 cm leaf
V&A (NAL L.893 and 894-1893)
VOLUME I NOT ILLUSTRATED

Three weeks after *The Golden Legend* (cat.no.O.15) was published, Morris issued the first book set in his second type – Troy, so named because it had been planned from the outset to make its first appearance in this title. As well as using Troy for the text, the smaller size of the same design (named Chaucer) was used in the table of contents and glossary.

The beauty of the edition is entirely the result of Morris's typographical and decorative gifts. There are no illustrations, but Morris makes superb use of corner and marginal decorations, inspired by Johann Zainer's woodcuts of 1473.

Commending the text to Quaritch's customers, Morris wrote that it made a thoroughly amusing story, instinct with medieval thought and manners: 'For though written at the end of the Middle Ages and dealing with classical mythology, it has no token of the coming of

the "Renaissance" but is purely mediaeval…Surely this is well worth reading, if only as a piece of undiluted Mediaevalism.'

These volumes were purchased by the Museum for £9 9s. from J.& J. Leighton.

O.17 *The History of Reynard the Foxe*, translated by William Caxton

Kelmscott Press, issued 25 January 1893
Vellum, 28.7 x 20.5 cm leaf
V&A (NAL L.1134-1893)

This was the third Caxton edition to be reprinted by Morris, who published it in the same format as *The Golden Legend* and *The Historyes of Troye*. His approach to editing Caxton's texts was explained by his son-in-law, H. Halliday Sparling, who is mentioned in the colophon as having corrected this book for press. Caxton's texts were to be taken as a basis, but were not to be looked upon as 'archaeologically sacrosanct'. They were to be collated with Caxton's originals and corrected where needed. Mistranslations were to be put right and omissions filled in, taking care to preserve Caxton's style and flavour.

Ten copies were printed on vellum, twice as many as were produced for *The Historyes of Troye*, although three hundred copies of each were printed on paper.

Purchased by the Museum from J.& J. Leighton for £16 10s.

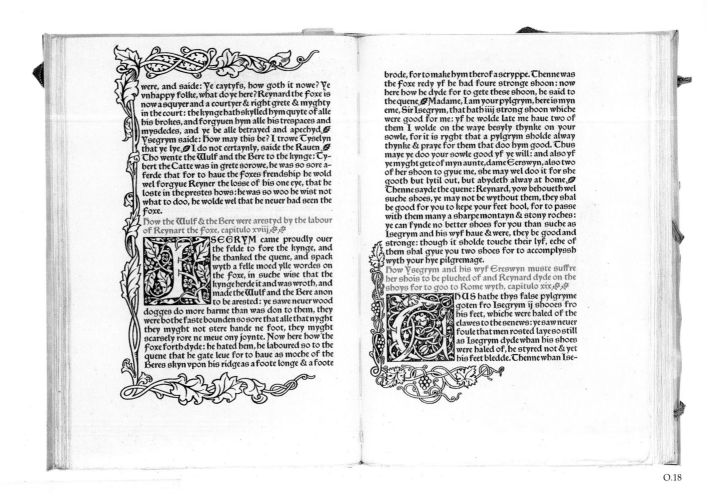

O.18

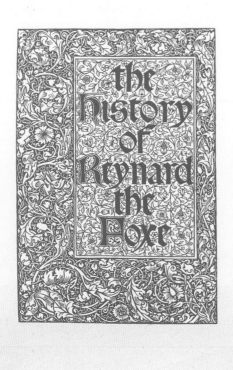

O.18 *The History of Reynard the Foxe,* translated by William Caxton

Kelmscott Press, issued 25 January 1893
Paper, 28.7 x 20.5 cm leaf
V&A (NAL L.896-1893)

Two facing pages of text from a copy printed on paper showing one of the many frames designed by Morris and also two of his decorated initial letters.

Purchased from J.& J.Leighton for £3 15s.

O.19 Proof of title-page for
The History of Reynard the Foxe

Designed by William Morris, 1893
Printed in red ink on paper, 41.25 x 27.3 cm
Sanford and Helen Berger Collection

This is the only Kelmscott Press title-page to have been proofed in colour. It is not clear why this design was proofed in red, but as another proof in red has survived with the inner lettered panel cut away, the purpose may have been to simulate the effect of a red frame surrounding the lettered panel printed in black. Apparently Morris decided that the effect was too strident for his taste. (For his reluctance to print large initials in red, see cat. no. O.14.)

O.19

O.20 *The History of Godefrey of Boloyne*
by Guilelmus, Archbishop of Tyrel

a Kelmscott Press book, issued 24 May 1893
Paper, 28.7 x 20.5 cm leaf
V&A (NAL L.897-1893). Purchased from J.& J. Leighton for £6.6s.

b Three border designs for
The History of Godefrey of Boloyne
William Morris
Ink and Chinese white, mounted together, 22.7 x 24.6 cm
V&A (D.1558 to 1560-1907)
Purchased from S.C.Cockerell

c Three proofs for borders for
The History of Godefrey of Boloyne
19.2 x 19.7 cm
V&A (E.1229-1912)
NOT ILLUSTRATED

Once again Morris chose a Caxton text, arguing that this one 'must from a literary point of view be considered one of Caxton's most important works'. He did not regard it as a romance, as it had been called by others; he viewed it as a very serious piece of history. He found Caxton's style vigorous and agreeable 'and altogether a delightful book to read'. It also inspired him to design a profusion of new ornaments. The decorative scheme was similar to that used in his two previous quartos (cat.nos.O.16–18).

He designed an intricate title-page, numerous borders varying in size from side and corner units to half- and three-quarter borders. In addition he drew six- and eight-line initials, most of them with floral or vine patterns. His second printer's mark made its first appearance in this book.

The total effect may have been too powerful for some Kelmscott subscribers; or perhaps too few of them shared Morris's delight in the text. For whatever reason, the edition never sold out, and in June 1897 Jane Morris gave the overstock to British public libraries.

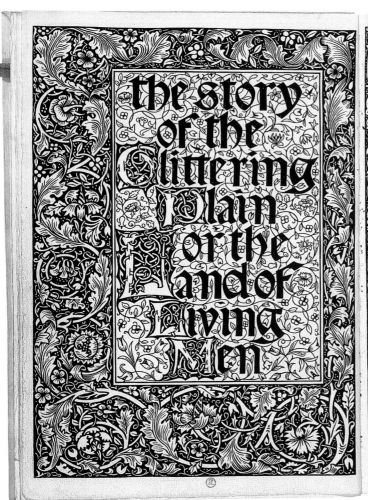

First years of the change

bed, & even sometimes more commonplace; in others, as in France, it lost order, virility, and purity of line. But for a long time yet it was alive and vigorous, & showed even greater capacity than before for adapting itself to the needs of a developing society: nor did the change of style affect all its furniture injuriously; some of the subsidiary arts as, e.g., Flemish tapestry & English wood-carving, rather gained than lost for many years.

AT last, with the close of the Fifteenth century, the Great Change became obvious; & we must remember that it was no superficial change of form, but a change of

48

spirit affecting every form inevitably. This change we have somewhat boastfully, and as regards the arts quite untruthfully, called the New Birth. But let us see what it means.

SOCIETY was preparing for a complete recasting of its elements: the Mediæval Society of Status was in process of transition into the modern Society of Contract. New classes were being formed to fit the new system of production which was at the bottom of this; political life began again with the new birth of bureaucracy; & political, as distinguished from natural, nationalities, were being hammered

49

A new Society

O.21

O.21 *Gothic Architecture* by William Morris

Kelmscott Press book; issued 21 October 1893
Paper, 14.3 x 10.4 cm leaf
V&A (NAL L.169-1893)

This was the first of six Kelmscott books produced in this small but elegant format. It was later used for four other texts written or translated by Morris.

He had given this lecture to the Arts and Crafts Exhibition Society in 1889. Unusually, this edition was not printed on the premises of the Kelmscott Press but at the New Gallery in London where the exhibition was held. One of the Kelmscott Albion presses was set up while the Arts and Crafts Exhibition Society held its annual show at the New Gallery during October and November 1893. According to the first Secretary of the Press, the crowds surrounding the pressman W. Collins were so enthusiastic that they imposed a severe strain on his Celtic modesty.

It seems that three editions of about five hundred copies each were printed at the New Gallery. This was exceptionally high figure for a Kelmscott edition; the separate printings made it possible to correct some of the misprints which occurred all too often in Kelmscott books. The Golden type was used after a trial setting in Chaucer type (used for most of the later books in this format).

Purchased from the Kelmscott Press for 2s. 6d.

O.23a

O.22 *Ballads and Narrative Poems*
by Dante Gabriel Rossetti

Kelmscott Press book, issued November 1893
Paper, 20.5 x 14.0 cm leaf
Private Collection

Early in 1893, Morris agreed to print two volumes of poems by his friend Rossetti, who had died in 1882. This volume was followed five months later by Rossetti's *Sonnets and Lyrical Poems*; the two volumes were printed in the same format, both were set in Golden type and were decorated with borders as well as six- and ten-line initials.

The two volumes were commissioned by the London firm of Ellis & Elvey where Morris's close friend F.S.Ellis was a partner. Ellis collaborated in many Kelmscott publications by taking on editorial duties. Proofs of these texts were read by the poet's younger brother W.M.Rossetti, who supervised this book with great care.

The pages exhibited include the first of three pressmarks designed by Morris for his Kelmscott editions.

O.23 *The Story of the Glittering Plain*
by William Morris

a Kelmscott Press book, issued
17 February 1894
Paper, 29.1 x 21.0 cm leaf
V&A (NAL L.579-1894)
Purchased from the Kelmscott Press for £5 5s.

b Design for title-page of
The Story of the Glittering Plain
William Morris, 1894
Ink and Chinese white, 35.25 x 25.2 cm
Inscribed: 'Reduce $\frac{1}{16}$ in width'
Sanford and Helen Berger Collection

This was the only text published in two separate editions by the Kelmscott Press. Morris originally planned to issue this book with illustrations by Walter Crane (see cat.no.O.13), but was forced to produce an unillustrated edition of his story in a different format as the first book from his press in May 1891.

In February 1894, this second version was published in a larger format, set in his Troy type with twenty-three illustrations drawn by Walter Crane and engraved on wood by A.Leverett.

As the sizes of type which Morris installed at his press were restricted to those suitable for text composition, they were not large enough for displayed lines; so he produced title-page designs in which he combined his talents as a decorator with his gift for designing larger letter forms.

In the fourth, fifth and sixth lines of the design for the title-page, Morris was disturbed to find a distracting vertical stress in the words 'Plain', 'the' and 'Land', created by the stems of the letters i, h and d falling so closely beneath each other. When his design was cut on wood, the three words were staggered to avoid this vertical stress.

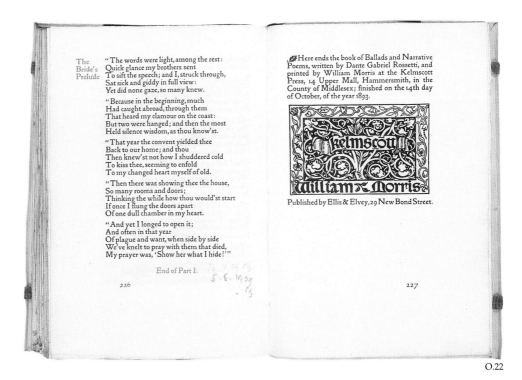

O.22

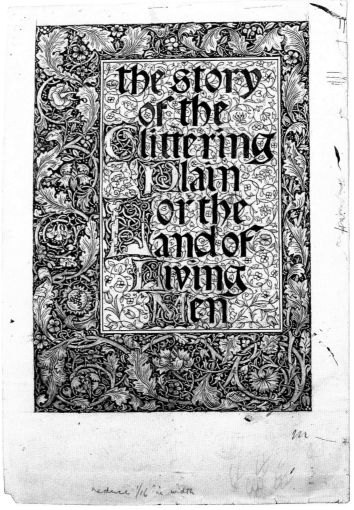

O.23b

O.24

O.25

O.24 *The Well at the World's End* by William Morris

Kelmscott Press book, issued 4 June 1896
Paper, 28.5 x 20.4 cm leaf
V&A (NAL L.688-1896)

This work was longer in production than any other Kelmscott book. Cockerell saw proofs on April 1892, and by October of that year, Morris was busy on the borders. The main reason for the delay was the trouble Morris experienced in finding an acceptable set of illustrations for his text. Both Charles Fairfax Murray and C.M.Gere were named as his choice before he commissioned Arthur J. Gaskin, who was, like Gere, an artist of the Birmingham School, and a most talented illustrator. He visited Kelmscott House in 1892 with samples of his work which Morris admired. An extensively illustrated edition was planned for which Gaskin received £250.

Unhappily, the outcome did not please Morris, who eventually settled for only four illustrations by his friend Burne-Jones; that shown here is 'The Chamber of Love in the Wilderness'. These were used at the head of each 'book' with the title below lettered by Morris, who also provided a great variety of borders, initials and a fourteen-line initial word; the text was set in Chaucer type from Longman's trade edition which was printed at the Chiswick Press while the Kelmscott edition was in production.

Purchased from the Kelmscott Press for £4 9s. 3d.

O.25 Wood block for *The Well at the World's End* by William Morris

27.8 x 19.5 x 2.5 cm
Inscribed
British Museum (1897-12-28-17)

Wood block engraved with a Morris border used on page 116. Powdered chalk has been applied to engraved portions of the border, so that the design can be 'read' in black and white, much as it would appear. The block is marked 'Border 7' and on the top edge is stamped with the name of its maker or supplier: 'J.SCOTT WHITEFRIARS ST EC.'

THE WORKS OF GEOFFREY CHAUCER

Kelmscott Press, 1896

This was the crowning Kelmscott Press achievement of Morris's collaboration with Burne-Jones. As undergraduates at Oxford they had counted Chaucer as one of their great discoveries. Later their admiration for him steadily grew.

Scenes from 'The Prioress's Tale' were painted by Burne-Jones on a wardrobe that he gave Morris as wedding present. Embroideries, stained glass and tile designs were based on *The Legend of Goode Wimmen*, and Morris showed his veneration of Chaucer in his poem *Jason* (1887) by calling him his master. The creation of the Chaucer Society in 1868 raised interest in his works and in 1878 Morris was asked to write an introduction to an edition of Chaucer's writings, but refused because only a small selection was planned. His heart was set on producing a complete edition from a carefully restored text, and with a wealth of illustrations by Burne-Jones. Eventually permission was obtained to use a text which the Reverend Walter W. Skeat had prepared for Oxford University Press.

At the outset, forty illustrations were envisaged. Their number rose to eighty-seven (for which eighty-five pencil

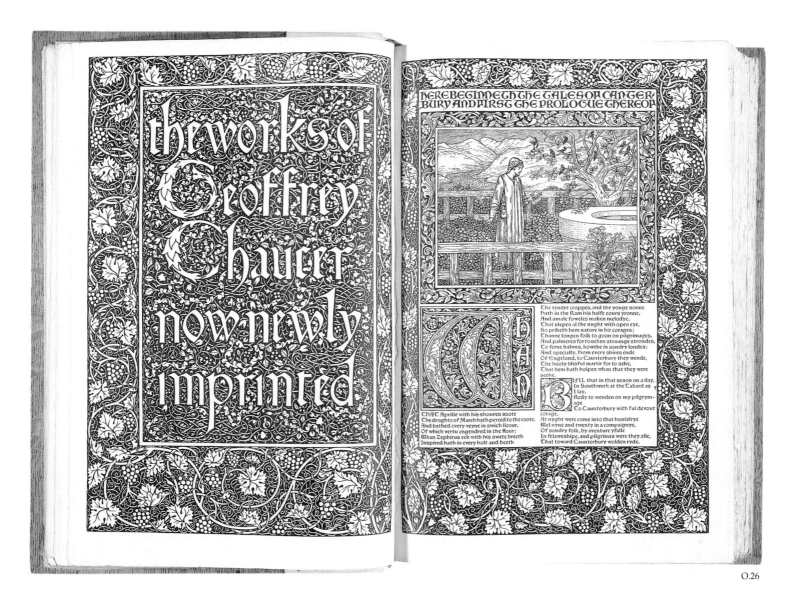

O.26

drawings survive at the Fitzwilliam Museum in Cambridge). Before these were cut on wood, their lines were considerably strengthened with great skill and sensitivity by Robert Catterson-Smith (see cat. no. O.32). Morris's drawings were also cut on wood by highly competent craftsmen, so the work of both friends was made more homogeneous, and better suited to the weight of line given to the Chaucer type used for the densely set double-column text.

Morris's typography was much enhanced by the large quantity of decorative designs and lettering that he drew for this edition. He supplied the title-page, twenty-six large initial words, scores of decorated initials – many of them used in earlier Kelmscott books – as well as fourteen large outer borders and eighteen frames for illustrations. This setting delighted Burne-Jones who 'loved to be snugly cased in borders and buttressed up by the vast initials – and once or twice when I have no big letter under me, I feel tottery and weak; if you drag me out of my encasings it will be like tearing a statue out of its niche and putting it in a museum.'

The two friends had the greatest mutual admiration for each other's part in the production. Morris called the illustrations 'magnificent and inimitable' and saw them

as 'the most harmonious decoration possible'. Burne-Jones regarded Morris as simply 'the greatest master of ornament in the world'. Both enjoyed immersing themselves in antiquity. As they sat together on Sundays while the illustrations were being drawn – or re-drawn, as so many were – Burne-Jones recalled 'we never got to speak of anyone later than the ninth century.'

Burne-Jones was too prim to illustrate the bawdier passages in some of Chaucer's tales, as Morris hoped he would. Despite this limitation, the artist showed himself capable of entering wholeheartedly into Morris's scheme, and painstaking in trying to interpret Chaucer accurately, though he sometimes failed. He preferred to deal with the more chivalric and courtly elements in the text. His greatest strengths were in the composition of his drawings and in his handling of figures against intricate backgrounds.

The Kelmscott Chaucer captured the public's imagination from the moment it was first announced. It remains the best-known Kelmscott edition and the most highly prized. Although it was rapidly sold out, it failed narrowly to cover its costs and was in effect subsidised by healthy profits made on smaller Kelmscott books.

O.26 *The Works of Geoffrey Chaucer*

Kelmscott Press book, issued 26 June 1896
Paper, 42.5 x 29.2 cm leaf
Cheltenham Art Gallery and Museums
Bought with the assistance of generous grants from the Trustees of the National Heritage Memorial Fund, the MGC/V&A Purchases Grant Fund, The British Library (from the Wolfson Foundation and the Wolfson Family Charitable Trust), The Pilgrim Trust, The J. Paul Getty Jr. Charitable Trust and the National Art Collections Fund

This copy was given to Emery Walker by William Morris. Apart from the illustrations engraved on wood after a design by Burne-Jones, all the decoration, lettering and type on these pages are the works of Morris.

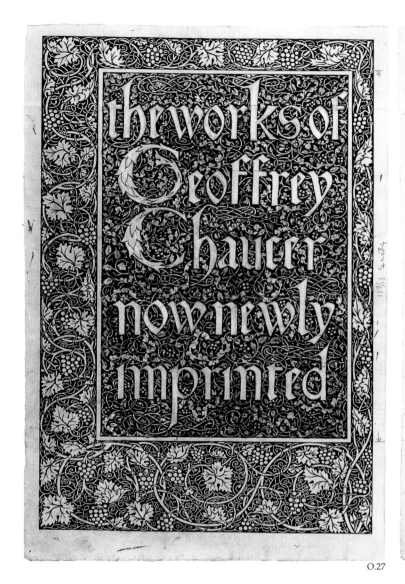

O.27

O.28

O.27 Design for title-page of
The Works of Geoffrey Chaucer

William Morris, February–May 1896
Ink and Chinese white, 42.3 x 29.0 cm
Pierpont Morgan Library, New York
(PML 76923M) Gift of John M. Crawford Jr.

This was Morris's last design for the Chaucer. He began
it on 19 February 1896 after Burne-Jones (whose illustrations were completed in December 1895) expressed
his anxiety over the delay. Morris finished this design
at the end of March; after some retouching in May, the
title-page was printed when the final sheet went
through the press.

O.28 Design for a large border for
The Works of Geoffrey Chaucer

William Morris, 1896
Ink and Chinese white, 41.8 x 32.2 cm
Inscribed
V&A (D.1552-1907)

One of Morris's fourteen designs for large borders drawn
in ink and Chinese white. This appears on page 470.
Long experience of designing textiles, carpets and wallpapers helped him to resolve the transitions from broad
to narrow spaces in the four segments of the design.

W. R. Lethaby saw Morris at work on borders:

*He would have two saucers, one of Indian ink, the other of
Chinese white. Then, making the slightest indications of the
main stems of the patterns he had in mind, with pencil, he
would begin at once his finished final ornaments by covering
a length of ground with one brush and painting the pattern
with the other. If a part did not satisfy him, the other brush
covered it up again, and again he set to put in his finished
ornament...The actual drawing with the brush was an agreeable sensation to him; the forms were led along and bent over
and rounded at the edges with definite pleasure; they were
stroked into place, as it were, with a sensation like that of
smoothing a cat...It was to express this sensuous pleasure
that he used to say that all good designing was felt in the
stomach.*

O.29 Wood block for a large border for
The Works of Geoffrey Chaucer

20.0 x 16.0 x 2.5 cm
Inscribed: 'Chaucer no.19', 'Reason'
British Museum (1897-12-28-73)

Because the same borders, frames and decorated letters
were used repeatedly throughout the Chaucer, they
were printed from copies known as electrotypes. These
were made from the wood blocks engraved by W.H.
Hooper after Morris's designs.

This block could not have been used for printing
because the space within the border has not been
cleared. Consequently the entire surface would have
been covered by ink when the rollers went over it. In

fact the surface of the block still has some remains of the graphite with which it was covered before an electrotype copy was made.

Electrotypes were produced from a wax mould of the surface of the wood block. Graphite prevented the surface of the block from sticking to the beeswax-based compound used for making the mould. Copper was deposited on the moulds through electricity developed by magnetism – a method known as galvanism.

Morris feared a loss of quality by using electrotype copies. Walker won him over by proofing on one sheet of paper two rows of the same decorated letters. One row was printed from the wood blocks, the other from electrotypes. In fact, Morris managed to put his finger on the electrotypes, but admitted he had done so almost by chance – and agreed to use electrotypes.

O.30 Wood block for
Edward Burne-Jones's illustration for
'The Legend of Goode Wimmen' for
The Works of Geoffrey Chaucer

12.6 x 16.5 x 2.5 cm
Inscribed on the back: 'Chaucer no.62, p.431'
British Museum (1897-11-17-96)

This block was used to print this illustration on page 431. It shows Hypsipyle and Medea in the foreground with the *Argos* in the background.

On the edges of the block can be seen cardboard wedges, which were used to keep the block in place within its electrotype frame. A further advantage of using electrotypes to assemble the more elaborately decorated pages in the Chaucer was that a metal electrotype mounted on a wooden base had great strength, and could withstand considerable pressure when blocks, type and other typographical elements were wedged within it.

O.31 Design for a frame for
The Works of Geoffrey Chaucer

William Morris, 1896
Ink and Chinese white, 19.4 x 26.9 cm
Inscribed: 'Frame 5', 'Mars'
V&A (D.172-1903)
NOT ILLUSTRATED

This is frame no. 5 from the set of eighteen frames designed to encase the Burne-Jones illustrations. The frame appears on page 24 of the Kelmscott Chaucer and surrounds Mars.

O.29

O.30

O.32

O.33

O.32 Design for 'The Tale of the Clerk of Oxenford' for *The Works of Geoffrey Chaucer*

Edward Burne-Jones, *c*.1895
Pencil, 13.0 x 17.0 cm
Fitzwilliam Museum, Cambridge
Given by Stanley Baldwin Esq. (1050.15)

A pivotal part in translating Burne-Jones's drawings onto woodcuts was played by Robert Catterson-Smith. Here is an extract from his explanation of the intermediary stages:

Emery Walker made a very pale print of a photograph (a platino) from Sir E.B.J.'s pencil drawing – I then stuck the print down on stout cardboard, and, in order to avoid the expansion of the paper I put the paste on the cardboard first and then applied the paper print very quickly, so quickly that it had no time to absorb moisture and so expand, then I immediately ran a hot smoothing iron over it which at once dried the paste. Next I gave the print a thin even wash of Chinese white with a little size in it. The result was to get rid of everything but the essential lines. Next I went over the pale lines with a very sharp pencil, copying and translating from the B.-J. drawing which was in front of me. When the pencil drawing was finished all trace of the photograph had disappeared. Next came the inking over, which was done with a fine round sable brush and very black Chinese ink which I bought in bottles. By putting a little size in the Chinese white as above mentioned, the ink was not absorbed by the white and so remained jet black – otherwise it would have become grey…When difficulties arose in the treatment of passages, I consulted B.J. – sometimes work by Albert Durer was consulted to see how he had dealt with passages. Some of the drawings were done over several times. Finally E.Walker made a photograph on the woodblock and [W.H.] Hooper cut it.

O.33 Proof with original border for *The Works of Geoffrey Chaucer*

Border by William Morris, 1896; proof from illustration by Edward Burne-Jones
Indian ink and Chinese white, 22.2 x 27.7 cm
V&A (D.1554-1907).
Purchased from S.C.Cockerell

One of eighteen frames, used on page 129 to encase a Burne-Jones illustration in the second part of 'The Tale of the Clerk of Oxenford' (see cat.no.O.32).

O.34 *The Works of Geoffrey Chaucer*

Kelmscott Press book, issued 26 June 1896
Paper, 42.5 x 29.2 cm leaf
V&A (NAL L.757-1896)

The illustrations on both pages are from designs by Burne-Jones. The decorated initials were designed by Morris. On the left page, two of the four three-line initials are of identical design; this presented no problem once Morris had agreed to use electrotypes for printing his borders and initials (see cat.no.O.29).

Purchased from the Kelmscott Press for £16 3s.

O.35 Initial word 'WHILHOM' for *The Works of Geoffrey Chaucer*

a Design for the above
William Morris, 1896
Ink and Chinese white,
14.4 x 21.5 cm
Inscribed:'Big letter for Chaucer', 'This width exactly', in the hand of Emery Walker
V&A (D.1553-1907)

b Proof of the above
From a wood block engraved by W.H.Hooper
10.5 x 13.0 cm
V&A (D.1553a-1907)

One of twenty-six large initial words drawn by Morris in ink and Chinese white. His design was subsequently redrawn by Robert Catterson-Smith, who cut the wood block after the design had been photograph-ically transferred on to its surface. The proof shows how sensitively Catterson-Smith modified and executed Morris's design.

Exhib. 1934 (279)

O.34

O.35a

O.35b

O.38

O.39

O.36 Three initial letters for
The Works of Geoffrey Chaucer

a Design for the above
William Morris, 1896
Ink and Chinese white, 6.1 x 14.1 cm
Inscribed
V&A (D.1561-1907)
NOT ILLUSTRATED

b Proof for the above
From wood block engraved by W.H.Hooper
6.2 x 16.9 cm

V&A (E.1183-1912)
NOT ILLUSTRATED

When Morris drew the initials G, R and A in ink and
Chinese white, he made them a trifle taller than the size
in which they were needed. So his drawing was
marked by Walker with a vertical line and with an
instruction to 'reduce to exact height of line'. The
reduced photograph would then have been retouched,
re-photographed, and cut on wood in much the same
way as described in cat.no.O.35.

Exhib. 1934 (279)

O.37 *The Works of Geoffrey Chaucer*

Kelmscott Press book, issued 26 June 1896
Vellum; special stamped pigskin binding;
42.5 x 29.2 cm leaf
The Syndics of Cambridge University Library
(Sel.1.16)

Late in February 1896, the Kelmscott Press announced
that it would accept orders for supplying the Chaucer
in four varieties of special bindings. Two were to be
executed to Morris's design by T.J. Cobden-Sanderson,
either in full white tooled pigskin, or in half pigskin
over oak boards; the other two were to be carried out
by J.& J. Leighton to a different design by Morris, in
either full or half pigskin over boards.

Because his health was failing, Morris only finished
one of these binding designs between December 1895
and January 1896, although he made a start on a second
design. He regarded white pigskin as a 'beautiful material for wearing and showing designs'. Forty-eight
copies were bound to his design at the Doves Bindery.
The majority were tooled by Douglas Cockerell with
variations in quality, both in the exactness with which
the design was followed, and in the strength with
which the tools were impressed into the pigskin bindings over the oak boards.

Morris took his inspiration for this design from a binding in his library by Ulrich Schreier (Augsburg 1478) on
a copy of a large Koberger Bible, close in size to the
Kelmscott Chaucer.

On the upper cover, the grape-vine border is related to
his own design for the title-page and the facing text-
page. The lower cover relates more closely to the
Schreier binding, with its diagonal bands forming large
lozenges. Within each lozenge are stylised oak leaves.
Many of Schreier's bindings combined cut-leather
work and tooling. The cut leather often had a criblée
background which seems to have inspired the small
dots on Morris's grape-vine border. His small tools in
the centre panel of the upper cover are also related to
those on Schreier's binding. Despite noting these similarities, Dr Paul Needham regards Morris's binding for
the Chaucer as 'a work of art in its own right, the lower
cover especially having a clarity and simplicity that
excels its model'.

O.38 Design for a binding tool made for
The Works of Geoffrey Chaucer

William Morris, *c*.1896
Pencil and watercolour, 9.0 x 16.1 cm
Inscribed: 'Well raised up' and other notes
V&A (E.195-1955)

One of a set of designs by Morris for tooling the
pigskin Chaucer bindings. This is endorsed in the
handwriting of the bookbinder, T.J.Cobden-Sanderson:
'Design by William Morris for detail for side of
Chaucer.' Another hand has added: 'One tool die sunk
as before.'

O.39 Metal tool for binding of
The Works of Geoffrey Chaucer

19.5 cm long, 2.5 cm wide
Society of Antiquaries of London (933)

Tool cut from original design (cat.no.O.38) used for a
pigskin binding of the Kelmscott *Chaucer*.

O

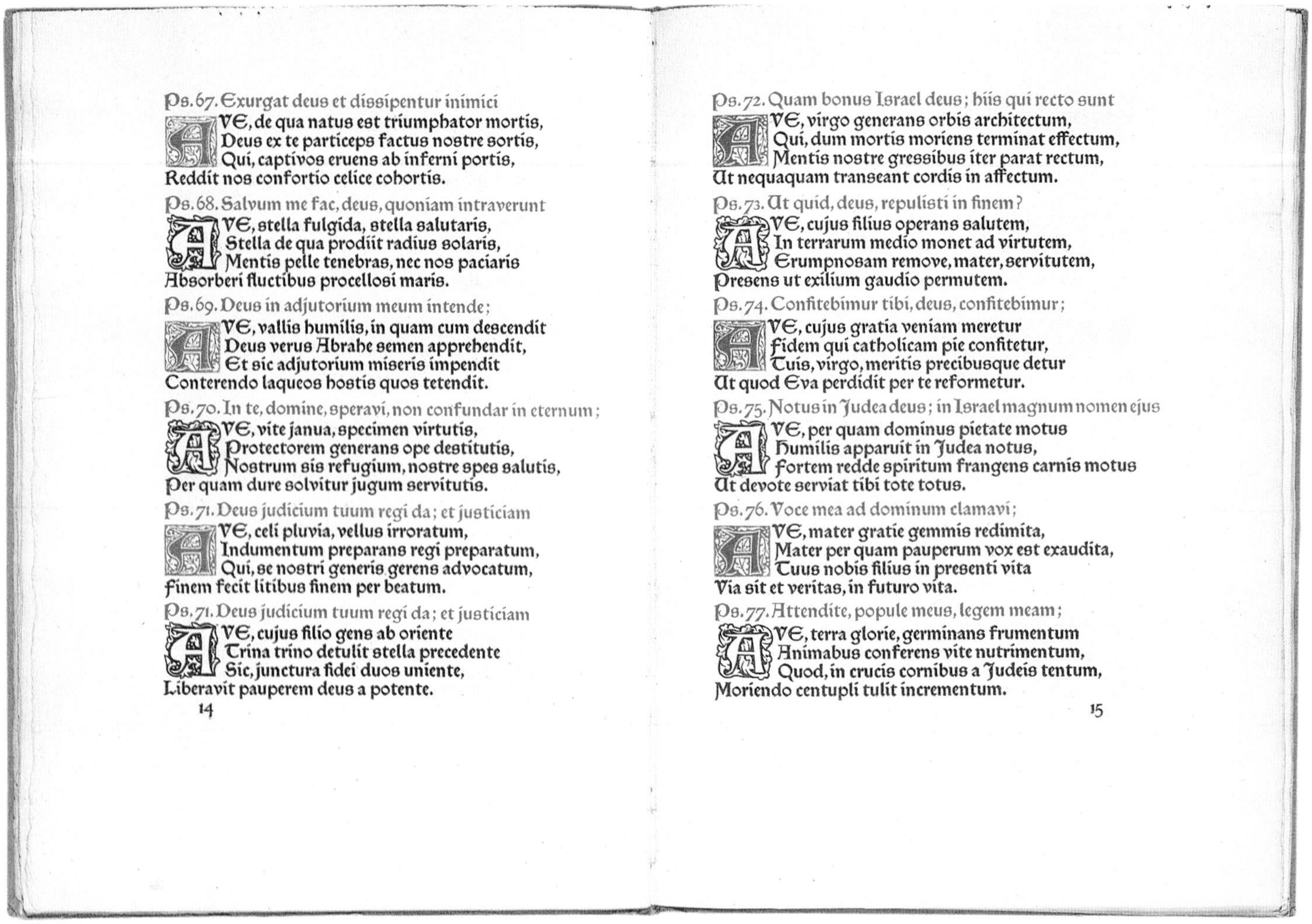
Ps. 67. Exurgat deus et dissipentur inimici
AVE, de qua natus est triumphator mortis,
Deus ex te particeps factus nostre sortis,
Qui, captivos eruens ab inferni portis,
Reddit nos confortio celice cohortis.
Ps. 68. Salvum me fac, deus, quoniam intraverunt
AVE, stella fulgida, stella salutaris,
Stella de qua prodiit radius solaris,
Mentis pelle tenebras, nec nos paciaris
Absorberi fluctibus procellosi maris.
Ps. 69. Deus in adjutorium meum intende;
AVE, vallis humilis, in quam cum descendit
Deus verus Abrahe semen apprehendit,
Et sic adjutorium miseris impendit
Conterendo laqueos hostis quos tetendit.
Ps. 70. In te, domine, speravi, non confundar in eternum;
AVE, vite janua, specimen virtutis,
Protectorem generans ope destitutis,
Nostrum sis refugium, nostre spes salutis,
Per quam dure solvitur jugum servitutis.
Ps. 71. Deus judicium tuum regi da; et justiciam
AVE, celi pluvia, vellus irroratum,
Indumentum preparans regi preparatum,
Qui, se nostri generis gerens advocatum,
Finem fecit litibus finem per beatum.
Ps. 71. Deus judicium tuum regi da; et justiciam
AVE, cujus filio gens ab oriente
Trina trino detulit stella precedente
Sic, junctura fidei duos uniente,
Liberavit pauperem deus a potente.
14

Ps. 72. Quam bonus Israel deus; hiis qui recto sunt
AVE, virgo generans orbis architectum,
Qui, dum mortis moriens terminat effectum,
Mentis nostre gressibus iter parat rectum,
Ut nequaquam transeant cordis in affectum.
Ps. 73. Ut quid, deus, repulisti in finem?
AVE, cujus filius operans salutem,
In terrarum medio monet ad virtutem,
Erumpnosam remove, mater, servitutem,
Presens ut exilium gaudio permutem.
Ps. 74. Confitebimur tibi, deus, confitebimur;
AVE, cujus gratia veniam meretur
Fidem qui catholicam pie confitetur,
Tuis, virgo, meritis precibusque detur
Ut quod Eva perdidit per te reformetur.
Ps. 75. Notus in Judea deus; in Israel magnum nomen ejus
AVE, per quam dominus pietate motus
Humilis apparuit in Judea notus,
Fortem redde spiritum frangens carnis motus
Ut devote serviat tibi tote totus.
Ps. 76. Voce mea ad dominum clamavi;
AVE, mater gratie gemmis redimita,
Mater per quam pauperum vox est exaudita,
Tuus nobis filius in presenti vita
Via sit et veritas, in futuro vita.
Ps. 77. Attendite, popule meus, legem meam;
AVE, terra glorie, germinans frumentum
Animabus conferens vite nutrimentum,
Quod, in crucis cornibus a Judeis tentum,
Moriendo centupli tulit incrementum.
15

O.41

O.40 Stamped calfskin impression of tools made for *The Works of Geoffrey Chaucer*

Bernard Middleton, February 1989
26.4 x 20.6 cm
Society of Antiquaries of London
NOT ILLUSTRATED

A modern impression from metal tools made for the Kelmscott *Chaucer*.

O.41 *Laudes Beatae Mariae Virginis*

Kelmscott Press book, issued 7 August 1896
Paper, 29.0 x 21.0 cm leaf
V&A (NAL L.1188-1907)

The first of two Kelmscott books printed in three colours; the second, *Love is Enough* (1898) by Morris, was published nearly eighteen months after his death.

Morris had the blue ink made to his own specification from ultramarine ash by Winsor & Newton. This firm also supplied a brilliant vermilion to the Kelmscott Press. According to Walker, the inferiority of the ingredients from which trade printing inks were made had been noticed by Mr Winsor, who set to work on making inks of pure colour and fine quality. His brilliant vermilion was later used by the Doves and Ashendene presses.

In May 1893 Morris had bought the early thirteenth-century manuscript from which the text of this edition was prepared anonymously by Sydney Cockerell. Morris referred to it as the 'Nottingham Psalter', but it is now associated with Reading Abbey whose dedication is marked in gold in the Calendar as *dedicatio ecclesiae*. The *Laudes* have elsewhere been attributed to Stephen Langton, Archbishop of Canterbury.

As every stanza opens with the word 'Ave', Morris was relieved that Walker had proved to him that electrotypes could provide perfect copies of woodcut initials (see cat. no. O.29).

Purchased by the Museum from Hodgson & Co. for £4.

Exhib. 1934 (268)

FROISSART'S CHRONICLES

by William Morris, Kelmscott Press, 1897

Since his days at college, Morris had retained a great enthusiasm for Lord Berners' translation of Froissart's Chronicles. As soon as his Troy type was delivered in January 1892, he had a single-column trial page of Froissart set up in his new type. Early in 1893 further trial pages were set in double-column using his Chaucer type. In March 1893 Morris showed some new initials for Froissart to his friends.

Burne-Jones offered in October 1893 to provide a big frontispiece for volume I, and some shields of arms; a drawing of Fame was intended for volume II, but if this offer had been accepted, it might have delayed completion of his promised frontispiece and illustration for *The Life and Death of Jason*, which appeared in July 1895. So Morris devoted some of his own energy and imagination to working on the decoration of specimen pages for a Kelmscott edition of Froissart.

An interview given in 1895 reported Morris as saying: 'No book that I could do would give me half the pleasure

O.42

that I am getting from the Froissart. I am simply revelling in it. It's such a noble and glorious work and every page [proof] as it leaves the press delights me more than I can say. I am taking great pains with it, and doing all I can to realise what I have long wished.' Unfortunately the venture had to be held in abeyance while the Chaucer absorbed the greater part of his presses' capacity.

Before he was able to carry out his plans, Morris died. A formal announcement that the *Froissart's Chronicles* would not be published was made in November 1896. By then about thirty-four pages of the work had been set up in type, but no sheets had been printed. His executors decided to print sixteen pages in an edition of thirty-two copies for distribution to his friends,

before the type was distributed. In addition, 160 copies were printed on vellum.

The six exhibits used give a tantalising impression of the manner in which Morris might have produced his edition of *Froissart's Chronicles*, if he had lived to complete it.

O.42 Two trial pages of the projected edition of Lord Berners' translation of *Froissart's Chronicles*

William Morris, 1896, issued 7 October 1897
Vellum, 42.1 x 56.4 cm
V&A (E.504-1903)

These pages show Morris experimenting with a new

decorative style. Having proved his ability to work within the constraints of rectilinear shapes, he now had the audacity to explore more exuberant forms of borders and initials, which captured the pageantry of Froissart's text.

The profile of the initial T on the right page is cusped, and is most skilfully integrated with the border immediately to its left. The cusping echoes the profile of the heraldic decoration at the foot of the left page, and is also visible in the initial F above. Two other cusped initials were designed for the Froissart: though they were never used, they were shown in the final Kelmscott book printed in 1898.

One of 160 vellum copies issued by the Kelmscott Press at one guinea each.

O.43

O.44

O.43 Large wood block for a border for *Froissart's Chronicles*, c.1892–6

40.0 x 27.8 x 2.5 cm
British Museum (1897-12-28-306)

Using the same technique described in cat.no.O.35., Morris's design for this large border was transferred on to wood; it was cut by C.E. Keates who had worked for the Kelmscott Press since 1892. His block and the smaller one cut by Spielmeyer were printed with great skill by Stephen Mowlem (see fig.104) with the help of an apprentice.

O.44 Album of sixteen pages relating to *Froissart's Chronicles*, compiled c.1897

Paper, some vellum; various sizes, image shown
42.4 x 28.5 cm
V&A (NAL 1995056850)
Bequeathed by Mrs Alan Thomas

This album was assembled and annotated by Sydney Cockerell. As Secretary of the Kelmscott Press and later as one of Morris's executors, he had a close knowledge of the project, and knew the individuals connected with it.

Supporting the evidence visible in Morris's splendid design for the opening page with its magnificent heraldic border, the album also contains a list of coats of arms, followed by Walker's notes on the arms and their tinctures. There is also a proof of the small border with several indications by Morris for details which were to be recut by Spielmeyer.

O.45 Proof for *Froissart's Chronicles* with rough pencil sketch by William Morris, c.1895

Paper, 41.8 x 28.5 cm
Sanford and Helen Berger Collection

This trial arrangement was discarded in favour of larger new initials and heraldic ornament. However, the sketch for decoration between the text columns resembles closely one of a set of six decorations in the first Kelmscott edition to appear in double column (*The Well at the World's End*, published on.4 June 1896).

O.46 Small wood block for border for *Froissart's Chronicles*, c.1892–6

21.4 x 28.0 x 2.5 cm
British Museum (1897-12-28-307)

The surface of the block shows that Morris's design, as well as part of the double-column text setting in Chaucer type, was transferred by photography on to the block. The cut-away areas have been filled with powdered chalk so that the effect of black and white can be easily judged. This block was engraved in April 1894 by W. Spielmeyer who had also worked on decorations for the Chaucer.

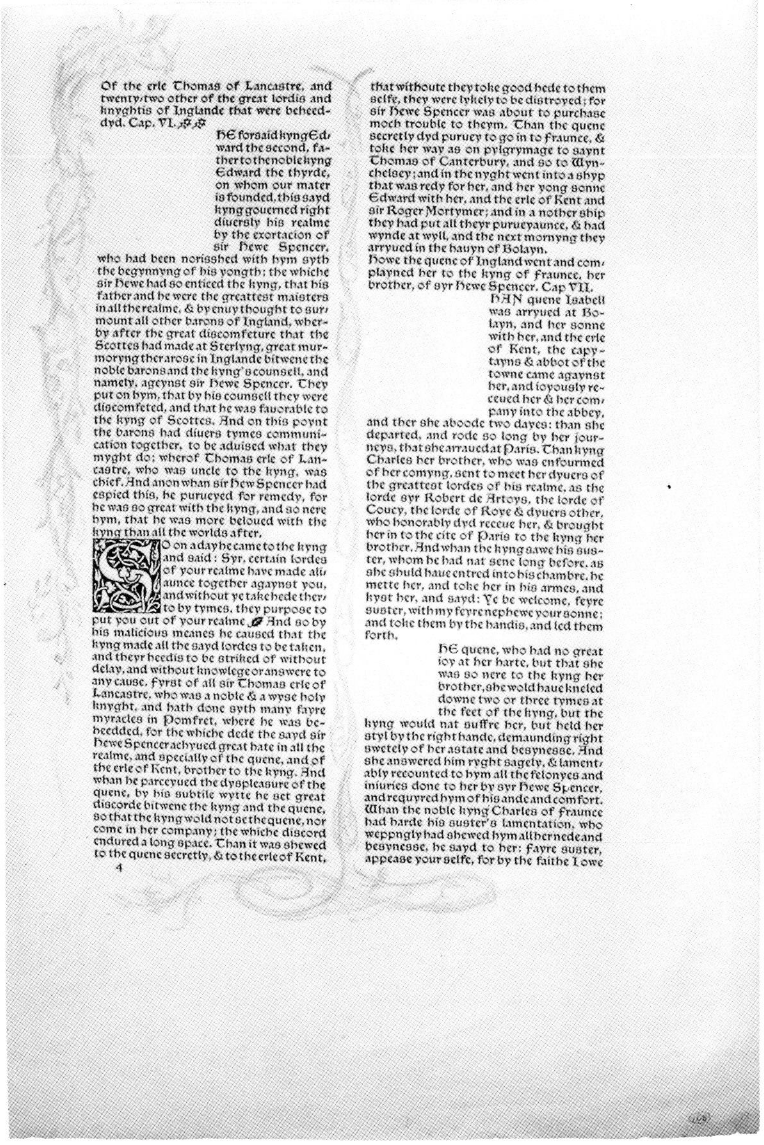

Of the erle Thomas of Lancastre, and twenty-two other of the great lordis and knyghtis of Inglande that were beheeddyd. Cap. VI.

HE forsaid kyng Edward the second, father to the noble kyng Edward the thyrde, on whom our mater is founded, this sayd kyng gouerned right diuersly his realme by the exortacion of sir Hewe Spencer, who had been norisshed with hym syth the begynnyng of his yongth; the whiche sir Hewe had so enticed the kyng, that his father and he were the greattest maisters in all the realme, & by enuy thought to surmount all other barons of Ingland, wherby after the great discomfeture that the Scottes had made at Sterlyng, great murmoryng ther arose in Inglande bitwene the noble barons and the kyng's counsell, and namely, ageynst sir Hewe Spencer. They put on hym, that by his counsell they were discomfeted, and that he was fauorable to the kyng of Scottes. And on this poynt the barons had diuers tymes communication together, to be aduised what they myght do; wherof Thomas erle of Lancastre, who was uncle to the kyng, was chief. And anon whan sir Hew Spencer had espied this, he purueyed for remedy, for he was so great with the kyng, and so nere hym, that he was more beloued with the kyng than all the worlds after.

SO on a day he came to the kyng and said: Syr, certain lordes of your realme have made aliaunce together agaynst you, and without ye take hede therto by tymes, they purpose to put you out of your realme. And so by his malicious meanes he caused that the kyng made all the sayd lordes to be taken, and theyr heedis to be striked of without delay, and without knowlege or answere to any cause. Fyrst of all sir Thomas erle of Lancastre, who was a noble & a wyse holy knyght, and hath done syth many fayre myracles in Pomfret, where he was beheedded, for the whiche dede the sayd sir Hewe Spencer achyued great hate in all the realme, and specially of the quene, and of the erle of Kent, brother to the kyng. And whan he parceyued the dyspleasure of the quene, by his subtile wytte he set great discorde bitwene the kyng and the quene, so that the kyng wold not se the quene, nor come in her company; the whiche discord endured a long space. Than it was shewed to the quene secretly, & to the erle of Kent,

4

that withoute they toke good hede to them selfe, they were lykely to be distroyed; for sir Hewe Spencer was about to purchase moch trouble to theym. Than the quene secretly dyd puruey to go in to Fraunce, & toke her way as on pylgrymage to saynt Thomas of Canterbury, and so to Wynchelsey; and in the nyght went into a shyp that was redy for her, and her yong sonne Edward with her, and the erle of Kent and sir Roger Mortymer; and in a nother ship they had put all theyr pureueyaunce, & had wynde at wyll, and the next mornyng they arryued in the hauyn of Bolayn.

Howe the quene of Ingland went and complayned her to the kyng of Fraunce, her brother, of syr Hewe Spencer. Cap VII.

HAN quene Isabell was arryued at Bolayn, and her sonne with her, and the erle of Kent, the capytayns & abbot of the towne came agaynst her, and ioyously receued her & her company into the abbey, and ther she aboode two dayes: than she departed, and rode so long by her journeys, that she arraued at Paris. Than kyng Charles her brother, who was enfourmed of her comyng, sent to meet her dyuers of the greattest lordes of his realme, as the lorde syr Robert de Artoys, the lorde of Coucy, the lorde of Roye & dyuers other, who honorably dyd receue her, & brought her in to the cite of Paris to the kyng her brother. And whan the kyng sawe his suster, whom he had nat sene long before, as she shuld haue entred into his chambre, he mette her, and toke her in his armes, and kyst her, and sayd: Ye be welcome, feyre suster, with my feyre nephewe your sonne; and toke them by the handis, and led them forth.

HE quene, who had no great ioy at her harte, but that she was so nere to the kyng her brother, she wold haue kneled downe two or three tymes at the feet of the kyng, but the kyng would nat suffre her, but held her styl by the right hande, demaunding right swetely of her astate and besynesse. And she answered him ryght sagely, & lamentably recounted to hym all the felonyes and iniuries done to her by syr Hewe Spencer, and requyred hym of his ande and comfort. Whan the noble kyng Charles of Fraunce had harde his suster's lamentation, who weppngly had shewed hym all her nede and besynesse, he sayd to her: Fayre suster, appease your selfe, for by the faithe I owe

O.45

Of the erle Thomas of Lancastre, and twenty-two other of the great lordis and knyghtis of Inglande that were beheeddyd. Cap. VI.

HE forsaid kyng Edward the second, father to the noble kyng Edward the thyrde, on whom our mater is founded, this sayd kyng gouerned right diuersly his realme by the exortacion of sir Hewe de Spencer, who had been norisshed with hym syth the begynnyng of his yongth; the whiche sir Hewe had so enticed the kyng that his father and he were the greattest maisters in all the realme, and by enuy thought to surmount all other barons of Ingland, wherby after the great discomfeture that the Scottes at Sterlyng, great murmoryng therin arose Inglande bitwene the noble barons and the kyng's counsell, & namely, ageynst sir Hewe Spencer. They put on hym that by his counsell they were discomfeted, & that he was fauorable to the kyng of Scottes. And on this poynt the barons had diuers tymes communication together, to be aduised what they myght do; wherof Thomas erle of Lancastre, who was uncle to the kyng, was chief. And anon whan sir Hew Spencer had espied this, he purueyed for remedy, for he was so great with the kyng, and so nere hym, that he was more beloued with the kyng than all the worlds after.

SO on a day he came to the kyng and said: "Syr, certain lordes of your realme have made aliaunce together agaynst you, & without ye take hede therto by tymes, they purpose to put you out of your realme". And so by his malicious meanes he caused that the kyng made all the sayd lordes to be taken, & theyr heedis to be striked of without delay, and without knowlege or answere to any cause. Fyrst of all sir Thomas erle of Lancastre, who was a noble and a wyse holy knyght, and hath done syth many fayre myracles in Pomfret, where he was beheedded, for the whiche dede the sayd sir Hewe Spencer achyued great hate in all the realme, and specially of the quene, & of the erle of Kent, brother to the kyng. And whan he parceyued the dyspleasure of the quene, by his subtile wytte he set great discorde bitwene the kyng and the quene, so that the kyng wold not se the quene, nor come in her company; the whiche

4

discord endured a long space. Than it was shewed to the quene secretly, & to the erle of Kent, that withoute they toke good hede to themselfe, they were lykely to be distroyed; for sir Hewe Spencer was about to purchase moch trouble to theym. Than the quene secretly dyd puruey to go in to Fraunce, & toke her way as on pylgrymage to saynt Thomas of Canterbury, and so to Wynchelsey; and in the nyght went into a shyp that was redy for her, and her yong sonne Edward with her, & the erle of Kent and sir Roger Mortymer; and in a nother ship they had put all theyr purueyaunce, and had wynde at wyll, and the next mornyng they arryued in the hauyn of Bolayn.

Howe the quene of Ingland went and complayned her to the kyng of Fraunce, her brother, of syr Hewe Spencer. Cap VII.

WHAN quene Isabell was arryued at Bolayn, and her sonne with her, and the erle of Kent, the capytayns & abbot of the towne came agaynst her, and ioyously receued her & her company into the abbey, and ther she aboode two dayes: than she departed, and rode so long by her journeys, that she arraued at Paris. Than kyng Charles her brother, who was enfourmed of her comyng, sent to meet her dyuers of the greattest lordes of his realme, as the lorde syr Robert de Artoys, the lorde of Coucy, the lorde of Roye & dyuers other, who honorably dyd receue her, & brought her in to the cite of Paris to the kyng her brother. And whan the kyng sawe his suster, whom he had nat sene long before, as she shuld haue entred into his chambre, he mette her, and toke her in his armes, and kyst her, and sayd: Ye be welcome, feyre suster, with my feyre nephewe your sonne; and toke them by the handis, and led them forth.

THE quene, who had no great ioy at her harte, but that she was so nere to the kyng her brother, she wold haue kneled downe two or three tymes at the feet of the kyng, but the kyng would nat suffre her, but held her styl by the right hande, demaunding right swetely of her astate & besynesse. And she answered him ryght sagely, and lamentably recounted to hym all the felonyes & iniuries done to her by syr Hewe Spencer, and requyred hym of his ayde & comfort. Whan the noble kyng Charles of Fraunce had harde his suster's lamentation, who wepyngly had shewed hym all her nede and besynesse, he sayd to her: "Fayre suster, appease your selfe, for

O.47

O.47 Proof for *Froissart Chronicles* with pencil sketch by William Morris, *c.*1895

Paper, 41.75 x 28.4 cm
Sanford and Helen Berger Collection

The text used in cat.no.O.45 was rearranged to accommodate a different disposition of initials, including a newly designed Y. This was one of four initials shown in the final Kelmscott book printed in 1898, when it was described by Cockerell as having been 'designed for the Froissart, but never used'. Instead of a central ornament between the columns, Morris experimented here with a scheme to place a single heraldic shield beneath the left column. It showed the style of decoration he intended to support a single stumpy shield (later replaced by a row of three shields).

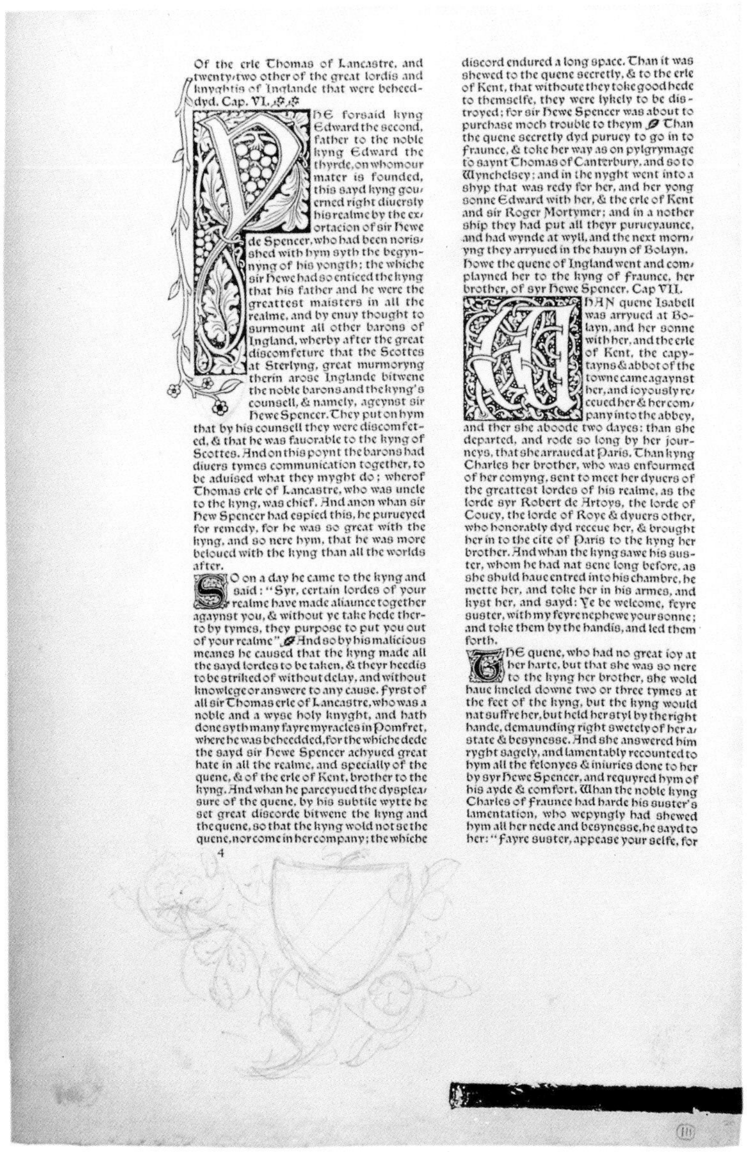

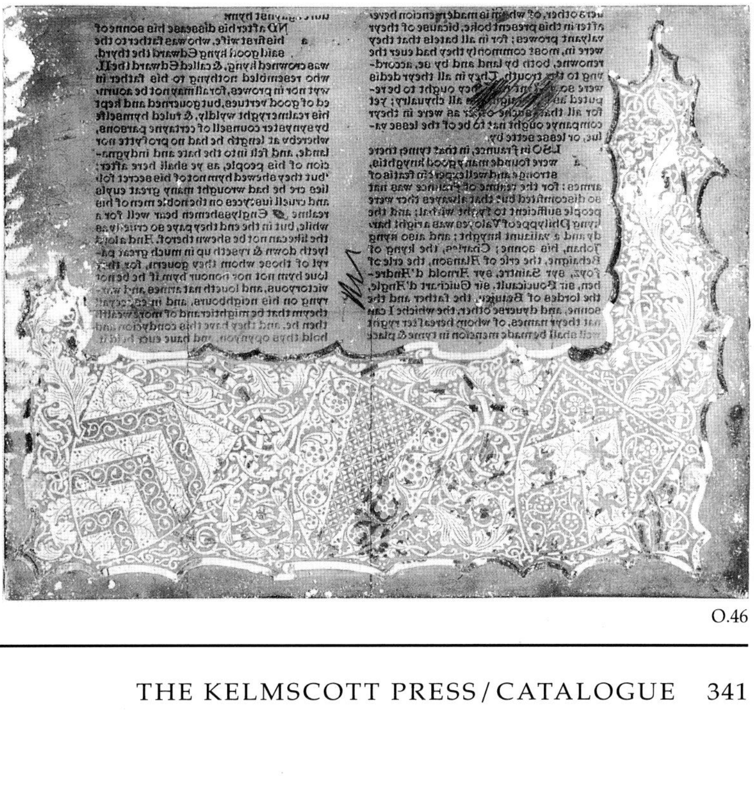

O.46

THE LEGACY

THE MORRIS
WHO READS US

Norman Kelvin

Of the many ways to begin viewing Morris, one recommending itself is to see how his life's work resonates in the last decade of the twentieth century; and to do so by starting with the figure of Morris constructed by his younger contemporaries in the 1890s, then to move back and see – guided by our own lights – how the Morris of the earlier decades leads to the one of the 1890s. We can, as it were, combine historical information with awareness of what we ourselves care about, as a first step towards making him a presence in our own *fin de siècle*. The next step will be to note that we have constructed a Morris who reads us as we read him.

To begin with the earlier decades is to begin, logically, with Morris's childhood, although this has been done many times, most recently and most impressively in Fiona MacCarthy's splendid 1994 biography of Morris. We can observe that as a boy Morris, who was born on 26 March 1834 into a family of newly acquired wealth, who had three younger brothers and four sisters, two of them older, and whose father died when he was eight, became quasi-isolated by temperament from his brothers, began to feel an ambivalent closeness and distance (for reasons of interests) towards his mother, and remained close to one older sister, Emma, only to be deprived early of her presence, when in 1850 she married and moved with her husband, a clergyman, to Derbyshire. Early on, Morris learned to take pleasure in quiet, solitary observational walks, first in the grounds of Woodford Hall, the family home (after he was six) and in adjacent Epping Forest, and later, as a schoolboy at Marlborough, in the countryside of Wiltshire. What he saw or conceived for himself on his walks was a blend of what Wordsworth saw in the Lake District and Thomas Hardy in Dorset. He saw and loved not wild nature without boundaries or human habitation, not the (psychologically) unbounded expanse of Emily Brontë's Yorkshire moors, but nature dotted with signs of human habitation, present and past – and largely past. However, he saw these signs not as did Wordsworth (for whom evidence of human habitation was also essential), in stone walls and in the smoke rising from a shepherd's cottage, but as Hardy did – in history and pre-history. Morris saw it for example as Silbury Hill, 'the tallest prehistoric structure in Europe', as Fiona MacCarthy observes, and as the medieval church near Avebury.

As he matured, the human presence implicit in cultivated nature and in Gothic architecture mattered more and more, and it was through love of them that he was to assess and interpret the external world when, later, he became an artist. And in his writing, love of a woman was to be joined with that of architecture and nature, and (it should be added) of history too, as the stories in which women appear occur usually in the past or future, almost never in the present.

Nature, architecture, history: for the boy, William Morris, they were not yet a setting for his own imagined loves; but he read of love. What he read, and he was a great reader, connected readily with what his observant eye saw in nature and architecture. It connected also with what his developing moral imagination seems to have required to make sense of history: to create a natural and architectural context for human society and then place in it a female protagonist and an autonomous male hero for whom love is initially a source of conflict or frustration. In particular, the 'Waverley' novels of Walter Scott, all of which Morris claimed he had read by the age of seven, provided not only history and its artefacts, including incidental references to architecture, but the image of the hero as the fashioner of history and art, and also the challenged lover of a woman until complications are resolved by either a tragic ending or marriage.

Morris at the age of seven probably did not observe this, but in the texts of Scott's novels, amidst much else, there is the image of woman not only as object of male desire (expressed in Romantic

ON PREVIOUS PAGE 343
Marie Stillman, *Kelmscott Manor*.

language and manner) but also as equal in capacity for desire. A possible residual memory of this, added to much else that must be inadequately described as temperament and experience, was to result in Morris's later elaboration of such an image of woman. It was to be his first break with his own age. Desire in a woman was never to be for him the terrifying phenomenon it was in both Victorian and *fin-de-siècle* literature; and his freedom from the furies haunting many of his male contemporaries was to become evident as early as the writing of *The Defence of Guenevere*, the title poem of the collection (his first) published in 1858. It was in his early poetry, too (as well as brief tales), that he was first to articulate his sense of relationships: the historic past and a detailed architectural setting as context for a male hero constructed as ambivalently autonomous: dependent on a close male friend, or, alternatively, imprisoned in a triangular relationship and dependent on the woman's choice; often, in Morris's work, not in favour of the hero.

Writing poetry and brief prose romances began when Morris entered Exeter College in 1853. During his years as an undergraduate (he received his BA in 1856) he also discovered in himself and gratified a need for male friendship, establishing close bonds with Edward Burne-Jones, Cormell Price, Robert Dixon and William Fulford – the first two friendships were to remain intact for a lifetime. There were also in these years opportunities for seeing new architecural splendours, giving him at once new aesthetic gratification and new knowledge, for at Oxford he was reading Ruskin (whose work was to be a major shaping force throughout his life). With Burne-Jones and Fulford he visited the cathedrals and churches of Abbeville, Amiens, Beauvais, Rouen and Chartres, among others. He joyed to see them, learned from them a great deal about medieval architecture and was later to become their guardian, along with those of England, against what he believed was the distorting animus of the nineteenth-century urge to restore buildings. In France, too, he saw new landscapes, describing them in his letters home in language echoing the Romantic celebration of nature and expressing an intensity of feeling that Pater was soon to recommend be reserved for art.

It was at the end of the trip that Morris and Burne-Jones dreamed of a fellowship – a community – of artists: the paradigm for what he was to strive for in both art and politics. At the time, however, it was a dream only; his first career decision was to become an architect, and he entered the Oxford office of the Gothic revivalist, George Edmund Street as an apprentice. The apprenticeship lasted through most of 1856, and though it ended with Morris's abandoning architecture as a profession, it exposed him to new possibilities in the applied arts, particularly with respect to integrating decorative elements into buildings. Equally important, the year in Street's office began what was to be a lifelong friendship with Philip Webb, chief clerk in the office and Morris's senior in all ways. At this time, the friendship was at least that of equals, though Webb in fact was Morris's teacher and therefore leader; and observing this is important as preparation for discussing the varying degrees of deference, support and acceptance of his own leadership that Morris's relationships with his friends were to require.

When, during 1856, Street moved his office to London, Morris accompanied him, and took rooms with Burne-Jones in Red Lion Square. Here there was another significant beginning: unable to find aesthetically pleasing furniture, Morris designed his own (it was painted by Burne-Jones, Rossetti and himself), so that the sensibility in Morris that required an acceptable domestic interior found expression also as a desire to design (and later make) things himself.

Soon after his settling in London, the elements in Morris's life-in-the-making began to assemble themselves, and the catalyst was love and marriage; marriage to Jane Burden, daughter of an Oxford stable-hand met in 1857 when Morris, as one of a group of young artists organised and led by Rossetti, was in Oxford painting frescoes in the Oxford Union. They married in 1859, and Morris commissioned Philip Webb to build a house (called Red House) at Bexleyheath, Upton, Kent. In 1860 the Morrises moved in, and here the continuing dissatisfaction with available furniture led to the furnishing and decorating of the house by Morris and his friends, with Webb designing most of the furniture and watching over its execution, and Edward Burne-Jones painting murals. Jane participated as well, embroidering wall hangings, and by so doing expressing a shared interest with her husband for, as Fiona MacCarthy has observed, an important part of Morris expressed itself in the feminine activity of needlework.

His dissatisfaction with available decorative materials led next to the founding of Morris,

Marshall, Faulkner and Co. in 1861. Its members were Rossetti, Burne-Jones, Ford Madox Brown, Philip Webb, Arthur Hughes and those indicated in the firm's name (one, Charles Faulkner, was another Oxford friend who was to remain close for a lifetime). The firm produced wallpapers, textile designs, stained glass, metalwork and furniture; and a reference to the last in the firm's circular reads in part: 'Under this head is included embroidery of all kinds, Stamped leather, and ornamental work in other such materials, besides every article necessary for domestic use.' Suggesting as it does a domestic interior in its entirety, the statement anticipates the 'Morris look' the firm was to make fashionable among the middle classes later in the century. It anticipates, too, the scope of the Arts and Crafts Movement that began in the 1880s and that was to confer upon an indifferent – or at best ambivalent – Morris the role not only of inspirer, but leader.

At the start, Morris, Burne-Jones, Rossetti and Madox Brown at least, shared equally in designing. Morris, however, gradually came to the fore, and also began to emerge as the complex individual he was to be: a man who spoke of fellowship but required in practice that he be the leader, dependent on able and loyal friends, and most comfortable in friendship sustained by a work activity with himself in charge – although (certainly consistent with this) holding forth in a convivial gathering or lecturing to an audience also pleased him. What he did not enjoy, also consistent, was going to the theatre and concerts, in other words, being an anonymous member of a spectator group. It may be no further surprise that when Morris spoke of the great learning experiences of his life, it was books or the tutelage of close friends he acknowledged most often; it seems seldom to have been hearing someone else lecture, except on a few occasions in the 1880s when he listened to Ernest Bax and Edward Aveling, his mentors in socialism; and, in 1888, to Emery Walker, also to become a mentor, in this case, in printing.

The early 1860s, when the firm had its early successes, were the years too in which Morris became a father: Jenny Morris was born in 1861 and May in 1862, and his success in the role of father, for indeed he was a success in this role, began. And what began, too, was his stumbling in the role of husband. It is stumbling set in a sharp light by the affair between Jane Morris and Rossetti, which started probably around 1867 and lasted (possibly at the end as a friendship without physical intimacy) until 1881, perhaps six months before Rossetti's death on Easter Sunday 1882.

In the mid-seventies, fatherhood was augmented by a new role, as Morris turned to the world beyond his home. The turning was also 'beyond', though it eventually relates to, his designing patterns for the firm; and beyond his achieving identity as a poet, having by 1870 published the three volumes of *The Earthly Paradise*, in addition to *The Defence of Guenevere and Other Poems* and *Jason*, the latter begun as one of the tales for *The Earthly Paradise*. He turned first to struggle over a major national issue, the threat of war with Russia, joining in 1876 the Eastern Question Association, which opposed entry into what was in fact a war in progress, the Russo-Turkish conflict. A year later, he turned also to public activity in defence (as he saw it) of England's architectural heritage, helping to found the Society for the Protection of Ancient Buildings.

In both organisations he was energetic, resourceful, committed. Moreover, he related to others as one among equals, not even as first among equals. In the Eastern Question Association, he was no more important than others on the executive committee, of which, as treasurer, he was a member. In the SPAB, founded to oppose restoration (as distinct from conservation) of buildings, he worked well with others; and also willingly accepted the professional judgement of architects who supported the SPAB's 'anti-scrape' policy.

Nevertheless, Morris did distinguish himself from some of the other leaders of the Eastern Question Association and the SPAB. He discovered in himself a desire, and a talent, to be a leader-as-teacher. He began what was to become a central activity – a way of relating to others who were not necessarily his fellow workers: he began to lecture. He began with his talk 'The Decorative Arts', delivered on 4 December 1877, and ended with one titled 'How We Live and How We Might Live' on 19 July 1896, but read by another, R. Catterson-Smith, since Morris, who died in October, was too ill by July to deliver it himself.

Despite his occasional grumbling and weariness with the topic on hand, the role of teacher-as-lecturer, thus leader, was to fulfil him. The majority of his lectures, throughout his lecturing career, were concerned with SPAB matters or what was to become his second chief topic and his political commitment – socialism. The audiences, for a long while, came on their own initiative. Attentive and appreciative, they gave him a kind of support. At the end, the audiences for the SPAB were like those at earlier meetings. As for the late audiences for socialism, they heard him at the Hammersmith Socialist Society (his last, smallest and most congenial socialist group). They were composed for the most part of loyal friends and employees of Morris and Co. (for several of whom attendance might have been prudence only). The point, however, is that some of those present at the late lectures on SPAB business or on socialism gave him the same affection, or attention and respect he had received earlier, and some at the very least, attention; and together, surely, enabled him to continue to feel he was both communicating with others and being supported by them.

As for the content of the lectures – as distinct from audience – those on socialism turn us to our own major interest here, though Morris's two chief interests in his lectures may be resolvable into one. The subject of these socialist lectures, which began in 1883, was usually socialism and art, or more precisely, socialism as a necessary condition for art. In saying this about the lectures that began in 1883, we begin to make apparent the connection between Morris and the aestheticism of the 1890s, though the ground for the link was anticipated with the sighting of a direction in Morris's writing by Walter Pater in 1868, when in a review article in the *Westminster Review* he praised *The Earthly Paradise* and Morris's earlier work as aesthetic poetry. It was in this article that Pater, digressing from Morris to aesthetic poetry in general, wrote the words he was to reprint in the Conclusion to the first edition of *The Renaissance* in 1873, that were to become at first the notorious and then the simply famous, avowal of aestheticism and of the Aesthetic Movement of the 1890s:

> Not the fruit of experience, but experience itself, is the end. A counted number of pulses
> only is given to us…How shall we be present always at the focus where the greatest num-
> ber of vital forces unite in their purest energy?…To burn always with this hard gemlike
> flame, to maintain this ecstasy, is success in life.

If we remember that all through the most active years of his commitment to socialism, 1883 to 1890, Morris continued to be a productive designer, we can see a link between the Morris who expressed the decorative impulse everywhere and the Morris who intervened in the life of the public on the level of civil society. This is so because the market for consumer goods – one of the spaces in which civil society exists – is the end-concern of producing wallpapers and fabrics, and Morris and Co. materials sold marvellously well among the middle classes, as Charles Harvey and Jon Press have shown in their study of Morris as businessman. There is a link, further, between the artist who thus helped define the culture of the society and the man who became, in the eyes of the same public that bought his wares, a political figure, remaining so, it might be added, to the end of his life.

Morris as designer leads also to Morris and the art and literature of the 1890s. A strong impulse among the visual artists of the decade was towards the decorative – from the flattened perspective and outlining of Aubrey Beardsley to the woodcuts of Shannon and Ricketts and Lucien Pissarro (working in London at this time). Among the young poets there was a strong tendency towards Romantic Pre-Raphaelitism, as in the early poems of W.B.Yeats, and towards perceiving symbolist antecedents in Pre-Raphaelite poetry, as in Yeats's work again and in that of the other members of the Rhymers' Club. Many of the young artists and poets of the decade were great admirers of Morris, and in this fact lies the central complication in the story; for he neither returned their admiration nor gave them any encouragement at all. The Morris they admired and to whom they looked for support and encouragement was the Morris they needed, and therefore constructed.

He was seen as one of the makers of early Modernism, as we define it now. He was seen, too, as someone who could be expected to approve and support the avant-garde; for had he not done as much in politics by supporting socialism, albeit his own conception of it? But it was because it was his own that there was a problem. Morris implicity belonged to the school of social radicalism beginning in modern times with Rousseau, that posits an essential human nature and asserts that needs, desires and expression of self have been distorted or suppressed by modern social conditions. Like Rousseau and Ruskin – and the early Marx – Morris believed the natural would never be able to express itself properly or adequately within existing society. Embracing the ideas of Ruskin (and of Pugin before him), Morris celebrated, as the icon for what was wanted, the medieval craftsman, achieving and expressing self in carving stone ornaments and illuminating manuscripts: in spontaneously gratifying the fundamental human desire to decorate.

Although Morris acknowledged that in the future people would require their own ideas about art, his fixed idea about the effect of capitalism on the arts encouraged him to deny that a radical departure from the recent past could begin in the 1890s. Moreover, his invented ideology and the position it required encouraged the exclusions inspired by his private affections. Thus, when he attempted to depict the decorative arts of the future in *News from Nowhere* (and occasionally in his lectures) he could conceive only of medieval forms and decorative ideas and of his own adaptations of these. That Morris's own patterns were original in that they continued to have the impact of the new, to be regarded as modern by the middle classes at the end of the century, complicates the situation by putting Morris-as-craftsman in contradiction to the Morris-as-political-theorist who denied, on grounds of theory, that there could be any art worth the name in the capitalist-dominated 1890s, a contradiction emphasised by the fact that many of the purchasers of the fabrics and wallpapers of Morris and Co. in the 1890s believed themselves not only up-to-date in the arts but forward-looking in politics.

In literature Morris's role is even more complex. He praised only narrative and incident, and created settings that are vaguely medieval, as in *The Wood beyond the World*, or pre-medieval, as in *The Roots of the Mountains* and *The House of the Wolfings*, to say nothing of the explicit re-invention of the fourteenth century as a model for English life in the twenty-first century in *News from Nowhere*. But he also, through the images of women he created, began, intentionally or not, to participate in the male response to the idea of the New Woman, response that included the *femme fatale* of Wilde's *Salomé*, the androgynous figures in Beardsley's drawings, George Gissing's *The Odd Women*, the self-destructive Sue Bridehead of *Jude the Obscure*, Ibsen's central figures in *A Doll's House* and *Hedda Gabler* (first staged in London in 1889 and 1890 respectively), as well as, a few years after the turn of the century, the women in Shaw's *Candida* and *Major Barbara*.

Most significantly, Morris's incarnations of the New Woman express no anxiety, in contrast to so many of the others of the 1890s, (literally) embodying as they do the efforts of male writers to come to terms with the representation of female desire as other than threatening. For the figures Morris created there is sufficient preparation in his socialist lectures; and they exist in all his romances, including *News from Nowhere*. Their athletic physicality and openness to air and sunshine make Morris one of the writers who in the 1890s affirmed and celebrated the human body; though the lack of evidence in his writing that he recognised he was partaking in a strained and conflicted movement makes his role even in this all-important matter complex and ambivalent.

Finally, what the young of the 1890s saw in Morris was 'really there'. His insistence on flattened forms in decoration, if rooted in his love of medieval design, anticipates Post-Impressionism, or more precisely Post-Impressionism embraces an approach to colour and form that is like Morris's approach to design, as Stella Tillyard has argued persuasively. The Morris who began by describing himself in 1868 as 'the idle singer of an empty day', thus giving aid and comfort to Walter Pater in his aestheticist interpretation of Morris, anticipates the later Morris, who in the early 1880s was already profoundly privileging art by implying over and over again in his socialist lectures and writings that the chief reason society needed to be changed was to give people the necessary conditions, rest and leisure, for creating and enjoying art. The young artists and writers of the 1890s were right to see the anti-bourgeois sentiment expressed in Morris's discourse on art and society as emblematic of their own feelings, however unable Morris himself was to recognise the kinship between what he felt and what they did.

What then is Morris's relevance for our Post-Modernist, post-naturalist, post-Marxist age? First, some assumptions and values of Modernist art that make Morris a problematic, if important, figure of the 1890s, have been abandoned. The Post-Modern, in its guise of eclectic user of the past, takes cognisance again, especially in its interest in popular literature, in narrative and incident: Morris's severe, blunt, but romance-oriented definition of the desirable in all literature other than the lyric poem. If we think of narrative and incident as structure, we can see too how his concept of what literature is – psychologically flat or at least dependent on dialogue and action for the suggestion of the complex – associates with his vivid sense of what pattern in wallpapers, textiles and, indeed, in the totality of furnishings in a room should be. Second, although in our *fin de siècle* the retreat from politics based on prophetic ideology has carried away with it the rationalist belief in the perfectibility of society and/or of humans as individuals, there remains the need to imagine utopias. Morris would have denied that his Marxism was fundamentally the expression of a utopian desire; but in his indifference to Marxist ideology – ideology as it was developing under the tutelage of German, French, English and indeed Russian revolutionaries in the 1890s – he shifted the emphasis of socialism in the late nineteenth century to, at best, what we have discovered in Marx's early thought and to what became the concern of the twentieth-century Frankfurt school of Marxist cultural historians. That is, the possibility that art is a central, profound and essential human concern and not part of a 'superstructure of society', inferior in ontological status to economic activity. It is a shift that opens the way to imagining new human perfections in society and individual life, new because brought about by new powers, those undreamed of by nineteenth-century Marxists in general.

Morris's outlook, however, appears to sit less comfortably with the global post-modern artistic-political vision and a society that has been radically transformed by electronic communication of information, promising – or threatening – to transform the very meaning of the art artefact and thus of the experiencing of art, as well as promising or threatening to equate the experiencing of virtual reality with the experiencing of reality itself. Morris, in this vision, is the brake; indeed the resistance to the dynamic of Post-Modernism at the end of the twentieth century. His essential *humanism* is at odds with whatever is anti-humanist, or post-humanist, including machines that shape thinking and feeling by establishing information itself as an almost autonomous and centralised phenomenon, product and commodity, thus threatening – not promising – to displace art defined as a humanist enterprise from the centre, leaving at best a radically transformed art that exists in a blur with other information and is indistinguishable from it.

Related to Morris's humanism was his detestation of the class distinctions in nineteenth-century English society. His awareness of the harshness and mean subtleties of class division, and of upper-class use of power, informed his strong feelings about the system, and accounts as much as anything for his enthusiastic but non-ideological embracing of nineteenth-century Marxism: non-ideological, that is, except for his assent to the doctrine of class conflict.

And derivative for Morris of his view of class division was his conception of work as pleasurable – a idea that intuitively broke with Marxism and its vision of labour abolished. For Morris, work is essential; but what is also essential is that it be carried on under social conditions that allow the natural pleasure in work to be experienced. And the idea that work is essential and naturally pleasurable leads us to the most radical of all Morris's ideas – his assertion that all work done with pleasure *is* art. Morris takes hold of Carlyle, Ruskin and Marx, and out of their ideas in combination makes something radically new.

Of special interest here, his view of pleasure as both a sensory phenomenon and a moral imperative permits us to see Morris's ideas as resonant with a continuity between Modernism and Post-Modernism. Modernism's aestheticising morality of art, and its Paterian equation of aesthetic experience with pleasure, even happiness, remain at the root of Post-Modernism, even as the latter enlarges and makes radically inclusive the range of cultural artefacts to be called art.

However, Modernism unknowingly but severely qualified the morality of pleasure, of art as pleasure, when it hierarchically privileged the aesthetic concept of 'organic form' and the artists who produced it. Moreover, this privileging led not only away from an egalitarian view of what is art and who is an artist but towards the homeomorphic political doctrine of the 'organic society' (e.g. fascism), as the cure for the fragmentation and 'decay of values' in modern society. For Morris, in contrast, though he stumbled over a truly egalitarian answer to the question, 'What is art?', the pursuit of pleasure led to the promotion of the open society. It led to a vision of social and political control so minimal that it has often been called by critics and interpreters an anarchist vision. In the late 1990s, it is Post-Modernism that expresses Morris's commitment. It is Post-Modernism that returns to politics by perceiving the desire for pleasure as the starting-point for imagining the good society for everyone; where the life of the senses is fully lived by all; where, that is, aesthetic sensibility, historically defined, is universally gratified; and where, in the process, the very idea of social and political control would be forced, once more in history, to try to reconcile itself with the idea that all should have the freedom to become themselves.

Morris had another moral–social principle, or vision, that resonates today: that for individuals to become themselves fully, the idea and practice of fellowship must flourish; a principle somewhat akin to Marx's early concept that self-realisation for a human is self-realisation as a species being.

And if by fellowship Morris sometimes meant being surrounded by dependents upon whom he could in turn depend, he at least incorporated into the idea of a psychological and physical space in which work is carried on the premise that authentic work is always pleasurable, is equated with art and is, finally, a social activity; one requiring, furthermore, a political frame that encourages it to be so. Today, as the image of the isolated artist wanes, and the old meaning of isolation disappears in the cyberspace in which we work, we move dangerously and perhaps unfortunately towards achieving in that arena a form of connectedness eerily embodying some of the meanings of fellowship based on work associated with visions like Morris's. The similarity, however, is very likely an illusion, in the old, moralistic meaning of illusion. The social and political control needed to keep the machines operating and linked with each other as easily suggest the coercive enforcement Morris denounced and warned against as they do the defining and maintaining of a space in which fellowship, or even its successor, can prosper.

Relationships, and the earlier discussion of Morris and the New Woman, bring into focus a special friendship of his; a friendship of many years but one that takes on itself the special colouration of the 1890s. I speak of his closeness to Georgiana Burne-Jones, the wife of his famously close friend, Edward Burne-Jones. Who was she, and what was she to Morris? Companion, soulmate, a person sympathetic on the whole to his politics, she was above all a woman of mind: a writer, a political participant, a friend of George Eliot. She was also the seemingly patient and enduring wife of a womanising husband; and a link through her sisters to Rudyard Kipling and Stanley Baldwin, both her nephews; as well as to the painter Edward Poynter, her brother-in-law. She was an active figure, one who affected public life in the 1890s, at least locally, and (of importance here) the life of William Morris. Their sympathetic response to each other, strongly suggested by what is left of their correspondence, is a significant fact about *him* in his relations with others. In enabling us to see or construct Morris in the 1890s, it stands alongside his self-abnegating role in his relationship with Jane Morris and his splendid fulfilment of the role of a father to Jenny (and to some degree to his other daughter, May). It demonstrates that despite his fantasies of female sex slaves in *The Well at the World's End*, one of his romances of the 1890s (it is the villains of course who enslave these scantily clad and barefoot figures), and despite his view of housework as particularly congenial work for women in *News from Nowhere*, Morris related to the power of mind in women: to intellectual equality, the unparalled equality in the last analysis. He was a man who celebrated beauty, and who demonstrated in his friendship with Georgiana Burne-Jones that he could recognise beauty of intellect, as well as of art object, face or human form.

His taking pleasure in the fact there was intellectual equality between himself and Georgiana Burne-Jones looms large in the image of Morris as a man of the 1890s present in the 1990s. It is a bridge, too, to the nature of his heroism, which was to confront honestly – with intellectual vigour – the public issues of the day and, from our perspective, unerringly identify the important issues. He was also, however, a series of enigmatic surfaces: surfaces like those that successfully represent ideas of beauty and social justice but are not transparent. There is never a confessional mode in Morris's poems, prose narratives, or even letters. That he successfully transcended loss and defeat in his relations with Jane Morris, turning the self to public action in earlier years when she took Rossetti as her lover; and to productive labour when in middle age she accepted Wilfrid Scawen Blunt in the role, is to speak again of surfaces. The feelings that accompanied his deferring to Rossetti and Blunt are concealed from us, and the surfaces we do see tell us only how Morris subtracted the sexual in love – as pleasure – from the potential of his own life and how, indeed courageously, he asked of art and political struggle the gratification of his desires. Whether he thus fulfilled them or restricted them we shall never know, but, again on the surface, apparent resignation was a fact; and so, too, was refusal to succumb to despair, to let it lead to inaction. That he seldom revealed more than surfaces, but also never gave way to whatever was painful under them, leaves finally a question: is it appropriate or accurate to speak of Morris as self-alienated because self-concealed, when he presented so sharp and clear an image of himself *in* his work and in the realm of public action? It is not a rhetorical question; like many such questions concerning Morris, through the answers we give to it we define ourselves.

Whatever answers we give, however, some last observations do not depend on them. In politics it is the performative nature of his lectures and essays that made the difference. He guided his listeners and readers away from economics as a social science, towards economics as a moral issue, and towards both recognition and confrontation of themselves as creative, sentient beings. In addition, whatever his own fears and failings, he asserted the absolute need for decency in all human intercourse. He failed in that decency in his relations with the immediate generation of artists about to take the place of his own in the 1890s; for those artists required of him, without his knowing it, a partial self-deconstruction for which he was not ready. But perhaps the best way to explain even this, if not justify it, is to say that despite the perception of him as a modernist by the writers and artists of the 1890s, he in fact skipped a cultural generation in defining himself through his enthusiasms and dislikes in the arts and belongs to Modernism only in special ways. His is a voice actually for Post-Modernism, or for post-Post-Modernism (a movement waiting not so much to be born as to be named). For we shall be asked to decide whether aesthetic experience is to be distinguished from other pleasurable kinds; whether there exists an authentic and enduring self, the bedrock of humanism; and finally, whether there can be survival of human society without decency. In the moral and aesthetic space in which we debate these questions Morris will be a presence, not to be ignored.

As for the last mentioned, decency, it is a fundamental fact of Morris's life and doctrine, looming large, whatever anti-climactic feeling may attend it in context here. It is always fragile, but if it can inform and thus sustain a life founded on pleasure in bodily activity, making, viewing, touching and listening, it will help transform pleasure into something larger than itself: a basis for community (as Terry Eagleton has also observed, from a different perspective). Morris's contemporaries in the 1890s must have sensed this possiblity in his vision. They transformed *him* into something larger than the sum of his parts. And the balance of the evidence for doing so, or not, is on their side, as we can see more clearly now than at any earlier time in this century. With whatever necessary reservations, we can happily do the same.

MORRIS IN CONTEXT

Clive Wainwright

Whenever the posthumous fame of someone, whether politician, scientist, soldier, artist or designer, grows to a certain level this fame eclipses in our eyes that of their contemporaries in the same field. Once this process has taken place it is very difficult objectively to compare their contribution to their particular field with that of others working in it at the same time. Galileo was not the only scientist in Pisa nor Mackintosh the only architect in Glasgow at the period when they flourished, but most of us would be hard put to it to name others. It is not always thus, for Monet, Cézanne and Sisley were all painting in Paris at the same time and do not eclipse one another, but until recently they collectively eclipsed several prominent academic painters of the period. When, however, the fame of one particular person has been established for several decades even though there is some fashion in these matters it is rare for one of their contemporaries suddenly to overtake them.

William Morris is just such a case; he is a household name and is today certainly the best-known nineteenth-century English designer, and to many people probably the only one they could readily name. This does not automatically make him the best or most innovative and interesting English designer of the second half of the nineteenth century, though if it happens that he was not the debate about who was would be fierce. Looking back from the late twentieth century in an attempt to arrive at an objective opinion of how historical figures viewed each other and were viewed by the population at large, and in the case of designers how their designs were viewed, is fraught with pitfalls. While the haphazard and sparse survival of the documentation, artefacts and indeed the names of designers during earlier periods is such that only a tentative attempt can be made, with the nineteenth century, however, such a vast mass of objects and documentation survives that the prospect of making sense of it is daunting indeed. For instance, the National Art Library has over 2,000 publications on the 1851 exhibition alone. The problem was perhaps best summed up in 1918 by Lytton Strachey in the preface to *Eminent Victorians*:

> Concerning the Age which has just passed, our fathers and our grandfathers have poured forth and accumulated so vast a quantity of information that the industry of a Ranke would be submerged by it, and the perspicacity of a Gibbon would quail before it. It is not by the direct method that the explorer of the past can hope to depict that singular epoch. If he is wise, he will adopt a subtler strategy…he will row out over the great ocean of material, and lower down into it, here and there, a little bucket, which will bring up to the light of day some characteristic specimen, from those far depths, to be examined with careful curiosity.

I shall dredge up in my bucket a few quotations and designs to make my points, but there are likely to be many others equally or, indeed, more appropriate.

Because of the survival of the Arts and Crafts Movement into the 1920s and the growth of the socialist movement, the name of Morris probably remained in the public mind, but it was the continuing existence of Morris and Co. itself that played the most important part. Nowhere is this more clearly demonstrated than in the catalogue of that important milestone of the Victorian Revival the 'Victorian Exhibition in aid of St Bartholomew's Hospital' which ran throughout June 1931 at 23A Bruton Street just off Bond Street. The exhibition was organised by a committee that included Albert Richardson, H.S. Goodhart-Rendel and Oliver Bernard, and was chaired by Sir Cecil Harcourt-Smith the Surveyor of the King's Works of Art who had been director of the Victoria and Albert Museum. But the importance for the Morris story is that Morris and Co. designed and furnished a:

Morris Boudoir Sitting Room. Morris furniture, wallpapers, chintzes, carpet, etc; Burne-Jones tapestry; De Morgan pottery, Benson metalwork and Powell glass from the designs of Philip Webb...When William Morris, the poet, newly married, and inspired by the influence of D.G.Rossetti, wished to build himself a house, his fastidious taste rejected the barbarous decorations of the period and forced him to design and make practically everything he needed. Out of this arose the famous decorative 'Morris Movement', where the dyeing, weaving, chintz-printing, stained glass and arras tapestry work instituted by him in 1861 still goes on.

The whole was arranged by H.C.Marillier, who had been the Managing Director of Morris and Co. since 1905 and had known Morris himself, thus we see him keeping the name of the firm before the public and setting it firmly at the heart of the Victorian Revival. The company would no doubt have been particularly keen to help had the suggestion of the *Yorkshire Daily Post* that 'A permanent Victorian Room should be established at the Victoria & Albert Museum – a room which would faithfully re-create the domestic background of our grandparents' lives' been taken up.

Three years later, in 1934, the Museum did hold a Morris exhibition. Then in 1936 Nikolaus Pevsner in his seminal book, *Pioneers of the Modern Movement from William Morris to Walter Gropius*, wrote:

Morris was the first artist (not the first thinker, for Ruskin had preceded him) to realise how precarious and decayed the social foundations of art had become during the centuries since the Renaissance, and especially during the years since the Industrial Revolution...Morris made up his mind to open a firm, the firm of Morris, Marshall & Faulkner, Fine Art Workmen in Painting, Carving, Furniture and Metals. This event marks the beginning of a new era in Western art.

The index is revealing; there are thirty-seven references to Morris, one to Dresser, one to Pugin and none to Owen Jones. Much has been written about *Pioneers*, for it is a remarkable book; Pevsner himself, when I once discussed it with him in the 1960s, readily admitted that he by then viewed the subject rather differently. He still, however, concluded one of his last books thus: 'So I may be excused if I do not continue this summary of nineteenth century architectural writing to the year 1900. There is a good reason, I think, why Morris should remain the end, although as I have shown in my earlier book [*Pioneers*], he is a beginning too' (*Some Architectural Writers of the Nineteenth Century*, London, 1972 p.288). *Pioneers*, however, shaped our thinking and the teaching of the history of the applied arts for forty years and the name of Morris was there in the title as the true harbinger of modern design.

The long shadow of *Pioneers* certainly lies over that key exhibition, *Victorian and Edwardian Decorative Arts*, in 1952 which was to lead in the 1960s to the opening of the Victorian Galleries at the Victoria and Albert Museum. The section of the catalogue on Morris reads thus:

Morris's whole life was a crusade against the debased standards of mid-Victorian mass-production which he traced to the influence of machine manufacture and the disappearance of honest and satisfying hand-craftsmanship. His own particular contribution was in the field of flat pattern-making in which his fertility was prodigious and his genius unsurpassed.

As we historians of the applied arts and architecture move out of the Post-Modern phase of the early 1990s into the sunlit uplands of the New Historicism, we have access to a far wider range of modern publications that analyse nineteenth-century design than did Pevsner. Even so, the coverage of Morris's contemporaries is still patchy, there are no analytical biographies of major architects and designers such as Owen Jones, G.E.Street, Pugin, William White, Philip Webb and J.P.Seddon. Then we have none for the design theorists such as Henry Cole and no analytical study of the growth of those collections in the South Kensington Museum that Cole so actively promoted and William Morris and his contemporaries so constantly used for inspiration. Even for Ruskin, from whom Morris absorbed more ideas than from any other source, though there are numerous recent studies of specific aspects of his career we only have the first volume of Tim Hilton's important biography. Yet with Morris, quite apart from Fiona MacCarthy's splendid and massive new biography, we have dozens of other books, several quite recent biographies and Norman Kelvin's magisterial edition of Morris's letters about to be completed. If sheer volume of publication is any guide Morris must be more significant than any of the other designers. This imbalance does make it very difficult directly to compare Morris with the people I have mentioned. The situation is gradually becoming easier year by year; we now have biographies of Burges, Butterfield, Dresser and Shaw, and Ruskin studies are undergoing a renaissance thanks to the Ruskin Programme at Lancaster University.

As this catalogue demonstrates, it is the multi-faceted nature of Morris's achievement that is so attractive to scholars in so many areas. Here was a man who could achieve a good standard in so many disciplines yet in most of these, as one would expect, he could not actually compete with the professionals. The English love the inspired amateur who is willing to have a go at anything and especially one who has sufficient wealth to subsidise his experiments as artist and architect. Had Morris persevered in Street's office he might have made a good architect or in Rossetti's studio a good painter. Street however had to make a go of architecture to make a living and Rossetti was in a similar position as a painter. Morris's poetry is interesting and good and was highly rated by many of his contemporaries, but today we realise that he was no Tennyson, Browning, Hopkins or even a Rossetti. His writings about art, architecture and design are crucial to any understanding of nineteenth-century culture, but he was no Ruskin, Jones, Arnold or Pugin. Similarly, his political writing is fascinating, but whether it was as sound theoretically as that of several of his contemporaries is in my opinion still an open question.

Let us now turn to Morris and design, first some of his writings. In his lecture, 'Hopes and Fears for Art', given at Birmingham in the late 1870s (published in 1883) Morris stated: 'That thing which I understand by real art is the expression by man of his pleasure in labour. I do not believe he can be happy in his labour without expressing that happiness; and especially is this so when he is at work at anything in which he specially excels'. Ruskin had been lecturing and writing about this very question since the late 1840s, for example in 1856 in the discussion after a lecture on this subject given by the headmaster of the very Government School of Art in Birmingham where Morris was to give his lecture Ruskin interjected, 'In no way therefore could good art ever become cheap in production…The Paper seemed to dwell wholly upon the advantage of art to the consumer, or only to the producer as a mercantile matter. He was sorry it did not show the effect of the production of art on the workman; surely the happiness of the workman was a thing which ought to be considered?' (George Wallis, *Recent Progress in Design as applied to Manufacture*, London, 1856, p.9). There are many other Ruskin books and essays which Morris would have read, indeed several, including *The Seven Lamps of Architecture* of 1849, were published earlier than 1856, but this statement by Ruskin is less well known today. Morris would have known Wallis, who shortly after this moved to the South Kensington Museum.

Here is Morris on the subject of furniture construction, this time in a lecture ('The Lesser Arts of Life') in 1882:

> For us to set to work to imitate the minor whims of the *blasé* and bankrupt French
> aristocracy of Louis XV's time, seems to me merely ridiculous. So I say our furniture should
> be good citizens furniture, solid well made in workmanship, and in design should have
> nothing about it that is not easily defensible, no monstrosities or extravagances, not even of
> beauty, lest we weary of it: as to matters of construction, it should not have to depend on
> the special skill of a very picked workman, or the superexcellence of his glue, but be made
> on the proper principles of the art of joinery.

In the 1840s Pugin in his writings was pursuing this very line and many examples could be given, he even went as far in one of his letters about furniture construction to Crace his cabinet maker as drawing a glue-pot and labelling it 'The modern joint' (see Atterbury and Wainwright, *Pugin*, London, 1994, p.256).

In his most influential book on design, *The True Principles of Pointed or Christian Architecture*, (1841), Pugin wrote, 'The strength of wood-work is attained by bracing the various pieces together on geometrical principles'. Interestingly, one of the few pieces of furniture that Morris himself designed is wholly indebted to Pugin. The table (cat.no.J.3) dates from about 1856 and is clearly directly inspired by the table designed by G.E.Street in about 1855 (cat.no.J.2) for Cuddesdon

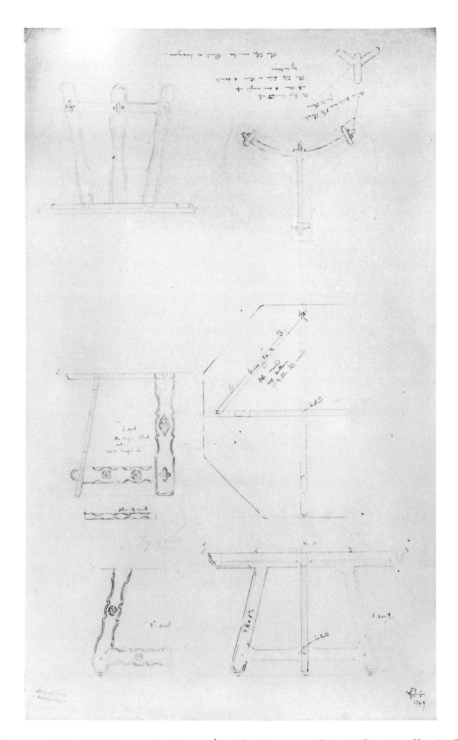

Fig.111 Design for a round table by
A.W.N.Pugin.

College near Oxford – it is no coincidence that Morris was working in Street's office in Oxford for the first half of 1856. But the Street table was inspired by one of Pugin's round tables of the late 1840s, and further to strengthen the connection the Cuddesdon table was made by George Myers who made several pieces of the Pugin furniture shown in the 1851 exhibition. Indeed, whilst Morris like his mentor Ruskin never paid public tribute to his debt to Pugin, Street was honest about his debt and in 1853 the year after Pugin's death wrote of Pugin: 'His tables did not depend upon crockets, finials and flying buttresses for all their character, but were real, simple, and properly constructional provisions for certain wants, with no more material consumed in their construction than was necessary for their solidity, and no sham or incongruous ornaments' ('On the Revival of the Ancient Style of Domestic Architecture', *The Ecclesiologist*, XIV, 1853, p.76). Morris would of course have known Street's article.

It was Street who also helped promote Morris's interest in a radical new departure just beginning in furniture design. In 1856 Street took Morris to Lille in northern France to see an exhibition of the designs for the new Cathedral in Lille. The competition had been won by Burges and his partner Clutton – Street had come second – and one of their drawings depicts an elaborately painted organ case which was Burges's first design for a piece of painted furniture. Even here the origin goes back to Pugin and to the painted case he designed in the late 1840s for Jesus College Chapel, Cambridge (see *Pugin*, 1994, pl.35). Burges soon had made several pieces of painted furniture, the most elaborate being for his early patron H.G.Yatman. Morris knew Burges, and in 1865 was to collaborate with him on a scheme of interior decoration at Oakwood Court in Yorkshire, and in the run up to the 1862 exhibition he and his circle began to experiment with painted furniture, including a painted chair for Morris's rooms in Red Lion Square. The earliest surviving piece is the Prioress's Tale Wardrobe designed by Webb and painted by Burne-Jones as a present for Morris, and for the 1862 exhibition itself Morris painted the celebrated St George Cabinet (cat.no.J.18).

Burges showed several painted pieces in the exhibition, including the Wines and Beers Cabinet. Burges, who was to publish far more on medieval art and architecture than Morris and had carefully studied the surviving pieces of early painted furniture in the cathedrals of Noyon and Bayeux, realised that in the Middle Ages they made painted furniture rather than just furniture that was painted. The distinction is a very real one that Webb and Morris had at this date not yet grasped. With a piece of painted furniture the programme of decoration is designed to fit the object and the figurative painted panels are contained within an architectonic framework of abstract patterns that act as frames, whereas the whole front of the Prioress's Tale Wardrobe is painted, like an easel painting so that when the door opens the picture itself splits in the middle. The doors of the St George Cabinet look as though they are easel paintings that have been painted in a studio and then attached

Fig.112 Wine and Beers Cabinet by William Burges.

Fig.113 Detail of above.

Fig.114 Yatman wool and flax wardrobe by William Burges.

to the cabinet. The Yatman pieces and the Wines and Beers follow the medieval tradition, and the doors have separate pictures on each with an architectonic frame.

The stands of the medieval pieces are designed as a integral part of the whole cabinet, but the St George Cabinet is a long rectangular box which lies on a stand like an elaborate coffin about to be removed for burial from its stand. To one contemporary observer, 'The chest is hardly better made than an ordinary egg-chest, or packing case…The price is fifty guineas' (*The Building News*, 8 Aug., 1862, p. 99). The stand itself is more interesting, but in construction and in the curved braces Webb is wholly indebted to Pugin. By contrast the Wines and Beers has a stand designed and painted as an integral part of the whole design.

Then there is the whole question of iconography, for following the Puginian rules of honesty the purpose of the piece should be expressed in the scenes painted upon it. Burges carefully followed this principle: one of the Yatman pieces is a writing desk, so writing and printing figures in the paintings; another Yatman piece is a wardrobe, so textile processes are shown, and the battle between the wines and beers is wholly appropriate for a drinks cabinet. Indeed, on the latter cabinet (fig.112), at the suggestion of Burges, to reinforce this point Poynter has painted portraits of Burges's friends labelled with their favourite drinks – fig.113 shows Whistler whose tipple was apparently gin sling. What has Chaucer's Prioress to do with the contents of a wardrobe or St George with the function of a cabinet?

Morris and Webb also benefited from Burges's scholarship in the technique they used in their painted pieces; they employed a medieval technique that Burges had used for his Yatman Cabinet or desk (now in the V&A). This was the technique described by Theophilus, 'Take tin leaf, not covered with varnish nor coloured with saffron, but simply as it is, and diligently polished, and with it cover the place on which you wish to paint. Then grind the colours to be laid on most carefully with linseed oil, and when very fine lay them on with a pencil and allow to dry' (*An Essay upon the Various Arts in Three Books...*, London, 1847, p.35). Morris and Webb used it inside the St George Cabinet and on the whole of the outside of the painted chest (cat.no.J.19) also shown in the 1862 exhibition.

The criticisms I have made when comparing the Morris painted pieces with the Burges ones were echoed by many of the critics writing about the 1862 exhibition. Most critics praised the design and construction of the Burges pieces, but attacked the Morris ones:

> The specimens exhibited by Mr. Burges in particular will well repay examination...Some painted and japanned furniture, exhibited by Messrs. Morris, Marshall, and Co., is simply preposterous. We believe that it is meant to be inexpensive; but some of the affixed prices scarcely bear out the assertion. We must totally decline to praise the design and execution of these specimens. The colouring in particular is crude and unpleasing, while the design is laboriously grotesque (*The Ecclesiologist*, XXIII, 1862, pp. 170–71).

In the event the South Kensington Museum bought the Wines and Beers Cabinet because it was a more successful design than any of the Morris pieces; the St George Cabinet was not acquired until the twentieth century. The architect and designer Charles Lock Eastlake, who was soon to publish his influential book *Hints on Household Taste*, wrote:

> It is a curious and interesting epidemic this 'moyen age' mania in our island at the present time: when and how did it arise? From Pugin's ashes or the writings of Ruskin?...We see evidences of it more or less in every church, in every home, in every shop we enter. It is pointing our windows, and inlaying our cabinets, and gothicizing the plates we eat from, the chairs on which we sit, the papers on our walls. It influences the bindings of our books, the colour of our carpets, the shape of our beer-jugs, picture frames, candlesticks-what not? As we strolled into the court devoted to messrs Morris and Co.'s mediaeval furniture, tapestries &c., who could believe that it represented manufactures of the 19th century – the age, *par excellence* of cog wheels and steam rams and rifled cannon? Six hundred years have passed since the style of yon cabinet was in vogue. (*London Society*, Aug. 1862, p.106)

Fig.115 *Brocatel* woven silk and cotton textile, designed by Morris or Henry Dearle, *c.*1888 (cat.no.M.88).

Fig.116 Printed cotton designed by Pugin, *c.*1850.

Fig. 117 Plate from Pugin's *Floriated Ornament*, published in 1849.

Fig. 118 E.W. Godwin, design for *Butterfly Brocade* woven silk, about 1874.

Fig. 119 Watercolour of naturalistic ornament by Christopher Dresser.

Let us look at another example in the field in which Morris excelled as a designer. In a lecture entitled 'Textiles' and published by the Arts and Crafts Society in 1893 he stated that, 'Never introduce any shading for the purpose of making an object look round…beautiful and logical form relieved from the ground by well-managed contrast or gradation, and lying flat on the ground will never weary the eye'. More than fifty years earlier, in his seminal book *True Principles*, Pugin had written, 'Flock papers are admirable substitutes for ancient hangings, but then they must consist of a pattern *without shadow*, with the forms relieved by the introduction of harmonious colours'. Pugin had not invented this idea, but, along with other theories relating to 'honest' design and construction, he brought it to the attention of the generation of designers who took up his ideas following his early death in 1852.

In *The Lesser Arts of Life* in 1882 Morris wrote, 'Lastly, love of nature in all its forms must be the ruling spirit of such works of art as we are considering', yet Pugin had written in 1849, '*Nature* supplied the mediaeval artists with all their forms and ideas; the same inexhaustible source is open to us: and if we go to the *fountain head*, we shall produce a multitude of beautiful designs in the same spirit of the old, but new in form' (*Floriated Ornament*, 1849). Let us compare a Morris textile – in both cases a silk brocatelle – (fig.115) with a Pugin one (fig.116). The illustrations of *Floriated Ornament* set new standards for the transformation of plant forms into flat pattern applicable to painted decoration, wallpapers and textiles. It and those that followed from the pens of Owen Jones, Bruce Talbert, Edward Godwin and Christopher Dresser built on Pugin's foundations and all were vital reference books to the Morris generation of designers. It is interesting to compare the naturalistic flat-pattern designs of these designers with those of Morris.

I am not, in all this discussion and quotation from other authors, accusing Morris of just copying others, but no designer works in a vacuum unaware of both what his predecessors and contemporaries have and are creating. Innovation in designs happens in fits and starts and then everyone builds on such innovation – the vital question is how much did Morris innovate? Are his designs actually better than those of Pugin, Jones and Dresser? You must judge for yourself from the original objects in the exhibition and from the illustrations in this catalogue. For me at least, Morris's flat-pattern designs, whether for textiles, wallpaper or stained glass, lack the bite and excitement that characterises the best designs of several of his contemporaries. As so clearly shown by Harvey and Press in their recent book, Morris was an extremely good businessman and good at marketing the Morris and Co. products to a fast-growing domestic market. Did he perhaps take a less radical line with his designs, knowing that by making them a little more anodyne and prettier they would appeal to a far wider middle-class market? Perhaps he was not even aware that he was not on the cutting edge of design?

Perhaps Morris did the same with his writing, much of which was first given as lectures. These essays and his lectures influenced two generations, so probably it does not matter that not all the ideas in them were his own – *he* popularised them by the sheer force of his personality, making them available to the widest possible audience. That the sheer magnetism of his personality and his conversation often made a more lasting impact than his actual ideas is clear from the reminiscences of those who knew him him. For instance, on 12 March 1869 Henry James met Morris: 'His talk is indeed wonderfully to the point and remarkable for clear good sense. He said no one thing that I remember, but I was struck with the very good judgement shewn in everything he uttered…All his designs are as good (or rather nearly so) as his poetry'. His ability to reorganise and reiterate the ideas of other people is nowhere more apparent than with his foundation of SPAB, and I consider this to be his most important contribution to our world today. Morris might well have agreed, for as Aymer Vallance wrote in 1897:

> Had Mr Morris been asked which one in preference to any other of his undertakings he considered his greatest and best, he would have had no hesitation in naming the Society for the Protection of Ancient Buildings…his attention was awakened to the urgency of the subject by his study of John Ruskin. Indeed so entirely do the opinions of the two writers agree on these points, that in many a passage Ruskin expresses himself in terms that, removed from the context, might well be mistaken by anyone not previously acquainted with it for an utterance of Morris and *vice versa*.

Here we see the post-Morris hagiographical engine in motion – how logically could one mistake things written by Morris for those written by Ruskin – Vallance is hinting that Morris's writings might be mistaken for Ruskin's even though the latter were written first. The 'Lamp of Memory' chapter in *Seven Lamps of Architecture* was published in 1849, nearly thirty years before the foundation of SPAB. Morris was quite open about his debt to Ruskin and wrote a letter to him about using quotations from him. Ruskin had written, 'I must not leave the truth unstated, that is again no question of expedience or feeling whether we shall preserve the buildings of past times or not. *We have no right whatever to touch them.* They are not ours. They belong partly to those who built them, and partly to all generations of mankind who are to follow us'. Morris, in a speech to SPAB at their twelfth annual meeting in July 1889, made use of Ruskin's powerful image of our responsibility to our descendants, though to my ear rather blunted the impact of Ruskin's words: 'These old buildings do not belong to us only; that they have belonged to our forefathers, and they will belong to our descendants unless we play them false. They are in no sense our property to do as we like with. We are only trustees for those who come after us'.

Interestingly, Morris was by no means the first to use this image – indeed he may well have been at a lecture of 1866 with the very Ruskinian title of 'New Lamps for Old Ones' on the subject of the restoration of old buildings. He could also have read the published version in *Building News*

Fig. 120 Owen Jones, design for
Stanhope woven silk textile, 1872.

Fig. 121 Woven silk textile designed by
B. J. Talbert, 1875–80.

for 8 June of the same year. The lecture was given by Morris's friend the architect J. P. Seddon at the Architectural Association. Seddon, who very much captured the tone of Ruskin's original, said, 'To preserve unmutilated the precious structures which have descended to them as heirlooms from the past – not to be wantonly altered to serve a passing purpose, but tenderly and reverentially cared for to hand down in no worse condition to generations yet to come'. It was, however, Morris not Ruskin or Seddon who *actually* brought the SPAB into being and it has always and still does play a major role in saving buildings.

To conclude, however, with the Morris designs that we all know so well; pause to look at the great number of modern reprints of his textiles and wallpapers that grace so many houses and hotels today and ask yourself how good are they? They might be the visual Muzak of the 1990s, Muzak is easy listening, Morris to our generation is certainly easy looking.

MORRIS AFTER MORRIS

Paul Greenhalgh

William Morris died on 3 October 1896. It was never likely that he would be allowed a quiet passing. Even as the two-wheeled harvest cart decked in willow branches delivered him up to Kelmscott churchyard, the processes of interpretation had begun as to what exactly his life had been about, and what his oeuvre implied for the future.

The *Daily News* for Monday 5 October 1896 observed in its obituary that, he 'was…distinguished in several distinct ways, no one of which had any obvious and distinct relation to any of the others'. As the nineteenth century had seemingly demonstrated that there was not one William Morris but several, so the twentieth was about to enjoy a host of Morrises. Indeed, with the man himself out of the way, the process of his cloning into many beings went ahead unencumbered and at a far faster pace. The several William Morrises existing at the level of practice – designer, artist, poet, political activist, cultural theorist, conservationist, ecologist – had been held in reasonable proximity before 1896 by the man himself. His careers and commitments cohered through him. After his death however, a process of fragmentation took place which gave rise to a number of independent versions of the man, some overtly opposed to others.

The practices were separated out by the subject specialists. In itself, this process was natural and quite usual. It matters little if, say, the lovers of textile or art theory have not corresponded with the conservationists or littérateurs. But what has mattered has been the tendency of apologists to break down – often unwittingly – what might be described as the *ethical* consistency of Morris. E. P. Thompson, in a seminal lecture of 1959, identified 'a quality which permeates all of [his] activities and gives to them a certain unity' (see London, ICA, 1984, p.129). This 'certain unity' is the *ethic*, the ideological and psychological underpinning of all Morris's activities. The *ethic* is the thread that holds together the beads, his practices. The breaking of this thread resulted in a disjuncture between the intellectual underpinning and the material outcomes. The way he thought about things – furniture, socialism, poetry, old buildings – was separated from the things themselves. The twentieth century is strewn with partial and compartmentalised understandings of the man and his work.

Morris's greatest contribution to the twentieth century has undoubtedly been in the visual arts and related areas. Even at this site of his greatest influence, however, the space that was created between his ethics and aesthetics has proven a key factor in our interpretation of him. This space, and others like it, stemmed initially from a widespread desire to separate his political life from the rest. The treatment of his politics should therefore be dealt with first.

Immediately after his death, numerous writers depicted his political life as little more than a passing buffoonery. One, writing in the *Pall Mall Gazette* of 5 October 1896 believed he 'imagined himself a practical politician', and claimed that he 'used to propound his creed with a vehemence of sincerity that was one quarter comic and three parts pathetic'. Another, in *The Times* published the same day, judged his politics to be 'the results of a warm heart and a mistaken enthusiasm; they indicate not the strength of the man, but his weakness, and are as nothing compared with the lasting work of his better genius'.

Substantial publications and exhibitions set a trend that came to hold sway. J. W. Mackail's *The Life of William Morris* of 1899, for example, barely mentions socialism, and *A Brief Sketch of the Morris Movement*, published by Morris and Co. in 1911, made a single reference to his 'Utopian propaganda', which was seen as being 'partly responsible for his untimely death'. In fact, Aymer Vallance's biography (1897), written with Morris's permission, was the only one published in the wake of his

PIONEERS OF THE
MODERN MOVEMENT

FROM WILLIAM MORRIS
TO WALTER GROPIUS

BY NIKOLAUS PEVSNER

LONDON: FABER & FABER

Fig. 122 Frontispiece from the first edition of Nikolaus Pevsner's *Pioneers of the Modern Movement*, 1936.

death, which contained extensive reference to his politics. Museums dealt with him little better. An important exhibition at the Victoria and Albert Museum in 1934, celebrating the centenary of his birth, ignored the subject.

The second half of the century has seen a steady reversal of this trend. As we commemorate the centenary of his death, we can say with some confidence that Morris's politics have been restored to him. The rehabilitation occurred after the Second World War in the form of corrective monographs and exhibitions. Notable landmarks in this regard are E. P. Thompson's *William Morris: Romantic to Revolutionary* (1955), Paul Meier's *William Morris: The Marxist Dreamer* (1978) and the Institute of Contemporary Arts exhibition *William Morris Today* (1984).

However, this late analysis and celebration of his politics has not necessarily led to a reintegration of them into the total oeuvre. Lauded or derided, the politics have remained isolated. Indeed, perhaps all persuasions fail to recognise what would have been a sad truth for Morris himself, that his socialism has had no significant impact in the political arena during the twentieth century. His intense idealism has not proved a useful model for real action; our natural habitat is still nowhere near Nowhere.

His poetry has fared even less well than his politics, regardless of the perspective taken on it. It has been a striking reversal, as his obituaries show that many Victorians considered his poetry to be his most important aspect. The *St James Budget* for Friday 9 October 1896 described him unequivocally as 'William Morris, the poet'. *The Times* made the claim that he was 'a poet, and one of our half dozen best poets, even when Tennyson and Browning were alive'. But in stating that he 'will always rank as one of the greatest poets of our era, besides being remembered as one of the ablest of the latter-day writers of prose romance', *The Globe* (5 Oct.1896) made an assertion that would be doubted even before the First World War and completely ignored after it.

Morris the theorist and practitioner in the visual arts has remained most fully alive. His influence has been wide and multifarious. For example, his views on the conservation of works of art of all kinds have been vital. The Society for the Protection of Ancient Buildings has provided a model for pressure groups and professional conservators throughout the century.

At the simplest and most direct level, he and his company provided us with a model of domestic decor. In 1903, C.L.Eastlake noted that '…it is certain that the picturesque element which has become conspicuous in the appointment of many English homes may be traced to the early efforts of William Morris and Burne-Jones' (*Magazine of Art*, 1903, p.37). Morris himself was a shrewd and able businessman who understood the needs of commercial life, and who left behind him an active and bullish company as Harvey and Press have shown. Largely through its own efforts, the 'Morris Movement' appeared to be embracing the world as described in the firm's 1911 publication, *A Brief Sketch of the Morris Movement*:

> The question is sometimes asked: 'Do people still buy Morris goods?' The answer is 'Yes',
> and in larger numbers than ever, as the influence of the Morris Movement penetrates
> further and further afield. India, Canada, America, Australia and the Continent all furnish
> their quota of admirers of the Morris style and lovers of his pure bright colours and
> vigorous designs.

Fig.123 One of the coronation thrones designed and embroidered by Morris & Co. for George V's coronation in 1910. Taken from a specially published brochure.

The commercial aspect partly explains the antipathy of the company towards his politics. Apparently socialism did not make economic sense. Throughout the twentieth century Morris and Co. products, as well as reproductions and derivations from them, have been continuously popular in the absence of any real political or ethical agenda.

Indeed, separated from its underlying ethic, the Morris 'look' proved susceptible to forms of appropriation far wider than the commercial. Most notably, it received the attentions of nationalists. Late nineteenth- and early twentieth-century Europe bristled with nationalist pride. The turmoil of a world going through social, political and economic modernisation led to a reaction in the form of a revival of ethnic values and vernacularism. As Eric Hobsbawm has observed, '…with the decline of real communities to which people had been used – village and kin, parish and barrio, gild, confraternity or whatever – their members felt a need for something to take their place' (Hobsbawm, p. 148).

Both large and small nations used the vernacular to identify and present themselves to the world. Morris and the Arts and Crafts Movement provided a model for this activity. Historian Nicola Gordon Bowe has asserted that

> The Arts and Crafts movement which had evolved in England from the Utopian socialism
> and romantic medievalism of Carlyle, Ruskin and William Morris, provided a natural focus
> for late nineteenth century nationalist aspirations towards identity (1993, p.183).

The vernacular revival occurred in most countries after 1890 and became a potent and sinister force in the twentieth century.

The English, for their part, brought 'olde Englande' to perfection. After 1896, in an atmosphere of increasing xenophobia and reactionism, Morris, coupled still to the Arts and Crafts Movement, was characterised as the epitome of English style. The official choice of Morris and Co. to decorate parts of the British Pavilion at the Paris Exposition of 1900 was in recognition of the company's ability to represent an acceptable vision of the nation: 'the building erected by the British Royal Commission on the Rue des Nations is typical of the best side of British domestic architecture and decoration, and therefore a fitting official exhibit of our nation…a bit of old England on the banks of the Seine' (*Magazine of Art*, 1900, p.549). In winning commissions to design various royal thrones, including George V's coronation throne, the company had positioned itself at the heart of the English establishment.

There is a powerful irony in all of this. The ideas and example of Morris were – and are – widely recognised as a key inspiration of various schools of thought within the Modern Movement in design. Internationalist, anti-historicist and mainly left-wing designers and theorists claimed him as

Fig.124 Section of the British Pavilion, Paris Exhibition, 1900, showing two of the *Holy Grail* tapestries woven for George McCulloch.

their own. As he and the Arts and Crafts were shuffled to the right in England, and others used him as a guide to ethnic nationalism, he was also inspiring a new generation of modernist radicals. This was most famously recognised by Nikolaus Pevsner in his volume *Pioneers of the Modern Movement: From William Morris to Walter Gropius* of 1936 (fig.122):

> The history of artistic theory between 1890 and the First World War proves the assertion on which the present work is based, namely, that the phase between Morris and Gropius is an historical unit. Morris laid the foundation of the Modern style; with Gropius its character was ultimately determined.

The radical applied arts movements that sprang up all over Europe at the turn of the century invariably conjoined Morris, John Ruskin and the Arts and Crafts Movements, and credited them with having established the theoretical agenda. International modernists in Austria, Belgium, Czechoslovakia, Germany, the Netherlands, Hungary, Italy, North America, Poland and Scandinavia began their careers in these movements. The view of Belgian designer Henry Van de Velde was typical. In *Le Nouveau* (1929) he wrote of his belief that 'The two great apostles of the new movement were John Ruskin and William Morris'.

The First Proclamation of the Weimar Bauhaus in 1919 explains fully why Pevsner made his famous connection: 'There is no essential difference between the artist and the craftsman…Let us create a new guild of craftsmen, without the class distinctions which raise an arrogant barrier between craftsman and artist' (*Bauhaus, 1919–1928*, exh. cat., MOMA, New York, 1938, p.16).

By closely associating Morris with Ruskin, however, the Modernists consequently attributed the latter's reactionism to the former. Admiration accepted, they were sceptical of what they perceived

to be a combination of historicism and anti-industrialism. Thus, Morris was generally characterised as leading 'a revolt against destiny' (W.D. Teague, 1940). John Gloag, a commentator on modern design for much of this century, was typical in believing him to have 'rejected the contemporary world, [he] would have nothing to do with the machine' (in W.J. Turner, *British Craftsmanship*, 1948, p.104). Pevsner himself saw his commitment to handicraft as an impediment; his modernism was 'only one half of [his] doctrine. The other half remained committed to nineteenth century style and nineteenth century prejudices'; Peter Rayner Banham eloquently summed up the position of Modern Movement thinkers in 1960:

> The human chain of pioneers of the Modern Movement that extends back from Gropius to William Morris, and beyond him to Ruskin, Pugin and William Blake, does not extend forward from Gropius. The precious vessel of handicraft aesthetics that had been passed from hand to hand, was dropped and broken, and no one bothered to pick up the pieces.

He was quite wrong in his latter assertion. Whilst Gropius and his colleagues were formulating their principles on modern design and creating the lineage that ultimately provided the world with the international style, others were inventing the philosophy of modern craft.

Craft has been made to mean so many things that it has come to mean very little. Suffice it to say here that our current understanding of the idea of craft derives heavily from the *fin-de-siècle* art world in general and Morris in particular. He brought a particular train of nineteenth-century thought to a conclusion by providing craft with a politicised rationale; for him it was an ideologically motivated approach to the making of things. Whilst many thinkers – not least Karl Marx – believed work to be the key site of political struggle, Morris separated himself from other left-wing thinkers by postulating creative work as *the* end, not a means *to* an end.

The modern studio crafts movement, which has been a distinct and separate element within the decorative and fine arts, follows this argument to its conclusion. The position is not anti-technology *per se*, but rather is an ideological opposition to capitalism and the systemic organisation of labour. Modern craft is not a set of genres, traditions or techniques. It is an ethically motivated approach to material culture and, as such, William Morris is vital to its intellectual formation (see Coleman, 1988). Following Morris's logic, Bernard Leach, the modern potter, affirmed that:

> We do not turn from science and the inventions of Western man as evils in themselves, but as powers which have not yet been fully used in the human interest…We live in a machine age: as craftsmen we have the choice of using it or as being regarded as mere survivals. Every craftsman should be free to decide the degree to which he can extend his power over material without loss of control. (Farleigh, 1945)

Over the last twenty-five years, the idea of the artist-craftsperson has expanded dramatically through all genres on an international basis and is one of the most energetic areas of visual culture. As the studio potter Alison Britton confirmed in 1991, 'the ideas of William Morris and John Ruskin are still a point of reference' (see M. Margetts, *International Crafts*, p.10).

A hundred years ago, in a letter to the *Manchester Examiner* (14 March 1883) Morris put the following question to an arrogant art-world and an alienated public: 'What business have we with art unless we can all share it?' (Briggs, 1962, p.139). The question, sweeping to one side any distinction between ethical and artistic life, showed that one can think in an all-inclusive manner without compromise or vaguery. It has lost none of its withering power. As we enter the next century, we should do well to remember that Morris was a single person, not a collection of isolated caricatures. Perhaps then we can finally make sense of what he said and did.

Fig. 125 Cover of a Morris & Co. catalogue published to celebrate the redecoratrion of the shop at George Street, Hanover Square, in the 1920s.

A FLOOD-LIT VIEW
OF THE NEW WINDOW

at

MORRIS and COMPANY

ART-WORKERS LTD.

17, St. George Street, Hanover Square, London, W.1

Telephones : Mayfair 1664, 1665.   Lift to all floors.

Charles Skipper & East Ltd., London.

NOTES
ON
AUTHORS

Stephen Astley works in the Designs section of the Collection of Prints, Drawings and Paintings at the V&A and is the author of various articles on design history.

Howard Batho is Curatorial Assistant in the Textiles and Dress Collection at the V&A, seconded to work on the 1996 *William Morris* exhibition. His interests lie in nineteenth- and twentieth-century art and design and he has published on twentieth-century textile subjects.

Mary Bennett was formerly a Keeper at the Walker Art Gallery, Liverpool, having begun her career at the William Morris Gallery, Walthamstow. She has organised major exhibitions on Madox Brown, Millais and Holman Hunt. Her publications include the catalogue of Pre-Raphaelite paintings in the Merseyside Collections and she is presently working on a catalogue raisonné of the works of Ford Madox Brown.

Frances Collard is curator with responsibility for British nineteenth-century objects in the Furniture and Woodwork Collections at the V&A. She has published on various aspects of nineteenth-century furniture design, including *Regency Furniture* (1985).

John Dreyfus was formerly Typographical Adviser to Cambridge University Press and to the Monotype Corporation. He is President of the Printing Historical Society and has published widely, including *Into Print* (1994).

Peter Faulkner is Reader in Modern English Literature in the School of English and American Studies at the University of Exeter. He has written widely on Morris's literary work and is editor of *The Journal of the William Morris Society*.

Paul Greenhalgh is Head of Research at the V&A. He was formerly Head of Art History at Camberwell College of Arts, a tutor at the Royal College of Art and a curator in the Ceramics and Glass Collections at the V&A. He has published a number of articles and books including *Ephemeral Vistas* (1988), *Modernism in Design* (1990) and *Quotations and Sources from Design and the Decorative Arts, 1800–1990* (1993).

Charles Harvey, see under Jon Press.

Martin Harrison writes and lectures widely on nineteenth-century stained glass and twentieth-century photography. He has published (with Bill Waters) *Burne-Jones* (1973) and *Victorian Stained Glass* (1980).

Lesley Hoskins is Archivist at Arthur Sanderson & Sons Ltd and Secretary of The Wallpaper History Society. Her publications include *The Papered Wall* (1994).

Norman Kelvin is Professor of English in the City College and the Graduate Center of the City University of New York. He is the editor of the four-volume edition of the *Collected Letters of William Morris*. He has published many articles and reviews on English and American literature.

Fiona MacCarthy is a design historian and critic who has written extensively on nineteenth- and twentieth-century design history. She is the author

of a number of biographies, including *Eric Gill* (1989) and *William Morris* (1994) which won the 1994 Wolfson History Prize.

Chris Miele works as an architectural historian in the Conservation Group of the Historic Buildings and Monuments Commission (English Heritage). He has written on the history of London and the early conservation movement, including a collection of Morris's writings on architecture (1996).

John Nash has studied and taught calligraphy and lettering since 1968 and was the first American chairman of the Society of Scribes and Illuminators. With Gerald Fleuss, he the author of *Practical Calligraphy* (1992). At present he is involved in inscriptional letter carving.

Jennifer Hawkins Opie is Deputy Curator in the Ceramics and Glass Collections at the V&A, specialising in nineteenth- and twentieth-century studies. She has contributed to and been responsible for many exhibitions and publications, including *Minton, 1798–1910* (1976), *The Poole Potteries* (1980), *Art and Design in Europe and America, 1800–1900* (1987).

Linda Parry is Deputy Curator in the Textile and Dress Collection at the V&A and the curator of the 1996 exhibition *William Morris*. Specialising in nineteenth-century textile history, her publications include *William Morris Textiles* (1983) and *Textiles of the Arts and Crafts Movement* (1988).

Jon Press is Professor of History at Bath College of Higher Education. **Charles Harvey** is Professor of Business History and Management and Director of the School of Management at Royal Holloway College, University of London. Together they are the authors of numerous books and articles on cultural and business history, including *William Morris: Design and Enterprise in Victorian England* (Manchester University Press, 1991), winner of the Wadsworth Prize for Business History in 1992.

Nicholas Salmon edited and introduced *William Morris: Political Writings* (1994). He has also edited two further volumes on Morris's journalism and historical writings (1996).

Eric Turner has been a curator in the Metalwork Department of the V&A for the last twenty years. He has published and lectured extensively, both nationally and internationally, on nineteenth- and twentieth-century metalwork subjects.

Clive Wainwright has worked at the V&A since 1966 and is currently Senior Research Fellow in Nineteenth-Century Studies. He has published widely on the applied arts and the history of collecting, including *The Romantic Interior: The British Collector at Home, 1750–1850* (1989), and was co-editor of *Pugin: A Gothic Passion*, which accompanied the 1994 V&A exhibition.

Raymond Watkinson is a past President of the William Morris Society and editor of the Society's *Journal*. He has published extensively on nineteenth-century art and design, including *William Morris as Designer* (1967), *Pre-Raphaelite Art and Design* (1970) and, with Teresa Newman, *Ford Madox Brown* (1991).

WILLIAM MORRIS OBJECTS IN THE VICTORIA AND ALBERT MUSEUM

compiled by Howard Batho

The following is a list of items in the Collections of the Victoria & Albert Museum which relate to William Morris, the firms of Morris, Marshall, Faulkner & Co. (1861–75), Morris & Co. (1875–1940) and the Kelmscott Press (1891–98). It contains details of objects and books as well as preliminary sketches, drawings, designs, proofs and other documentation concerning both identified and unknown subjects. Drawings, caricatures and contemporary photographs of the Morris family are also included.

The list is arranged by V&A Collection. Further catalogue information for objects is held by each Collection and all enquires regarding access to the material for study purposes should be made to the relevant Collection.

Objects included in the catalogue sections of this publication are indicated with the V&A museum number in **bold**.

The following abbreviations have been used to denote individuals and firms:

WASB	W. A. S. Benson
EB	Elizabeth Burden
EBJ	Edward Burne-Jones
JHD	John Henry Dearle
WDeM	William De Morgan
CFM	Charles Fairfax Murray
KF	Kate Faulkner
FH	Frederick Hollyer
WHH	W. H. Hooper
GJ	George Jack
KK	Kathleen Kersey
FMB	Ford Madox Brown
M&Co	Morris & Co.
MMF&Co	Morris, Marshall, Faulkner & Co.
MM	May Morris
WM	William Morris
RNS	Richard Norman Shaw
DGR	Dante Gabriel Rossetti
EW	Emery Walker
GW	George Wardle
PW	Philip Webb

CERAMICS AND GLASS COLLECTION

Object is followed by title, designer, date of design, manufacturer and date of production (if different from date of design). Arranged chronologically by year of acquisition.

TILES AND TABLEWARE

Two tiles, *Woman in robe playing an oboe*, EBJ, *c*.1860. Made by M&Co, C.324-1927

Two tiles, *Woman in cloak playing an oboe*, EBJ, *c*.1860. Made by M&Co, C.325-1927

Dish, *Star flower*, KF for M&Co, 1880, **C.324-1930**

Two tiles, *Beauty and the Beast*, EBJ, 1863. Made by MMF&Co, 1863 to early 1870s, **C.54-1931**

Two tiles, *Imago Philomela de Atheni Martyris*, EBJ, 1862. Made by MMF&Co, until 1868 or early 1870s, **C.55-1931**

Tile, KF or JHD, 1875–80. Made by M&Co, **C.56-1931**

Tile, *Bough*, WM *c*.1870. Made by MMF&Co, early 1870s, **C.57-1931**

Tile, *Daisy*, WM, 1862. Made by MMF&Co, 1870s, **C.58-1931**

Tile, *Primrose*, WM 1862–5. Made by MMF&Co, 1862 to early 1870s, **C.59-1931**

Panel of tiles, *Sleeping Beauty with Swan* border tiles, EBJ and WM, 1862–5. Made by MMF&Co, 1864-5, **Circ.520-1953**

Tile, *Peony*, KF c.1877. Made by M&Co, *c*.1880, **Circ.614-1954**

Two tiles, *Imago Phyllidis Martyris* with *Scroll* border, EBJ and WM, 1864 and 1870, Made by MMF&Co, 1868–1870s, **Circ.530-1962**

Imago Amadeus as above, Circ.531-1962

Four tiles, Figures of medieval minstrels, EBJ or CFM after WM. Made by MMF&Co, 1872 , **Circ.104-1965**

Tile panel, WM, 1876. Made by WdeM, **C.36-1972**

Four tiles, *Pink and Hawthorn*, WM, 1887. Made by WDeM, **C.39 to C-1975**

Tile, *Longden*, PW 1870. Made by MMF&Co, **C.219-1976**

Tile, *Tulip and Trellis*, WM, 1870. Made by WDeM, **C.220-1976**

Tile, *Geoffrey Chaucer*, EBJ, 1863. Made by MMF&Co, **C.61-1979**

Four tiles, WM, *c*.1875. Made by M&Co, **C.62 to C-1979**

Tile, *Scroll*, WM or PW, *c*.1870. Made by MMF&Co, **C.25-1995**

Six items of table glass, PW *c*.1860–3 for James Powell & Sons, sold by MMF&Co, C.259,260-1926, **C.261-1926**, C.262-1926,**C.263-1926**, C.264-1926

Eight items of table glass, PW *c*.1860–3 for James Powell & Sons, sold by MMF&Co, **C.79-1939**, C.79A-1939, C.80-1939, **C.80A-1939**, **C.81-1939**, C.81A-1939, C.82&A-1939

One item of table glass, PW or TG Jackson 1913 for James Powell & Sons, sold by M&Co, C.523-1934

Five items of table glass, PW late 19th century for James Powell & Sons, sold by M&Co., Circ.457 to D-1947

STAINED GLASS

Arranged chronologically by year of acquisition and by groups.

Three panels, Chaucer's *Legend of Good Women*, EBJ for MMF&Co, *c*.1864, **774 to 776-1864**

Four panels, *The Holy Grail*, EBJ for M&Co, 1866, C.623 to 626-1920

Three panels, Minstrels, WM for M&Co, *c*.1874, C.677-1923, **C.678-1923**, C.679-1923

Three panels, Poets: *Lucretius, Homer and Aeschylus*, EBJ for M&Co, *c*.1874, C.680-1923, **C.681-1923**, C.682-1923

Six panels, *The Legend of St George*, DGR for MMF&Co, *c*.1862, **C.315 to 320-1927**

One single panel and four panels in series, *King René's Honeymoon*, FMB, EBJ and DGR for MMF&Co, *c*.1863, C.197-1918, **Circ.516 to 519-1953**

Six panels from Chaucer's *Legend of Good Women*, EBJ, 1864. These copies made by Mr Glasby, 1909, Circ.49 to 54-1954

Miscellaneous panels

Head of Penelope, EBJ for MMF&Co, *c*.1864, **773-1864**

Elaine, EBJ for M&Co, 1870, **C.321-1927**

Jacob Petrarch, WM and EBJ for MMF&Co, *c*.1862, C.322-1927

The Prince, EBJ for MMF&Co, *c*.1864 , **C.323-1927**

Merchant's Daughter, EBJ for MMF&Co, *c*.1864 , **C.323A-1927**

Baptism of Christ, EBJ for MMF&Co, *c*.1862, **C.440-1940**

Call of St Peter, EBJ for James Powell & Sons, *c*.1860 , C.62-1976

Panel, possibly from Red House, PW for James Powell & Sons, *c*.1859–60 , **C.63-1979**

FURNITURE AND WOODWORK COLLECTION

Listed chronologically by year of acquisition.

Cabinet, *The Legend of St George*, PW 1861–2, painted by WM. MMF&Co, **341-1906**

Piano, Priestly of Berners Street, painted by EBJ, *c*.1860, W.43-1926

Corner cupboard, PW for EBJ, *c*.1870, W.44-1926

Table, PW for MMF&Co, 1860, **W.45-1926**

Cabinet, *King René's Honeymoon*, J.P. Seddon for T.Seddon 1861–2, **W.10-1927**

Grand Piano, EBJ. John Broadwood painted by KF, 1884–5, **W.23-1927**

Cabinet, GJ for M&Co, *c*.1890, W.42-1929

Sideboard, painted by EBJ, *c*.1860, **W.10-1953**

Secretaire, GJ for M&Co, *c*.1893, **Circ.40-1953**

Four painted panels, WM, DGR or EBJ,
c.1857,
Circ.128,129-1953, Circ.310,311-1960

Armchair, possibly RNS for M&Co, 1876,
Circ.24-1958

Bed, possibly M&Co, c.1875,
Circ.238-1958

Cabinet top and bottom, WASB for M&Co,
c.1899, Circ.19-1959 & W.39-1970

Sussex armchair, PW for MMF&Co 1860,
Circ.288-1960

Saville armchair, GJ for M&Co, c.1890,
Circ.401-1960

Child's chair, M&Co, c.1879, Circ.215-1961

Bergere armchair, GJ for M&Co, c.1893,
Circ.249toB-1961

Adjustable-back chair, PW for MMF&Co,
from c.1866, **Circ.250-1961**

Rossetti chair, possibly DGR for
MMF&Co, from c.1863, **Circ.304-1961**

Adjustable-back chair, PW for MMF&Co
from c.1866, Circ.642-1962

Cabinet, GJ for M&Co, c.1900,
Circ.135-1963

Sideboard, PW, 1862, MMF&Co,
Circ.540-1963

Chest, PW, 1862, MMF&Co, **W.35-1978**

Two chairs, M&Co, c.1901, W.2&3-1980

Armchair, M&Co, c.1901, W.4-1980

Chair, FMB, c.1857-8, **W.13-1985**

METALWORK, SILVER AND JEWELLERY COLLECTION

Pair of candlesticks, PW for MMF&Co,
1861, **M.1130&A-1926**

Table lamp, WASB, c.1890. Sold through
M&Co, **Circ.21 to C-1961**

NATIONAL ART LIBRARY

*The following list of NAL items relating to
William Morris is selective. It is limited to
Kelmscott Press publications and associated
material and manuscripts concerning William
Morris, the firms and his circle of friends and
colleagues. Material not listed here includes,
for example, the firm's catalogues and
Morris's published lectures. Further details
regarding the Morris material held by the
NAL can be obtained from the Library's card
catalogue and microfiche.*

KELMSCOTT PRESS PUBLICATIONS
Listed chronologically by year of publication.

Morris, William
The Story of the Glittering Plain, 1891,
L.1620-1893

Morris, William
Poems by the Way, 1891, L.1622-1893

Blunt, Wilfred Scawen
The Love Lyrics and Songs of Proteus, 1892,
L.888-1893

Morris, William
*The Defence of Guenevere, and Other
Poems*, 1892, L.889-1893

Morris, William
A Dream of John Ball and a King's Lesson,
1892, L.884-1893

Voragine, Jacobus de
The Golden Legend (3 vols.), 1892,
L.890,891,892-1893

Le Fevre, Raoul
The Recuyell of the Historyes of Troye
(2 vols), 1892, **L.893,894-1893**

Mackail, John William
Biblia Innocentium, 1892, L.1594-1893

Caxton, William (trans.)
The History of Reynard the Foxe, 1893,
L.1134-1893 and **L.896-1893**

Shakespeare, William
The Poems of William Shakespeare, edited
by F.S.Ellis, 1893, L.1595-1893

Morris, William
News from Nowhere, 1893, **L.883-1893**

[Lull, Ramon]
The Order of Chivalry and *L'Ordene de
Chevalerie*, with a translation by
William Morris, edited by F.S.Ellis,
1893, L.885 and 886-1893

Cavendish, George
*The Life of Thomas Wolsey, Cardinal
Archbishop of York*, 1893, L.1621-1893

[Guilelmus, Archbishop of Tyre]
The History of Godefrey of Boloyne, 1893,
L.897-1893

More, Sir Thomas
Utopia, 1893, L.1292-1893

Tennyson, Alfred Lord
Maud, a Monodrama, 1893, L.1051-1907

Morris, William
Gothic Architecture, 1893, **L.1169-1893**

Meinhold, William
Sidona the Sorceress, 1893, L.1221-1893

Morris, William (trans.)
The Tale of King Florus and the Fair Jehane,
1893, L.579-1894

Morris, William
The Story of the Glittering Plain, 1894,
L.579-1894

Morris, William (trans.)
Of the Friendship of Amis and Amile, 1894,
L.1247-1894

Swinburn, Algernon Charles
Atlanta in Calydon, a Tragedy, 1894,
L.1334-1894

Morris, William
The Wood Beyond the World, 1894,
L.1421-1894

Perceval, le Gallois
Syr Perecyvelle of Gales, 1895,
L.575-1895

Morris, William
The Life and Death of Jason, 1895,
L.794-1895

Morris, William
The Well at the World's End, 1896,
L.688-1896

Chaucer, Geoffrey
The Works of Geoffrey Chaucer, edited by
F.S.Ellis, 1896, **L.757-1896**

Mary, The Blessed Virgin
Laudes Beatae Mariae Virginis, printed
from a 13th-century English psalter,
1896, **L.1188-1907**

Spenser, Edmund
*The Shepheardes Calandar Conteyning
Twelve Aeglogues*, 1896, L.1322-1896

Cockerell, Sydney Carlyle
*Some German Woodcuts of the Fifteenth
Century*, edited by S.C.Cockerell, 1898,
L.23-1898

Morris, William
*A note by William Morris on his aims in
founding the Kelmscott Press*, 1898,
L.204-1898

SPECIMEN PAGES AND PROOF SHEETS FOR KELMSCOTT PRESS PUBLICATIONS
*Material is listed chronologically by publica-
tion date of the Kelmscott Press publication
for which it was designed.*

The Golden Legend, 1892
Trial proof sheets,
L.507-1921, **L.2634C-1939**

The History of Godefrey of Boloyne, 1893
Specimen page, Circ.118-1933

The Tale of King Florus, 1893
Proof sheets, L.2640,2641-1939

The Story of the Glittering Plain, 1894
Proof sheet, L.2639C-1939

Of the Friendship of Amis and Amile, 1894
Proof sheet, L.2642-1939

The Tale of Beowulf, 1895
Specimen pages, Circ.117,121,122-1933

The Well at the World's End, 1896
Proof sheet, L.506-1921

The Story of Sigurd the Volsung, 1898
Proof sheets,
L.2634A-1939, L.2639A&B-1939

The Sundering Flood, 1898
Proof sheets,
L.2634D-1939, L.2639D-1939

Love is Enough, 1898
Proof sheet, L.2634B-1939

Froissart's Chronicles, compiled c.1897
Album of sheets, **1995956850**

Miscellaneous

Proofs for letters,
Circ.272 to 274-1920, Circ.276-1920

MANUSCRIPTS

Letter from PW to Mr Rigby regarding
PW's drawings of animals for the
tapestry *The Forest*, 8 October 1901,
Ms.L.2559-1933

MM Embroidery Department Day Book
for M&Co, 1892-6, Ms.L.2636-1939

Fourteen items of ephemera including
specimens of printing and greeting
cards printed by the Kelmscott Press,
Ms.L.2652 to 2665-1939

Illuminated manuscript *A Book of Verse* by
WM, 1870, **Ms.L.131-1953**

Three bills and two letters to A.A.Ionides
from M&Co for 1883-4 redecoration of
1 Holland Park, **Ms.L.885-1954**

Twenty letters from WM to Wilfred
Scawen Blunt, 1 letter from L.Debney,
1 letter from JHD. 2 bills to W.S.Blunt.
1885-1896, Ms.L.2385-1954

Bound volume including medieval Latin
verse copied by WM, late 19th century;
letter from DGR to JM regarding
photography session, 5 July 1865,
Ms.L.138-1955

Typescripts of letters from WM to Thomas
Wardle, 1875, 1877, 1896, **Ms.L2387-
1956**

Letters to S.C.Cockerell including
photographs and press cuttings,
1871-1900, Ms.L.696,697-1957

Letters from PW to WM and others,
Ms.L.687-1958

Letters from PW to S.C.Cockerell and
others, 1891-1915, Ms.L.688 to 690-1958

Letters and memoranda from Warrington
Taylor, business manager of M&Co to
WM, PW and DGR, 1866-69,
Ms.L.691-1958

Letters to Sir S.C.Cockerell from JM, WM,
EBJ, Arthur Hughes, Mrs Marie
Stillman and others (1893-1938),
Ms.L.692-1958

Letters from Lady Burne-Jones and others
to S.C.Cockerell, 1896-1947,
Ms.L.693,694-1958

Note by WM referring to embroidered
Icelandic valance, c.1884,
Ms.L.2768-1963

Letter from WM to WDeM regarding an
attempt to involve William Carlyle in
SPAB, 3 April 1877, Ms.L.23-1983

Five letters from George Wardle to
MMF&Co regarding the decoration and
architecture of Norfolk and Suffolk
churches, 1865-6, **Box I 86 DD**

NATIONAL ART LIBRARY ARCHIVE OF ART AND DESIGN

Art and Crafts Exhibition Society papers,
1886-1984. On loan from the Society of
Designer-Craftsmen, AAD/1980/1

Morris & Co embroidery patterns,
AAD/1990/6

NATIONAL ART LIBRARY V&A ARCHIVE

The V&A Archive holds the Museum's
official correspondence files. These
include a report by William Morris, in
his capacity as an Art Referee on
textiles offered to the Museum by Sir
J.C.Robinson, and correspondence
between the Museum and Morris & Co.

PRINTS, DRAWINGS AND PAINTINGS COLLECTION

MATERIAL FOR LITERATURE, PRE-KELMSCOTT PRESS

Illustrations for The Story of Cupid and Psyche part of The Earthly Paradise, an edition projected by William Morris, 1866, but abandoned.

Drawings for illustrations, EBJ, c.1866, **E.30-1955**, E.31-1955

Proofs for illustrations by EBJ, probably engraved by WM, c.1866, E.1810 to 1813-1920, **E.1814-1920**, E.1815 to 1835-1920, **E.1836-1920**, E.1837 to 1843-1920, E.573 to 578-1921, E.2398-1921

Proof of vignette on title-page for *The Earthly Paradise, A Poem* by William Morris. Published by F.S.Ellis, 1868. Engraved by WM from EBJ illustration, E.1014-1949

MATERIAL RELATING TO BOOKS PUBLISHED BY THE KELMSCOTT PRESS

Items are listed in publication order of the book for which the object was designed. Unless otherwise stated, designs for borders, ornaments, frames, words and letters are by William Morris, illustrations by Edward Burne-Jones and proofs from engravings cut by W.H.Hooper.

The Story of the Glittering Plain, 1891
Proofs for borders,
E.1709-1920, E.1778-1920

Poems by the Way, 1891
Proof of page, E.1779-1920

The Defence of Guenevere, and Other Poems, 1892, proofs for borders, E.1710 to 1712-1920, E.1780-1920, E.1788-1920

A Dream of John Ball and a King's Lesson, 1892, proofs for illustrations, Circ.283-1920, E.1781-1920

The Golden Legend, 1892
Proofs for illustrations, Circ.285,286-1920, E.1782,1783-1920, **E.1784-1920**

The History of Reynarde the Foxe, 1893
Proofs of pages,
E.1777-1920, E.1787-1920

News from Nowhere, 1893
Proofs for border,
E.1230-1912, E.1713-1920

The Order of Chivalry, 1893
Proof for illustration, E.579-1921

The History of Godefrey of Boloyne, 1893
Designs for borders,
D.1558 to 1560-1907
Proofs for borders,
E.1234 to 1247-1912, **E.1229-1912**

Maud, 1893
Design for border, D.1556-1907

Sidonia the Sorceress, 1893
Proof for page, E.1714-1920

Sonnets and Lyrical Poems, 1894
Proof for title-page, E.1273-1920

The Story of the Glittering Plain, 1894
Proofs for borders, E.1233-1912, E.1718 to 1719-1920

Of the Friendship of Amis and Amile, 1894
Proof for title-page, E.1272-1912

The Tale of the Emperor Coustans and of Over Sea, 1894
Proof for border, E.1708-1920

Syr Perceyvelle of Gales, 1895
Drawings for illustrations,
E.1274-1912, E.32-1955

The Well at the World's End, 1896
Drawings for illustrations,
E.33 to 36-1955
Proofs for borders, E.1231,1232-1912, E.1715 to 1717-1920

The Works of Geoffrey Chaucer, 1896
Designs for borders, letters and initials, **D.172-1903**, D.1552-1907, **D.1553-1907, D.1561-1907**, E.194-1955, **E.195-1955**
Proofs for borders,
D.1553A-1907, D.1554-1907
Drawings for illustrations
De Consolatione Philosophiae, E.44-1955
The Knyghtes Tale, E.37-1955
The Legend of Goode Wimmen, E.45-1955
The Parlement of Foules, E.43-1955
The Romaunt of the Rose, E.42-1955
The Tale of the Clerk of Oxenford, E.41-1955
The Tale of the Wife of Bath, E.38 to 40-1955
Troilus and Criseyde, E.46-1955
Proofs for illustrations
Unidentified, E.390,391-1901
The Frankelyens Tale,
E.1267 to 1269-1912
The Knyghtes Tale, E.1257,1259-1912, E.581-1921, E.622-1923, Circ.636-1923
The Man of the Law's Tale, E.624-1923
The Prioress's Tale, E.1261,1262-1912
The Romaunt of the Rose,
E.1270,1271-1912, E.623-1923
The Tale of the Wife of Bath,
E.1263 to 1266-1912, E.1785-1920
The Prologue, E.1225-1912

The Earthly Paradise, 1897
Design for border, D.1557-1907
Drawings for illustrations
(not published), E.2892 to 2895-1927,

The Water of the Wonderous Isles, 1897
Design for ornament, D.1555-1907
Designs for words, E.889-1939

Sire Degrevaunt, 1897
Drawing for illustration, E.47-1955

The Story of Sigurd the Volsungs, 1898
Drawings for illustrations,
E.48 to 51-1955
Proof trial pages, E.2991 to 2993-1910

Love is Enough, 1898
Proofs for pages and ornaments,
E.1844 to 1846-1920
Proofs for illustrations,
E.2990-1910, E.1275-1912, Circ.284-1920

Material for unpublished works

The Beginning of the World,
an illustrated edition of J.W. Mackail's, *Biblia Innocentium* (1892), drawings for illustrations, E.1683 to 1707-1920

Froissart's Chronicles
Trial proof page, **E.504-1903**

Unidentified proofs

Proofs for words and letters, D.1562,1563-1907, E.1183 to 1213-1912, E.1215 to 1228-1912, Circ.268 to 271-1920, Circ.275-1920, E.1720 to 1756-1920, E.563 to 568-1921

Proofs for borders and frames, Circ.277 to 282-1920, Circ.284-1920, E.1757 to 1776-1920, E.569 to 572-1921

Proofs for illustrations, E.584 to 587-1921

DESIGNS FOR INTERIOR DECORATIVE SCHEMES

The Green Dining Room, South Kensington Museum, London, 1866–67

Studies for figures, EBJ, 1866–7, E.2897 to 2905-1927

Designs for ceiling decoration PW and WM, 1866–7, **E.1169, 1170-1940**

Design for decoration of wall and cornice, PW, 1866, **E.5096-1960**

St James's Palace, London, 1881

Design for painted decoration, the Blue Room, WM, 1881, **E.289-1939**

Elevation sketch for the Throne Room and Blue Room, WM, 1881, **E.53-1940**

Elevation sketch for the Blue Room, probably PW, 1881, **E.54-1940**

ARCHITECTURAL DRAWINGS

Architectural drawings for Red House, PW, 1859, E.58-1916, **E.59 to 61-1916**, E.62-1916, **E.63,64-1916**, E.65 to 68-1916, E.69 to 71-1916

DESIGNS FOR FURNITURE

Design for the inside of a grand piano, EBJ, 1879-90, E.690-1927

Engraving by O. Lacour after the finished decoration for the above, E.960-1896

Four designs for the doors of the cabinet, *The Legend of St George*, WM, 1861, **E.2787 to 2790-1927**

DRAWINGS, CARTOONS AND STUDIES FOR STAINED GLASS

Listed by designer and chronologically by year of acquisition. Object type – cartoon, design or study is followed (where known) by title or subject, church for which the design was first used and the date.

Ford Madox Brown

Design for *St Oswald*. St Oswald's Church, Durham, 1864–5, 231&B to E-1894

Design for *John Holbrook*. Cambridge (Peterhouse), 1872, 647-1894

Studies, draped figure and a hand holding a book, 780-1894

Design for *St Oswald crowned King of Bernicia*. St Oswald's Church, Durham, September 1864–5, **E.1853-1910**

Design for *Gideon*. St Martin's Church, Scarborough, 1862, E.2906-1927

Designs for *The Legend of St Editha*. Tamworth Church, Staffordshire, 1873, E.2911 to 2913-1927

Edward Burne-Jones

Design for *The Tree of Life*. The American Episcopal Church of St Paul at Rome, 1892, 584-1898

Designs for *Emblems of the Four Evangelists*. Castle Howard Chapel, Yorkshire, 1872, 585-1898

Design for *The Last Judgement*. St Philip's Church, Birmingham, 1897, 1000-1901

Cartoon for *Eunice*. Abbey Church, Paisley, Renfrewshire, 1876, 1001-1901

Design for *Christ amongst the Candlesticks*. Abbey Church, Paisley, Renfrewshire, 1876, 1002-1901

Design for *Justitia*. Cambridge (Jesus College), 1875/6, 1003-1901

Design for *Timiditas*. Cambridge (Jesus College), 1875/6, 1004-1901

Design for *Christ and St Mary Magdalene in the Garden*. Church of Jesus at Troutbeck, Cumberland, 1872, 1005-1901

Design for *St Gregory*. Church of St Mary the Virgin, Speldhurst, Kent, 1006-1901

Photographic enlargement for *The Nativity*. St Philip's Church, Birmingham, 1887–8, E.224-1911

Photographic enlargement for *The Crucifixion*. St Philip's Church, Birmingham, 1887–8, E.225-1911

Design for *St Barbara*. Whitelands College, Putney, London, 1891, E.691-1920

Studies for *King René's Honeymoon* (sculpture). 1862 Exhibition, E.2883,2884-1927

Cartoon for *Chorus Angelorum*. Possibly for All Saints Church, Middleton Cheney, Northamptonshire 1864–6, E.2907-1927

Design for *Adam and Eve*. All Saints Church, Middleton Cheney, Northamptonshire, 1870, **E.2908-1927**

Design for *The Fall of Man*. Cambridge (Jesus College), 1873, E.2909-1927

Design for *The Virgin Mary*. St Mary the Virgin, Speldhurst, Kent. 1872, E.2910-1928

Study of a female head, 1889, E.603-1929

Design for *St George and St Sabra and the Annunciation*, E.887,888-1939

Drawing for *St James as Bishop*. Westminster (Savoy Chapel), 1870, E.1844-1946

Edward Burne-Jones for James Powell & Sons

Cartoon for *The Good Shepherd*. Congregational Church, Maidstone, 1862, **E.1317-1970**

Three cartoons for *The Tower of Babel, Solomon and the Queen of Sheba* and *Adam and Eve*. Bradfield College, Berkshire, 1857, **E.1318 to 1320-1970**

Two cartoons for *Christ in Glory* and *The Third Day of Creation*. Waltham Abbey, Essex, 1861, **E.1321,1322-1970**

Charles Joseph Faulkner

Four designs for *The Story of Dives and Lazarus*. 1860s, not designed for MMF&Co, **E.1162,1163-1940**, E.1164,1165-1940

Peter Paul Marshall

Design for *St Michael and the Dragon*. St Michael and All Angels, Brighton, *c*.1862, **E.1166-1940**

Design for *Joshua*. St Martin's Church, Scarborough, *c*.1862, E.1167-1940

Design for *The Prophet Daniel*. *c*.1863, E.1168-1940

William Morris

Design for background for *St Mary the Virgin*. St Martin's Church, Marple, Cheshire, 1873, **E.2791-1927**

Design for woman playing a lute, 1872–4, E.2806-1927

Design for *The Recoginition of Tristram*. Harden Hall, Bingley, Yorkshire, 1862, E.572-1940

Design for *Ezekiel*. Bradford Cathedral, 1863, E.1845-1946

Design for *Charlemagne*, *c*.1865, E.449-1949

William Morris drawings, possibly for stained glass, E.2792 to **E.2805-1927**. Subjects identified:
Nympha Florum (E.2792),
Goode Wimmen (E.2793) and
Lucretia (E.2794, 2801)

Dante Gabriel Rossetti

Four cartoons for *The Story of St George and the Dragon*. Bradford Cathedral, Yorkshire, 1861–2, E.1840 to 1843-1946

Drawing, possibly for stained glass, *St Augustine*, E.1844-1946

Design for *Sermon on the Mount*. All Saints Church, Selsley, Gloucestershire, 1862, **E.2916-1927**

George Wardle

Drawings of painted decorations in East Anglian churches, *c*.1862–3, 3437 to 3442, **3489, 3490&A**, 3491 to 3516, 4598 to **4611**, 4775 to 4784, 4889 to 4897, 4972 to **4982**

Drawings of panels, figures and stained glass in East Anglian churches, E.1400 to 1446-1933

Drawings of stained-glass windows and architecural details of French and Dutch churches, *c*.1864, E.1447 to 1458-1933, E.1465,1466,1470-1933

Original designs for stained glass, possibly intended for MMF&Co, E.1460 to 1464-1933

Bound volume of drawings of painted decorations in East Anglian Churches. Made for MMF&Co, 1865–6, E.317 to 404-1939

Philip Webb

Designs for *The Symbols of the Evangelists*, *c*.1865–70, E.2917 to 2931-1927

Design for *The Pelican in her Piety*. St Michael and All Angels, Brighton, 1862, E.2932-1927

Design with tree with an axe in the trunk. Unitarian Chapel, Leeds, *c*.1875, E.2933-1927

Two designs each with a fish and sun above, E.2934,2935-1927

Design with rose in centre and a fleur-de-lis, E.2936-1927

Design for *Flaming Star* from *Signs of the Zodiac*. Royal Agricultural College, Cirencester, Gloucestershire, 1865, **E.2937-1927**

Design for *Dog Barking at Moon* from *Signs of the Zodiac*. Royal Agricultural College, Cirencester, Gloucestershire, 1865, **E.2938-1927**

Design for *Ram and Crab* from *Signs of the Zodiac*. Royal Agricultural College, Cirencester, Gloucestershire, 1865, E.2939-1927

Design for *Banners of the Tribes of Israel*. All Saints Church, Middleton Cheney, Northamptonshire, 1865, **E.2940-1927**

Designs with angel, trefoil and symbol of St Luke, E.2941,2942-1927

Designs for *Pelican in her Piety* and *Agnus Dei*, E.2943,2944-1927

Tracing of a drawing with eagle above a sea full of fish, E.2945-1927

Designs with shields of arms, E.2946 to 2950A-1927

Designs with heraldic panels, E.2951 to 2953-1927

Design for *Adam naming the animals*. All Saints Church, Selsley, Gloucestershire, 1862, **E.1289-1931**

Designs for table glass

Fourteen designs for table glass. PW for James Powell & Sons, *c*.1860–62. Probably sold through MMF&Co, E.326 to 329-1944, **E.330-1944**, E.331,332-1944, **E.333-1944**, E.334 to 339-1944,

One sheet of designs for table glass. PW for James Powell and Sons, 1860, **E.340-1944**

DESIGNS FOR TEXTILES

Identified embroidery designs

Listed chronologically by year of acquisition.

Design for *Artichoke*, WM, *c*.1880, 65-1898

Design for an altar-cloth, Busbridge Church, Surrey, E.288-1939

Design for an embroidery for the Battye family, MM, E.30-1940

Design for a panel, *Lotus*, WM, *c*.1875–80, E.32-1940

Design for the Royal School of Needlework, WM, *c*.1875, **E.41-1940**

Design for the *Bay Leaf* cushion, EB, E.42-1940

Drawing for the *Bay Leaf* cushion, EB, E.43-1940

Drawing for embroidered panel, *Acanthus*, WM, *c*.1878, E.55-1940

Design for a super-frontal, PW, 1898–9, **E.58-1940**

Preliminary design for above, E.59-1940

Working drawings for *Romaunt of the Rose*, WM and EBJ, *c*.1872, E.63,64-1940

Design for embroidered panel, *Flamma Troiae*, WM, *c*.1860, **E.571-1940**

Design for an embroidered panel, *King Arthur*, EBJ, c.1863, E.449-1949

Designs, tracings and drawings for various embroideries of various subjects and types drawn by WM, MM and others, E.1467,1468-1933, E.838-1937, E.316-1939, E.27 to 29-1940, E.31-1940, E.35 to 37-1940, E.39-1940, E.46-1940, E.50-1940, E.52-1940, E.56-1940, E.66,67-1940, E.956 to 961-1954, E.962-1954, Circ.492-1967

Designs for printed textiles

Rose and Thistle, WM, 1881, **E.293-1939**

Wreathnet, WM, 1882, **E.308-1939**

Evenlode, WM, 1883, E.543-1939

Columbine or *Bluebell*, WM, 1876, **E.44-1940**

Design for a damask, 1878–82, not put into production, E.49-1940

Rosebud, JHD, *c*.1905, E.60-1940

Sketch design probably for *Utrecht* velvet E.961-1954

Rose, WM, *c*.1883, **E.1075-1988**

Designs for woven textiles

Violet and Columbine, WM, 1883, **E.304-1939**

Bird and Vine, WM,1879, **E.40-1940**

DESIGNS FOR CARPETS AND RUGS

Identified designs for carpets

Redcar, WM, *c*.1881, **E.144-1919**

Designs for Naworth Castle, WM, 1881, **E.287-1939, E.47&48-1940**

Sketches and designs for unidentified carpet projects

E.290,291-1939, E.294-1939, **E.295,296-1939**, E.297-1939, **E.298-1939**, E.299,300-1939, **E.301-1939**, E.302,303-1939, E.305 to 307-1939, E.309 to 311-1939, E.315-1939, E.33-1940

TAPESTRY DESIGNS

Identified tapestry designs

Cartoon for *The Goose Girl*, Walter Crane, 1883, 155-1898

Cartoon for *The Adoration*, after EBJ, 1888, **E.5012-1919**

Cartoon for *Acanthus and Vine*, WM, 1879, **E.3472-1932**

Design. *The Seasons or the Orchard*, M&Co after Morris, *c*.1890, **E.544-1939**

Design with acanthus and peacocks, WM, 1879–81, **E.620-1939**

Design for *Acanthus and Vine*, WM, 1879, **E.45-1940**

Tracing from E.5012-1919 above. JHD or EBJ, E.51-1940

Drawing for *The Forest*, JHD, *c*.1877, E.1172-1940

Drawings for *The Seasons*, *c*.1890, E.1173(1to5)-1940

Unidentified tapestry designs

E.621-1939, E.34-1940, E.57-1940, E.61-1940

Sketches by EBJ, possibly preliminary designs for tapestries, E.1845 to 1848-1919, E.996-1976, E.1000-1976, E.1001-1976

Designs for textiles, intended technique unknown

E.292-1939, E.312 to 314-1939, E.316-1939

DRAWINGS AND DESIGNS FOR TILES

Study for *Cinderella*, EBJ, *c*.1862, E.2877-1927

Study for *Beauty and the Beast*, EBJ, *c*.1862, E.2890-1927

Ten copy drawings of six tiles of *Beauty and the Beast*, EBJ, *c*.1862–5, E.1290 to 1292-1931, **E.1293-1927**, E.1294 to 1296-1931, **E.1297, 1298-1931**, E.1299-1931

Nine tracings of six tiles of *Cinderella*, EBJ, 1862–5, E.1300 to 1308-1931

Four copy drawings of *Sleeping Beauty*, EBJ, 1862–5, E.1309 to 1312-1931

DESIGNS FOR WALLPAPERS

Acorn, WM, *c*.1879, E.38-1940

Mermaid holding fishes, EBJ *c*.1880 E.62-1940

Grafton, WM, *c*.1883, E.955-1954

Acanthus, WM, 1874, Circ.297-1955

Vine, WM, 1873–4, E.1074-1988

PORTRAITS, CARICATURES, SELF-PORTRAITS

Portrait of MM by EBJ, 1886, E.886-1939

Self-portrait. WM, dated July 29th 1856, **E.376-1946**

Self-portrait. WM, 1856, **E.377-1946**

Caricature of WM from the back. EBJ, *c*.1870, **E.449-1976**

Caricature of WM reading poetry to EBJ, *c*.1865, **E.450-197**

EDWARD BURNE-JONES SKETCH BOOKS

Containing studies for textiles, stained glass and mural decoration, 1857 to 1874, E.1 to 8-1955, **E.9-1955**, E.10-1955

PHOTOGRAPHS

Subject is followed by photographer and date if known.

Photographs of William Morris

William Morris by FH, 1874, Ph.7714-1938

William Morris by FH, 1884, Ph.7715 to 7717-1938

William Morris by Ellis & Green, *c*.1868–70, **Ph.1780-1939**

William Morris, *c*.1876, **Ph.1808-1939**

William Morris by EW, 1889, Ph.1809-1939

William Morris, Ph.1811-1939

Family and group photographs

William Morris with Edward Burne-Jones by FH, 1874, Ph.7711-1938

Children of Morris and Burne-Jones. FH, 1874, Ph.7815-1938, Ph.1783 to 1786-1939

Morris and Burne-Jones families. FH, 1874, Ph.7816-1938, Ph.1812-1939, **Ph.1813-1939**

May Morris. FH, Ph.7821-1938

Album of photographs of Jane Morris. John R. Parsons, 1865, with later prints by EW, **Ph.1735 to 1752-1939**

WM and unidentified group, Ph.1814-1939

Jane Morris, c.1914. Harry F. Phillips, Leek, Ph.1815-1939

William Morris with the Hammersmith Branch of the Socialist League, c.1885, **Ph.1817-1939**, Ph.1817A-1939, Ph.1820-1939

William Morris with the Hammersmith Socialist Society, c.1890, Ph.1821-1939

William Morris with workers of the Kelmscott Press, c.1893, **Ph.1819-1939**

Houses

Eight interior and exterior photographs of Red House, late 19th century (Purchased from Pollard 33/4977), Ph.527 to 534-1934

Eleven interior and exterior photographs of Red House, c.1910–11, Ph.1789 to 1800-1939

Three interior photographs of Kelmscott House. EW, 1896, **Ph.1&2-1972**, Ph.3-1973

Album of photographs, Kelmscott Manor, 1931. Photographs by Miss Netta Peacock, Ph.1760 to 1779-1939

Three photographs of Kelmscott Manor, Ph.1803 to 1805-1939

WALLPAPER

Designs are listed alphabetically with the designer and exact date of registration or first year of production.
Wallpaper samples are single loose sheets or bound in one of three volumes of Morris & Co. wallpaper pattern books. The volumes contain the following:

WALLPAPER PATTERN BOOK
published by Morris & Co, printed by Jeffrey & Co, E.633 to 749-1915

WALLPAPER PATTERN BOOK
published by Morris & Co, printed by Jeffrey & Co, E.750 to 858-1915

WALLPAPER PATTERN BOOK
published by Morris & Co, printed by Jeffrey & Co, 1880-1917, E.2734 to 2866-1980

Wallpapers E.1401 to 1432-1979 are reprints by Arthur Sanderson & Son Ltd, c.1955

Acanthus, WM, 1875
E.726,795,801-1915, **E.494-1919**, E.495,496-1919, Circ.24-1955, Circ.281-1959, E.2857 to 2860-1980

Acorn, WM, 1879
E.816-1915, E.518 to 520-1919, E.38-1940, Circ.282-1959

Anemone, JHD, 1897
E.734 to 738-1915

Apple, WM, 1877
E.2217-1913, E.806 to 808-1915, E.506 to 508-1919

Arbutus, KK, 1903
E.1413-1979

Arcadia, MM, c.1886
E.633 to 636-1915, E.555,556-1919

Artichoke, JHD, 1888–9
E.1406-1979, E.2830,2831-1980

Autumn Flowers, WM, 1888
E.2214,2215-1913, E.657,658,709,727,733-1915, E.567,568-1919, E.2772 to 2776-1980

Bachelor's Button, WM, 1892
E.2219-1913, E.696 to 698-1915, E.596 to 601-1919, Circ.44-1954

Bird and Anemone, WM, 1882
E.827,828-1915, **E.530-1919**, E.531-1919, C.21669

Bird and Pomegranate, KK, c.1926
E.1426-1979

Blackberry, JHD, 1903
E.1415-1979, E.2793,2794,2839-1980

Blackthorn, WM, 1892
E.2232-1913, Circ.22A-1953, E.602-1919, E.2781-1980

Blossom, KF, 21 September 1885
E.1427-1979, E.2767-1980

Borage, WM, 1888–9
E.660 to 663-1915, E.569-1919

Bower, WM, 1877
E.809-1915, E.509-1919, E.2762-1980, C.19463

Bramble, KF, 17 January 1879
E.1414-1979

Branch, WM, c.1871
E.3699-1915, E.467-1919, Circ.274-1959

Brentwood, JHD, 1913
E.1417-1979

Brocade, adapted from a Portuguese design, 1911, E.1425-1979

Bruges, WM, 1888
E.651 to 656,718-1915, E.560-1919, **E.561-1919**, E.562 to 566-1919, E.2777-1980

Carnation, KF, 1880
E.818-1915, Circ.46-1954

Ceiling, WM, 1877
E.692,810,823,832-1915, **E.510-1919**, E.511-1919, E.2737-1980

Celandine, JHD, c.1896
E.2213-1913, E.728-1915, E.2765-1980

Christchurch, WM, 1882
E.833-1915, E.2758-1980

Chrysanthemum, WM, 1877
E.2173-1889, E.802-1915, E.504,505-1919, E.350-1972, E.2782,2783-1980

Clover, JHD,1903
E.1412-1979, E.2778,2779-1980

Compton, WM, 1896
E.2216-1913, E.720,722-1915, E.606,607-1919, Circ.290-1959, E.2818 to 2819-1980

Daffodil, JHD, 1903
E.1419-1979, E.2780,2792-1980

Daisy, WM, 1864
E.2222-1913, E.750 to 752,794-1915, E.441-1919, **E.442-1919**, E.443,444-1919, E.3718,3720-1927, E.2739 to 2742-1980

Diaper, WM, 1868-70
E.659,760,761,771,773,774,788,789-1915, E.454 to 457-1919, **E.458-1919**, E.459 to 462-1919, E.3704-1927

Double Bough, WM, 1890
E.2221-1913, E.683 to 685, 687,688,691,705-1915, E.585 to 591-1919, E.2755,2841 to 2847-1980

Flora, WM, 1891
E.690,713-1915, E.593-1919, E.2763,2764-1980

Flowering Scroll, JHD, 1908
E.1431-1979

Foliage, JHD, 1899
E.1421-1979, E.2796,2797-1980

Fritillary, WM, 1885
E.2211-1913, E.853 to 856-1915, E.542 to 548-1919, Circ.283-1957

Fruit, WM, 1866
E.2210-1913, E.752-1915, E.445-1919, **E.446-1919**, E.447 to 449-1919, E.3710 to 3712 -1927, Circ.248-1964, E.2743 to 2746,2840-1980, C.21666

Garden, JHD, 1899
E.1424-1979, E.2805-1980

Garden Tulip, WM, 1885
E.857,858-1915, E.549 to 552-1919, E.2802 to 2804-1980

Golden Lily, JHD, 1897
E.1407-1979, E.2815 to 2817-1980

Grafton, WM, 1883
E.650,831-1915, E.533,534-1919

Granville, JHD, 1896
E.724,725-1915, E.2835,2836-1980

Hammersmith, WM, 1890
E.674,675-1915, E.579-1919, E.2799-1980

Harebell, JHD, 1911
E.1420-1979

Honeysuckle, WM or MM, 1883
E.667 to 669,830-1915, E.532-1919, E.2788 to 2791-1980

Horn Poppy, MM, 21 September 1885
E.707,845 to 852-1915

Hyacinth, JHD, c.1900–12
E.1416-1979

Indian, WM, c.1868–70
E.748,757 to 759-1915, **E.3706-1927**, E.3707 to 3709-1927

Iris, JHD, c.1887
E.2220-1913, E.642,643,699,703-1915, E.2785 to 2787-1980

Jasmine, WM, 1872
E.770,772,793-1915, **E.475-1919**, E.476,477-1919, Circ.23-1954, E.2751 to 2753-1980

Larkspur, WM, 1872 and a second version 1875
E.2218-1913, E.768 to 770,778,790,791, 839-1915, **E.468-1919**, E.469 to 471-1919, **E.472-1919**, E.473,474-1919, E.2771-1980

Lechlade, WM, 1893
E.704,706-1915, E.603,604-1919, E.2828,2829-1980

Leicester, JHD, c.1912
E.1404-1979

Lily, WM, 1874
E.776-1915, E.484-1919, Circ.276-1959, E.2754,2766-1980

Lily Border, unknown, c.1915
E.1408-1979

Lily and Pomegranate, WM, 1886
E.2224,2225-1913, E,637,638-1915, E.553,554-1919, E.2852,2853-1980

Loop Trail, KF, 1877
E.803 to 805,843-1915

Mallow, KF, 1879
E.811 to 813,826,829,834,844-1915

Marigold, WM, 1875
E.3469 & A-1913, E.719,775,777,796, 797-1915, E.820,825-1915, E.478 to 483-1919, Circ.27-1959

Meadow Sweet, JHD, 1904
E.1429-1979, E.2812 to 2814-1980

Merton, KF, 1888
E.646 to 648-1915

Michaelmas Daisy, JHD, c.1912
E.1403-1979

Myrtle, WM, 1899
Circ.27-1954, E.2784-1980

Net Ceiling, WM, 1895
E.721,723-1915, E.608-1919, E.2735,2736, 2866-1980

Norwich, WM, 1889
E.665,666-1915, E.570 to 574-1919, E.2223-1913, Circ.26-1954, E.2849 to 2851-1980

Oak Tree, JHD, 1896
E.729 to 732-1915, Circ.88-1968

Orange Border, unknown, c.1915
E.1409-1979

Orchard, JHD, 1899
E.1402-1979, E.2768 to 2770-1980

Persian, JHD, 1904
E.1411-1979, E.2837,2838-1980

Pimpernel, WM, 1876
E.798,799-1915, **E.497-1919**, E.498,499-1919, Circ.280-1959, Circ.249-1964, E.2854 to 2856-1980

Pink and Rose, WM, c.1890
E.678 to 682,686,708,717-1915, E.580 to 584-1919, E.2848-1980

Planet, JHD, 1903
E.1401-1979, E.2757-1980

Poppy, WM, 1880
E.640,819,821,824-1915, **E.521-1919**, E.522 to 527-1919

Powdered, WM, 1874
E.649,780-1915, E.487-1919, Circ.19-1954, Circ.277-1959, E.2759 to 2761-1980

Queen Anne, WM, c.1868–70
E.762 to 764,784,781-1915, E.3721,3722-1927

Rambler, JHD, 1908
E.1430-1979

Rose, WM, 1877
E.502, 503-1919, E.2806,2807-1980, C.20566

St James's, WM, 1881
E.528-1919, E.529-1919, Circ.25-1954, E.2861,2862-1980

St James's Ceiling, WM, 1881
E.693,695-1915, **E.594-1919**, E.595-1919

Scroll, WM, c.1871
E.3470-1913, E.639,766-1915, E.463 to 465-1927, E.3698-1927, Circ.279-1959, E.2808 to 2810-1980

Seaweed, JHD, 1901
E.1418-1979, E.2756-1980

Single Stem, JHD, c.1905
E.710,714-1915, E.2825 to 2827-1980

Spray, adapted from historical sample, c.1871
E.2807-1927, E.3713,3714-1927

Sprig, unknown, 1901
E.1428-1979

Spring Thicket, JHD, 1894
E.711,715,716-1915, E.605-1919, E.2832 to 2834-1980

Sunflower, WM, 1879
E.676,677,814,815,817,821-1915, E.512-1919, **E.513-1919**, E.514 to 517-1919, E.2863,2864-1980

Sweet Briar, JHD, 1912, E.1405-1979

The Wreath or *New Ceiling*, WM, 1883
E.535-1919, Circ.288-1959

Thistle, JHD, 1897
E.2209-1913, E.743 to 747-1915, E.1432-1979

Tom Tit, JHD, 1897
E.739 to 742-1915

Tree Freize, JHD, 1903
E.1423-1979, E.2734-1980

Trellis, WM, 1864
E.836-1915, E.450,451-1919, **E.452-1919**, E.453-1919, E.3700 to 3703-1927, Circ.247-1964, E.2747 to 2750-1980, E.2795, 2811-1980

Triple Net, WM, 1891, E.689-1915, E.592-1919

Tulip Frieze, JHD, 1903
E.1422-1979, E.2738-1980

Venetian, WM, c.1871
E.749,754 to 756,783 to 785,834-1915, E.3715 to 3717-1927

Verdure, KK, 1913, E.1410-1979

Vine, WM, 1874
E.485-1919, E.486-1919, E.2800,2801,2865-1980

VR, 1887. Reprint from original block by Sandersons, c.1981
Circ.16-1961, E.1138-1988

Wallflower, WM, 1890
E.670 to 673-1915, E.575 to 578-1919

Wild Tulip, WM, 1884
E.837,840 to 842-1915, E.536,537-1919, **E.538-1919**, E.539 to 541-1919, C.21670, E.2820 to 2824-1980

Willow, WM, 1874
E.779,782,786,787,792-1915, E.488 to 493-1919, Circ.285-1959

Willow Bough, WM, 1887
E.641,644,645-1915, **E.557-1919**, E.558,559-1919, Circ.18-1954, Circ.297-1955, Circ.281-1959

Woodland Weeds, JHD, c.1905
E.712-1915, Circ.252-1954, E.2798-1980

Wreath, WM, 1876
E.500,501-1919

MISCELLANEOUS

Printed panel in memory of Rev. T. Sadler, Unitarian Minister at Rosslyn Hill Chapel, Hampstead, E.1789-1920

St John's Church and Parsonage, Keswick, engraving, E.2349-1928

TEXTILES AND DRESS COLLECTION

PRINTED AND WOVEN TEXTILES

Designs are listed alphabetically. Designed by William Morris unless otherwise stated. Date is for registration of design.
Samples found in the three V&A Morris & Co. textile pattern books are listed with the museum number of the relevant pattern book.

PATTERN BOOK OF PRINTED VELVETEENS, Morris & Co, 1890s, **T.660-1919**

WORKING PATTERN BOOK, Morris & Co, 20th century, **T.30-1940**

SWATCH BOOK OF PRINTED TEXTILES, Morris & Co, 1925-1940, **T.34-1982**

Printed textiles

Acanthus, 25 April 1876
T.660-1919, T.30-1940, Circ.7&A-1966

Acorn, Adapted from historical design, before 1912, Circ.446-1953

African Marigold, 7 October 1876
T.640 to 642-1919, T.30-1940, Circ.411,412-1953, Circ.42-1954, Circ.486-1965, Circ.492-1965, T.34-1982

Avon, possibly JHD, c.1887
T.597, 598-1919, T.30-1940

Bird and Anemone, Before April 1881
T.650 to 656-1919, T.30-1940, Circ.417-1953, Circ.273-1961, T.34-1982

Bluebell or *Columbine*, 1876
T.588-1919, T.30-1940, Circ.417-1953, **Circ.44-1956,** Circ.273-1961, T.34-1982

Borage, 1883
T.48,49-1919, T.30-1940, Circ.418-1953, T.159-1962, Circ.526-1962, T.7-1979

Bourne, JHD, c.1905
T.30-1940, T.34-1982

Brentwood, JHD, 1913
T.30-1940

Briar or *Sweet Briar*, JHD, c.1906
T.30-1940, T.12-1954

Brother Rabbit, 20 May 1882
T.50-1912, T.645, 646-1919, **T.647, 648-1919**, T.649-1919, T.30-1940, T.342-1980, T.34-1982

Carnation, KF, 15 October 1875
T.44-1919, T.591-1919, T.30-1940, **T.248-1984**

Cherwell, JHD, 1887
T.660-1919, T.30-1940, T.62-1946, T.34-1982

Coiling Trail, copied by WM from a Bannister Hall 1830s textile, c.1868, T.34-1982

Colne, KK, c.1905
T.595-1919, T.30-1940

Compton, JHD, 27 February 1896
T.615,616-1919, T.30-1940, Circ.78-1956, T.2&A-1978 (repro), T.34-1982

Corncockle, 22 April 1883
T.36-1919, T.590-1919, T.30-1940, T.168-1973, Circ.84-1953, Circ.87-1953, T.34-1982

Cray, 1884
T.34,35-1919, T.52-1919, T.612 to 613-1919, T.30-1940, Circ.86-1933, Circ. 80, 81-1953, Circ.82-1953, Circ.426-1953, T.291-1975, T.4 to B-1978 (repro) T.34-1982

Daffodil, JHD, c.1891
T.623,624-1919, T.30-1940, Circ.431,432-1953, Circ.287-1955, **T.34-1982**

Eden, JHD, c.1905.
T.30-1940, T.24-1955, Circ.288-1955, T.34-1982

Evenlode, 2 September 1883
T.46-1912, T.596-1919, Circ.88-1933, Circ.93-1933, T.333-1985, T.30-1940

Eyebright, 23 November 1883
T.51-1912, T.46,47-1919, T.30-1940, Circ.420 to 423-1953, T.34-1982

Florence, JHD, c.1890
T.660-1919, T.30-1940

Flowerpot, 18 October 1883
T.52-1912, T.51-1919, T.30-1940, T.34-1982

Haddon, adapted from 19th century Indian textile design, after 1915
T.34-1982

Honeysuckle, 11 October 1876
L.C.C. Loan 46, T.53,54-1919, T.630 to 633-1919, Circ.87-1933, Circ.96-1933, Circ.196-1934, T.385-1934, T.30-1940, Circ,413 to 415-1953, Circ.289&A-1955, Circ.290&A-1955, Circ.487 to 490-1965, **Circ.491-1965**, T.34-1982

Indian Diaper, before December 1875
T.585-1919, T.30-1940, Circ.45-1956

Iris, 25 April 1876
T.45-1919, T.141-1919, T.30-1940

Jasmine Trellis, 1868-70
T.30-1940, **T.70-1953**, Circ.105-1966

Kennet, 18 October 1883
T.48-1912, T.604 to 606-1919, Circ.123-1953, T.30-1940, T.34-1982

Large Stem, Copied by WM from a Bannister Hall 1830s textile, c.1868
T.34-1982

Larkspur, 15 April 1875
T.30-1940, Circ.493,494-1965

Lea, 2 February 1885
T.55-1912, T.607 to 611-1919, T.614-1919, T.30-1940, T.30-1940, T.85-1953, T.34-1982, **T.105-1985**

Little Chintz, 1876
T.40-1919, T.30-1940, T.34-1982

Lodden, 1884
T.39-1912, T.54-1912, T.30-1940, T.34-1982

Marigold, 15 April 1875
T.638,639-1919, T.30-1940, Circ.483 to 485-1965, Circ.495-1965, **Circ.496-1965**, T.167-1973, T.34-1982

Medway, 21 September 1885
T.599,600-1919, Circ.85-1933, T.30-1940, Circ.428 to 430-1953, T.34-1982

Peony, KF, 22 June 1877
T.587-1919, T.30-1940, T.71-1953, Circ.47-1956,T.34-1982

Persian, JHD, 1895–1900, T.30-1940

Pomegranate, 22 June 1877
T.592-1919, T.30-1940

Powdered, c.1902
T.30-1940, T.34-1982

Rose, 8 December 1883
T.53-1912, T.38-1919, T.30-1940, Circ.425-1953, Circ.43-1954

Rosebud, JHD, c.1905
T.30-1940, T.166-1980

Rose and Thistle, before April 1881
T.32,33-1919, T.634 to 636-1919, **T.637-1919**, T.30-1940, Circ.83-1953, Circ.416-1955

Severn, JHD, 1887–90
T.660-1919, T.30-1940

Shannon, JHD, after 1892
T.30-1940

Small Stem, copied by WM from a Bannister Hall 1830s printed textile, c.1868
T.37-1979, T.34-1982

Snakeshead, 1876
T.37-1919, T.643,644-1919, T.30-1940, T.141-1919, Circ.371-1955, Circ.46-1956

Strawberry Thief, 11 May 1883
L.C.C. Loan 47, T.47-1912, **T.586-1919**, Circ.90-1933, Circ.94&A-1933, Circ.95-1933, T.30-1940, Circ.419-1953, Circ.372-1955, T.166 & A-1973, T.1-1978

Strawberry Thief, printing blocks. Twenty-four blocks, c.1883,
T.125&A-1980, **T.125B to S-1980**, T.15 to C-1981

Striped Twill, JHD or KK, c.1906
T.186-1982

Sweet Briar, JHD, c.1912
T.34-1982

Tangley, adapted from early 19th century textile design, after 1915
T.34-1982

Trail, JHD, c.1891
T.589-1919, T.30-1940, **Circ.432-1953**

Trent, JHD, 1888
T.55-1919, T.619 to 622-1919, T.30-1940, Circ.79-1953

Tulip, 15 April 1875
T.42,43-1919, T.625 to 629-1919, T.30-1940, Circ.406-1953, Circ.408&A-1953, Circ.409&A-1953, **Circ.410-1953,** Circ.410A-1953, Circ.20,21-1954

Tulip and Willow, 1873
T.593-1919, T.30-1940, Circ.89-1933, **Circ.91-1933**, Circ.92-1933

Utrecht, 1871
T.30-1940, **T.210-1953**, Circ.446-1953

Wandle, 28 July 1884
T.45-1912, T.594-1919, Circ.199-1934, **T.425-1934**, T.30-1940, **Circ.427-1953,** Circ.173-1956

Wey, c.1883
T.49-1912, T.41-1919, T.601 to 603-1919, T.30-1940, T.660-1919, T.30-1940, T.87-1980, **T.87A-1980**

Windrush, 18 October 1883
T.30,31-1919, T.617,618-1919, T.30-1940, **Circ.424-1953**

Willow, c.1895
T.30-1940, T.209-1953, T.34-1982

Wreathnet, 1882
T.50-1919, T.30-1940

Yare, JHD, after 1892, T.30-1940, T.34-1982

Woven textiles

Acanthus, 25 April 1876
T.28-1919, T.30-1940, Circ.433-1953, Circ.446-1954, T.22,23-1968

Alva, adapted from historical textile, 1905-10, T.30-1940

Anemone, 8 February 1876, T.30-1940

Apple, JHD, 1895–1900
T.497-1934, T.30-1940, T.56-1946

Bird, 1878, T.73-1919, **T.30-1940**,
Circ.250D&E-1961, Circ.501-1962,
Circ.501A-1962, T.211-1983 (repro)

Bird and Vine, 15 May 1879
T.14-1919, T.15 to 17-1919, T.30-1940

Brocatel, WM or JHD, *c*.1888
T.30-1940, T.61-1946, **Circ.86-1953,
Circ.125-1953**, Circ.444,445-1953

Campion, 8 March 1883, T.19-1919, T.30-
1940, Circ.384&A, 385&A, 386&A,
387&A-1962, Circ.47,48-1962

Carnation, JHD, *c*.1905, T.30-1940

Cedric, JHD, *c*.1905, T.30-1940

Cross Twigs, JHD, *c*.1898
T.20-1919, T.30-1940, T.58-1946

Crown Imperial, 18 November 1876
T.30-1940, T.22-1919, T.157 to H-1986
(modern repro)

Diagonal Trail, JHD, *c*.1893
T.30-1940, T.18-1919

Dove and Rose, 1879
T.25,26-1919, T.64,65-1919, T.30-1940,
T.59-1946, **Circ.126-1953**, Circ.610-1954,

Elmcote, JHD, *c*.1900, T.30-1940

Flower Garden, 1879, T.66, 67-1919, T.30-
1940, Circ.94-1953, Circ.442,443-1953,
Circ.80-1966, **Circ.80A-1966**

Flowering Net, JHD, *c*.1906, T.30-1940

Golden Bough, WM or JHD, *c*.1888
T.21-1919, T.496-1934, T.30-1940, T.57-
1946, Circ.95-1953, T.356-1971

Golden Stem, JHD, *c*.1890, T.30-1940

Gothic, see *Musgrove*

Granada, 1884
T.33-1912, **T.4-1919**

Hamilton, JHD, probably based on a
historical design, 1912-14, T.30-1940

Helena, JHD, *c*.1890
T.30-1940, T.60-1946

Honeycomb, 11 February 1886
T.29-1919, T.30-1940

Indian Diaper, before December 1887
T.30-1940

Isaphan, *c*.1888, T.9,10-1919, T.30-1940,
T.111-1953, Circ.127-1953

Ixia, JHD, 1905-10
T.30-1940

Kennet, 18 October 1883, **T.69-1919**, T.30-
1940, T.50-1946, Circ.123-1953

Madras Muslin, 1881
T.657-1919, T.658,659-1919, T.30-1940

Mohair Damask, 18 November 1876
T.30-1940, T.9-1953, T.22, 23-1968

Musgrove, adapted from historical design,
before 1910, T.30-1940, T.19-1968

Oak, 1881, **T.74-1919**, T.30-1940, T.52-1946,
Circ.124-1953, Circ.439 to 441-1953,
Circ.611-1954, Circ.86-1957 (repro.)

Poppy, JHD, 1895-1900, T.30-1940

Peacock and Dragon, 1878, T.6 to 8-1919,
T.64-1933, T.64A-1933, T.65&A-1933,
T.30-1940, Circ.434,435-1953

Persian Brocatel, JHD, *c*.1890
T.68-1919, T.30-1940

Pineapple, adapted from a historical
design, T.30-1940

Pomegranate, JHD, 1895–1900, T.30-1940

Rose and Lily, JHD, *c*.1893
T.70-1919, T.30-1940, T.51-1946, T.54, 55-
1946, Circ.93-1953, T.122-1953,
Circ.139-1953, Circ.436,437-1953

St James, August 1881, T.2-1919, T.75,76-
1919, T.30-1940, T.53-1946, Circ.438-1953

Sistine, adapted from a '15th century
design', before 1912
T.30-1940, T.311-1975, Circ.612-1954

Small Figure, possibly JHD, *c*.1890
T.30-1940

Squirrel, JHD, *c*.1898
T.30-1940, Circ.106-1964

Sunflower, JHD, *c*.1890, T.30-1940, T.93-1985

Swivel Damask, 1877, T.27-1919, T.30-1940,
Circ.447-1954, T.21-1968

Trinitas, adapted from a historical design,
1912–14, T.30-1940

Tulip, JHD, 1895–1900
T.30-1940, T.110-1953

Tulip and Net, JHD, 1888–89
T.57-1934, T.30-1940

Tulip and Rose, 20 January 1876
T.30-1940, T.20-1968, Circ.390&B to
C-1970, **Circ.390A-1970**, T.110-1972

Venetian, adapted from a historical design,
1905–10, T.30-1940

Violet and Columbine, 7 April 1883, T.11 to
13-1919, T.30-1940, T.674 to E- 1974

Vine, JHD, *c*.1890, T.30-1940

Vine and Pomegranate, WM or KF, *c*.1877
T.23,24-1919, T.30-1940, **Circ.383-1962**

Wreath, JHD, *c*.1910, T.30-1940

Wreathnet, 1882, T.30-1940

EMBROIDERIES
Listed chonologically by year of acquisition.

Bell pull, WM or FMB, 1865, **T.5-1919**

Tray cover, 1890s, T.120-1939

Firescreen or cushion cover, WM,
c.1878–80, **T.68-1939**

Firescreen panel, PW or MM, 1885–90,
T.69-1939

Trial sample for pelmet, WM, 1881–2,
T.87-1946

Embroidered screen, JHD, *c*.1885–90,
Circ.848-1956

Four unfinished embroidery kits, MM,
c.1890, Circ.300, **301,302,**303-1960

Panel, *c*.1895, T.61-1976

Embroidered figure, *King Arthur*,
EBJ, 1863, **T.118-1985**

Embroidered figure, *Morgan Le Fay*,
EBJ, 1863, T.119-1985

Embroidered figure, *Merlin*, EBJ, 1863,
T.121-1985

Panel depicting *Phyllis*, WM or EBJ,
c.1860–63, **T.122-1985**

Unworked embroidery silks, 1870s–80s,
T.123-1985

Panel depicting a Pomegranate Tree, WM,
c.1860, **T.124-1985**

Table cloth, MM, *c*.1890-95, **T.426-1993**

EMBROIDERED HANGINGS

Acanthus, WM, *c*.1880, **T.66-1939**

Vine, WM, *c*.1880, T.67-1939

Acanthus, WM, *c*.1880, Circ.524-1953

The Musicians, EBJ and WM, *c*.1875,
T.121-1953

Lotus, WM, 1875–1880, **T.192-1953**

Sunflower, WM, *c*.1876, **Circ.196-1961**

The Orchard, MM, 1896, Circ.206-1964

Embroidered curtains, WM, 1890s,
Circ.81&A-1966

Superfrontal, PW, 1898-99, **T.379-1970**

Hangings, MM or WM, 1890-95,
T.364&A-1976

Artichoke, WM, 1877, **T.166-1978**

Honeysuckle, WM, *c*.1876, T.262-1978

Acanthus, WM, *c*.1880, **T.153-1979**

The Owl and *The Pigeon*, JHD, *c*.1895,
T.369&A-1982

TAPESTRIES

Angeli Laudantes, WM and JHD, 1894,
153-1898

The Seasons or *Orchard*, WM and JHD
c.1890, **154-1898**

Tapestry border, reproductions, 1911–14,
Morris & Co,
Circ.53-1911, Circ.301-1911, **Circ.423-
1911**, Circ.152-1912, **Circ.1914-1 to 3**

The Forest, WM, PW, JHD, 1887,
T.111-1926

Panel, JHD, 1890–1910, Circ.238-1965

Pomona, EBJ and JHD, *c*.1900, **T.33-1981**

Tapestry panel, scrolling acanthus leaf,
WM or JHD, *c*.1890, **T.111-1986**

Angeli Ministrantes, WM and JHD, 1894,
T.459-1993

CARPETS AND
FLOOR COVERINGS

Linoleum
Two samples of linoleum, 1875,
Circ.527-1953, T.81-1978

Machine-woven carpets
Listed alphabetically by design.

Artichoke, WM, 1875–80, T.342-1978,
T.188-1984

Bellflowers, WM, 1875–80, T.103-1953

Daisy or *Grass*, WM, 1870–75, Circ.39-1954

Lily, WM, *c*.1875, Circ.526-1953,
Circ.65&A-1959, **Circ.65B-1959**

Rose WM, 31 March 1876,
Circ.382-1962, T.344-1978

Tulip and Lily, WM, *c*.1875, Circ.117,118-
1953, T.16&A-1972, **T.101-1953**

Four unidentified carpets, Circ.8-1954,
Circ.38-1954. Circ.343-1978, T.346-1978

Hand-knotted carpets
Redcar, WM, *c*.1881, **T.3-1919**

Bullerswood. WM with JHD, 1889,
T.31-1923

Rug, WM, *c*.1879-81, **T.104-1953**

Carbook, WM, 1881–3, **Circ.458-1965**

Hammersmith rug, JHD, *c*.1890, T.425-1993

LOOMS
Miniature tapestry loom, **156-1893**
Miniature carpet loom, **283-1893**

SELECT BIBLIOGRAPHY

Any detailed study of William Morris must include his own writings. These were gathered together in the first instance for publication by his daughter May with later compilations (see first section, 'Books by Morris'). Making one's way through the twenty-four volumes of May's *Collected Works* alone is not a practical prospect for those who wish to have a general pen-portrait of the man, or to place his life and work in context. Fortunately, this is covered in numerous publications. The following four-part list (arranged chronologically) presents the most useful titles for the non-specialist, with writings by Morris, general books about him and then specific sources on those aspects of Morris's career as a designer and manufacturer that provide the main content of this catalogue. In order to place the present exhibition and publication in context, a list of the major Morris exhibition catalogues is also included.

BOOKS BY MORRIS

Morris, May (ed.), *The Collected Works of William Morris*, 24 vols., London, 1910–15. Reissued Bristol, 1992

Morris, May (ed.), *William Morris: Artist, Writer, Socialist*, 2 vols., Oxford, 1936

Henderson, Philip (ed.), *The Letters of William Morris to his Family and Friends*, London, 1950

Briggs, Asa (ed.), *William Morris: Selected Writings and Designs*, London, 1962

LeMire, Eugene D. (ed.), *The Unpublished Lectures of William Morris*, Detroit, 1969

Morton, A.L. (ed.), *Three Works by William Morris*, London, 1968

Morton, A.L. (ed.), *The Political Writings of William Morris*, London, 1973

Kelvin, Norman (ed.), *The Collected Letters of William Morris*, Princeton: I (1848–80), 1984; II (1881–88), 1987; III (1889–96), 1996

Boos, Florence (ed.), *William Morris's Socialist Diary*, London, 1985

Faulkner, Peter (ed.), *William Morris: Selected Poems*, Manchester, 1992

Naylor, Gillian (ed.), *Morris by Himself*, 1988

Wilmer, Clive (ed.), *'News from Nowhere' and other Writings by William Morris*, Hammersmith, 1994

Salmon, Nicholas (ed.), *William Morris: Political Writings*, Bristol, 1994

Salmon, Nicholas (ed.), *William Morris: Journalism*, Bristol, 1996.

Miele, Chris (ed.), *William Morris: Architecture*, Bristol, 1996

Poulson, Christine (ed.), *William Morris: Art and Design*, Bristol, 1996

GENERAL BOOKS ON MORRIS

Vallance, Aymer, *William Morris: His Art, his Writings and his Public Life*, London, 1897; reissued 1986

Mackail, J.W., *The Life of William Morris*, London, 1899

Thompson, E.P., *William Morris: Romantic to Revolutionary*, London, 1955; revised edn, 1977

Henderson, Philip, *William Morris, His Life, Work and Friends*, London, 1967

Thompson, Paul, *The Work of William Morris*, London, 1967; revised edn 1991

Faulkner, Peter, *William Morris: The Critical Heritage*, London, 1973

Lindsay, Jack, *William Morris: His Life and Work*, London, 1975

Faulkner, Peter, *Against the Age: An Introduction to William Morris*, 1980

Stansky, Peter, *William Morris*, Oxford, 1983

Stansky, Peter, *Redesigning the World: William Morris, the 1880s, and the Arts and Crafts Movement*, Princeton, 1985

Marsh, Jan, *Jane and May Morris*, London, 1986

Poulson, Christine, *William Morris*, London, 1989

Latham, Davis, and Latham, Sheila, *An Annotated Critical Bibliography of William Morris*, London, 1990

Harvey, Charles, and Press, Jon, *William Morris, Design and Enterprise in Victorian Britain*, Manchester, 1991

MacCarthy, Fiona, *William Morris: A Life for Our Time*, London, 1994

PAINTING AND THE DECORATIVE ARTS

Surviving documentation in the form of contemporary accounts, magazine articles and catalogues (Morris & Co. published on a range of subjects between 1910 and 1914) and the art objects themselves, have provided the main inspiration for the catalogue section of this book. Whereas the following list includes those widely used, a number of individual references appear in the text. Some titles are not exclusive to their chapter headings.

General

PRIMARY SOURCES

Only primary sources used consistently are listed separately here. For a more comprehensive catalogue, K.L. Goodwin's A Preliminary Handlist of Manuscripts and Documents of William Morris (William Morris Society, 1983) includes most of those in accessible collections.

Early notebook with designs, sketches and a draft letter to clients: British Library (see cat.no.D.3)

Minute book for Morris, Marshall, Faulkner & Co.: Sanford and Helen Berger Collection (see cat.no.D.1) with a copy at Hammersmith and Fulham Archives and Local History Centre

Account book of Ford Madox Brown: Private Collection with a copy at the Walker Art Gallery, Liverpool

Account book of Philip Webb with MMF&Co.: Private Collection (see cat.no.D.4)

Account book of Edward Burne-Jones with MMF&Co. (2 vols.): Fitzwilliam Museum, Cambridge

Burne-Jones Papers: Fitzwilliam Museum, Cambridge

Correspondence (Warington Taylor) with William Morris, Philip Webb and Dante Gabriel Rossetti: NAL, V&A Museum

Correspondence (Philip Webb) with William Morris and others: NAL, V&A Museum

Correspondence between Thomas Wardle and William Morris: Perkins Library, Duke University, Durham, North Carolina, with typescript copy in the NAL, V&A Museum

Miscellaneous diaries by Morris and Morris family correspondence: British Library

Memorials of William Morris by George Wardle, 1897: British Library

Album of photographs of Morris & Co. stained glass: Birmingham Museums and Art Gallery

J.W. Mackail's unpublished notes for *The Life of William Morris* (1899): William Morris Gallery, Walthamstow

Typed list of work undertaken by S.&S. Dunn for Morris & Co.: William Morris Gallery, Walthamstow

Metford Warner, Draft Paper to be read at the Design Club, 1909: NAL V&A Museum

PUBLISHED SOURCES

Day, Lewis F., 'The Art of William Morris', *Art Journal*, Easter Art Annual extra number, 1899

Holman Hunt, W., *Pre-Raphaelitism and the Pre-Raphaelite Brotherhood* (2 vols.), London, 1905

G.B-J [Georgiana Burne-Jones], *Memorials of Edward Burne-Jones*, London, 1912

Crow, G.H., 'William Morris, Designer', *The Studio*, special Winter number, 1934

Lethaby, W.R., *Philip Webb and His Work*, London, 1935

Doughty, Oswald, and Wahl, John Robert, *Letters of Dante Gabriel Rossetti*, 3 vols., Oxford, 1965–7

Watkinson, Raymond, *William Morris as Designer*, London, 1967

Waters, Bill, and Harrison, Martin, *Burne-Jones*, London, 1973

Christian, John, *Edward Burne-Jones*, Arts Council, London, 1975

Fitzgerald, Penelope, *Edward Burne-Jones: A Biography*, London, 1975

Surtees, Virginia (ed.), *The Diary of Ford Madox Brown*, 1981

Morris, Barbara, *Inspiration for Design, the Influences of the Victoria and Albert Museum*, London, 1986

MacDonald, Sally, 'For "Swine of Discretion": Design For Living', *Museums' Journal*, Dec. 1986, pp. 123–9

Gere, Charlotte, *Nineteenth-Century Decoration, the Art of the Interior*, London, 1989

Watkinson, Ray, and Newman, Teresa, *Ford Madox Brown*, 1991

Gere, Charlotte, and Whiteway, Michael, *Nineteenth-Century Design from Pugin to Mackintosh*, London 1993

Gere, J.A., Pre-Raphaelite *Drawings in the British Museum*, London 1994

Harvey, Charles, and Press, Jon, 'The Ionides Family and 1 Holland Park', *Journal of the Decorative Arts Society*, 18, 1994, pp.2–14

Hartley, Eeyan, 'Morris & Co. in a Baroque Setting', *The Journal of the William Morris Society*, XI, no. 2, Spring 1995

Painting

Surtees, Virginia, *The Paintings and Drawings of Dante Gabriel Rossetti (1828–1882): A Catalogue Raisonné*, London, 1971

Tate Gallery, *The Pre-Raphaelites*, exhibition catalogue, London, 1984

Watkinson, Ray, 'Red House Redecorated', *The Journal of the William Morris Society*, VII, no.4, Spring 1988, pp.10–15

Church Decoration and Stained Glass

Sewter, A.C., *The Stained Glass of William Morris and his Circle*, New Haven, 1974/5

Harrison, Martin, *Victorian Stained-Glass*, London, 1980

Domestic Decoration

Anon, 'Decorations at Westminster Hospital', *The Builder*, 11 Jan. 1879, p.51

Weaver, Lawrence,'Rounton Grange, Yorkshire', *Country Life*, 26 June 1915, pp.906–12

Mitchell, Charles, 'William Morris at St James's Palace', *The Architectural Review*, Jan. 1947

Kirk, Sheila, and Curry, Rosemary J., *Philip Webb in the North*, Middlesbrough, 1984

Furniture

Anon, 'Madox Brown's Designs for Furniture', *The Artist*, XXII, May 1898, pp.41–51

Tait, E.M., 'The Pioneer of Art Furniture. Madox Brown's Furniture Designs', *The Furnisher*, 1900–1, pp.61–3

Pevsner, Nikolaus, 'Colonel Gillum and the Pre-Raphaelites', *The Burlington Magazine*, XCV, no. 600, 1953, pp. 73-81

Ormond, Richard, 'Holman Hunt's Egyptian Chairs', *Apollo*, July 1965, pp. 55–68

Jervis, Simon, '"Sussex" Chairs in 1820', *Furniture History*, X, 1974, p. 99

Surtees, Virginia, *The Diaries of George Price Boyce*, London, 1980

Kirkham, Pat, 'William Morris's Early Furniture', *The*

Journal of the William Morris Society, IV, no. 3, Summer 1981, pp. 25–8

Carruthers, Annette, ' "…like Incubi and Succubi": A Table by Webb or Morris', *Craft History*, II, April 1989, pp. 55-61

Tiles and Tableware

Williamson, George C., *Murray Marks and his Friends*, London, 1919

Morris, Barbara, *Victorian Table Glass and Ornaments*, London 1978

Myers, Richard and Hilary, 'London Agents for Dutch Tiles' and 'Wightwick Manor', *Glazed Expressions*, Tiles and Architectural Ceramics Society, Autumn/Winter 1981

Myers, Richard and Hilary, 'Morris & Co. Ceramic Tiles', *Journal of the Tiles and Architectural Ceramics Society*, I, 1982, pp.17–22.

Van Lemmen, Hans, '19th Century Dutch Tiles', *Journal of the Tiles and Architectural Ceramics Society*, I, 1982

Catleugh, Jon, *William De Morgan Tiles*, London, 1983

Rudoe, Judy, and Coutts, Howard, 'The Tableglass Designs of Philip Webb and T.G. Jackson for James Powell & Sons, Whitefriars Glassworks', *Journal of the Decorative Arts Society*, 1992, pp. 24–41

Wallpapers

Lubbock, P. (ed.), *Letters of Henry James*, London 1920

Floud, Peter, 'The Wallpaper Designs of William Morris', *The Penrose Annual*, LIV, 1960

Clark, Fiona, *William Morris: Wallpapers and Chintzes*, London, 1973

Lynn, C., *Wallpapers in America from the Seventeenth Century to World War I*, New York, 1980

Gere, C., *Nineteenth Century Decoration: The Art of the Interior*, London, 1989

Thorndycraft, D., 'A Royal Commission: Morris & Co. at St James's Palace', unpub. MA dissertation, Royal Holloway College, London, 1993

Sanderson, Arthur, & Sons Ltd, *Catalogue of Block-printed Wallpapers*, London, 1993

Tibbles, T., 'Speke Hall and Frederick Leyland. Antiquarian Refinements', *Apollo*, May 1994

Textiles

Floud, Peter, 'Dating Morris Patterns', *The Architectural Review*, July 1959

Parry, Linda, *William Morris Textiles*, London, 1983

Dufty, A.R., *Morris Embroideries: The Prototypes*, London, 1984

Parry, Linda, *Textiles of the Arts and Crafts Society*, London, 1988

Calligraphy and the Kelmscott Press

Sparling, H.H., *The Kelmscott Press and William Morris, Master Craftsman*, 1924

Dunlap, Joseph, *The Book That Never Was*, New York, 1971

Dunlap, Joseph, 'The Road to Kelmscott', Doctoral Thesis, Colombia University, New York, 1972

Isherwood, Andrew, *An Introduction to the Kelmscott Press*, V&A, London, 1986

Peterson, W.S., (ed.), *The Ideal Book: Essays and Lectures on the Arts of the Book by William Morris*, California, 1982

Peterson, W.S., *A Bibliography of the Kelmscott Press*, Oxford, 1984

Dreyfus, John, *Morris and the Printed Book*, William Morris Society, London, 1989

Peterson, W.S., *The Kelmscott Press: A History of William Morris's Typographical Adventure*, Oxford, 1991

Legacy

Teague, Walter Dorwin, *Design This Day: The Technique of Order in the Machine Age*, London, 1947

Farleigh, J. (ed.), *Fifteen Craftsmen on their Crafts*, London, 1945

Banham, Rayner, *Theory and Design in the First Machine Age*, London, 1960

Thompson, E.P., *The Communism of William Morris*, London 1965 (Shortened version published in *William Morris Today*, ICA, London 1984, see below)

Edel, Leon, *Henry James Letters*, London, 1974

Van de Velde, Henry, 'Le Nouveau', in *Deblaiment d'Art*, Brusssels, 1979

Parry, Linda, 'Morris and Company in the Twentieth Century', *The Journal of the William Morris Society*, VI, no. 4, Winter 1985–6

Hobsbawn, E.J., *The Age of Empire: 1875–1914*, London, 1987

Coleman, Roger, *The Art of Work: An Epitaph to Skill*, London, 1988

Britton, Alison, 'Sustaining Alternatives', in Margetts, Martina, (ed.), *International Crafts*, London, 1991

Bowe, N. Gordon (ed.), *Art and the National Dream. The Search for Vernacular Expression in Turn-of-the-Century Design*, Dublin, 1993

Forest, Neil, 'Reclaiming the Role of Craft in Architecture', in Hickey, G.A. (ed.), *Making and Metaphor: A Discussion of Meaning in Contemporary Craft*, CCFCS, Canada, 1994

EXHIBITION CATALOGUES

London, Victoria and Albert Museum, *William Morris Centenary Exhibition*, 1934

London, Victoria and Albert Museum, *Victorian and Edwardian Decorative Arts*, 1952

London, Victoria and Albert Museum, *Morris & Co. Centenary Exhibition*, 1961

Stanford, Connecticut, Stanford University Art Gallery, *Morris & Co.*, 1975

New York, Pierpont Morgan Library, *William Morris and the Art of the Book*, 1976

Zurich, Bellerive Museum, *William Morris*, 1978

Fitzwilliam Museum, Cambridge, *Morris & Company in Cambridge*, 1980

Farnham, Surrey, West Surrey College of Art and Design, *William Morris and Kelmscott*, 1981

Birmingham, City Museums and Art Gallery, *Textiles by William Morris and Morris & Co., 1861–1940*, 1981

Berkeley, California, The Bancroft Library and the University Art Museum, *William Morris, The Sanford and Helen Berger Collection*, 1984

Manchester, Whitworth Art Gallery, *William Morris and the Middle Ages*, 1984

London, Institute of Contemporary Arts, *William Morris Today*, 1984

Tokyo, Isetan Museum of Art and Osaka, Daimaru Museum, *William Morris*, 1989

Toronto, Art Gallery of Ontario, *The Earthly Paradise, Arts and Crafts by William Morris and his Circle from Canadian Collections*, 1993

Adelaide, the Art Gallery of South Australia, *Morris & Company, Pre-Raphaelite and the Arts and Crafts Movement*, 1994

LIST OF LENDERS TO THE EXHIBITION

The Museum is extremely grateful for their generous help.

Sanford and Helen Berger

Birmingham Museums and Art Gallery

The Bodleian Library, University of Oxford

Ivor Braka Limited – London

The British Library Board

British Library of Political and Economic Science, London School of Economics

The Trustees of the British Museum

The Castle Howard Collection

The Syndics of Cambridge University Library

Cheltenham Art Gallery and Museums

Brian Clarke

All Saints Church, Dedworth, Windsor

John Dreyfus

The Syndics of the Fitzwilliam Museum, Cambridge

J. Paul Getty KBE, Wormsley Library

Hammersmith and Fulham Archives and Local History Centre

Mr and Mrs Christopher Hampton

St Nicholas, Beaudesert, Henley-in-Arden Parish Church, Warwickshire

The Vicar and Church Wardens of St John's Church, Hollington

International Institute of Social History (IISH), Amsterdam

The Master and Fellows of Jesus College, Cambridge

The Parish of Kentish Town

Hans van Lemmen

The Patron and Governors of the Lord Leycester Hospital, Warwick

The Trustees of the United Reformed Church, Maidstone

Maltwood Art Museum and Gallery, University of Victoria, British Columbia

Marx Memorial Library

National Trust, Wightwick Manor

Norfolk Museums Service (Norwich Castle Museum)

The Pierpont Morgan Library

Public Record Office, London, UK

The Vicar and Church Wardens of the Parish of St Martin-on-the-Hill, Scarborough

Collection of the Guild of St George, The Ruskin Gallery, Sheffield

St Bride Printing Library

Arthur Sanderson & Sons Ltd

Society of Antiquaries of London

Society of Antiquaries of London (Kelmscott Manor)

The Society for the Protection of Ancient Buildings

The Tate Gallery, London

Francesca and Massimo Valsecchi

Whitworth Art Gallery, University of Manchester

William Morris Gallery (London Borough of Waltham Forest)

William Morris Society, Kelmscott House, London

Williamson Art Gallery and Museum, Birkenhead, Wirral

PHOTO CREDITS

The photographic credit is listed first; ownership, if different, follows.

V&A = By courtesy of the Board of Trustees of the Victoria & Albert Museum

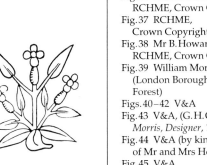

Fig. 1 V&A
Fig. 2 By courtesy of The National Portrait Gallery
Fig. 3 Hammersmith and Fulham Archives and Local History Centre
Fig. 4 Sotheby's (Mr and Mrs Christopher Hampton)
Fig. 5 V&A
Fig. 6 Cyril Band (copyright of the Oxford Union Society)
Fig. 7 V&A (Lewis F. Day *The Art of William Morris*, 1899)
Fig. 8 V&A (Morris & Co catalogue)
Fig. 9 V&A (St Michael and All Angels, Brighton)
Fig. 10 V&A
Fig. 11 William Morris Gallery (London Borough of Waltham Forest)
Fig. 12 V&A
Fig. 13 William Morris Gallery (London Borough of Waltham Forest)
Fig. 14 V&A
Fig. 15 By permission of The British Library
Fig. 16 V&A (Private Collection)
Fig. 17 V&A (G.H.Crow *William Morris, Designer*, 1934)
Fig. 18 V&A (Morris & Co catalogue)
Fig. 19 V&A (G.H.Crow *William Morris, Designer*, 1934)
Figs. 20–21 V&A
Figs. 22–23 William Morris Gallery (London Borough of Waltham Forest)
Fig. 24 Marx Memorial Library
Fig. 25 William Morris Gallery (London Borough of Waltham Forest)
Fig. 26 V&A, May Morris (*The Collected Works of William Morris* Vol. II, 1910–15)
Fig. 27 V&A
Fig. 28 William Morris Gallery (London Borough of Waltham Forest)
Figs. 29–30 By permission of The British Library
Fig. 31 IISH, Amsterdam
Fig. 32 Derek Parker
Fig. 33 Greater London Record Office
Fig. 34 A. F. Kersting
Fig. 35 V&A (by permission of The Society for the Protection of Ancient Buildings)
Fig. 36 Richard Dennis, RCHME, Crown Copyright
Fig. 37 RCHME, Crown Copyright
Fig. 38 Mr B. Howarth Loomes. RCHME, Crown Copyright
Fig. 39 William Morris Gallery (London Borough of Waltham Forest)
Figs. 40–42 V&A
Fig. 43 V&A, (G.H.Crow *William Morris, Designer*, 1934)
Fig. 44 V&A (by kind permission of Mr and Mrs Hollamby)
Fig. 45 V&A

Fig. 46 V&A (Society of Antiquaries of London, Kelmscott Manor)
Fig. 47 V&A
Fig. 48 V&A (the Vicar and Church-Wardens of St Martin-on-the-Hill, Scarborough)
Fig. 49–50 V&A (St Michael and All Angels, Brighton)
Fig. 51 Birmingham Museums and Art Gallery
Fig. 52 V&A (by kind permission of All Saints Church, Middleton Cheney)
Figs. 53–54 V&A (the Masters and Fellows of Jesus College Chapel)
Fig. 55 V&A (St Michael and All Angels, Brighton)
Figs. 56–58 V&A (by kind permission of Mr and Mrs Hollamby)
Fig. 59 RCHME, Crown Copyright
Figs. 60–61 V&A
Fig. 62 Country Life Picture Library
Fig. 63 V&A (*The British Architect*, 21 November 1884)
Figs. 64–66 RCHME, Crown Copyright
Fig. 67 V&A (GBJ *Memorials of EBJ*, 1912)
Fig. 68 V&A
Fig. 69 Copyright © 1991 By The Metropolitan Museum of Art
Fig. 70 Ashmolean Museum, Oxford
Fig. 71 Hulton Deutsch Collection
Fig. 72 Haslam & Whiteway Ltd
Fig. 73 V&A
Fig. 74 V&A (Morris & Co. catalogue)
Fig. 75 RCHME, Crown Copyright
Fig. 76 V&A (William Morris Gallery, London Borough of Waltham Forest)
Fig. 77–78 Haslam & Whiteway Ltd
Fig. 79–81 V&A (by kind permission of Mr and Mrs Hollamby)
Fig. 82 V&A (by kind permission of the Vicar and Church Wardens of St John the Baptist, Findon)
Fig. 83 V&A
Fig. 84 Birmingham Museums and Art Gallery
Fig. 85 Country Life Picture Library
Fig. 86 RCHME, Crown Copyright
Fig. 87 V&A
Fig. 88 RCHME, Crown Copyright
Fig. 89 V&A
Fig. 90 British Library
Fig. 91 Society of Antiquaries of London, Kelmscott Manor
Fig. 92 Tate Gallery, London
Fig. 93 V&A, (Lewis F. Day *The Art of William Morris*, 1899)
Fig. 94–95 V&A (Morris & Co catalogue)

Fig. 96 St Bride Printing Library
Fig. 97 V&A (Bullerswood School)
Fig. 98 Birmingham Museums and Art Gallery
Fig. 99 V&A, (Private Collection)
Fig. 100 The Pierpont Morgan Library, New York MA 4011
Fig. 101 The Bodleian Library, University of Oxford MS. Eng. misc. d. 265
Fig. 102 British Museum
Fig. 103 The Pierpont Morgan Library, New York
Fig. 104 V&A
Fig. 105 St Bride Printing Library
Fig. 106 Cheltenham Art Gallery and Museums (Emery Walker Library)
Fig. 107 V&A (Society of Antiquaries of London, Kelmscott Manor)
Fig. 108 Trustees of the National Library of Scotland (MS 2922)
Fig. 109 V&A (G.H.Crow *William Morris, Designer*, 1934)
Fig. 110 Sotheby's
Figs. 111–113 V&A
Fig. 114 H. Blairman & Sons
Figs. 115–116 V&A
Fig. 117 Private Collection
Fig. 118–121 Haslam & Whiteway Ltd
Fig. 122 V&A (from *Pioneers of the Modern Movement*, N. Pevsner, Faber & Faber Ltd, 1936)
Fig. 123 V&A (Morris & Co. catalogue)
Fig. 124 V&A (exhibition catalogue)
Fig. 125 V&A (Morris & Co. catalogue)

A.1 V&A (Sanford and Helen Berger Collection)
A.2 V&A (William Morris Gallery, London Borough of Waltham Forest)
A.3–A.5 Tate Gallery, London
A.6 V&A (Society of Antiquaries, London, Kelmscott Manor)
A.7–8 V&A
A.9 V&A (Private Collection)
A.10–12 Birmingham Museums and Art Gallery
A.13–14 V&A
A.15 V&A: British Museum
A.16–17a British Museum
A.18 British Museum
A.20 Fitzwilliam Museum, Cambridge
A.22 British Museum
A.23 V&A
A.25 V&A (William Morris Society, Kelmscott House, London)

D.1 V&A (Sanford and Helen Berger Collection)
D.2 V&A (Private Collection)
D.3 By permission of The British Library
D.4 V&A (Private Collection)
D.5 Fitzwilliam Museum, Cambridge

D.6 British Museum
D.7 V&A

E.3 Christie's Images (J. Paul Getty KBE – Wormsley Library)
E.5 William Morris Gallery (London Borough of Waltham Forest)
E.6–8 IISH, Amsterdam
E.9 By permission of The British Library
E.10 V&A (Marx Memorial Library)
E.11 Hammersmith and Fulham Archives and Local History Centre
E.12 V&A

F.4–7 V&A (by permission of The Society for the Protection of Ancient Buildings)
F.9 By permission of the Ruskin Gallery, Collection of the Guild of St George, Sheffield.
F.10–13 V&A (by permission of The Society for the Protection of Ancient Buildings)
F.14 By permission of The British Library
F.15 Public Record Office, London, UK
F.16 V&A (Sanford and Helen Berger Collection)

G.1–3 V&A
G.5 V&A
G.6 Fitzwilliam Museum, Cambridge
G.7 V&A (Sanford and Helen Berger Collection)
G.8 British Museum
G.9 V&A (William Morris Gallery, London Borough of Waltham Forest)
G.11–13 Fitzwilliam Museum, Cambridge
G.14 Tate Gallery, London
G.15 V&A (Sanford and Helen Berger Collection)
G.16 V&A (Sanford and Helen Berger Collection)

H.1 V&A (The United Reformed Church in Maidstone): V&A
H.2–3 V&A
H.4 Tate Gallery, London
H.5 V&A
H.6 Birmingham Museums and Art Gallery
H.7 V&A (William Morris Gallery, London Borough of Waltham Forest)
H.8–10 V&A
H.11 Tate Gallery, London
H.12 Fitzwilliam Museum, Cambridge
H.13–15 V&A
H.16 Williamson Art Gallery and Museum, Birkenhead, Wirral
H.17–20 V&A
H.21 V&A (All Saints Church, Dedworth, Windsor)
H.22 Brian Clarke
H.23 V&A (Sanford and Helen Berger Collection)

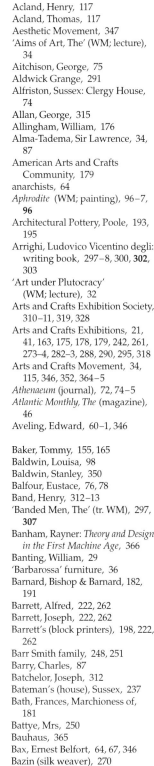